Public Management and Governance

Public Management and Governance is the leading text in international public management and governance and an ideal introduction to all aspects of this field. It combines rigorous insight from pre-eminent scholars around the world with a clear structure and supportive, thoughtful, and intuitive pedagogy. This revised and updated fourth edition responds to the significant changes in the external environment, as well as the field itself. It includes six new chapters covering aspects of increasing importance:

- Public management and governance developments in non-OECD countries
- Risk and resilience
- Innovation in public management and governance
- Digital public management
- Digital public governance
- Behavioural approaches to public policy

Throughout the new edition, there is a wealth of new content on emergent topics such as collaborative leadership, diversity and inclusion, complexity theory and evidence-informed policy. Each chapter is supplemented with discussion questions, group and individual exercises, case studies and recommendations on further reading; this edition also includes more international cases. This highly respected text is an essential resource for all students on undergraduate and postgraduate courses in public management, public administration, government, and public policy as well as for policymakers and practitioners seeking an up-to-date guide to the field.

Tony Bovaird is Emeritus Professor of Public Management and Policy at the University of Birmingham and Chief Executive of Governance International. He has published widely in strategic management, public policy evaluation, and public services management.

Elke Loeffler is Senior Lecturer and Director of Strategic Partnerships (CPRL) at the Open University and Director of Governance International. She has published widely in public governance, quality management in the public sector and user and community co-production of public services.

Public Management and Governance

Fourth Edition

**Edited by Tony Bovaird
and Elke Loeffler**

Routledge
Taylor & Francis Group

LONDON AND NEW YORK

Designed cover image: guvendemir

Fourth edition published 2024
by Routledge
4 Park Square, Milton Park, Abingdon, Oxon, OX14 4RN

and by Routledge
605 Third Avenue, New York, NY 10158

Routledge is an imprint of the Taylor & Francis Group, an informa business

First edition published by Routledge 2003
Third edition published by Routledge 2015

British Library Cataloguing-in-Publication Data
A catalogue record for this book is available from the British Library

Library of Congress Cataloging-in-Publication Data
A catalog record has been requested for this book

ISBN: 9781032253732 (hbk)
ISBN: 9781032232591 (pbk)
ISBN: 9781003282839 (ebk)

DOI: 10.4324/9781003282839

Typeset in Goudy
by Deanta Global Publishing Services, Chennai, India

Access the Support Material: www.routledge.com/9781032232591

Contents

Figures

Tables

Case examples

Contributors

Rachel Ashworth has served as Dean and Head of Cardiff Business School since September 2018 and is a Professor in Public Services Management. Her research focuses on accountability and governance, equality, diversity and inclusion, and organisational change in public services. Her current projects focus on mainstreaming equality in public policy, the implementation of Public Value, and governance reform in emergency services. She has published in journals including *Journal of Public Administration, Research and Theory, Journal of Management Studies, British Journal of Management, Public Administration, Policy and Politics*, and *Public Management Review*.

Arman Behrooz is a second-year student in the Public Administration and Organizational Science research Masters at Utrecht University. Previously he completed his Bachelor of Arts in Social Sciences at the University of Toronto, with a focus on sociology, human geography, and Middle Eastern civilizations. Although exploring a variety of topics relating to public administration throughout his two-year master's programme, Arman's research interests include digital governance and public sector innovation. He is currently developing his thesis project on the effects of phenomenon-based budgeting on public sector capacity to engage with anticipatory innovation in collaboration with the OPSI in OECD.

Annette Boaz is Professor of Health and Social Care Policy at the London School of Hygiene and Tropical Medicine. She has more than 25 years of experience in supporting the use of evidence across a range of policy domains. She was part of one of the largest UK investments in the evidence use landscape, the ESRC Centre for Evidence Based Policy and Practice and a Founding Editor of the journal *Evidence & Policy*. She has undertaken an international leadership role in promoting the use of evidence through the Transforming Evidence initiative, recently publishing a new book on evidence use, *What Works Now: Evidence-informed policy and practice* (Boaz, Davies, Fraser and Nutley, Policy Press 2019).

Geert Bouckaert is Professor of Public Management at the KU Leuven Public Governance Institute in Leuven, Belgium. He is Past-President of the International Institute of Administrative Sciences (IIAS) and of the European Group for Public Administration (EGPA). He was vice-chair of the UN/ECOSOC Committee of Experts for Public Administration (CEPA). His main research interests are in public sector reform, trust, performance management and measurement, and financial management in the public sector.

Tony Bovaird is Emeritus Professor of Public Management and Policy at INLOGOV, University of Birmingham and Chief Executive of Governance International. He directed the meta-evaluation of the UK Local Government Modernisation Agenda on

behalf of the Department of Communities and Local Government and led an evaluation for the Cabinet Office of the UK Civil Service Reform Programme. He has undertaken research for OECD, European Commission, UK central government, National
Audit Office, Local Government Association and many other public agencies in the
UK and internationally. His current research with Elke Loeffler focuses on improving
local governance through user and community co-production and better partnership
working, including projects for the EU Presidency, AHRC Connected Communities
programme, the Scottish and Welsh Governments and the Bertelsmann Foundation. He
is on the Editorial Board of the *International Public Management Journal* and *Complexity,
Governance and Networks*.

James L. Chan is a Professor Emeritus of Accounting at the University of Illinois at Chicago,
where he was head of the Department of Accounting and the Ernst & Young Professor.
In his long academic career, he also held visiting appointments at ten other universities,
including the University of Chicago, as the Emmett Dedmon Visiting Professor in Public
Policy, and Peking University, as Distinguished Overseas Professor. Chan has published
over 100 papers and other writings mostly in government accounting, finance and management. He was chairman of the Government and Nonprofit Section in the American
Accounting Association, and co-founded the Comparative International Government
Accounting Research (CIGAR) Network. Upon his retirement in 2008, he received two
life-time contribution and achievement awards. Professor Chan complemented his academic interests with practical experiences, serving on the staff and task forces of standard-
setting bodies and consulting with the IMF and other leading international organizations
and with governments in the United States and China. Chinese by birth, he received all
his degrees in accountancy from the University of Illinois at Urbana-Champaign.

Joep Crompvoets is Professor of Information Management in the Public Sector and
Research Manager at the Public Governance Institute of KU Leuven University in
Leuven, Belgium. Previously, he was staff member of the research institute CSIC in Spain
and lecturer at Wageningen University (Netherlands). His main research interests are
e-governance, public sector innovation, data infrastructures, GIS and data sciences.

Howard Davis is an independent researcher and academic. He has served as Professor of
Social and Local Policy and Co-Director of the Centre for Communities and Social
Justice at Coventry University and Director of The Local Government Centre, Warwick
Business School, as well as positions at Birmingham and Canterbury Christ Church
Universities. He is currently working with colleagues at Kwansei Gakuin University.
He has led a large number of projects advising on and evaluating the modernisation and
improvement of public services – commissioned by both national and local governments.
He also has many years of international working with particular reference to improving
the delivery of local and public services. His experience includes membership of a wide
range of governmental and partnership bodies and a variety of local authority transformation and programme boards. His UK and international research interests and publications cover local government, community wellbeing and governance, ethics, structures,
performance, innovation and inspection of public services.

Caroline Fischer is an Assistant Professor for Public Administration and Digital
Transformation at the University of Twente. Caroline obtained her PhD from the
University of Potsdam with a dissertation on public sector knowledge management. In
general, her work often employs a micro-level perspective to public administration with

an emphasis on motivation, values, attitudes and behaviour of public servants as well as citizens. She is particularly interested in topics related to error, risk, crisis and learning, and human resource management in the public sector, as well technological developments in government.

Carsten Greve is Professor of Public Management and Governance at the Department of Organization, Copenhagen Business School, where he is also Head of Department. He has written widely on public management reform and public-private partnerships.

Jean Hartley is Professor of Public Leadership at The Open University Business School, where she undertakes research on leadership and leadership development by politicians, public servants and civic activists, and particularly on leadership with political astuteness by managers. Jean co-edited the *The Routledge Companion to Leadership*. She also researches innovation in governance and public services and has co-written *Valuing Public Innovation*, and has writes on and researches about public value. Jean is also the Academic Director of the Open University's multi-disciplinary Centre for Policing Research and Learning.

Utz Helmuth is a Managing Director with the consultancy PwC Strategy&. He has been leading multiple large scale organizational transformations, including the development and implementation of new target operating models and processes. Prior to joining Strategy&, he was a visiting scholar at Georgetown University and worked as a project manager at the Institute for Systemic Management and Public Governance at the University of St. Gallen. He also holds a doctor's degree from the University of St. Gallen, based on research into performance management, on which he has undertaken a number of research projects and published several studies. He also served as vice-chairman of eCH's section on business process management – a standards committee for the Swiss government.

Peter M. Jackson was Dean of Social Science and Pro-Vice Chancellor at the University of Leicester, UK. More recently, he was Director of Enterprise for the College of Social Science and Professor of Economics and Strategy in the University of Leicester's School of Management. He had a continuing interest in public finance and public sector management for over 40 years. Since starting out his career as an economist with HM Treasury, he made major contributions to debates on public expenditure management and control and on approaches to measuring the performance of public sector organisations. His most recent work focused on public value, public sector efficiency and productivity and public private partnerships. In 2001 he was appointed as specialist adviser to the Finance Committee of the Scottish Parliament, assisting in its inquiry into the Private Finance Initiative. [Sadly, Peter died shortly after revising his chapter but before publication – the editors wish to record their huge appreciation of his contribution to the four editions of this textbook].

Janne Kalucza is an IT manager specializing in digital process management and a lecturer in business psychology and statistics. She obtained her PhD from the University of Hamburg with a dissertation on administrative burden and digitalisation in the public sector. Her research interests include approaches to behavioural public administration, the impact of digitalisation on bureaucratic processes, and experimental methodology.

Erik Hans Klijn is a Professor in the Department of Public Administration and Sociology, Erasmus School of Social and Behavioral Sciences, Erasmus University Rotterdam. His research and teaching activities focus on complex decision-making and management in networks, and Public Private Partnerships. In the last decade his research has extended to branding and the impact of media on complex decision-making. He has published extensively in international journals and received a honorary doctorate from the university of Gent for his work on network governance in 2019. He served as president of the International Research Society of Public Management (IRSPM) from 2012 until 2018.

Eva Knies is Professor of Strategic Human Resource Management at Utrecht University School of Governance in the Netherlands. Her research interests include Human Resource Management and leadership in the public sector, public service performance, and employee well-being. Knies is co-editor of the *Research Handbook on HRM in the Public Sector* (with Steijn) and the book *Managing for Public Service Performance* (with Leisink, Andersen, Brewer, Jacobsen, and Vandenabeele). She is a co-chair of the Study Group on Public Personnel Policies of the European Group for Public Administration.

Christopher Koliba is the Edwin O. Stene Distinguished Professor of Public Administration, Policy & Governance at the School of Public Administration and Affairs at the University of Kansas. He is also Professor Emeritus in the Community Development and Applied Economics Department and Co-Founder of the Socio-Ecological Gaming and Simulation Lab at the University of Vermont (UVM). He was a Fulbright Scholar at the University of Colombo, Sri Lanka, in 2015. His research interests include comparative governance network analysis, network performance and accountability, organizational learning and development, and environmental governance. His current research focuses on development of complex adaptive systems models and network analysis of critical infrastructure networks of watersheds, energy grids, food systems, and transportation planning. He is lead author of *Governance Networks in Public Administration and Public Policy* (2019, 2nd edition, Routledge).

Joop Koppenjan is Professor Emeritus in Public Administration at the Erasmus University Rotterdam. His research interests include public policy, policy networks, public private partnerships and public management, with a focus on governance, stakeholder involvement, public values and sustainability. He has (co-)authored various books and book chapters and numerous articles in peer reviewed journals. Together with Erik Hans Klijn he published the monograph *Governance Networks in the Public Sector* (Routledge, 2016). In 2019 he published the edited volume *Smart Hybridity, Potentials and Challenges of New Governance Arrangements* (Eleven, 2019, together with co-editors Philip H. Karré and Katrien Termeer). Website: https://www.eur.nl/people/joop-koppenjan/

George Addo Larbi has recently retired from the World Bank Group, where he held positions including Practice Manager for Governance and Lead Governance Specialist in Africa, East and South Asia. He is currently an Honorary Senior Fellow at the International Development Department, School of Government and Society, University of Birmingham (where he was a Senior Lecturer, prior to joining the World Bank Group in 2006) and also provides advisory and consultancy services on public sector management and governance issues. He has published several articles, books, and reports on public sector governance issues in refereed journals, including *Public Administration and Development*, *International Review of Administrative Sciences*, *Public Management Review*, and *Journal of*

International Development. His book publications include: Larbi, G.A. and Y. Bangura (2006), *Public Sector Reforms in Developing Countries: Capacity Challenges to Improve Public Services* (Palgrave Macmillan) and Batley, R. and Larbi, G.A. (2004), *The Changing Role of Government: Reform of Public Services in Developing Countries* (Palgrave Macmillan). George holds a PhD degree in Public Policy/Development Administration from the University of Birmingham.

Edwin Lau is Head of the Infrastructure and Public Procurement Division in the OECD Public Governance Directorate. His division provides data, analysis and guidance on strengthening strategic and value for money outcomes through reinforced infrastructure planning, coordination and delivery, in particular to deliver on climate and resilience objectives. He also oversees projects on public procurement and public private partnerships. Edwin previously led OECD divisions on budgeting and public expenditure and on public sector reform, including the OECD statistical publication *Government at a Glance*, and the Observatory for Public Sector Innovation. Edwin worked in the US Office of Management and Budget in the 1990s, and holds a Master's degree from the Harvard University Kennedy School of Government and a diplôme d'études approfondies from Sciences Po in Paris.

Veiko Lember is Senior Research Fellow in Public Management and Policy at Ragnar Nurkse Department of Innovation and Governance, Tallinn University of Technology, Estonia, and Visiting Professor at Public Governance Institute, KU Leuven, Belgium. He is also a co-coordinator of the Erasmus Mundus joint Master's Programme of Public Sector Innovation and E-Governance (with KU Leuven, University of Münster and Tallinn University of Technology). In 2017–2022 he served as a member of the Steering Committee of the European Group for Public Administration (EGPA). Veiko's main research interests are in public sector innovation, digital governance, public-private partnerships, citizen co-production, public procurement of innovation, technology transfer, and innovation policy governance. His most recent book with Tiina Randma-Liiv is *Engaging Citizens in Policy Making: e-Participation Practices in Europe* (Edward Elgar, 2022).

Elke Loeffler is Senior Lecturer and Director of Strategic Partnerships at the Centre for Policing Research and Learning at the Open University Business School. She is also Director of Governance International (an international consulting and research company with nonprofit status in the UK) where she provides accredited co-production training programmes. Elke is an Associate of the Institute of Local Government Studies at the University of Birmingham, a Steering Group Member of the European Group of Public Administration (EGPA), and a Board member of the International Research Society for Public Management (IRSPM). Previously she was a staff member of the Public Management Service (now GOV) of OECD. Elke is an editorial board member of the *International Review of Administrative Sciences*, *Public Money and Management* and *der moderne staat*. She graduated in political science and economics in Germany and the US and received her PhD at the German University of Administrative Sciences, Speyer.

Zhiming Ma is an Associate Professor of Accounting at Guanghua School of Management, Peking University, China. He obtained his PhD in accounting from The Hong Kong University of Science and Technology, and his Bachelor's and Master's degrees in economics from Peking University. His research interests centre on debt contracting, auditing, and government accounting. His publications have appeared in *Journal of Accounting and Economics*, *Journal of Financial Economics*, *Contemporary Accounting Research*, *Journal of Financial and*

Quantitative Analysis, Review of Accounting Studies, and Accounting, Organizations and Society. He also serves on the editorial board of *Accounting and Business Research.*

Nick Manning retired as Head of Governance and Public Sector Management at the World Bank in December 2013. He led the development and implementation of the Bank's updated approach to public sector management. Nick was previously the World Bank Manager for Public Sector and Governance for Latin America and the Caribbean. He has also served as Head of the Public Sector Management and Performance Division at the OECD and as the World Bank Lead Public Sector Management Specialist for South Asia. He has held advisory positions on public management for the Commonwealth Secretariat and for UNDP in Lebanon. Nick began his public sector career in local government in the UK and before moving to international advisory work was Head of Strategic Planning for an inner London Borough. He holds various honorary academic, research and advisory positions and has published extensively on public management reform and development and on public sector developments within the OECD.

Steve Martin is Professor of Public Policy and Management at Cardiff University and Director of the Wales for Public Policy (www.wcpp.org.uk). His current research focuses on evidence use by policy makers. He has written widely on public sector reform and public service improvement and served as an adviser to the European Commission, Council of Europe, and numerous UK government departments, public bodies and local government organisations. He is a former editor of *Policy & Politics* and currently a member of the Editorial Boards of *Public Money & Management, Policy & Politics,* and *Local Government Studies.*

Albert Meijer is Professor of Public Innovation at Utrecht University School of Governance. His research focuses on transparency, open government data, coproduction and social media. He is co-editor-in-chief of the journal *Information Polity,* chair of the Permanent Study Group on E-government of the European Group for Public Administration and Director of the Governance Lab Utrecht. He has published frequently in journals such as *Public Management Review, Public Administration Review* and *Government Information Quarterly.* Recently, he published the book *Public Management in an Information Age* (Bloomsbury Publishing, with co-authors Alex Ingrams and Stavros Zouridis).

Sandra Nutley is Professor Emeritus at the School of Management, University of St Andrews. Her research focuses on understanding and improving research use and public service performance improvement. She has published widely in both these areas and has served as an expert adviser for a range of government departments and other public bodies. She was the founding Director of the Research Unit for Research Utilisation (www.ruru.ac.uk) – a research collaboration that investigates the use of social science research in public policy and service delivery settings. Sandra's publications include a trilogy of books on the use of research evidence: *What Works: Evidence-based policy and practice in public services* (Davies, Nutley and Smith, Policy Press 2000); *Using Evidence: How Research can Inform Public Services* (Nutley, Walter and Davies, The Policy Press, 2007); and *What Works Now? Evidence-informed policy and practice* (Boaz, Davies, Fraser and Nutley, Policy Press 2019).

Suzanne J. Piotrowski is a Professor of Public Affairs and Administration at Rutgers University–Newark and Director of the Transparency and Governance Center (TGC). She researches freedom of information, transparency, and open government issues with a strong focus on connecting with communities of practice. In 2020, she became a co-principal investigator on a $2.3 million Smart and Connected Cities National Science Foundation Grant to make public services more equitable and efficient in the City of Newark, New Jersey. In 2022, MIT Press' Information Policy Series published her co-authored project, *The Power of Partnership in Open Government? Multistakeholder Governance Reform and the Open Government Partnership*.

Adrian Ritz is Professor of Public Management and Director of the KPM Center for Public Management at the University of Bern, Switzerland. His main research areas are in the fields of public management, public leadership, motivation, and human resources management in the public sector. He has published articles in the most relevant journals in the field. His co-authored German book *Public Management* (Springer) is now in its 6th edition. He is also President of the advisory board of the Swiss Paraplegic Research Corporation and a board member of the Swiss Paraplegic Foundation (SPS).

Alasdair Roberts is Professor of Public Policy at the University of Massachusetts Amherst. He is a fellow of the U.S. National Academy of Public Administration. In 2022, he received the ASPA Riggs Award for Lifetime Achievement in International and Comparative Public Administration. In 2014 he received Canada's Grace-Pépin Access to Information Award for his research on the right to information. His most recent book, *Superstates: Empires of the Twenty-First Century*, was published by Polity Books in 2023.

Kuno Schedler is Professor for Public Management at the University of St. Gallen in Switzerland. He is Director of the Institute for Systemic Management and Public Governance at the University of St. Gallen. His research currently focuses on rationalities in organizations, service model innovation, digital government and smart criminal justice. He has been involved as an expert in several reform projects within the public sector, from which he draws practical insights for his scholarly work.

Slobodan Tomic is a Lecturer in Public Management at the School of Business and Society, University of York, UK. His academic interests include all aspects of public administration and public policy, especially those that have to do with regulatory governance. His previous research has focused on the analysis of integrity institutions and policies, particularly oversight bodies, which he has investigated both in OECD and non-OECD contexts, with a particular interest in how they manage institutional autonomy when politicisation pressures are anticipated. He has worked on several projects with international organisations, including on civil service and autonomous agencies reform.

Jacob Torfing is a Full Professor in Politics and Institutions at the Department of Social Sciences and Business, Roskilde University, Denmark, and Professor 2 at the Social Science Faculty, Nord University, Norway. He is the founder and co-director of the Roskilde School of Governance. He recently acquired the high Danish doctoral degree of Doctor Scientiarum Administrationis. His recent interests include public sector reform, collaborative governance, public innovation and co-creation.

Wouter Van Dooren is Professor of Public Administration in the Research Group on Politics & Public Governance at the Antwerp Management School. His research interests include public governance, performance information, accountability and learning, and productive conflict in public participation.

Sandra van Thiel is Professor of Public Management at the Department of Public Administration and Sociology, Erasmus University Rotterdam. Her research focuses on executive agencies, public management and research methods. Publications include *Government Agencies* (with Koen Verhoest, Geert Bouckaert and Per Laegreid), the *Palgrave Handbook on Public Administration and Public Management in Europe* (with Edoardo Ongaro) and *Research Methods in Public Administration and Public Management*. She is a frequent consultant for various governments and public sector organizations, in the Netherlands and internationally. She is the editor-in-chief of the *International Journal of Public Sector Management*.

Lois M. Warner is an Associate Teaching Professor of Public Affairs and Administration at Rutgers University-Newark, and Director of Institutional Assessment. Prof. Warner teaches courses in the undergraduate, graduate and executive graduate programs, including Ethical Public Service, and Administrative Ethics. She researches the use of multimedia and open educational resources in public administration education and conducts workshops on these topics at major international conferences.

Foreword

This book has been written with the aim of giving readers a clear picture of the current state of play and the most important emerging issues in public management and governance. We intend that it will help students of public issues to be better informed and help policymakers and managers who work in public services (whether in public, voluntary or private sectors) to be more effective.

The book is also written to help readers to understand what it means to become better citizens and, as such, to help to change the current practice of public management and governance. In this way, we hope that the ideas in the book will help readers to make a greater contribution to their neighbourhoods, their local authorities, their regions and the countries in which they live – and perhaps even to the quality of life of citizens elsewhere in the world.

In this fourth edition, the importance of government shines out even more clearly than before, as the world during the past few years has looked to its political leaders and public service managers for help through a savage economic recession, citizen revolts against governments perceived as ineffective and unresponsive, major threats to world security and the global environment, and a devastating health pandemic. However, the weaknesses of government in the face of these challenges have also come through strongly. We hope the book will play a part in helping the next generation of leaders and managers to cope with such threats and ensure that public management and governance become a byword for success and wellbeing, not simply the name of a textbook.

Finally, it is with sadness that we record the death of some previous authors (Chris Bellamy, Andrew Erridge, Peter Jackson, Christopher Pollitt), who contributed so whole-heartedly to the success of previous editions. And we welcome our host of new authors who have taken on the mantle of making the study of public management and governance not only worthy but exciting.

Structure of the book

The book comprises three main parts:

1 *From Public Management to Governance*, setting out the role of the public sector, public management and public governance, and how these have evolved in recent years in different contexts.
2 *Public Management*, exploring the main managerial functions which contribute to the running of public services.

3 *Public Governance*, exploring the ways in which organizations in the public domain work together with their partners, stakeholders, citizens and networks to influence the outcomes of public policies.

4 *... and finally*, looking to what the future may hold for public management and governance.

Logical though we believe this to be, we know from our own reading habits, as well as the even more inexplicable habits of our colleagues and past students, that many readers will find their own wholly idiosyncratic pathway through this book. To help make this process just a little more systematic, we have provided multiple cross-references to other chapters throughout.

Some thanks

We have had enormous help, as always, from our fellow authors in this book, to whom we are hugely grateful for their patient and imaginative responses to our demands. However, there are others who stand behind them to whom we are also greatly indebted – particularly, the reviewers who fed back how the book works on their courses, and the many students who have told us how they have used previous editions.

Part I

From public management to governance

Part I forms an introduction to the key themes of the book and locates the public sector in its political, social and economic context.

Chapter 1 examines what is "public" about the public sector and about public services. It distinguishes public management from the wider issues of public governance.

Chapter 2 explores recent changes in the context of public policy, identifies the major paradigm shifts in public policy making in recent decades and examines the changing role of politics in public governance.

Chapter 3 examines the size and scope of the public sector. It compares trends in the size and composition of public expenditure across OECD countries and looks at some of the forces that shape these trends. It then considers the implications of these trends for public sector management.

Chapter 4 examines the objectives and results of that generation of public sector reforms which has occurred since the 1980s, the different reform trajectories across OECD countries, and some of the risks and unintended consequences of public sector reform.

Chapter 5 looks beyond OECD countries and examines public management and governance developments in other parts of the world.

Chapter 6 discusses one of the major methodological innovations of recent years, exploring behavioural approaches to public management and governance.

DOI: 10.4324/9781003282839-1

1 Understanding public management and governance

Tony Bovaird and Elke Loeffler

Why study public management and governance?

Welcome to this fourth edition of *Public Management and Governance*. We aim to provide you with up-to-date state-of-the-art knowledge on what the public sector is doing, why it is doing it and how it might do it better. We hope also to challenge you to think for yourself how your society should be governed – one of the questions that has fascinated people for thousands of years – and how your governors should be managed – a question that is much more recent. Along the way we hope that you will have fun as well. Above all, we will be introducing you to the ideas of some of the leading analysts of the public sector and public services around the world, so that you can weigh up their arguments and develop your own.

So what's in store? A book full of analysis of worthy but boring public sector activities? Actually, issues of public management and public governance are often very interesting (see Box 1.1). That's why they attract some highly talented and dedicated people, who might otherwise earn a great deal more money in other jobs. However, we also want to warn readers of this book that it can no longer be taken for granted that the activities of public management and governance are always 'worthy' – sometimes they are conducted by "sharks" rather than by "suits" (see Box 1.2).

Consequently, nowadays public managers have to earn our respect and gratitude, rather than simply assume it. And the players in the public policy arena have to earn the trust of those for whom they claim to be working, rather than claiming legitimacy simply on the grounds that they were elected or that they are part of a prestigious profession. So this fourth edition of *Public Management and Governance* suggests some tough questions for you to ask to see if that trust has indeed been earned – and gives you some ammunition for the debate.

Learning objectives

The key learning objectives in this chapter are:

- To be aware of the different meanings of "public"
- To understand the main differences between public management and public governance
- To understand the motives for studying public management and public governance

DOI: 10.4324/9781003282839-2

Box 1.1 Public management and governance issues are interesting…

Public policy on global warming

The more I think about it, the more fatalistic I become … I suspect the newspapers echo public opinion on this subject. Just about all national papers now accept global warming, but they still object to anything required to deal with it. Low-energy light bulbs will cause old folk to fall down stairs. Higher petrol duties or road charges will be unfair to the poor (although most poor people don't own cars). Restrictions on cheap air travel breach the time-honoured British right to celebrate summer by vomiting over waiters in Faliraki. Wind turbines are ugly. And so on. Does anyone really think that, barring technological miracles, we have the slightest chance of averting calamity?

Source: Peter Wilby, Eat canapé, avoid catastrophe, *New Statesman*, 14 September 2009, p. 10.

Box 1.2 …But not necessarily "worthy"

The Great Chicago Sell-Off

When Chicago needed some extra income to support its public services in 2008 and sold 36,000 parking spaces for 75 years to an investment conglomerate (including a megabank, an international venture capital firm and a Middle Eastern investment authority) they did more than just outsource a current public service. Parking meter prices immediately went through the roof (quadrupling or more in the first year), and already by 2019 the investors, who paid the city $1.15b, had made a profit of $500m and looked forward to 64 more profitable years. Estimates suggested the city was underpaid by at least a factor of ten times. However, even worse, the city has now lost control over what it can do with and on its streets. If a meter is removed or cannot be used (e.g. due to road construction or repair, a fair, a street parade, etc.), the city has to pay the lost income. For 75 years, any plans to manage or change parking spaces in Chicago, e.g. by allowing bars, cafes and restaurants to replace parking spaces by outdoor tables, have effectively been ruled infeasible. And the city has had to fork out $20m annually due to street closures.

Source: Mike Kampf-Lassin (2022), "The Great Chicago Sell-Off", *Jacobin*, 45: 147–148.

What do we mean by "public"?

Box 1.3 The public domain

The essential task of the public domain can be interpreted as enabling authoritative public choice about collective activity and purpose. In short, it is about clarifying, constituting and achieving a public purpose. It has the ultimate responsibility for constituting a society as a political community which has the capacity to make public choices. Producing a "public" which is able to enter into dialogue and decide about the needs of the community ... is the uniquely demanding challenge facing the public domain.

Source: Ranson and Stewart (1994, pp. 59–60).

Before we go further, we should explore what we mean by "public". We start with a clear statement from Ranson and Stewart (Box 1.3) as to what constitutes the public domain. (They wrote in the context of local government, but their analysis applies quite generally.)

This short passage explains how the public domain is the arena in which public choice is exercised in order to achieve a collective purpose. This is the arena which this book explores.

Ranson and Stewart also introduce another meaning of the word "public" – the group (or groups) of people who inhabit the public domain. They clearly identify the political concept of "a public which is able to enter into dialogue and decide about the needs of the community", which we might contrast with the marketing concept of different "publics", each of whom expects to be treated differently by public services and public managers.

Another common usage of "public" is to distinguish between the "public sector" and the "private sector", which essentially revolves around differences of ownership (collective ownership, in the name of all citizens, versus individual ownership) and motive (social purpose versus profit). This meaning is particularly relevant when public managers claim that the public sector is different from the private sector and that therefore private sector management methods would not work in their agency – see Allison (1994) on the concept that public and private management are alike in all unimportant respects! However, there are other, wider meanings of "public". For example, "public services" are sometimes delivered by private or third sector contractors, rather than public agencies. Here, the concept of "public" generally means that the providers have to observe and satisfy some form of "public service obligation". Again, "public issues" are those which cannot simply be left to the decision-making of private individuals – they typically necessitate mobilising the resources of public and voluntary sector organisations or regulating the behaviour of private firms or individuals or groups in civil society.

We shall examine each of these dimensions of "public" in this book. Consequently, we shall take the word "public" to be part of the problematic, i.e. the set of concepts to be explored in this text, rather than defining it unambiguously here at the outset.

Public management and governance: Some key issues

So, what is public management? And what is public governance? While most people will immediately assume they have a general grasp of what public management entails, fewer will have a feel for what is meant by public governance. Moreover, we want to argue that both concepts actually cover quite a complex set of ideas.

We shall take *public management* to be a set of approaches and tools to optimise the use of resources in and by public service organisations in order to coordinate organisational efforts, so that organisational objectives can be accomplished and public needs are satisfied (adapted from Noordegraaf 2015, p. 20). It therefore covers the set of activities undertaken by managers in two very different contexts:

- in public *sector* organisations
- in public *service* organisations, whether in public, voluntary or private sectors

This raises a number of issues that we will consider later:

- What distinguishes "public management" from "public administration"?
- What is "public" about public services?
- Are "public services" always in the "public sector"?
- Is public management only about public services?

We take *public governance* to mean "how an organisation works with its partners, stakeholders and networks to influence the outcomes of public policies". (You will find other approaches to defining "governance" in Chapter 15.) The concept of *public governance* raises a different set of questions, such as:

- Who has the right to make and influence decisions in the public domain?
- What principles should be followed in making decisions in the public domain?
- How can we ensure that collective activities in the public domain result in improved welfare for those stakeholders to whom we accord the highest priority?

This chapter addresses these issues and sets the stage for the rest of the book.

Is "public management" different from public administration?

In the middle of the twentieth century, the study of the work of civil servants and other public officials (including their interface with politicians who passed legislation and set public policy) was usually labelled "public administration". As such, there is no doubt that "public administration" conjured up an image of bureaucracy, life-long secure employment, 'muddling through' and lack of enterprise – dark suits, grey faces and dull day jobs.

From the 1980s onwards, however, a new phrase began to be heard and even achieved dominance in some circles – "public management". This was interpreted to mean different things by different authors, but it almost always was characterised by a different set of symbols from those associated with public administration – it was thought to be about budget management not just budget holding (see Chapter 9), a contract culture (including contracts with private sector providers of services (see Chapter 8) and employment contracts for staff, which were for fixed periods and might well not be renewed (see Chapter 10), entrepreneurship and risk taking and accountability for performance (see Chapter 12).

These differences can be (and often were) exaggerated. However, it appears that the expectations of many stakeholders in the public domain did alter – they began to expect behaviour more in keeping with the image of the public manager and less with that of the public administrator.

What is "public" about public services?

In everyday discussion, we often refer to "public services" as though they were "what the public sector does". However, a moment's reflection shows that this tidy approach doesn't make much sense any longer, at least in most countries (see Chapters 4 and 5).

After all, we have for a long time become used to seeing private firms mending holes in our roads and repairing the council's housing stock. More recently it has become commonplace in many areas to see private firms collecting our bins and running our leisure centres. Moreover, whatever country we live in, there are very few services that are never run by the private sector – in the UK it has long been possible to find some places that have private provision of hospitals, schools, child protection, home helps for the elderly and disabled, housing benefit payments and a local council's Director of Finance. (Indeed, in the UK we even had, for a while, provision of the post of Director-General of the BBC by a private company.)

Furthermore, there are some things that are done by the public sector that might cause raised eyebrows if described as "public services" – such as running a telephone company (as the city of Hull did for many decades) or a city centre restaurant (as Coventry did up to the 1980s).

So what *is* public about public services? There is no single answer to this prize question – but neither is there a lack of contenders to win the prize (see Box 1.4). The answer you come up with is very likely to relate to the discipline in which you were trained and to your ideological position.

For welfare economists, the answer is quite subtle but nevertheless quite precise – public services are those which merit public intervention because of market failure (see Chapter 3). In other words, any good or service that would result in suboptimal social welfare if it were provided in a free market should be regulated in some way by the public sector and in this way qualifies as a "public service".

This definition of "public services" is attractively rigorous but unfortunately very wide-ranging. Almost all services, under this definition, exhibit some degree of "publicness", since the provision of most goods and services in the real world is subject to market failure for one or more of the common reasons – chronic disequilibrium, imperfect competition, asymmetric information in supply or in consumption, externalities, discrimination based on criteria other than cost or technical ability to satisfy user requirements, uncertainty, non-rivalry in consumption, non-excludability in supply or users' ignorance of their own best interest. Consequently, this yields a definition of "public services" that is only occasionally useful – for example, it suggests that all theatres and cinemas are worthy of public intervention (since they are at least partly non-rival in consumption), whereas anyone who has sat through a performance of most Broadway or West End musicals knows that there are real limits to the justifiable level of public subsidy to many theatrical events.

Box 1.4 Characteristics of public services

- focus on democratic accountability, fairness and public interest
- restricted by regulation/legal frameworks
- need to respond to socio-political demands, political pressure and public discourse
- exposure to (expert and non-expert!) public/political/media scrutiny
- need for rationing, not maximising 'sales'
- monopolistic, not responding to customers
- 'non-excludable' (i.e. automatically available to everyone)
- successes and failures have 'externalities' (knock-on benefits or costs)
- performance not defined by simple bottom line or shareholder value
- multiple, complex, long-term outcomes, affected by external factors

---

An alternative approach to defining the scope of "public services" comes from politics. It suggests that "public services" are those which are so important for the re-election of politicians or, more realistically, of political parties, that they are given a public subsidy. Under this perspective, where a service is so important in political decision-making that politicians are prepared to spend some of their budget on it, then its "publicness" must be respected. However, the attractive simplicity of this stance has again been bought at the expense of mind-numbing expansion of the definition of what is potentially a "public service". There are very few goods or services that are never important electorally. However invisible is the widget in the sprocket in the camshaft in the car that is bought by international customers who have no interest in the producer or its location, when it is proposed that a local widget factory should be closed and the widgets should be produced elsewhere (especially if it is "abroad"), so that local politicians are goaded into proposing public subsidies to keep the production going in its present location, then that widget becomes a "public good" under this definition.

A third approach, which similarly sounds like common sense, focuses on all those goods where providers are placed under a "public service obligation" when they are given the right to supply the service. This approach defines as a public service all those services in which Parliament has decreed a need for regulation. However, this approach probably results in a definition of "public service" that is too narrow. For example, there is a legal public service obligation imposed on the providers of all electricity, gas and water utilities and on broadcasters but not on the provision of leisure centres – yet the latter services may form a major part of the quality of life of certain groups, particularly young people and families with young children, and as such may be widely supported by politicians as important services to be provided in the public sector or through public subsidy.

What is public governance?

Trying to define public governance seems to open Pandora's box. Although there is a general acknowledgement that public governance is different from public management, the academic literature on governance (which each year increases exponentially) offers a myriad of definitions. Indeed, even the authors of different chapters in this volume offer different ideas of what is "public governance".

The definition of governance is not, in itself, of critical importance, particularly because many practitioners are widely familiar with governance in practice, although they may find it difficult to recognise it in the forms discussed by academics (see Chapter 15). Nevertheless, we have given a definition above, because we believe it helps to focus discussion.

Whereas in public management a lot of attention is usually paid to the measurement of results (both individual and organisational) in terms of outputs, public governance pays a lot of attention to how different organisations interact in order to achieve a higher level of desired results – the quality-of-life outcomes for citizens and stakeholders. Moreover, in public governance, the ways in which decisions are reached – the processes by which different stakeholders interact – are also seen to have major importance in themselves, whatever the outputs or outcomes achieved. In other words, the current public governance debate places a new emphasis on the old truths that "what matters is not what we do, but how people feel about what we do" and that "processes matter" or, put differently, "the ends do not justify the means". These contrasting emphases – on ends AND means - make "good public governance" exceptionally difficult but may well represent non-negotiable demands by the public in modern society.

The difference between a managerial and a governance approach is illustrated in Case Example 1.1.

Case Example 1.1 Differences between managerial and governance approaches

Whereas public-management-oriented change agents tend to focus their efforts on improving street cleaning and refuse collection services, a local governance approach emphasises the role of citizens in respecting the communal desire that no-one should throw litter or allow dog-fouling on the streets in the first place and that materials should be recycled, not simply thrown away. This involves education (not only in the schools, since "litter-bugs" come in all sizes and ages), advertising campaigns, encouragement of people to show their disgust when dirty behaviour occurs and the provision of proper waste facilities (including those for dog waste) which will help to prevent litter and dog-fouling problems occurring in the first place.

Box 1.5 Corporate governance and sustainability

Governance involves ensuring that Boards are focused on the long-term sustainability of their business. They should be confident that their business models will deliver this – with appropriate risk mitigations as necessary – and that performance indicators and incentives reinforce the desired behaviours.

Source: CIMA (2010, p. 1).

Whereas the governance discussion in the public sector is relatively recent (see Chapter 4), there has been a debate in the private sector for some time on one aspect of governance – *corporate governance*, which refers to issues of control and decision-making powers within organisations (not just private companies) – see Box 1.5.

Subsequently, international organisations have issued guidelines as to how to improve corporate governance (OECD Watch 2017). Although many reforms were implemented in OECD countries, the fallout around the collapse of Enron in the United States in 2001 showed that corporate governance is not only a matter of drafting a stricter legal framework but also of respecting societal values – in the words of Solomon (2007, p. 5), "corporate governance checks and balances serve only to detect, not cure, unethical activity".

Another longstanding governance debate surrounds the issue of *global governance* from the field of international relations, focusing on how to cope with problems that transcend the borders of nation states (such as climate change migration, sex tourism and trafficking or the exploitation of child workers), given the lack of a world government. Some commentators have remained optimistic about the possibilities – e.g. senior UN staff have argued that globalisation needs to be "managed" and have proposed to "govern" globalisation and "make it work for the poor" or simply to achieve "globalisation for all".

However, pessimists suggest that globalisation means that governments everywhere have become powerless and that managing globalisation is an oxymoron, since globalisation is shaped by markets in a "race to the bottom", not by governments. Some have suggested that this powerlessness is reinforced by the coming of the Internet age – that there is no governance against the "electronic herd" (Friedmann, 2000).

Moreover, the events following 9/11, 2001, in New York City have cast a further, more troubled, light on the idea that global activities (such as terrorism) can be "fought" through collective international action. A recent international research project (Papaconstantinou and Pisani-Ferry, 2022, p. 325) has concluded that "Global interdependence is undergoing a fundamental transformation. What was once regarded as a unified system is fast morphing into a multi-polar regime characterised by the coexistence of alternative policy preferences".

Recently, Irwin (2020) has argued that the COVID-19 pandemic has added further momentum to the deglobalisation trend, which is evident in declines in world trade, export bans on "critical" goods such as medical equipment, personal protective equipment and pharmaceuticals and protectionism to avoid "trade dependence", and suggests that the absence of a coordinated and cooperative international response could accelerate destructive "beggar-thy-neighbour" policies not seen since the 1930s.

Whereas governance is a positivistic concept, analysing "what is", *good governance* is obviously a normative concept, analysing "what ought to be". Even though particular international organisations like the United Nations and the Council of Europe have excelled in providing rather abstract definitions of the characteristics of "good governance", we believe that this concept is highly context-dependent. This means that instead of using a simple operational blueprint or definition, the meaning of "good governance" must be negotiated and agreed upon by the various stakeholders in a geographical area or in a policy network.

"Good governance" raises issues such as:

- stakeholder engagement
- the equalities agenda (gender, ethnic groups, age, religion, etc.)
- due process and fair treatment
- ethical and honest behaviour
- transparency
- accountability
- sustainability

Importantly, the implementation of all of the governance principles agreed upon between stakeholders has to be evaluated – ideally, by those same stakeholders.

However, there is as yet no theoretical reason to suppose that all of the principles which we would wish to espouse under the label "good governance" are actually achievable simultaneously. This "good governance impossibility theorem" (mirroring the "general equilibrium impossibility theory", which shows that it is impossible for markets to deliver all of the welfare characteristics which economists have traditionally held dear) is troubling – if valid, it means that politicians need to trade off some principles of good governance against others to which they give a lower priority. This is not a debate that has yet surfaced explicitly in many countries – and it is one that we must suspect politicians will be keen to avoid.

The final section of the book, from Chapter 15 onwards, goes into these public governance issues in greater depth.

What is the role of public management within public governance?

The concepts of public management and public governance are not mutually incompatible. Nevertheless, not all practices of public management are part of public governance, and not all aspects of public governance are part of public management.

For example, some practices of public management revolve around the best way to provide computer support and training to staff of a public agency. There are few public governance dimensions to this decision, which is a common concern for most organisations in all sectors. On the other side, there are issues of co-production of public service between family members and social care staff paid by the local authority, who come together to look after the welfare of a young person with special educational needs and disabilities – the division of roles within the family in liaising with and helping shape decisions by the formal care system is a public governance issue but need not (and usually will not) involve intervention from any public manager.

Consequently, we suggest in this book that the realms of public management and public governance are separate but interconnected. One is not a precursor to the other, nor superior to the other – they do and should co-exist and should work together, through appropriate mechanisms, in order to raise the quality of life of people in the polity.

Of course, not all aspects of public management and public governance can co-exist. When taken to extremes, or interpreted from very contrasting standpoints, contradictions between public management and public governance can indeed be detected. For example, Rod Rhodes (1997, p. 55), writing from a governance perspective, characterises the "New Public Management" (NPM) (one branch of public management) as having four weaknesses: Its intra-organisational focus, its obsession with objectives, its focus on results and the contradiction between competition and "steering" (which often requires collaboration) at its heart. While each of these elements of NPM, if treated in a suitably wide framework, can be reconciled with a governance perspective, an extreme NPM proponent who insists that her/his view of the world is the only way to understand reform of the public sector is bound to antagonise a proponent of the governance perspective (*and vice versa*).

So why should you study public management and governance?

Finally, we want to make a claim for this book that we hope will encourage you to read it with more enthusiasm – and to read more of it than you otherwise might. We want to claim that the study of public management and governance will not only make you a more informed student and a more effective manager (whatever sector you work in), but that it will also make you a more engaged citizen. You should be able to make a greater contribution to the neighbourhood, the local authority, the region and the country in which you live. You may even be able to make a contribution to the quality of life of many citizens elsewhere in the world. And if you decide you do NOT want to know more about public management and governance – just remember that you will be making it more difficult for all those people who will therefore have to work harder to substitute for the contribution you might have made.

So our greatest hope is that, however you use this book, it will help you to find out more about and care more about what it means to be an active citizen, influencing the decisions made in the public domain.

Structure of the book

The book has four main parts:

- an *introductory* part, setting out the role of the public sector, public management and public governance and how these have evolved in recent years in different contexts
- a second part on *public management for public service organisations*, exploring the main managerial functions that contribute to running public services
- a section on *governance* as an emerging theme in the public domain
- and a final part which explores what the future might hold for public management and governance

Questions for review and discussion

1   How would you define public services? Show how this question would be answered by authors from different schools of thought, and try to come up with your own definition.
2   In many cities across the world, food poverty has become a serious problem. Think of a public management and a public governance solution to this problem. Why are they different?

Reader exercises

1   How do you think the image of the public sector has changed in the last five years? Have you personally experienced significant changes to public services, especially since the start of the COVID-19 pandemic? If yes, have these changes shown that the public sector is able to deal effectively with problem issues? If not, why do you think this was so?
2   Does ownership matter – i.e. does the efficiency or effectiveness of a service depend on whether it is in the public or private sector? Why? How would you collect evidence to support your view – and to try to refute it?
3   Find someone in your organisation who read the first, second or third edition of this book (from 2003, 2009 and 2015, respectively). Explore with them how its key themes have changed since they read it – e.g. by comparing chapter headings or summaries in particular chapters.

Class exercises

1 In groups, identify the main differences between "public management" and "private management" and between "public governance" and "corporate governance". Thinking about the news over the past month, identify instances where these concepts might help in deciding who has been responsible for things that have been going wrong in your area or your country. (Now try answering the question in terms of things that have been going right in your area or your country. If you find this difficult, what light does this throw on how the media shape debates on public management and public governance?)

2 In groups, identify some public services in your area that are provided by private sector firms. Each group should identify ways in which these services are less "public" than those that are provided by the public sector. Then compare your answers in a plenary session.

Further reading

Tony Bovaird (2005), 'Public governance: Balancing stakeholder power in a network society'. *International Review of Administrative Sciences*, 71(2): 217–228.

Edoardo Ongaro and Sandra van Thiel (eds.) (2017), *The Palgrave Handbook of Public Administration and Management in Europe*. Cham, Switzerland: Palgrave Macmillan, in Particular Parts I and II.

Kuno Schedler (ed.) (2022), *Elgar Encyclopedia of Public Management*. Cheltenham and Massachusetts: Edward Elgar, in Particular, Part I.

References

Graham Allison (1994), 'Public and private management: Are they fundamentally alike in all unimportant respects?' In F.S. Lane (Ed.), *Current Issues in Public Administration* (5th ed.). New York: St Martin's Press, pp. 14–29.

CIMA (2010), *Corporate governance: developments in the UK*. London: Chartered Institute of Management Accountants.

Thomas Friedmann (2000), *The Lexus and the Olive Tree: Understanding Globalisation*. London: HarperCollins.

Douglas A. Irwin (2020), *The Pandemic Adds Momentum to the Deglobalization*. Trend. (Available at: https://www.piie.com/blogs/realtime-economics/pandemic-adds-momentum-deglobalization-trend).

Mirko Noordegraaf (2015), *Public Management: Performance, Professionalism and Politics*, Palgrave. London and New York: Macmillan.

OECD Watch (2017), *Calling for Corporate Accountability: A Guide to the 2011 OECD Guidelines for Mulitinational Enterprises*. Amsterdam: OECD Watch.

George Papaconstantinou and Jean Pisani-Ferry (2022), 'Main take-aways'. In George Papaconstantinou and Jean Pisani-Ferry (Eds.), *New World, New Rules? Final Report on the Transformation of Global Governance Project 2018–2021*. Florence: European University Institute, pp. 325–340.

Stuart Ranson and John Stewart (1994), *Management for the Public Domain: Enabling the Learning Society*. Basingstoke: Macmillan.

Rod Rhodes (1997), *Understanding Governance: Policy Networks, Governance, Reflexivity and Accountability*. Buckingham: Open University Press.

2 The changing context of public policy

Tony Bovaird and Elke Loeffler

Introduction

Public expenditure in most parts of the world increased rapidly after 1945, as the "welfare state" in its various forms became widespread. However, by the early 1980s, budget deficits provided a major motive for public sector reforms in many parts of the world – reforms that covered both the content of public policy and the way in which public policy was made. In the following 25 years, many governments, at least in the OECD countries, achieved more favourable budget positions (see Chapter 3). However, from 2008, the most severe economic recession in the world economy since the 1930s ushered in a period of financial austerity in public sectors which has persisted in many countries to the time of writing (mid-2023).

Meanwhile, other challenges have emerged since the 1980s to drive reforms in public policy. These new pressures on governments consist of a mixture of external factors (such as the COVID-19 pandemic, global climate change, the ageing society, the information society and the "tabloid society") and internal factors (including the consequences, both planned and unplanned, arising from the "first generation" of public sector reforms, as outlined in Chapter 4). These new pressures have emphasised the quality of life implications of public policies and the governance aspects of public sector organisations. They have typically pushed the public sector in a different direction to the managerial reforms of the 1980s and 1990s. In particular, they have re-emphasised the role of politicians in making tough policy decisions (e.g. on lockdown during COVID), the role of populist politicians in spreading "fake news" and increasing social divisiveness and the importance of an engaged civic society for effective public policies.

Learning objectives

The key learning objectives in this chapter are:

- To identify recent changes in the context of public policy
- To identify the major paradigm shifts in public policy-making in recent decades
- To identify the changing role of politics in public policy

DOI: 10.4324/9781003282839-3

Recent changes in the context of public policy

Most policies have spending implications. If money becomes scarce, policy-makers have less space to manoeuvre. However, financial crises also have an upside – they put pressure on public organisations to become more efficient. In particular, the fiscal crises in most OECD countries in the 1980s (lasting in some until the 1990s) were a key trigger for public sector reforms (see Chapter 4). As these crises receded in many OECD countries before and after the millennium, the financial imperative for public sector reforms remained, but in weaker form, only to reappear in savage form after the global financial crash of 2008.

As well as economic and financial factors, other pressures on governments have remained important, consisting of a mixture of external factors and internal factors. We can map the external factors against the so-called 'PESTEL' headings – political, economic/financial, social, technological, environmental and legal/legislative (see Box 2.1). Many of these external factors have operated for decades, while others have become significantly more important recently, particularly the global health pandemic. The first factor to make a major impact was the global environmental crisis, particularly since the Rio Summit in 1992 (in spite of the growth of "climate change denial" in many governments in the last decades, sometimes driven by desperate attempts to cope with the short-term effects of financial austerity, while shutting their eyes to the long-term potential disasters facing them). The "costs of an ageing society", including the increase in pension costs, have also become a major public policy issue around the world, reinforcing the concern with public sector spending deficits. However, increasingly interest has grown in many countries in the quality of health (not just health care), the quality of life of children, particularly the prevalence of child poverty (not just the quality of public services for children), and the quality of life of the elderly (not just the quality of their social care).

Box 2.1 External factors driving public policy reforms

Political

- new political and social movements in many countries – and internationally – which contest the neo-liberal world view, especially in relation to world trade, the global environment, gender and racial discrimination and attitudes to civil liberties
- rise of populist leaders, advocating radical nationalist and anti-establishment agendas
- loss of popular legitimacy by some long-established public leadership elites, such as political party leaders, local politicians, etc.
- changing expectations, fuelled by globalisation (particularly through tourism and the mass media), about the quality of services that governments should be able to deliver, given what is currently available in other countries
- changing expectations that there will be widespread and intensive engagement with all relevant stakeholders, but particularly citizens, during policy-making and policy implementation processes

- changing expectations about the extent to which public services should be "personalised" to the needs of individual citizens
- increased insistence by key stakeholders (and particularly the media) that new levels of public accountability are necessary, with associated transparency of decision-making and openness of information systems

Economic/financial

- decreasing proportions of the population within the "economically active" category as conventionally defined, with knock-on effects on household income levels and government tax revenues
- economic recession from 2008 in most OECD countries, and many other parts of the world, generally producing falling tax revenues, increasing welfare payments and rising budget deficits for governments, followed since 2020 by COVID-19 lockdown/slowdown and, since February 2022, the energy and cost-of-living crises, sparked partly by the Russian invasion of Ukraine
- increasing (or continuing) resistance by citizens to paying higher rates of tax
- weakening roles of trade unions as labour markets become more flexible (although their resistance to cost of living crises may reverse this)

Social

- traditional institutions such as the family and social class have changed their forms and their meanings in significant ways, so that old assumptions about family behaviour and class attitudes can no longer be taken for granted in policy-making
- traditional sources of social authority and control – police, clergy, teachers etc. – are no longer as respected or influential as formerly
- changing expectations about the core values in society – just as the 1980s saw traditional values such as public duty and individual responsibility being replaced by values of individual self-realisation and rights, so in the 1990s there was a slow return to the understanding that caring and compassion are vital characteristics of a "good society" and that "social capital" is vital to a successful public sector. In the current era of fiscal austerity there is some evidence of growing selfishness, e.g. hostility to welfare benefit recipients, asylum seekers, and economic migrants
- the ageing society, which means that much higher proportions of the population are in high need of health and social care
- changing perceptions about the minimum quality of life for certain vulnerable groups that is acceptable in a well-ordered society – especially in relation to child poverty, minimum wages for the low paid and the quality of life of elderly people (especially those living alone)
- a revolt against conceptions of "difference", whether of gender, race, physical or mental (dis)abilities, as "given" rather than socially constructed, so that disadvantaged groups with increased expectations are seeking new political settlements
- changing perceptions about which behaviours towards vulnerable people are socially acceptable in a well-ordered society – particularly in relation to child abuse, child poverty, domestic violence and levels of anti-social behaviour

- the growing realisation that public services not only alter the material conditions experienced by users and other citizens but also affect the emotional lives of users, citizens and staff, affecting their ability to form fulfilling social relationships within a more cohesive society
- the growing desire by many citizens to realign the balance between paid work, domestic work and leisure time, particularly to tackle some of the gendered inequalities embedded within the current (im)balance of these activities
- the new level of scrutiny that the "tabloid society" provides to the decisions made by politicians and by public officials (and also scrutiny of their private lives), often concentrating more on the "people story" side of these decisions rather than the logic of the arguments

Technological

- technological changes, particularly in ICT, which have meant that public policies can now take advantage of major innovations in ways of delivering services (e.g. through artificial intelligence) and also that the policy-making process itself can be much more interactive than before
- the information society, in which a much higher proportion of the population can make use of new ICT technologies
- increased concern about the efficacy and reliability of "hi-tech" solutions
- renewed interest in "alternative health care" and in "alternative technologies"
- increased risks of hacking and cyber-crime and concern about privacy, data security, growth in the "surveillance society" and misuse of 'big data'
- Misuse of artificial intelligence (AI) and 'decision-making by algorithm'

Environmental

- increasing concerns with global warming and the impact of climate change, e.g. through flooding, hurricanes, "deep freezes"
- willingness to take some serious steps to reduce the usage of non-renewable energy sources and to recycle waste materials, e.g. through a "Green New Deal"
- increasing pressure for governments (and increasingly private firms and third sector organisations, too) to demonstrate the environmental impact of all new legislation, policies and major projects

Legal /legislative

- increasing influence of supra-national bodies – e.g. UN, World Bank, IMF, WTO, EU – in driving legislative or policy change at national level
- growing public discontent in some countries about influence of supra-national or foreign governments on domestic policy (e.g. concern in developing countries with IMF-imposed reforms and in Greece about EU-imposed fiscal austerity and in the UK about "EU-imposed laws")
- increasing legal challenge in the courts to decisions made by government, by citizens, by businesses and by other levels of government

Many of these external factors have tended to push most governments in rather similar directions – e.g. the concern with climate change means most governments have had to prepare "net zero by 20XX" plans, the longstanding slowdown in economic growth has generated austerity programmes, child poverty has driven many governments towards "workfare" programmes (encouraging parents to accept work, even if low-paid, either through incentives such as tax breaks or sanctions such as threatening withdrawal of benefits), the ageing society means that the pensions policies of most OECD countries are now under threat, the information society means that e-government is a major theme everywhere, and the "tabloid society" has driven governments in most countries to take public relations (now generally known as "spin") much more seriously than (even) before.

However, the internal factors that are driving changes in public policy tend to be more context-specific. For example, in many countries governments are contracting out a high proportion of public services and also looking to the private sector for advice and consultancy on many policy-relevant issues. This is sometimes because of the superior access to capital finance enjoyed by the private sector, and sometimes because of the perception that the private sector has greater expertise in certain functions. This has had a number of important policy implications: for example, a new generation of public sector employees no longer expects to enjoy a "job for life", which increases the flexibility of policy-making (but probably also means higher salaries have to be paid and, where greater mobility occurs, may lead to a loss of "institutional memory").

Moreover, in some countries where governments have gone far down the road of contracting out public services to the private sector (see Chapter 8), there have emerged new and serious concerns about fraud and corruption in privately run public services (see Chapter 27). In other countries such as Germany the reverse trend can be observed: Many local authorities have reduced the outsourcing of public services. Here, the inflexible accounting system in the public sector had been a major reason for contracting out public services to private sector companies. However, this often meant that the local council lost influence over how public services were provided, budgets were less transparent and "creative accounting" became more common. Also, most German local authorities by 2009 had introduced resource accounting, which reduces the emphasis on balancing current year cash budgets, so that the benefit-cost ratio of outsourcing appeared less attractive.

Again, the concerns about fragmented and disjointed public policies and governmental structures (often the consequence of "managing at arm's length" or "agencification" – see Chapter 17) have encouraged governments to find more mechanisms for coordination and integration, but in different ways in different countries. While it is widely agreed that today's "wicked" problems can no longer be solved by a single policy or by a single actor, governmental responses have differed significantly, from the emphasis on "joined up government" in the UK and "whole of government" approaches in Australia, to the "seamless services" agenda in the USA and the "one stop shop" initiatives for citizens and investors now seen in many countries.

Public policy at a time of austerity

Since the onset of widespread economic recession in 2008, and subsequent fiscal austerity, two economic issues have appeared to have exercised particularly strong influence over public opinion and public policy – government spending deficits and the national debt (or, more precisely, growth in or the rate of decline in the national debt).

The arguments in this debate, though often crude and ill-informed, have often seemed to revolve around some widely shared assumptions. Indeed, a casual observer might assume that some of the old and long-since discredited "golden rules" of economic policy ("maintain a balanced budget", "keep your currency linked to gold") had been replaced by new golden rules. Yet this is not the case. Let us consider some of the common assumptions behind this policy debate and notice how ill-founded they are.

New golden rule – proposal no. 1: Don't run a budget deficit – and, if you have a deficit, you must get it down. Sounds reasonable? Yet the USA Federal Reserve spent more than $4 trillion in its three rounds of bond buying from 2008 to 2014 (known as "quantitative easing" or QE), contributing a large element of the USA government deficit, and as a result almost certainly prevented a more dire economic situation. Indeed, the growth in US net private worth has been greater than this, halting a precipitate decline occasioned by the housing market collapse of 2007 and the stock market collapse of 2008 (see http://online.wsj.com/articles/SB10001424052702303824204579423183397213204). Moreover, subsequently economic growth was significantly faster in the US than in the Eurozone, which insisted on tight austerity measures and budget deficit reduction plans in all of its members. Was this policy ill-advised? Admittedly, QE does have some complicated consequences (see https://www.bbc.co.uk/news/business-15198789) – it makes subsequent government borrowing more expensive, makes pension schemes more expensive and raises the value of shares and property relative to cash savings, which redistributes wealth towards more wealthy people. We have seen further rounds of major QE since the COVID-19 pandemic and the Russian invasion of Ukraine, which appear, once again, to have staved off severe economic downtowns in most countries – but the final balance of these interventions has still to be seen.

New golden rule – proposal no. 2: Don't allow national debt to rise above a certain level – although, confusingly, the level specified tends to vary between rule proposers. The argument is that this could make a country vulnerable to people wanting to cash in that debt. Logical? Well, not in theory, if most of the national debt is held by local people, so it actually represents their assets! Nor does it make sense if the debt has been accumulated in order to invest in valuable assets – for example, as we discussed above, "quantitative easing" refloated the US economy after 2009 and drove up asset values in housing and industry, so that it increased US economic net worth and could be argued to have actually paid for itself. In any case the US and Denmark have had similar rates of economic growth (2.0% p.a. from 2013 to 2021, IMF data, see https://en.wikipedia.org/wiki/List_of_countries_by_real_GDP_growth_rate#List_(2013–2021)), but the ratio of national debt in the US was 107% in 2021 and only 33% in Denmark. So how reliable a rule is that? Actually, this suggests an alternative golden rule – anyone who talks about "debt" without mentioning in the same sentence the value of corresponding assets should be wholly ignored until they get the point!

What does this add up to? Well, it is essentially a warning that most of the conventional wisdom on economic policy is misinformed. There is likely to be only one golden rule in economic policy – the appropriate spending and tax balance in your country, and in your local authority, depends on your circumstances, NOT on any rules.

Changing paradigms of public policy

In the 1980s, the drivers of change, particularly the financial pressures, pushed most Western countries towards a focus on making the public sector "lean and more competitive while, at the same time, trying to make public administration more responsive to citizens' needs by offering value for money, choice flexibility, and transparency" (OECD, 1993: 9). This was later known as "new public management" (Hood, 1991) (see Box 2.2).

Box 2.2 Elements of New Public Management (or NPM)

- emphasis on performance management
- more flexible and devolved financial management
- more devolved personnel management with increasing use of performance-related pay and personalised contracts
- more responsiveness to users and other customers in public services
- greater decentralisation of authority and responsibility from central to lower levels of government
- greater recourse to the use of market-type mechanisms, such as internal markets, user charges, vouchers, franchising and contracting out
- privatisation of market-oriented public enterprises

Source: OECD (1993: 13).

Whereas some scholars considered this reform movement as a global paradigm change (e.g. Osborne and Gaebler, 1992: 325 and 328), others were more sceptical of the transferability of Westminster-type managerialism to Western Europe and other countries. Certainly, the credence given to the NPM paradigm by public sector practitioners in a major country such as Germany has remained rather low throughout the past three decades.

In NPM, managers were given a much greater role in policy-making than previously in the "old public administration" (PA), essentially at the expense of politicians and service professionals. While this clearly helped to redress the traditional balance in the many countries where management had been rather undervalued in the public sector, it quickly led many commentators to question whether this rebalancing had gone too far. In particular, it led to a vision of the public sector that often seemed peculiarly empty of political values and political debate.

As Chapters 4 and 5 show, different countries responded to the challenges in different ways, depending on a variety of factors. However, one factor in most of these responses was a concern with the governance dimension of public policy and the governance of public sector organisations (see Chapter 15). This governance-oriented response tended to emphasise:

- the importance of "wicked problems" that cut across neat service lines, so that "quality of life" improvements are more important than "quality of service" improvements
- the need for these "wicked problems" to be tackled cooperatively, because they cannot be solved by only one agency – thus the need for multi-stakeholder networking; for example, evidence indicates that clinical care may account for only 20% of health outcomes, while socioeconomic, behavioral, and environmental factors determine the rest (PCIC, 2023)
- the need for agreed "rules of the game" that stakeholders will stick to in their interactions with one another, so that they can trust each other in building new joint approaches to the problems they are tackling – extending "corporate governance" principles into the sphere of "public governance"

- the critical importance of certain principles that should be embedded in all interactions which stakeholders have with each other, including transparency, integrity, honesty, fairness and respect for diversity

Of course, the set of responses described above have developed gradually rather than overnight. Indeed, many of today's wicked problems are the emerging and unresolved problems from yesterday. Also, in many cases, fiscal pressures have deepened and have become mixed with the new demands on governments. Which pressures are dominant and which are less relevant depend essentially on the setting (see Chapters 4 and 5). As public policy contexts become more differentiated in the future, the variety of governance reforms is likely to be much greater than in the NPM era.

Pollitt and Bouckaert (2017: 19) also use the concept of the "Neo-Weberian State" (NWS) to describe a public sector model characteristic of stable and prosperous Western European democracies such as Germany, France and the Nordic group. NWS consists of key "Weberian" characteristics such as the central role of the state and the preservation of a public service with a distinct status, to which they add principles such as citizen-orientation and performance management. While Pollitt and Bouckaert argue that NWS is a hybrid concept which consists of rather contradictory Weberian and neo-characteristics, Byrkjeflot et al. (2018) consider that it is more useful to distinguish between "degrees of Weberianism". After all, the Weberian state was originally conceived as an ideal-type, not a depiction of reality.

These challenges put public agencies under pressure to adapt. Whereas some agencies respond to the new environment quickly or even proactively, others change more slowly or not at all. As a result, old and new structures and management approaches are often found side by side (Hood, 1991). This messy situation is multiplied by the many different kinds of reform going on – some of which are described in Parts II and III in this book. Figure 2.1

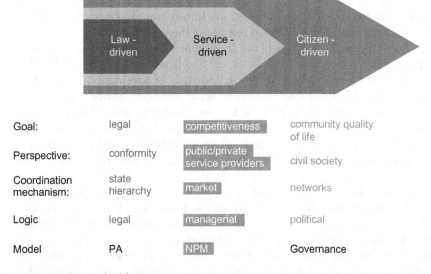

Figure 2.1 Types of public agencies.

Source: Translated and adapted from Gerhard Banner (2002).

shows the main directions of reform as a movement from law-driven ("*Rechtsstaat*") to service-driven to citizen-driven agencies, but with each of these co-existing with each other to some degree in any given agency. The importance of the different goals and logics and how different coordination mechanisms (also referred to as "modes of governance") are linked with each other is often context- and service-specific. As Rod Rhodes (1997) suggests, "it's the mix that matters".

Of course, it is not enough to diagnose what is happening in the public policy system. It is necessary also to decide what to do next. Pollitt and Bouckaert (2017: 115) suggest that there are four trajectories (the "4Ms") for public sector reforms:

- *maintenance* of existing administrative structures and processes – usually involving small, incremental changes
- *modernisation* of the system, by seeking out opportunities for improved services and better regulation through major changes to keep the state machine fully professional and up-to-date. This option has one variant that emphasises the need for deregulation and "empowerment" of lower levels of managers, while another variant emphasises the need for citizen participation and stakeholder engagement
- *marketisation* of the system, by introducing as many market-type mechanisms as possible (e.g. through competition and performance management)
- *minimisation* of the administrative system, by divesting the state of as many tasks as possible, e.g. through privatisation, contracting out and cutting "red-tape"

This latter option has been referred to by some academics as the "hollowing out of the state", and they typically add other mechanisms such as the loss of national government powers to international organisations such as the WTO or the European Union. For much of the 1980s and early 1990s, this option haunted the public policy arena as a spectre threatening the extinction of the public sector as we know it. However, such fears have now somewhat abated. The debate is now rather which (plural) roles the state should play, which (plural) reform modes it should adopt and in which context. As the analysis of Pollitt and Bouckaert demonstrates, different regimes at different times have leaned towards one or other of these trajectories but few have consistently followed just one of them.

Moreover, a major theoretical critique of the "hollowing out of the state" and "network governance" perspectives comes from Mark Bevir and Rod Rhodes (e.g. Bevir and Rhodes, 2003). In their work, they undertake a "decentred" analysis of governance, i.e. one that does not accept the "truth" of any single narrative about what governance is and how it evolves over time. They attempt to "unpack the institutions of governance through a study of the various contingent meanings that inform the actions of the relevant individuals" (Bevir, 2003: 209). They point out, for example, that the network governance narrative is only one of several that provides insight into the current state of governance around the world.

Taking these various lines of argument into account, we would argue that the dilemma outlined in the "hollowing out of the state" debate misinterprets the issue at stake. The most important question is not whether the state will remain more powerful than other players but which set of formal (legal) and informal rules, structures and processes will be needed so that the state, the private and third sectors, citizens and other important stakeholders can each believe that they exercise power over decisions by the other stakeholders, in ways that protect their interests and allow the creation of win-win situations for all parties concerned. And if this is not possible, what changes are necessary to these political rules, structures and processes in order to ensure acceptable minimum outcomes (both in terms of quality of life and in terms of quality of governance processes), from the viewpoint of key stakeholders, which we would interpret as meaning, in particular, the most disadvantaged and vulnerable groups in society?

The politics of public policy

The role of politics in the public sector, which might seem in theory to be central, has for a long time been under pressure from two other major sources – the professional groupings who tend to believe that they are uniquely well informed about policy and the managerial cadres who tend to believe that they are uniquely expert in getting the various professional groupings to work together effectively. More recently, a third set of actors has tried to push its way onto this already crowded stage – the groups of citizens and other stakeholders who have been told that they alone know best what they want, at least in terms of services that directly affect their quality of life. So, is there still room for politicians to play a role upon this stage?

First, it is important to recognise that politicians can play a number of roles – leadership of their polity (at a variety of levels), catalyst for and driver of policy and behaviour change for their society, strategy-making for the organisation, partnership building with other organisations and with other stakeholders (including other communities, other countries and even other political parties), watchdog over the decisions made within their polity, lobbyist in relation to decisions made in other polities (including national, regional and local levels) and last, but not least, representation of and advocate for their constituents. Not all of these roles are equally supported by the bureaucratic structures of the public sector – in particular, constituency roles and advocacy for particular citizens tend to be rather poorly supported by officials, being largely regarded as "political" and therefore for political parties to support – a paradox, since the legitimacy of all politicians springs from their election from a constituency or by citizens more generally.

How does this role differ in different contexts? Not only do the fundamental roles of politicians alter, as we move from the global to the local stage, but so do the relative priorities between these roles, often influenced by who are the dominant stakeholders with whom politicians have to interact in their area. Furthermore, political roles vary, depending on the balance in the polity between representational and participative democracy.

Starting at the global level, *global politics* is mainly about security, trade and environment, and is played out by heads of state and ministers. However, many of these decisions have major implications at national, regional, local and neighbourhood levels – e.g. the "peace dividend" can be a bonus for national social programmes (more government funds are available) but very bad for local employment where army and naval bases are closed. Again, global environmental strategy involves clashing national interests ("carbon guzzlers" and oil/gas producers versus the rest), while global environmental improvement often entails "think global, act local" approaches. So national and local politicians cannot ignore the global level in their policy-making, even though their role may essentially be lobbying for their own interests.

National politics is often the most ideologically driven, as it is the main forum for debating the ideas that determine election results (national and local) and subsequent legislation. Consequently, here we see frequent clashes between ideological viewpoints, between national power groupings (which can variously be categorised as classes, "fractions of capital", dominant coalitions of stakeholders, communities of interest, etc.) and between the "political" sensitivities of party politicians and the "technical" recipes favoured by the "technocracy". Policy-making at this level has a strong emphasis on injecting "political fla-vour" into professionally designed strategies.

Regional politics has different connotations in each country. In some countries, there is a clear desire to allow expression to feelings of separate identity, as well as differing priorities – e.g. in Spain's *autonomias* and the devolved assemblies in Scotland, Wales and Northern Ireland in the UK. In other cases, regional government has been deliber-ately formulated as a counterweight to central government (e.g. in the US since 1776 and, nearly 200 years later, in the post-1945 German constitution, largely fashioned in the US mould). At the regional level, politicians tend to be in a half-way house between national and local politics. Where the region is strong (e.g. US states, some powerful Spanish *autonomias* such as the Basque Country and Catalonia, some German *Länder* such as Bavaria and Baden-Württemberg), then regional politicians can have a national and even international significance. Where regions are weak (e.g. Spanish *autonomias* such as Murcia, the regions in France and in many Central and Eastern European countries), regional policies may play merely a "gap-filling" role between cen-tre and localities.

Local politics still usually has some ideological flavour but this is often idiosyncratic (local political parties often deviate in their views from their national parties) and less important than stances on local issues. The role of the strategic politician locally is partly to lead the local community towards new goals, partly to help the locality to compete against other areas and partly to represent the community where policies from other levels of government are not helpful locally. Clearly, many local politicians are non-strategic, worried only about "patch politics" and working for their constituents to improve the outcomes from public services and from dealings with other agencies. This means that many officials experience local politics as an irritant in policy implementation rather than a contribution to the policy-making process, which may explain why many have such a negative view of it.

Neighbourhood politics is usually far from the ideological level and is dominated by local issues – often pitting local politicians against their own party colleagues and leaders. Indeed, neighbourhood politics often involves balancing of interests within and between neigh-bourhoods, forging coalitions on issues and across interest groups that have little parallel at any higher level of politics – NIMBYism (the "Not In My Back Yard" syndrome) is the most obvious example of this. Consequently, highly rational strategies, cooked up by well-informed professionals and backed by top politicians in the local council and nationally, may still fail because they "don't go down well on the street".

Clearly, there is still a major role for political input into policy-making, even in this era of highly professionalised "public management" and partnership-based "network governance". However, the autonomy of political decisions should not be exaggerated. There are many different pressure points by which other stakeholders can drive politi-cians down roads that they do not personally like very much. Indeed, political platforms are usually designed to take on board the interests of a wide coalition of stakeholders. At worst, it can mean that politicians seek to "please everyone, all the time" – then strategic policy-making becomes next to impossible. Only if politicians are prepared to weather adverse comment, when they follow strategic policies they believe in, can they claim to exercise political leadership and help their organisations and partnerships to manage strategically.

Summary

In the 1980s, fiscal pressures were hugely important as drivers of change in public policy.

After almost two decades of economic growth up to 2008, fiscal pressures reasserted themselves and, in many countries, remained strong drivers of public policy, until the COVID-19 pandemic and the energy crisis subsequent to the war in Ukraine reinforced these pressures. However, throughout the past 40 years, many other major changes in the political, economic, social, technological, environmental and (international) legislative fields have impacted on public policy-making, the implications of many of which are only slowly becoming evident.

The paradigms of public policy-making have changed significantly during the past three decades – the "old public administration" was partly replaced by the "new public management", which in turn has been partly supplanted by the "public governance" perspective. However, current public policy-making in most countries still has strong elements of all three approaches – and it is not clear whether or how these will converge to produce a more "unitary" approach in the future. In any case, further perspectives will no doubt emerge that will partly borrow from, and partly replace, these perspectives.

Politics is integral to policy-making, but the role of politicians, which has never been as clear as suggested in the conventional model of democratic decision-making ("the primacy of politics"), is today even more complex, given the roles that are played in public decision-making by professional groups, managers, engaged citizens and other stakeholders.

Questions for review and discussion

1 Which of the main groups of factors driving changes in public policy (listed in Box 2.1) have been of most importance in your country in the last five years? Is this likely to continue in the next five years?
2 What are the main paradigms of public policy-making and what are the main differences between them?
3 How consistent with each other are the analyses of the characteristics of NPM which are to be found in different chapters of this book (e.g. Chapters 2, 4, 5, 9, 19)?

Reader exercises

1 Get a copy of a serious newspaper, such as *The Guardian*, *Le Monde* or *Frankfurter Allgemeine Zeitung*. Try to find examples where factors listed in Box 2.1 are cited as influencing current government policy decisions.
2 In the same newspaper, identify some politicians whose activities are described in detail. Identify the roles that they are playing. How many of these roles would you describe as "policy-making" roles? And at what geographical level is this policy being decided?
3 In the same newspaper, identify instances where the term "debt" has been used without any reference to associated "assets" and where the term "budget deficit" has been used without any reference to "consequent changes in economic growth and net worth".

Class exercise

Divide into groups. Each group should identify the four major policy areas (at national or international level) where it believes current government policy needs to change. For each of these, the group should suggest how such changes might be initiated in the current political climate.

The groups should then come together and compare notes. Where there are commonalities between the lists, suggesting that there is some consensus between the groups on the need for change, discuss why these policies have not yet been altered.

Further reading

Paul Cairney (2020), *Understanding public policy: Theories and issues*. London: Bloomsbury.

Christopher Pollitt and Geert Bouckaert (2017), *Public management reform: A comparative analysis - into the age of austerity* (4th ed.). Oxford: Oxford University Press.

References

Gerhard Banner (2002), 'Zehn Jahre kommunale Verwaltungsmodernisierung – Was wurde erreicht und was kommt danach?' In Erik Meurer and Günther Stephan (Eds.), *Rechnungswesen und, Controlling*, 4(June): 7/313–42, Freiburg (Haufe Verlag).

Mark Bevir (2003), 'A decentred theory of governance'. In Henrik Paul Bang (Ed.), *Governance as social and political communication*. Manchester: Manchester University Press, pp. 200–221.

Mark Bevir and Rod Rhodes (2003), 'Decentring British governance: From bureaucracy to networks'. In Henrik Paul Bang (Ed.), *Governance as social and political communication*. Manchester: Manchester University Press, pp. 61–78.

Haldor Byrkjeflot, Paul du Gay and Carsten Greve (2018), 'What is the "neo-Weberian State" as a regime of public administration?' In E. Ongaro and S. Van Thiel (Eds.), *The Palgrave Handbook of Public Administration and Management in Europe*. London: Palgrave Macmillan. https://doi.org/10 .1057/978-1-137-55269-3_50.

Christopher Hood (1991), 'A public management for all seasons?' *Public Administration*, 69(1): 3–19.

OECD (1993), *Public management developments, survey 1993*. Paris: OECD.

David Osborne and Ted Gaebler (1992), *Reinventing government: How the entrepreneurial spirit is transforming the public sector*. Reading, MA: Addison-Wesley.

PCIC (2023), *Social determinants of health*. https://pcictx.org/population-health/social-determinants-of-health#:~:text=From%20the%20University%20of%20Wisconsin,%25%20(see%20Figure%20 1).

Christopher Pollitt and Geert Bouckaert (2017), *Public management reform: A comparative analysis - into the age of austerity* (4th ed.). Oxford: Oxford University Press.

R. A. W. Rhodes (1997), 'It's the mix that matters: From marketization to diplomacy'. *Australian Journal of Public Administration*, 56(2): 40–53.

3 The changing role of public spending

Peter M. Jackson

Introduction

What is the right size for the public sector; is public spending too big or too small; is the composition of public spending wrong? These simple questions do not have simple answers. It all depends. The answers depend upon the questioner's vision of the purpose of the state; her ideological stance; how she weighs up the costs and benefits of two imperfect social institutions – the state and the market. Different perspectives will, in a diverse society, produce different answers. It is these differences and their resolution that are the stuff of politics.

In this chapter the perspective that will be presented is that of the economist, in particular the political economist. By its nature it will be a partial contribution to what is a complex debate. Those who provide simple, either/or, contributions do not understand the nature of the issue.

Learning objectives

This chapter will look at the following issues:

- The economic role and scope of the state
- The trends in public spending and some of the forces that shape them
- The changing composition of public spending
- The implications for public management

The entangled public sector

The implicit framework that underpins much of public sector economics and public management views the public sector as an autonomous and exogenous entity within an economy. The public sector is assumed to exist separate from the market (private) sector. Choices and decisions made in the private sector are based upon individuals' tastes and preferences. Public choices are shaped by some conception of collective preferences and are made by political agents, acting on behalf of the citizens of a country, in a non-market setting.

It is, however, important to look beyond this simple, private sector/public sector dualism. What is the relationship between the two sectors? Public sector (or more precisely "state") involvement in the private sector is one of intervention. The state, using its monopoly of legitimate powers (Weber, 1922: 78), intervenes to control private/market activities. The state controls, regulates, and corrects those private decisions which have the potential to

DOI: 10.4324/9781003282839-4

impose negative or adverse impacts upon other members of society. In addition to intervening in the affairs of the private sector the public sector also creates the "rules of the game" (i.e. laws) that enable market exchanges and that protect private property rights. The public sector is also a producer of goods and services. Whether a good or service should be produced by the public or the private sector depends upon the characteristics of the good/service and upon individuals' ideological preferences.

The world, however, is more complex than the simple dualism suggested in public management texts. The public sector is embedded in a socio-economic milieu and has a symbiotic relationship with the private sector. This is the perspective found in Polanyi (1957: 250): "economies are embedded and enmeshed in institutions, economic and non-economic". Rather than seeing resource allocation decisions being taken either through the market *or* the state, it is more useful to think of the two sectors, at times, cooperating – each complements the other. Rather than a simple linear relationship existing between the two sectors, it is better described as one of complexity, non-linearity, and entanglement. Changes in one sector can, through complex positive and negative feedback mechanisms, have unexpected consequences for the other. This presents challenges to policy makers, who are often taken by surprise at the unintended consequences of a policy intervention.

The notion of the embedded and entangled public sector does not replace the private/public sector dualism. Rather it enriches it. Thus, we can imagine a continuum between, at one end, a pure market economy with no public sector (i.e. pure laissez-faire) and, at the other end, a pure public sector or collective economy, with no market sector (often thought of as a fully planned "command and control" economy). The structure of real economies lies between these two extremes, depending upon the dominant political ideology prevailing at the time.

The framework of the entangled public sector gives deeper insights into several fundamental questions such as:

• How does the public sector influence economic growth?
• How does the interaction between the public and private sector influence the development of the welfare state?
• What social forces shape government decision making?
• What is the role of ideas, institutions, and culture in shaping socio-economic policies?

The state and the market are intertwined. They are connected. States do not exist as exogenous agents lying somewhere outside of the economy. States have a role to play in facilitating economic processes and decisions. It is within this complex environment of state and market entanglement that public sector management takes place. Also, the departments of central and local government along with the various agencies of government are themselves entangled, thereby adding to the complexities and challenges of public sector management.

(Note: some readers might object to concepts such as the "state", the "public sector", and the "government" being used as if they are interchangeable. They are correct to do so. In the meantime we think of them as "non-market actors" endowed with the authority to make and enforce laws, to raise taxes, and to borrow.)

The economic role of the state

The state in a mixed capitalist economy is ubiquitous. Zoning in cities; anti-monopoly or competition policies; safety legislation to protect consumers and employees; measures to control pollution and to safeguard the biodiversity of the natural environment; contract enforcement legislation and bankruptcy laws are only a small number of examples of how the state is woven into the fabric of society. How are these and other economic activities of the state justified?

In *The Wealth of Nations* (1776), Adam Smith set out what he regarded to be the minimum activities of a state. These are the provision of essential "public goods" such as the protection of the state from external threats ("defence of the realm") and the internal protection of the population by the provision of law and order. The state should also define and enforce private property rights, enforce contracts, and make provisions for education along with "certain public works and institutions".

The borders of the state have, however, shifted over time to incorporate new activities. This reflects changes in events, differing political philosophies, and, more recently, a deeper understanding of the pathologies of capitalist economies. These changes have influenced the location and shape of the boundaries of the state. Institutions are, however, dynamic. They are subject to innovation and evolve over time, reshaping the contours of the state.

Consider some of the changes that have taken place over the past 150 years. Industrialization was accompanied by the movement and concentration of the population into cities and urban areas. This was accompanied by a breakdown of traditional systems of social protection, for which the state gradually took responsibility, culminating in the emergence of the "welfare state", which was introduced first by Bismarck in late 19th-century Germany and in the UK by the 1945 Atlee government, following the Beveridge Report of 1942, which recommended tackling of the "5 giants" of want, disease, ignorance, squalor, and idleness. This was the basis of the "welfare state" and many of the new social policies that emerged, together with the public spending required to implement them.

Industrialization created new jobs and increases in real income. This in turn generated the increase in tax revenues necessary to finance the social reforms. In the early 20th century differences in per capita public expenditure between countries were explained by differences in the population, the degree of urbanization, social organization, the level of industrialization, and the degree of openness of the economy. More open economies faced risks from higher imports and risks to workers' jobs.

Tackling the "5 giants" meant that the number and size of spending departments in central and local government grew, along with employment in the public sector. The state was now a producer, a regulator, a protector, and an enabler. These additional functions and roles not only added to the state's external and internal complexity and entanglement but also increased public expenditure.

Economic foundations of government intervention

Why are some production and consumption activities organized within markets, whilst others use non-market forms such as the public sector, voluntary organizations, charities, or not for profits? Markets are often favoured because, it is argued, they are more efficient in allocating scarce resources compared to other organizational forms. Markets use prices to coordinate the billions of transactions that occur in any single day. Markets ensure that an economy's resources are allocated to their best use, in accordance with individuals' preferences. Pro-market advocates claim that government interventions will reduce greatly the market system's efficiency and effectiveness. They favour a minimal state.

Whilst there is a logic to the pro-marketers' argument, it only applies to perfect markets. Also, it requires very strict and demanding assumptions. First, there must be a very large number of producers and consumers; the decisions of any single producer or consumer will not impact on market prices. Consumers' preferences are fixed and determined external to the market system, and the product sold on each market is homogeneous. There must be a set of well-defined and enforceable property rights and contracts, along with zero transaction costs. A complete set of markets including future and insurance markets and markets for products not yet imagined must exist. There are no gaps in any individual's information or knowledge; all risks are known and computable; there are no information biases or distorted information; and there are no gaps or holes in markets. The decisions of one economic agent are assumed to have no material impact on others, and producers are assumed not to collude. This very lengthy and strong set of assumptions forms the foundations of perfect or efficient markets.

The consumer and her preferences are sovereign, i.e. the consumer is free to choose alternatives that are in her own best interests and is free from interventions or directions from government or anyone else. It is this freedom and liberty bestowed by the market system that is cherished and highly valued by libertarians, neoliberals, and the new public management in its simplest forms.

A moment's reflection soon concludes that these assumptions are unlikely to exist in practice. Monopolies and other observed forms of market structure violate the assumptions. Producers have an incentive to collude, and, in some instances, consumers will form purchasing consortia. A complete set of future and insurance markets does not exist either because there are technical problems setting them up or because they are too expensive to establish. Transactions costs are not zero and information is not complete, unbiased, or equally distributed (think of "fake news").

Market failure is a situation where the market system fails to behave as a set of perfectly competitive markets would. It can have important negative consequences. This creates a potential role for government. Acting to achieve what is best in the "public interest", government can intervene in the market system to create a more efficient allocation of resources. Monopolists, or a few firms who dominate a market (oligopolists), are in a strong position to exploit consumers and to transfer income from consumers to shareholders. Government can act as a countervailing power by introducing competition policies that will protect the interests of consumers and ensure a more efficient allocation of resources.

When markets fail to exist, as in the case of most futures and insurance markets, the government could step in as "insurer of last resort". Examples include the collective provision of insurance to deal with the costs of natural events such as earthquakes, landslides, or flooding. Some government action during the COVID-19 pandemic falls into this category.

Some industries are categorized as "natural monopolies", which are characterized by high fixed costs; economies of scale in both production and consumption; no close substitutes; and high barriers to entry. Economies of scale in consumption and production arise from network effects – once investment in a distribution network has taken place then the marginal cost of adding an extra consumer is almost zero. Examples of natural monopolies include gas, water, electricity, and telecommunications. Natural monopolies, like all monopolies, if left to the market will create an inefficient allocation of resources. Government can prevent this by taking the natural monopoly into public ownership (i.e. "nationalization") or regulating its market by using price controls.

Many market decisions made by individuals (consumers and producers) have material impacts on others. These impacts are called "externalities" and can be positive (good) or negative (bad). Externalities are sometimes called unpriced effects because there are no markets to trade the externalities. This is another example of a market failure. In the case of a negative externality, such as pollution, producers dump pollutants into the atmosphere, the sea, or waterways. They do not pay for dumping their pollutants and so the outputs of the products they produce (along with the levels of pollution) are greater than they would be if they were charged. The atmosphere, the sea, and the waterways are examples of "common pool resources". Because there are no well-defined property rights to common pool resources they tend to be overused (exploited). This is called the "tragedy of the commons". Pollution, excessive uncontrolled use of natural resources, as in the case of overfishing, tree felling in the Amazon rainforest, over-hunting of rare but highly valued species, and the destruction of natural habitats resulting in the narrowing of biodiversity are examples of tragedies from market failure. In such cases, decisions that seem to be rational to the individual decision maker are not rational for the group as a whole – i.e. an outcome is created that no single person desires. This should also include future generations, who will inherit a world that is not of their making without having a voice in today's decisions. To deal with these tragedies means finding a collective solution, but collective solutions generally do not come from voluntary actions. Consequently, governments can establish and enforce collective solutions where the market fails to do so. Government policies could make the polluters pay, e.g. through a pollution tax; or establish markets, e.g. for carbon credits, or regulate resource use, e.g. by forbidding use of some polluting fuels.

A current example of external benefits is those that arise from a mass vaccination programme, e.g. for COVID-19. Leaving the decision to be vaccinated to individuals will, most likely, result in few people choosing vaccination, especially if they have to pay. Everyone calculates rationally that "if everyone else gets vaccinated, then the chances of me contracting COVID are low. I can save money and inconvenience by not being vaccinated – I can get a 'free ride' on the decisions made by others". If this seems rational to one individual, then it seems rational for all, and the result is that no-one, or a only very small number of people, will get vaccinated. Consequently, the virus will spread and deaths from the virus will increase. In a situation like this the government can, to protect the population, make the vaccines and testing kits free, and mandate practices (enforceable in law) such as mask wearing and social distancing. It can also provide the public with information and in the limit take the decision to "lock down".

In 1954 the Nobel Prize-winning economist Paul Samuelson introduced the concept of "public goods". Pure public goods are non-excludable and non-rival. They are non-excludable because they do not have well defined property rights, and they are non-rival because one person's consumption of them does not reduce the amount available to all other consumers. The market fails to provide pure public goods because no one has an incentive to pay for them (non-excludability) and, therefore, no producer will have an incentive to produce them. If, however, there is a demand for such goods and the market fails to produce them, then how is this demand to be satisfied? A voluntary solution would require a group of consumers to get together and commission a producer. But there is an incentive for some group members to opt out when it comes to paying their share of the costs ("free riders" again). Consequently, voluntary solutions, like markets, are likely to fail. The public sector can overcome these problems by providing the public good and financing it from compulsory taxation.

Because the pure public goods concept is a theoretical construct, there are very few examples of these goods, but national defence and street lighting (a local public good) are very close to the definition. My consumption of the benefits of street lighting does not diminish the benefits available to my neighbours. Street lighting is non-excludable and non-rival, as too is national defence.

Finally, Richard Musgrave (1959) defined "merit goods" (which are also called "positive freedom goods") as those which provide benefits that should be available to all individuals, irrespective of their personal circumstances (income, race, gender, age etc.). Examples of such goods are education, health care and social care. These goods have strong positive externalities, and on that basis alone could justify government provision, but there are also social justice arguments to support the case for government provision. Individuals who, however, are not satisfied with the level or quality of merit goods provided by the public sector often have the option of accessing these goods from the market.

"Demerit goods" (bads) refer to activities such as gambling, excessive consumption of alcohol, sugar, or salt, and the use of certain classes of drugs. These activities are deemed to be bad for individuals' health and wellbeing and should, therefore, be discouraged. The agency which has the legitimate power to do something about these issues is the government. It can use taxation, legislation, regulation and persuasion via information campaigns to discourage the production or consumption of demerit goods. This area of government intervention is highly controversial. Some regard such government intervention to be intrusive and a threat to freedom of choice and individual liberties. They seek to curb the spread of the "paternalistic state".

There is also a category of markets which most citizens will wish government to outlaw. These are called "noxious" or "repugnant" markets. The types of commodities or services traded in these markets are arms, drugs, toxic waste, child labour, human body parts, child prostitution and endangered exotic species. Modern day slavery would be included in this group. Only government has the legislative power to combat these kinds of practices.

Market failures are ubiquitous. This, however, does not imply that government should intervene to correct all market failures. It simply signals a potential role for government. Before government gets involved the failure needs to be of substantial significance to the wellbeing and rights of members of society – and the intervention needs to be likely to work and devoid of potential net-negative side effects. The decision to get involved will reflect society's set of preferences and what is defined to be in the public interest.

Capitalist market-based economies are inherently unstable. They are never in equilibrium and imbalances and instabilities are revealed as unemployment, inflation, and balance of payments difficulties. These market system ("macro-economic") pathologies can also be thought of as another kind of market failure, where the entire market system fails to achieve equilibrium at full employment. Keynes argued successfully that governments can intervene through the management of aggregate demand and reduce unemployment and moderate inflationary price rises. Demand can be stimulated or reduced by changing tax and public expenditure levels (fiscal policy) or by changing interest rates and/or the money supply (monetary policy). However, the most effective levels and mix of macro-economic policy levers continue to be hotly disputed on both ideological and technical levels.

Finally, what about the distribution of income and wealth that emerges from a competitive market system? This will depend upon the initial distribution of rights within the economy, especially property rights. If the initial distribution is not socially just, then the market-based distribution will also not be just.

The distribution of incomes also depends upon individuals' rights to access markets and opportunities. There are, however, many barriers including various forms of discrimination based, for example, on gender, race, religion or age. Government can do much to change the final distribution of income and wealth. It could extend rights to those denied them, it can legislate against forms of discrimination, and it can use the fiscal system. The use of a progressive tax system, that is, one where the marginal rate of tax is higher for high income earners, will reduce income inequalities. If the tax system is coupled with public expenditure policies that focus grants, subsidies, and other social expenditures on those of lower incomes then redistribution of purchasing power (income) can be significant.

The case for government intervention given above, and summarized in Box 3.1, is partial and only deals with the problems of a capitalist system, as seen through the lens of the economist. Other disciplines focus on other aspects. Also, it only sets out a potential case for government intervention – how a government chooses to respond to market failures and inequalities depends upon political preferences, social values, and ideological considerations, as well as economic analysis. Nor is the state endowed with superior knowledge to guide its decisions. Just as markets fail, so too do governments, for similar reasons. In the final analysis a choice must be made between two highly imperfect systems, the market and the state, or more likely a mix of the two.

Why do public sector managers need to know about the underlying economic logic of government intervention? It places the rationale for many of the activities of the state in the context of wider political economy controversies and highlights the policy trade-offs between efficiency and equity. Moreover, the nature of the goods and services that are provided by government is generally much more complex than those traded on markets. This is important when considering specific issues such as measuring the performance of a government department. What does value for money or effectiveness mean in such a context (see also Chapter 12)?

Box 3.1 The role of the state is...

...allocative

- Correcting market failures through regulation, taxation, subsidies and providing goods and services.

...distributional

- Achieving a just and fair society by regulation; adjusting rights; giving access to markets in the face of discrimination, progressive taxation, and subsidies.

...stabilization

- Controlling economic growth, unemployment, and inflation by fiscal and monetary policies.

Source: Musgrave (1959).

The size, composition and growth of the state

Public expenditure data record how much government spends upon its activities. This expenditure represents the purchase of public sector inputs (labour, capital and consumables) that are required to produce the goods, services, and policies of government. In this section high level total public expenditure will be examined. To understand the details of each public service it is necessary to drill down to the service's micro-processes, as discussed in some later chapters.

The boundaries of the state have changed over time and differ from one country to another. These variations reflect different policy responses, differences in beliefs about what constitutes "the good society", and social and demographic differences. Variations in real incomes per capita indicate the availability of tax revenues to finance public services. There is no suggestion that these factors *determine* public expenditure. Rather, they might be taken into consideration when decision makers are making public choices.

In 1870 the public sectors of the world were relatively small compared to market activities. Laissez-faire prevailed, and government was confined to the core activities that had been set out by Adam Smith. Defence spending increased during the world conflicts of 1914–18 and 1939–45 but returned to normal levels following the peace. The 1950s and 1960s were years of post-war reconstruction and infrastructure building. The UK established the foundations of the welfare state, as did many other countries, especially Japan. During the years of the Cold War, western nations strengthened their spending on defence, while the growth in real per capita incomes, up to the early 1970s, provided resources for an expansion in public services such as education, health care, and personal social services.

Table 3.1 shows the growth in the relative sizes of the public sectors in some high- and low-income countries, from 1870 until 2020, measured by public expenditure as a percentage of GDP. Of course, international comparisons of public expenditure over time are fraught with problems and pitfalls. Differences exist in the definitions of categories of spending and of accounting conventions. Therefore, the exact number in the tables is not important, but rather the general patterns and changes over time.

For each country over the past 150 years the relative size of public spend has increased. The institution of government has become a feature of importance in the lives of citizens.

The years 1950 to 1980, referred to as the "golden age of public sector intervention", were the age of Keynesianism. During the 1970s, however, the tide started to turn against Keynesian policies. It was argued that the public sector had become too large and was partly the cause of poor economic performance. Commentary at the time argued that public expenditure and public deficits forced up interest rates and crowded out private sector spending, especially on investment. Moreover, advocates for a smaller public sector emphasized the distortionary effects of taxation which had negative impacts on entrepreneurship and

Table 3.1 Public expenditure % GDP 1870–2020

	1870	1900	1910	1930	1940	1950	1960	1970	1980	1990	2000	2010	2020
France	13.2	11.4	10.6	18.6		24.1	22.8	20.5	45.9	49.6	51.7	56.6	62.4
Germany		17.9	19.5	16.3		27.2	22.9	39.5	48.2	44.7	45.1	47.9	51.1
UK	7.1	10.8	8.1	18.7	28.4	33.1	33.1	42.0	47.6	41.1	36.8	50.6	50.3
Canada	4.9	6.1	6.0	7.7	18.6	14.9	14.9	36.1	41.6	48.8	41.1	43.8	52.5
Japan		1.1	3.1	2.9	4.0	15.9	18.4	20.3	33.5	30.1	37.3	39.8	46.7
USA	3.8	2.7	2.2	3.6	8.9	13.4	28.3	32.3	34.3	37.2	33.9	42.5	46.2
Brazil		15.5	13.1	11.2	10.8	8.7	13.7	11.4	6.8		35.3	40.4	42.7
Russia		23.8		12.7	5.5	6.1					32.8	38.5	38.8
India	6.3	7.2	6.1	5.5	5.3	5.3	11.2	11.7	17.5	27.2	27.1	27.3	31.1
China										30.1	17.1	22.7	36.9

Notes: High-income countries: France, Germany, UK, Canada, Japan, USA.

Low-income countries: Brazil, Russia, India, China.

Sources: World Bank; IMF; author's calculation.

economic growth. Politicians and public sector bureaucrats, involved in policy decisions, were thought to pursue their own self-interests rather than those of citizens, resulting in poor policy choices (Tullock, 1967). Overall, the public sector was deemed to be inefficient, lacking the appropriate incentives and managerial skills required to deliver value for money. However, there was little evidence to support many of these claims.

The 1980s were dominated by the Thatcher governments (1979–90) in the UK and the Reagan administrations (1981–89) in the USA. Both of these governments were elected on manifestos that promised to roll back the frontiers of the state and to improve the efficiency and effectiveness of government departments. During this period many of the foundations of the new public management were laid. Thatcher and Reagan were influenced by neoliberal advisors such as Friedrich Hayek and Milton Friedman, both of whom were critical of Keynesian thinking.

Were the frontiers rolled back? The evidence in Table 3.1 suggests "no" – from 1980 until 2000 there was a degree of stability in the ratio of public spending to GDP for high income countries, while it actually increased in lower income countries.

However, there is some evidence that the shape of the public sector in the UK changed. The privatization of most of the UK's nationalized industries that began in the early 1980s generated about £70 billion of revenue. This is recorded in the national accounts as negative public sector capital spending, which means that the state appears to have shrunk slightly. Another element of the privatization policy was to contract out to the private sector some activities that had been provided in-house. Thus, competitive tenders were invited for cleaning, laundry, maintenance, secretarial services, car parking, grass cutting, and similar services (see Chapter 8). Contracting out was concentrated in the NHS and local government. Cost savings from contracting out were difficult to identify, and there existed the issue of whether the quality of the services was maintained.

Many other countries also introduced privatization policies, as well as eliminating many of the regulations that impacted on the private sector, which reduced both compliance and implementation costs.

Over the past 20 years the relative size of the state has grown for all countries. This is in part accounted for by the 2007–8 financial crisis, which caused a fall in levels of real GDP, followed by years of sluggish growth, and then the COVID-19 pandemic, which required significant emergency increases in public spending beyond the levels that had been planned.

It is important also to look at the composition of public spending, which is divided into current expenditure on goods and services (wages and salaries, consumables, interest on debt), capital spending and transfer payments. The element of public spending which has grown fastest is transfer payments, which represents mainly the transfer of incomes, via a progressive tax system, from those on high incomes to those on low incomes as part of the government's distributive role. Transfer payments, plus a progressive tax system and the provision of positive freedom goods, are aimed at reducing the vertical inequities in society.

For the EU-27 countries, transfer payments, in the form of social protection expenditure, increased from an average 36.6% of total public spending in 1995 to 41.4% in 2019. This includes state pensions, benefits paid to the unemployed, the sick and disabled, family and child support benefits and housing (rent) subsidies. Almost 50% of all transfer payments are allocated to state old age pensions. The drivers of transfer payments are the number of beneficiaries, the take-up rate, changes in the real value of the benefits, and a change in the architecture of benefit programmes.

The number of public sector employees is another indicator of the size of the public sector. Public services, like services in general, tend to be labour intensive. The public sector is a major employer and many public sector jobs demand professional and highly skilled labour with an educational attainment level that is above average. Public sector employment in the UK, as a proportion of total employment, was 4.9% in 1870, rose to a high of 29.5% in 1980, slowly declined to 22.5% in 2010, and then, in the years of austerity, fell rapidly to 17.5% in 2021. Austerity had strong impacts on employment levels in UK health services, education, police, and the armed forces. Between 2001 and 2021 armed forces personnel fell by 73%. These reductions in the number of public sector employees need to be seen in the context of population growth. The UK population increased by 14% between 2000 and 2020, from 59 million to 67 million. Similar changes in public employment, though not to the same extent, can be found in other high-income countries. Many commentators have suggested that this indicates lower standards of public service per capita in these countries.

The years 2010 to 2022 have been called the "decade of lost pay" in the public sector. Various forms of pay restraint have resulted in large reductions in the real incomes of public employees. This is now showing up as recruitment problems.

The impact of the pandemic

The COVID-19 pandemic of 2019 is the worst public health event to have hit the world since the Spanish flu pandemic of 1918.

Such catastrophic events, which also include wars, famines, and natural disasters, demand intervention on a scale that only government can provide.

In the UK, and also in other mainly industrialized countries, the government intervened with a package of measures in an attempt to arrest the spread of the virus, to minimize the number of deaths, and to protect the economy from the pandemic's impact. These interventions had impacts on the public finances on the expenditure and the tax sides. The UK Office for Budget Responsibility has estimated the total cost of the pandemic support mechanisms to be about £315 billion, almost all of which (£313 billion) will be incurred in 2020–2 – other estimates are even higher. Pandemic-related expenditure caused a year-on-year increase of 23.5% in public spending and took it over £1 trillion for the first time.

UK public sector borrowing during 2020–1 rose by £323 billion to 15.1% of GDP. Interest payments on the debt rose to £39 billion (1.8% of GDP). The ratio of public debt to GDP increased from 82% in 2020 to 95% in 2021, which is the highest since the 1960s. The increase in borrowing was not all due to the expenditure increases. The pandemic caused a massive reduction of 11.3% (2020–1) in GDP, which was the greatest fall in GDP since the great frost of 1709. As incomes fell, so too did tax revenues, by £36 billion (2020–1).

The majority of the 2020–1 expenditure increase was allocated to the NHS (£75 billion), the Coronavirus Job Retention Scheme (the "furlough" scheme), the Self Employment Income Support Scheme (£122 billion), and the Bounce Back Loan Scheme (£58 billion). The additional NHS spending was used to pay for additional treatment costs, the purchase of personal protection equipment, and the vaccine programme.

The state and economic growth

The state has a role to play in promoting long-term economic growth by designing the framework for a national industrial policy. This does not mean the government spotting winners and investing in them. Rather, it means providing a coordination role and joining up the interests of the different industrial partners. It means investing in expensive "blue sky" research carried out by universities and having a well-educated work force that is trained in essential basic and advanced technical skills. These are all areas where the market, if left alone, is likely to fail, because firms underinvest in training and research. Mariana Mazzucato (2011), in her book *The Entrepreneurial State*, explores several cases in which, contrary to conventional wisdom, the state acts as a risk taker rather than a risk averse, rule-bound bureaucratic machine. Mazzucato shows that it is often the public sector that takes the big risks, leaving the private sector to take the lower risks in contrast to the traditional entrepreneurial image. It was the public sector that took risks and funded the basic science which underpins the iPhone, the internet, GPS, and touch screen displays. This is a system in which the public sector socializes risks whilst rewards are privatized. The state has a role to play working in partnership with the private sector to create new technologies, new materials, and new markets and thus a new dynamic environment for growth and prosperity. In Box 3.2 a range of different images of government are set out.

Box 3.2 Images of government

Government as:

- Producer
- Consumer
- Coordinator
- Employer
- Protector
- Enabler
- Risk taker
- Regulator
- Controller
- Legislator
- Innovator
- Insurer
- Entrepreneur

Conclusion

The old tropes "market vs state", "private sector good, public sector bad", are no longer useful to describe the relationships between the public and private sectors. Today's economies are mixed. They are a complex entanglement of relationships, which include those between the public and private sectors along with many other forms of organization. It is within the context of these symbiotic, non-linear, and often ambiguous relationships that public sector management takes place.

Questions for review and discussion

1　What are the main causes of "market failure" in your country at this time? Which state interventions are most likely to correct them and why?

2   What are the main causes of "government failure"? How might market solutions com-
    pensate for government failure?
3   How compelling do you find the economist's reasons for state interventions? What
    other reasons do you think need to be added from the perspectives of other disciplines?

Reader exercises

1   Choose a public service in your country in which you have a special interest. Find sta-
    tistics on the level of expenditure on this public service, the level of employment, and
    the level of usage over the past ten years:
    •   Are the trends in line with changes in the number of clients? What factors are most
        likely to drive the costs of this service?
    •   What other factors might explain these changes?
2   Why have governments around the world taken such an active role in combating
    COVID-19? What does this suggest about the potential role which governments might
    take in the post-COVID recovery?

Class exercise

Divide into three groups. Each group should consider the images of government set out in
Box 3.2 above. Give examples of the government activities that correspond to these images.
Are some of the images traded off against one another – if so, which and how? Which of
these images should be given higher priority in your country, and why? The groups should
present their arguments to each other in a plenary session.

Further reading

Kenneth J Arrow (1969), 'The organisation of economic activity: Issues pertinent to the choice
    of market vs non-market allocation'. In *The analysis and evaluation of public expenditures*. Joint
    Economic Committee, 91st Congress, 1st session. Washington DC.
James M Buchanan and Richard A Musgrave (1999), *Public finance and public choice; two contrasting
    visions of the state*. Cambridge, MA: MIT Press.
Richard Swedberg (2003), 'Politics and the economy, chapter VII'. In R. Swedberg (Ed.), *Principles of
    economic sociology*. Princeton, NJ and Oxford: Princeton University Press, pp. 158–188.

References

Mariana Mazzucato (2011), *The entrepreneurial state*. London: Demos.
Richard A Musgrave (1959), *The theory of public finance*. New York: McGraw-Hill.
Karl Polanyi (1957), 'The economy as instituted process'. In K. Polanyi (Ed.), et al., *Trade and market
    in the early empires: Economies in history and theory*. New York: Free Press, pp. 243–269.
Gordon Tullock (1967), 'The welfare costs of tariffs, monopolies and theft'. *Western Economic Journal*,
    (June): 224–232.
Max Weber (1922/78), *Economy and society*. Berkeley and Los Angeles, CA: University of California
    Press.

4 Public sector reforms across OECD countries

Edwin Lau and Nick Manning

Introduction

The last century has seen unprecedented growth in the volume and complexity of expectations placed on the public sector and its staff. In response, public sector management has seen significant and widespread change across the OECD.

While public management practices diverge widely across countries, unprecedented globalisation in the twenty-first century has resulted in all governments facing many shared and interlinked challenges, from the recent COVID-19 pandemic and energy crises to the longer-term challenges of climate change, digitalisation and the rise of social media. While the technical menus available to reformers have been broadly comparable, the opportunities and constraints facing reformers have varied significantly. The result has been some rather diverse public sector responses. Pressure for reform continues, but early rhetorical promises of dramatic efficiency and service delivery improvements are now treated with more caution.

Learning objectives

This chapter will help you to:

- Understand the origin and development of different paradigms of public management, from traditional 'bureaucratic' administration, through 'new public management' to 'public governance'.
- Compare the approaches to these paradigms across countries.
- Identify the risks of public sector reform.

A rhetoric of inevitability but a reality of some divergence

The public sector management reform plot is composed of three intertwined stories:

1. Changing beliefs concerning how to deliver the complex and often hard to measure products of the public sector – whether through 'command and control' hierarchies, markets or collaborative networks.
2. Changing fashions concerning the 'foundations' of public sector behaviour and performance – whether it be centralised recruitment for technical and apolitical competence, managerial capacity to drive desired results, competition or user choice, independent and incentivised agencies, innovation for front-line problem-solving or increased engagement of citizens and businesses to co-create solutions.

DOI: 10.4324/9781003282839-5

3.   Changing units of analysis – whether through focus on individual public agencies and specific public services, improvements to the public sector as a whole or, at the international level, response to global challenges, e.g. climate change.

Within these stories, reformers often claim that history is on their side and that a new model will sweep all before it. In reality, each new 'revolutionary' reform represents a series of adjustments, compromises and even recycling of earlier ideas in order to find a set of practices that meet the needs and mood of the day – and we seem no nearer to a 'final' public management model.

In the nineteenth century, patronage and political influence led to a wave of meritocratic reforms that established vertically integrated hierarchies with centralised recruitment to create an apolitical public service. In the UK, the Northcote-Trevelyan report of 1854 recommended open recruitment, slowly putting an end to most forms of patronage. In the US, the 1883 federal Pendleton Civil Service Reform Act targeted the previous spoils system. It placed most federal employees on a system of merit-based appointments and established the United States Civil Service Commission. In continental Europe, France decided in 1875 that the *Conseil d'Etat* (an administrative body) had the right to judge the legality of a policy decision taken at a political level.

The stylised result was that public sector institutions ran on seemingly mechanical principles, providing a constraint on political institutions and ensuring legal constraints on the execution of political directives. An idealised apolitical bureaucratic world, based on hierarchy and using centralised recruitment with merit protection as a protection against patronage, continued until the middle of the twentieth century: Sayre (1958: 102) suggests that the late 1930s was, at least in the US, the 'high noon of orthodoxy' in which 'administration was perceived as a self-contained world, with its own separate values, rules, and methods', maintaining professional standards enforced from within the public service.

Max Weber noted that a modern bureaucracy acts, in principle, as a lasting, impartial, rule-abiding and non-partisan executor of laws and regulations, which are devised by the political leadership (Weber, 1978). Weber observed that these traits were more likely to be found in hierarchical organisational structures staffed by career officials operating within stable and comprehensive sets of rules. However, while Weber made these observations in Western Europe, Western Europe did not invent rational bureaucracy, as shown by the long history of bureaucracy in China and India.

'Managerialism' pushed back against the notion that improvement in delivery was obtained by improving large sets of formal rules, and that performance was best enhanced by self-policed professional standards. It was driven by a belief that institutions perform as well as they are managed – and that there was a distinctive skill set that good managers acquired, whether in the public or private sector. Efficiency in delivering results, of whatever nature (e.g. public sector provision of services, policy, regulation or taxation) would only be as good as the quality of managers, and the flexibility that deregulation gave them to exercise these skills. After all, managerialism is a 'set of beliefs and practices, (that) will prove an effective solvent for ... economic and social ills' (Pollitt, 1990: 1).

This theme was picked up and developed in a set of ideas which Hood labelled 'New Public Management' (NPM) (Hood, 1991). NPM sought to extend private sector management practices and introduced the idea of developing quasi-contracts within the public sector in which disaggregated entities were given budgets to provide specified outputs. Thus, it was NPM, more than managerialism, which challenged the long-standing notion that the basic organising principle of the public sector was hierarchy; many elements of the public sector were instead organised as a set of internal trading operations. NPM led to considerable contracting out of services to the private sector (see Chapter 8); if desired outputs could be specified internally, then they could also be set out in tender documents. Thus, NPM sought to create markets where none existed before.

Making markets requires that the customer has information about the product. The logic of the 'marketizers' has been that government – acting as the proxy for the public as consumers – should know whether targets were being achieved. One logical extension of this is the 'choice' agenda where service users can choose the most attractive schools or hospitals on the basis of their performance. This is highly demanding, requiring that informed users make choices, that public funds follow those choices and that entities whose services are not in demand are allowed to fail.

Most recently, discussion concerning public management recognises that many complex, multi-faceted problems (e.g. providing community care for the frail elderly) rely on networks of providers who must coordinate at the local level and recognise that they are providing services, not simple products, making their specification problematic, as intangibles, such as meeting the highly differentiated needs of individuals, are difficult to standardise and price.

This requires recognising service recipients as active partners ('co-production' – see Chapter 23). A large-scale survey of European senior public sector managers rated 'collaboration and cooperation amongst different public sector actors' second only to digital government as a key reform trend (Hammerschmid et al., 2013). This implies that reform is less about better implementation or improved efficiency and rather more about engaging the public to create public value. A key challenge here is how to evaluate and incentivise agencies and individuals when they are part of a complex network of services and where the outcomes that they aim to achieve together often cannot be specified in advance. From this more recent perspective, innovation is given a high value, incentivising some experiments and risk-taking by public employees (OECD, 2013b).

Most recently, the 2030 Sustainable Development Goals adopted by the United Nations, together with pressure from citizens, civil society and investors, have led to increased awareness of the need to integrate environmental, social and governance (ESG) objectives into public decision-making, while the COVID-19 pandemic, climate-related disasters and wars in Syria and Ukraine have increased concern for public sector resilience to ensure the rapid resumption of essential goods and services in times of crisis.

Technological uncertainty and information uncertainty generated by 'fake news' have also contributed to declines of trust in government and the need to strengthen government foresight and fight against mis- and dis-information, making the task of ensuring value for money more complex for governments. Coupled with some very visible failures of market-based models, these concerns have reduced the influence of NPM.

To underscore that reform trends do not always represent a linear movement, (Pollitt and Bouckaert, 2017) highlight many examples of maintaining traditional hierarchies within the public sector, à la Weber, with more responsive managerial cultures, and more professional managers, instilled within administrations that remain a Sayre-like 'separate world' – they refer to this as the 'Neo-Weberian State'.

Table 4.1 summarises the management models evident at different times and places within the public sector. While there has been increasing interest in the options to the right of the table, there is no consistent movement and certainly no inevitability about any of the options.

Table 4.1 Macro models of public sector management

Broad mechanism	Hierarchy	Markets	Network
Foundations	Centralisation of recruitment with merit protection as a protection against patronage; Managerial skills and flexibility for managers in their use of inputs and in managing staff	NPM, emphasis on quasi-contracts within the public sector and specification of target results; Flexible agencies accountable for specified outputs	Choice agenda informed by performance information; Acknowledge complexity; focus on services and outcomes; public sector innovation and experimentation; Open government; public-private collaboration, e.g. Responsible Business Conduct
Approach	Neo-Weberian approach maintains hierarchy while emphasising professional management	Competition and performance incentives	Focus on delivering public value
The unit of analysis	Ministerial portfolios; Public sector	Individual agencies; economic sectors	Communities
Points of continuing attention	Management information and 'intelligence' – what is getting done?; Professional standard-setting and self-regulation	Targets – are we doing what we said?	Transparent results, voice and public ranking – do the public know what is being achieved?; Choice and competition – can money follow client choice – can we create a public sector 'failure regime'?; Tackling 'wicked' (complex, multi-faceted) social problems; integrating ESG criteria in decision-making; including service recipients as active partners ('co-production'); behavioural insights; foresight and resilience in face of uncertainty

What's on the micro technical menu?

Over the last century, the more micro technical menus of how money, people and organisations are managed, and how risk is shared between actors responsible for producing public services, have been extended. While the choices made at a particular time in a particular place might vary, the overall menu is likely to be familiar to most public managers across the OECD. Table 4.2 sets out the most recent developments in these management menus.

The growth in managerial options has laid particular emphasis on budgetary practices, the management of compensation and careers, and the development of performance metrics (sometimes within 'performance standards' and with targets, linked to incentives or sanctions), generally with some increased managerial autonomy for the subordinate (see Chapter 12).

While the scope, types and uses of performance measurement vary enormously across OECD countries, most countries have sought to shift emphasis from controlling the mix of inputs and processes *ex ante* towards *ex post* monitoring and evaluation of outputs and outcomes. Relaxation of input controls gives managers more flexibility to improve performance, while in return they are held accountable for results. This has led to the development of stronger processes of *external control* (e.g. through inspection and audit – see Chapter 14) on outputs, emphasising that results are (at least) as important as the means that delivered them. In parallel, *internal management control* for probity and compliance has also been strengthened, as local managers' discretion increases.

With regard to budgeting, many countries include performance information in their budgets, but few use it in their budgetary decision-making process and even fewer use it for the allocation of resources. Performance budgeting practitioners recognise that the allocation of resources can rarely be directly linked to the degree to which output targets are met – e.g. through automatic mechanisms for rewarding successful agencies. Although performance measures increasingly inform political judgements, the problems in attempting to use measures to allocate resources automatically are generally overwhelming (Robinson, 2007). In practice, the OECD has found that there are few or no consequences to poor performance identified through performance budgeting processes (OECD, 2019b).

The use of performance information in budget decision-making is growing fastest in the adoption of spending reviews which use performance evaluations to better manage aggregate expenditures, align expenditures with government priorities or improve effectiveness within programmes and policies (Box 4.1). Their use by OECD countries has clearly increased since the 2008 global economic crisis. Spending review objectives can be adjusted, enabling governments to re-purpose each review to focus on a government-wide set of priorities or objectives, rather than simply promoting incremental performance improvements.

Performance management systems are not an end in themselves – they can motivate public servants to be more attentive to public purposes and results – but this can nearly always be done better by using performance information for dialogue, e.g. between the executive and Parliamentary budget committees, heads of agencies and the centre of government or ministries of finance, managers and staff, rather than for control (see Chapter 12).

Table 4.2 Current technical management trends

The control of money: reforming public expenditure management and financial accountability

Budget practices and procedures	• Use of fiscal rules (expenditure, budget balance, debt and revenue) and establishment of independent fiscal institutions • Medium-term perspective in budget preparation and flexibility (e.g. carry-over of unused funds) • Fiscal transparency and citizen budgets • Spending reviews • Budgeting for government priorities such as green, gender or wellbeing objectives
Accounting	• Accruals accounting with extended cost calculation supported by performance measurement • Integration of ESG and resilience measures
Audit	• Adding audit criterion 'Most Economically Advantageous Tender' (MEAT) • Value for money audits, including performance audit and evaluation • Improved alignment of audit and organisation performance criteria and data

The control of people: reforming human resource management in the public sector

Workforce size and composition	• Defining and recruiting according to competency needs • Greater use of lateral entry – particularly for senior staff • Workforce diversity and representation, especially for senior staff
Compensation and careers	• Decentralisation of the employer and personnel management function • More explicit codes of conduct and codes of ethics • Performance management based on key performance indicators; limited introduction of performance-related pay • Moves towards defined contribution pension schemes • Creation of senior civil service or equivalent • Consideration of non-pay incentives (flexitime, telework, wellbeing)

The control of organisations: restructuring the public sector for better regulation, service delivery and inter-governmental relations

Regulatory management	• Growth in independent regulators • Creation of central bodies for regulatory management • 'Agile' regulatory approaches; regulatory sandboxes
Inter-governmental decentralisation	• Some functional and fiscal decentralisation to sub-national governments • Inter-governmental coordination arrangements
Organisational diversification	• Unbundling – creation of 'arm's-length' agencies, as well as 'de-agencification'/re-integration of agencies to reassert political control • Delegation of managerial authority within central ministries and departments

Sharing risks and approaches with private actors: employing alternative service delivery mechanisms

Public procurement and public private partnerships (PPPs)	• Increased out-sourcing but (later) also in-sourcing • E-procurement • Infrastructure governance to improve choices concerning PPPs, public infrastructure procurement and blended finance models • Pre-tender engagement • Green procurement

(Continued)

Table 4.2 Current technical management trends (Continued)

Empowering citizens: introducing demand-side reforms

Market-type mechanisms	• Market-based approaches to delivering public services (including introduction of user charges and some use of vouchers) and concessions • Market-based approaches to delivering internal government services • Market-based approaches to setting regulatory standards or prices
Open government	• 'Passive' openness: provision of information about services and entitlements through charters; Freedom of Information legislation • 'Active' openness: open government data; open services; open policy-making/innovative forms of citizen engagement (Citizen Assemblies) and user and community co-production • Extension of offices of ombudsman • Fight against mis- and dis-information
Digital government	• Integrated service delivery, in particular through one stop shops and mobile services, based on aligned infrastructure and legal frameworks • Shared back office services • Applications, data storage and computing power through public, private and hybrid cloud computing/data centres • Promoting the development of new services built on open data

Note: This table draws on Joumard, Kongsrud et al., 2004; OECD, 2005a, b, 2007, 2009a, 2011; 7; OECD, 2013a, European Commission, 2013, Hawkesworth and Klepsvik, 2013, OECD, 2019a.

Box 4.1 Spending reviews

Spending reviews are a specific kind of evaluation which is centrally conducted to develop, assess, recommend and adopt policy options by analysing a government's existing expenditure. A 2020 OECD survey shows that the number of OECD countries using spending reviews has more than doubled since 2011, and nearly all are currently considering undertaking such reviews.

Spending reviews can either focus on reallocating resources to higher priority programmes, e.g. Australia's Comprehensive Expenditure Reviews, Canada's Programme Review and Strategic Review, Spending Reviews in Denmark and the UK and the Netherland's Interdepartmental Policy review. Or they can focus on how to improve the efficiency of existing programmes, e.g. Finland's Productivity Program (2005–11) or Korea's Self-Assessment of the Budgetary Program.

Lessons from the global crisis led to more proactive recovery measures in most OECD countries following the 2020 COVID-19 pandemic, enabled by historically low interest rates. However, these efforts have worsened the fiscal position of most countries. Recent developments, e.g. the establishment of fiscal rules, have been bolstered by the establishment of independent fiscal institutions – currently 30 of the 38 OECD countries have independent fiscal institutions (OECD, 2021c), and these are actually required by the European Union.

Box 4.2 Open government data

Open Government Data has emerged across OECD countries as a key way to ensure greater transparency and accountability, to inform citizen choice and to stimulate economic growth by encouraging new services based on public data (Ubaldi, 2013). It is one of the main pillars of the Open Government Partnership, an international initiative to increase governments' commitment for greater openness.

The G8 Summit in 2013 released an Open Data Charter which consists of five principles:

- Releasing data for innovation
- Releasing data for improved governance
- Useable by all
- Quality and quantity
- Open data by default

OECD countries continue to strengthen efforts for open government – where businesses, civil society organisations and citizens have increased power to know what has been decided (*transparency*), to obtain their legitimate service entitlement (*accessibility*) and to be heard (*consultation and participation*) (OECD, 2005a). Over 90% of OECD countries have adopted Freedom of Information (FOI) legislation which establishes rights of access to information. More 'active' forms of openness involve publishing government datasets ('Open Data'); giving citizens greater opportunities to engage in the design and delivery of services ('Open Services'); and engaging with citizens in policy-making ('Open Decisions') (European Commission, 2013). More recently, governments at different levels have experimented with yet more innovative forms of participation, such as Citizen Assemblies – e.g. on vaccination in France, on abortion rights in Ireland and on the impact of digital technologies in Canada.

By involving citizens, the notion of open government takes the previous 'citizen-centred' service delivery approach, in which governments anticipate citizen needs, one step further by making government itself more 'citizen-driven' and participative, in ways that are strongly enabled by new technologies such as social media. Open Data (Box 4.2), for example, implicitly recognises that making government data more open only has an impact on improved governance and public sector innovation if that data can be re-used by others outside of government to interact with the public sector and to create new services. For this to happen, data sets need to be open, shareable, open-format and machine-readable in order to allow mass processing (Ubaldi, 2013).

While regulations imposed on businesses and citizens have become more complex in many fields, administrative simplification efforts (e.g. creation of one-stop-shops) have helped people comply with these regulations and to access government services more easily. Consultation and participation in the development of regulation (e.g. through regulatory impact assessments) and the creation of ombudsman offices have provided citizens with a right at least to be listened to, even if redress options vary significantly (Box 4.3).

Box 4.3 Regulatory quality and performance

Since the 1990s, the focus on regulatory reform has shifted from deregulation or elimi-nating regulations to creating a regulatory environment favourable to competition, with goals such as shaping market conditions and meeting the public interest. This requires a whole-of-government approach and consensus around common objectives. Some countries have used task forces to help establish principles for better regulation, e.g. the UK's Better Regulation Task Force (1998) and the Council of Australian Governments (2007). Ireland, Finland, Canada and several other countries have also established principles of better regulation (OECD, 2011).

OECD (2021a) adopted a Recommendation for Agile Regulatory Governance to Harness Innovation. This recognises the need to adapt regulatory policy and gov-ernance in the face of high levels of uncertainty and disruptions brought about by rapid innovation and technological change. For example, in 2015 the UK Financial Conduct Authority (FCA) launched a new programme on regulatory sandboxes to allow businesses to test new ideas in the market with real consumers (OECD, 2021b).

In parallel, governments are looking at structural approaches to improve agility and respon-siveness. Many countries, including France, Canada, Italy, Japan, Korea, Spain, Turkey and the UK, have *decentralised* some responsibilities to lower levels of government, in the hope of making service providers more responsive to users. Increased application of vouchers (e.g. for public housing or education), individual budgets (e.g. for people with learning or physi-cal disabilities in the UK or for people with long-term care needs in the Netherlands) and user charges (e.g. for car users in congested cities) provide powerful mechanisms for reveal-ing public preferences.

In some countries, giving government responsibilities to bodies at arm's length from government (e.g. the UK executive agencies, and the development of 'ZBO' organisations in the Netherlands) has significantly altered the traditional picture of direct hierarchical control by a minister (see Chapter 17). These agencies can have varying degrees of man-agement autonomy, combined with contract-like accountability for results – interestingly, making them more responsive to politically defined targets. These reforms, however, have also been criticised for a resulting loss of political control, and governments are seeking new governance models to align institutional arrangements with agency mandates and citizen preferences (de Kruif and van Thiel, 2018). In sum, the diversity of organisational forms – although it has always existed – has increased in recent years and now provides a choice of structures that can, in principle, be tailored to particular political and customer needs.

Why do reform strategies differ?

Despite the shared understanding of micro technical approaches, OECD countries have taken strikingly different strategic directions towards improving responsiveness and perfor-mance. Why have different selections been made from the managerial menus at different times and, when selected, introduced at different speeds?

The obvious explanation is that there is insufficient evidence to know which overall managerial model produces the best result under particular circumstances. It is certainly par-adoxical that rigorous cost-benefit analysis – a core principle of the performance movement

– has rarely been applied to public management reforms. Reasons include the difficulty of measuring reform 'results' (OECD, 2009b), political pressures to take action (and to be seen to be taking action) and the existence of a large market of reform-promoting consultants. Reformers have a distinctly limited evidence base, leaving reforms hostage to academic fashion and short-term political and populist concerns. Recent work in OECD countries to review the effectiveness of reforms has suggested mixed results (Ingrams et al., 2020).

Even when a clear macro reform approach is identified, it will be strongly influenced by administrative traditions, administrative systems and political contexts. Single-party majority governments are well positioned to drive through complex reform programmes that would create tensions within coalition governments, whereas the latter's reforms may better survive changes in government, but may also be less responsive to changing political needs that may risk renegotiating hard-won political agreements. Coordinating public management reforms across government is easier if a powerful central agency can drive reform. Federal countries (e.g. Germany, Belgium, the USA and Canada), where authority is divided vertically between levels of government, tend to be less able to drive through comprehensive and uniform reforms than unitary systems (e.g. New Zealand, the UK, the Netherlands, France). However, the lack of uniformity in federal systems can provide also a natural testing ground for reforms.

Administrative cultures are a second major factor determining reform paths. The '*Rechtsstaat*' ('rule of law' or legal state) model (of which the Napoleonic tradition is an important subtype) is typified by a culture of 'correctness and legal control' (Pollitt and Bouckaert, 2017: 61), possibly making it less malleable to performance-oriented reforms than 'public interest' systems. In Continental Europe, legislative authority still provides the key legitimising mechanism in public administration, together with an independent administrative court system and the ethos of a professional civil service. Consequently, managerialist ideas generally must show that they are compatible with the existing legal framework.

By contrast, the Westminster 'public interest' or 'civic culture' tradition attaches much higher value to pragmatic and flexible decision-making for the public benefit. Here, governments are regarded as a somewhat necessary evil that must be held to account at all times. Enforcing the law is an implicit rather than explicit principle in the work of public servants. Public servants are regarded as employees more or less like any other, except that their employer happens to be the state. This tradition appears to be peculiarly compatible with more radical reform efforts.

Risks of reform

One obvious risk arising from the increasing volatility in public sector management across the OECD is that the pace of change is itself damaging (Wynen et al., 2019). A review of US government reforms concludes that a deluge of reforms not only did little to improve performance but may have created confusion over intent, distracting from organisational missions and resources (Light, 2006). Reforms may involve costs such as the distraction of time and energy from core tasks, the loss of staff morale and motivation, negative productivity consequences and the costs of remedying problems in reform design.

Moreover, shortening institutional memories may increase the risk of reform overload. The spread of term contracts for senior officials and higher rates of staff turnover increase the likelihood that lessons from previous reforms are rapidly forgotten. One UK study concluded that the 'constant re-organisation of departmental boundaries and structures … weakened the confidence of … staff and reduced policy quality' (Hood et al., 2002: 11). Moreover, successive reforms create a risk of 'reform fatigue', threatening the successful implementation of future reforms.

A second risk regards unintended consequences of transparency. While government's openness to public scrutiny seems a fundamental tenet of democratic governance, at least in the short-term, transparency may reduce civil servants' willingness and ability to experiment and fail – a necessary factor for innovation. Transparency may also undermine the quality of policy-making itself (see Chapter 25). For example, applying FOI rules to senior public servants' emails can deter them from providing 'free, frank and fearless' advice to ministers. In extreme cases, increasing public scrutiny may in fact promote informal communications and an incomplete audit trail, so that key information is no longer preserved as a public record. Moreover, 'excessive transparency' can compromise policy negotiations, prompting officials to 'posture' for their constituencies, rather than pursing the 'right' policy in the public interest.

A third risk concerns the potential 'gaming' effects of performance management. If agents know the control mechanism used, they will be tempted to find ways of short-circuiting it to make their performance appear more favourable. Bevan and Hood (2005) studied gaming behaviour in the UK health sector, ranging from 'hitting the target but missing the point' to outright cheating. Of course, gaming can be significantly reduced by making it harder for agents to predict the control mechanism, e.g. by randomising performance measures, by reducing their specificity or by increasing uncertainty about when and how the measurement will take place. Better monitoring could also help to detect gaming risks, especially if combined with reinforced face-to-face scrutiny.

The fourth and final risk is that too many eggs are being placed in the reform basket. In particular, there is a persistent hope that reforming how government does its business will reverse what is seen as a long-term decline in trust in government. The evidence is patchy and in many countries possibly a simple reflection of immediate concerns about the economy (Manning and Wetzel, 2010). A 2021 OECD survey found that, on average, 4 out of 10 people trust their national government while 4 out of 10 do not (OECD, 2022).

The relationship between management reform and public trust is far from clear – some reforms, such as *codes of conduct*, may be taken by citizens as signals of potential wrongdoing, rather than of more careful scrutiny. Similarly *choice* concerning the provider of public services, seen as positive by some reformers, can be interpreted by the public as indicating inadequate standards by some providers. Trust in government in OECD countries may be declining for reasons not susceptible to public management reform, e.g. the decreased relevance of national governments in the face of global security concerns.

The final risk is that governments will be caught on a reform treadmill – always promising more, while deepening public disillusionment. It appears that the hard work across the OECD in improving public sector performance for the last 30 years has bought no significant 'trust dividend'. One reason may be the focus on reform of processes, rather than the results achieved, so a cynical public is convinced that government is incapable of 'getting it right'. Moreover, there is also a growing public who feel 'left out' and forgotten by government. The OECD survey found that most people feel that their government is reliable in delivering public services – even during the COVID pandemic – but doubt that a poorly performing public service would be improved if many people complained about it (OECD, 2022).

Research has demonstrated some linkages between governance quality and life satisfaction (Helliwell, 2014). Improving the understanding of the impact of reform – and communicating reform successes – could be a first step in rebuilding trust. Moreover, the off-putting (and often over-promising) terminology of reform may itself be part of the problem – a more modest approach may be more convincing to the public.

Summary: Where does this leave us?

Continuing fiscal pressures suggest that OECD governments will inevitably find themselves pushed to greater efforts to do more with less. Government concerns for improved responsiveness and performance are doubtless here to stay as key concerns for the future public management reform agenda. That agenda is more complex as the distinction between public and private service provision has blurred. It remains to be seen whether 'Open Government' initiatives will indeed change administrative cultures and bring in external actors, including citizens, to collaborate and 'co-produce' policies and services with public administrators.

Not all answers to the challenges on the horizon may be found within public management reform. First, making painful choices about who gets what from the state (e.g. limiting access to certain treatments) will be inevitable and such prioritisation cannot be limited to technical exercises and will require strong political buy-in. The cost-saving potential of making the machinery of government more efficient may have been overstated (it is always easier to announce efficiency savings in the future, than service reductions in the present). Second, rather than attempting to improve public sector performance further, governments are likely to increasingly rely on private and third sector service provision – although the need to ensure energy continuity and data sovereignty (and to contain private profits viewed as excessive) may limit this trend. Thirdly, preliminary trust data seem to show that, beyond efficient and effective services, citizens expect governments to be prepared for and ready to respond to rapid developments such as pandemics, conflicts, cybersecurity and climate-related disasters. This demands government capacity for greater resilience, risk management, agility and strategic foresight. Finally, governments may look to broader governance questions (political party financing, lobbying and conflict of interest, policing, education policy, etc.) in order to address trust deficits.

Public management reform will undoubtedly continue to play a significant role in the hunt for public service improvements. However, some of the gloss of the first generation of reforms has rubbed off, and there is growing recognition of the unintended consequences of reform. A growing number of countries are looking at how they can adapt their public sectors to demographic and fiscal changes in order to do *better* for less, breaking down hierarchies and encouraging public sector innovation, e.g. by focusing on the problem-solving skills of public servants and enabling them to take greater risks.

Overall, it seems likely that experience of past reforms will tilt reformers towards more caution in their future efforts. Perhaps, reformers will pilot reforms more often before scaling them up, target them more carefully towards sectors where they are most promising and consider more carefully the return on resources invested in reforms. Ultimately, however, the public sector is about much more than delivering services efficiently – and its broader political significance in society will ensure that the drive to institute reforms will continue, even if perhaps more cautiously than in the recent past.

Questions for review and discussion

1   Compare the current reform agenda of your national government in specific policies (e.g. health reform, labour market reform) with the three paradigms of public sector reforms outlined in this chapter and try to identify which paradigm is most dominant.

2   Consider a public sector reform which has failed. In your view, what were the greatest risks to this reform and which strategies should have been taken to mitigate the identified risks?

Reader exercises

1   Interview an official or an elected politician at national or local level in your country, asking them:
a. What are the main challenges facing the public sector at present?
b. To what extent can improved public management help to deal with these challenges?
c. What lessons should be learnt from past public sector reforms?

2   Choose one public agency in your country and try to find statistical evidence for both levels of efficiency savings and levels of service improvement during the past five years. How do your findings relate to the claims made by that agency for how it has pursued improvements during that time?

Class exercise

1   Working in groups of people from the same country, identify the main reform themes over the past five years. Trace how each of these reforms has changed during this period and how often these changes were based on evidence of success or failure of the reform. Present your conclusions to the whole class and identify how many reforms have run the full course from proposal, to implementation to evaluation – and how many have ceased before full evaluation.

Further reading

Christopher Pollitt and Geert Bouckaert (2017), *Public Management Reform: A Comparative Analysis*, 4th edition. Oxford: Oxford University Press.

References

Gwyn Bevan and Christopher Hood (2005), *What's Measured Is What Matters: Targets and Gaming in the English Public Health Care System*. London: Economic and Social Research Council.
G. Hammerschmid, S. Van de Walle, et al. (2013), *Public Administration Reform in Europe: Views and Experiences from Senior Executives in 10 Countries*. Brussels: European Commission.
I. Hawkesworth and K. Klepsvik (2013), 'Budgeting Levers, Strategic Agility and the Use of Performance Budgeting in 2011/12', *OECD Journal on Budgeting*, 13(1), 105–140.
J. Helliwell (2014), 'Good Governance and National Well-Being: What Are the Linkages?', *OECD OLIS GOV/PGC(2014)11*.
Christopher Hood (1991), 'A Public Management for All Seasons?' *Public Administration*, 69(Spring), 3–19.
Christopher Hood, Martin Lodge, et al. (2002), *Civil Service Policy-Making Competencies in the German BMWi and the British DTI*. London: Industry Forum.
Alex Ingrams, Suzanne Piotrowski and Daniel Berliner (2020), 'Learning from Our Mistakes: Public Management Reform and the Hope of Open Government', *Perspectives on Public Management and Governance*, 3(4 December), 257–272. https://doi.org/10.1093/ppmgov/gvaa001.
I. Joumard, P. M. Kongsrud, et al. (2004), 'Enhancing the Cost Effectiveness of Public Spending: Experience in OECD Countries', *OECD Economic Studies*, 2003(2), 109–161.

Johan A. M. de Kruijf and Sandra van Thiel (2018), 'Political Control of Arm's-Length Agencies: One Standard Does Not Fit All', *International Public Management Journal*, 21(3), 461–476. https://doi.org/10.1080/10967494.2016.1269857.

P. C. Light (2006), 'The Tides of Reform Revisited: Patterns in Making Government Work, 1945–2002', *Public Administration Review*, 66(1), 6–19.

Nick Manning and D. Wetzel (2010), 'Tales of the Unexpected: Re-building Trust in Government', in O. Canuto and M. Giugale (Eds.), *The Day after Tomorrow: A Handbook on the Future of Economic Policy in the Developing World*. Washington, DC: World Bank (pp. 163–181).

OECD (2005a), *Modernising Government: The Way Forward*. Paris: OECD.

OECD (2005b), *The OECD Human Resources Working Party: A Summary Retrospective and an Agenda for Action*. Paris: OECD.

OECD (2007), *Towards Better Measurement of Government*. Paris: OECD (http://www.oecd.org/dataoecd/11/61/38134037.pdf).

OECD (2009a), *Government at a Glance*. Paris: OECD.

OECD (2009b), *Measuring Government Activity*. Paris: OECD.

OECD (2011), *Government at a Glance*. Paris: OECD.

OECD (2013a), *Government at a Glance*. Paris: OECD.

OECD (2013b), *Innovation for Better Public Services*, OECD OLIS GOV/PGC(2013)3/REV1. Paris: OECD.

OECD (2019a), *Budgeting and Public Expenditures in OECD Countries 2019*. Paris: OECD.

OECD (2019b), *OECD Good Practices for Performance Budgeting*. Paris: OECD Publishing.

OECD (2021a), *Recommendation on Enhanced Access and Sharing of Data*. Paris: OECD.

OECD (2021b), *Regulatory Challenges Raised by Innovation and the Regulatory Responses*. Paris: OECD.

OECD (2021c), *OECD Independent Fiscal Institutions Database (2021) Version 2.0*. http://www.oecd.org/gov/budgeting/oecd-independent-fiscal-institutions-database.xlsx.

OECD (2022), *Building Trust to Reinforce Democracy: Key Findings from the 2021 OECD Survey on Drivers of Trust in Public Institutions*. Paris: OECD.

Christopher Pollitt (1990), *Managerialism and the Public Services: The Anglo-American Experience*. Oxford: Blackwell.

Christopher Pollitt and Geert Bouckaert (2017), *Public Management Reform: A Comparative Analysis - Into the Age of Austerity*, 4th edition. Oxford: Oxford University Press.

M. Robinson (ed.) (2007), *Performance Budgeting: Linking Funding and Results*. Washington, DC: IMF.

W. S. Sayre (1958), 'Premises of Public Administration: Past and Emerging', *Public Administration Review*, 18(2), 102–105.

B. Ubaldi (2013), *Open Government Data: Towards Empirical Analysis of Open Government Data Initiatives*. OECD Working Papers on Public Governance, No. 22. Paris: OECD. http://doi.org/10.1787/5k46bj4f03s7-en.

Max Weber (1978, originally 1964), *Economy and Society* (Vol. 2). Berkeley, CA: University of California Press.

Wynen Jan, Koen Verhoest and Bjorn Kleizen (2019), 'Are Public Organizations Suffering from Repetitive Change Injury? A Panel Study of the Damaging Effect of Intense Reform Sequences', *Governance*, 32(4), 695–713.

5 Public management and governance trends in non-OECD countries

George Addo Larbi

Introduction

This chapter will review and explore the key elements of public management and governance reforms in a range of non-OECD regions and countries. It will not attempt to present a comprehensive coverage of reforms in non-OECD countries but will use examples from several regions, and several countries within those regions, to illustrate issues such as: what are the public management and governance practices and trends in non-OECD countries? What is the future of public management and governance in non-OECD countries and what should they do differently? What lessons can be teased out from reforms in non-OECD countries and what examples can be given of effectiveness?

Learning objectives

This chapter is intended to help readers:

- Understand the evolution of public management and governance reforms in non-OECD countries.
- Compare the approaches to reform across these countries and tease out some lessons.
- Reflect upon the potential future patterns of public management and governance reforms in these countries.

Evolution of reform paradigms in non-OECD countries

The New Public Management (NPM) model became a dominant template for reforms in most non-OECD/developing countries from the late 1980s for over two decades, following examples from OECD countries such as Australia, New Zealand and the UK, benefitting from the financial and technical support of donor agencies and governments (see Chapter 4). While some progress was made in some countries, institutional and capacity challenges often hindered the implementation of these reforms and undermined the results and confidence in the NPM model (Larbi, 2006; Batley and Larbi, 2004; Brinkerhoff and Brinkerhoff, 2015). A review of NPM, with its marketization approach to public services and emphasis on shrinking government and the role of the state, suggests that it was not effective in addressing broad societal issues such as poverty reduction, gender and social inclusion,

DOI: 10.4324/9781003282839-6

and broad access to service delivery. Consequently, the later generation of reforms shifted towards wider public governance models in several of these countries.

The emergence of major global challenges and shocks, such as climate change and the ongoing COVID-19 pandemic, has underlined the need for capable and functioning governments and institutions to address these challenges and formulate and translate public policies into services and outcomes that matter for their citizens. The search for solutions for new and old challenges/problems means public management and governance in non-OECD countries have continued to evolve beyond the NPM model of reforms towards a wider model of public governance, often including such themes as Centre of Government (CoG) reforms, the use of digitalization/technology, the role of citizens, and the deepening of decentralization, while still keeping some core elements of NPM, such as 'value for money', the contracting out of services, and performance management/results orientation.

There is therefore acknowledgement that markets fail to deliver public goods but also that state failures need to be fixed through continuous reforms and institutional strengthening. Neither state nor market working on their own can address broad societal challenges and deliver outcomes for citizens. Reforms need to continue to address persistent and perennial inefficiencies and abuses in the use of public resources and the declining trust in government. Governments and public institutions must be prepared to work together in more joined-up ways, to work better with non-state actors, and to take advantage of technological innovations and solutions.

Reforms to improve public service performance, coordination, and accountability for results from the centre

Public management and governance reforms and practices in non-OECD countries have often followed trends in OECD countries, albeit with some unique characteristics in terms of the forms and functions they take – but with mixed results. This section will briefly give examples to illustrate the forms these reforms have taken. A common theme in public sector management reforms in non-OECD countries over the past decade or so has been the desire to reform the CoG and to drive results on key strategic government programmes and improve coordination from the centre (e.g. Ghana, Kenya, and Malaysia); a continuing focus on improving performance through various instruments (e.g. performance contracts and performance management, as in Rwanda and the Philippines); delegating and decentralizing decision-making from the centre to sub-national governments (e.g. Kenya and Nepal); and the use of technology to improve various aspects of public services, such as public financial management and procurement (e.g. in Bangladesh and Rwanda); and online service delivery and one-stop shops.

Reforms to drive results and achieve better coordination from the centre have taken various institutional designs and forms including:

- Delivery units
- CoG reforms
- Performance contracts, normally in the office of the president or prime minister with key central ministries or institutions like planning and finance ministries

These reforms are usually modelled along the lines of similar reforms in OECD countries. Reforms are premised on the idea that a well-functioning CoG provides incentives for the implementation of government policies and programmes, and stimulates public sector performance with systematic monitoring and evaluation systems to reinforce accountability to the chief executive (World Bank, 2018a). Examples from three countries, Kenya, Philippines, and Rwanda, will illustrate these types of reforms in the public service of non-OECD countries.

Kenya's Presidential Delivery Unit: The drive for enhanced efficiency and effectiveness in delivering public services and implementing government's flagship programmes led to the establishment of Government Delivery Units (GDUs) in several African countries such as Kenya and Ghana, following models pioneered in the UK. Kenya's Presidential Delivery Unit (PDU) was created in 2014 and focused on what are called 'the Big 4' areas: (1) universal health care (target – 100% universal health coverage by 2022); (2) affordable housing (target – 500,000 affordable housing units for low-income population; (3) manufacturing (increasing manufacturing); and (4) food security (target – 100% food and nutrition security) (Government of Kenya, 2020). Kenya's 'Big 4' is anchored on its long-term Vision 2030, which is also aligned with the UN SDGs. Implementation has followed a three-pronged approach: (1) delivering flagship projects under the 'Big 4'; (2) tracking and reporting on the flagship projects through a government performance tracking system; and (3) interactive communication of progress made with citizens (e.g. use of social media, beneficiary stories, mainstream media, and a public portal).

Kenya's PDU has had mixed results, as in several other African countries that have embarked on similar reforms. Despite the very good intentions and noble expected outcomes, challenges in implementation have affected results. These challenges included the lack of an institutionalized performance culture within the public service, resource constraints (symptomatic of the fiscal situation facing several African countries, even for their flagship projects), and lack of prioritization of projects within ministries and agencies (e.g. at one point the PDU was tracking up to 700,000 projects which is far too many for strategic focus). The overall conclusion is that Kenya's case illustrates the potential of GDUs but that there were mixed results, as in several such units in Africa, which undermines their relevance. GDUs may be more relevant and sustainable if they sharply focus on carefully prioritized flagship government programmes and also lead to tangible development outcomes and dividends to citizens.

Linking long-term development plans to the performance of public service institutions: The desire of governments in non-OECD countries to improve performance and results has also been related to the long-term development agendas of countries. Countries such as Bangladesh, Kenya, the Philippines, Malaysia and Rwanda have adopted long-term economic development plans with a vision to transition to the next level of economic development. However, such transitions need to be accompanied and supported by reforms aimed at improving governance and modernizing and strengthening public sector institutions and management, especially the public service or bureaucracy that are largely responsible for the implementation of government policies and programmes. Research by Kauffman and Art (2002) found a strong correlation between per capita income and quality of governance. There is some evidence that strong public institutions like the civil service underpin successful economic growth and development, and recent research has shown the relationship between a merit-based civil service and economic growth.

In the case of the Philippines, its long-term development plan, the AmBisyon *Natin 2040* and the Philippine Development Plan 2017–22, acknowledge the important facilitative role that the government will have to play. The role of the civil service is central to this. The importance of reforming the civil service/bureaucracy to improve its performance and support the achievement of the ambitions of economic development and growth is well acknowledged in several non-OECD countries, as illustrated below by the cases of the Philippines (see https://2040/neda.gov.ph) and Rwanda.

Embedding performance culture in the Philippines' public service: A major part of the reform of the public service in most countries is the introduction of performance management and, in some cases, performance contracts, both at the organizational/departmental level and at individual staff level. In the case of the Philippines, a performance management tool was developed at both agency and individual level to help translate plans into programmes and activities. A performance-based incentive system (PBIS) was introduced earlier in 2012 and in 2016, the compensation and position frameworks were revised with the objective of strengthening the PBIS by recognizing and rewarding government personnel with greater roles and responsibility for achieving performance targets and delivering results. A results-based performance management system was developed to integrate the efforts of government agencies relative to the National Leadership Agenda and formed the basis for determining performance-based allowances and other incentives. While progress has been made in embedding a performance culture within the public service with the greater use of performance information in the budget process and other decision-making processes, a few challenges to implementation emerged. These included poor target setting for output and outcomes indicators (in some cases under-targeting by agencies), difficulty of measuring performance, and accountability for sector level performance (see www.pemna.org).

Rwanda – driving results through performance contracts: Rwanda is another country that has used performance contracts, driven from the centre (Office of the President), to reform and improve public services in the context of its Vision 2020 and the Economic Development and Poverty Reduction Strategy (EDPRS). The EDPRS was aimed, inter alia, at transforming Rwanda into a middle-income country, reducing poverty by 20% and increasing life expectancy from 49 to 66 years by 2020. After very slow progress in the initial five years, national government acknowledged the need to improve the performance of the public service to bring the EDPRS on track. This involved the launch of an aggressive performance contracting programme called 'imihigho' which derives its name and basis from a historical tradition of making commitments in public in communities, keeping those commitments, and being held accountable for them. Under the leadership of the president, district mayors across the country set development targets for their districts. Mayors, prepared action plans based on the national development agenda and, following extensive consultations with their communities, made public commitments to deliver on them (see World Bank, 2018a). These commitments were formalized into performance contracts with well-defined measurement indicators and signed at a public ceremony with the president by the mayors of all districts. There is a formal process for reviewing the progress and performance of districts in achieving their development targets with rewards and incentives, as well as sanctions that are enforced. The 'imihigho' programme has encouraged competitiveness among districts, increased community and stakeholder participation and ownership of development programmes in their districts and communities, and instilled a culture of regular performance evaluation. After the success of the 'imihigho' programme at the district level, Rwanda expanded the performance contact system to other parts of the public service and has made good progress in achieving its development objectives.

COVID-19 and the need for effective inter-agency coordination and reforms

As noted earlier, CoG reforms have become more prominent because of the increasing responsibilities and complexities of government, which makes more pertinent the need to strengthen inter-agency coordination and collaboration with other actors (e.g. private and NGO sectors) to deliver services and results. This has been even more evident during the COVID-19 pandemic, given the involvement of central agencies, state and non-state actors, and different levels of government in responding to the pandemic. Indeed, all cross-cutting initiatives such as responding to health pandemics or climate change, or implementing the UN SDGs, make reforms to strengthen the CoG necessary. In the case of the SDGs, one of the many challenges facing countries in implementation is ensuring appropriate governance and coordination structures across ministries and levels of government. As an OECD survey notes, the implementation of the SDGs will necessarily entail making difficult trade-offs requiring the involvement of different ministries, departments, agencies, and CoGs to find the balance between sometimes competing goals. The survey found that 'coordinating across ministries was the biggest challenge listed by centres of governments' in delivering on the SDGs (OECD, 2017: 5).

CoG coordination challenges and good practices are also illustrated by how governments responded to the COVID-19 pandemic. Coordination from the CoG was necessary during the pandemic because it involved multi-level institutions across government (e.g. health, education, interior/security, local government, social welfare). For example, education authorities had to work with teachers' unions, health authorities, and local governments during the lockdowns to ensure the effective delivery of online classes to students (Kunicova, 2020). COVID-19 has been a major disruption globally but has also provided opportunities for the reform of governance and institutions towards more effective governments, better prepared for pandemic responses in the future. This merits further research in how countries and their governments responded and what lessons this suggests for future preparedness. Anecdotal evidence suggests that responses to COVID-19 by governments in both OECD and non-OECD countries exposed and exacerbated some coordination failures at the CoG, with instances of weak accountabilities, lack of transparency, patronage and corruption (e.g. in procurement), and inefficient use of resources (see International Budget Partnership, 2021). One clear lesson from responding to the COVID-19 pandemic, ongoing climate change, and the implementation of the SDGs is that they all require change in the mindset of bureaucrats and in the overall governance culture of a country, with acknowledgement that the government alone cannot deal with such challenges and will require cooperation and partnership with civil society, NGOs, the private sector, and local governments, i.e. a joined-up effort.

Reforms to improve the use of public resources/'value for money'

Public financial management (PFM) plays a key role in the sound allocation and use of public resources and macroeconomic management. PFM reforms have been ongoing for several decades in a number of non-OECD countries, often following models from OECD countries such as use of a medium-term expenditure framework (MTEF) and performance budgeting. While some of the aspects of PFM reforms (e.g. accounting and financial reporting, internal and external audit and oversight) have been relatively successful even in some challenging contexts (e.g. Bangladesh, see Box 5.1), the policy, planning and budgeting aspects have been relatively less successful, partly because they are more complex and politically sensitive, given the multiple interests involved.

PFM modernization can have a substantial impact on the effectiveness, efficiency, and transparency of public spending. Recent reforms include strengthening the capability to respond to natural disasters, climate change, and health pandemics. COVID-19 radically disrupted existing PFM and fiscal policies, with countries having to tear up their existing budgets and fiscal policies and introduce fiscal measures to deal with the pandemic, including support to health systems (e.g. PPEs and vaccines), households (e.g. cash transfers and lower tax rates), and businesses (e.g. tax exemptions/deferrals, and loans/grants) in both OECD and non-OCED countries (see World Bank, 2021a). Reforms have become necessary, as normal PFM and government business practices and processes such as planning, budgeting, procurement, and other decision-making tools are not fit for purpose when responding to emergencies like COVID-19, climate change, and natural disasters, particularly as laws, rules, and regulations in many developing countries and some developed countries are often not flexible enough to adapt quickly to emergencies.

Box 5.1 Public financial management reforms in Bangladesh

Bangladesh has improved on most governance indicators in the past ten years even though its overall scores are still lower than the regional averages. The world governance indicators show steady improvement that indicates the success of earlier reforms to strengthen PFM, transparency, anti-corruption, and rule of law. Part of the PFM reforms has been digital payment systems and the Integrated Budget and Accounting System (*iBAS++*) which is being used in all line ministries and directorates for budget preparation and management. At the end of 2021, *iBAS++* had been rolled out to all 540 accounts offices throughout the country under the Controller General of Accounts (CGA), all offices under Controller General of Defense Finance (CGDF), all Self Accounting Offices (SAEs), and foreign missions.

The Finance Division has embraced an electronic funds transfer (EFT) system which has enabled the salaries of government employees and pensioners to be automatically paid to their bank accounts from the *iBAS++*. This is a good step towards a paperless office, which will contribute to addressing climate issues. Building on this, the government was able to pay cash assistance to 5 million beneficiaries affected by COVID-19 through EFT to their individual bank accounts and mobile money wallets (BKASH, ROCKET, and others). Efforts are ongoing to cascade digital payments to vendors using online bill submission, and this should usher in an era of greater transparency in government payment systems and build trust in vendors to support service delivery.

Acknowledgement: The contribution of Winston Cole (Lead Governance Specialist, World Bank) to this box is acknowledged with thanks.

In reforming PFM systems to respond to disasters, a World Bank team developed the Disaster Resilient and Responsive Public Financial Management (DRR-PFM) Assessment tool which provides a good framework for how central finance agencies can use risk analysis to inform their risk reduction, response, and recovery planning (World Bank, 2022c). This covers key PFM functions such as planning and budgeting, public investment and asset management, budget execution and control, public procurement, audit, and oversight, as well as the three cross-cutting themes of institutional arrangements, IT systems and records, and social inclusion. Even though the DRR-PFM assessment tool was originally developed for and used in nine Caribbean countries, it provides good practice guidance to other countries on how PFM could be reformed to respond to disasters and emergencies.

In more recent years, PFM reforms in some non-OECD countries are being informed by climate change and natural disaster concerns, in acknowledgement that PFM practices that are appropriate during normal operations may be ill-suited for disaster response and other emergencies. For example, in Bangladesh the government adopted a Climate Fiscal Framework in 2014 to provide a roadmap to integrate national climate strategies with the resource allocation system and medium-term budget framework. In both Bangladesh and Bhutan national public investment projects are screened for climate policy alignment, climate impacts, and climate-related risks. Moreover, climate budget reports are produced to provide analysis of climate-related expenditures. Bhutan is developing a climate budget tagging system to enhance reporting and spending on climate change mitigation and resilience. Overall, reforming governance and public institutions to respond to climate change in both OECD and non-OECD countries has been a challenge as such reforms are slow and lag behind climate change science due to a number of factors, including bureaucratic and administrative bottlenecks, and vested interests with enormous financial and economic influence over policy and decision-making.

Use of technology to improve access to information and services

For over a decade, technology has played a major role in the reform of public services in both OECD and non-OECD countries (see also Chapters 11 and 20), particularly in human resources management and public financial management and procurement. First generation reforms have included integrated financial management information systems (e.g. Ghana, Kenya, Liberia) and human resource management information systems. In more recent years, new technologies, including artificial intelligence, digitization and use of big data, are driving a new generation of reforms in public services by modernizing and updating systems and introducing e-procurement (e.g. Bangladesh and Rwanda). Online delivery of public service, like the payment of taxes and issuing of passports, driving licenses, and ID cards, is increasingly being digitized in many non-OECD countries, following more advanced developments in OECD countries. The COVID-19 pandemic drove governments and service providers to be more agile by moving services online and enabling home-based work. At the same time, it exposed public service and government weaknesses and business continuity challenges, with major disruption of services initially in many countries, and this has reinforced the need to scale up the use of technologies in public services. This became more apparent when workers and students had to work remotely from home during COVID-19 induced lockdowns. It exposed the digital divide between poor and rich communities in the same country, and between rich and poor countries. For example, in education not all students could access online learning. Moreover, in several countries, the bulk of public servants could not work or attend meetings remotely, due to inadequate internet connectivity and lack of access to hardware such as computers.

Technology is a major area of investment to drive reform in public services through the automation of simple procedures and processes and more platforms for online services and one-stop shops. However, enabling digital transformation will require continuous training and improved technical skills for public services and a conducive and appropriate legal and regulatory environment that encourages innovation, balanced with data security and privacy issues (see World Bank, 2016, 2022b).

Decentralization is a recurrent theme in many non-OECD countries

Some countries have deepened and broadened decentralization reforms (e.g. Kenya's devolution reforms since 2013 and Nepal's fiscal federalism reforms). A review of progress and developments in decentralization in ten African countries (Botswana, Burkina Faso, Ethiopia, Ghana, Mali, Mozambique, Nigeria, South Africa, Tanzania, and Uganda) over a decade ago found mixed results from these decentralization processes in Africa, with considerable achievements in some areas and more limited advances in others (see also Dafflon and Madies, 2013). Decentralization in some African countries (e.g. Kenya, Uganda, Nigeria) and some Asian countries (e.g. Nepal and the Philippines) has advanced considerably in the devolution and deconcentrating of legal authority to sub-national governments (see Boxes 5.2 and 5.3). In some countries with histories of conflict, decentralization has been used to promote and consolidate national stability (e.g. Kenya, Nepal).

Box 5.2 The transition from unitary to federal government in Nepal

Following the promulgation of a new federal constitution in 2015, Nepal embarked on ambitious reforms to shift the country from a unitary to a federal system of government. The reform was unprecedented both in scale and scope, adopting a 'big bang' approach to state restructuring with the creation of three tiers of government at the federal, provincial, and local levels, with significant decentralization of decision-making and resources to sub-national governments. This involved the creation of 7 provinces and the consolidation of about 3,400 Village Development Committees in 75 existing districts into 753 new local government units in 2017. This was followed by a series of local government elections in 2017 and then provincial and federal elections later in 2017–2018. The emergence of sub-national governments (SNGs) in Nepal with the authority to manage resources carries important implications for service delivery and for fostering a transparent and inclusive path to governance and development, key to addressing a root cause of conflict and fragility (World Bank, 2021b, 2018b).

Several laws and institutions have been put in place to implement federalism mandated by the constitution by devolving functions, funds, and functionaries to SNGs. These include the Intergovernmental Fiscal Arrangement Act (IFAA), National Natural Resources and Fiscal Commission Act (NNRFCA), and Local Government Operation Act (LGOA). The NNRFC oversees the design of the fiscal transfers formula for SNGs, which guides the distribution of tax revenue and natural resource royalties to SNGs through conditional and equalization grants.

Box 5.3 Kenya's devolution reforms

Kenya's 2010 constitution provided a framework for the devolution and major restructuring of the state in response to several decades of grievances, including the centralization of state powers and resources in national government and significant regional disparities in economic and social development. The restructuring of the Kenya state under the Constitution of 2010 was designed to respond to the grievances with three key objectives:

- Decentralization of political power, public sector functions, and public finances
- Ensuring a more equitable spatial distribution of resources among regions
- Promoting more accountable, participatory, and responsive government at all levels

Elections held in 2013 and 2017 ushered in 47 county governments headed by an elected county governor, and elected county assemblies to provide oversight of the county executive. An elected president heads a national executive. There is a bi-cameral legislature (National Assembly and Senate), with the Senate protecting the interest of the county governments.

A recent assessment of devolution suggests that devolution has led to the establish-ment of institutions and systems for the delivery of devolved services; provided a plat-form that is expected to enhance equity in Kenya with overall disparity decreasing; and, by and large, met the expectations of Kenyans. However, there are still signifi-cant challenges to implementation and achieving desired outcomes, including ambi-guities in financing and service provision, with the national government still heavily involved in the delivery of devolved services, governance, and coordination. Quality of service delivery is mixed and varies widely between richer urban counties and poor rural counties. While overall regional disparities have been decreasing, these persist in economic and educational outcomes and in health service delivery (Muwonge et al., 2022).

Overall, devolution has been a positive development in Kenya with improvement in citizen participation, e.g. in county planning and budgeting activities, as required by law. The fiscal framework for the sharing of revenue between national and county governments has been a major achievement. However, more work needs to be done on implementation as part of the long-term agenda to sustain devolution.

International experience in devolution and decentralization suggests that while these can improve the efficiency and accountability of public service delivery, this is likely only to happen under specific conditions, including sufficient sub-national government autonomy and capacity to deliver services (specific to local needs), strong accountability, good gov-ernance, a sufficient degree of expenditure and revenue decentralization, and the political commitment of key actors to the reform.

What is the future of public management and governance in non-OECD countries?

The multi-faceted challenges faced by governments around the world call for effective, capable, and agile governments anchored on strong institutions, which are able to respond to these challenges. These complex challenges are a reminder that government and the state still matter. However, going forward, it is likely to be a different kind of government and state that will matter to citizens in dealing with crisis – government that listens and can be trusted by citizens, the private sector, and communities. Such a government needs to be able to convince citizens to change their behaviour radically (e.g. by taking preventive action in a pandemic and by reducing their carbon footprint) and to convince the private sector to leverage finance and investments to create jobs, innovate, and finance long-term infrastructure and other development challenges. It is clear that the *status quo* is not sustainable, and governments and the public sector will have to change through meaningful and sustained reforms (see World Bank, 2022a).

Better coordinated and collaborative government: The implementation of public management and governance reforms in most non-OECD countries not only faces capability challenges but also administrative/bureaucratic bottlenecks and institutionalized behaviours that undermine reforms, create opportunities for corruption, and create distance between government and citizens. This underlines the decline in trust in government in many non-OECD countries (as also in some OECD countries) (see 2021 Trust Edelman Trust Barometer, Global Report).

In a period of unprecedented upheavals and change, governments need to be humble and to develop the capability to learn and adapt to changing contexts and situations. This requires government and the public bureaucracies to be agile and to think ahead, reforming existing institutions or creating new ones to respond to new challenges. For example, the monitoring of CO_2 emission targets under climate change commitments will require institutions that can monitor emissions and understand the science of climate change. Responding to health and other emergencies requires agility, better coordination between levels of government, and better collaboration with different actors, including communities, the private sector, and civil society.

Citizen demands and government capability to respond: There are increasing demands on governments to deliver public services, to create an enabling environment for private sector investments, and to create opportunities for employment/jobs, especially for the bulging youth population in most non-OECD developing countries. Future governments need to be more responsive to citizens' needs and to work better with the private sector, while at the same time having the capacity to regulate what the private sector does.

The increasing role of technology and innovation in governance and public sector reforms: Information technology/digitalization and social media are fast changing the nature of accountability between citizens and government. In some sense, there is now too much information and misinformation, which makes it difficult for ordinary citizens to distinguish between truth and falsehood. On a more positive note, the growth of social media, and the speed at which information is shared and spread beyond traditional media, make it increasingly difficult for government to hide information from citizens, so ushering in greater transparency. Governments can increase the use of social media and information technology to share information with citizens and to get feedback from them on service delivery and public policy options. Technology will also play an increasingly greater role in public service delivery and in government business, building on the positive developments of an increase in online service delivery and remote working prior to and during COVID-19 (World Bank, 2022b). These latter developments should not be lost post-COVID-19 but will require significant investments by governments, the private sector, and development/aid agencies in both hardware and software and on the extension of 'last mile connectivity' to remote, poor, and rural communities.

Continuous improvement in public finances: COVID-19 and the ongoing Russia–Ukraine war have imposed unprecedented fiscal strains on governments globally, and this has worsened an already bad debt situation in several non-OECD countries in Africa and Asia. Debt transparency is increasingly becoming important, and governments will need to give a high priority to managing debt at sustainable levels and prudence in public finances. More importantly, they will need to strengthen public finance institutions, including agencies collecting revenues to be able to fund public services and investments.

Conclusions: What can we learn from non-OECD countries?

Public management and governance reforms in non-OECD countries have continued to evolve beyond the NPM model, in search of solutions to new and old challenges. While some NPM-type reforms (e.g. performance management and performance contracts) remain relevant and ongoing, this chapter has illustrated how relatively new reforms in some non-OECD countries are factoring new challenges like climate change and emergencies into governance and public sector reforms.

The implementation of reforms remains a perennial challenge, due to low capability to deal with the complexity of issues, bureaucratic bottlenecks, and political economy considerations. There is some evidence that where leadership and commitment are present, progress is made to overcome most of the challenges in implementation, and that course-correction actions can be taken in reforms, as shown in the case of Rwanda.

The difficulties facing governments and the public sector in general in non-OCED countries are illustrated by the multi-faceted challenges of climate change, health pandemics such as COVID-19, and conflicts (in some countries). These, in some cases, are compounded by tight fiscal space and high indebtedness. All these call for agile, effective, and capable governments that are both responsive and trusted by citizens and the private sector. This in turn means governments in non-OECD countries need to re-invent and re-imagine themselves through reforms to be able to cope and produce outcomes demanded by citizens. There is need for a more collaborative approach to governance and in delivering services and meeting the expectations of citizens. Governments need to assess their capabilities together with what the private sector, NGOs, and communities can contribute to meeting the challenges faced by citizens.

It is apparent that coordination across government, both inter-ministerial and inter-governmental coordination, is a major issue both in OECD and non-OCED countries. CoG reforms are increasingly being used in non-OECD countries to help address the issue of coordination and to focus on achieving results in key strategic areas, as seen in the case of Kenya. In a resource constrained world, the pressures to demonstrate results and 'value for money' remain strong, which remains one of the key legacies of NPM.

Technology/digitalization is a major driver for innovation in both OECD and non-OECD countries. While OECD countries may be more advanced in technological innovation, some non-OECD countries are leapfrogging and making impressive advances in the use of technology, especially in public service delivery (e.g. digitalization of services).

Questions for review

1 What are the key drivers of reforms in non-OECD countries, and what are the key challenges?
2 Give examples of where technology/digitalization is having a positive impact on governance and public management in non-OECD countries.

Reader exercises

1 What do you see as the future trends of governance and public management reforms in non-OECD countries? How do you think this is likely to vary between countries or groups of countries?

2   In what ways do you consider that technology may be used in the future to improve public management and governance? Can you find examples of where some of these approaches are already being used in non-OECD countries?

Class exercises

1   In groups, discuss how many reforms outlined in this chapter can be classified as essentially about public management practices and how many as governance reforms. In plenary session, compare your answers.
2   Discuss how climate change and COVID-19 have influenced governance and public management reforms in the different countries represented in your class and suggest patterns which emerge.

Further reading

Brinkerhoff, D.W. and Brinkerhoff, J.M. (2015), "Public Sector Management Reform in Developing Countries: Perspectives Beyond NPM Orthodoxy". *Public Administration and Development*, 35(4), 222–237.

Larbi, G.A. (2006), "Applying New Public Management in Developing Countries". In Bangura, Y. and Larbi, G.A. (eds.) *Public Sector Reform in Developing Countries: Capacity Challenges to Improve Services*. Basingstoke: Palgrave Macmillan, pp. 25–52.

References

21st Annual Edelman Trust Barometer (2021), *Global Report 2021*.

Batley, R. and Larbi, G.A. (2004), *The Changing Role of Government: The Reform of Public Services in Developing Countries*. Basingstoke: Palgrave Macmillan.

Brinkerhoff, D.W. and Brinkerhoff, J.M. (2015), "Public Sector Management Reform in Developing Countries: Perspectives Beyond NPM Orthodoxy". *Public Administration and Development*, 35(4), 222–237.

Dafflon, Bernard and Madies, Thiery, eds (2013), *Political Economy of Decentralization in Sub-Saharan Africa*. Washington DC: The World Bank/Agence Francaise de Development.

Government of Kenya (2020), *The Big 4 Agenda: Implementation Progress Report, January 2021 to December 2019*.

International Budget Partnership (2021), *Managing Covid Funds: The Accountability Gap*. Available at: www.internationalbudget.org.

Kaufmann, D. and Kraay, A. (2002), *Growth Without Governance*. World Bank Policy Research Paper No. 2928. World Development Research Group. Washington, DC: World Bank.

Kunicova, Jana (2020), "Driving COVID-19". *Response from the Centre: Institutional Mechanisms to Ensure Whole-of-Government Coordination*. World Bank Group. Available at https://openknowledge .worldbank.org/bitstream/handle/10986/34786/Driving-the-COVID-19-Response-from-the -Center-Institutional-Mechanisms-to-Ensure-Whole-of-Government-Coordination.pdf?sequence =1&isAllowed=y.

Larbi, G.A. (2006), "Applying New Public Management in Developing Countries". In Bangura, Y. and Larbi, G.A. (eds.) *Public Sector Reform in Developing Countries: Capacity Challenges to Improve Services*. Basingstoke: Palgrave Macmillan, pp. 25–52.

Muwonge, A., Williamson, T.S., Owuor, C., and Kinuthia, M. (2022), *Making Devolution work for Service Delivery in Kenya*. Washington, DC: World Bank Group.

OECD (2017), *Getting Governments Organised to Deliver on the Sustainable Development Goals: Summary Report and Next Steps*. Available at https://www.oecd.org/gov/SDGs-Summary-Report -WEB.pdf.

World Bank (2016), *World Development Report 2016: Digital Dividends*. Washington, DC: World Bank.

World Bank (2018a), *Improving Public Sector Performance Through Innovation and Inter-Agency Coordination*. Malaysia: World Bank Group Global Knowledge and Research Hub.

World Bank (2018b), *A New Approach to a Federal Nepal*. Washington, DC: World Bank.

World Bank (2021a), *A Review of Fiscal Policy Responses to COVID-19*. MTI Insight. Washington, DC: World Bank.

World Bank (2021b), *Federalism and Public Expenditure for Human Development in Nepal: An Emerging Agenda*. Washington, DC: World Bank.

World Bank (2022a), *The Future of Government: Re-imagining Government for Good Governance*. Global Practice. Washington, DC: World Bank.

World Bank (2022b), *Tech Savy: Advancing GovTech Reforms in Public Administration*. Washington, DC: World Bank.

World Bank (2022c), *Disaster Resilient and Responsive Public Financial Management: An Assessment Tool*. Washington, DC: World Bank.

6 Behavioural approaches to public management and governance

Janne Kalucza and Caroline Fischer

'For the man who wishes to explore the pure science of administration, it will dictate at least a thorough grounding in social psychology.'

(Herbert Simon, 1947: 202)

Introduction

This chapter will explore the distinctive features of the behavioural approach to public administration scholarship, an approach which has become increasingly popular in the past decade and which provides new insights into the behaviour and motivation of stakeholders involved in public administration.

Learning objectives

1. Students will understand the distinctive features of the behavioural approach to public administration.
2. Students will be able to identify advantages and disadvantages of behavioural research designs.
3. Students will have a basic understanding of experimental methods in public administration research to test administrative behaviours in a controlled environment.
4. Students will be able to reflect on behavioural perspectives and theories that inform public administration.
5. Students will be able to identify administrative behaviours and behavioural assumptions underlying public policies and service delivery in public administration contexts.

What is behavioural science?

As the term suggests, behavioural science is concerned with human behaviour. While we can ask big questions about the overarching connection of complex issues at the macro-level of government or society at large, a behavioural scientist would argue that in the end it all boils down to human decision-making, interpersonal interaction, and individual behaviour. Public administration scholars have always been interested in the individual interacting with administrative structures, both from the 'inside' perspective of public employees, and

DOI: 10.4324/9781003282839-7

from the 'outside' perspective of citizens. However, the explicit term 'behavioural public administration' (BPA) has only recently been coined, and it encompasses advances in experimentation and measurement in research of public management and governance based on the principles of psychological research.

So, what does this fancy term mean in practice? It suggests that researchers are able to answer classic questions and puzzles about behaviour through the use of research methods for studying individual behaviour and its determinants, which are established within the study of psychology, but are new(er) to the study of other disciplines and much newer to public administration – see Box 6.1. As psychology is a field that is largely concerned with quantitative methods, this approach emphasizes experimental methods, in particular, as a methodological approach to studying public management and governance.

Some of the most common themes in BPA research are how citizens use performance information to evaluate public administrations, the impact of transparency on decision-making, and what influences trust by citizens in government (Li and van Ryzin, 2017). Within this chapter, we will give several specific examples of research within BPA, to demonstrate the range of experimental studies from the research lab to the real world and from the individual human being to the organizational context.

Box 6.1 Behavioural approaches to society and organizations

What other disciplines have behavioural subfields and are concerned with behaviour in public administration contexts? There are well-established literatures on behavioural economics, organizational behaviour, political psychology, and organization and work psychology. They all have in common that they focus on the analysis of micro-level motivation, intentions, and behaviour of individuals and combine it with the organizational and societal level. The role of the individual can vary greatly between and within these subfields – from a citizen in general, or a voter or user of a public service in particular, to an employee in general or a politician or civil servant in particular. While psychology, for example, starts from its core – the individual level – and opens up to include environmental measures, political science or organization studies tend to start from the analysis of the meso-level (organization, groups, parties) or the macro-level (whole political system, society) and then incorporate individual level analyses later on. Within behavioural public administration scholarship, we find multiple starting levels of analysis, all recognizing the importance of individual behaviour.

Methodological advancements in experimentation and measurement

The increase in the interest in and use of experimental methods is not by chance. Experiments allow researchers to test causal relationships. Their strength lies in the opportunity to strategically manipulate some contextual factors, while keeping others constant, and then observe how the changes influence individual behaviour. We will look at two key aspects of experimental methods in more detail in this chapter: establishing counterfactuals and testing validity.

In our day-to-day life we might ask ourselves from time to time 'What if I had made a different decision? How might my life have looked like if things had turned out differently?'

However, because time moves linearly for us, we do not know. We can only observe one possible outcome. In experiments, behavioural scientists aim to model several possible trajectories of events starting at the same point of departure by changing small details and analysing the effects these changes produce. Researchers are able to compare two or more scenarios by using a control group and one or more experimental groups. Individuals in the control group experience the 'normal' trajectory of time, in which no change happens. The experimental group experiences the 'counterfactual' trajectory of time in which the researchers introduce a new or different stimulus as compared to individuals in the control group. Afterwards, researchers can do what we cannot do in our daily life, see whether things turned out differently in the varying scenarios and whether this was due to their meddling or because of other influencing factors.

To make sure changes in the outcome can be attributed to their intervention, behavioural scientists use different features of experiments such as randomization, within or between subject designs, and the level of artificiality. Randomization can be used in allocating participants to their treatment groups or when deciding the order stimuli are presented in. This should ensure that characteristics of the individuals like previous experience or personality do not impact the results of the experiment systematically. When designing experiments, researchers usually need to decide whether they want to compare different groups to each other ('between person design') or compare the state of the same person before and after an intervention ('within person design'). While a within person design allows us to observe the direct impact of an intervention on a person's attitudes or behaviours, measuring the variables we are interested in before confronting the individual with an intervention might give away our intention to change the variable and create a demand-effect in which the individual behaves differently after the intervention because they think they are expected to do so in the experimental environment. In a between person design we do not have this issue as we compare different people in different scenarios. However, when we find a difference in individual behaviour in the different scenarios, it might also be because the people in our different groups differ in important characteristics that are more relevant than our intervention in explaining the difference in behaviours. In the decision about which design approach to take, behavioural scientists need to weigh these advantages and disadvantages in relation to their research question.

In the end, a lot of the magic of experiments boils down to control and the question of whether it was really the researcher's intervention that changed the trajectory of outcomes or some other factor coming into play. This is where the 'wiggle room' that researchers have in the manipulation of the level of artificiality comes in and leads us to the question of validity. Validity, like objectivity and reliability, is a quality criterion of (quantitative) research methods. It concerns whether a researcher has really measured, or manipulated, what they aimed to measure or manipulate. In experimentation, the balance of external and internal validity is one central criterion for deciding on the context the experiment will be based in. When behavioural scientists want to favour internal validity, to ensure it is their stimulus and nothing else that causes a change, they have to perform their experiment in a lab. There, they have a lot of control, but also a high level of artificiality. This trade-off also works the other way around. When researchers are willing to give up some control, they can move their experiment to the field and decrease artificiality, while increasing the external validity of their research and the applicability of the findings for practice. In the next section, we will present three examples of experiments along this range of artificiality: lab experiments, survey experiments, and field experiments.

First, however, let's focus on the advancements in measurement which behavioural public administration scholars have contributed to public administration scholarship. While measuring attitudes with explicit questions is already common in surveys in public administration research, BPA has introduced the measurement of implicit attitudes, cognition, and emotions. Implicit attitudes, in comparison to explicit ones, are what we do not necessarily know about ourselves consciously – for example, they might be based on societal or cultural stereotypes we do not want to hold explicitly, but that our brain jumps to, when we are forced to make very fast judgements. Behavioural scientists try to measure these implicit attitudes and cognition by using tools such as the Implicit Association Test, in which participants are asked to pair words of categories such as gender and career intention. Based on their reaction time, researchers can estimate how closely participants associate certain categories with each other. An even newer territory of methodological advancement is the use of emotional measurement in research of public management and governance. While it is possible to ask participants about their feelings explicitly, we as humans are not always in tune with our emotions and might not realize how small changes in our mood influence our behaviour. The selection of research we will present in more detail in the following sections also encompasses some examples of these advancements in measurement.

Taken together, BPA can contribute valuably to the classic debate in public administration scholarship on methodological rigour vs. practical relevance through the use of its key elements, showing that it is possible to combine rigorous methodological analysis with impact for the field (Zhu et al., 2019). However, we need to consider the so-called replication crisis in the field of psychology in which a lot of classic (experimental) findings could not be replicated to prove them valid outside their original research design settings. Clearly, single experimental results are not sufficient to build robust evidence, and continuous replication and publication of null-results (studies not supporting the suggested hypotheses) are needed. In this connection, BPA scholarship especially benefits from an 'open science' approach. For example, the preregistration of research designs is becoming more common for experimental research in BPA and more scholars are publishing their datasets and the accompanying code for statistical analysis. Simultaneously, journals increasingly ask for this level of openness. Preregistrations are useful to deter researchers from just working with their data, without having any theoretical idea beforehand about which specific relationships they are looking for, and then writing a story about the data after they have found something interesting (so-called HARKing – hypothesizing after results are known). Preregistration also helps to avoid researchers changing their data analysis approach until they find a statistically significant result (so-called p-hacking), as researchers making use of preregistrations usually have to publish their hypotheses and data analysis plan before collecting the data. Open data and code, alongside journal publications, are useful in reviewing analyses and discovering mistakes, and open the possibility of replicating studies with new datasets, to produce more robust results, as well as aiding both qualitative and quantitative forms of research synthesis, such as literature reviews and meta-analyses. Recent research, based on the meta analysis of statistically significant findings in BPA research published in top public administration journals, found little or no significant bias towards the publication of statistically significant results supporting the hypotheses being researched in the different studies, so the findings are not solely the result of the selective reporting of significant results (Vogel and Xu, 2021). This makes it more likely that the findings of BPA studies are indeed reliable.

Diverse methods: Lab, survey, field

As described earlier, experiments can take many forms. All these forms – be it a lab experiment, a survey experiment, a field experiment, or even quasi or natural experiments –come with different advantages and disadvantages. This section showcases in more detail methodological features of three types of 'real experiments' (meaning using randomized treatment and control groups, in contrast to quasi-experiments) – namely, collecting data in the lab, by using surveys, and in the field, and then in Box 6.2 we discuss the difficulties of using experiments to understand likely future behaviour.

According to a recent systematic review (Li and van Ryzin, 2017), survey experiments are the most often used types of experiments in public administration research – they are conducted and published about twice as often as lab and field experiments. A majority of survey experiments focus on the perspective of citizens and use them as participants, whereas lab experiments mostly build on student samples, and field experiments more often focus on public servants or other professionals. Putting these three types of experiments on a continuum of strong manipulation control (high internal validity) to a more naturalistic setting (high external validity), lab experiments are best able to isolate and test causal effects of a set of variables (high internal validity), whereas field experiments tend to offer more external validity. Survey experiments often constitute a compromise between these two extremes, partly explaining their popularity among BPA researchers.

Lab experiments: The case of emotion measurement

The strength of lab experiments is that they offer a controlled environment that enables high internal validity. However, the majority of public administration research for a long time preferred external over internal validity, obtained for example through the representativeness of an analysed sample (Tepe and Prokop, 2017). The advantage of collecting data in the lab is the opportunity to measure reactions to a treatment that can barely be observed or self-reported, for example through physiological measurements of implicit attitudes and cognition.

One stream of BPA research, building on that advantage, studies emotional responses of citizens and public servants to certain situations, such as stress at work or an unpleasant encounter with the administration. Emotions are mental states that trigger physiological, behavioural, and cognitive reactions.

For example, Hattke et al. (2020) analysed citizens' emotional reactions to bureaucratic red tape. 'Red tape' describes dysfunctional rules that might cause administrative delay and burden to those caught by those rules. The researchers measured emotions relying on physiological measures such as facial reactions, electrodermal activity, and heart rate. They found that individuals show negative emotional responses when confronted with bureaucratic red tape – for example, confusion, frustration, and anger. They showed that red tape is an affective rather than a cognitive phenomenon.

Survey experiments: the case of measuring motivation and behavioural intentions

Some authors argue that surveys have become the *modus operandi* in public administration research, since they are 'quick and cheap' and can easily be administered to a large and realistic population. Therefore, self-reported behaviour in surveys and survey experiments is an often-used efficient alternative to lab or field experiments. Technologies utilized in survey sampling, with the rise of online access panels (e.g. YouGov) and platform labour markets (e.g. Amazon's Mechanical Turk), have certainly fuelled that development.

One stream of BPA research, building on these opportunities and the advantages of survey experiments, focuses on the work motivation of public servants. Work motivation is a psychological process that determines and directs the intended and actual behaviour of workers. As such, it is not directly observable, which makes it ideal to study through self-reporting by the study population.

For example, Fischer (2022) analysed the motivation to perform a specific type of work behaviour in public organizations, namely the sharing of knowledge. In a survey experiment she found that two tested incentives, building on *achievement motivation* (when an individual is motivated by getting a reward for high performance – in this case, a positive performance appraisal) and *appreciation motivation* (when an individual is motivated by the appreciation of co-workers), both positively affected workers' intention to share their own knowledge with co-workers for specific types of knowledge that were easy to codify ('explicit knowledge'). However, she could not prove such an effect on the sharing of more implicit types of knowledge, concluding that motivation is not the most important driver to change the behaviour of public servants towards sharing implicit knowledge (where ability and opportunity to share knowledge might be more important).

Field experiments: The case of implementing nudges in the real world

Field experiments involve participants from the relevant study population (e.g. public servants instead of students), use authentic treatments in a natural setting, and lead to real-world outcomes. Although it is harder to control contextual influences in field experiments, they are closer to the actual situation in which the behaviour will occur and can better capture real-world complexity. They also often capture real behaviour instead of behavioural intentions or the artificial behaviour of a participant in the lab. Examples of treatments in field experiments could be training delivered to a specific group of people (e.g. transformational leadership training to supervisors in public organizations), pieces of information or data (e.g. explaining the advantages of recycling waste to citizens), or the introduction of a new process (e.g. automated decision-making).

One very topical stream of research (often promoted by Behavioural Insights teams, see Case Example 6.1) that builds on the idea of testing real-world interventions explores the effect of 'nudges' to change behaviour to an intended behaviour, e.g. to get citizens to act 'in the public interest' (usually as defined by the government). Nudges are subtle cues that aim to change the choice architecture of an individual, by making a certain behaviour more attractive, faster, easier, or the default (Thaler and Sunstein, 2009). However, in contrast to classic strategies of public administration to achieve citizens' compliance with policies, such as legislation and law enforcement, nudges do not rely on forbidding an unwanted behaviour or changing economic incentives, e.g. by offering rewards.

Due to the COVID-19 pandemic, studies on vaccination uptake have become popular again. For example, Keppeler et al. (2022) tested the effect of an official mailing campaign inviting citizens to get their jab, in a large-scale field experiment with 27,000 participants. Building on the idea of psychological ownership to reduce the free-riding behaviour in the production of a public good – in this case, herd immunity against the virus – they changed the wording of the vaccination offer by adding possessive pronouns, e.g. 'your vaccination', 'your personal contribution', and 'your personal protection'. This psychological ownership-based nudge increased vaccination uptake significantly (by 39 per cent).

Box 6.2 The difficulties of measuring real behaviour in a fictitious context

Experiments aim to capture the real-world impact of a treatment. However, while they are usually able to deliver high internal validity, they are often criticized for lacking external validity, especially because they measure a rather artificial behaviour (lab experiments) or just intentions or self-reported behaviour (survey experiments). Hence, the *authenticity and level of abstraction* of a treatment are an issue that is often discussed.

Think back to our example of collecting physiological measures to determine emotions. Participants might just be nervous from being in a lab. Therefore, it is important to collect baseline measures for every individual in such a situation and to compare changes within one individual. However, in other cases it is harder to control for the influence of the lab setting, e.g. when risk aversion is tested in dice games. These kinds of tests often try to mimic a real-world situation by implementing real-world consequences for the participants, such as the opportunity really to win money. However, due to ethical reasons, there is not much room to incentivize participants differently, aside from ensuring, of course, that participants should never face negative consequences from participating in the research.

Survey experiments by definition have to rely on capturing the self-reported perceptions of respondents rather than their real behaviour. Clearly there is a need to make 'vignette settings' (the descriptions of the experimental situation to which the participant is asked to respond) as concrete and realistic as possible. It is important, too, to deal with the criticism that participants may easily state their intentions to behave in a way that they would never actually demonstrate in reality. One way to overcome this is to use the effort which participants put into giving an answer as a sign of the honesty and therefore validity of the answer they give. So-called 'real-effort tasks' involve cognitive, creative, or physical effort from participants. For example, participants may be asked to count errors, write an essay, or sort out values in a table. The basic idea is that the greater the effort that one puts into such a task, the likelier it is that one would actually perform the behaviour one has stated in the survey.

Although field experiments are closer to an authentic setting, the awareness of the participants that they are part of an experiment might bias their decisions and reactions anyway. Moreover, in field research there are ethical implications arising from manipulating real-world behaviour. Is it, for example, acceptable to give a certain training programme or reward or opportunity to only some participants and not to others, in order to test their effect? Is it acceptable to influence the decisions of citizens on how to vote, in order to test the impact of a certain campaign instrument? Is it acceptable to add to the burden of public servants, for example by sending in fake job applications to a real job opening in order to test for potential discriminatory candidate selection behaviour? There can never be universally applicable answers to these questions – the specific potential contribution to our knowledge base of a certain study has to be weighed against the costs and burden that it entails. These ethical considerations might therefore entail stepwise approaches in BPA, as, for example, in clinical trials of new drugs, which start with a small sample of volunteers, proceed with increasing sample sizes if early results are encouraging, and only at the end are tested through a randomized control trial with a large sample, as the final determinant of whether or not they are safe and effective.

Case Example 6.1 Behavioural insight teams around the world

Behavioural public administration research produces knowledge for public administration as a design science, helping policy-makers to develop evidence-based policies. Much of this evidence is produced not only in universities or other research organizations but also in the public sector itself – in so-called policy labs, nudge units, or similar teams existing at federal or local levels or provided by a non-profit organization. The British Behavioural Insights team (https://www.bi.team/) was founded in the heart of the British government in 2010 and has in the meantime grown into a global non-profit organization with branches in, among others, Latin America, the Caribbean and Singapore, and in 2012 it supported the foundation of the Behavioral Insights Unit of New South Wales in Australia (https://www.nsw.gov.au/behavioural-insights-unit). The US nudge unit was the Social and Behavioral Sciences Team (https://sbst.gov/), formed as a subgroup of the National Science and Technology Council in 2015 but inactive from 2017 to 2022 (during the Trump administration).

An organization that was founded as a non-governmental and non-profit organization from the beginning is the Swiss *staatslabor* (https://www.staatslabor.ch/en), launched in 2017. The *staatslabor* understands its role as a platform to connect experts, civil society, and the government and to be a lab for policy innovations. For example, it experiments with public health-related campaigns, such as 'Dry January' to prevent excessive alcohol consumption, or participation processes like 'Innovation Champions', not only consulting youth citizens in the political process but enabling actual co-production by them in public service delivery. It has worked with several public sector entities to introduce 'intrapreneurship' programmes, which aim to enable civil servants to use methods such as user-centred design to improve their services.

> Our work at *staatslabor* aims to make the public sector bolder, more collaborative, and more open. In our experience there are scores of pioneering civil servants everywhere who share those aims. We work with them to help them bring the best ideas and methods to bear on their challenges so they can better serve the public.
>
> (Danny Buerkli, co-director of *staatslabor*)

Diverse focus points of research: The individual, the organizations, society

One of the most pertinent critiques of the BPA stream is its focus on the micro-level. Moynihan (2018) warns that public administration as a field might lose its identity and relevance for practice when neglecting macro and meso-level questions and focusing just on the research questions that can most easily be answered using experimental research. However, since this warning, the BPA research field has developed and nowadays incorporates more research projects that fruitfully combine these different analytical levels (Jilke et al., 2019). This section showcases behavioural research at these different analytical levels and in different empirical contexts.

Micro-interventions on the individual level

Vogel and Willems (2020) focused on the idea that knowing about the social impact of one's work can raise a person's motivation for that job, because one feels needed and can do something good for society. They built on that assumption to tackle the problem of public employees who are frustrated with their jobs and might have forgotten about their initial motivation to enter their profession. They argue that micro-interventions to remind these employees about the difference that they make to society or to a specific group of citizens could refuel their motivation and job satisfaction. Participants in their study were asked to reflect on how their work contributes to a community or to society in general. They found that these reminders about the value of their work enhanced employees' willingness to recommend their jobs to others, decreased their intention to leave, increased their positive attitude to their jobs, and decreased their negative perceptions. By using an intervention that referred to an outcome at the macro-level (societal impact) to influence micro-level perceptions and behavioural intentions, the authors combined two different analytical levels in a fruitful way. Moreover, these micro-interventions are small and easy to implement managerial measures that can easily be translated into concrete recommendations for practice. Hence, the study also shows that a fruitful combination of methodological rigour and practical relevance is possible.

How national culture influences the perception of meso-level behaviour

Research at the 'meso-level' – the group or organizational level – is central to public administration research, since all governance activities rely at least partly on collective decision-making. Meso-level topics often studied through a behavioural approach include the transparency of governmental decision-making and of the service delivery process. Transparency is here understood as the openness of the state in making information about public organizations and their behaviour available, so that external actors can monitor them. Governmental transparency is often seen as a determinant of better governance (see Chapter 15). Behavioural research on this topic is characterized by diverse foci. Research looks both at impacts on the micro-level (e.g. how individuals use government information) and the macro-level (e.g. how transparency can reduce corruption), as well as determinants on the micro-level (e.g. journalists requesting information) and the macro-level (e.g. the existence of freedom of information laws, national culture). For example, Grimmelikhuijsen et al. (2013) study the effect of transparency on trust in government in a cross-country comparison between the Netherlands and South Korea. Experiments suggest that in both countries transparency has a slightly negative effect on trust in government and that this negative effect is stronger in South Korea. The national culture of South Korea is assumed to be characterized by higher power distance (the extent to which the less powerful members of a country accept that power is distributed unequally) and stronger long-term orientation, so these results are claimed to show that cultural values influence how citizens perceive government transparency and whether they appreciate it. In this way, the authors suggest how a macro-level variable (national culture) influences a meso-level behaviour (transparency) and impacts a micro-level outcome (trust).

Summary

Behavioural public administration combines psychological research methods with core research themes within public management and governance. It has advanced the field, not only by diversifying the methodological toolbox of researchers, but also by introducing a sharp and unapologetic focus on the individual as a level of analysis, influencing what research questions can be posed and answered. Research within BPA has flourished since its relatively recent introduction, promoting the use of open science principles, and opening the discipline for interdisciplinary endeavours with other micro-level disciplines, such as behavioural economics in the research on nudging. Field experiments promise direct practical impact, since results are often closer to practical application than in macro-level research. However, BPA as a field also needs critical discussion both about the size of the impacts (both explicit and implicit) achieved through experimental research and about the ethical dimension of influencing individuals both in the lab and in the real world. In future, BPA can benefit from integrating more critical and theory-based approaches into the currently largely method-driven research endeavours and developing a framework for much needed mixed-methods designs, integrating qualitative and quantitative research methods.

Questions for review and discussion

1   What are the particular contributions which make BPA distinctive from other approaches to public management and governance?
2   What has been the impact of the 'experimental turn' in public administration for the field? List at least two positive developments and two drawbacks, then consider how it might be possible to mitigate the negative consequences of the experimental turn.

Reader exercises

1   What is 'behaviour'? Please distinguish in your definition the individual, organizational, and societal levels. Study the newspapers from your home town or country and find examples that mention the individual level behaviours of public servants or citizens, the organizational behaviours of public agencies, and the macro-level behaviours at the societal level.
2   Describe two key characteristics of BPA research. Search within the recent publications of a public administration journal of your own choice (e.g. JPART, PAR, or PMR) for a BPA study and identify whether they exhibit these two characteristics.

Class exercises

1   The practical relevance of BPA research often stems from showing how to achieve an intended behaviour change and so result in better outcomes. For example, BPA research finds that citizens are more likely to separate their trash accurately into recycling trashcans which are easy to reach and designed attractively and when citizens are informed about the consequences of their behaviour, such as negative effects on the environment or waste disposal workers. In groups, think about the public trashcans in the home towns of different group members. How are they designed and positioned? Identify potential ways of making recycling easier and more attractive for local people. In the plenary, vote on which group has come up with the ideas most likely to be successful.
2   Individually, go to https://implicit.harvard.edu/implicit/ and take an Implicit Association Test of your choice. As a group, discuss how you evaluate such measurements of implicit assocations in terms of experimental design characteristics such as the level of artificiality. Additionally, if you are comfortable to share your results, reflect on how the results you obtained reflect your explicit views on the same topic and why they might be different.

Further reading

Bhanot, SP and Linos E (2019) Behavioral Public Administration: Past, Present, and Future. *Public Administration Review* 80: 168–171.

Grimmelikhuijsen S, Jilke S, Olsen AL and Tummers L (2017) Behavioral Public Administration: Combining Insights from Public Administration and Psychology. *Public Administration Review* 77(1): 45–56.

James O, Jilke SR and van Ryzin GG (eds.) (2017) *Experiments in Public Management Research.* Cambridge: Cambridge University Press.

Riccucci NM (2010) *Public Administration: Traditions of Inquiry and Philosophies of Knowledge.* Washington, DC: Georgetown University Press.

References

Fischer C (2022) Incentives Can't Buy Me Knowledge: The Missing Effects of Appreciation and Aligned Performance Appraisals on Knowledge Sharing of Public Employees. *Review of Public Personnel Administration* 42(2): 368–389.

Grimmelikhuijsen S, Porumbescu G, Hong B and Im T (2013) The Effect of Transparency on Trust in Government: A Cross-National Comparative Experiment. *Public Administration Review* 73(4): 575–586.

Hattke F, Hensel D and Kalucza J (2020) Emotional Responses to Bureaucratic Red Tape. *Public Administration Review* 80(1): 53–63.

Jilke S, Olsen AL, Resh W and Siddiki S (2019) Microbrook, Mesobrook, Macrobrook. *Perspectives on Public Management and Governance* 2(4): 245–253.

Keppeler F, Sievert M and Jilke S (2022) Increasing COVID-19 Vaccination Intentions: A Field Experiment on Psychological Ownership. *Behavioural Public Policy*: 1–20.

Li II and van Ryzin GG (2017) A Systematic Review of Experimental Studies in Public Management Journals. In James O, Jilke SR and van Ryzin GG (eds.), *Experiments in Public Management Research.* Cambridge: Cambridge University Press, p. 2036.

Moynihan D (2018) A Great Schism Approaching? Towards a Micro and Macro Public Administration. *Journal of Behavioral Public Administration* 1(1): 1–8.

Simon HA (1947) A Comment on "the Science of Public Administration". *Public Administration Review* 7(3): 200–203.

Tepe M and Prokop C (2017) Laboratory Experiments: Their Potential for Public Management Research. In James O, Jilke SR and van Ryzin GG (eds.), *Experiments in Public Management Research.* Cambridge: Cambridge University Press, pp. 139–164.

Thaler R H and Sunstein C S (2009) *Nudge: Improving Decisions About Health, Wealth and Happiness.* New Haven and London: Yale University Press.

Vogel D and Willems J (2020) The Effects of Making Public Service Employees Aware of Their Prosocial and Societal Impact: A Microintervention. *Journal of Public Administration Research and Theory* 30(3): 485–503.

Vogel D and Xu C (2021) Everything Hacked? What Is the Evidential Value of the Experimental Public Administration Literature? *Journal of Behavioral Public Administration* 4(2). DOI: 10.1080/14719037.2022.2083848

Zhu L, Witko C and Meier KJ (2019) The Public Administration Manifesto II: Matching Methods to Theory and Substance. *Journal of Public Administration Research and Theory* 29(2): 287–298.

Part II

Public management

The second part of this book explores the main managerial functions which contribute to the running of public services and the management of public sector organisations.

The main management functions considered are strategic management and marketing (Chapter 7), contracting and partnering (Chapter 8), financial management (Chapter 9), human resource management (Chapter 10), information and communications technology (ICT) management (Chapter 11), performance measurement and management (Chapter 12), process and quality management (Chapter 13) and public service inspection and audit (Chapter 14).

While each of these management functions is shown to have acquired greater importance and to have developed increased momentum during the era of New Public Management, each chapter also maps the more recent evolution of these functions within the rather different framework of public governance.

DOI: 10.4324/9781003282839-8

7 Strategic management and marketing in public service organizations

Tony Bovaird

Introduction

In this chapter we explore how public service organizations can develop appropriate strategies, matching the outcomes they wish to achieve, and choose the right marketing approaches to convince their various stakeholders to work with them in pursuing those outcomes.

Learning objectives

This chapter is intended to help readers:

- To understand what "strategy" and "strategic management" mean in a public service context
- To be able to develop corporate and service unit strategies
- To understand the difference between strategic management and strategic planning
- To understand the role of marketing in public sector and public service contexts
- To prepare a marketing plan for their service or unit
- To understand the political dimension to public service strategy making and marketing
- To understand the limitations of public service strategic management and marketing

What's strategic?

Now everyone wants to have a strategy. To be without a strategy is to appear directionless and incompetent – whether it's a strategy for the organization as a whole, for the corporate centre, for service delivery units, for consultation with stakeholders, for introducing changes to front office opening hours, for office paper recycling… Sadly, by the time a word has come to mean everything, it means nothing. So, can we rescue any meaning for this much over-used word "strategy"?

Johnson et al. (2008) suggest that we can at least map out the characteristics that distinguish strategic decisions from non-strategic ones (Box 7.1). Thus strategic decisions help to determine what the organization does *not* do (its "scope" – what it says "yes" to, and what it says "no" to), how well it fits the requirements of its customers and adopts the

DOI: 10.4324/9781003282839-9

technologies available to it in the marketplace, what it does particularly well, how well it appeals to its stakeholders, how it balances long- and short-term considerations and how it manages the potential knock-on effects of the narrow-minded and selfish decisions made in separate "silos" of the organization. In this reading, a decision is strategic if it meets one of these criteria – if not, the decision can be characterized as *operational* or *tactical*, rather than *strategic*. However, "strategic" should not be confused with "important" – strategic and operational decisions are *both* important and both can only be effective if aligned with each other.

Box 7.1 Strategic decisions are concerned with:

- the scope of an organization's activities
- searching for fit with the organization's environment by making major resource changes or repositioning its activities
- creating opportunities by building on an organization's resources and competences
- values and expectations of those who have power in and around the organization
- the long-term direction for the organization
- achieving some advantage for the organization over rivals

Source: Adapted from Johnson et al. (2008).

The building blocks: "Strategy", "strategic plans", "strategic management"

So what is "strategy"? It is perhaps surprising, given how often the word is used, that it has no widely agreed definition. Perhaps we ought to start with an antidote to most definitions, after Karl Weick (1979): "A 'strategy' is an after-the-event rationalization by top management of what they (often wrongly) believe their organization has recently been doing". A warning not to believe everything we are told about strategy!

Mintzberg suggests five different meanings (Box 7.2), each of which can be appropriate in different circumstances. Since these meanings are already in wide currency, it would be unwise to insist that only one of these meanings makes sense.

Many people think of a "strategy" immediately as a strategic plan (often a written document). However, it is clear that "strategic management" is more than making and implementing strategic plans. As Box 7.2 suggests, we can also explore strategy from other conceptual standpoints – the "ploy-making" of highly competitive organizations (as studied in games theory), the "pattern-making" of organizations that wish to give a sense of purpose and coherence to their different activities, the "positioning" of the organization to achieve "fit" with other stakeholders in its environment (studied in marketing) and the "paradigm-changing" (or "transformational") activities that try positively to influence culture (a key focus of organization studies). To this list of alternative ways of perceiving strategy we might add strategy as "pull" (or "stretch") – the focus on improvement of the organization's core competences so that it can do better what it already does well.

> **Box 7.2 What is a "strategy"?**
>
> - **plan**: some sort of consciously intended course of action, a guideline to deal with a situation
> - **ploy**: a specific manoeuvre intended to outwit an opponent or competitor
> - **pattern**: a pattern in a stream of actions
> - **position**: a means of locating an organization in an "environment" – the mediating force or "match" between an organization and its environment
> - **perspective/paradigm**: an ingrained way of perceiving the world
>
> Source: Henry Mintzberg (1987).

Corporate and service strategies

Public sector strategies at corporate and service unit level typically have several elements:

- the *outcomes strategy*: Who is it all for? And for which outcomes? This spells out our priorities – which services do we intend to produce, for which users and with which outcomes?
- the *production and delivery strategy*: How are we going to produce and deliver the services which meet the needs and demands of our priority users, making best use of both our internal capabilities and those of other potential providers? What resources need to be mobilized and made available, including the right level of staffing and financial resources, and how are they to be allocated efficiently and effectively?
- the *governance strategy* to determine the overall corporate purposes and the principles on which relevant stakeholders agree for how they will work together to meet these purposes

A corporate strategy, rather than simply building up from and replicating the contents of all the organization's service unit strategies, generally focuses on laying down broad guidelines to which the more detailed service unit strategies should conform. In particular, it often determines the governance strategy for the organization, while the service unit strategies tend to focus strongly on the production and delivery approach for each separate service. The outcomes strategy, on the other hand, often has both a corporate element (e.g. who are the priority citizens to be served by this agency?) and also a service unit element (e.g. who are the priority service users to be targeted by each separate service?).

In the next sections, we explore the development, selection and implementation of corporate and service unit strategies. In Table 7.1, we summarize briefly their key elements, including the outcomes strategy component, the production and service delivery component and the governance strategy component.

Analysing the external environment

In analysing the external environment, we seek to understand the factors influencing external stakeholders and the consequent opportunities and threats that face the organization.

Table 7.1 Developing corporate and service unit strategies

	Element of corporate or service unit strategy			Overall corporate or service unit strategy
Key strategic management activities	**Outcomes strategy** ("Which outcomes for which stakeholders?")	**Production and delivery strategy** ("Which pathways to achieve these outcomes?")	**Governance strategy** ("Observing which principles, set by whom?")	
Environmental analysis	Analysis of external environment of organization	Analysis of internal environment of organization		Combining analyses of internal and external environments
Stakeholder analysis	Analysis of key external stakeholders and service users	Analysis of key internal stakeholders	Agreement on priority stakeholders and service users	Agreement on priority stakeholders and service users
Determining purposes and outcomes	Analysis of key outcomes desired by external stakeholders	Analysis of key outcomes desired by internal stakeholders	Agreement on overall purposes	Agreement on overall purposes

There are three main elements to this analysis of the external environment:

- stakeholder mapping
- PESTEL analysis and risk assessment
- "Five Forces" analysis

Stakeholder mapping requires us to identify the stakeholders most important to the organization or programme, so they can be prioritized. This is typically done in a "stakeholder power/interest matrix" – in Figure 7.1 we have illustrated this with reference to the stakeholders of the development aid programme of the UK government. Stakeholders with high power over the programme and high interest in it are clearly critically important (e.g. the UK Foreign, Commonwealth and Development Office (FCDO) or the governments of countries receiving aid from the UK, who have to "play ball" for the aid to be effective) – they should be given central roles in the programme's decision-making. At the other extreme, organizations with neither power over nor interest in the programme will often be largely neglected (subject to giving them the level of information required by law – and perhaps rather more, just to be safe). The "general public", too, often appears to fit in this cell. Of course, if sufficiently large numbers of the general public grow disaffected, and become organized, they can suddenly move to one of the other cells.

However, the lesson from Figure 7.1 is clear – not all stakeholders are equal and a public sector organization must decide how to allocate its resources to work most closely with those stakeholders to whom it gives priority.

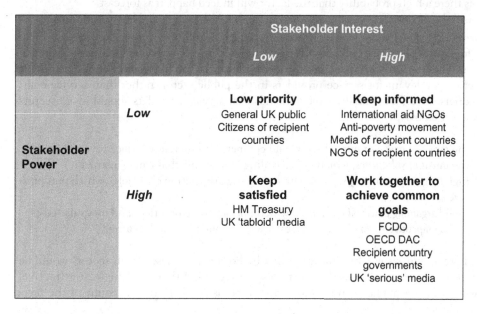

		Stakeholder Interest	
		Low	*High*
Stakeholder Power	*Low*	**Low priority** General UK public Citizens of recipient countries	**Keep informed** International aid NGOs Anti-poverty movement Media of recipient countries NGOs of recipient countries
	High	**Keep satisfied** HM Treasury UK 'tabloid' media	**Work together to achieve common goals** FCDO OECD DAC Recipient country governments UK 'serious' media

Figure 7.1 Stakeholder power/interest matrix for UK development aid programme.
Source: Author.

PESTEL analysis sets out a statement of the main factors that are likely to impact on external stakeholders in the future, separated out into:

- political factors
- economic factors
- social factors
- technological factors
- environmental and ecological factors
- legal factors

This analysis is notoriously simple to do, to the extent that one can very easily end up with a document that is ludicrously long, detailing a huge list of potentially relevant factors. This is clearly impractical, so some sort of filter must be applied to ensure that only the most relevant factors are analysed. However, this still entails a wide and imaginative search for all potentially relevant factors, so they can be filtered. Of course, in practice, this search will be subject to "blind spots", prejudices and plain ignorance, so PESTEL analysis cannot ever pretend to be fully comprehensive. *Risk assessment*, which is the most common filter applied to the factors (see Chapter 24), typically attempts to estimate in advance the following risks:

- will the factor have a high impact, if it occurs soon?
- will the factor have increasing impact over time?
- is the impact likely to be negative on external stakeholders? (This takes account of the fact that many stakeholders are risk averse, placing more importance on potential costs and losses than on potential benefits and gains)

- is there a high probability that the factor will indeed happen as forecast?
- will the factor affect our organization more than other comparable organizations?

The final piece in the external environment jigsaw is the *"Five Forces"* analysis of Michael Porter. This explores what sectors the organization might like to work in – or not. It therefore is relevant for service providers in the public sector, rather than service commissioners. Five Forces analysis recommends that service providers should avoid sectors characterized by:

1   the *threat of new entrants*, which would compete and therefore reduce revenue
2   the *threat of substitutes*, which puts a ceiling on revenue that can be earned
3   high *bargaining power of suppliers* (including the distribution channels), which puts pressure on costs
4   high *bargaining power of customers*, which puts a ceiling on prices and may raise costs
5   high *competitive rivalry*, which drives down revenue that can be earned

Five Forces analysis was originally applied by Porter to analyse which sectors would be regarded by a private firm as the most competitive – and therefore the least attractive. However, in the public sector context the analysis needs to take account of the facts that:

- public sector organizations do not always have a choice about which sector they work in (so this analysis is irrelevant for organizations which can only work in specified sectors set out in the legislation, or for organizations prohibited, either legally or politically, from working in some sectors)
- public sector organizations are not always competitive in their intent
- other stakeholders (particularly government) impact on choice of sector

Consequently, Five Forces analysis has a different role in external environmental analysis by public sector organizations. First, they need to consider the bargaining power of stakeholders other than just suppliers and customers, particularly *partners* (which might either increase costs or decrease revenue) and the likelihood of interference by *other levels of government* (which again could affect costs or revenue, or might even rule out any work at all in the sector), since both of these may make a sector less attractive.

Secondly, public sector use of the Five Forces model should explore collaboration as well as competitive rivalry in a sector, asking in relation to each of the Five Forces: "How does it affect the sector's ability to work in collaboration?"

Finally, public sector commissioners will use the Five Forces very differently from public service providers – they will often wish to manage the market for a service by:

- promoting new entrants, who can bring innovation and compete to bring down costs
- restricting the power of suppliers, in order to keep down the costs of the service
- promoting greater bargaining power on the part of service users
- finding substitutes, to promote lower-cost approaches to meeting need
- promoting provider rivalry and tackling collusion, to get lower costs and better quality

Analysing the internal environment

In developing the production and delivery strategy for a public organization, we need to understand the factors influencing internal stakeholders and the consequent strengths and weaknesses of the organization, compared to other organizations.

There are four main elements to this analysis:

- value chain analysis
- core competence analysis
- organizational culture analysis
- competitor and collaborator analysis

Value chain analysis explores the ways in which the organization creates value for its stake-holders and distributes this value between them. This requires a definition of "value". Mark Moore (1995: 47) suggests that "public value" is evident

> partly in terms of the satisfaction of individuals who [enjoy desirable outcomes] … and partly in terms of the satisfactions of citizens who have seen a collective need, fash-ioned a public response to that need, and thereby participated in the construction of a community.

While helpful, this remains rather vague. Bovaird and Loeffler (2012: 1126–1127) suggest that public value, or "value-added in the public sector", has several dimensions:

- *user value*
- *value to wider groups* (e.g. the family of service users, or supply chain of service providers)
- *social value* (creating social cohesion or generating social interaction)
- *environmental value* (ensuring environmental sustainability of all policies)
- *political value* (support to the democratic process, e.g. through co-planning of services with users and other stakeholders)

Accepting this multi-dimensional concept of value, we need to understand how a public sector organization can create value. In the past, the model typically used to do this was the value chain, which explores how different core and support activities result in value-added for different stakeholders and how these activities can be reconfigured to improve the stra-tegic capabilities of the organization and thereby increase the value-added; for more detail on this technique, see Chapter 13. In Chapter 15 on public governance, a rather different public value model is explored, which focuses on how politically defined needs and govern-ance principles, behaviour change, co-production and commissioned services can impact on quality-of-life outcomes.

Core competence analysis, like the value chain, explores the strategic capabilities of the organization, but focuses on the underlying competences that allow the organization to outdo rivals in bringing benefits to customers. A core competence resides in the organiza-tion, not in individuals or in the technology alone (Box 7.3). There are many different ways in which core competences can be developed – in Box 7.4, some examples of common core competences are illustrated.

Box 7.3 A core competence is…

… a bundle of skills and technologies that enables an organization to provide a particular benefit to customers.

Source: Hamel and Prahalad (1994: 199).

Box 7.4 Some examples of core competences

- *Speed*: The ability to respond quickly to customers and to incorporate new ideas and technologies quickly into services.
- *Consistency*: The ability to produce a service that unfailingly satisfies customers' expectations.
- *Foresight*: The ability to see the environment clearly and thus to anticipate and respond to customers' evolving needs and wants.
- *Agility*: The ability to adapt simultaneously to many different environments.
- *Innovativeness*: The ability to generate new ideas and to combine existing elements to create new sources of value.

Source: Adapted from Hamel and Prahalad (1994).

As in the value chain, a key lesson from the analysis is that an organization should focus only on those activities for which it has a core competence. Other activities should either be dropped, or (if they are important to delivering value to customers) outsourced. In this way, core competences become the fundamental building blocks of the organization – this has become known as the "resource-based view of strategy" (Bryson et al., 2007). Hamel and Prahalad (1994) suggest that private firms should aim to have many core competences. However, given the constraints imposed by legislation on what they must do (and cannot do), public sector organizations may not find it possible to have even one core competence. Consequently, they may have to remain relatively unfocused in their work – in danger of being less effective than more focused private and third sectors organizations.

One key capability in an effective organization is its ability to integrate all the activities in the value chain – this can be a core competence in itself. Consequently, outsourcing of some activities to agencies with superior capabilities is not unambiguously the right answer, if the organization is poor at integrating externally sourced activities. However, this argument could lead to complacency in the face of unfortunate levels of internal inefficiency.

The resource-based view of strategy suggests that the overall service system can be made more cost-effective by a variety of strategic approaches, including strategies based on resource advantage, efficiency improvement through better resource utilization, relationship advantage, intra-organizational capabilities, core competences and dynamic capabilities and building capacity for user and citizen co-production of outcomes (Bovaird, 2012a).

Organizational culture analysis explores the underlying taken-for-granted assumptions and norms in the organization. There are two well-established ways of exploring organizational cultures – one is the "four cultures" approach of Charles Handy (Box 7.5) and the other is the "cultural web" of Whittington et al. (2022).

The "four cultures" approach is a valuable way of distinguishing between very different types of organizational culture. However, Handy recognizes that most organizations may have several cultures simultaneously – a role culture is likely to predominate in "steady state" parts of the organization (such as payroll), a task culture in the innovative parts of the organization (such as new service development), but a power culture in those parts of the organization that deal with frequent crisis, where a strong and consistent "hand on the tiller" is needed (e.g. in the boardroom).

Box 7.5 The "four cultures"

Power culture: All power rests with one individual at the centre of the organization (the "spider at the centre of the web, pulling all the skeins") – typical of those organizations dominated by a founder, a major figure in the profession or a "control freak".

Role culture: All individuals play a clear, standardized role within their own "silo", reporting to a line manager and managing staff below them in the hierarchy, but they do not exercise initiative and do not communicate outside of the line management structure – this culture is often found in large bureaucracies.

Task culture: Individuals undertake tasks in multidisciplinary, cross-departmental groups, as well as within a line management structure – often the culture aspired to by professional staff in public service organizations.

Person culture: Individuals tend to work alone, with only passing reference to line managers and teams – this tends to be typical of academics, small consultancies, research and development staff ("nerds") in technically orientated organizations, and inspectors working in the field.

Source: Adapted from Handy (1993).

A more action-oriented approach to understanding and changing organizational culture comes from the "cultural web", which seeks to establish what the *paradigm* of the organization is – the "set of assumptions held in common and taken for granted" in the organization (Whittington et al., 2022) – and requires mapping of six elements:

1 the *stories* within the organization, e.g. who are the heroes/villains?
2 the *routines and rituals*, e.g. how are regular budget crises handled?
3 the *symbols* of the organization, e.g. who has their own car parking space?
4 the *power base* in the organization, e.g. who really makes the decisions?
5 the *structure* of the organization, e.g. how many layers in the hierarchy?
6 the *control* system, e.g. how does the organization stop things happening?

Mapping of the cultural web is, of course, only the beginning. Leaders must take active steps to change inappropriate aspects of the culture. Typically, they start with more visible parts of the culture – the structures and control system. However, for culture change to take root, it is necessary to ensure that the stories, rituals and routines and the symbols are altered as well. The difficulty of this much harder (and longer) task – which entails winning "hearts and minds" – has given rise to the often-quoted saying "Culture eats strategy for breakfast".

Before engaging in such a battle, leaders need to be confident of what a better culture would look like. Some private sector studies suggest that high performing organizations tend to have highly adaptable cultures, which not only respond positively to change but actually celebrate change and seek out innovation. Most studies of the public sector indicate that such attitudes are rare in people and even rarer in organizations as a whole. This possibly remains the single greatest challenge to public sector strategic management.

Taken together, these analyses of the internal environment help us to decide how to balance in-house provision with external provision. Where our competitors are better than us, we have the choice of improving, outsourcing or working with them in "strategic partnerships" (using their strengths to make our services better). The latter two options are often unwelcome to public sector staff and politicians. However, if the alternative is to continue to do a worse job, then they may become acceptable. Again, the most difficult part of the analysis is to ask "How well will the organizations involved gel together in practice – will they achieve synergies working with each other?" – see Chapter 8 on contracting and Chapter 16 on partnerships.

Developing and evaluating strategic options

Taken together, the analyses of external and internal factors allow an analytically rigorous strengths, weaknesses, opportunities and threats (SWOT) analysis to be compiled for the organization.

This SWOT analysis then needs to be turned into a series of strategic options for doing things better in the future – building on strengths, reducing weaknesses, seizing opportunities, countering threats.

The notion of a "strategic option" is often seen as any change that might be made in the existing elements of a strategy. However, a more rigorous approach suggests that a strategic option should be a coherent alternative strategy in itself (Box 7.6). To be coherent, all the decisions on each strategic element in Box 7.6 need to be mutually reinforcing. So a strategic option is not just a change in *one* of these elements.

Box 7.6 A strategic option

This is a connected series of decisions on:

- service outcomes (*"which outcomes for which stakeholders?"*)
- service production and delivery, including appropriate resources and technologies (*"which pathways to achieve these outcomes?"*)
- governance (*"which principles, set by whom and policed by whom?"*)

For an organization to be successful, it must devise a full range of strategic options and evaluate which is the most appropriate. Of course, this requires imaginative and creative people, who can map out these alternative "futures" for the organization – and such people are not always easy to find, nor do organizations (especially bureaucracies) always allow "creatives" to play such important roles.

Option evaluation is then necessary (unless top management has already decided which option it prefers, in which case the evaluation is more of a "show trial" for the undesired options). The evaluation process can use three sets of criteria – feasibility, suitability and acceptability – to test out the strategic options before selecting one of them (Whittington et al., 2022).

The *feasibility* of the options includes financial, technological, staffing and managerial feasibility. However, when an otherwise highly desirable option appears to be infeasible, this should not be accepted without a fight. Most feasibility constraints can be removed or circumvented with appropriate effort – or funding. Only when the constraint itself has been tested and proved binding can a feasibility test be accepted as final.

The *suitability* of the options is typically tested to see if the proposed portfolio of services provides a coherent set of activities, giving a good fit between what the external environment requires and what the organization can do well. The "Boston Matrix", for example, from the perspective of a public service provider (Figure 7.2) could rank services by their growth in demand (or need) and by their "net social value" (e.g. their contribution to the needs of high-priority users, or to high-level outcomes). Clearly, "dead duck" services are candidates for closure, to provide more resources for the "star" services, to repackage and relaunch the "bread and butter" services and to pilot "question mark" services (so that they can later become star services or dropped as failed experiments).

The second suitability test is the "Needs and Provision Matrix" (Figure 7.3), from the perspective of public sector commissioners (i.e. those organizations that decide on what needs to be provided, and for whom, rather than being providers themselves). This suggests that in-house provision should only occur where need is high and is not met by other agencies. The assumption is that a commissioning organization must make the most of its scarce resources to encourage the widest possible provision from all agencies in the field, only using its own resources for direct provision when all other avenues have been explored.

The *acceptability* of the options needs to be tested against stakeholder objectives. In private firms this would include rate of return on investment, shareholder value-added, etc. In the public sector, these objectives are likely to be more complex – and there are usually many more stakeholders as well. The priority objectives and desired outcomes must be decided in the outcomes strategy, subject to the principles set out in the governance

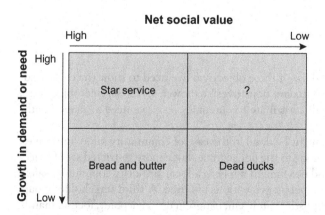

Figure 7.2 Public sector Boston matrix.

Need

		High	Low
Provision by other agencies	High	*Arrange for targeted in-house provision*	*No intervention*
	Low	*Arrange for extensive in-house provision*	*Encourage provision by others*

Figure 7.3 Need and provision matrix.

Source: Adapted from Walsh (1993).

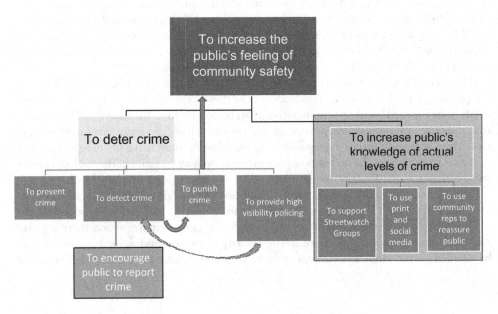

Figure 7.4 Maps from three stakeholders.

Source: Adapted from Bovaird (2012b).

strategy. In order to make practical use of these objectives, we need to show the cause-and-effect chain linking high level "outcome objectives" to lower level "service objectives", whose achievement we believe will contribute to outcomes – i.e. we need a "map of pathways to outcomes".

Figure 7.4 illustrates how this might be done in the case of community safety initiatives. The overall strategy map might belong to the police force, but a more restricted set of objectives (those inset in the right-hand box) might apply to a local authority community safety service, which focuses on changing public perceptions of crime. A third stakeholder group, perhaps representing the more simplistic "catch 'em, bang 'em up" viewpoint, focuses mainly on the arrows connecting detection and punishment – unlike the other two stakeholders, it sees "high visibility policing" as valuable only if it helps to detect crime, which is the sole mechanism it proposes to improve perception of community safety. Where there are unproven or (as here) disputed links in the logic of these "cause-and-effect" chains between objectives, then we need a more evidence-informed approach to setting strategy in this area (see Bovaird, 2012b, and Chapter 28). This approach also reminds us of the potential importance of pathways to outcomes which focus more on social, community or market mechanisms – often neglected by public service commissioners.

The performance of each of the strategic options can be reported in a *Balanced Scorecard* (Kaplan and Norton, 1996), in order that their relative merits can be assessed. This sets performance indicators for each of the main organizational objectives, which in the public service domain are usually grouped under such headings as "citizen and user results", "process improvement results", "organizational learning and development results" and "financial results". Although this technique was originally devised for reporting in the private sector, it has now also become popular in public sector organizations in the UK and USA. (Performance indicators in the public sector are considered more fully in Chapter 12.)

So far we have essentially been discussing the strategy of one public service organization. In practice, no public service organization can expect to be successful without close interaction with many other agencies – most need to work in partnership with others (see Chapter 16), so that the partnership, too, has a strategy. In practice, this often focuses on how the partners will interact (the governance strategy of the partnership) and what outcomes it will seek which are different from those of the individual partners.

Strategic management, strategic planning and strategic thinking

Strategy is often seen as being about "strategic plans". The idea of strategic planning is quite old, going back to the town and country planning movement (e.g. the "worker colonies" of Owen, Cadbury, Salt, Guell, etc., the "garden cities" of Howard and the "machine for city living" of Le Corbusier) and, later, industrial planning, starting in the Soviet Union in the late 1920s and spreading to many other countries after 1945. Ironically, these "public sector" planning roots then gave rise, from the 1950s onwards, to private sector forms of planning, particularly budgetary planning and "manpower" planning, which in turn spread to many public sector organizations. Eventually, the idea of overall corporate plans for an organization, and separate business or service plans for organizational units became strong in both private and public sectors.

While this can be a productive approach, it suggests that strategy making is a linear process, based on rational planning – a "determination of the long-term goals of an enterprise and the adoption of courses of action and the allocation of resources necessary for carrying out these goals" (Chandler, 1962).

In the 1980s, a very different view of strategic management began to emerge. Mintzberg (1992), for example, suggested that very few planned, intended strategies actually get implemented – most end up in the bin. Moreover, many strategies that do get realized were never planned – they might, for example, have been imposed by a dominant politician or chief executive or loomed from an unexpected opportunity. Mintzberg particularly emphasized "emergent strategies" – those that are grounded in the practice of staff, rather than planned by top managers, and are adopted implicitly, often unseen, because they work better than the official "planned strategies". As James Joyce (1932) observed: "a plan was by them adopted (whether by having preconsidered or as the maturation of experience)".

Of course, not all the emergent strategies that creep out of the woodwork are desirable – it depends on which stakeholder they help. So, for example, public sector staff are sometimes accused of taking an unhelpful ("that's more than my job's worth") approach. This is often an emergent strategy, flatly contradicting the explicit customer-oriented strategies of their organization – but it works for such staff (while they get away with it). More sinisterly, corrupt practices sometimes originate as an emergent strategy – e.g. when officials short-circuit their own procedures and give a licence to a local business more quickly than normal on payment of a "back-hander".

Nevertheless, emergent strategies have the potentially desirable characteristic that they may correspond better to the needs of the environment in which they emerge. After all, they are generally developed by front-line staff who are especially close to service users. Where it is difficult to get staff to take part formally in service improvement programmes, emergent strategies that naturally develop "bottom-up" may be all the more valuable.

Nevertheless, the formalizing role of planning may be important – it allows an organization to test emergent strategies, once they become noticed. Those that are not in the best interests of the organization can then be stamped out, while those that are valuable can be incorporated into the planned intended strategy. However, Mintzberg's critique throws serious doubt on the "plan fetishism" that has long been a characteristic of many countries' public sectors, where every agency and all its units have to have a plan, often with overelaborate performance management and external inspection.

Strategic management in a political environment

It is important that we do not fall into the trap of believing that there is no difference between strategic management in public, private and voluntary sectors, although many of the techniques used may be similar. Some key differences spring from the political context in which public sector organizations work, including:

- the role of politicians, who often openly clash on major strategic issues
- the interaction between politicians and other stakeholders, e.g. the media
- the pressure for "short-termist" decision-making arising from regular elections

Strategic management involves difficult decision-making. It normally means *selectivity – not doing some things* – and *focus –* prioritizing the activities and target groups that matter most. This usually brings adverse comments from some stakeholders (much more commonly made public than in private and third sectors). Opposition politicians often see it as their role to contest publicly and vocally almost all strategic decisions made by the ruling group, usually mobilizing opposition from any groups disadvantaged by the decision (even groups to which they are not normally sympathetic). Only if the organization is prepared to weather these adverse comments can it hope to manage strategically.

For strategic direction to be maintained, the ruling group needs to be steadfast in defending its main strategic decisions. However, there are many pressure points by means of which politicians can be driven to make inconsistent decisions or to reverse strategic decisions already taken. These pressures can come from:

- political parties
- policy networks
- the civil service or managerial systems
- professional groups

- charities or voluntary organizations (at national or local level)
- community groups
- the media
- sponsors who provide funding for a party or an individual

The platforms of political parties are usually designed to take on board the interests of a wide coalition of stakeholders. At worst, this can mean that politicians seek to "please everyone, all the time". In these circumstances, strategic management becomes next to impossible. However, even where politicians start out by plotting a clear and principled course, relatively minor changes in their coalition of stakeholders can undermine strategies.

The need to maintain political coalitions also explains why highly rational strategies, cooked up by well-informed professionals and backed by top politicians, may still fail because they "don't go down well on the street". Since politicians are regularly subjected to this street test, in the form of elections, their strategies are likely to be over-influenced by the short-term and narrow factors that sway voters at a given time. Further, the unfavourable reaction of the financial markets to government policies whose credibility they regard as highly suspect can bring down a government – or, at least, a UK prime minister and Chancellor of the Exchequer, as Liz Truss and Kwasi Kwarteng discovered in 2022.

Strategic management and innovation

Finally, it is important to consider the interaction of strategic management and innovation. We stressed above that a healthy organizational culture is, above all, adaptable and innovation-seeking. However, innovation can be disruptive and even destabilizing. How can strategic management embed innovative attitudes, balance their potentially damaging effects and overcome bureaucratic inertia?

Public sector organizations can innovate in many ways, including:

- new services
- new customers ("target groups")
- new service production processes
- new procurement processes
- new partnership arrangements with the rest of the public sector, with the voluntary sector and with the private sector
- new decision making processes ("addressing the democratic deficit")
- new governance structures and processes
- new goals and ambitions for the organization
- new organizational culture

Given the importance of many of these, "no change" is normally not an option. However, being strategic means being selective and focused. Not all of these innovative directions can be pursued effectively at once – that way madness lies, as in the UK tendency towards "*initiativitis*" (see Box 7.7). So perhaps public sector strategy makers will have to accept that, just as "no change" is not an option, "all change" is also not an option.

> ### Box 7.7 "Initiativitis" may mean less gets done
>
> [The] damaging combination of an absence of a strategic plan and the lack of cor-
> porate grip has created the space for a multiplicity of strategies, plans and processes
> which has created unnecessary complexity and confusion …
>
>   The result has been the sense among some staff that changes are simply the
> next "initiative" which they can safely ignore. We were told that in some parts of
> the council there is now a culture of what was described to us as "organizational
> disobedience".
>
> Source: Kerslake (2014: 39).

The role of marketing in a public sector context

We now explore a key activity in the design and implementation of strategy, namely marketing. Marketing is often thought of as essentially commercial (i.e. oriented towards making
profits). This clearly is not relevant to most aspects of public sector organizations. However,
attention to the markets for its services is indeed relevant.

Fortunately, there is no reason to believe that marketing can only be viewed in such
pejorative terms as "pressure selling", "hype" or "advertising through subliminal influencing" with all their negative connotations. The growing literature on public sector marketing
attests that it is now more accepted as legitimate but still has to justify its role. This chapter
therefore looks at how marketing can contribute to more cost-effective public sector organizations and higher-quality public services.

The definitions in Box 7.8 show that marketing can be defined in ways compatible with
public service values. The Chartered Institute of Marketing definition, in particular, is relevant (as long as we leave out the word "profitably").

To make this clearer, in Box 7.9 we contrast two polar extremes – a *product orientation*, as
might typically be evidenced by professionals who are convinced that they know better than
anyone what service should be provided, and a *service orientation*, as advocated by marketing
specialists.

Clearly, "customers" in a public sector context include many different stakeholders, all of
whose needs must be considered. Here we can refer back to the types of value-added in the
public sector identified earlier in this chapter – value-added for users, for wider social groups,
for society as a whole ("social value-added"), for the polity ("political value-added") and for
the environment. Marketing can be employed to explore how to increase value-added for all
the stakeholders involved in all these types of public value.

However, there are a number of very different modes in which marketing can be used
(Box 7.10). Some of these modes fundamentally seek to serve the user's interest (positive
marketing, some variants of anti-marketing), while some seek to serve society's interest
(social marketing) and some seek to serve the interests of target users at the expense of non-
target users (demarketing).

Box 7.8 Definitions of marketing

"Marketing is the establishment of mutually satisfying exchange relationships" (Baker, 1976).

"Marketing is the management process responsible for identifying, anticipating and satisfying customer requirements profitably" (Chartered Institute of Marketing).

Box 7.9 Product orientation versus market orientation

Product orientation

- emphasis on getting the "product" right in professional terms
- product is developed first, then there is an attempt to attract customers
- organization is inward-looking, its production needs come first
- success is measured primarily in terms of professional esteem, with a secondary emphasis on the number of customers attracted
- and if the service fails? "We did our best, we produced a really good service – but the market failed – it didn't appreciate us"

Service orientation

- emphasis on doing what the customer wants
- services are developed to meet expressed and potential wants in a coordinated way
- the organization is outward-looking, the customers' needs come first
- success is measured by both the number and satisfaction level of customers (i.e. "quality" as well as quantity)
- the customer is central to everything the organization does (i.e. there is a culture of "customer obsession")
- and if the service fails? "Our fault – we failed to meet the market's requirements"

Box 7.10 Modes of marketing

- positive marketing: Encouraging target groups to use particular goods, services or organizations because they will meet their needs
- social marketing: Advancing a social, environmental or political viewpoint or cause because it will meet society's needs
- anti-marketing: Encouraging target groups to cease using particular goods, services or organizations, either because it is against their interest or because it is against society's interest
- demarketing: Deterring non-target groups from service uptake

Source: Adapted from Sheaff (1991).

One of the key issues that emerges from this discussion is "who is the customer?" – this feeds directly into the decisions on outcomes strategy discussed earlier in this chapter. There are many potential customers for the public sector, including:

- people currently receiving the service
- people waiting for it
- people needing the service but not actively seeking it
- people who may need the service in the future
- people refused the service
- carers of people needing the service (both those receiving it and not receiving it)
- taxpayers
- citizens (particularly those who wish to see people in need being well looked after)
- referrers of potential clients of the service

In the rest of this chapter, we speak of all of these as "customers", but a detailed marketing plan will normally try to differentiate the needs of each of these different customers and tailor the service to those different needs. (Moreover, the service user, in some cases, may not consider her/himself to be a beneficiary or "customer" at all, e.g. prisoners.)

Preparing a marketing plan

In this section, we will consider how marketing plans can be constructed in public sector organizations.

There is clearly a very strong connection between strategic management and the marketing plans of any organization (or organizational unit such as a service department). Typically, each constituent service unit of the organization is expected to prepare a service strategy, nested within and aligned to the corporate strategy, but with a marketing plan which goes into greater detail on the target groups (market segments) for its services and the marketing mix which will ensure its services are appropriate for those market segments.

Analysing market segments

People in different market segments will normally prefer different services or different designs of a given service. The most typical criteria for drawing up market segments in the public sector are demographic (gender, age, household composition), socio-economic (class, socio-economic group), economic or social disadvantage (pensioners, unemployed, low income, disability groups, ethnic minorities, isolated people, etc.) and geographic (neighbourhood, ward, town, region, etc.). However, more recently there has been greater interest in using such criteria as lifestyle and tastes (often using psychographics) (Twenge, 2023). Each of these approaches naturally tends to miss some of the important differences between individuals, although each allows a move away from treating all customers as a mass market. Another form of market segmentation looks at the customers' attitude to the service provided (unaware, hostile, aware, interested, wavering towards action, tester, occasional user, loyal).

Each of these approaches is useful for a particular form of marketing initiative, but the critically important issue is to prioritize between these market segments in order to determine which segments should form the target or priority groups for the public agency. This is one of the fundamental political tasks in any public sector organization.

Deciding the marketing mix

In order to implement the chosen strategic option, the marketing plan needs to set out decisions on key operational issues (the "marketing mix"), as illustrated in Figure 7.5. The elements of the marketing mix are closely interrelated and therefore need to be carefully aligned with each other:

- The *product* (or *service*) needs to be designed with the needs of the customer in mind. Design features need to include not only the core features of the service itself but also the way in which it is delivered, including such "customer care" aspects as the availability of the service (e.g. opening hours), reliability (e.g. how often is the service defective?) and responsiveness to customers' needs (e.g. does the service take account of differences in gender, age, ethnicity, (dis)ability, etc.?). A key element of service design is market research, which should be central to public services management, whether conducted by surveys, focus groups or other methods.
- The *promotion* of the service has to be suitable for the target group, so that over time the users become aware of the service, interested, keen to use it and then take action to try it out (summarized in the AIDA pneumonic – **a**wareness, **i**nterest, **d**esire, **a**ction). The mix of promotional methods needs to be carefully thought out, including advertising, special sales promotions, sponsorship deals and public relations campaigns. In recent years, particular attention has been given to "nudge" techniques, which frame problems and issues in such a way as to influence the target group towards desired behaviours (Thaler and Sunstein, 2008; John et al., 2011; and see Chapter 6 and https://www.bi.team).
- The *place* in which the service is available has to be suitable for the target service user (e.g. comfortable to use and accessible, perhaps through co-location with local shops or

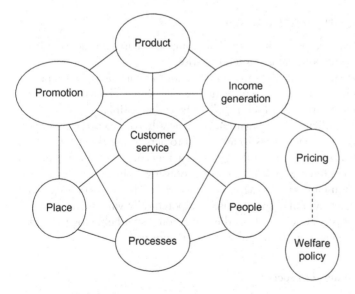

Figure 7.5 The expanded marketing mix for public services.

Source: Adapted from Christopher et al. (2002).

other public services, and appropriate transport has to be available – or services can be provided virtually, e.g. over the internet or through a call centre).

- The *processes* used to assess eligibility and to deliver the service have to be clear and understandable for the target group (including easy-to-use forms, with translation available if required) and should be designed to minimize time taken and hassle.
- The *people* who supply the service have to be welcoming and empathetic to the target group and well trained in giving the service.
- The *income generation* activities of the organization have to be consistent with its principles and efficiently organized so that the net income is maximized. Sources of income might include fundraising by volunteers, donations, sponsorship, sales of associated services (e.g. from a charity shop), merchandizing, sales of advertising space or pricing.
- The *prices* charged have to be appropriate to the target group's means (which will partly be determined by overall national *welfare policy*, to which an organization must conform and to which it contributes), proportionate to the benefits given and consistent with the income generation plan. This may entail giving concessions (which may require income assessment, with its problems of stigma, deterrence to usage and high costs).

Clearly, there will be considerable overlap between outcomes strategies and the operational marketing plans – for example, the decision on the portfolio of services to be offered belongs to both, although it is handled at a finer level of detail in marketing plans. Again, promotion is just one branch of marketing communications, by means of which the organization seeks to keep in touch with its various customers. (This is considered in more detail in Chapter 22, on stakeholder engagement.) Moreover, marketing plans and service delivery plans will often have strong overlaps (e.g. making sure that proper transport arrangements are in place is part of the "place" factor in the marketing plan, but also part of the "logistics" factor in the service delivery plan).

Marketing in a politically driven organization

Marketing is never easy in any context but it is especially complicated in a political environment, where a number of thorny political issues tend to arise.

First, marketing, like strategic management in general, requires clear statements of priorities, particularly about which target groups are priorities for each policy. This means telling many groups that they are *not* priorities – which is politically embarrassing.

Second, promotion of the policies of an organization generally tries to show them in a positive light and promotion of services tries to attract customers to use them – but such promotion can be interpreted as "selling" the ruling group's achievements to the population and can therefore be accused of having "political" motives or using "spin".

Third, pricing of services is usually seen as highly controversial and changes of prices tend to be made relatively infrequently, removing the use of a potentially valuable tool in the marketing mix for significant periods, even where there are grounds for believing that price increases would not be so unpopular with the public as politicians fear.

Targeting the most disadvantaged in society

The first political issue highlighted in the previous section is by far the most important. We might expect, given the rhetoric of the public sector over recent decades, that it has particularly targeted and helped the most disadvantaged groups in society. However, this cannot be assumed, as Le Grand pointed out more than 30 years ago:

Almost all public expenditure in social services in Britain benefits the better off to a greater degree than the poor ... [even in] services whose aims are at least in part egalitarian, such as the NHS, higher education, public transport, and the aggregate complex of housing policies.

(Le Grand, 1982)

He goes on to suggest that there persist substantial inequalities in public expenditure, however it is measured, and to show how, in many policy areas, public expenditure has failed to reduce inequality significantly in terms of:

- inequalities in public expenditure per user
- inequalities in public expenditure per unit of need
- inequalities in the opportunity to use public services
- inequalities in access to services (including cost of access and time taken to get access)
- inequalities in outcomes

However, Lupton et al. (2013) conclude that, more recently, UK public spending may have been more effective in improving the lot of the worst off in society. They show that, in general terms, where New Labour spent money between 1997 and 2010, outcomes improved, but remained unchanged where no policy effort or extra money was spent. Outcomes improved most for the people explicitly targeted by policy – families with children and pensioners (Lupton et al., 2013: 61), which could be seen as the most important indicator of success for policies on inequality.

More generally, Le Grand's rather pessimistic conclusions about the weakness of targeting public spending in the UK may not apply everywhere – research by Doerrenberg and Peichl (2012) provides evidence that government social spending has effectively reduced inequality across OECD countries, taken as a whole – a 1% increase in government spending was linked to a 0.3% drop in inequality. However, a more recent paper (Anderson et al., 2018) finds no clear evidence that higher government spending has played a significant role in reducing income poverty in low- and middle-income countries (although it has perhaps worked better for countries in Sub-Saharan Africa than for countries in Eastern Europe and Central Asia).

The lesson is clear – if politicians cannot or will not address directly the need to target public expenditure and public services at the most disadvantaged, then it seems likely that public service marketing will remain a relatively weak tool for achieving the purposes of government – and those purposes will be much harder to achieve.

Limitations of marketing

While marketing can help public sector organizations to work more effectively to please their customers, there remain significant limitations to its use in the public sector.

First, it is often artificial to regard all those who come into contact with the public sector as its customers. The relationship between the state and some of its subjects (e.g. prisoners, child abusers) is characterized by relations of dominance and punishment rather than exchange and mutual reward. Marketing is less relevant in these circumstances.

Second, the manipulation of public tastes and preferences to make the public sector's services more desirable is questionable in the public sector. This largely rules out some approaches from private sector marketing, which create demand for unnecessary services and encourage behaviours based on "base desires" and unworthy motives such as power and greed or which emphasize style rather than performance.

Third, there are areas where individuals making their own choice will not contribute to the highest good of their society – e.g. because of spillover effects from their decisions, the poor quality of information on which they act, their lack of understanding of their own (long-term) best interest or for other reasons. In the many cases where these "market failures" are likely to exist (see Chapter 3), then collective decisions based on political processes will remain superior to "customer" decisions influenced by marketing.

In general, then, the balance between marketing and political decision-making as a way of mediating between service users, citizens and service producers is one that will always be hard to find and is likely to shift over time. While marketing may have played too small a role in traditional public administration up to the 1980s, it has perhaps been in danger of encroaching too far in some areas of public policy since then.

Summary

This chapter has argued that both strategic planning and strategic management are important but strategic management is essential, whereas strategic planning may have a more limited role. It has considered a range of techniques for understanding the external and internal environment of organizations and for identifying and evaluating strategic options.

It has also linked these strategies to the marketing plans needed to ensure that they are implemented, choosing an appropriate marketing mix.

Moreover, innovation is the lifeblood of good strategic management, with constant development and testing of new strategic options. "No change" is not an option (but neither is "all change"!).

Political processes are intrinsic to good strategic management in the public sector, but some aspects of political decision-making can make strategic management difficult. Nevertheless, marketing in a political environment can help to force political decision-makers to be more open, e.g. about their priority target groups, but we must also be sensitive to the limitations of marketing when applied in the public domain.

Questions for review and discussion

1   How do you think strategic plans in the public sector would differ if they were initially drawn up by politicians and then considered for approval by professionals and managers in the public sector?
2   In what circumstances might realized strategies be more likely to stem from planned intended strategies than from emergent processes? Why?
3   Why does the term "marketing" often appear to have a pejorative meaning? Is this justified in relation to public service marketing?

Reader exercises

1   Find a strategic plan for a public sector organization with which you are familiar.
    How well has it analysed its external and internal environments? Does it indicate the strategic options it considered before it chose its preferred strategy? Does it make clear the evaluation criteria on the basis of which its preferred strategy was chosen?
2   Choose a public sector organization that you know. Consider one of its services: Try to identify the main elements of the marketing mix. Can you suggest some changes to the marketing mix that would make this organization more accessible to vulnerable groups?

Class exercises

1   In groups, identify some organizations you know, in public, voluntary and private sectors, which have the core competences listed in Box 7.4. Compare your results, identifying any sector differences which appear to emerge.

2   Divide into groups. Each group should identify the main elements of the marketing mix in the higher education system and propose changes that would help to increase enrolment of students from disadvantaged backgrounds in this system. Compare notes and identify the reasons behind the main differences in each of your proposals.

Further reading

John Bryson (2018), *Strategic planning for public and nonprofit organizations: A guide to strengthening and sustaining organizational achievement* (5th ed.). Hoboken, NJ: Wiley.

Paul Joyce and Anne Drumaux (eds.) (2018), *Strategic management in public organisations: European practices and perspectives.* London: Routledge.

Philip Kotler and Nancy Lee (2006), *Marketing in the public sector: A roadmap for improved performance.* Upper Saddle River, NJ: Wharton School Publishing.

Kieron Walsh (1993), *Marketing in local government.* Harlow: Longman.

Richard Whittington, Patrick Regner, Duncan Angwin, Gerry Johnson and Kevan Scholes (2022), *Exploring strategy* (13th ed.). Harlow: Pearson.

References

Edward Anderson, Maria Ana Jalles d'Orey, Maren Duvendack and Lucio Esposito (2018), 'Does government spending affect income poverty? A meta-regression analysis', *World Development*, 103: 60–71.

Michael Baker (1976), 'Evolution of the marketing concept', in Michael Baker (ed.), *Marketing theory and practice.* London: Macmillan, pp. 3–25.

Tony Bovaird (2012a), 'Capacity building and local government: Organisational responses to the need for greater human capacity', *Comparative Public Administration*, 11 ("Integrated human capacity building in the age of decentralization"), edited by Akira Nakamura, Osamu Koike and Masao Kikuchi. Tokyo: Local Autonomy College.

Tony Bovaird (2012b), 'Attributing outcomes to social policy interventions–"gold standard" or "fool's gold" in public policy and management?', *Social Policy and Administration*, 48(1): 1–23.

Tony Bovaird and Elke Loeffler (2012), 'From engagement to co-production: The contribution of users and communities to outcomes and public value', *Voluntas*, 23(4): 1119–1138.

John Bryson, Fran Ackermann and Colin Eden (2007), 'Putting the resource-based view of strategy and distinctive competencies to work in public organizations', *Public Administration Review*, 67(4): 702–717.

Alfred Chandler (1962), *Strategy and structure.* Cambridge, MA: MIT Press.

Chartered Institute of Marketing (2009), *Marketing and the 7Ps: A brief summary of marketing and how it works.* Maidenhead: CIM.

Martin Christopher, Adrian Payne and David Ballantyne (2002), *Relationship marketing: Creating stakeholder value* (2nd ed.). Oxford: Butterworth Heinemann.

Philipp Doerrenberg and Andreas Peichl (2012), *The impact of redistributive policies on inequality in OECD countries.* Bonn: Institute for the Study of Labor (IZA).

Gary Hamel and C.K. Prahalad (1994), *Competing for the future.* Boston, MA: Harvard Business School Press.

Charles Handy (1993), *Understanding organisations* (4th ed.). Harmondsworth: Penguin.

Julian Le Grand (1982), *The strategy of equality: Redistribution and the social services.* London: Allen & Unwin.

Peter John, Sarah Cotterill, Alice Moseley, Liz Richardson, Graham Smith, Gerry Stoker and Corinne Wales (2011), *Nudge, nudge, think, think: Using experiments to change civic behaviour.* London: Bloomsbury.

Gerry Johnson, Kevan Scholes and Richard Whittington (2008), *Exploring corporate strategy: Text and cases* (8th ed.). Harlow: FT Prentice Hall.

James Joyce (1922), *Ulysses.* Revised version (1932), Hamburg: The Odyssey Press.

Robert S. Kaplan and David P. Norton (1996), *The balanced scorecard: Translating strategy into action.* Boston, MA: Harvard Business School Press.

Bob Kerslake (2014), *The way forward: An independent review of the governance and organisational capabilities of Birmingham City Council.* London: HMSO.

Ruth Lupton, John Hills, Kitty Stewart and Polly Vizard (2013), *Labour's Social Policy Record: Policy, Spending and Outcomes 1997-2010.* London: CASE, LSE.

Henry Mintzberg (1987), 'The strategy concept 1: Five Ps for strategy', *California Management Review,* 30(1): 11–24.

Henry Mintzberg (1992), 'Mintzberg on the rise and fall of strategic planning', *Long Range Planning,* 25(4): 99–104.

Mark H. Moore (1995), *Creating public value: Strategic management in government.* Cambridge, MA: Harvard University Press.

Rod Sheaff (1991), *Marketing for health services.* Buckingham: Open University Press.

Richard H. Thaler and Cass R. Sunstein (2008), *Nudge: Improving decisions about health, wealth and happiness.* New Haven and London: Yale University Press.

Jean M. Twenge (2023), *Generations: The real differences between Gen Z, `millenials, Gen X, Boomers and Silents … and what they mean for the future.* New York: Atria.

Kieron Walsh (1993), *Marketing in local government.* London: FT Prentice Hall.

Karl Weick (1979), *The social psychology of organizing.* Reading, MA: Addison-Wesley.

8 Contracting and partnering for public services

Carsten Greve

Introduction

This chapter examines the debate surrounding contracting for services, public-private partnerships (PPPs) and empirical evidence on the effectiveness of government policies. These policies have been introduced in countries throughout the world so there is much experience to draw upon (Bovaird, 2016; Hodge and Greve, 2019).

In general, there has been a shift from competing for contracted services through competitive tendering towards more complex arrangements, which include managing multiple contracts, managing relationships through the supply chain and developing accountable partnerships (Greve, 2008). These latter include public-private partnerships (see Chapter 16), and partnerships with users and communities ('user and community co-production of services' – see Chapter 23). This chapter will examine the merits of contracting and partnerships as mechanisms for managing the delivery of externalized services.

Learning objectives

- To understand the meaning of contracting;
- To understand why contracting for services has been increasing;
- To be able to identify the pros and cons of contracting out specific services;
- To understand the links between contracting, competition and partnerships;
- To understand how contracting could be used to pursue the wider socio-economic goals (public value) of government.

The rise of contracting for services: From competition to partnership

Competition

Many OECD governments have been committed to reducing the size and role of the public sector, often believing that it was less efficient than the private sector in delivering public services. This led to a fundamental shift away from direct service provision through the hierarchy of public sector organizations towards market-based competition and contractual relationships between public sector organizations and private or non-profit organizations. The ideas associated with the New Public Management (NPM) were dominant partly because

DOI: 10.4324/9781003282839-10

they succeeded in linking with other influential strands of thought, in particular the growing critique of the public sector and bureaucracy in the management and organization literature (see Chapters 3 and 4).

The ideas of cost reduction (economy) and efficiency are central to the argument in favour of competitive tendering, and a number of subsequent studies (e.g. Petersen, Hjelmar and Vrangbaek, 2018) described the issue of cost-saving from contracting. OECD (2022) sees contracting and public procurement as the cornerstone of strategic governance. Public procurement has been defined by OECD as

> the process of identifying what is needed; determining who the best person or organiza-
> tion is to supply this need, and ensuring what is needed is delivered to the right place
> at the right time, for the best price and that all this is done in a fair and open manner.
> (OECD, 2015: 6)

Governments can thereby avoid accusations of favouritism and fraud, and the openness of the system will encourage more suppliers to participate, thus increasing competition, which can in turn reduce prices, improve quality and lead to greater innovation among suppliers.

European Union procurement rules have influenced member countries' approach to contracting. Usually these services were previously delivered by staff of the public agency (the 'in-house' provider), which was now required to compete against outside bidders. This involved setting up a direct service organization (DSO), separate from the client (but usually run by the previous managers of the service), which was responsible for the competitive tendering process. As Box 8.1 illustrates, OECD now has specific recommendations for public procurement. These public procurement recommendations should ensure a level playing field for all potential providers of service.

Partnership

Partnership has come to dominate the agenda on public-private relations in recent years. While competition was the hallmark the New Public Management, partnership relations with suppliers appeared as a key element as an alternative. Partnership is 'any arrangement in which the production of a given service is shared between two or more organizations' (Alford and O'Flynn, 2012: 20).

Box 8.1 OECD principles for public procurement

- transparency;
- integrity;
- access;
- balance;
- participation;
- efficiency;
- e-procurement;
- capacity;
- evaluation;
- risk management;

- accountability;
- integration.

Source: OECD. Public Procurement Toolbox. https://www.oecd.org/governance/procurement/toolbox/principlestools/

By emphasizing cooperation and collaboration, policy initiatives set out to change the nature of the procurement function and of the relationship between government departments and suppliers. By moving away from the competitive market model represented by the New Public Management, partnership working with suppliers can build social capital, leading to reduced transaction costs, increased outputs and improved outcomes (e.g. greater social cohesion). Social capital research (see Erridge and Greer, 2002: 504–507) suggests that increased interaction and exchange can:

- lead to the development of trust and the creation of norms and sanctions that reduce transaction costs;
- improve access to resources among network members;
- create identity, building a sense of 'belonging' and shared action;
- have positive ripple effects within society by encouraging participation and creating greater social cohesion.

Government policies in many countries have reinforced this more participative, collaborative approach, with an approach to contracting that facilitates the effective delivery of more complex services.

Improved relationships within the network of the supply chain have provided an opportunity for interested stakeholders to work together more closely, set out common and clear objectives to address community problems and tackle issues such as the environment or quality of life for disadvantaged groups. For example, collaborative supply relations have facilitated close engagement between government departments, registered charities and local schools and communities in the implementation of local environmental projects. Under this arrangement, partnership stakeholders collaborate to share information, set up performance measures, report on the progress of environmental projects and disseminate good practice in an effort to improve the environment in local communities. The contracting arrangements in a collaborative setting often become more complex. A famous in-depth case study of how the US Coast Guard tried to introduce a comprehensive contract for buying and maintaining a system of new boats, aircraft and communications and control architecture for its fleet demonstrated major challenges to complex contracting (Brown, Potoski and Van Slyke, 2013). The 24 billion USD contract proved too complex to handle for the US Coast Guard in the end. Managing complex contracts is different from the single stand-alone contract for a very specific service and requires that government contractors know how to align values with existing institutions as well as understanding the markets in which they are operating.

The scope and nature of service contracting

Across the OECD in 2019, governmental public procurement spent an average of 12.9% of GDP on contracted services (OECD, 2021). Under COVID-19 public procurement rose to 14.9% of GDP in 2020. The debate about the effectiveness of contracting out has been going on for years. A systematic review of international studies of economic and quality effects revealed the following: (1) Cost-savings documented in the studies showed a decreasing trend over time. (2) Cost-savings tend to be greater in so-called 'technical services', that are relatively easy to measure (e.g. cleaning, garbage collection) than in more complex social services. (3) Economic effects measured from contracting out appear to be twice as high in Anglo-Saxon countries as in other countries (Petersen, Hjelmar and Vrangbaek, 2018).

Choosing between public or private sector suppliers

What is the theoretical rationale for choosing between keeping a task in-house or contracting it out to external providers? Various theories of contracting provide some of the background for why a service may be organized in one sector rather than the other. Dominant theories have been transaction cost economics, developed by Oliver Williamson, and principal-Agent theory (see Box 8.2). The increase in the contracting out of services previously delivered directly by public sector organizations reflects a partial move away from the predominant form of service delivery, namely internal bureaucracy, to alternative forms of delivery.

Box 8.2 Theories of internal and external service provision

Transaction cost economics

In his extensive writings, Oliver Williamson has argued that the make-or-buy decision should be determined by comparison of the transaction costs of internal versus external provision. It is cheaper to buy one-off services – such as building a school – than it is to maintain all of the necessary construction staff and plant in-house. On the other hand, in-house provision is well-suited to services that are provided frequently, that involve a non-trivial degree of uncertainty and that need significant transaction-specific investments.

Principal-agent theory

Donahue (1989) points out that successful contracting requires that the agents tasked with performing a particular function can be readily controlled by their principal (the client). This requires that exact specifications can be drawn up, outputs can be easily measured and inadequate suppliers are quickly replaced. Donahue cites waste collection as exemplifying the benefits of contracting, concluding that: 'Contractors chosen by fair and honest bid contests typically out-perform public monopolies' (p. 68).

Contestable markets

Many of the criticisms of public providers hinge upon the absence of competitive forces, which allows public providers to be inefficient monopolies. From this perspective, the

---

remedy is clear – where possible, competitive pressures should be created by giving service users as wide a choice as possible from a broad range of alternative providers, giving rise to a mixed and vibrant economy of provision. Contracting-out *per se* would simply replace public monopolies by private monopolies. This is the reasoning that underpins a government's desire to create and manage markets in which existing suppliers find their position contested by new suppliers.

Functional matching

The fourth perspective suggests that the public, private and voluntary sectors are good at doing different things. Based on a clear understanding of the different strengths of the different sectors, public agencies can allocate functions to the most suitable sectors.

Source: Adapted from Entwistle et al. (2002: 10–11).

These theoretical considerations suggest that internal providers have an advantage in the provision of services where:

- future needs and priorities cannot be predicted with certainty, so that any service specification undertaken now is likely to need significant variations in the future;
- outputs are diffuse and difficult to measure, so that the degree of achievement of any output-based specification is difficult to determine;
- the service will not require assets that will be under-employed if only used for in-house provision;
- flexibility and responsiveness, local knowledge and the exercise of political judgement are required.

Partnerships in public service delivery

The partnership approach has become an influential approach to contracting as we have seen. There are many conceptual definitions of what a partnership is, beyond the most basic feature of two or more organizations collaborating. One way of categorizing partnerships was provided by Brinkerhoff and Brinkerhoff (2011) who distinguished between (1) policy PPPs, (2) service delivery PPPs, (3) infrastructure PPPs (sometimes also referred to as the private finance initiative or PFI), (4) capacity building PPPs and (5) economic development PPPs. It can also be useful to separate the different levels on which PPPs are operating. Greve and Hodge (2013: 4) argued that PPPs could be seen as:

1) a project;
2) an organizational form;
3) a policy;
4) a governance tool or governance style;
5) a phenomenon within a broader historical and cultural context (which means that a partnership may mean different things in China than in the US).

Klijn (2022) has suggested that PPPs can be viewed in the following way:

1) PPP as a monitoring game, where the orientation is towards economics and the conditions for opportunistic behaviour;
2) PPP as a collaboration, with an orientation towards complex interactions between partners;
3) PPP as sensemaking, which tries to reconcile the partners' different frames of meaning.

Bovaird (2006) analyses three case studies to illustrate how market relationships have changed in a multi-stakeholder procurement environment, each representing one form of the new procurement approaches that are emerging (Box 8.3):

- relational contracting;
- partnership procurement;
- distributed commissioning.

Partnering with the private sector was pursued more vigorously, especially through PPPs, to fund infrastructure capital projects. Donahue and Zeckhauser (2011) focus on a number of areas where public sector actors and private sector actors can collaborate, including a case study on the maintenance of Central Park in New York City.

The shift towards PPPs has been described as a 'movement'. Hodge and Greve (2022) reviewed the available evidence and the challenges of performance of infrastructure PPPs. They identified 24 different objectives or promises made by governments in relation to infrastructure PPPs. These were grouped under six headings: Financial, project delivery, cultural change, policy, governance and economic. On performance, Hodge and Greve (2022: 52) stated: 'We noted some of the existing empirical PPP evidence focusing on Value for Money performance and confirmed that mixed results exist internationally'. A systematic literature review found that infrastructure PPPs are on average more costly than traditional procurement and provide similar Value for Money as traditional procurement. This lack of PPP success is markedly different from the usual positive judgements made by governments promoting PPPs. Evaluations are mostly done by governments or consultancy companies. Although many evaluations show that PPP projects are finished on time and on budget, fewer independent and research-based evaluations exist.

Six challenges exist according to Hodge (2010) with regard to the evaluation of PPPs:

(1) the topic of PPP evaluation is not always precise;
(2) PPPs have multiple objectives;
(3) many academic disciplines can be used (for example, economics and public policy) which have their own methodology and standards;
(4) evaluators have several roles to play, for example seeking scientific certainty or digging out performance information for politicians;
(5) value for money is often used as a standard, but still lacks a rigorous evidence base;
(6) reviewing international studies accurately requires a solid evaluation approach that is not always used.

The European Commission has pushed both competitive and collaborative approaches. Competition has been a central element of its public procurement policies, including the Services Directive, which aims to break down barriers to cross-border trade in services between EU member states, so that service providers, particularly small and medium-sized enterprises, will find it easier to set up business and offer services in other member states and to provide services across the boundaries of member states.

Box 8.3 Case studies on stakeholder relationships in PPPs

Relational contracting for Revenues and Benefits service: Consultants of the company Unisys were encouraged to work informally with staff working in the Revenues and Benefits section of the London Borough of Harrow to identify barriers to more effective and efficient working and to explore staff reactions to different options for change. A bottom-up approach was adopted, which allowed a new approach to emerge that built on existing knowledge bases in the department, was consistent with the most positive aspects of departmental culture and allowed local priorities to be incorporated in the resulting systems. Simultaneously, the consultants came to recognize new ways of solving problems by marrying their technical expertise with the service knowledge held by front-line staff. The contract was simply to improve the quality of the service while making savings – it did not revolve around the delivery of a fixed specification.

Partnership procurement of Dudley Community Health Unit: The original idea of the Primary Health Trust and the local authority was 'Let's build a local Mental Health Unit'. It then became a 'one-stop shop' for all primary health services in the local area, so that the business case was health-driven. Later the concept was extended to incorporate social services and the local library and was developed as a PFI project. Mill Group was chosen as the preferred developer and facility manager because it agreed to a flexible 'relational contract'. In spite of the complexity of this joint procurement process, the building was completed on time, on budget and on specification. At no stage did a 'variations management game' emerge, in which contractors sought to profit excessively from variations to the specification which were found over time to be desirable. Nevertheless, with hindsight, the underlying concept was probably under-ambitious – in this co-location model, the services are 'next door' to each other, rather than being truly joint and seamless, in their commissioning and delivery.

Distributed commissioning: A local Community Trust took advantage of the redevelopment of old military barracks in the rural village of Caterham, which had long-standing housing and social problems. The Trust managed to broker a planning agreement with the private developer, who was suspicious at first that the arrangement was an attempt to lower densities and profit margins on the site, but eventually agreed to contribute over £2 million for social facilities and believed it had made a bigger profit on the development than if it had gone for traditional middle-income housing. The Community Trust has used its funds to establish a range of economic, social, educational, cultural and sports facilities on the site and to manage them so that they respond to wider community needs in the area (including a skate park, community theatre group, craft workshops, sports teams, etc.). The Trust also negotiates with major service providers in the area on behalf of villagers. Local villagers, initially suspicious of being swamped by 'incomers', have played a major part in the evolution of the new community activities, which have significantly improved the quality of life for local villagers. In this way, the commissioning of local public services has been distributed to a local group of people, rather than simply being decided by the local council.

Source: Adapted from Bovaird (2006).

However, the EU has also promoted a more collaborative approach – it suggests that there should be greater dialogue between purchasers and suppliers, arguing that a more cooperative approach can reduce costs through working with suppliers to identify inefficiencies in the supply chain, while improved supply market intelligence and a better use of resources can lead to commercial gains without competition. This 'competitive dialogue' approach attempts to combine the advantages of competition and collaboration by allowing 'market testing' at the early stage of the service design and procurement process, while getting the advantages of close collaborative working with the final shortlist of potential partners, before making the final procurement decision.

Infrastructure PPPs, privately financed, have increasingly become the vehicle for providing the infrastructure to deliver government policy through, for example, the building and equipping of schools, hospitals, transport systems, water and sewerage systems. However, there is no uniform pattern of provision, with a mixed economy of provision between public, private and voluntary sectors being adopted as appropriate for each project. The global financial crisis renewed the need to look at the role of PPPs and examine the relationship between the sectors (Greve and Hodge, 2013).

International developments in contracting and partnering for public services

The use of contracting and PPPs has grown internationally, involving broadly similar approaches in most cases, although the drivers differ in each country, and the processes are adapted to the particular constitutional, legal and governance arrangements of each country.

Contracting for public services is now an integrated part of public service delivery in most European countries because of the use of European Union procurement rules. Moreover, the greater use of contracting for public services across EU borders has resulted in frequent investigations by the European Commission and occasional critical judgements by the European Court of Justice, but rarely penalties to match the offence. Donahue and Zeckhauser (2011) have identified a wider trend towards 'collaborative governance' in the EU.

Internationally, the interest in PPPs has surged. PPPs for infrastructure development are used regularly in countries like Australia, Canada, Ireland, Germany, Spain and the USA. PPPs are also of interest to international organizations like the United Nations and the World Bank (Hodge and Greve, 2019). The international attraction of PPPs to governments is obvious: They offer control and ownership, combined with capital and efficiency from the private sector (Boardman and Vining, 2010: 159). A number of studies of how the PPP policy was implemented in various parts of the world have now surfaced. Liebe (2022) examines the implementation of PPP policy in the European Union and notes the interaction between the European Commission and the European Investment Bank. Mihov (2022) uses the theoretical lenses of institutional work and policy transfer theory to analyse how infrastructure PPP policy was implemented in Germany through several decades. What started out as a fascination with the British Private Finance Initiative model developed into a specifically German institutionalized version of an infrastructure PPP model and then scepticism and abandonment of the pure private finance aspect of the PPP model towards a more mixed economy approach.

Outside Europe, there is considerable experience with transport and other infrastructure projects in Australia and Canada. There are around 150 PPP projects in Canada.

In Australia, PPP projects have involved the Sydney harbour tunnel and the Melbourne CityLink project. Projects are often reported as being on time and on budget. Some projects are less successful, which may be because of poor contract and project management. The essential questions in infrastructure PPPs are whether risks are shared or not, and how benefits and costs are shared. An infrastructure PPP project that works must be aligned with the proper institutional conditions: a robust legislative framework, a clear PPP policy from the government, a shared concept of reasonable contract conditions and the availability of competent private partners. Among the criteria appropriate for judging PPPs are value for money, risk sharing, budget documentation and transparency and political support. One of the key issues is the economics of PPPs. Economists are not just interested in on-time and on-budget delivery, but also look to benefit-cost analysis, the proper discount rates for PPP projects and the social benefit of PPPs compared to other types of projects (either private or public).

OECD has investigated PPPs on a number of occasions. The recommendation from OECD and other international organizations is that PPP is not a panacea to all problems, but that successful PPP projects require careful planning and institutional design skills to work. OECD also believes that the issue of risk sharing remains perhaps the most crucial aspect of a PPP deal. Furthermore, the competencies in contract management from the public sector side must be upgraded (most private sector organizations already have these skills). OECD (2017) has grouped PPP policy as one element of a general approach to the governance of infrastructure.

Contracting for wider socio-economic goals (public value) of government

Policy on contracting, through the structures and procedures mentioned above, partly reflects the market model supported by public choice theorists, but also new arrangements of collaboration between public, private and non-profit sectors. In a classic text, Self (1993) argues that the market model is inconsistent with the public interest on three grounds:

1　public choice encourages the individual to maximize economic opportunities and personal wealth, whereas public interest requires identification or sympathy with others' needs;
2　political liberty cannot be treated as the dependent variable of a strong, autonomous market system; rather a balancing of the roles of the state and the market is required;
3　the market system makes no distinction between individuals' 'wants' and common 'needs' essential for a tolerable life.

Of course, there is always a danger that the dominant voices heard in supply chain debates will be commercial interests, usually large and powerful corporations which may ignore other issues, such as environmental damage, unfair employment conditions or exploitation of poorer producers. This suggests that public sector organizations should provide moral leadership by incorporating this broader social dimension into contracting decisions.

Policy areas usually considered include unemployment, social exclusion, protection of minorities, income distribution and economic development, particularly in relation to small firms and environmental policy. Environmental sustainability is likely to be important for future procurement policy as the world focuses on 'green growth'.

There are a number of methods through which the objectives of these policies could be achieved. Contractual clauses may be included, requiring contractors to comply with wider government goals such as combating discrimination on grounds of sex, race, religion or disability. 'Green' sourcing protects natural resources and the environment in which citizens live. OECD has recognized many of these points in its more comprehensive and balanced recommendations for public procurement and in the recommendations for the governance of infrastructure. A strategic commissioning approach has also been used in the UK to secure a more holistic way of procuring public services (see Chapters 7 and 15; Bovaird, Briggs and Willis, 2014). The debate is also reflected in the wider trend of public value that is influential in the literature on public management and governance (O'Flynn, 2021).

Given that the New Public Management model has come under criticism, there is a task for governments to ensure that the public interest is paramount. An example of a successful use of public procurement to promote employment is highlighted in Box 8.4.

Box 8.4 The Northern Ireland Unemployment Pilot Project

Northern Ireland has historically suffered from much higher levels of unemployment than other regions of the UK. The new 2002 Public Procurement Policy in Northern Ireland included a pilot project that was seen as an opportunity to redress this imbalance by taking advantage of the high level of public sector infrastructural investment and procurement of goods and services in the region. A condition was included in selected contracts for construction and services requiring contractors to submit a social policy statement and employment plan, outlining how they would meet the requirement actively to seek to employ people from the long-term-unemployed target group. On award of contract, the winning contractor was required to implement the proposals. The pilot project was monitored over a two-year period, and a final evaluation report was submitted in 2005.

The pilot project led to the recruitment of 51 new employees from the target group, of whom 46 were retained by the contractors. Those who have left employment will have benefited from their experience of work. The creation of these jobs was achieved with very little additional direct cost. The overall 'project cost per job created' during the evaluation period was £900,000, against a construction industry benchmark of £1 million.

The employment plan process has quickly become an embedded part of the culture of contracting with government amongst construction contractors, those most involved to date. The survey issued to all contractors at the end of the pilot project showed that almost two-thirds believed that the inclusion of the employment plan as part of the contract did not dissuade them from tendering for the contract. The procedures generally operated successfully, although there were a small number of instances of non-compliance. The Water Service provides an example of best practice, with 4 projects within the pilot, resulting in 13 people from the target group being employed at a project cost per job created of £720,000. There was clearly commitment to the pilot from the top of the organization, project managers were fully informed and committed, arrangements for regular monitoring reports were agreed with contractors, and arrangements were made by contractors to link up with an FE college to provide potential employees.

Source: Adapted from Erridge (2007).

Summary

This chapter has found that competitive contracting under NPM has resulted in some transfer of service provision from the public to the private sector, although the overall effect is still limited. Where services are delivered by the private sector, there is some evidence of savings and improved quality, but these must be weighed against higher transaction costs, incidences of contractor failure and inequality effects on public sector employees.

Governments internationally have pursued partnership with the private sector, adopting a more collaborative approach but backed by an increase in inspection and audit (see Chapter 14). While there is therefore a common recognition of the necessity of using private sector expertise and finance, governments also seem to recognize the distinctive contribution that public sector employees can make. However, this attitude does not persist where these employees are felt to be resistant, or where the services they provide are deemed to have failed (whether schools, hospitals or local authorities).

This suggests that the core problem that governments have sought to address through contracting is the perceived failure of public agencies to manage the delivery of public services efficiently and effectively. Increasingly, the solution is being found in a mixed economy of public, private and voluntary provision and through PPPs.

There are some key areas where we cannot yet be sure of the lessons emerging on contracting out and partnership working, and where, therefore, further research is needed. These include, in particular:

- can a more collaborative approach be developed through amending the rules and regulations on procurement policy even further?
- what are the drivers, forms and outcomes of contracting, in particular in PPPs, across different countries with varying constitutional, legal and governance arrangements?
- how can public value be pursued and reached through contracting and collaboration with the private sector?

Acknowledgement

The versions of this chapter which appeared in earlier editions of *Public Management and Governance* were authored or co-authored by Professor Andrew Erridge of Ulster University. He sadly died before the preparation of this revised chapter, but we wish to recognize his outstanding contribution over the years.

Questions for review and discussion

1 Should social and employment rights be protected through the contracting process by the insertion of relevant clauses in contracts? What are the benefits and risks of allowing such concerns to be embedded in contracts?
2 Why is it easier to use market-based contracting approaches in simple repetitive services than in complex, professionally based activities? Discuss which services fall into these categories in (1) a major metropolitan local authority in your country, and (2) an executive agency of central or regional government in your country.
3 What are the main factors that make local authorities reluctant to contract out services to, or partner with, the private sector? What steps do you consider central government might take to encourage local government to make more use of effective opportunities for contracting out or partnering?

Reader exercise

Select at least three articles on using private sector contractors or private finance to provide public services that have recently appeared in news media. What arguments and/or evidence do they provide in relation to the issues discussed in this chapter?

Class exercise

Identify in class some public services that have been contracted out. In groups, discuss the extent to which the contracting out of these services has more successfully met:

• the needs of those for whom the service is provided;
• the needs of the providers (i.e. the managers and employees);
• the government's political and managerial goals;
• the government's social, economic and environmental goals.

Further reading

John Alford and Janine O'Flynn (2012), *Rethinking public service delivery: Managing with external providers*. London: Palgrave MacMillan.
Tony Bovaird (2016), 'The ins and outs of outsourcing and insourcing: What have we learned from the past 30 years?' *Public Money and Management* 36(1), 67–74.
Carsten Greve and Graeme Hodge (eds.) (2019), *The logic of public-private partnerships*. Chelthenham: Edward Elgar.

References

Anthony Boardman and Aidan Vining (2010), 'Assessing the economic worth of public-private partnerships'. In Graeme Hodge, Carsten Greve and Anthony Boardman (eds.), *International handbook on public-private partnerships*. Chelthenham: Edward Elgar, pp. 159–186.
Tony Bovaird (2006), 'Developing new relationships with the 'market' in the procurement of public services'. *Public Administration* 84(1), 81–102.
Tony Bovaird, Ian Briggs and Martin Willis (2014), 'Strategic commissioning for local public services: Service improvement cycle or just going round in circles?' *Local Government Studies* 40(4), 553–559.
Tony Bovaird (2016), 'The ins and outs of outsourcing and insourcing: What have we learned from the past 30 years?' *Public Money and Management* 36(1), 67–74.
Derrick Brinkerhoff and Jenifer Brinkerhoff (2011), 'Public-private partnerships: Perspectives on purposes, publicness and good governance'. *Public Administration and Development* 31(1), 2–14.
Trevor L. Brown, Matthew Potoski and David M. Van Slyke (2013), *Complex contracting. Government purchasing in the wake of the US coast guard's deepwater program*. Cambridge: Cambridge University Press.
John D Donahue (1989). *The privatization decision*. New York, NY: Basic Books.
John Donahue and Richard Zeckhauser (2011), *Collaborative governance*. Princeton, NJ: Princeton University Press.
Tom Entwistle, Steve Martin and Gareth Enticott (2002), *Make or buy: The value of internal service providers in local government*. Project Report. London: PSNet.
Andrew Erridge (2007), 'Public procurement, public value and the NI unemployment pilot project', *Public Administration*, 85(4): 1023–1043.
Andrew Erridge and Jonathan Greer (2002), 'Partnerships and public procurement: Building social capital through supply relations'. *Public Administration* 80(3), 503–522.

Carsten Greve (2008), *Contracting for public services*. London: Routledge.

Carsten Greve and Graeme Hodge (eds.) (2013), *Rethinking public-private partnerships: Strategies for turbulent times*. London: Routledge.

Graeme Hodge (2010), 'Reviewing public-private partnerships: Some thoughts on evaluation'. In Graeme Hodge, Carsten Greve and Anthony Boardman (eds.) *International handbook on public-private partnerships*. Chelthenham: Edward Elgar, pp. 81–112.

Graeme Hodge and Carsten Greve (2020), *The logic of public-private partnerships*. Chelthenham: Edward Elgar.

Graeme Hodge and Carsten Greve (eds.) (2022), *A research agenda for public-prvate partnerships and the governance of infrastructure*. Chelthenham: Edward Elgar.

Erik-Hans Klijn (2022), 'Theories of public-private partnerships'. In Graeme Hodge and Carsten Greve (eds.), *A research agenda on public-private partnerships and the governance of infrastructure*. Chelthenham: Edward Elgar, pp. 33–52.

Moritz Liebe (2022), 'The determinants of uptake in Europe: A mixed methods approach'. In Graeme Hodge and Carsten Greve (eds.), *A research agenda for public-private partnerships and the governance of infrastructure*. Chelthenham: Edward Elgar, pp. 275–300.

Micaela Mihov (2022), 'Institutional work in policy transfer: A case study of PPP adoption in Germany'. In Graeme Hodge and Carsten Greve (eds.), *A research agenda for public-private partnerships and the governance of infrastructure*. Chelthenham: Edward Elgar, pp. 301–326.

OECD (2015), *Recommendation of the council on public procurement*. Paris: OECD.

OECD (2017), *The governance of infrastructure*. Paris: OECD.

OECD (2021), *Governance at a Glance*. Paris: OECD.

OECD (2022), Public procurement toolbox. Available at www.oecd.org/governance/procurement/toolbox. Accessed 20 October 2022.

Janine O'Flynn (2021), 'Where to for public value? Taking stock and moving on'. *International Journal of Public Administration* 44(10), 867–877.

Ole Helby Petersen, Ulf Hjelmar and Karsten Vrangbæk (2018), 'Is contracting out of public services still the great panacea? A systematic review of studies on economic and quality effects from 2000 to 2014'. *Social Policy and Administration* 52(1), 130–157.

Peter Self (1993), *Government by the market?* London: Macmillan.

9 Conceptual revolutions in public financial management

James L. Chan and Zhiming Ma

Introduction

Governments and nations ignore public financial management (PFM) at their peril. Public money often enables government to do many good things, but sometimes also bad things; conversely lack of money constrains government actions. Mismanagement of the people's money hurts service delivery and undermines public confidence. At stake is no less than a nation's future. Unfortunately, while the importance of money may be obvious, its good management is often overlooked or taken for granted. But what is sound public financial management? It is the opposite of the following scenario:

> What is budgeted is often not disbursed, and what is disbursed often does not arrive. Salaries go unpaid for months, operating funds do not materialize, and government debts remain unsettled. At the same time, the executive branch makes unbudgeted expenditures throughout the year. These loose practices make public spending data extremely spotty — and the data that does exist is often inaccurate or even falsified.
>
> (Thomas, 2001: 39)

The implication is that sound public financial management follows a continuous cycle of well-designed activities in a fiscal period. *Financial management* refers to the execution of the approved budget by means of financial transactions for collecting revenues, spending, investing and borrowing. The entire process of *fiscal administration* consists of budget preparation, submission and approval, followed by financial management as defined earlier. This process ideally is preceded by informed fiscal policy making and followed by evaluation for improving performance and planning.

Actual activities in these steps depend on the meanings given to the words: public, financial, management. *Public* can refer to government units at various levels of aggregation, state-owned enterprises, social service institutions, local government and even public-private partnerships. (These can all be considered as part of the *public sector*. Most chapters of this textbook consider public service organizations, including some belonging to the private or third sectors; these organizations have rather different financial management conventions and practices than those of public sector organizations, the subject of this chapter.) *Financial items* range from cash to claims against and by others, and even to economic resources and moral obligations. *Management* covers any activity for getting things done.

As financial systems and procedures are covered elsewhere (see Further Reading), this chapter compares three models of public financial management based on three conceptual revolutions in public administration/management and governance. The first model regards

DOI: 10.4324/9781003282839-11

public laws as the source of authority and rationality as the essence of management; the second places public value ahead of cost; and the third stresses organizational survival through stakeholders' cooperation. These models will likely rise and recede in importance in response to the needs of different times and places.

Learning objectives

After studying this chapter, you should be able to:

- Describe the main features and premises of the three models.
- Identify the revolutionary ideas that contributed to their emergence.
- Explain the concepts behind financial management procedures and techniques.
- Critique existing and proposed financial management practices.

The Wilson–Weber classical model

The classical model applies Woodrow Wilson's vision of public administration and Max Weber's characterization of bureaucracy to government finance. Active in the late 19th century and early 20th century, Wilson was an American political scientist who became US president, and Max Weber was an influential German sociologist. Their spirit continues to permeate contemporary textbooks and professional references (e.g. Mikesell, 2017; Allen et al., 2013).

Wilson's view of public administration as "a field of business" also aptly describes government's fiscal function. Being separate from politics and "incognito to the outside world", this instrument of public policy is full of mere technical details, confusing particulars and minute distinctions (Wilson, 1887). It is conducted by a Weberian bureaucracy with the following attributes: jurisdiction and function prescribed by public laws and rules, staffed by career officials and civil servants, organized as a hierarchy and recognized for its professionalism and expertise (Gerth and Mills, 1946).

Essential features

The classical model of public financial management has the following essential features:

> It construes the keywords narrowly: "public" refers to government executive departments; "financial" is about cash; and "management" concerns spending appropriations. For example, the 1787 Constitution of the United States famously states: "No money shall be drawn from the Treasury, but in consequence of Appropriations made by Law, and a regular Statement and Account of the Receipts and Expenditures of all public Money shall be published from time to time" (Article I, Section IX, Clause 7). Thus empowered, the US Congress monopolized the power of the purse until 1921, when the age of executive budgeting began, although Congress has continued its oversight of presidential spending and enacted a large body of budget laws and rules. (Refer to Lienert and Jung (2004) for a comparative analysis of Western budget laws.)

A budget commonly refers to proposed annual expenditures for a future period, which tends to be current base plus an increment. Line items in the approved budget authorize the purchase of inputs, such as personnel and equipment. Operating and capital expenditures, measured in terms of cash, are not necessarily differentiated. At the government level, a budgeted annual deficit, i.e. expenditures in excess of revenues, is prohibited. Actual deficits are absorbed by prior surpluses or financed by authorized borrowing. Financial management as budget execution ensures spending is only for authorized purposes and does not exceed the available balance in the applicable appropriation. Words are equally important as numbers. Budget laws and rules enunciate budget concepts and designate who does what in the budget process, as well as dealing with taxes and other revenues, debts, procurement, treasury management, accounting and auditing, and other functions.

Advances in the past century

During the 20th century, as government expenditures, revenues and debts expanded greatly to address economic crises and development, fight wars and maintain peace, fiscal administration grew in scope and complexity. Extensive research and development led many of the subsequent advances.

Government budget concepts grew in sophistication. Budget requests were expressed as functions and programmes in addition to organizational units, in order to align resource allocation with policy objectives. In order to better gauge the economic impacts of fiscal policy, the scope of the government budget expanded to cover the whole of government. Government budgets also took into account credits extended to and by the government. As governments acquired other forms of financial and capital resources and incurred long-term obligations, the balance sheet as a statement of assets and liabilities rose in prominence to capture the cumulative ("accrued") effects of past actions, including but not limited to deficit financing. If this trend continues, the next conceptual breakthrough will likely be accrual budgeting, which could transform the budget document from focusing only on flows into (eventually) a comprehensive prospective statement of both stock and flow measures.

Budget preparation has also undergone revolutionary changes since the 1950s. Changing priorities undermined incremental budgeting. New methods – planning programming budgeting system (PPBS), zero base budgeting (ZBB), participatory budgeting, performance budgeting, among other innovations – were used to prepare expenditure budgets. The golden rule, which permits debt financing of capital expenditures, narrows deficit prohibition to the operating budget. The acceptance of an active role of government in stabilizing the economy gives rise to tolerant fiscal rules that relate deficits and debts to the size of the economy. The medium-term fiscal framework and long-term fiscal sustainability are introduced to reinforce fiscal resilience under conditions of uncertainty.

Financial management has also experienced major advances. Financial integrity is now a common concern. Safeguards ranging from prevention of embezzlement to prohibition of kickbacks and pay-to-play are incorporated into laws. Governments diversify revenue sources, develop revenue forecasting techniques, and use tax incentives to boost economic development. As governments borrow in invisible and indirect ways, calls for accrual accounting and full disclosure grow louder. Making sure that government has adequate financial resources to pay off all maturing liabilities is a critical responsibility. This requires the careful structuring of its portfolio of financial assets, including cash and investments in securities. Public financial investments have become so large and complex as to require the creation of special institutions, such as sovereign wealth funds, development banks and private-public partnerships. Such investments have extended to economic resources (e.g. natural resources) and intangibles (e.g.

intellectual property). However, it is politically controversial to tighten control over other lev-els of government and quasi-public institutions.

Generalizability

The adoption of these advances in public financial management around the world is too varied to generalize in this chapter. Instead, the next section covers the United States and China, two countries with vastly different political economies and cultural traditions. If they share anything in common in their public financial management practices, one could have some confidence in the generalizability of the classical model. In particular, we suggest that you ask of a country's public finance system: (1) Is it substantively rational in the sense of contributing to the achievement of national goals? (2) Is it procedurally rational in the sense of methodically executing the steps of planning, performance and assessment?

The United States is arguably the most powerful country in the world today and intends to stay that way. The American economy is driven primarily by the private sector, with the public sector playing a compensatory role. The general pattern of American public financial management is sketched in Case Example 9.1, subject to the following peculiarities. In the federal government, Congress is often accused of micro-managing executive agencies, where chief financial officers are less powerful than budget directors. While requiring bureaucrats to exercise strict budgetary control, politicians have lost control over the federal budget, as evidenced by continuous deficits and mounting debts over 50 years. Financial discipline is often compromised in fighting wars and rebuilding war-torn nations. In many states and local governments, elected officials occupy top fiscal positions as treasurers, comptrollers and auditors. In some jurisdictions, the people vote on budgets, tax limits and bond issues. Professional associations of fiscal officers develop national norms in part to compensate for diversity in state finance laws. It appears that Americans honour the classical model of pub-lic financial management through the ways in which they consciously breach it, as well as by their compliance.

Case Example 9.1 American government financial management

Americans tend to view financial management as a technocratic function that begins when the political process of budgeting ends. Due to its federal structure, the United States has 51 fiscal systems: 50 state systems plus 1 for the federal government.

Federal financial management. The 1921 Budget and Accounting Act created the modern budgeting system, and the 1990 Chief Financial Officers Act updated finan-cial management practices. The Office of Management and Budget sets policies for implementation by the Treasury Department and agency CFOs. The Government Accountability Office, the legislative watchdog, conducts performance and financial audits. While the president submits the federal budget, Congress holds the ultimate power over the purse strings and oversees the operations of all federal agencies and programmes. In recent decades, federal agencies faced repeated threats of shutdown for lack of authorized funds (recall the US Constitution quoted earlier). The Treasury Department, aided by agency CFOs, collects revenues, disburses cash and borrows money subject to debt limitations imposed by Congress. Three parallel accounting systems are in operation: the cash system for managing liquidity, the budgetary system for year-round control and the accrual system for preparing annual financial reports. Through grants and contracts, the federal government influences state and local financial practices.

State and local financial management. Besides managing their own finances, American states oversee the finances of local governments, totalling 80,000 with half of them operating schools. State laws typically require balanced operating budgets, leaving the capital budgets to be financed by bonds and intergovernmental grants. Financial managers' actions are regulated by laws and rules, disciplined by bond rating agencies and guided by norms sanctioned by professional associations.

Since its economic reforms and "opening" in the late 1970s, *China* has been modernizing its public financial management. The governing Communist Party holds the government and fiscal administration responsible for contributing to the achievement of national strategic goals. Discipline and rationality permeate an elaborate top-down chain of means and ends. Fiscal policy is designed to support the series of five-year socioeconomic development plans, continued from the central planning era. Central government makes uniform national policy, often after local demonstration projects. However, varying regional conditions, multiple layers of government and the large and complex organizational structure together necessitate local flexibility in policy implementation. Current practices reflect a delicate balance between traditional and contemporary approaches, as well as combining unique Chinese ways and international norms predicated on Western experiences.

Case Example 9.2 Chinese public financial management

In support of the development of a market economy, China officially adopted a public finance framework in 1998 and periodically revised the comprehensive budget law (most recently in 2018) to codify or require fiscal policies and practices. Specifically:

Budget concepts and process. The unified budget encompasses the government's general and special funds, as well as funds for social security and state-owned capital operations. Budgets are balanced over economic cycles to realize medium-term fiscal policy objectives. Deadlines for executive submission and legislative approval of budgets are specified in law.

Budget control. The focus of the budget process has shifted from prohibiting off-budget funds to hardening constraints to prevent unauthorized expenditures. Advanced information technology is used to standardize and streamline the budget execution process.

Treasury management and intergovernmental transfers. After establishing the single treasury account and centralizing the funds disbursement system, the Ministry of Finance has improved the distribution of funds to local governments. Transfers for increasing fiscal capacity have increased in relation to earmarked grants.

Debt and risk management. Central government continues to issue debt in conducting macro-fiscal policy. Subject to legislative approval and central government rules, local governments are now permitted to issue bonds directly on their own credit. Regulation of the expanding government bond market is strengthened, along with improved credit rating and monitoring mechanisms.

Government accounting and financial reporting. Government accounting now consists of the old cash-based budget accounting and the new addition of accrual financial accounting. Since 2013, the Ministry of Finance has mobilized central government ministries and virtually all provincial and municipal governments in preparing accrual-based consolidated financial statements. The next step is the publication of comprehensive annual financial reports, since budgets, final accounts and audit reports, with certain exceptions, are already made public.

In summary, though institutional details differ, both China and the United States adhere to the same rationalist logic of maintaining a competent public financial management system to implement fiscal policies, but the effects are faster and greater in China, due to its central authority and larger public sector (read Case Example 9.5 for another Sino-American comparison).

Advice on implementing the advanced classical model is available in Allen et al. (2013) and the IMF PFM Blog (see Further Reading).

In conclusion, the Wilson–Weber model presents a conservative establishmentarian point of view of public financial management. Laws are to be obeyed not challenged; civil servants are not to get involved in politics; administrators should focus on the means and not question the ends. This classical model is necessary to operate the machinery of government, but it does not reflect a wider range of perspectives about what public financial management could be or should be. The next two sections present a second model that focuses on public welfare and a third model that points out the multiple *publics* putting demands on government.

The Wilde–Moore public value model

By accepting public law and pledging political neutrality, public professionals ethically serve politicians under virtually any political and economic system. After politicians have determined the ends, professionals come up with the rational – economic, efficient and effective – means. This has led to two contending views of public management, with very different implications for the financial function. For contrast, both views are presented below.

New Public Management

When neoliberalism gained currency in the 1980s, New Public Management (NPM) and New Public Financial Management (NPFM) became fashionable in academic circles and influential in practitioner communities (Pollitt and Bouckaert, 2017; Olson et al., 1998). Governments practicing NPM and NPFM privatize state-owned or -controlled enterprises and cut government payrolls to make the public sector small. For example, in the US, the national government outsources weapon production to the military-industrial complex, and local governments hire contractors to collect garbage and even operate prisons. Citizens, treated as customers, are charged fees whenever possible, bureaucracies become competitive business units, and cost centres turn into revenue centres. Budget-maximizing bureau chiefs are reformed into cost-conscious and revenue-hungry entrepreneurs stressing performance measured as outputs and outcomes. Government officials follow universalized rules of economic rationality, downplaying anachronistic laws and rules as "red tape". Public services are priced at their full cost. Business-like accrual accounting and consolidated financial statements in annual reporting are codified as International Public Sector Accounting Principles (IPSAS) for global adoption. The UK government even replaced its own standards with international corporate financial reporting standards (see Case Example 9.3).

Case Example 9.3 UK resource accounting and budgeting

Since the early 1990s, UK central government has done its financial planning on the accrual basis ("resource accounting"). Departments have replaced cash budgets with current operating and capital expenditure subject to consolidated expenditure limits calculated by estimating future costs, including the cost of using capital assets. The system also separates programme budgets for providing goods and services from administrative running costs. However, after 30 years under this system, the large reduction in the number of civil servants did not significantly cut running costs or even paybill costs (Hood and Dixon, 2015).

Since 2009 the UK central government has produced consolidated "whole of government" accounts (WGA), encompassing local governments and nearly 10,000 organizations throughout the public sector. In 2011, another initiative was launched to align budgeting, accounting and reporting systems. While WGA provide the context for viewing the financial situation of individual departments and government units, their usefulness for managing their financial affairs has not been persuasively demonstrated.

By now the popularity of NPM has waned (Steccolini, 2019), even though its effects linger and managerialism is still alive and manifested in other ways (Pollitt, 2016). But even during its heyday, the ideological basis and claimed benefits of NPM were questioned, and Mark Moore, a Harvard public management professor, advocated an alternative model.

"Accounting" for public value

Moore (1995, 2013) champions the creation, recognition and reporting of public value, i.e. the benefits of government to the whole community. See Case Example 9.4 for how it was done in the USA. Irish playwright Oscar Wilde defined a cynic as a person who knows the price of everything and the value of nothing, so we attach his name to this model.

Case Example 9.4 Creating, recognizing and reporting public value

In 1939, Clarence Ridley and Herbert Simon published a pamphlet entitled "Specifications of the Annual Municipal Report". It distinguished outcomes (e.g. clean streets) from outputs (e.g. the amounts of garbage removed).

Moore (2013) illustrates the recognition of public value and the construction of value chains, and he presents templates, though without numbers, of public value accounts and balanced scorecards of public services by American state and local governments. At the state level are the revenue department of Minnesota, a welfare and employment project in Illinois, a social service agency in Massachusetts and a political accountability entity in Oregon. At the municipality level are the city government of the District of Columbia, New York City police department and Seattle solid waste utility.

From the other side of the world comes an example of reporting public value at the community level: the Murray Darling Basin Authority responsible for managing water resources in southeast Australia produced a comprehensive economic and social condition report.

At the international level, the United Nations, whose 2030 Agenda for Sustainable Development has 17 Sustainable Development Goals (SDGs), publishes a *World Social Report* each year with a theme related to human conditions around the world. In 2016 it was social exclusion, in 2020 socioeconomic inequality due to technological innovation, climate change, urbanization and international migration.

Public value in public management as discussed above has a number of biases and limitations. The unfavourable consequences of government actions are often obscured or ignored. One should also not overlook the human toll resulting from the actions of governments in powerful nations in the past. For five centuries, European colonial powers destroyed civilizations and robbed wealth from the Americas, Africa, Asia and elsewhere. The American government appropriated lands belonging to Native Americans and protected slavery, and the US-led war on terrorism in the past 20 years devastated Afghanistan and Iraq. Official accounting of the losses suffered by the victims remains rare and incomplete.

For guidance on how to account for public value, consult Moore (2013), Steccolini (2019) and Bracci et al. (2021).

Next, we turn to a model that unpacks the public into multiple *publics* and examines both the costs and benefits of government decisions and actions.

The Barnard–Simon stakeholder model

The field of public financial management needs a model that takes into account *all* of the political, economic and social interests at stake. In recent financial crises, financial institutions and bondholders were protected at the expense of many others' interests. Even in ordinary times, the equitable distribution of government costs and benefits is a perennial issue. This issue is ignored in the classical economic theory of the firm, in which stockholders hire managers to maximize the firm's profit and the owners' wealth by treating everyone else as means to this end.

A behavioural theory of government

In contrast, influenced by Barnard (1938), Simon proposed a revolutionary organization theory. Chester Barnard (1886–1961) was a thoughtful American manager, and Herbert Simon (1916–2001) was an American polymath who pioneered the behavioural approach to public administration. Simon started with a simplified model of government with three groups: elected legislators who appoint administrators, who in turn hire civil servants to execute the legislative agenda. Simon (1947) argues that, unlike their corporate counterparts, these public managers adopt a "satisficing" approach, seeking only satisfactory solutions, because they have only bounded rationality due to imperfect information and finite information-processing capacity.

The Barnard–Simon organization theory has been generalized to view government as a coalition of stakeholders for increasing their individual and collective well-being. In this view of governance, the politicians, public managers and public employees are internal stakeholders. The continuation of their governing authority depends on their ability to hold together the organizational coalition of diverse external stakeholders. These include: (1) the beneficiary publics – recipients and co-producers of services, grantees, borrowers and targets of government regulation; (2) the benefactor publics – voters, taxpayers and fee payers; (3) financial resource-providing grantors and bondholders; and (4) service-providing contractors. Using their superior knowledge about the production functions of public services, managers offer inducements adequate to attract the inputs, termed "contributions", of each type of external stakeholders (see Table 9.1). These stakeholders decide to accept or reject the offers, leading to their entering, staying or exiting the coalition. The management's goal

Table 9.1 Government as a coalition of stakeholders

Stakeholders	Contributions by stakeholders	Inducements to stakeholders
Internal stakeholders		
Politicians	Authority, policy guidance, monitoring of performance	Power, prestige, services to constituency, likelihood of renewal of mandate
Administrators	Knowledge of means to achieve ends; skills in negotiation, persuasion and implementation	Financial and non-financial compensation and benefits, career advancement opportunities
Employees	Skills in implementation	Employment
External stakeholders		
Voters	Legitimacy	Services for the general welfare and to individuals (which may require co-production by recipients)
Taxpayers	Tax dollars	
Service recipients, customers	Fees	
Grantees	Goods and services otherwise unaffordable	Financial resources with or without conditions or restrictions
Borrowers	Investment in and consumption of goods and services that also benefit the society ("merit goods" – see Chapter 3)	Loans (to be repaid with or without interest) not otherwise available
Insured or guaranteed groups	Fees to receive protection	Financial protection
The regulated	Compliance	Protection
Grantors	Financial resources with or without conditions or restrictions	Securing of services they consider desirable to their target groups or the general population
Bond holders	Financing (for fixed periods)	Interest payments, principal repayment
Contractors	Goods and services	Payments or promises of payment

Sources: Simon (1947), Salamon (2002), the authors.

at any time, and over time, is to find terms of engagement attractive to each of the diverse stakeholders, so that a state of equilibrium is attained, as evidenced by the continuing cooperation of the stakeholders whose interests are intertwined. If it fails to do so, the coalition runs the risk of falling apart. It is also possible, of course, that these deals may not be fair to those stakeholders with weak negotiating power.

Financial executives shoulder special responsibility to negotiate and enforce the financial terms – amount, timing and certainty of payment claims – in the contracts and other agreements with all stakeholders, so that organizational equilibrium is maintained over time. Organizational sustainability is expressed by: (1) *financial liquidity* indicated by adequate cash to meet financial obligations whenever due; (2) *financial solvency* indicated by adequate financial resources, including cash, to cover financial obligations whenever due; (3) *economic viability* indicated by the capacity in terms of scarce resources to produce goods and services in both the short and long terms. Failure to maintain the values of these indicators in their acceptable ranges could have serious consequences in terms of their financial and human toll, as financial crises in history have demonstrated.

It is therefore the financial executives' job to design and maintain the organization's accounting systems. These systems include an internally oriented management information system for detecting and solving problems by planning and control, and an externally oriented financial accounting system to keep accurate scores based on transactions with the external stakeholders identified above. Through these accounting systems we monitor the organization's fiscal health, which is also affected by the inter-connected financial and economic system it belongs to. Therefore, systemic risk is of great concern to individual institutions' managements. It is their responsibility to prevent financial crises and to solve the crises that come despite their best efforts.

Incidence of costs and benefits

Recognizing that unequal bargaining power may result in inequity, some public organizations take affirmative actions to reduce economic and social injustice. Financial support is often needed to realize these good intentions, e.g. paying reparations for historical wrongs, such as slavery and appropriation of native lands. Employers face financial pressure directly in meeting demands for a living wage, parental leave, generous pensions, and indirectly in agreeing to work rules that improve employee safety and health. The COVID-19 pandemic has exposed the gaps in public health care between the rich and the poor within and between many countries, prompting unprecedented government public health and economic measures (see Case Example 9.5).

Case Example 9.5 The role of public money in the COVID-19 pandemic

In this global public health crisis, governments around the world have spent a lot of money in different ways and to different effects.

For example, in 2020–2021, the US government committed over $4 trillion to save the economy, to reboot an unfunded public health system and to provide free hospitalizations, tests and vaccinations. The federal government also restricted travel and issued guidelines and selective mandates for local enforcement. Providing scientific information and relying on voluntary compliance is the main American strategy for fighting the pandemic.

In contrast, after a slow start and initial missteps, China waged an all-out campaign against the virus with orders from the central government. The government spent several billions on emergency COVID care and transferred rescue funds to localities on an expedited basis. The primary strategy was effective but involved drastic isolation of infected areas, including entire cities, wherever and whenever necessary. "Neighbourhood watch" citizens enforced quarantines. A nationwide tracking system using high-tech gadgets now keeps the population safe as the economy bounces back.

Consequently, during 2020 and 2021, China with a population of 1,447 million had 133,000 cases and 5,699 deaths; the US with 334 million people had 56,800,000 cases and 824,175 deaths.

The Chinese people spared the Chinese government from larger public expenditure, while saving many lives. In contrast, the American people obliged the US government to spend much more money, with much less effect.

Public money in different countries matters in different ways and to different degrees.

Sources: Wang and Xu (2021), WHO (2022).

With contributions from Hanyu Xiao and Xiao-hu Wang.

The Barnard–Simon stakeholder model is applicable to institutional networks for solving large and complex societal and global problems (see Chapters 15–18). Continuing the pandemic example, aided by government guidance and funding, public, non-profit sector and private sector organizations are often cooperating in providing care, tracking and slowing down infections and developing and distributing vaccines in a tightly knit intertwined system. Similar partnerships are required to address the causes and effects of financial crises and global warming. In all of these collective efforts, government plays a leading role in making public policies and organizing the relevant partners to solve the problems. In this context, a government financial executive plays the role of the managing partner in crafting, negotiating and administering agreements among network members. Lacking direct authority over network members, she relies on provisions in the network's charter to enforce a code of conduct.

Institutional networks rely on common data specifications, such as generally accepted accounting and auditing standards, to facilitate information sharing. When a network is sufficiently large and formal, a secretariat becomes necessary, in which the financial executives administer the financial terms of the network agreements. Important to worldwide public financial management are the UN Development Programme, the International Monetary Fund, the World Bank, the Organization for Economic Cooperation and Development, the European Union and regional development banks. Collectively they provide considerable funding and technical assistance to improve public financial management practices, especially in developing nations and transitional economies.

For inspiration on putting the stakeholder model into practice, consult Sunder (1997), Salamon (2002), Heller (2003), Ashworth and Newman (2023).

The future of public financial management

This chapter offers a comparative analysis of three conceptual revolutions in the intellectual history of modern public financial management: The classical Wilson–Weber model regards; public law as the source of authority and a rational bureaucracy as its execution arm. The idealistic Wilde–Moore model places public value ahead of government costs. The realistic Barnard–Simon model advocates the striving for organizational survival through harmonizing the interests of various stakeholders. By adapting to meet future needs, these models are likely to persist over the 21st century.

Scholars have interpreted public financial management in various ways – the point, however, is to change it for the better. That requires dealing with several big issues looming on the horizon: (1) the effects of advances in information technology, including cryptocurrencies, on public and private financial systems; (2) the high cost and (mis)management of security and military functions of government; (3) the challenge to the value premises of Western "best practices" posed by Eastern values; and finally (4) reforming national and global fiscal and monetary systems to tackle the effects of climate change, pandemics and other existential threats to humanity.

In the uncertain future, the vulnerable world will need imaginative thinkers and competent leaders to use the power of public money wisely to create an inclusive and equitable society.

Acknowledgement

We appreciate the guidance of the editors and suggestions by Danny Chow, Andrew Massey, Ileana Steccolini, Xiao-Hu Wang and Hanyu Xiao. We are solely responsible for any remaining shortcomings and errors.

Questions for review and discussion

1 What is revolutionary about the underlying paradigms of the three models of public financial management?
2 What are the premises, significant features and limitations of the three models?
3 How do the three models of public financial management complement each other?
4 What future conceptual revolutions are likely to happen in public financial management?

Propositions for class debates

1 "Money spent on perfecting public financial management in poor countries is better used in helping the poor and sick".
2 "Equity, instead of efficiency, should be the criterion for evaluating the performance of public organizations".
3 "Artificial intelligence will eliminate the chief financial officer's job".
4 "Public and private financial management are fundamentally alike in all unimportant respects".

Further reading

E. Bracci, et al (2021). Accounting for (public) value(s): reconsidering publicness in accounting research and practice. *Accounting, Auditing & Accountability Journal* 34(7): 1513–1526.

International Monetary Fund, *Public financial management*. Blog, https://blog-pfm.imf.org/.

P. Heller (2003), *Who will pay?* Washington, DC: IMF.

R. Ashworth (2023), "Changing equalities: Politics, policies and practice" in Tony Bovaird and Elke Loeffler (Eds), Public Management and Governance (4th edition). London: Routledge (Chapter 26 in this volume).

O. Olson, et al (1998), *Global warning*. Oslo: Cappelen Akademisk Forlag.

S. Sunder (1997), *Theory of accounting and control*. Cincinnati, OH: South-Western Publishing.

References

R. Allen, et al (eds.) (2013), *The international handbook of public financial management*. Hampshire: Palgrave Macmillan.

C.I. Barnard (1938), *The functions of the executive*. Cambridge, MA: Harvard University Press.

G.H. Gerth and C.W. Mills (1946), *From Max Weber: Essays in sociology*. Oxford: Oxford University Press, pp. 191–244.

J.L. Mikesell (2017), *Fiscal administration*, 10th edition. Wadsworth, CA: Belmont.

I. Lienert and M.K. Jung (2004), "The legal framework for budget systems", *OECD Journal on Budgeting*, 4(3): 11–473.

C. Hood and R. Dixon (2015), *A government that worked better and cost Less?* Oxford: Oxford University Press.

M. Moore (1995), *Creating public value*. Cambridge, MA: Harvard University Press.

M. Moore (2013), *Recognizing public value*. Cambridge, MA: Harvard University Press.

C. Pollitt (2016), "Managerialism redux?", *Financial Accountability and Management*, 32(4), pp. 429–447.

C. Pollitt and G. Bouckaert (2017), *Public management reform*, 4th edition. Oxford: Oxford University Press.

L.M. Salamon (2002), *The tools of government*. Oxford: Oxford University Press.

H.A. Simon (1947), *Administrative behaviour*. New York: Free Press.

I. Steccolini (2019), "Accounting and the post-new public management", *Accounting, Auditing and Accountability Journal*, 32(1), pp. 255–279.

M.A. Thomas (2001), "Getting debt relief right", *Foreign Affairs*, 80(5), pp. 36–45.

X.H. Wang and J.Y. Xu (2021), "The central government's capacity building role in policy implementation in China", *Public Money and Management*, 42(2), pp. 57–58.

W. Wilson (1887), "The study of administration", *Political Science Quarterly*, 2(2), pp. 197–222.

World Health Organization (WHO) (2022, January 7), "Covid-19 dashboard", https://covid19.who.int/.

10 Human resource management in public service organizations

Adrian Ritz and Eva Knies

Introduction

Human resource management (HRM) in public service organizations is a core function because public service organizations are highly labour-intensive. However, politicians in government debating human resource (HR) policies often regard the public workforce as an everlasting resource in terms of quantity and quality, overlooking the great challenges that public employers face in modernizing their HRM and their organizational cultures, while maintaining a reasonably stable institutional environment.

Many of these challenges are not faced by public service organizations alone – most organizations in Western societies face an ageing work population, increasingly competitive labour market conditions, and blurring boundaries between public, private, and non-profit sector organizations. However, the ways in which public sector organizations are able to tackle HRM reform are often different, depending on the degree of the organization's 'publicness'. At the same time, they have to be aware of the opportunities for collaboration and exchange with private and non-profit organizations delivering public services.

Consequently, the HRM approach explored in this chapter builds on general HRM insights, while at the same time considering characteristics specific to the public sector, with the ultimate goal of creating and delivering public value through people, in which public HRM can be a key driver.

This chapter first defines the concept of HRM, then discusses public-private differences in HRM systems and explains our model of strategic public HRM. We then give examples of HRM practices for implementing strategic public HRM and, finally, outline the key issues and new challenges facing public HRM.

Learning objectives

- To understand human resource management in public service organizations
- To demonstrate how public-sector specific characteristics shape HRM
- To comprehend strategic HRM as enabler of the public HRM value chain
- To be aware of HRM practices that specifically fit a public sector context
- To explore the key issues and new challenges that public HRM faces today

DOI: 10.4324/9781003282839-12

What is HRM?

HRM refers to the management of work and people. It is a field that builds on insights from different disciplines, including psychology, sociology, and economics. HRM has its roots in the 1980s when two landmark books were published that marked the transition from personnel management to HRM – Fombrun et al. (1984) considered the Michigan model, while Beer et al. (1984) presented the Harvard model. Although there are marked differences between the two approaches (see Box 10.1), they have in common a broader perspective than traditional approaches like personnel management, which mainly focused on the administrative role of personnel departments in recruitment, development, compensation, etc. A major development was that both models acknowledge that employees are an important resource for achieving strategic goals.

This strategic focus is also visible in a more recent, often-used model: the HRM value chain (Wright and Nishii, 2013). This model advocates alignment between the overall organizational strategy and HRM policies and practices and the importance of supporting and facilitating employees' attitudes (e.g. satisfaction, work engagement, and commitment) and behaviours (e.g. in-role and extra-role) which are of crucial importance for achieving organizational goals. Wright and Nishii also acknowledge that HRM as intended by top management is not necessarily translated, as desired, into the perceptions of employees. They point to the role of HRM implementation (mostly by line managers) in the translation from policies to practice. Their terminology of intended, actual/implemented, and perceived HRM is now commonly used in the field.

General conceptual models of HRM are often assumed to be applicable in different types of contexts (e.g. country, sector, organization). However, although the underlying principles can be translated to various contexts, it is well established that context matters, not only for HRM itself but also for its effect on various outcomes. Given that many of the prominent HRM models were developed and empirically tested in a private sector context, we need to acknowledge that HRM in a public sector context is not 'business as usual'. Consequently, in this chapter we discuss the distinctiveness of public HRM, building on the literatures around both HRM and public administration and management.

Box 10.1 Harvard and Michigan models of HRM

The *Harvard model* by Beer et al. (1984) posits that HRM policy choices (e.g. regarding employee influence and work systems) are influenced by stakeholder interests (e.g. shareholders, employee groups, trade unions, government, and communities) and situational factors (e.g. business strategy and workforce characteristics). HRM policy choices in turn affect HRM outcomes (e.g. commitment and competence) and long-term consequences. The latter are considered to be threefold: individual well-being, organizational effectiveness, and societal well-being.

The *Michigan model* by Fombrun et al. (1984) puts performance centre stage and proposes that the HRM practice of employee selection is an important determinant of performance, which in turn will be followed by appraisal, which leads to either rewards and/or development. The main idea of this model is 'fit'; *strategic fit* concerning the alignment between business strategy and HRM policies and *internal fit* concerning the alignment of individual HRM practices to a consistent and coherent HRM bundle.

Beer et al. (2015) point to four differences between the models:

- The Michigan model is concerned with returns to shareholders, while the Harvard model acknowledges a range of stakeholders.
- The so-called 'soft' Harvard model applies a social systems perspective ('human'), while the 'hard' Michigan model takes an individual, primarily economic perspective ('resource management').
- The Michigan model defines outcomes from the perspective of shareholders ('performance'), the Harvard model takes a balanced perspective on outcomes.
- The scope of the situational factors included in the models differs.

What is specific about public HRM?

Is public HRM different from private sector HRM and, if so, what are its specific characteristics? This long-standing issue has to be discussed with reference to the institutional frame influencing public HRM. A major difference is the *systemic approach* that public HRM most often follows. It is strongly characterized by planned processes at the level of strategic and operational HRM (e.g. career plans) and a variety of diverse and pluralistic outcomes and values (e.g. performance vs. equality), quite different from one-sided 'profit maximization as value' inherent to private sector HRM.

The institutional frame defining these cornerstones of public HRM is the *political-administrative system* with its political actors (e.g. parliament), the legal frame (e.g. rule of law), and the managerial level, which implements political policies and regulations (e.g. HR managers). Therefore, the starting point of public HRM is normative political decisions, from both outside the organization (the legislative level) and inside (for those public organizations with elected or appointed political leadership). Politics therefore define the cornerstones of the public employment system and the institutional framework for managing public employees.

Consequently, the history of public HRM is intrinsically linked to the unique *legal environment* in which it develops. We can distinguish two types of legal environments shaping public personnel systems (Ripoll and Ritz, 2022). The first is the *common law tradition* of Westminster-type countries, which does not distinguish between public and private legal spheres. This leads to a comparatively low differentiation between state and society, low codification of legal norms, and public servants in senior civil service positions who are generalists, primarily legitimized by job functions rather than acquired qualifications. In contrast, the Continental European *rule of law (civil law) tradition* distinguishes clearly between public and private law, with codified statutes to reinforce the distinction. Consequently, there is a hierarchy between state and society, with the state being at the centre of society. This leads public officials to define themselves as representatives of a higher authority, with a high status in society – and they primarily have a public law educational background.

These different administrative traditions strongly influence public employment practices (Ripoll and Ritz, 2022) – see Box 10.2. For example, public employees in countries from the Napoleonic administrative system are more *career-based* and have centralist HRM decision-making. In these career-based systems (e.g. France, Germany, Japan, Spain) there is a marked differentiation between private and public sector employment – the latter is linked to the promotion of collective values and a public service ethos, through the development of experienced, homogeneous, and lifetime public servants, who are chosen by early competitive selection procedures. In contrast, functional HRM systems in Westminster-type countries (e.g. UK, the Netherlands, and Switzerland) or Scandinavian participatory systems (e.g. Sweden or Finland) are *position-based* and much more decentralized. Public employment in these countries is much more open to exchange of values and practices between public and private sectors and allows higher mobility of employees across sectors.

Box 10.2 Three types of public HRM systems

We distinguish three types of HRM systems based on different legal environments and administrative traditions:

Hierarchical HRM system: Continental European countries with a 'rule of law' tradition and a HRM model focused on formal roles, legal qualifications, centralist decision-making structures, and a preference for career-based selection and promotion.

Functional HRM system: Westminster-type countries with a common law tradition and a HRM model focused on diverse qualifications, employee mobility, achievement of efficiency and effectiveness, and a preference for position-based selection and promotion.

Participatory HRM system: Scandinavian countries with a HRM model focused on decentralization, autonomy, and empowerment of decision-making at all levels of an organization, and a preference for position-based selection and promotion.

Notwithstanding important international differences, most legal environments have faced similar pressures in recent decades. During the 1990s, the *NPM* paradigm (see Chapter 4) criticized the public HRM system as preventing public managers from doing their job effectively. Relying on competition and efficiency criteria, NPM promoted private sector styles of management in public HRM, specifically including:

- The stimulation of civil servants' motivation and performance through pay-for-performance or similar compensation systems
- The expansion of 'at-will' employment systems to increase flexibility in hiring, promoting, and releasing public employees
- The decentralization of HRM policy to agencies (Kellough, 2017)

After years of continuous reforms, NPM was widely challenged because of its negative side effects in the public sector, and the '*New Public Governance*' model (see Chapters 4 and 15), based on collaboration and policy effectiveness criteria, gained popularity – acknowledging, like NPM, the problems with traditional public HRM, but introducing 'new' solutions based on collective co-production, interdependency of organizations and actors, and intrinsic, prosocial, and public service motivations (Boruvka and Perry, 2020; Ritz et al., 2016a).

There has therefore been a *general reform trend* from traditional HR administration, with origins in Weberian bureaucracy, towards modernized HRM systems. The traditional values of political neutrality, transparency, legality, equality, expertise, and accuracy of administrative behaviour are being complemented by values such as efficiency and effectiveness, collaboration, pragmatism, flexibility, and agility. Public employers are both adapting to changing environments by implementing reforms but also keeping elements from preceding eras, and aligning them to new challenges. As a result, today's public HRM is generally characterized by a *hybrid model of HRM*, strengthening values such as:

- Strategy and results orientation, based on hiring competition, performance-orientation, and differentiated employment regimes
- Collaboration across organizational units and integrating public service values and principles of legality and equality into HRM policies and strategies

Strategic public HRM

When applying strategic HRM to the public sphere, there is a need to extend the scope of the concept of 'performance'. In the private sphere, performance primarily refers to gaining competitive advantage or profit generation. By contrast, in the public sphere performance means focusing on the mission of an organization, creating and delivering public value, which is seen to encompass a broad set of performance dimensions or values such as efficiency, effectiveness, accountability, equity, and resilience (see Chapter 12). Building on both general HRM insights and the distinctive nature of HRM in the public sector, Figure 10.1 sets out a contextualized version of the HRM value chain (Vandenabeele et al., 2013; Knies and Steijn, 2021; Ripoll and Ritz, 2022).

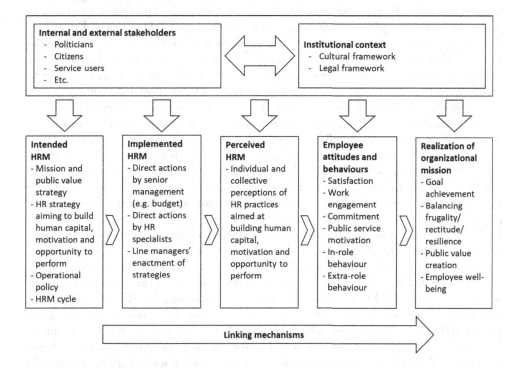

Figure 10.1 Public HRM value chain.

Source: Knies and Steijn (2021: 8).

This public HRM value chain builds on the Harvard model (Beer et al., 1984) by distinguishing multiple strategic outcomes: goal achievement; balancing frugality, rectitude, and resilience; public value creation; and employee well-being. In particular, it acknowledges that various public values are at play. From an HRM perspective, employee well-being is defined as a goal in itself and not only a means to an end. In addition, not only the outcomes, but also employees' attitudes and behaviours are contextualized. For example, employees' public service motivation (PSM) is centre stage, as this is an important driver of their behaviour. Finally, it recognizes the importance of the wider organizational context (as in the Harvard model) – both the influence of internal and external stakeholders (e.g. politicians, citizens, communities, and service users) and the cultural and legal frameworks.

A large body of the HRM literature specifies what makes HRM effective in achieving multiple strategic goals. Gratton and Truss (2003) identified three principles of effective HRM: vertical alignment, horizontal alignment, and implementation/action.

First, *vertical alignment* refers to the alignment of HRM policies and practices with the overall organizational strategy. It is argued that before designing HRM practices, organizations need to identify what kind of attitudes and behaviours are likely to contribute to reaching the organizational outcomes expected from employees. This implies that designing HRM requires in-depth knowledge of the value chain and underlying processes of an organization. A best practice approach, copying the strategy of other organizations, will not deliver the same results. Applying the principle of vertical alignment to a public sector context is not as straightforward as in a private sector context, in which organizations generally have a single bottom line (i.e. financial performance). In the public sector, organizations tend to have multiple and sometimes even conflicting outcomes. This makes it complex to define the required employee attitudes and behaviours and the HRM practices that support these. For example, police forces typically have the aim to protect public safety, enforce the law, and, when necessary, help people who are at risk of becoming a victim of crime. These multiple goals require a broad range of behaviours from police officers, from repressive to preventive action. In order to support and facilitate these behaviours, HRM practices such as training and development need to be aimed at a broad range of knowledge and skills.

Secondly, *horizontal alignment* refers to the alignment of individual HRM practices so that they form a coherent bundle. Research shows that implementing bundles of HRM practices can create synergy, so that the effect of the bundle is larger than the sum of the effects of individual practices. It is also key to avoid so-called 'deadly combinations', where one HRM practice cancels out the positive effects of another – for example, the use of high levels of PSM as a criterion when selecting new staff, while at the same time using pay-for-performance practices that crowd out PSM. A field experiment conducted by Bellé et al. (2015) among nurses in Italy showed that monetary incentives for activities with a prosocial impact could crowd out employee image motivation.

Third, the *principle of action/implementation* refers to the fact that the implementation, as well as the design, of HRM policies and practices matters. In many organizations, both public and private, HRM devolution has resulted in increasing HRM responsibilities for line managers, so they are primarily responsible for leading the transfer from intended to perceived HRM – and employees' perceptions of HRM not only depend on managers' implementation of HRM policies and practices, but also on their leadership behaviours. Some leadership behaviours (e.g. transformational and transactional leadership) are relevant in both public and private organizations, while other types of behaviours (e.g. accountability, rule-following, political loyalty, and network governance leadership) are specific to public sector leadership (Tummers and Knies, 2016). A key challenge in public organizations, especially in countries with closed career systems, is that line managers are often promoted because of their seniority or professional expertise in a certain field rather than because of good leadership skills, which can affect the quality of HRM implementation.

HRM practices

As discussed above, effective public HRM requires that the implementation of HRM policies and practices is aligned with the overall organizational strategy. We distinguish five major HRM practices in a 'HRM cycle' (Riccucci et al., 2019; Ripoll and Ritz, 2022):

- *Workforce planning*: At this first stage of the HRM cycle, managers connect the organizational missions, goals, and strategies with its human capital, either simply to fill internal vacancies (i.e. succession planning) or to restructure work, determine critical skills and competencies, develop training programmes, and review administrative capabilities (i.e. workforce planning) (Riccucci et al., 2019). Workforce needs assessment is key and takes into account contextual developments (such as technological development and labour supply), balances them with the HRM strategy, and identifies gaps or areas for improvement.
- *Recruitment*: In recruitment, public organizations first attract applicants, then assess their qualities, and finally select preferred candidates. Recruitment processes start attracting candidates with effective employer branding and, further, with communicating job postings to the labour market based on the workforce needs assessment. Public employers can decide to offer incentives to increase applications or appeal to public values motivation or public service motivation (see Box 10.3), which helps to explain why individuals join public-service oriented organizations (Perry and Wise, 1990; Ritz et al., 2016a). The selection process begins with verifying individuals' credentials and screening all applications, evaluating qualifications through interviews, work tests, and/ or job simulations in order to select the preferred candidate. Recruitment might appear to be a mechanical and apolitical process, but it is actually a hot topic in public administration because of its direct link to diversity and representation. Over the years, 'elite men' have dominated most bureaucracies in developed countries, so other segments of the population were excluded from the public sector.
- *Performance management*: Performance management is a continuous cycle of goal setting, monitoring and feedback, developing, rating, and rewarding. Performance appraisal or rating is at the heart of performance management, but it is also very challenging, because it is impossible to reach full objectivity. In public HRM performance appraisal is regularly undermined by the setting of ambiguous goals, ignorance or neglect of external influences on individuals' performance, and inappropriate (or non-existent) monetary incentives. Public organizations need to give special attention to a wider range of potential benefits (e.g. pension systems, work-life balance, intrinsic rewards, flexible work arrangements) to reward well-performing employees.
- *Development*: Public employers need to develop employees' skills, competencies, and motivation so that they contribute better to the desired outcomes, address challenges, and help to develop the organization. Employees need training to develop new or update existing skills and abilities. The career perspectives of people with highly specialized functions are sometimes static and limited, which can be exacerbated by low levels of employee turnover. This is particularly important in career-based systems, where public servants obtain a life-long position and have less incentive to adapt their competencies to changing environments. In the public sector, HR development has to be understood

as an effective strategy for rewarding intrinsically motivated individuals. This means that the psychological contract between employer and employee has to change from a combination of job security (from the employer) with loyalty (from the employee) to a combination of high intensity on- and off-the-job development (from the employer) with high employee engagement and performance.

- *Release*: The relationship between a public organization and an employee is based on the expectations of the organization (in a formal contract or informal 'psychological' contract) and the contributions of the employee to satisfy these expectations. Although sometimes legally specified, the terms of employment are more usually agreed through collective bargaining (Riccucci et al., 2019). Nevertheless, they may not be respected by either the employee or the employer and both sides can terminate employment, given justified reasons. Releasing public personnel based on structural, performance, or qualification issues is much easier in position-based and liberalized public employment systems (although it is still not very common). In career-based systems, it is standard for the employer to have to offer an alternative job to the employee released from a job, except in the case of misconduct.

Public organizations tend to emphasize HRM practices that support the well-being of employees, whereas private organizations tend to take a performance-oriented approach. Indeed, comparative studies show that public organizations typically use more 'soft' HRM practices, aimed at equal opportunities, welfare management, and training and development, whereas private organizations prioritize 'hard' HRM practices, aimed at appraisal and performance and compensation and benefits. However, an empirical study in eight European countries by Knies et al. (2022) found that the traditional public sector investment in employee well-being continues to be distinctive only for HRM practices aimed at equal opportunities. Private sector organizations, on the other hand, make greater use of performance-oriented HRM practices, including compensation and benefits, the use of performance appraisal data, and modern development and career management practices. This implies that some traditional differences between public and private HRM have faded, although others remain.

Box 10.3 Public service motivation

Motivation in the public sector is strongly linked to the institutional setting. In organizations delivering public services the fit between public service values and opportunities for employees to satisfy their needs is decisive for high quality service and high performance. The concept of public service motivation (PSM) applies specifically to public employees, although it also applies to public service-related jobs in other sectors. PSM can be defined as the desire to behave in accordance with motives that are grounded in the public interest in order to serve society (Ritz et al., 2016b). The concept is often used in staff surveys. It builds upon instrumental, value-based, and pro-social motives and comprises four dimensions which have been empirically tested (Perry, 1996; Kim et al., 2012):

1) Attraction to public policy-making/attraction to public service
2) Commitment to the public interest/commitment to public values
3) Compassion
4) Self-sacrifice

Key issues and challenges for public HRM

Public sector organizations need to adapt their HRM strategies in order to promote public values and legitimacy, constantly balancing the key institutional values of a public sector organization, and the new trends and challenges in society and economy (Ripoll and Ritz, 2020), such as:

- *Diversity and representation*: Diversity and its management have increasingly gained relevance in public strategic HRM. Two major paradigms can be distinguished (Ashikali et al., 2021). On the one hand, the *discrimination and fairness perspective* mainly aims to prevent negative diversity outcomes. It focuses on equal employment opportunity practices, fair treatment, the absence of discrimination in the employment process, and the elimination of social exclusion. On the other hand, the *synergy perspective* focuses on realizing the potential performance benefits of diversity when used as a resource in order to improve organizational effectiveness, creativity, and innovation. Moreover, the synergy perspective treats diversity as a resource to improve interaction with diverse clients and citizens. A representative workforce allows bureaucracy to represent better and actively non-dominant groups within society and thereby to increase the organization's legitimacy.
- *Equal opportunity*: Public HRM is heavily focused on equal and fair treatment of all employees in all employment decisions, such as hiring, promotion, and compensation, through an appropriate political and legal environment. Especially in hiring and compensation decisions, public organizations need to be role-model employers in the equal treatment of women and men, people from all ethnic groups, people with different sexual orientations, etc. Equal employment opportunity and its implications for HRM practices also influence the ultimate goals of strategic HRM, such as employee satisfaction, motivation, engagement, and performance.
- *Employer attractiveness*: The interest of individuals in being employed by a public organization is of key importance for strategic HRM in a competitive labour market with increasing workforce mobility between sectors. Individuals' decisions to apply for, accept, and eventually to leave a job are likely to be based on the fit between an organization's characteristics and their own traits and motivations. One highly relevant factor has always been the job security offered to loyal employees. While the qualifications and promotion opportunities offered by an employer in exchange for employee engagement have gained in importance, high job security remains one of the most relevant attractions of public sector jobs across the world. When this is missing, it may become difficult to attract qualified staff and other incentives must be competitive with private sector jobs.
- *Digitalization*: Public organizations increasingly rely on information technology (IT) over the entire HRM cycle, but particularly in dealing with selection or appraisal, given the privacy policies affecting them. Moreover, new technologies require constant upskilling and reskilling of employees. Due to the increase in IT use, public organizations are now more prone to cyber-attacks, which demands greater cyber-security, including relevant skills in both the IT and non-IT workforce. In addition, digitalization fundamentally challenges public HRM as existing job profiles will disappear and new ones need to be developed.
- *New work*: Work environments are changing all over the world. The concept of 'New Work', relevant to public as well as private HRM, considers how employers can offer

more flexible work environments in an increasingly digitalized world from four main perspectives: spatial (e.g. mobile offices), time (e.g. work scheduling), structural (e.g. holacracy), and contractual (e.g. self-employment). New Work has strong implications for organizational culture and leadership in government offices. Administrative cultures oriented towards hierarchy, rule following, and presentism of employees are heavily challenged. Critics of the 'New Work', however, question the outcomes of highly flexible work environments for low-qualified people and for the well-functioning of self-organization, and point to the paradox of urging people to become competitive entrepreneurs while seeing themselves as members of an organization.

- *New leadership and employee roles:* Following these 'New Work' developments and the move from bureaucratic hierarchy to more collaborative cultures, the traditional roles of public leaders and employees become challenged. In an increasingly networked world, with governments facing wicked problems, bureaucrats now need to bridge boundaries in a multi-partner work environment. This requires lateral leadership and boundary-spanning, policy entrepreneurship, and collaborative skills, joint working within and partnership working between siloed public organizational units, co-production with citizens who are 'experts by lived experience', greater 'people skills' promoting personal relationships, the capacity to learn quickly from others, and distributed leadership promoting changing roles when necessary (Needham and Mangan, 2014).

Summary

Highly labour-intensive organizations such as public service organizations largely depend on HRM. In this chapter, we have shown that the public HRM approach builds on general HRM insights, while at the same time incorporating characteristics specific to the public sector, with the ultimate purpose of creating and delivering public value through human resources. The public HRM approach is distinct from generic models of HRM, as it is strongly characterized by planned processes at the level of strategic and operational HRM (e.g. career plans) and a variety of diverse and pluralistic performance outcomes. Strategic HRM in the public sphere extends the scope of performance, focusing on the mission of a public organization encompassing a broad set of values such as efficiency, effectiveness, accountability, equity, and resilience. Keys to success are the fit between organizational policies set by the political-administrative system and HRM practices and the alignment between the implementation of HRM strategies and HRM practices. HRM practices are designed to implement HRM strategies and help to cultivate the abilities, motivations, and opportunities of public employees, so that they are engaged and satisfied and can achieve the intended goals. Finally, this chapter presents key issues and new challenges that public HRM faces today, such as diversity and representation, pro-social motives, employer attractiveness, digitalization, new work, etc.

Questions for review and discussion

1 What is the difference between the Harvard and Michigan models of HRM, and how are these models related to public HRM? Select an organization with which you are familiar, and discuss which of the two models is most relevant to it.
2 What is specifically 'public' about the value chain model of public HRM?
3 Which of the three types of the HRM system (Box 10.2) is most typical of public service organizations in your country? Can you think of examples of the other types – or of organizations which have a mix of these?

Reader exercises

1 Looking at the public service organization for which you work or with which you are familiar, what changes to the diversity of the workforce do you believe to be appropriate? Identify the HRM practices which most need to change in order to achieve this change.
2 Interview a member of staff of a public sector organization in your area. Explore their reaction to the key issues and challenges identified above – which of these do they think their organization has successfully tackled – and why?

Class exercises

1 Select a public organization and find relevant information about HRM on their website or in their annual report. Try to determine how this organization is performing in terms of vertical alignment, horizontal alignment, and implementation/action. What is going well, and which elements could be strengthened – and how?
2 Look at the differences between public and private HRM and select two people from your private or professional environment, working either for the public or private sector. Discuss in small groups how you think that these people are influenced in their identity, values, and behaviours by the specific institutional environment.
3 Look at current job advertisements from public service organizations on the internet. What challenges are identified, and how do employers suggest that new employees should be able to respond to these challenges? Are these suggestions convincing?
4 Do you agree that there has been convergence of public and private HRM over the past ten years? Identify in small groups the arguments for a convergence and the arguments against, then report back to the plenary group.

Further reading

Boselie, P.; Van Harten, J.; Veld, M. (2021), "A human resource management review on public management and public administration research: Stop right there… before we go any further…". *Public Management Review*, 23(4), 483–500.
Breaugh, J.; Hammerschmid, G. (2021), "Different systems, different civil service, different HRM: A comparison of HRM approaches in Anglo-Saxon and Rechtsstaat systems". In: B. Steijn and E. Knies (Eds.), *Research Handbook of HRM in the Public Sector*. Cheltenham: Edward Elgar, pp. 292–306.
Knies, E.; Steijn, B. (2021), "Introduction to the research handbook on HRM in the public sector". In: B. Steijn and E. Knies (Eds.), *Research Handbook on HRM in the Public Sector*. Cheltenham: Edward Elgar, p. 112.
Ritz, A.; Brewer, G.A.; Neumann, O. (2016a), "Public service motivation: A systematic literature review and outlook". *Public Administration Review*, 76(3), 414–426.

References

Ashikali, Tanachia; Groeneveld, Sandra; Ritz, Adrian (2021), "Managing a diverse workforce". Forthcoming. In: Peter Leisink and Lotte B. Andersen et al. (Eds.), *Managing for Public Service Performance* (forthcoming). Oxford: Oxford University Press.
Beer, Michael; Boselie, Paul; Brewster, Chris (2015), "Back to the future: Implications for the field of HRM of the multistakeholder perspective proposed 30 years ago". *Human Resource Management*, 54(3), 427–438.

Beer, Michael; Spector, Bert; Lawrence, Paul R.; Mills, D.; Quinn, Walton; Richard, E. (1984), *Managing Human Assets*. New York: Free Press. Available online at http://www.loc.gov/catdir/description/simon032/84014996.html.

Bellé, Nicola (2015), "Performance-related pay and the crowding out of motivation in the public sector: A randomized field experiment". *Public Administration Review*, 75(2), 230–241.

Boruvka, Elise; Perry, James L. (2020), "Understanding evolving public motivational practices: An institutional analysis". *Governance*, 33(3), 565–584.

Fombrun, Charles J.; Tichy, Noel M.; Devanna, Mary Anne (1984), *Strategic Human Resource Management*. New York: Wiley.

Gratton, Lynda; Truss, Catherine (2003), "The three-dimensional people strategy: Putting human resources policies into action". *Academy of Management Perspectives*, 17(3), 74–86.

Kellough, J. Edward (2017), "Public personnel management: A cornerstone of effective government". In: Norma M Riccucci (Ed.), *Public Personnel Management Current Concerns, Future Challenges* (6th edition). New York London: Routledge (pp.1–11).

Kim, Sangmook; Vandenabeele, Wouter; Wright, Bradley E.; Andersen, Lotte Bøgh; Cerase, Francesco Paolo; Christensen, Robert K. et al. (2012), "Investigating the structure and meaning of public service motivation across populations: Developing an international instrument and addressing issues of measurement invariance". *Journal of Public Administration Research and Theory*, 23(1), 79–102.

Knies, Eva; Borst, Rick T.; Leisink, Peter; Farndale, Elaine (2022), "The distinctiveness of public sector HRM: A four-wave trend analysis". *Human Resource Management Journal*, n/a. DOI: 10.1111/1748-8583.12440.

Knies, Eva; Steijn, Bram (2021), "Introduction to the research handbook on HRM in the public sector". In: Bram Steijn and Eva Knies (Eds.), *Research Handbook of HRM in the Public Sector*. Cheltenham: Edward Elgar, pp. 1–13.

Needham, Catherine; Mangan, Catherine (2014), "The 21st century public servant". Available online at https://21stcenturypublicservant.files.wordpress.com/2014/11/21-century-report-4-pg-report.pdf.

Perry, James L. (1996), "Measuring public service motivation: An assessment of construct reliability and validity". *Journal of Public Administration Research and Theory*, 6(1), 5–22.

Perry, James L.; Wise, Lois Recascino (1990), "The motivational bases of public service", *Public Administration Review*, 50(3), 367–373.

Riccucci, Norma M.; Naff, Katherine C.; Hamidullah, Madinah F. (2019), *Personnel Management in Government: Politics and Process*. London: Routledge.

Ripoll, Guillem; Ritz, Adrian (2022), "Public personnel management". In: Kuno Schedler (Ed.), *Encyclopedia of Public Management*. Cheltenham: Edward Elgar, pp. 166–171.

Ritz, Adrian; Brewer, Gene A.; Neumann, Oliver (2016a), "Public service motivation: A systematic literature review and outlook". *Public Administration Review*, 76(3), 414–426.

Ritz, Adrian; Neumann, Oliver; Vandenabeele, Wouter (2016b), "Motivation in the public sector". In: Thomas R. Klassen, Denita Cepiku and T.J. Lah (Eds.), *The Routledge Handbook of Global Public Policy and Administration (Routledge International Handbooks)*. Florence: Taylor and Francis, pp. 346–359.

Tummers, Lars G.; Knies, Eva (2016), "Measuring public leadership. Developing sclaes for four key public leadership roles". *Public Administration*, 94(2), 433–451. DOI: 10.1111/padm.12224.

Vandenabeele, Wouter; Leisink, Peter; Knies, Eva (2013), "Public value creation and strategic human resource management: Public service motivation as a linking mechanism". In: Peter Leisink, Paul Boselie, Maarten Van Bottenburg and Dian M. Hosking (Eds.), *Managing Social Issues: A Public Values Perspective*. Cheltenham: Edward Elgar Publishing, pp. 37–54.

Wright, Patrick M.; Nishii, Lisa H. (2013), "Strategic HRM and organizational behaviour: Integrating multiple levels of analysis". In: David E. Guest, Jaap Paauwe and Patrick M. Wright (Eds.), *HRM and Performance: Achievements and Challenges*. Chicester: Wiley, pp. 97–110.

11 Public services and management in the digital age

Veiko Lember and Joep Crompvoets

Introduction

It is widely accepted that today we live in a digital age. Digital technologies function as the key enabling technology of modern times, underlying its deep impact on how the public sector and societies in general function. Historically, governments have always relied on a bundle of various technologies to organize and deliver public services. While cadastral maps and bookkeeping techniques were then among the early key information technologies enabling, for example, tax collection, today much tax collection depends on digital technologies from the interconnected information systems to predictive algorithms.

Ever since the early use of computers after WWII and the creation of the Internet in the 1960s and especially the world wide web in the 1990s, digital technologies have become ubiquitous in the public sector. According to Gartner, in 2022, governments across the globe are expected to invest a staggering $557.3 billion into digital technologies. Governments are today developing and using sophisticated systems of digital technologies to redesign public services, co-create public value with citizens and influence the behaviour of people and private organizations. Relatedly, collecting, sharing, analysing and minimizing the harm from using the ever-increasing mass of data has become a key public management challenge.

The uptake and use of digital technologies have significantly shaped public service provision and public management in general. From the perspective of citizens and private organizations, recent technological innovations have improved access to information and intensified knowledge exchange, as well as enhanced connectivity, openness and transparency on all levels. A number of governments have empowered citizens with 'right to information' legislation. In many countries, citizens today are more aware of their rights, have better access to public services and consequently have higher expectations of service levels (matching their expectations of private sector organizations), including customization and other benefits. Citizens and businesses therefore can expect better and more individualized services, faster processes, more transparency and participation and the reduction of administrative burdens.

From the public sector perspective, digitalization provides new options to make public services more efficient and effective while responding to the ever-present economic and budgetary pressures. At the same time, the digital capabilities that underlie the opportunities for efficiency in public service delivery have also become a central building block for national security, maintaining state authority and advancing international competitiveness. Moreover, the increasing reliance on digitalization has created a new context for public management.

DOI: 10.4324/9781003282839-13

However, the increasing use of digital technologies in public services does not automatically create new public value, as it can also destroy it. Competing political and citizen value considerations, the prevalence of short-term cost saving goals or limited in-house technological capacity can all mean that the use of digital technologies can lead to severe negative consequences. As technological change is always an open-ended process that is riddled with value and other conflicts, digital services and processes may sometimes not only disempower citizens, but as 'weapons of math destruction' amplify the real-world biases and discriminatory practices (O'Neil, 2016).

Learning objectives

The key learning objectives of this chapter are:

- To understand the significance of digital technologies in public services
- To understand trends in how digital technologies are used in public services
- To reflect critically on the effects of digital technologies on public services and management

Digital public services

Public services are services offered to the general public and/or in the public interest with the main purpose of developing public value (see also Chapter 1). Modern digital technologies have provided governments with new opportunities for developing and organizing public services for creating public value. There has been a rapid increase in access to government services across the world (see Box 11.1). In addition, redesigning easy-to-use online services has made it possible for governments to increase citizen compliance without using coercion or financial incentives (e.g. in declaring taxes). Also, digital technology has empowered ordinary citizens by offering them a way to co-create public services, make their voices heard and challenge government leaders about their ability and willingness to address public concerns and requests. At the same time, private companies increasingly provide services and solutions that rely upon government data. The increased connectivity of citizens and businesses, the possibility for people to work together, to perform tasks and to distribute workload regardless of distance and boundaries, as well as the open availability of previously non-published information and data mean that an increasing number of government tasks can also be performed – completely or in part – by citizens, companies and others. It is no longer governments alone (the 'visible hand') or the market alone (the 'invisible hand') that can respond to societal needs; now all and any partnerships and groups ('many hands') can more easily contribute to public value.

Box 11.1 Rapid evolution of digital public services in Bangladesh

Bangladesh is one of the countries that has in the last decade made significant investments into digital public services. After launching its 'Digital Bangladesh' strategy, the number of active people online has climbed up from 3% in 2008 to 70% (116 million people) in 2021. The key programme of the strategy – Access to Information – has developed a network of more than 5,800 digital centres. The idea of the network is that people would not need to travel more than 4 km to access digitally over 150 key public services.

Source: UNDP (2022).

Technological innovations are often associated with positive and radical change in public service delivery, but this is not always the case. Some digital projects may lead to little change in the actual service processes, while in other cases the use of digital technologies may lead to radical institutional changes. To better understand the significance of digital technologies for public services and management, the following three approaches offer a useful distinction (see also OECD, 2019):

- *Digitization* – analogue solutions put into digital or machine-readable format, e.g. allowing forms to be downloaded, printed, filled out and returned as pdf formats instead of paper formats, which requires very little or almost no change on part of the public service.
- *Digitalization* – process and organizational re-thinking, taking advantage of all sorts of digital opportunities; leads to new activities or assumes institutional or process change (e.g. new kind of services, service re-design or new collaborative practices) and aims at providing more public value.
- *Digital transformation* – profound institutional, societal and economic changes that are related to the uptake and use of digital technologies; often long-term cumulative processes resulting from unplanned or second-order effects.

While digitization mostly characterized the early days of digital public services, the digitalization of public services is at the heart of contemporary public service change efforts. These efforts build on a mix of old and new service delivery principles that characterize how the existing and emerging technological opportunities are exploited – at least in policy rhetoric – to develop digital public services (see Box 11.2). Meanwhile, the level of more thorough-going digital transformation of the public sector is still open for debate.

Box 11.2 Principles of digital government

Digital-by-default: Public agencies should design and deliver services *digitally* as the preferred option (while still keeping other channels open for those who are disconnected by choice or necessity).

Once only: Public agencies should ensure that citizens and businesses supply the *same information only once to a public agency*.

Inclusiveness: Public agencies should design digital public services that are *inclusive by default* and *cater for different needs*, such as those of the elderly and people with disabilities.

Openness and transparency: Public agencies should *share information and data* between themselves and enable citizens and businesses to *access, monitor* and *correct* their own data; enable users to *monitor administrative processes* that involve them; and *engage with* and *open up to stakeholders* in the design and delivery of services.

Interoperability: Public services should be designed to work *seamlessly* across organizational borders, relying on the free movement of data and digital services.

Trustworthiness and cybersecurity: All initiatives should go beyond mere compliance with the legal framework on *personal data protection* and *privacy*, and *IT security*, by integrating those elements in the design phase. These are important pre-conditions for *increasing trust* in the take-up and use of digital services.

The technologies underlying digital services are often categorized into front-end and back-end technologies. The application of front-end technologies requires a different skill set compared to the back-end ones. While back-end processes focus more on the logic of processes and technical problem solving, front-end processes place more emphasis on the design and usability of services. The front-end and back-end are often connected to each other through an application programming interface (API), a sort of digital 'waiter' that allows applications to communicate with each other. The API also enables external stakeholders such as private firms, citizens or voluntary organizations to develop front-end solutions and services that rely on government data.

In this context, 'front-end' refers to all technologies allowing or facilitating users to somehow see the (web) content or interact (by interfaces) with the content. Front-end technologies enable the use of digital public services by service users, including:

- *Identification (ID) systems*: Technologies providing proof of legal identity that is often required for – or simplifies the process of – accessing basic rights, services, opportunities and protections. Governments have created a variety of functional ID systems to manage identification, authentication and authorization for specific sectors or uses, such as voting, taxation, social protection, travel, etc. India, for example, runs Adhaar, the world's largest centralized mandatory public ID system based on biometric and demographic data. On the other hand, Japan and the US, among other countries, have no mandatory centralized ID system and make use of many different digital ID systems.
- *Portals*: Technologies providing a single point of entry to various public and private services, so that it is easier for users to find what they are looking for. Such portals act as doorways, allowing the otherwise complex underlying functionalities to be presented and used in a much more user-friendly manner. In the UK, for example, the ease of finding information has been the key digitalization aim for the past decade, leading to the creation of the central gov.uk portal that replaced hundreds of old webpages.
- *Apps*: Technologies designed to run on a mobile device such as a phone, tablet or watch, performing a specific function directly for an end user or, in some cases, for another application (e.g. authenticator). Apps were originally intended for productivity assistance, such as email, calendar and contact databases, but the public demand for apps caused rapid expansion into other areas such as mobile games, factory automation, GPS and location-based services, order-tracking and ticket purchases, so that there are now millions of apps available – including government apps. In Denmark, for example, all

residents are obliged to receive and read messages from the government digitally, for which the government has created a digital post app.

- *Artificial intelligence (AI)-powered digital assistants*: Intelligent virtual assistants or intelligent personal assistants are technologies that can perform tasks or services for an individual based on commands or questions. Contrary to the pre-programmed information systems, these virtual assistants are based on machine-learning algorithms that are trained on historical datasets to provide answers or make decisions without explicitly being programmed to do so. The term 'chatbot' is sometimes used to refer to these technologies generally or specifically accessed by online chat.

'Back-end', on the other hand, refers to technologies dealing with all behind-the-scenes activities including the rapid, frequent and reliable delivery of the databases, large/complex applications and/or micro-services. Back-end technologies enable the smooth performance of the provision, storage and/or management of digital services using the Internet, hardware (servers, computers), software, data warehouses, data infrastructures, platforms and/or process management tools. In Estonia, for example, one of the backbones of digital public services is its unique data exchange system called X-Road, which in 2022 connects more than 1,500 otherwise decentralized public and private information systems and which facilitates close to 3 billion inquiries a year across these information systems, serving more than 3,000 digitally accessible services (see https://www.x-tee.ee/factsheets/EE/#eng).

Key trends in the digitalization of public services

Next to the rapid technological advancements in software, hardware and computational power in recent decades, the current developments in digital public service delivery have been influenced by the vastly improved availability of data. This includes not only the ability to use 'old' data sources such as office files or government registries at a much greater speed, but also the ability to harness new data sources, such as social media or digital images. The following examples characterize some of the recent key trends in digital public services:

- **Automation.** The quest for greater efficiency through automation has always been the main driver of introducing new ICTs into the public sector – digital technologies simply happen to be the latest example of this evolution (Agar, 2003). Compared to the previous eras, where automation mostly concerned discrete processes (e.g. payroll calculations), the exponentially increased computation power and the Internet have now enabled governments to collect, store, analyse, manipulate and exchange data to automate the entire public service delivery chains. The recent welfare-to-work reform in Australia provides a characteristic example of this evolution, where traditional face-to-face employment counselling is to be fully automated, with clients expected in most cases to interact only with the so-called 'chatbots' (Considine et al., 2022).
- **Service integration**. Similarly, service integration has long been another 'holy grail' for governments, where digital technologies are expected to enable more coherent and coordinated public service delivery (Dunleavy et al., 2006). Due to vastly improved data exchange between various service stakeholders, governments now have a more holistic overview of their service users, which both reduces the time and effort needed for service delivery and potentially enables more informed decision-making.

Digitalization also creates new value creation opportunities and inter-organizational structures that rely on real-time machine-to-machine coordination. For example, many governments have started to integrate similar services around different life moments (see Box 11.3). This approach bundles together various formal procedures and related services that previously had to be initiated and processed separately. As governments today possess a lot of data on residents, they are increasingly well positioned to offer these services pro-actively, that is, pushing services to citizens before the latter even realize the need for them.

Box 11.3 Singapore's *Moments of Life* concept

Singapore is widely considered a global leader in digital government. One of its central digitalization efforts has been the creation and implementation of the *Moments of Life* (LifeSG) concept that anchors public services to citizens' key moments in life (e.g. birth, education, housing, family, career or retirement). It integrates and bundles government services from various agencies into a single convenient process with the aim of making it easier for citizens to discover and access relevant services.

Initially starting out with a small pilot focused on the key moment of starting a family, the government aimed to overcome the fragmented user experience of services by organizing them around citizens' journeys instead of the setup of government agencies. It required extensive inter-agency collaboration and mutual adjustment of their policies, processes and operations. On a process level, the main design methods used were journey mapping, user interviews and co-creation workshops with different stakeholders. The key user insights generated through this process were used to define those moments of life which services could be anchored around and accessed online in one place.

Source: Ganesan et al. (2019).

- **Building ecosystems**. The digital era has enabled novel ways to connect different public service stakeholders. The ecosystem approach has deepened the inter-dependency within the public sector as well as between the public and private sectors in terms of horizontal and vertical partnerships. For example, Google Maps and other similar private platforms depend on and run their services on open data provided by government cadastral agencies. On the other hand, an increasing number of public services (e.g. life-event services) depend on data and functionalities provided by other, be they public or private, organizations. As a result, modular strategies have emerged where digital public services are developed by re-using already existing digital components (e.g. payment platforms, open software code or canonical registries), often developed or owned by stakeholders who are external to a specific service delivery. This has led some to argue that we have entered into the era of government-as-a-platform.
- **Predictive government.** While the true anticipatory power of predictive algorithms is very much debatable, governments across the world have started to invest in developing and commissioning algorithmic solutions that could, for example, predict criminal recidivism, job performance or at-risk kids (Narayanan, 2019). Using various sorts of historical data to train the algorithms in finding certain behavioural patterns, these types of predictive algorithms are believed to provide options for preventing harm and to enable more anticipatory, individualized and contextualized service delivery. This

overall quest to develop predictive capabilities goes hand-in-hand with exploiting other AI-powered technologies, such as face recognition at borders, translating speech to text in national parliaments or grading essays in schools.

- **Harnessing social media**. Social media has not only enabled billions of people globally to connect to each other, but also to establish direct relationships with their governments. Social (information) sharing, content creation, content curation and open platforms are among the more widely used social media applications (Mergel, 2016). Social media have become an important new data source for governments to sense the dynamics of change in society, to inform about and collect feedback on public services and also exercise control over their citizens and manipulate social sentiment. Social media have created many novel opportunities to self-organize and co-create public services (e.g. from providing real-time information during crises such as floods or earthquakes to developing peer-to-peer and self-sustaining communities).

- **Do-It-Yourself-Government.** There is a new wave of technology-induced co-production practices that have recently emerged around the globe and that promise to change the way citizens are engaged with and provide input for public services. In Mexico City, which has one of the largest public-transportation systems in the world with 14 million rides per day, the citizens were able to co-produce the city's first ever complete public transportation map within just two weeks by sharing their travel data through a mobile app (OECD, 2017). Taken to the extreme, this digitally enabled 'prosumption' trend can shift the full control of service provision to citizens without the need for direct or even indirect government participation (e.g. peer-to-peer energy networks or community-owned taxi platforms providing public transport functions).

The above overview of key digital technologies and trends is nowhere near exhaustive. Every new technical invention necessitates further innovations to keep the technological systems in balance (Kranzberg, 1986). There is thus a constant need for new and auxiliary innovations in order to keep the digital services running as expected. For example, as the centrality of data in modern digital services is increasing, the need for advanced cybersecurity and privacy-preserving technologies has also increased. This is why one can witness numerous new experiments with blockchain and other similar technologies constantly emerging. Also, these and other digitalization trends assume that governments keep developing highly functional and resilient data infrastructures, a task that has proven to be a challenging one (Greenway et al., 2021).

Digitalization and public management

Although it is questionable to what extent public management as such can fundamentally change, the use of digital technologies in and around public sector has created a new context for it. That is, what management is about, how managers manage and what values determine the practice of management (Lynn, 2012).

One of the key questions in public management is how to structure public sector organizations – who actually does the management, and how much delegation and control is exercised at different levels in the public service organization. In many public service areas, especially in mass service organizations such as employment, tax or social security agencies, the pace of digitalization has evolved hand-in-hand with clear centralization tendencies. Zouridis et al. (2020), for example, captured this tendency as the rise of system-level bureaucracy, where the previously decentralized decision-making authority in large service organizations has increasingly shifted into the hands of the system-level bureaucrats such as managers, lawyers, IT architects and data analysts. This trend builds on radically better access to the ever-more granular information from the centre of organizations and on the enhanced capabilities of those organizational centres to codify and prescript the expected decision-making actions into software. This tendency, as a result, has redefined who constitutes the core organization of the digital-era public service organizations (e.g. employment councillors working directly with clients vs. system architects working in the central back-office) and how tasks are divided between humans and machines (e.g. through prescriptive algorithms). Put simply, today technologists play a much more central role in public management and service provision than before.

Yet, digitalization has not only enabled the centralization of the decision-making authority to the top, but it has also reinforced some of the decentralization tendencies common to the early Internet-era visions. Within organizations, more and more public services are developed and implemented by ad hoc inter-disciplinary teams, making the overall organizational structures much more fluid than before. These teams often make use of agile and design methods that rely on constant iterations, short feedback cycles and modularized processes rather than traditional top-down policy design and implementation cycles (Mergel et al., 2021). At the same time, many governments have delegated the provision of and control over the key digital public services and infrastructure to private technology providers (e.g. private cloud services or COVID-19 mobile tracing platforms). The tendency to outsource critical digital service components to the private sector has reinforced the old and raised new questions about how the division of tasks between public and private sectors should be organized, how to hold private sector stakeholders accountable and how to maintain the sovereignty of states vis-à-vis powerful digital giants. What seems to be clear is that due to the increased organizational and technological inter-dependencies, the digital age increasingly assumes both high-level in-house technological knowledge as well as network and contracting management capabilities from public managers in order to govern the ever-more technology-dependent relationships with the external service stakeholders (see e.g. Dickson and Yates, 2021).

Another central question revolves around the craft and processes of management – has the digital age somehow changed what managers do? Due to the centrality of digital technologies, there has been a rapid influx of new professions into the public sector, e.g. digital entrepreneurs, software engineers, cybersecurity specialists, user experience designers, process managers, data scientists and others. These professions also bring new knowledge domains, leadership styles and management practices into the public sector. The new managerial styles create not only new opportunities for public service provision, but also new kinds of conflicts (e.g. rapid and experimental service development culture vs. dominant public sector accountability regimes). To make the most out of digitalization opportunities, public managers need to be able to secure access to a whole range of new digital competences. It is, however, increasingly challenging for public managers to attract and keep specialists such as data scientists or software engineers in the public sector, especially as the current global digital race provides wide and often more lucrative options for these professionals in the private sector. Thus, the ability to create a unique public sector ethos or mission mystique among the digitalization specialists, and keep them in the public sector, has become a key leadership and personnel management task.

Lastly, one needs to understand if and how public management institutions, i.e. the values that determine responsible practice and legitimacy, have been shaped by digitalization trends. As argued above, there are various service delivery principles that have (re)emerged in the digital era. Design thinking, for example, has become a central building block of digital public services, increasingly codified into horizontal public service standards (see, for example, the UK government's design principles https://www.gov.uk/guidance/government-design-principles). Focus on user needs, opening up the public sector working processes, iterative and data-informed development processes and constant testing with users are some of the 'new' values that have come to inform what the responsible service delivery practice should be (Greenway et al., 2021). Governments also try to adjust their procurement, personnel, financing and collaboration routines accordingly to support the take-up of digital technologies. All of these changes bring new values to the fore and, thus, shape what the responsible and legitimate practice of public service delivery looks like in the digital age. And of course, with these practices have also surfaced new value conflicts. The emerging experimental and data-informed service planning and delivery practices, for example, force governments to constantly find compromises between values such as individual privacy and user experience.

Digitalization is never neutral

Not only is the relationship between digitalization, public services and management a complex one, it is often controversial. As Melvin Kranzberg (1986) once observed, 'technology is neither good or bad, nor is it neutral'. Technologies tend to amplify the processes, practices and structures for which they are adopted (Zuboff, 2019) and, therefore, the adoption of new technologies without critically reflecting upon and re-thinking the underlining institutional practices usually fails to improve public services. In the worst cases, it can even destroy public value (see Box 11.4).

Box 11.4 Robodebt: Automated decision-making going wrong

In 2015, the government of Australia launched a new policy initiative to strengthen the integrity of its welfare system and reduce overpayments made to social security recipients. Enabled by new online service delivery as well as data analytics, storage and sharing capabilities, the government decided to fully automate the oversight of potential overpayments. As the number of processed inquires increased from 20,000 a year to 20,000 a week, the new initiative was expected to save the government $3.7 billion for the fiscal year 2016/17 alone.

However, it turned out to be one of the biggest policy failures in Australia, now known as the Robodebt scandal. Hundreds of thousands of social security recipients were unlawfully penalized, causing them severe psychological and financial stress. Resulting from several court rulings, the government had to pay back over $1 billion to more than 400,000 people. The root of the problems was not in the IT systems, but in the fact that the automated process was aimed at serving hidden policy goals (reduction of budgetary deficit), was based on a problematic choice of calculation methods and shifted the responsibility of proof (in relation to the alleged overpayments) from the government to vulnerable and uninformed citizens.

Source: Whiteford (2021).

Digitalization forces public managers to deal with various new and old challenges, such as the digital divide, privacy loss, data (in)justice and increasing power imbalances. Developing digital services also means that significant trade-offs have to be made between various legitimate, yet competing values. Yet these value considerations often remain unarticulated, hidden or are framed as purely technical issues. As the example above shows, there always exist different policy agendas and value positions that inform policy-makers' decisions to launch certain kinds of digitalization projects and not others. There are also different design preferences and choices that shape how digitalization eventually affects service users and outcomes. Often service users do not engage with digital services as anticipated, or come up with unexpected ways of using new technologies that might run against the plans and aims of the policy-makers and service designers.

It thus matters who is involved in the digitalization decision-making processes and who has the power to influence the agenda and decisions. As the use of digital technologies increases, it is vital to make sure that public service stakeholders from local residents to advocacy coalitions become part of imagining what digital services ought to deliver and how. Moreover, to make use successfully of the digital opportunities and manage different value conflicts, strong public sector in-house service, data and technology capabilities remain key. These capabilities need to be supported by high-level budgeting, personnel, procurement and other organizational capabilities adjusted to the digital era needs. It is no coincidence that countries with highly functional digital public services such as Denmark, Finland or the Republic of Korea all have, simultaneously, well-performing basic bureaucratic structures and public management systems.

Summary

Over the past decades, digital technologies have provided a myriad of new options for re-thinking public service delivery. From the early attempts to speed up information exchange and migrating services online to re-designing the entire eco-system of service provision, governments have gradually learned how to create new public value through digitalization. As governments increasingly invest in new digital and data capabilities, digitalization has also shaped the structure, craft and institutions of public management. Digitalization constantly challenges existing public service and management routines, providing governments with new options to abandon poorly functioning processes. But there also exists a considerable gap between what digitalization visions and technological opportunities promise and what governments actually do and can accomplish. Digitalization can serve many different aims, some of which enjoy popular support, but some of which remain hidden and problematic. This is why digital public service delivery will remain as much about understanding and shaping the institutions and practices that underlie the services as about mastering technology.

Questions for review and discussion

1   What are the key digitalization principles and trends shaping contemporary public management and public service delivery?
2   How does digitalization in the public sector shape public management? Can we talk of an emerging 'public management paradigm for the digital age'?

Reader exercises

1   Pick two different public sector organizations in your country and try to find evidence for their service digitalization developments. What are the similarities and differences? What could explain the differences?

2 Think of a digital public service that you recently used. How well did the service exemplify the key digitalization principles in Box 11.2? What are the main areas needing improvement? In what sense did the service add or destroy public value?
3 Digital public services are often delivered in a partnership between public and private sector. What speaks for and against increasing the role of private firms in delivering digital public services?

Class exercise

In groups, choose a public service you are familiar with and that is currently characterized by a low level of digitalization. Each group should think of what new value digitalization could create for this particular service and devise a plan for how the service could be (fully) digitalized – what principles, trends and management practices could be used to enhance the value of the service? Discuss the potential implications and value trade-offs which might arise from the implementation of the digitalization plan and how you would address these.

Further reading

For a historical account, see Agar, J., 2003. *The Government Machine: A Revolutionary History of the Computer*. Boston: MIT Press.
For recent evidence how digital technologies are shaping public management in the digital age, see Tan, E. and Crompvoets, J., 2022. *The New Digital Era Governance: How New Digital Technologies are Shaping Public Governance*. Wageningen, Netherlands: Wageningen Academic Publishers.
For reflections from relevant practitioners, see Greenway, A., Terrett, B., Bracken, M. and Loosemore, T., 2021. *Digital Transformation at Scale: Why the Strategy Is Delivery*. London: London Publishing Partnerships.

References

Considine, M., McGann, M., Ball, S. and Nguyen, P., 2022. Can robots understand welfare? Exploring machine bureaucracies in welfare-to-work. *Journal of Social Policy*, 51(3): 519–534.
Dickson, H. and Yates, S., 2021. From external provision to technological outsourcing: Lessons for public sector automation from the outsourcing literature. *Public Management Review*. https://doi.org/10.1080/14719037.2021.1972681.
Dunleavy, P., Margetts, H., Bastow, S. and Tinkler, J., 2006. New public management is dead—Long live digital-era governance. *Journal of Public Administration Research and Theory*, 16(3), 467–494.
Ganesan, V., Lam, Y. and Lin, D.-Y., 2019. *How Singapore is Harnessing Design to Transform Government Services*. Available at: https://www.mckinsey.com/industries/public-sector/our-insights/how-singapore-is-harnessing-design-to-transform-government-services.
Greenway, A., Terrett, B., Bracken, M. and Loosemore, T., 2021. *Digital Transformation at Scale: Why the Strategy is Delivery*. London: London Publishing Partnerships.
Kranzberg, M., 1986. Technology and history: "Kranzberg's laws". *Technology and Culture*, 27(3), 544–560.
Lynn, L.E., 2012. Public management. In B.G. Peters und J. Pierre, eds. *Handbook of Public Administration*. London: Sage, 17–31.
Mergel, I., 2016. Social media in the public sector. In D. Bearfield and M. Dubnick, eds. *Encyclopedia of Public Administration and Public Policy*, Vol. 3. New York: Routledge, 3018–3021.
Mergel, I., Ganapati, S. and Whitford, A.B., 2021. Agile: A new way of governing. *Public Administration Review*, 81(1), 161–165.

Narayanan, A., 2019. *How to Recognize AI Snake Oil*. Arthur Miller Lecture on Science and Ethics. Available at: https://www.cs.princeton.edu/~arvindn/talks/MIT-STS-AI-snakeoil.pdf.

OECD, 2017. *Observatory of Public Sector Innovation*. Paris: OECD.

OECD, 2019. *Going Digital: Shaping Policies, Improving Lives*. Paris: OECD.

O'Neil, C., 2016. *Weapons of Math Destruction: How Big Data Increases Inequality and Threatens Democracy*. Allen Lane.

UNDP Chief Digital Office, 2022. Inclusive by design: Accelerating digital transformation for the global goals. Policy Brief, New York.

Whiteford, P., 2021. Debt by design: The anatomy of a social policy fiasco – Or was it something worse? *Australian Journal of Public Administration*, 80(2), 340–360.

Zouridis, S., Van Eck, M. and Bovens, M., 2020. Automated discretion. In T. Evans and P.L. Hupe, eds. *Discretion and the quest for controlled freedom*. Cham, Switzerland: Palgrave Macmillan, 313–329.

Zuboff, S., 2019. *The Age of Surveillance Capitalism: The Fight for a Human Future at the New Frontier of Power*. London: Profile Books.

12 Performance measurement and management in public sector organizations

Geert Bouckaert and Wouter Van Dooren

Introduction

> *Sir Humphrey*: Minister, you said you wanted the administration figures reduced, didn't you? *Jim Hacker*: Yes. *Sir Humphrey*: So we reduced the figures. *Jim Hacker*: But only the figures, not the number of administrators. *Sir Humphrey*: Well, of course not. *Jim Hacker*: Well, that is not what I meant. *Sir Humphrey*: Well, really, Minister, one is not a mind-reader, is one? You said reduce the figures, so we reduced the figures.
>
> (*Yes Minister* 2.1 'The Compassionate Society', 1981)

This chapter aims to explore the concept, the potential, and the practice of performance measurement and management in public sector organizations. Management by numbers is a longstanding but contested practice, as demonstrated by the *Yes Minister* quote. It shows that performance management is both about measurement and management. It is about gathering and using information for action (Bouckaert & Halligan, 2008; Hatry, 1999; Van Dooren & Van de Walle, 2008).

Learning objectives

This chapter will look at the following key issues:

- The evolution of performance measurement and management in the public sector
- The key concepts in performance measurement
- The key concepts in performance management
- Some traps and lessons learned in performance management

The evolution of performance management

Since the 1980s, the *New Public Management* (NPM) has actively emphasized performance measurement as a management tool in government (OECD, 1997). Accurate performance information is needed to implement NPM-inspired management instruments such as

DOI: 10.4324/9781003282839-14

performance pay, performance contracts, or performance budgets (Christensen & Lægreid, 2016). However, NPM did not originate the idea of measuring government performance. In both Europe and the United States, there had already been longstanding performance measurement initiatives (Van Dooren & Van de Walle, 2008; Williams, 2003). The roots of the performance movement in the USA can be traced back to the progressive and scientific management movements in the early 20th century (Bouckaert, 1990). As early as 1949, the first Hoover Commission in the United States aimed at shifting the attention of the budget from inputs towards functions, activity cost, and accomplishments. New planning and budgeting approaches such as the Planning, Programming and Budgeting System (PPBS) in the 1960s, management by objectives (MBO) in the early 1970s (see Chapter 7) and zero-based budgeting (ZBB) in the late 1970s emerged (A. T.-K. Ho et al., 2019). These planning and budgeting approaches leaned heavily on the availability of performance information. Too heavily, argued Wildawsky (1969). The barrage of performance indicators to cover the budget with indicators was, in his view, making a mockery of serious policy analysis.

The performance movement lost steam in the 1980s. The fiscal crises of the 1980s led politicians to being preoccupied with savings and cutback management (A. T.-K. Ho et al., 2019). In early 1990s, interest in performance management reemerged. Politicians like US president Bill Clinton, UK prime minister Tony Blair, and German Bundeskanzler Gerhard Schröder promised a third way between big and small government. A government that works better and costs less. To support this agenda, performance measurement had to demonstrate 'what works' in order to target public expenditure. Minimizing the public sector was no longer the dominant public management reform strategy (Pollitt & Bouckaert, 2017). Outcomes and quality concerns gained importance in many countries.

In the 2000s, performance management had become a driver for NPM reform in many countries. In Australia the Public Service Commission evolved from 'Sharpening the Focus: Managing Performance in the APS' (2006) to 'Challenges of Evidence-Based Policymaking' (2009). In Canada, the 1996 planning, reporting and accountability structure (PRAS) was replaced in 2005 by the management, resources and results structure (MRRS). In the Netherlands a new performance-driven policy information architecture was approved in 2006, in combination with a 'comply or explain' policy of implementation. Many low- to middle-income countries also implemented performance management systems, often coupled with a performance budget. The performance budgets were often compiled with technical assistance from international organizations such as the Asian Development Bank and the World Bank (de Jong, 2019). Examples of performance budgeting can be found in amongst others the Philippines, Indonesia, Mexico, Kenya, Tunisia, and China.

In the 2010s, the limits of New Public Management became apparent. Competitive pressures and NPM's narrow focus on efficiency led to a corrosion of public services. The post-New Public Management emphasizes more collaboration instead of more competition and a focus on public value instead of on private values. The global financial crisis of 2010 and the COVID-19 pandemic of 2020 showed the importance of a resilient government that cooperates across boundaries. The implications for performance measurement and management are unclear. It seems that the post-NPM paradigm pushes performance measurement systems towards measurement and indicators of quality-of-life, whole of government, trust, and quality-of-governance (see Chapter 15). Public service requires inter-organizational collaboration and co-production with service users and citizens. Performance management increasingly becomes performance governance.

Key concepts in performance measurement

The input-output-impact model of performance measurement

This section will look at how different types of performance can be measured. There are several levels at which performance measurement can operate – it may refer to the measurement of inputs, outputs, or outcomes, and it may focus on economy, efficiency, or effectiveness. We can integrate these concepts into an input-output model of the policy and management cycle – see Figure 12.1 (Van Dooren et al., 2015).

The input-output-impact model gives a systemic overview of the aspirations of a public programme. Within the polis, societal conditions (1) are translated into societal needs (2). Not all societal conditions lead to the formulation of needs that government programmes are supposed to address. For a long time, many Western societies did not translate poverty and poor sanitary conditions into a need for policy. This changed in the early twentieth century under the pressure of social activists. The next step in the policy cycle is to infer more concrete objectives (3) from these general needs. Good objectives are *relevant*. They address the societal needs adequately. When the societal need is affordable housing, an objective of granting renovation subsidies may not be relevant when most of the affordability issues are in the rental sector.

Once the objectives are defined, inputs can be allocated, activities can be developed and outputs can be delivered (4, 5, 6). Personnel, infrastructure, and ICTs are some typical

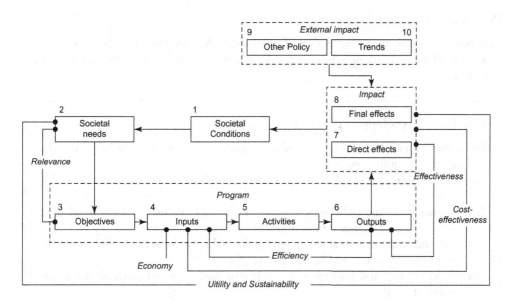

Figure 12.1 The policy and management cycle.

Source: Van Dooren et al. (2015: 21).

inputs. Inputs should be acquired economically. A computer with the same specifications should cost the same across programmes. With these inputs, activities are undertaken. For example, a school will organize lessons and a library will shelve books that may be lent out. The activities result in outputs (e.g., number of students passing exams or number of books on loan). The programme management should be concerned that the inputs yield the right amount and quality of outputs by organizing the activities in the best possible way. Therefore, the manager's feedback loop focuses primarily on inputs and outputs (6 to 3 and 4). When outputs are provided at low costs, the programme is efficient.

Once the outputs (i.e., the products and services) are provided, we can expect to see an impact in society. We can make a distinction between direct effects (7) and final effects (8). This distinction reflects an important division between the ends ultimately desired and the interim accomplishments that are expected to lead to those end results (although, of course, they may not). An output of a mental hospital may be the number of patients treated. The direct effect may be the number of patients that can get by without medicine. The final effect may be the number of discharged patients that can live independently.

Since a long time may elapse between the delivery of outputs and the occurrence of the end outcomes, the causality between the output and final effect may be difficult to establish. The impact of external factors will be hard to disentangle from the impact of a programme. Hence, the external effects should also be assessed. Two kinds of external effects can be distinguished. There are sometimes countervailing effects of other policies (9) and general trend effects such as growth of the economy or global warming (10). The effect of good education, for instance, is a thriving society with confident citizens. An inadequate health and nutrition policy, however, may run counter to the education policy. An economic downturn may lead to insecurity and stress in society. The policymaker's feedback loop is the confrontation of the effects with the objectives, which closes the circle.

Performance indicators

Performance indicators are variables that tell us how close we have come to reaching our objectives. Different kinds of indicators can be derived from the input-output-impact model – see Box 12.1.

Box 12.1 A typology of performance indicators

Input indicators: e.g. number of employees, money spent, number of hospital beds, number of public buses.

Output indicators: e.g. number of pupils taught, number of discharged patients, vehicle miles.

Intermediate outcome indicators: e.g. new knowledge, increased skills, number of recovered patients, user satisfaction with services.

End outcome indicators: e.g. increased grades achieved in schools, reductions in unemployment, increased health and well-being.

Societal environmental indicators: e.g. age structure, economic indicators such as growth of GDP.

The combination of the boxes in the input-output-outcome model allows the formulation of ratio-indicators.

Economy is an input/input ratio as cost divided by the input, e.g., the cost per employee, the costs per office. As with any indicator, interpretation is key. A low cost per employee for instance could refer to a young work force, a high level of technology, or a low pay structure.

Productivity or efficiency is an output divided by an input, e.g., bus hours on the road per employee (for public transport), shop or restaurant visits per food inspector, patrol hours per police officer per day. It is possible to consider one input, e.g., labour, which allows assessing labour productivity. It is also possible to have a combination of all input indicators, which results in a total factor productivity index. Usually, the only index of all inputs that is available is cost, which leads to the specific efficiency indicator of *unit cost* (e.g., cost per discharged patient, cost per crime cleared). Since *all* the costs of all the inputs used to obtain an output need to be calculated in financial terms, this can only be properly calculated if the organization has a reliable cost accounting system.

Effectiveness is effect divided by output, e.g., number of complaints received about dirty streets per kilometre of street that receives regular cleaning. The distinction between direct and long-term effects should be taken into consideration. Paradoxically, better street cleaning may lead to more complaints in the short run because expectations are raised.

Cost-effectiveness is outcome divided by cost, e.g., cost per unemployed person moving into employment can be an outcome measure for job counselling. As with the effectiveness indicators, the impact of external factors should be taken into consideration. People can find jobs for many reasons. Maybe a large labour-intensive investment has changed the local labour market? Or maybe a fiscal reform has given people an additional incentive to take up jobs even though they feel they are overqualified.

Performance standards

A performance measurement system that focuses on the different steps in the input-output model should provide an organization with sufficient information to plan, monitor, and evaluate both policy and management. The next step is to lay down standards that establish how well (or how badly) the organization is performing. A minimum standard is the value of a performance indicator that must be met.

Standards may be set in different ways:

- Mostly, the standards are set by comparison, usually either between time periods or across units. Time series analysis compares past performance with current performance. Cross-section analysis compares with other organizations, programmes, or countries.
- Another method is to use a scientific norm, e.g. for the maximum quantities of chemicals allowed in the food chain or vaccination levels needed to eradicate a disease and attain herd immunity.
- Politicians sometimes set a popular standard as a symbol of ambitious policies. Sweden for instance was a forerunner in the *vision zero* policy regarding traffic casualties. Although most people will understand that having no traffic casualties at all is not realistic, the zero-target should point us towards the enduring importance of addressing the issue.
- Performance standards are often a mixture of negotiation and science. The goal of the climate agreements to keep global warming below 1.5 degrees is an example of a norm that is both scientifically supported and negotiated.

The process of comparing performance across organizations is known as *benchmarking*. Where benchmarking is used to derive scorecards and 'league tables', it requires a high degree of comparability and a culture of transparency between the organizations to be compared – otherwise the comparisons are likely to be regarded as unfair (especially by those at the lower end). This is even more serious if these league tables trigger media attention or government action – e.g. intervention by a higher level of government or loss of budgets. Benchmarks seldom tell us *why* differences occur. Moreover, scorecards may often leave out the most interesting comparisons – e.g. with high performing organizations that are not comparable on most dimensions, but where their high performance is potentially transferable, or with those organizations which are moving upwards from the lower end of the scale.

Key concepts in performance management

The use of performance information

Performance measurement only becomes valuable when it is followed by the action of managers or policymakers – it is only justified if it is used (see Case Example 12.1). Performance management can be broadly defined as 'acting upon performance information'. In this section we will examine some of the most important uses of performance information in public sector management. Performance information can be used for different purposes in policy and management. We distinguish between three broad categories: to learn, to steer and control, and to give account (Van Dooren et al., 2015: 120) – see Table 12.1.

Table 12.1 Uses of performance information

	To learn	To steer and control	To give account
Key question	How to improve policy or management?	How to guide activities?	How to explain performance?
Orientation	Change/future	Control/present	Survival/past

Source: Adapted from Van Dooren et al., 2015: 120.

Case Example 12.1 CitiStat in Baltimore

The story of Baltimore's CitiStat shows how the uses of performance information shift over time. CitiStat was initiated in the early 2000s by Mayor O'Malley, who was elected on a platform to combat crime. Inspired by New York's CompStat system, he implemented a dashboard that shows crime statistics on a map of Baltimore. The performance indicators were primarily used for accountability. In 2004, CitiStat won the Harvard Innovation in Government award (Harvard University, 2004). The jury report called the system 'nothing short of confrontational'.

In bi-weekly meetings, the manager of each city agency must stand at a podium and answer questions from a panel led by the Mayor or his appointed inquisitor (sic) … During the meeting, various images are projected onto two screens behind the manager: graphs of performance, recent images of job sites, and even the manager's face. In Mayor O'Malley's words, CitiStat 'puts a face on the problem'.

Accountability is the primary use of the performance indicators. Many cities followed the lead of CitiStat and built similar systems (Behn, 2013). Yet, despite its initial success, CitiStat ran out of steam in the 2010s (Wogan, 2017). Senior managers compared the CitiStat meetings to the Spanish Inquisition and reports of data manipulation were rife. The numbers gaming and the intimidation in CitiStat meetings figured prominently in season 3 of HBO's *The Wire*, a show on urban life in Baltimore that inspired dedicated university courses. The credibility of the CitiStat system was affected, fewer reports were published, and fewer meetings scheduled. Today, the CitiStat system still exists, but the use of the performance indicators has shifted away from personal accountability to cross cutting policy issues such as homelessness and blight. The use of performance indicators shifts from accountability to learning. In recent years, CitiStat is also part of an open data platform, which adds a co-productive dimension to the focus on learning. The city should not only learn from, but also with communities.

First, performance information may be collected to find out what works and why (not). The main function here is *learning*. The key question is how policy or management can be improved. Learning requires an open, critical attitude that supports dialogue and sense-making (Moynihan, 2008). The use of performance information is future-oriented. The question is how to do things differently.

Secondly, the *steering and control* function of performance information is about monitoring goal-attainment on a day-to-day basis and taking corrective actions if needed. Typical applications are management scorecards and dashboards that monitor the performance of the organization or programme. Steering and control is occupied with the present rather than future or past performance.

The third purpose is *to give an account*. The key question here is how to explain performance levels to external account holders (Willems & Van Dooren, 2012). The NPM agenda has transformed accountability mechanisms from a focus on legality (spend resources lawfully) to a focus on results (demonstrate what is achieved). The purpose of accountability for results was to put external pressure on public organizations. The orientation is not so much change or control, but survival. Performance management is mainly about explaining past performance.

Target setting is of key importance in an accountability relationship. Targets are a specific value of a performance indicator to be reached by a specific date. While targets have the advantage of providing more clarity to front-line staff and middle managers, they can generate gaming, which can not only waste resources but also render the whole information system unreliable (Bevan & Hood, 2007). One way to prevent this is to apply a 'comply or explain' policy, as in the Netherlands (Bouckaert & Halligan, 2008: 283).

Performance reporting

Performance reporting is multifaceted. There is no one way of representing performance. Several authors have sought to propose models for performance in a comprehensive way. One of the best-known models is the balanced scorecard, reporting on financial performance, customer performance, internal processes, and innovation/growth/learning. The balanced scorecard calls for so-called strategy maps of the cause-and-effect relationships (Kaplan & Norton, 2004; Bovaird, 2012). Since the perception of 'good performance' tends to differ substantially between different stakeholders (see Chapter 5), the balanced scorecard can represent the perspectives of a variety of key stakeholders. The balanced scorecard was initially developed for the private sector, but consultancies made efforts to spread this model in the public sector. In addition, other private sector indicator models have been transferred, sometimes transformed, to the public sector. Examples are the models of the International Standards Organisation (ISO) and the European Foundation for Quality Management (EFQM).

Some specific public sector models have been created such as the Canadian Management Accountability Framework (MAF) which was developed by the Treasury Board Secretariat. The most successful European public sector model has been the Common Assessment Framework (CAF), launched in 2000 by the European Public Administration Network, the meeting of top civil servants of the member states of the European Union. The CAF was designed as the first European quality management instrument specifically tailored for and developed by the public sector itself. CAF is a general model for public sector organization. It is based on the EFQM model and follows the input-output-impact logic of performance (CAF Resource Centre, 2019) – see Figure 12.2. It proposes to collect indicators on five organizational dimensions that enable results: leadership, human resources, strategy and planning practices, and partnerships. The results dimensions reflect the development of the staff of the organization, the satisfaction of citizens, social and environmental responsibility, and key performance results. The model proposes a feedback loop where reflection on results fosters innovation and learning.

The shift of performance management to performance governance, mentioned earlier, has also an impact on the reporting frameworks. Performance indicators increasingly relate to frameworks that reflect collaborative challenges of society. A notable example is the Sustainable Development Goals (SDG) of the United Nations (Bouckaert et al., 2016). The SDG framework includes goals on amongst others climate action, poverty, and clean water. Performance governance to address these goals requires measurement efforts far beyond a single organization or public programme (United Nations, 2021).

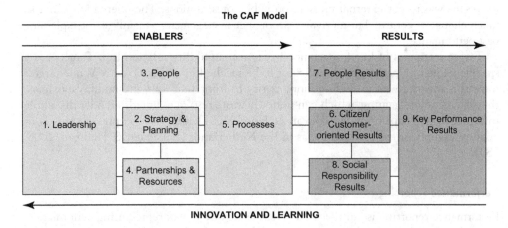

Figure 12.2 The CAF model.

Source: CAF Resource Centre (2019).

Some traps and lessons in performance management

Performance measurement provides interesting possibilities for enhancing public sector management and policymaking. However, there are also several traps (Van Dooren et al., 2015).

Lack of interest from politicians and/or citizens. The ownership of performance management initiatives usually lies within the administration. Politicians and the public often appear uninterested in the routine performance information that is provided – at least, until things go wrong. One response to this frustrating situation is to tailor performance measurement to the demand, implying that citizens and politicians should become involved in defining performance indicators that interest them. There is an increasing need to develop demand-driven performance information and indicators, in a dynamic context of constructing information to support reforms (Moynihan, 2008). We should also pay attention to non-routine feedback from performance measurement systems in our assessment of the value of performance management (Kroll, 2013).

Vagueness and ambiguity of goals. Ambiguity is often inherent in politics, and indeed may well be politically rational. Ambiguity allows for political cooperation (Stone, 1997). Making objectives and indicators clearer and more concrete might lead to political conflict when different stakeholders have different values and expectations. Reducing homelessness is such an ambiguous goal. When it is measured by the number of people living in the street, we miss out on people in temporary accommodation or young people involuntarily living in their parents' home. By making goals concrete, such value trade-offs become apparent and, depending on the context, politically sensitive.

Administrative overload. Performance measurement requires considerable data collection efforts. These efforts are typically made by the frontline workers, while the benefits of better oversight accrue at the top of the organization. To limit the burden on the frontline, automatic data collection and 'big data' strategies should be pursued. In addition, frontline workers can be involved in defining and interpreting performance measures.

Use and non-use. Measuring is not sufficient to guarantee the use of performance information. There are many reasons for non-use such as the bad quality of data, psychological, cultural, and institutional barriers, or a lack of incorporation in policy, financial, and contract cycles (Van Dooren et al., 2015).

Attention to heuristics. In recent years, the behavioural sciences have occupied a central place in the social sciences (James et al., 2020). Insights from cognitive and social psychology have come to show how cognitive heuristics shape human decision-making. The decision-making of citizens and public officials based on performance measurement is no exception. The academic literature has shown how heuristics are influencing performance management (see Box 12.2).

Box 12.2 Behavioural public performance: Some examples

Olsen (2015) presented the same hospital data in terms of patient dissatisfaction rather than patient satisfaction. A 90 percent satisfaction rate produced more positive perceptions of the performance of the hospital than when framed as a 10 percent dissatisfaction rate. Equivalent results are seen differently due to the positive or negative frame (*equivalence framing*).

Hong (2019) examined performance improvement efforts among public agencies and found that comparisons between organizations matter more for agencies which perform below average because they want to avoid being viewed negatively. For suc-cessful agencies, historical comparisons are more important because they want to maintain their own standards (*comparison effects, negativity bias*).

Baekgaard and Serritzlew (2016) studied the impact of prior preferences in relation to public or private ownership on the interpretation of hospital performance reports. The treatment and control group received the same performance reports, but the treatment group were given information on whether a hospital was public or private. The results offer strong support for the role of governance preferences in shaping the use of performance information (*motivated reasoning*).

Window dressing and gaming. Organizations have an interest in portraying a reputable image of themselves (Boon et al., 2021). This is particularly the case when performance informa-tion is used for accountability purposes. Consequently, when missing performance targets entails sanctions, organizations will be tempted to cheat in their performance reporting (Bevan & Hood, 2007).

The risk of data corruption is higher when organizations see performance measurement as imposed externally. Local government, for example, tends to see, and resist, central govern-ment attempts at control through performance measurement and reporting. Schools con-fronted with league tables may 'teach for the test' rather than to impart knowledge. Reported crime detection rates may be increased by spending more time getting convicted criminals to confess to their past crimes rather than trying to solve current crimes. The performance figures of a drug offenders' rehabilitation agency may be raised by directing activity towards the easy cases and refusing to accept the more difficult cases. All these abuses can be partly tackled by effective data auditing, a common approach to safeguard the accuracy, reliability, and comparability of performance information. However, when incentives are high, abuse will become more ingenious to escape detection. The way forward then is to de-incentivize performance management systems and evolve from accountability-based to learning-based performance management (Van Dooren & Hoffmann, 2018).

Summary

Performance management has value, but is not without its problems. Performance measure-ment and management in the public sector have evolved over time, with many ups and downs – they now attempt to cover a much wider range of concepts than 40 years ago, from inputs through outputs to outcomes and trust, and addressing issues of economy, efficiency, cost-effectiveness, and quality. The uses range from learning, to steering and control, and accountability. There remain significant difficulties but important lessons have been learnt.

Performance measurement is only useful if it is perceived as having improved policy or management. Clearly, performance data must be reliable and should cover the dimensions of performance that really matter. Performance management has often been about the 'hard' data, whereas quality management is often considered as a 'soft' management issue (see Chapter 13). Yet a narrow focus on costs and efficiency at the expense of service quality and outcomes can be dangerous. There is now an understanding in many other OECD countries that performance management also includes quality management, outcomes, and increasing the levels of trust.

Finally, performance governance is probably especially necessary in turbulent and crisis-ridden environments where user and community co-production will be indispensable to deliver services. Performance measurement can support management and policymaking in governing across the boundaries of organizations and policy fields.

Questions for review and discussion

1   What are the main types of performance that need to be measured and reported in the public sector? Who cares about these performance measures – and why do they care?
2   How can an organization decide whether its performance management system produces benefits at least as great as the costs it imposes?

Reader exercises

1   Take an annual report from a public agency with which you are familiar. Identify the performance indicators reported in it. Classify them according to the categories in Figure 12.1. Do you think that the balance between these types of performance indicator is appropriate for this agency?
2   Take one of the performance indicators identified in the previous reader exercise.
Consider how an individual, a unit, or a whole organization might find ways of influencing the reported level of that indicator in order to make their work look more successful. For each of these possible abuses, suggest ways in which that kind of behaviour could be made less easy or less likely to succeed.

Class exercises

1   Identify a case currently in the media where a public agency appears to have been changing its practices or its reporting approach in order to improve its 'league table' position, without necessarily improving its actual level of performance. Discuss how the performance measurement and reporting system might be changed in order to make such behaviour less likely in the future, while still producing useful information for the stakeholders who wish to hold this agency to account.
2   Discuss how your class, your tutor, and your college assess performance – of students, of staff, and of the organization as a whole. What are the major limitations in this performance assessment? How could they be tackled?

Further reading

Bouckaert, G., & Halligan, J. (2008). *Managing Performance, International Comparisons*. Routledge.
Van Dooren, W., Geert, B., & John, H. (2015). *Performance Management in the Public Sector* (2nd edition). Routledge.
James, O., Olsen, A. L., Moynihan, D. P., & Ryzin, G. G. V. (2020). *Behavioral Public Performance: How People Make Sense of Government Metrics*. Cambridge University Press.

References

Baekgaard, M., & Serritzlew, S. (2016). Interpreting Performance Information: Motivated Reasoning or Unbiased Comprehension. *Public Administration Review*, 76(1), 73–82. https://doi.org/10.1111/puar.12406.
Behn, R. D. (2013). *The PerformanceStat Potential: A Leadership Strategy for Producing Results*. Brookings Institution Press.

Bevan, Gwyn and Christopher Hood (2007), "What's Measured is What Matters: Targets and Gaming in Healthcare in England, *Public Administration* 84(3): 517–538.

Boon, J., Salomonsen, H. H., & Verhoest, K. (2021). A Reputation for What, to Whom, and in Which Task Environment: A Commentary. *Regulation and Governance*, 15(2), 428–441. https://doi.org/10.1111/rego.12290.

Bouckaert, G. (1990). 'Public Productivity as a Classical Movement', 'The History of the Productivity Movement'. *Public Productivity and Management Review*, XIV(1 Fall), 33–34, 53–89.

Bouckaert, G., & Halligan, J. (2008). *Managing Performance: International Comparisons*. Routledge.

Bouckaert, G., Loretan, R., & Troupin, S. (2016). Public Administration and the Sustainable Development Goals. *Session of the United Nations Committee of Experts on Public Administration*.

Bovaird, T. (2012), "Attributing outcomes to social policy interventions – 'gold standard' or 'fool's gold' in public policy and management?" *Social Policy and Administration*, 48(1): 1–23.

CAF Resource Centre. (2019). *Common Assessment Framework. The European Model for Improving Public Organisations through Self-Assessment.* European Instiute for Public Administration.

Christensen, T., & Lægreid, P. (2016). *The Ashgate Research Companion to New Public Management.* Routledge.

de Jong, M. (2019). Budget Reform Dynamics and Conceptualization of Reform Space. In A. T. Ho, M. de Jong, & Z. Zhao (Eds.), *Performance Budgeting Reform: Theories and International Practices* (pp. 28–49). Routledge.

Harvard University. (2004). *Award: CitiStat*. Innovations in American Government Awards. https://ash.harvard.edu/news/citistat.

Hatry, H. P. (1999). *Performance Measurement: Getting Results*. Urban Institute Press.

Ho, A. T.-K., De Jong, M., & Zhao, Z. (2019). *Performance Budgeting Reform: Theories and International Practices*. Routledge. https://www.routledge.com/Performance-Budgeting-Reform-Theories-and-International-Practices/Ho-Jong-Zhao/p/book/9781138483293.

Hong, S. (2019). A Behavioral Model of Public Organizations: Bounded Rationality, Performance Feedback, and Negativity Bias. *Journal of Public Administration Research and Theory*, 29(1), 1 17. https://doi.org/10.1093/jopart/muy048.

James, O., Olsen, A. L., Moynihan, D. P., & Ryzin, G. G. V. (2020). *Behavioral Public Performance: How People Make Sense of Government Metrics*. Cambridge University Press. https://www.cambridge.org/core/elements/behavioral-public-performance/88B464A24F25362F03D1DD1FBA9090F8.

Kaplan, R. S., and Norton, D. P. (2004), *Strategy Maps: Converting Intangible Assets into Tangible Outcomes*. Boston: Harvard Business School Press.

Kroll, A. (2013). The Other Type of Performance Information: Nonroutine Feedback, Its Relevance and Use. *Public Administration Review*, 73(2), 265–276. https://doi.org/10.1111/j.1540-6210.2012.02648.x.

Moynihan, D. P. (2008). *The Dynamics of Performance Management: Constructing Information and Reform*. Georgetown University Press.

OECD. (1997). *In search of results: Performance management practices*. Paris: Organisation for Economic Co-operation and Development.

Olsen, A. L. (2015). Citizen (Dis)Satisfaction: An Experimental Equivalence Framing Study. *Public Administration Review*, 75(3), 469–478. https://doi.org/10.1111/puar.12337.

Pollitt, C., & Bouckaert, G. (2017). *Public Management Reform: A Comparative Analysis - Into the Age of Austerity* (4th edition). Oxford University Press.

Stone, D. (1997). *Policy Paradox: The Art of Political Decisionmaking*. W.W. Norton and Company.

United Nations. (2021, August). *National Institutional Arrangements for Implementation of the Sustainable Development Goals: A Five-Year Stocktaking, World Public Sector Report 2021*. Division for Public Institutions and Digital Government, Department of Economic and Social Affairs.

Van Dooren, W., Bouckaert, G., & Halligan, J. (2015). *Performance Management in the Public Sector*. Routledge. http://anet.ua.ac.be/record/opacirua/c:irua:123038/N.

Van Dooren, W., & Hoffmann, C. (2018). Performance Management in Europe: An Idea Whose Time Has Come and Gone? In E. Ongaro & S. Van Thiel (Eds.), *The Palgrave Handbook of Public Administration and Management in Europe* (pp. 207–225). Palgrave Macmillan UK. https://doi.org/10.1057/978-1-137-55269-3_10.

Van Dooren, W., & Van de Walle, S. (2008). *Performance Information in the Public Sector: How It Is Used*. Palgrave Macmillan.

Wildavsky, A. (1969). Rescuing Policy Analysis from PPBS. *Public Administration Review, 29*(2), 189–202.

Willems, T., & Van Dooren, W. (2012). Coming to Terms with Accountability: Combining Multiple Forums and Functions. *Public Management Review, 14*(7), 1011–1036.

Williams, D. W. (2003). Measuring Government in the Early Twentieth Century. *Public Administration Review, 63*(6), 643–659.

Wogan, J. (2017, March 22). How Stat Got Stuck—In the Place That Made It Famous. *Governing*. https://www.governing.com/archive/gov-baltimore-citistat-statestat-maryland.html.

13 Process and quality management in public service organisations

Kuno Schedler and Utz Helmuth

Introduction

Business process thinking and quality management found their way into public services, with a focus on customers, efficiency and performance improvement, from the 1980s onwards. In this chapter, we will show that both process and quality management offer many advantages, particularly in eliminating wasteful activities in public service organisations, helping to redesign processes so that they are more directly oriented to adding value to the organisation's external customers, and improving the performance and impact of public administration.

Learning objectives

This chapter will help you:

- To understand the origin, nature and effectiveness of process management
- To learn how processes are measured and optimised
- To become aware of different perspectives on processes and quality management
- To understand what 'customer centricity' entails

Process-oriented organisations

More and more public (and private) sector organisations stress the importance of outcomes and the 'production process' to achieve them, instead of the pure hierarchical alignment of functions. This perspective has considerable organisational consequences. In a so-called 90°-rotation, the vertical view of the organisation (top-down line management) has changed into a horizontal view (input-output relationships) (see Figure 13.1). This organisational form is called a *process-oriented organisation*.

Following the establishment of process thinking in many companies in the 1980s, a second wave in the 1990s, particularly identified with Hammer und Champy (1993), promoted the idea of a re-engineering of processes to make them more customer-oriented ('business process re-engineering'). In the following, we will use the simplified term 'process management'.

This private sector discourse must be adapted appropriately when transferred to a public service context, as public agencies are subject to quite different requirements and regulations. However, all organisations face increasing expectations on their efficiency, customer orientation and service quality.

DOI: 10.4324/9781003282839-15

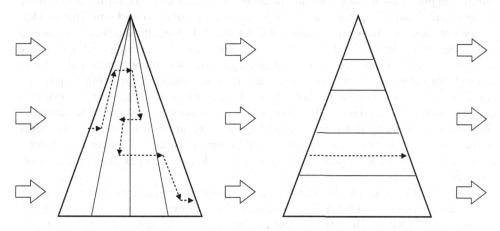

Figure 13.1 90° rotation from hierarchical to process-oriented organisation.

Through the development of uniform communication protocols, data and database standards, the triumphal march of IT is smoothing the way for business process orientation in public agencies (see also Chapters 11 and 20). Firstly, different departments in different locations can now access the same data simultaneously. Secondly, electronic data management considerably reduces times for decision-making and process throughput. Furthermore, through the internet, customers can link up to processes within public agencies and receive services directly, without having to go through intermediaries or other interfaces, which can greatly speed up and streamline the public service being offered to customers.

The nature of a process

> **What is a business process?**
>
> The logical organization of people, materials, energy, equipment, and procedures into work activities designed to produce a specified end result.
>
> (Gabriel A. Pall, 1987)

What exactly is a process? In terms of the 'process-oriented organisation' outlined earlier, one should imagine a business process as a recipe for achieving results in organisations. As in a cookbook, it documents in a step-by-step fashion who has to undertake which activities in order to achieve a particular goal, i.e. to create value. A business process proceeds chronologically from input to output, i.e. from the supply of resources to the delivery of the service. The fundamental components are 'events as triggers' and the activities that follow them. These activities are often assigned to organisational functions (also called organisational 'roles').

For public sector organisations the shape of processes is often pre-defined by legal norms. These are there to guarantee legal rights and protect the individual liberty of citizens in their contact with the government (Egli, 2022). For example, most processes executing building applications include time limits for possible legal objections. Shortening these 'waiting times' may be a process improvement from the point of view of some stakeholders but may impact negatively on the rights of those affected. A significant share of perceived citizen benefit lies in this legal binding of government action to existing rules and norms. In many cases, this means that certain government processes cannot be privatised or outsourced. For example, in most European countries it is considered impossible to privatise the imprisonment of criminals, as only the public sector is seen as legitimate for this process. However, this has the corollary that, where outsourcing is explored, it is sometimes considered an advantage that private or third sector organisations may have more flexibility in the processes which they use to provide a public service. However, if these different processes might possibly breach public governance principles, affected stakeholders may object strongly.

Lenk (2012) suggests a further distinction between well-structured production processes (e.g. dealing with a tax return) and open-ended decision-making processes (e.g. dealing with a building application). The latter processes grant considerable *degrees of freedom to administrative officers*. Both types of process occur in public agencies but only the former is suitable for full process mapping and standardisation. Moreover, in the case of decision-making processes, team-based work styles may be preferable to sequential process cycles, e.g. the setting up of a virtual roundtable or discussion forum controlled by architects for processing a building application.

The process chain considers the interaction between involved parties, e.g. different professional groups, managers and citizens. In public services, it is rarely appropriate to model the supply chain management as simply a vertical, continuous sequence of activities linking suppliers to their customers. Often service users and other citizens are involved in several stages of the 'supply chain', e.g. in co-designing or co-managing or co-delivering certain activities (see Chapter 23). Consequently, customers and other stakeholders of public agencies need to be modelled in separate strands (or 'swim lanes', as we shall call them later).

Analysing and optimising a business process

The *first stage* in process analysis is the mapping of processes. This helps not only to identify weaknesses in processes, and the potential for optimising them, but to document them for quality assurance or for replicating them elsewhere.

The *second stage* is to consider alternative process chains for achieving the same or greater customer benefits. This can be done by reconfiguring existing processes or by 'de novo analysis' (e.g. in business process re-engineering). A key element of service redesign is to determine the information required. In the cookbook metaphor, different dishes and preparation methods have to be chosen, depending on whether a dish is intended for a vegetarian, child or sick person. Table 13.1 provides an overview of possible information to be considered in process mapping and analysis. Determining the relevant information, including the intended objectives and target groups of the process, is key. However, a manager who wants a brief overview of which organisation units are involved in a process will require different information to a leader responsible for administrative reforms. As most processes in public administration involve several organisational units, comprehensive information is usually not at hand and has to be collected in advance or in a special workshop.

For the recording of information, a combination of written survey and interviews has proved to be of value. Questionnaires help to establish in a structured manner the basic features of a process, such as the people involved, activity sequences and information flows.

Table 13.1 Information dimensions for the structured recording of processes

Feature of the process	Information likely to be required
Stakeholders involved in process	Internal organisation units, customers, other external parties
Resources and events used in the process	Input, output, activities, media, data, IT, environmental conditions in which the process is carried out
Sequential aspects	Sequence of activities, frequencies of different activities, throughput times for different activities
Quality of the process	Importance of the process for the value-added to the customer, frequency of service failures or customer complaints or need for customer revisits/retreatment

Subsequently, the person doing the recording should have the opportunity to clarify potential ambiguities with the staff concerned.

A multiplicity of recorded information inevitably leads to the question of how this information can be meaningfully reproduced. A simple description in text form, as in a cooking recipe, quickly meets with limitations. An alternative is the graphical depiction of business processes, as introduced originally by Fritz Nordsieck (1932), which makes apparent at first glance the process sequence and the parties involved. Through formal symbols, rules and abstractions, further information can be depicted in such business process diagrams. Moreover, diagrams expedite comparisons between business processes. Different audiences are likely to need different kinds of diagram. Highly formalised business process diagrams designed to help the software programmer will probably not be understood by top managers. Subsets can help here, showing different levels of detail to different stakeholders, which represent different windows into the underlying process using a selection of the information available.

Figure 13.2 illustrates a subset for the process of an ID application in a Swiss city, using the internationally common and non-proprietary standard methodology of *Business Process Modelling Notation (BPMN)*. For purposes of modelling, BPMN uses flow objects, connecting objects and artifacts. *Flow objects* describe *what* is happening: In the form of circular *events*, they describe the start, interruption and end of a process. Rectangular *activities* stand for the tasks in a process ('open letter') and show sub-processes (marked by '+'). Diamond-shaped *gateways* mark the diverging and converging of processes. *Connecting objects* join flow objects through arrows. Unbroken arrows indicate the process flow, broken arrows information flows between different organisations, and broken lines represent associations. Finally, the example also shows *artifacts* in the form of *data objects*, which are used to describe more closely data used by activities. These are symbolised by a sheet of paper with the upper right-hand corner folded over. The various parties involved are separated from one another by swim lanes (within an organisation) or pools for different organisations.

The *third stage* in process analysis is process optimisation – choosing the right option for process improvement. Every optimisation is inevitably a normative action and is directed towards a chosen goal. Such goals can take very different shapes according to the stakeholder concerned. While politics normally insist on its primacy ('the political administration should push through its policies'), the general legal framework demands that decisions of the administration should above all be correct in terms of the law, which should be the same for all. Customers, too, push for their own needs ('decisions should be made quickly and take into account our special circumstances'). The definition of the goal of process optimisation is

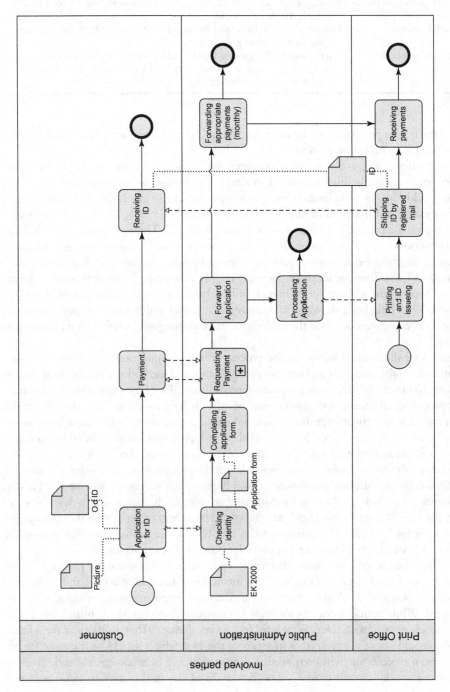

Figure 13.2 Process map for the application for a Swiss ID (simplified illustration).

therefore often a contentious decision, in which contending interests have to be weighed up against each other.

In the following, we will focus on (i) effectiveness as the degree to which a goal is achieved and (ii) efficiency as an input/output ratio.

Box 13.1 Examples of ineffective and inefficient public processes

Ineffective processes:

- High variation in service quality
- Unusually high death rate (health care)
- High crime rate (security institutions)
- Poor results in the OECD *Pisa* study (school system)
- Low research ranking of a university (higher education system)
- High number of successful appeals or complaints against administrative decisions (e.g. for building permits)

Inefficient processes:

- High number of activities which have to be redone
- Arbitrary process flow due to unclear responsibilities
- Many signatures needed for each draft (responsibilities too spread out)
- Work that is not value-adding (duplicated examinations in health care)
- Outmoded teaching methods (getting all students to write out standard notes)
- Delays in treating high priority cases (no triage system when customers register)
- Unnecessarily expensive purchasing (corrupt preference for 'cronies')

An indicator that reflects both the effectiveness and the efficiency of a process is the *total throughput time*. This incorporates not only the actual processing, but also post-processing times that are caused by quality failure, appeals, etc. If a file remains untouched for too long, then additional clarifications have to be made, or if a decision is contested due to flaws in the process, then this lengthens the total throughput time.

Digitisation and automation are powerful drivers for significant reductions of throughput times. The Consular of Passport and Visa (CPV) Division of the Ministry of External Affairs of India was able to reduce the average time of 45 days for passport issuance to 5 days by implementing a new IT system and service setup, while the number of passports issued annually tripled (PwC, 2014).

Table 13.2 cites several process-oriented process optimisation initiatives that are well suited to the public sector.

How to achieve impactful change

The search for efficiency needs itself to be efficient: Re-organising processes is costly and should be subject to efficiency considerations, too. In practice, process improvements programmes surprisingly often lose track and impact, generating countless process documentations that are rarely touched again.

Table 13.2 Overview on process optimisation approaches

Initiatives	Implementation
Omit	Seek and cancel unnecessary work steps
Standardise	Standardise work steps with comparable content, thus making them transferable
Improve use of resources	Are all resources used in such a way that the total throughput time is reduced? Are any areas under-capitalised, thus causing generally higher costs through uneconomical maintenance measures (e.g. highly outdated ICT equipment or transport fleet)?
Replace with other processes	Does it make sense to replace a process with another, thus avoiding duplicate work?
Do activities in parallel	Reduce the process duration for the customer through the simultaneous processing of several sub-processes
Outsource	Transfer processes that are uneconomical and/or do not reach a critical number of cases to other administrative units or external service providers
Avoid doubling back	Implement quality measures so that post-processing becomes superfluous
Collaboration	For complex, non-sequential decision-making processes, design collaboration such that relevant stakeholders are integrated from the outset

If processes in organisations are changed, managers are faced with a great challenge. Each existing system defines routines, power and responsibilities to which employees have become accustomed. Change triggers uncertainty, as both managers and employees cannot completely foresee what the future system will bring for them. So how can social processes that are triggered by process optimisation be managed?

Empirical investigations into the management of change processes do not provide a consistent picture, although it appears that participatory management tends to have positive effects on performance and job satisfaction – albeit to a more limited extent than commonly assumed (Wagner, 1994). In a qualitative study in the British public service, Thomas and Davies (2005) showed that employees boycott changes in their work organisation resulting from the introduction of New Public Management if they do not understand their background. The authors conclude that resistance of employees derives not only from changes seen as unfounded and pushed through by repressive management but above all from changes which call into question the identity of those affected. Conversely, in an investigation into the introduction of a new computer system, Symon (2005) points out that resistance, although damaging for the employer, can in itself create a sense of identity again for those affected.

In practice, *four simple recommendations* are likely to generate better results:

1 **Prioritise:** Start first with high frequency, repetitive processes, like tax or drivers' licence applications. Devoting significant resources to optimising a very rare process is likely to be less efficient than optimising one with many cases, especially if those cases relate to high priority groups.
2 **Focus on impact:** Focus on the desired end-state, concentrating on improvements that generate impact, not academic documentation of existing processes. Consider using customer journey mapping (see below).
3 **Cross the bridge step by step:** Organise optimisations in meaningful waves. As re-engineering is itself a time- and resource-consuming process, organise it sequentially, manage resources carefully and build further waves on top of the motivating effects of previous successes.

4 **Align expectations** between leaders and key stakeholders: To cope with resistance, agree with leaders upfront which 'level of noise' is acceptable and what support you can expect. Identify and involve allied staff members – 'the critical few' – e.g. from successful first optimisations that can help you to promote the exercise.

Customer focus in process management

Customer orientation and customer satisfaction have been important pillars of the New Public Management since the 1990s. However, the original concept of 'passive customers' changed over time, particularly under the influence of the New Public Governance paradigm. It became clear that many public services can only achieve public value if citizens are enabled to actively participate in the process. Arnberg (1996) speaks of 'pro-sumers' who simultaneously co-produce the public value of the services they consume (see Chapter 23). Road safety is produced by drivers and pedestrians, not by the police. Rehabilitation after an accident has to be implemented by the patient, albeit under guidance of medical staff. Students develop their knowledge themselves (the professor cannot learn for them but provides them with sources of knowledge). Citizens should participate in the shaping of their city and in political decisions on their environment – up to and including participatory budgeting (Ewens and van der Voet, 2019). In this context, public services now actively record the needs of their customers, e.g. through citizen surveys and customer feedback systems. At the same time, new administrative processes are being designed to provide more benefits for citizens. The impact on society, specifically on citizens, is thus the starting point for many process optimisations, with the new process being designed 'backwards' from the desired result, with a view to maximising service quality for the citizen.

A central element of the customer-oriented organisation is co-ordination between public agencies (Schedler and Proeller, 2010). While traditional bureaucracies primarily focus on optimising their internal (legal) processes, a customer-oriented administration is expected to organise contact experiences that allow citizens to access services as easily as possible, e.g. observing the 'once-only' principle, whereby citizens only have to give required information to one organisation involved in a service. This is especially important where citizens or businesses confront complicated administrative processes. In various countries, so-called 'one-stop shops' have been created, partly to help all citizens get better quality service and partly to guide socially weaker and less educated citizens more clearly to the support services to which they are entitled. Moreover, such one-stop shops are also a tried and tested means to attract potential investors to a location, as in Box 13.2.

Box 13.2 Invest South Africa One-Stop Shop

The InvestSA One-Stop Shop initiative is geared towards providing investors with services to fast-track projects and reduce government red tape when establishing a business. It is part of the government's drive to become investor friendly, improving the business environment by lowering the cost of doing business and making the process easier. One-Stop Shops house government entities such as the South African Revenue Services (to help with customs and tax), Home Affairs, Environmental Affairs, Eskom and the Companies and Intellectual Properties Commission under one roof.

URL: http://www.investsa.gov.za/one-stop-shop/ (online 18 December 2021).

In more recent times, public services have moved towards putting the customer perspective in the foreground, using the term 'customer centricity' in analogy to the private sector. 'Customer journey mapping', originally propagated by consultancies to the public sector, is now increasingly used in practice to help public agencies understand how their customers interact with public services (Buijs, Bergmans, and El Hasnaoui, 2021) – see Box 13.3. In this way, a longstanding concern is approached through new design thinking methods, although it is basically still process optimisation for improving the quality of public services experienced by citizens.

Box 13.3 How does customer journey mapping work?

Step 1: Define what effect an administrative contact should have for the citizen and the state. What is the purpose of the contact?

Step 2: Note all moments when the citizen is in contact with your administration during a service process. How does the citizen experience your organisation?

Step 3: Identify 'pain points' and 'moments of delight' from the citizen's perspective. At which points does the process simply not work for the citizen? When does the citizen get annoyed? When does it run like clockwork?

Step 4: Go through the customer journey yourself! Take the role of the citizen and contact your own administrative office. How do you experience your own organisation?

Step 5: Visualise the customer journey in a graphic and use it to show where the journey needs to be improved.

From process to quality management

The concept of quality is an ambivalent one in both private and public sectors. It has evolved over time, starting from an industrial notion of technical goodness to an increasingly human approach of creating benefits for the recipients of a service. Bovaird and Loeffler (2015, 163) summarise five different perspectives on quality, each of which will require a different approach to measuring the quality achieved:

- Quality as 'conformance to specification' (a meaning deriving from an engineering perspective and from the 'contract culture')
- Quality as 'fitness for purpose' (or 'meeting organisational objectives', essentially deriving from a systems perspective)
- Quality as 'aligning inputs, processes, outputs and outcomes' (deriving from the strategic management perspective)
- Quality as 'meeting customer expectations' (or 'exceeding customer expectations', deriving from consumer psychology)
- Quality as 'passionate emotional involvement' – quality as that 'which lies beyond language and number' (the social psychology approach)

Quality therefore is a multidimensional concept, especially in public services. In contrast to products, not only is the quality of the end product important but also the quality of the process. For example, patients in a hospital wish not only to get well as soon as possible but also to be treated with respect and empathy while in hospital.

Many associate the concept of quality with the achievement of public governance principles – the fundamental requirements of a well-functioning state: e.g. equality, rule of law, integration, peace, freedom (see Chapter 15). In public management, however, the focus is more on operational aspects of quality, in full awareness of the fact that, in the political environment of the state, achievement of an acceptable quality of public governance is a basic need that must be satisfied first. Customer needs are at the centre of this operational concept of quality, which therefore organically builds on process management. The primary goal of quality management in the private sector is customer satisfaction ('fulfilment of customer requirements'). This can also be transferred to public administration: According to the model of the three-stage legitimisation of administrative action (Schedler and Felix, 2000), the administration creates its legitimacy at the individual level through high performance quality, which ultimately leads to citizen acceptance of administrative decisions and finally to the active participation of the citizens. Customer satisfaction in the public domain may, however, have complicated effects – dissatisfied citizens may also be stimulated to become actively engaged.

The quality promise: Citizen and service charters

In the 1990s, the UK government realised that people were becoming convinced that performance indicators from the NPM approach were not sufficient to judge government activities. Rather, the administration must make a quality promise for every service, which can be monitored by the individual citizen. This should create pressure on the providers of public services to actually deliver the promised quality. These 'citizen's charters' focused on the fundamental principles (Bovaird & Loeffler, 2015) of:

- Information and openness
- Choice
- Courtesy and helpfulness
- Well-publicised complaints procedures
- Value for money

The idea of such charters gained international attention over time (see Case Example 13.1), in some places becoming a fashionable political priority. The basic idea that the quality of public services should also be communicated as a promise to the citizens has survived in various places, especially in easily measurable service areas such as public transport.

Case Example 13.1 The service charter of the Kenya National Library Service

Kenya National Library Service (KNLS) Board is a corporate body of the Kenya government that was established by an Act of Parliament (1965) to provide library and information services to the Kenyan public. The service charter sets down what KNLS is and what it does, and its commitment to provide Kenyan communities with the highest quality and accessible services that available resources will allow.

On the KNLS website, citizens can transparently view and download the service charter. The website also offers 'customer complaints resolution', which shows how complaints can be submitted and how the KNLS deals with these complaints.

Source: https://knls.ac.ke/service-charter/ (3 January 2022).

With the increasing importance of digital services, governments have also defined service standards to ensure consistent experiences when using public services online. For example, the UK Government Digital Service (2019 – https://www.gov.uk/service-manual/service-standard) has a mandatory 14-point Service Standard to ensure a co-ordinated approach to service design and delivery, including principles and approaches around understanding user needs, problem-solving, omni-channel, simplicity, inclusiveness, agility, openness and reliability.

Quality assurance: The main concepts in quality management

In addition to the measurement of service quality, the question of how quality can be produced or assured is central to public management. Here, too, public administration draws on the private sector when the most common approaches there are transferred to the public sector. Starting from a very generalist approach to total quality management (Cohen and Brand, 1993) two approaches in particular have become prominent in the public sector: Quality improvement based on quality excellence models (EFQM and CAF) and quality assurance based on the standard of the DIN EN ISO 9000 series of quality standards.

The European Foundation for Quality Management (EFQM) introduced a framework for assessing applications for the European Quality Award (today: EFQM Excellence Award) in 1992, which has since gained a high level of recognition in both the private and public sectors. The EFQM is financed through membership fees, training, publications and fees for external assessments.

In order to make the model even more usable for the public sector, a high-level working group of public officials developed the so-called Common Assessment Framework (EIPA, 2022) which was introduced in EU member states in 2000 and revised several times since then – see Figure 13.3. The framework is based on the EFQM model with its nine elements, but also incorporates experiences from a German quality award for public agencies. The 9 criteria are subdivided into 28 sub-criteria, which provide the framework for self-assessment.

It is noticeable in both EFQM and CAF that quality is understood in a very comprehensive sense. Basically, all central aspects of management in public organisations are found in some form, which is consistent with the idea of total quality management. While both the EFQM and CAF model provide a systematic framework for quality improvement in organisations they do not define specific standards which need to be met.

In contrast, the documents in the DIN EN ISO 9000 series (https://www.iso.org/iso-9001-quality-management.html) of the International Standard Setting Organization (ISO) provide a tool for quality assurance. The norm DIN EN ISO 9001:2015 stipulates the minimum standards for quality systems which conform with the overall DIN EN ISO 9001:2015

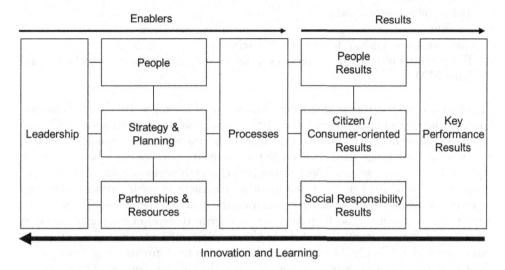

Figure 13.3 The Common Assessment Framework.

norms. This is the basis for external certification. In the private sector, according to the ISO website, more than 1 million companies in over 170 countries are certified with ISO 9001. Many public agencies have also been certified with ISO 9001C (Brito, Pais, dos Santos and Figueiredo, 2020; Lopez-Lemus, 2021).

DIN EN ISO 9000 provides seven principles for developing and implementing a quality system (ISO, 2015):

QMP1 – customer focus
QMP2 – leadership
QMP3 – engagement of people
QMP4 – process approach
QMP5 – improvement
QMP6 – evidence-based decision-making
QMP7 – relationship management

Apart from the DIN ISO 9001:2015 certification, there is now a plethora of sector-specific accreditation programmes, in particular for the education, social and health sectors. These include assessments by accreditation agencies to assess conformance with specific standards.

The value of quality management in public management

Quality management implicitly or explicitly plays a major role in modern public management. While private sector concepts can serve as a model, they must be adapted to the specific requirements of the public sector, similarly to how the Common Assessment Framework was adapted from the EFQM model. The values that make the public sector valuable to citizens must be at the forefront of quality management systems. Elg et al. (2017) explicitly name four central aspects that must be given special attention for the public sector:

- Rights and access of citizens
- Equality
- Coerciveness as a unique feature of public services
- The potential of high-quality services to improve legitimacy (see also Schedler and Felix, 2000)

The introduction of quality management systems usually has a positive effect in practice. A recent study from Portugal (Brito et al., 2020) shows that municipalities with ISO 9000 certification perform better in the areas of knowledge management, customer satisfaction and organisational image than non-certified municipalities, indicating a lasting positive impact of quality management. López-Lemus (2021) also shows for Mexico that the application of ISO 9000:2015 standards led to an improvement in public services. However, the extent of the improvement depends largely on the managers themselves: The influence of the public managers on public policy, the experience (tenure) of the public managers and the interest and commitment of the public managers influence the success of quality management. Hchaichi (2021) reports a similar result for the introduction of quality management in Tunisian state-owned enterprises, where the cultural elements of trust, loyalty, communication and social cohesion were identified as the basis for successful implementation. Managers who involved their employees in the TQM process were more successful. A prerequisite, however, is that the concepts and the instruments of quality management must be known by all those involved.

The great benefit of quality management systems is undoubtedly the structured approach to improving the performance of the public service organisation. Quality measurement presupposes that organisations define and explicitly formulate their performance and quality dimensions so that an indicator system can be developed on this basis. Citizen charters make these quality dimensions – the administration's quality promises – transparent to the public and introduce a feedback system that quickly reveals quality deficiencies and, in some cases, sanctions them quasi-automatically (e.g. if citizens receive compensation where standards are not met). Finally, the quality management models (EFQM, CAF, ISO 9001, etc.), define those areas of management that are important for ensuring good operational quality of the administration and that need to be worked on systematically. The widespread use of quality management has led to the development of an international 'quality ecosystem' in which organisations supplying and buying quality management systems, certification bodies and consultancies are integrated. They derive an economic benefit from quality management and therefore actively manage it. The consequent advantages of a functioning quality management system for public agencies and their customers (citizens) seem obvious to us.

Summary

Process and quality management form a pair of concepts that positively influence each other. Process management adds a new perspective to the traditional hierarchical view of public administration. Following the 90°-rotation, administrative action is analysed as steps towards the creation of public value – steps that cross organisational units and hierarchical levels. Optimising processes in public administration leads to better performance and quality. A customer perspective turns technical process optimisation into customer-centric processes, using 'customer journey mapping' as a method. Quality management models and frameworks help public managers to get a holistic view in organising their administration to create the best possible quality for citizens. In contrast to the private sector, the performance and quality of public organisations are assessed not only in operational (economic) terms but also as equality, sustainability, legitimacy and the rule of law.

Questions for review and discussion

1 Distinguish between activities, processes and services. How are they related to customer benefit?
2 Why might democratic and legal requirements limit the possibilities of process optimisation?
3 What are the different characteristics of quality management in the public sector and how are they related to key public sector values?

Reader exercises

1 Think of the last activity which you undertook with a public agency (e.g. making a passport application, applying for a grant or social welfare benefit). Suggest how the process could have been made more efficient and more effective.
2 Why do you think those improvements have not already been introduced?
3 Identify potential benefits and also potential pitfalls of quality excellence frameworks (such as the Common Assessment Framework) for public sector organisations.

Class exercises

1 Divide into groups of four to six. Each group should identify one key process in your university/school that leads to an important end-result and which students must undertake as part of their studies (e.g. passing an exam, submitting high quality assignments, making tutorial presentations). Carry out a process mapping for this process and suggest ways in which the process might be improved to add value to the students and to the administrators of the programme. Then do a customer journey mapping. Each group should present its findings to the other groups.
2 In groups, develop a citizen charter for the public sports facilities of your university or your local community. Compare group suggestions in a plenary session.

Further reading

Champy, J. and Hammer, M. (1993), *Reengineering the corporation*. New York: Harper Business.
Chase, R. B., Jacobs, F. R. and Aquilano, N. J. (2007), *Operations Management for Competitive Advantage*, Ch. 5, 11th International Edition. Boston, MA: McGraw Hill.

References

Arnberg, M. (1996), 'The role of client choice in improving public sector performance'. In OECD (Ed.), *Responsive government: Service quality initiatives* (pp. 245–264). Paris: OECD.
Bovaird, T. and Loeffler, E. (2015), 'Quality management in public sector organizations'. In T. Bovaird and E. Loeffler (Eds.), *Public management and governance*, 3rd edition. London: Routledge, pp. 162–177.

Brito, E., Pais, L., dos Santos, N. R. and Figueiredo, C. (2020), 'Knowledge management, customer satisfaction and organizational image discriminating certified from non-certified (ISO 9001) municipalities'. *International Journal of Quality & Reliability Management*, 37(3): 451–469. doi:10.1108/ijqrm-10-2018-0281.

Buijs, J. C. A. M., Bergmans, R. F. M. and El Hasnaoui, R. (2021), 'Analysis of the customer journey at the pension provider APG using self-service and data hub concepts'. In: J. vom Brocke, J. Mendling and M. Rosemann (Eds.), *Business process management cases vol. 2: Digital transformation - strategy, processes and execution* (pp. 111–124). Berlin, Heidelberg: Springer Berlin Heidelberg.

Cohen, S. and Brand, R. (1993), *Total quality management in government*. San Francisco, CA: Jossey-Bass.

Egli, P. (2022), 'Rechtsstaat and rule of law'. In K. Schedler (Ed.), *Encyclopedia of public management* (forthcoming). Cheltenham: Edward Elgar.

EIPA (2022), *The common assessment framework*. Retrieved from https://www.eipa.eu/caf-resource -centre/.

Elg, M., Wihlborg, E. and Ornerheim, M. (2017), 'Public quality - For whom and how? Integrating public core values with quality management'. *Total Quality Management & Business Excellence*, 28(3–4): 379–389. doi:10.1080/14783363.2015.1087841.

Ewens, H. and van der Voet, J. (2019), 'Organizational complexity and participatory innovation: Participatory budgeting in local government'. *Public Management Review*, 21(12): 1848–1866. doi: 10.1080/14719037.2019.1577908.

Hammer, M. and Champy, J. (1993), *Reengineering the corporation*. New York: Harper Business.

Hchaichi, R. (2021), 'The key success factors of total quality management implementation in state-owned enterprise'. *International Journal of Public Administration* (early access), 12. doi:10.1080/019 00692.2021.1993902.

ISO (2015), *Quality management principles*. Vernier: International Organization for Standardization.

Lenk, K. (2012), 'The nuts and bolts of administrative action in an information age'. In I. Snellen, M. Thaens and W. VanDeDonk (Eds.), *Public administration in the information age: Revisited*. Amsterdam: IOS Press, pp. 221–234.

Lopez-Lemus, J. A. (2021), 'ISO 9001 and the public service: An investigation of the effect of the QMS on the quality of public service organizations'. *International Journal of Organizational Analysis*. doi:10.1108/ijoa-05-2021-2753.

Nordsieck, F. (1932), *Die Schaubildliche Erfassung und Untersuchung der Betriebsorganisation*. Stuttgart: Poeschel.

Pall, G. A. (1987), *Quality process management*. Englewood Cliffs, NJ: Prentice-Hall.

PwC (2014), *Select case studies*. Government and Public Sector Consulting India (available at: https:// www.pwc.in/assets/pdfs/industries/government/select-case-studies-government-and-public-sector -consulting.pdf)

Schedler, K. and Felix, J. (2000), 'Quality in public management: The customer perspective'. *International Public Management Journal*, 3: 125–143.

Schedler, K. and Proeller, I. (2010), *Outcome-oriented public management: A responsibility-based approach to the new public management*. Charlotte, NC: IAP.

Symon, G. (2005), 'Exploring resistance from a rhetorical perspective'. *Organization Studies*, 26(11): 1641–1663.

Thomas, R. and Davies, A. (2005), 'Theorizing the micro-politics of resistance: New public management and managerial identities in the UK public services'. *Organization Studies*, 26(5): 683–706.

Wagner, J. A. (1994), 'Participation's effects on performance and satisfaction: A reconsideration of research evidence'. *Academy of Management Review*, 19(2): 312–330.

14 Regulatory inspection and public audit

Slobodan Tomic

Introduction

This chapter is about inspection and audit, methods by which government seeks to assure and improve the quality of public services and the integrity of public service organisations.

Inspection is an 'outward-looking' activity, usually performed on the spot, that aims to check whether inspected subjects – inspectees – comply with policy rules. Those rules generally relate to compliance with legal standards, e.g. on safety, health, product quality or the service delivery process.

Public audit is 'inward-looking' and directed towards public authorities rather than non-public actors. It investigates whether public funds are spent in a legal manner and whether public actions are cost-effective.

Learning objectives

- To recognise the different roles and purposes of regulatory inspection and public audit
- To understand the methods and potential effects of regulatory inspection
- To understand the methods and potential effects of public audit
- To recognise the limitations of regulatory inspection and public audit

Inspection in the public sector

Inspection is based on the belief that there is less chance of rules being broken when there is a fear of discovery and penalties being applied. It implies that we cannot rely on the assumption that people behave nobly as 'knights in shining armour' and that their compliance with law will be self-regulated. Therefore, punishments for breaking the law must be enforced in order to deter rule-breaking behaviour, and inspections make such violations detectable. Inspection also enables policy learning, based on up-to-date information from the field, which is often not directly available to policy professionals. Consequently, inspections are common in most parts of the public sector – see Box 14.1 for examples.

DOI: 10.4324/9781003282839-16

Who carries out inspections and how?

Inspection is typically done by public sector staff in inspectorates and regulatory agencies. Public service inspectorates are typically part of the central or state government ministries, with the task of ensuring that public service providers are complying with laws, policies and expected quality standards. Some inspectorates have a centuries-long history – for example, labour inspectorates were established in many countries in the 19th and early 20th centuries.

Private inspection agencies are also sometimes engaged in public inspections. They do so where public actors do not possess the necessary expertise, (e.g. the use of sophisticated data analytics to highlight potentially 'rogue' behaviour) or where public inspection agencies are suspected of conflicts of interest or political interference (e.g. the international sports anti-doping regime now uses private inspectors in certain countries).

Box 14.1 Some examples of inspectorates of public services

England and Wales

Her Majesty's Inspectorate of Constabulary and Fire and Rescue Services (HMICFRS)

- Responsible for inspection of police forces and fire and rescue services of England and Wales

Office for Standards in Education, Children's Services and Skills *(OFSTED)*

- A non-ministerial department of the UK government, reporting to Parliament and responsible for inspecting state schools and other educational institutions and also childcare, adoption and fostering agencies

New Zealand

Office of the Inspectorate, Department of Corrections

- Carries out prison inspections and thematic reviews
- Considers complaints from prisoners and offenders in the community
- Examines all deaths of people in custody
- Conducts other investigations and monitors situations where concerns emerge

Chile

The Labour Directorate (Dirección del Trabajo)

- Ensures compliance with labour, hygiene, pension schemes and safety standards in workplace
- Monitors, through field inspections, compliance with labour and pension-scheme laws
- Mediates labour-related disputes, in court and beyond
- Having own legal status, reports to the President of the Republic through the Ministry of Labour and Social Provision for Pensions for Retirement

---

Other public actors who may be responsible for inspections include regulatory agencies, institutions that have a more recent origin, particularly outside the United States. They differ from inspectorates in two main ways: first, they are often organisationally separate from the locus of political power and operate as autonomous institutions (although this is not always the case – in some countries they are still subsumed under ministries, as shown in Table 14.1). Second, inspection is not the only prominent task that regulatory agencies are charged with – they also manage tasks such as the design of regulatory standards, the development and implementation of regulatory policies and strategies and sometimes scientific research and development. Regulatory inspection typically checks whether a regulated subject, whether in the private, public or third sector, complies with legal standards, e.g. on safety, health, product quality or the service delivery process.

Sometimes, in response to changes in policy or technology, new inspection activities are created within existing inspectorates or regulatory agencies. For instance, alongside its traditional on-spot inspections of bookmakers and casino premises, the UK Gambling Commission now also carries out 'online' inspections, by checking on the websites of bookmakers/casinos to ensure that the way they deal with customers is compliant with the prescribed regulations (e.g. on anti-money-laundering measures, fair trading, protection of the vulnerable and other regulations).

Although the need for inspection is widely recognised, not all inspectorates are popular. OFSTED – the UK's regulator for standards in education – has long been heavily criticised for a range of reasons (Craven and Tooley, 2016), including its unnecessarily aggressive approach, its lack of insight into the way teachers work and its lack of success in protecting children from abuse and racism in schools.

Inspection enforcement styles

Inspections are usually conducted through on-site visits. During those visits, an inspector checks whether the inspectee(s) adheres to the prescribed procedure and/or quality standards. What makes on-site inspection different from other forms of control, such as continuous oversight or desk-based analysis of documents and reports submitted by an inspectee, is its unpredictability. Inspections generally do not occur at regular intervals and in a pattern known in advance to the inspectee, and may even be unannounced in advance. This element of surprise is supposed to reduce the extent of inspectees' non-compliance.

Inspection patterns are determined at the 'design' end of inspection. In the most rudimentary form, inspections are random, with no pattern to who will be inspected or when. However, there are more advanced forms of inspection, based on some sort of informed choice, such as:

- The regulator's, or inspector's intuition, sometimes drawing on prior experience.
- Risk prioritisation – inspected targets are chosen according to estimation of the probability and/or impact of a potential breach.
- Data analysis, primarily of the patterns in prior breaches; more sophisticated data analytics could draw on 'big data', shifting trends in the sector, real-time collated data from the field, the experiences of customers/citizens dealing with the inspectees and other indicators.

The way inspections are conducted can vary across inspectorates, even when they undertake similar or identical tasks. The concept of 'enforcement style' (Kagan, 1989; May and

Table 14.1 Examples of regulatory authorities across the world that conduct regulatory inspection

USA, Food and Drug Administration (FDA)

Probably the most prominent food and medicines regulator in the world. It has its own inspectorate carrying out inspection of the quality of food and medicines on the market.

New Zealand, Employment New Zealand – a labour inspectorate which:
- ensures compliance with employment standards;
- investigates breaches, carrying out appropriate enforcement action;
- provides resolution assistance around complaints of breach of employment standards;
- takes other steps in collaboration with industry and sector leadership and other key parties to enhance employment standards compliance.

Australia (New South Wales), Environmental Protection Agency (NEPA)

Australia, as a federal country, has environmental regulators at state level. As in many other countries, the regulation and enforcement of environmental protection is shared between the state regulator for environmental protection and local authorities, which often carry out part of environmental inspections. The New South Wales Environmental Protection Agency, for example, sets out regulatory standards for environmental protection, collaborating with and providing guidance for local authorities as to how the former should carry out inspections of environmental hazards and pollution within their geographical jurisdiction.

UK, Gambling Commission

The UK regulator for the gambling market, set up in 2007, as an independent regulatory agency operating at arm's length from government. Its inspectors visit on-site bookmakers' premises in order to check whether they are applying money-laundering regulations, rules against gambling by minors, and other mandatory regulations.

Chile, Nuclear Energy Commission (La Comisión Chilena de Energía Nuclear - CCHEN)

CCHEN is the Chilean nuclear energy regulator which, amongst other tasks, is responsible for supervision and inspection of nuclear and radioactive sources and their operators. Its mission is to protect people and the environment in relation to the management of radioactive waste and radiological issues. Unlike most other regulatory agencies it is not structurally separated from the government but a part of the Chilean Ministry of Energy.

India, Central Drugs Standard Control Organisation (CDSCO)

CDSCO regulates cosmetics, pharmaceuticals, and medical devices in India and conducts inspections of the production of medicine and pharmaceuticals. Unlike other so-called Independent Regulatory Agencies, which are outside governmental hierarchy, CDSCO is part of the Indian Ministry of Health.

South Korea, Financial Supervisory Service (FSS)

The FSS is South Korea's integrated supervisory authority, responsible for ensuring that banks, nonbank financial companies, financial investment services providers, and insurance companies comply with dedicated standards related to the safety and stability of the financial system. In addition to conducting prudential supervision of capital markets, it also inspects the work of financial market actors in order to ensure consumer protection. The FSS also checks the audits done by accounting firms to make sure that they are independent and reliable, i.e. that they provide accurate and credible information about the state of financial actors operating on the domestic financial market.

Singapore, Building and Construction Authority (BCA)

The BCA is the Singaporean regulator for safety, quality, inclusiveness, sustainability and productivity of construction sites and buildings. Its mission is to ensure that buildings in Singapore are designed, constructed and maintained to high standards of safety. The BCA creates rules for and advises on sustainability standards in construction, and inspects compliance with those and other safety and construction rules.

Winter, 2011) denotes the way an inspector engages with an inspectee, from the initial contact through the consideration of a potential breach to the subsequent imposition of a sanction, if a breach has been established.

The classic distinction in the analysis of enforcement styles at the 'receiving end' of inspections is between punitive and persuasive enforcement styles (Kagan, 1989). The punitive style, also labelled 'legalistic', 'deterrent' or 'adversarial', is based on the strict application of sanctions. Once a regulatee is caught breaching a regulation, the inspector issues a fine without weighing whether the breach has happened as a result of insufficient understanding of the regulation, the inspectee's low capacity for compliance or another 'benign' reason. The persuasive (also called 'advisory' or 'educational') enforcement style, is more facilitative and flexible – inspectors approach violators in a non-punitive way with the aim of understanding what the source of the violation has been. In this style, the inspector will possibly give the violator a 'second chance', if it has been established that the non-compliance has not been 'malign'.

According to conventional wisdom, the punitive enforcement style is better suited for 'immoral calculators' – inspectees who deliberately violate regulations. Knowing they might be punished can, arguably, deter them from breaking a regulation. Of course, the deterrence effect will also depend on the severity of the sanction, as well as monitoring frequency. A punitive approach may be particularly fitting in situations where risk or damage is high, such as in disaster-prone areas, e.g. a breach that might lead to a chemical accident, a health hazard, an outbreak of food poisoning and the like. In situations where sporadic breaches bear little risk of severe consequences, it would make sense to apply the persuasive enforcement style, particularly when inspectees need more clarity, advice and capacity development to be better prepared for following the regulations.

Recently, refined frameworks of enforcement style have been developed. They include highlighting 'intermediary' styles between punitiveness and persuasion, or adding other dimensions to the punitiveness/persuasion dimension, such as flexibility – how flexibly inspectors can and do apply rules when deciding how to deal with an inspectee (McAllister, 2010: 63). Another dimension that has been suggested is zealotry – how much effort an inspector puts into looking for violations or the frequency of scanning for breaches (Tomic, 2018). Adding such dimensions can enable us to capture more pertinent aspects of enforcement style.

While, intuitively, we may see one enforcement style as more fitting than another, we still lack substantial evidence to determine which enforcement style is more effective and under what conditions. Part of the challenge lies in defining and measuring 'better performance'. Does this mean improved compliance rates among regulatees, or greater 'policy smartness' that inspectees could develop from inspection-based learning? Whether and when there is a 'best enforcement style' is an issue yet to be settled, but a notable trend in regulatory governance over the past few decades has been the increasing popularity of mixed approaches. The most prominent framework in this regard is 'responsive regulation' (Ayres and Braithwaite, 1992).

Responsive regulation is a regulatory strategy that involves a graduated series of sanctions against repeat breaches of regulations. This system uses lenient sanctions at first, such as warnings, but if the regulatee repeats the violation, the sanction is escalated, to a pecuniary fine, business suspension or closure or even a criminal penalty. Responsive regulation is considered by many as a regulatory strategy more fitting than the 'linear' application of one enforcement style, because it avoids unfair sanctioning of a breach by someone not well informed or lacking the capacity to ensure compliance, whilst not risking mid- and long-term that such a non-punitive approach will spiral into 'anarchic' non-compliance. Anecdotal evidence and various empirical studies confirm that responsive regulation might have crucial advantages over the alternative enforcement strategies and style.

Still, this approach has its limitations – e.g. if sanctions do not escalate appropriately or if there are not enough resources dedicated to inspection, responsive regulation may not be effective (Baldwin and Black, 2008). Additionally, responsive regulation may not be able to effectively communicate moral messages to those being regulated (Parker, 2006), which is sometimes seen as equally or more important than achieving direct compliance.

Overall, there are two key takeaways from this section. First, there are various inspection/ enforcement styles, differing in terms of punitiveness but also in other possible dimensions such as flexibility or inspection zealotry. Second, many contemporary regulatory strategies are based on a mixed approach that combines punitive and persuasive elements such as in the case of responsive regulation, which is applied in a wide range of regulated areas.

Challenges to and negative sides of inspection

Inspection is an important tool for ensuring compliance with rules and standards, but it can sometimes be ineffective. For instance, people may 'game' the system by formally meeting the inspection requirements, while not actually meeting the underlying regulatory purpose. Teachers, for example, might 'stage manage' their performance for inspectors, without actually adopting the intended behaviours that would enhance students' learning outcomes. Or a construction worker might wear a helmet as mandated by law, but at the same time exhibit other reckless behaviours that endanger themselves and others. If not revised over time and in light of feedback from the ground and policy evaluation, inspections can create cultures of 'fetishisation of inspection' where 'ticking the box' is offered as proof of 'compliance' (so-called creative compliance) without much regard for its underlying purpose (Blanc, 2012: 79; Baldwin et al., 2011: 70–71).

Further, inspection can be burdensome and costly. Organisations need to invest resources (time, staff, operational capacities) to keep track of the regulation, undertake the steps necessary to follow the prescribed standards and often submit reports to the regulator about compliance. Excessive regulation and rules ('red tape') are clearly inefficient, but sometimes even 'proportionate' inspection may push organisations which have an exaggerated fear of the potential penalties from inspection to spend more time and resources than necessary in ensuring compliance.

Moreover, organisations can feel unreasonably intimidated by inspections (or audits), especially if repeated and frequent and characterised by a punitive enforcement style. This can be very stressful for individuals within the organisations. This problem is becoming increasingly recognised among some inspectorates and auditors. The National Audit Office in England, for instance, has introduced empathy training for its auditors to 'ease' the interaction with the auditees and make them feel less intimidated during on-site encounters. There are tasks and policy sectors where a punitive inspection style – even an intimidating approach one might argue – might play a positive role in preventing reckless inspectee behaviour that could lead to major disasters (e.g. a nuclear accident). Nonetheless, in other cases, there is significant scope for the inspector(s) to choose a less or more intimidating approach. One important consideration is to what extent an inspection style can be adjusted; sometimes the nature of the tasks and risks involved leave little space for adjustment – and the law can be quite prescriptive leaving little or no discretion to the inspector/agency to depart from one prescribed style.

Finally, inspections can be abused. This may particularly apply in states with a tradition of 'bureaucratic extortion', where inspections can be deployed 'excessively' or in a selectively targeted way to extract benefits from the inspectees. In developing and transitional countries, particularly in highly politicised contexts, with pervasive party patronage, the inspection may be used as a 'disciplining tool' against regime opponents, e.g. businesses that do not support the regime or that donate to the opposition. This might be problematic particularly in contexts of low administrative capacity, as not only are existing resources employed to carry out selective and unfair inspection but they then cannot be effectively employed where they are actually needed (Amengual, 2016).

According to the traditional 'business climate' argument, timely and high-quality inspection may facilitate business investment, by providing 'accreditation' of the organisations concerned. On the other hand, unclear and burdensome inspection can deter market investments by increasing business costs, and unfairly deployed inspection can produce market disadvantages for unfairly targeted businesses (Blanc, 2012: 9–14).

Public sector audit

Audit is another prominent form of regulatory control that has been used in both the corporate world and public management for many years. Unlike regulatory inspection, public audit is 'inward-looking' and directed towards public authorities rather than non-public actors. Public sector audit refers to control over whether public funds are spent in a legal and purposeful manner. Audited authorities can include a range of organisations, from executive governmental department (ministries), through public enterprises, hospitals, schools, regulatory and other agencies, to local authorities.

Supreme audit institutions (SAIs) are institutions responsible for public sector audits. Most countries in the world have a dedicated SAI, and many were established in the late 1980s or early 1990s with the rise of New Public Management (NPM), which, as a doctrine, places central importance on performance measurement and oversight across the public sector by institutions not directly controlled by the government (Hood, 1990). SAIs are usually autonomous from government, although the level of separation can vary from country to country, with some governments having considerable control over SAI staff and budgets. Some examples are given in Table 14.2. In line with the guidance from the SAI and any national legislation, auditors are appointed for each public sector organisation – e.g. in the UK the National Audit Office audits all central government departments but the 'Big 4' private sector accounting firms undertake a large proportion of the audits of other public sector bodies, including all local authorities and police forces.

We can distinguish a number of different types of audits. The most common type is the financial audit, which checks whether the audited funds were spent in a legal way. This includes, for instance, checking whether tendering procedures were followed or whether the funds spent throughout a project were allocated, discharged and reimbursed in line with the relevant expenditure standards and rules. Another type of audit, performance audit, has become increasingly important in recent years. This type of audit evaluates whether publicly funded projects and programmes bring value for money (VfM) (see Table 14.3), i.e. whether their budgets were not only spent legally, but also maximised the value obtained from the funds (Downe and Martin, 2015; Jackson, 2024; 34–35; Lau and Manning 2024: 41). Performance audits explore whether programmes and projects have achieved their goals efficiently and contributed to the public good, sometimes expressed as achieving public value.

Table 14.2 Examples of SAIs

Country	SAI name	Mission & key tasks	Status, independence, appointment procedure
Brazil	Federal Court of Auditors (TCU - Tribunal de Contas da União)	TCU conducts accounting, financial, budgetary, performance and equity audits and inspections to verify the legality and legitimacy of governmental actions. It audits the accounts of public administration bodies at the federal level and persons responsible for federal public assets. It audits accounts relevant to any illegal loss to the public treasury, due to neglect, misapplication or corruption. It sanctions public officials where legal violations are established in relation to the federal budget.	TCU is a collegiate body, with a constitutional status. The Court comprises nine Ministers, six of whom are appointed by the federal Congress and the others recommended by the President of the Republic. The Court also has four civil servants as auditors, non-political appointees. TCU also has an autonomous and independent office of Public Prosecution to uphold the legal order, whose senior staff are appointed by the President of the Republic.
Jamaica	The Auditor General	It conducts independent audits on the use of public resources, and provides reports on these audits, submitting them, together with annual reports, to Parliament.	It has constitutional status, according to which it is appointed by the Governor General on the advice of the Jamaican Prime Minister. Unlike the Brazilian TCU, or other SAIs with a collegiate model, the Auditor General acts as final decision maker.
England	The National Audit Office (NAO)	It carries out audits of central government departments, government agencies and non-departmental public bodies. This includes value for money (VFM) audits into the administration of public policy. Its reports are reviewed by the Public Accounts Committee of the UK Parliament.	Independent Parliamentary Body that reports to the Comptroller and Auditor General, an officer of the UK Parliament, who is appointed by Her Majesty the Queen, upon the Prime Minister's address to Parliament. The Public Accounts Commission is responsible for the appointment of the non-executive members of the NAO Board and its external auditor.

Note: Data as of 2022, as per official national legislation.

Table 14.3 A definition of value for money

Value for Money (VfM):
"An independent evidence-based investigation which examines and reports on whether economy, effectiveness and efficiency has been achieved in the use of public funds" (Northern Ireland Audit Office, UK)

The public audit cycle: From auditee selection through report submission to policy recommendations and sanctioning

After an audit organisation has selected which institutions and projects to examine, it gathers relevant documents from each one, including records of spending and evidence. A team of specialists from the audit body investigates these. When they finish, the auditor sends a report to show if the audited body followed budget expenditure regulations during the programme. If not, the auditor can propose or impose fines or other sanctions. The type and strength of the sanctions will depend on several factors, such as the kind of violation committed and the legal framework in that state. In some states, the audit body decides what sanctions to apply; in other states, sanctions are applied by the court or parliament to which the audit body forwards its reports. Sanctions can range from warnings to pronouncements of budget expenditure violations (a typical 'naming and shaming' measure), and might further involve prosecuting misdemeanours and even criminal charges/fines.

Audit reports are important because they help to hold public officials accountable. However, auditors may also help to improve policies. After a performance audit is conducted, the audit body often draws up a list of improvement recommendations, highlighting what the audited bodies can learn from the audit.

The effects of inspection and public audit

Inspection effects can be positive or negative. Auditors can play an important role in ensuring that taxpayers' money is well spent. By conducting financial audits and performance audits, they can help organisations save money and provide better public services. However, it is unclear whether these savings come at a cost to other parts of the government or to citizens themselves. For example, some budgetary savings, which appear positive in themselves, may simply shift costs to other programmes (e.g. when substance abuse centres are closed but police and courts have to deal subsequently with higher crime rates). Alternatively, the burden may be shifted to citizens, through reduced protection and benefits, the costs of which are not calculated in the audit. It is important to consider all of these potential consequences when assessing the effects of an audit body's work.

In many cases, improvements have been found in the behaviour of auditees, which often follows the recommendations of auditors based on their finished audit reports (Bonollo, 2019: 471–475). However, such improvements are not always associated with the removal of malfunctions and a reduction in corruption. Sometimes, auditees do indeed adopt the majority of audit recommendations but they may selectively aim for low-hanging fruit, adopting those recommendations that are the least demanding or lead to least-change resource or performance improvements. At the same time, the fact that an auditee has adopted a majority of an auditor's recommendations in the past may make future audits less stringent – this means that the simple count of 'implemented audit recommendations' is a poor indicator of whether audits have led to improvements in value for money. Studies have found that the adoption of a auditor's recommendation, or set of recommendations, usually has only a marginal effect on correcting the main malfunctions in the work of the audited institution (Morin, 2008, 2014).

Sometimes it is difficult to credit an organisation's improvement to an audit report, even though the latter might have been a key trigger. audit reports often point to internal organisational weaknesses and suggest ways of pooling resources and reducing inefficiencies, actions which are often subsequently actioned by managers. However, audited organisations can portray these actions as resulting from their own reflection and perceptiveness, not external advice (Van der Meer, 1999; Bonollo, 2019: 474).

What the future holds for regulatory inspection and public audit: Trends and challenges

What is the future for regulatory inspection and audit? Providing firm predictions is usually ungratifying. However, by looking at some environmental and situational factors (see Chapter 2), as well as wider governance trends (see Chapters 4, 5 and 15), we can get a better idea of how the work of regulatory inspection and public audit might evolve in the future.

The future of regulatory inspection and audit will be shaped by a number of factors, including the increasing financial pressures facing governments, the impact of digitisation and technology on the way organisations operate and the way regulators inspect them, and changing perceptions of risk and inspection priorities.

Increasing financial pressure on governments is likely to lead to a squeeze on resources available for regulatory inspection, with agencies having to make difficult decisions about where to allocate limited funds. This could mean that regulators are less able to conduct in-depth inspections and instead focus on areas that present the greatest risk to public safety.

Regulators and auditors themselves might also be subjected to higher accountability expectations. They may find that they need to justify their actions and performance to the public in the same way that those they inspect and audit have to. In the context of shrinking budgets, regulatory agencies will be under increasing pressure to justify the costs of their work. This is likely to lead to a more focussed approach, concentrating on areas where they can have the greatest impact and paying less attention to areas that are considered low risk, or where rigorous inspections and audits are difficult.

To prove themselves accountable, i.e. justify their conduct to the wider audience, inspectors and auditors may start to make their work more transparent. They may also place a stronger emphasis on public communication, including moving to open data. The drive towards more efficient inspection and audit strategies may result in a shift towards increasingly punitive enforcement styles, as these may be seen to bring more tangible and immediate benefits than the conciliatory style, whose benefits may be longer term and less visible, even if rather greater.

Expectations may also be raised that regulatory inspection and public audit will play a more active role in assisting and developing useful and efficient systems for the delivery of public services. In other words, in future audit bodies may be compelled to serve more as innovation consultants to public organisations, advising on where to allocate money and how to increase public service efficiencies and budget savings. At the same time, given the expected rise in public pressure for resource savings, auditors may generate more powerful pressures on public organisations, which may find it harder to ignore or circumvent audit reports. Balancing such roles would be challenging for audit bodies, though, as one requires a confrontational approach and the other a more collaborative engagement.

The development of digital tools and resources is also likely to have an impact on regulatory inspection and public audit, allowing inspectors to carry out their work more effectively. For example, online databases of regulations and guidance documents could help inspectors to quickly identify relevant information, while online mapping tools could help them to plan their visits. In addition, social media could be used to gather information from citizens about potential breaches or contraventions. Inspectors may be able to use digital sensors to detect breaches in safety protocols, or software that can automatically flag irregularities in financial records.

The increasing focus on safety standards is also likely to have an impact on regulatory inspection. In particular, agencies are likely to place greater emphasis on inspecting activities seen as posing a high risk of harm, e.g. food premises or social care homes or dangerous workplaces. This will be a particularly prominent priority in the wake of the global COVID-19 pandemic and the nuclear scare related to the war in Ukraine. In addition, agencies may place greater emphasis on developing risk-based inspection programmes, resulting in a more targeted and efficient approach to regulatory inspection.

So far, the role of audit bodies and regulatory inspectors has been to point out redundancies and inefficiencies among audited and inspected organisations. In the future, they may need more specialised skills in order to analyse and suggest improvements within particular areas. For instance, they may need more staff versed in the details of IT systems, healthcare procedures or defence weaponry, all of which are areas of high public spending.

Questions for review and discussion

1   What is your view of the proposition that: 'Inspectorates are outdated institutions, relics of the past'?
2   What would the world look like without regulatory inspection? And without state audit bodies?
3   What lessons for 'value for money' audit should be learnt from Chapter 14 (on performance management)?

Reader exercises

1   Have you engaged with any inspectorate or regulatory inspection in your life? If yes, what was the enforcement style they used? If no, can you think of interactions which you have had with public services where you think inspections or value for money audits needed to be undertaken? Give your reasons.
2   What difference does it make if an inspectorate or audit agency is an independent public organisation, separated from the government, civil service and political interference? Where such separation is not ensured, what safeguards should be put in place to protect the agency from inappropriate interference?

Class exercises

1   In groups, identify interactions which group members have had with public services which were unsatisfactory and where you think inspections or value for money audits might have helped to improve the experience. Choose two of these examples to report back to the plenary session on weaknesses of current inspection and audit practice. In plenary session, based on these reports, debate the extent to which current public service inspections and audits need to be extended or improved.
2   Split into groups to consider the proposition: 'Technology and automation will take over most of the current job of inspectors and auditors'. One set of groups should prepare arguments supporting the proposition and the other arguments opposing it. In plenary session, each group should summarise its case and then the class should vote on the proposition.
3   Undertake class exercise 2 again, but this time considering the proposition: 'Citizens and citizen engagement will be increasingly taking up some of the current functions of regulatory inspections and state auditors'.

Recommended reading

Ayres, I., & Braithwaite, J. (1992). *Responsive regulation: Transcending the deregulation debate*. Oxford University Press.
Blanc, F. (2012). *Inspection reforms: Why, how, and with what results* (p. 41). OECD.
Bonollo, E. (2019). "Measuring supreme audit institutions' outcomes: Current literature and future insights", *Public Money & Management*, 39(7), 468–477.
May, P. J., & Winter, S. C. (2011). "Regulatory enforcement styles and compliance", *Explaining Compliance: Business Responses to Regulation*, 10, 222–244.

References

Amengual, M. (2016). *Politicised enforcement in Argentina: Labor and environmental regulation*. Cambridge University Press.
Baldwin, R., & Black, J. (2008). "Really responsive regulation", *The Modern Law Review*, 71(1), 59–94.
Baldwin, R., Cave, M., & Lodge, M. (2011). *Understanding regulation: Theory, strategy, and practice*. Oxford University Press.
Craven, B. M., & Tooley, J. N. (2016). "Safeguarding children: Ofsted and regulatory failure", *Economic Affairs*, 36(1), 64–79.
Downe, J., & Martin, S. (2015). "Public services inspection", in Bovaird, T. and E. Loeffler (eds.), *Public management and governance*, 3rd edition. Routledge, pp. 193–204.
Hood, C. (1990). "De-Sir Humphreyfying the Westminster model of bureaucracy: A new style of governance?", *Governance*, 3(2), 205–214.
Jackson, P. M. (2024). "The changing role of public spending", in Bovaird, T. and E Loeffler (eds.), *Public management and governance*, 4th edition. Routledge, pp. 27–38.
Kagan, R. A. (1989). "Editor's introduction: Understanding regulatory enforcement", *Law & Policy*, 11(2), 89–119.
Lau, E., & Manning, N. (2024). "Public sector reforms across OECD countries", in Bovaird, T. and E Loeffler (eds.), *Public management and governance*, 4th edition. Routledge, pp. 39–52.
May, P. J., & Winter, S. C. (2011). "Regulatory enforcement styles and compliance", *Explaining Compliance: Business Responses to Regulation*, 222–244.
McAllister, L. K. (2010). "Dimensions of enforcement style: Factoring in regulatory autonomy and capacity", *Law & Policy*, 32(1), 61–78.
Morin, D. (2008). "Auditors general's universe revisited", *Managerial Auditing Journal*, 23(7), 697–720.
Morin, D. (2014). "Auditors general's impact on administrations: A pan-Canadian study (2001–2011)", *Managerial Auditing Journal*, 29(5), 395–426.
Parker, C. (2006). "The 'compliance' trap: The moral message in responsive regulatory enforcement", *Law & Society Review*, 40(3), 591–622.
Tomic, S. (2018). "Legal independence vs. leaders' reputation: Exploring drivers of ethics commissions' conduct in new democracies", *Public Administration*, 96(3), 544–560.
Van der Meer, F. B. (1999). "Evaluation and the social construction of impacts", *Evaluation*, 58(4), 387–406.

Part III

Public governance

The third part of this book focuses explicitly on governance as an emerging trend in the public domain. It examines a number of themes central to public governance and suggests how they are interlinked with public management and how these themes may evolve in the future, if public governance continues to acquire increasing importance.

Chapter 15 examines the relationship between governance and government. It suggests that the growing interest in public governance has arisen at least partly because of the modern necessity for governments to work in partnership with external stakeholders to achieve public value, which necessitates a strong focus on quality-of-life outcomes while ensuring that all stakeholders conform clearly and carefully to widely-shared principles of behaviour constraining how those outcomes are to be achieved ('the ends do not justify the means').

The subsequent chapters explore how public policy makers and managers have moved from being largely concerned with the management of public organizations to a wider conception of their role: Partnership working across public and private sectors (Chapter 16); managing at "arm's length" through different organizational forms (Chapter 17); managing "wicked problems" through complex adaptive governance networks (Chapter 18), and through innovation (Chapter 19); how e-governance both widens the scope for greater and more successful stakeholder involvement but also raises ethical challenges (Chapter 20); how public leadership involves a range of actors, both formal (such as politicians or public managers and professionals), but also informal leaders from any sector seeking an impact on the public domain (Chapter 21); how public agencies are finding new ways to engage with citizens (Chapter 22) and how this can often lead to service user and community co-production of public services and outcomes (Chapter 23); managing risk and resilience in the public domain (Chapter 24); the implications of the growing demand for transparency in government (Chapter 25); the changing agenda for management of equalities (Chapter 26); new concerns with and approaches to ethics and standards of conduct in public sector organizations (Chapter 27); and evidence-informed approaches to developing and refining policy and practice in the public domain (Chapter 28).

DOI: 10.4324/9781003282839-17

15 Public governance for public value

Elke Loeffler

Introduction

There is now a huge academic literature on public governance, public policy networks and network management in the public sector – and new variations on these ideas keep being invented – but much confusion remains about these concepts and, for most practitioners, they don't mean much at all. Does this mean that "good governance" is simply an abstract invention of political scientists and international organizations and of little importance in practice?

We want to argue that the reality is quite the opposite – governance is really of critical importance. However, it is indeed the case that most public managers and citizens are not interested in fancy "wish-lists" of governance principles – it is specific governance issues such as sustainability or social inclusion and the quality of life of citizens that get their attention.

As this chapter will show, public decision-making and the delivery of public services have undergone fundamental changes in the last decades. This is partly because we now have a more fragmented state, with far more public agencies (see Chapters 2, 4 and 17). It is also partly because citizens now expect different types of information (see Chapter 11), better communication (see Chapter 6) and, in some limited (but sometimes very vocal) cases, are keener to engage in public decision-making processes (see Chapter 22). Perhaps most important of all, it has come about because of "wicked" policy problems (see Chapter 18), which make partnership working (see Chapter 16) and co-production with citizens and communities (see Chapter 23) key for all public sector organizations and other public service providers.

As a result, public organizations no longer just have to be good at getting their organizational management systems right – e.g. financial management, human resource management, ICT and performance management – but they also have to manage their most important external stakeholders well in order to achieve the desired policy outcomes.

Learning objectives

This chapter will help readers:

- To define key concepts in public governance
- To identify the most important stakeholders in public governance
- To distinguish specific forms of public governance

DOI: 10.4324/9781003282839-18

- To identify the key principles of public governance
- To understand how to use a public value framework to put public governance into practice and evaluate its achievements

Sorting it all out: Key governance concepts

Governance is not a new term. Indeed, it was first used in France in the fourteenth century where it meant "seat of government" (Pierre and Peters, 2000: 1). The term became much more popular when the World Bank "reinvented" governance in a World Bank Report of 1989 (see Box 15.1). This use of the term governance signalled a new approach to development, based on the belief that prosperity is not possible without a minimum level of rule-of-law and democracy and that even "independent" agents, such as private firms, voluntary organizations and citizens themselves, can only achieve the outcomes they desire if they accept and develop appropriate rules for their *interdependence*. At the same time, use of the seemingly apolitical term "governance" was valuable in preventing criticism that the World Bank was trying to interfere in the political decisions made by debtor countries.

Box 15.1 Definitions of public governance

The exercise of political power to manage a nation's affairs.

(World Bank, 1989: 60)

Public governance is how an organization works with its partners, stakeholders and networks to influence the outcomes of public policies.

(Governance International, UK, https://www.govint.org/)

The interactive processes through which society and the economy are steered towards collectively negotiated objectives.

(Ansell and Torfing, 2022: 4)

Today, governance is a highly topical issue for international organizations – the United Nations, OECD and the Council of Europe all produce policy-relevant advice and research on governance issues. For example, in 2015 the UN General Assembly adopted the 2030 Agenda for Sustainable Development, with 17 sustainable development goals (SDGs) at its core (www.sdgs.un.org), which contained goals for better quality of life outcomes (e.g. "no poverty", "zero hunger"), better public services (e.g. "quality education", "clean water and sanitation") and core governance principles (e.g. "gender equality", "sustainable cities and communities"). Moreover, these concerns have now permeated the business world – in July 2022, 5 million articles on "ESG" principles were published online, discussing how organizations (mainly in the private sector) are monitoring and dealing with the "environmental, social and corporate governance" risks which affect and are affected by their businesses and investments (Minguela, 2022) (although some of this activity may simply be "greenwashing" – itself highlighting how important these issues have become).

More recently, the OECD (2022) has proposed a model of "anticipatory innovative governance", aimed at reinforcing governments' capacity to tackle future challenges based on organizational learning and experimentation with innovative solutions. Case Example 15.1 shows how this model has been applied to assess public governance in Finland.

In contrast to this enthusiasm for governance amongst international organizations, and national aid donors dealing with developing countries, the concept of good governance is given much less priority by most of the "older" EU member countries (except perhaps in formal speeches at political gatherings). This can be seen, for example, by the fact that there are very few staff in public organizations with the job title "governance officer" – and where such a post exists (as in some UK public sector organizations), it is often a relatively junior post, limited to undertaking "tick-box exercises" for reassuring regulators and auditors. It appears that governments find it more congenial to recommend good governance to others than to deal with uncomfortable governance issues themselves. In particular, in times of austerity there is an even greater reluctance to invest in "fuzzy" governance initiatives.

Case Example 15.1: Assessment of the Finnish public governance system

Finland has been systematically developing its public governance system over the last decade. During 2020–22 the government worked with the OECD and European Commission to undertake a comprehensive assessment based on the OECD anticipatory innovation governance model, which identified six main challenge areas for Finland's governance:

- overcoming the strategic foresight impact gap by integrating futures and foresight with core strategic processes, innovation and experimentation
- opening up the development of policy alternatives connected to future challenges by systematically involving citizens and other stakeholders in future-oriented policy creation
- strengthening the capacity of public servants to reflect and act on future policy challenges by increasing access to and experience with anticipatory innovation approaches and tools
- ensuring that traditional government policy steering mechanisms – strategic, budgetary and legal – allow for (and do not inhibit) the exploration of policy alternatives and tackling of complex problems
- using anticipatory governance mechanisms to allow complex and long-term policy issues to be collectively understood and sustained across the policy cycle
- countering government silos and creating new ways of collaboration to address emerging problems in a cross-governmental manner

Source: Adapted from OECD (2022), chapter 6.

Many governmental and non-governmental organizations have also focused on the attributes that they believe constitute "good governance" (see Box 15.2). While these normative governance conceptions often consist of long wish lists of governance principles, Grindle (2004) proposes "good enough governance" as a more realistic goal for many countries faced with the goal of reducing poverty which involves prioritizing strategic governance principles and being explicit about trade-offs.

It might be thought that the multiplicity of views on what constitutes governance in a positive and normative sense make it a less than useful concept. However, almost all definitions contain some common elements (Bovaird and Loeffler, 2002), which show that governance:

- assumes a multiple stakeholder scenario where collective problems can no longer be solved only by public authorities but require the collaboration of other players (citizens, business, voluntary sector, media, etc.) – and in which practices such as mediation, arbitration and self-regulation may often be even more effective than public action
- recognizes the importance of both formal rules (constitutions, laws, regulations) and informal rules (codes of ethics, customs, traditions) but assumes that negotiation between stakeholders seeking to use their power can alter the importance of these rules in specific situations
- no longer focuses only on market structures as steering mechanisms, as in conventional "New Public Management" approaches, but also considers hierarchies (such as bureaucracies) and cooperative networks as potential facilitating structures in appropriate circumstances
- employs reasoning not only in terms of the logic of ends and means, inputs and outputs, but recognizes that some characteristics of key social interaction processes (transparency, integrity, inclusion, etc.) are valuable in themselves
- is inherently political, concerned as it is with the interplay of stakeholders seeking to exercise power over each other in order to further their own interests – and therefore cannot be left just to managerialist or professional decision-making elites

---

Box 15.2 Definitions of "good governance"

> Good governance has eight major characteristics. It is participatory, consensus oriented, accountable, transparent, responsive, effective and efficient, equitable and inclusive and follows the rule of law. It assures that corruption is minimized, the views of minorities are taken into account and that the voices of the most vulnerable in society are heard in decision-making. It is also responsive to the present and future needs of society.
>
> (United Nations Economic and Social Commission for Asia and the Pacific, https://www.unescap.org/sites/default/files/good-governance.pdf)

Six core principles underpin the Good Governance Standard for Public Services in the UK:

> focusing on the organisation's purpose and on outcomes for citizens and service users, performing effectively in clearly defined roles, promoting values for the whole organization, developing the capacity and capability of the governing body to be effective, taking informed and transparent decisions and managing risk, engaging stakeholders and making accountability real.
>
> (OPM and CIPFA, 2004)

> Good governance has to be defined as context-specific. Given that it is impossible fully to implement all desirable governance principles at the same time, stakeholders need to agree on strategic governance priorities.
>
> (Governance International, UK, https://www.govint.org/)

The big challenge in practice is how to bring about "good governance". The definitions above make it clear that it cannot be achieved by good government alone. For example, in order to reduce crime it is important that the police service has sufficient resources, that it is efficiently managed and that it behaves in a fair and honest way and avoids racial and gender discrimination. If these prerequisites are not in place, crime levels can get out of hand in particular areas and inappropriate police responses may result in riots, an increase in lawlessness and unwillingness to give the police information. However, the long-term solution to the problem of crime may not be within the power of the police or achievable even by means of better designed interventions on the part of government or other public sector organizations. At the root of the problem may be issues such as insufficient work and stimulating leisure opportunities for young people, insufficient integration of specific groups or simply a high rate of unemployment in a particular area. In this case, good governance requires the cooperation of all relevant stakeholders in tackling the underlying problem. This is likely to include actions by various public organizations such as schools, the NHS and local authorities – but also by community groups, etc. As Case Example 15.2 shows, the police may even involve businesses in order to become more effective in tackling crime.

Case Example 15.2 Police train shop assistants to cut shop-lifting

Under a pilot scheme in the London Borough of Camden, police officers gave six staff members of two local stores from the Dixons group of electrical products the same training as the Metropolitan Police's 765 part-time officers. The trial was judged to be highly successful. Antony Rumming, 22, a Dixons team leader in Camden, said that the training had helped him to catch 20 potential fraudsters in the last year. "It helps knowing what they are going to do and the patterns involved", he said. A recent survey estimated that retail crime costs the industry £2.25 billion annually. The police have already announced further measures to give civilians special roles in major investigations, including murder inquiries.

Source: Adapted from *The Guardian*, Saturday, 30 October 2004.

So, government may no longer necessarily be the central actor but only one actor in the policy process. As Rod Rhodes (1997: 57) puts it:

> the state becomes a collection of inter-organizational networks made up of governmental and societal actors with no sovereign actor able to steer or regulate. A key challenge for government is to enable these networks and seek out new forms of co-operation.

In other words, the importance of public governance means that the question "How much state?" must be complemented by the follow-up question "Which state?" This suggests that we have to deal with the state as the interaction of multiple stakeholders, each of whom has some responsibility to influence and shape decisions in the public sphere, rather than seeing themselves as purely "autonomous agents". As Liam Byrne (2022: 24) puts it, "the quality of our independence rests on the quality of our interdependence".

Consequently, the move from government to governance requires all stakeholders to play a much more imaginative role in shaping the decisions in their communities or policy networks and contributing to publicly desirable outcomes. This is exemplified in relation to local governance in Table 15.1.

Important stakeholders in public governance

If governance is much more than government, does this mean that governments no longer have an important role to play in local politics and service delivery? Or, as the public governance experts Jon Pierre and Guy Peters (2000) ask provocatively: "Does government still matter?"

Perhaps more meaningful governance questions would be rather: When does government still matter? What functions could public organizations share with other stakeholders – and which can they *not* share? What are the roles of different stakeholders, including the public sector, in solving different problems in society?

The concept of stakeholders originally just included people who have a stake (or share) in a particular issue, service or organization – i.e. those who are *affected* in some way by the actions of the organization. However, the concept of stakeholder is nowadays usually widened to cover also people whose actions *affect* the organization concerned. Stakeholders can be groups of people, organizations or individuals.

Typically, public governance issues are likely to involve such key stakeholders as:

* citizens (as individuals)
* communities (of place, interest)
* community organizations that are loosely organized
* non-profit organizations (including charities and major non-governmental organizations), which are often quite tightly organized
* business
* media
* public agencies (e.g. different levels of government, including international levels)
* elected politicians
* trade unions
* parliaments and local councils

Obviously the stakeholders who are most important in any public governance issue will vary, depending on the policy area, the geographic area and the community concerned.

In order to solve "wicked" policy problems successfully it is important to identify the most relevant stakeholders – one powerful way to do this is by drawing up a stakeholder power-interest matrix (see Figure 7.1 in Chapter 7). The first step is to have a buzz session with all stakeholders who are believed to have a stake in the organization concerned, or to be affected by the organization's actions. The second step is to allocate these stakeholders into one of four categories by determining:

* their power over your organization/service/project (are they powerful enough to do your organization harm? Or are they so weak that your organization does not care much what they think about your organization?)
* the interest they have in your organization/service/project

The position of stakeholders in the matrix will help managers to understand how best to engage with them.

Table 15.1 The move from local government to local governance

Local government needs to consider not only…	…but increasingly
Organizational leadership	*Leadership of networks and partnerships*
Developing organizations	Developing communities
Ensuring policy coherence across organizational departments and services	Ensuring policy coherence across organizational and sectoral borders and levels of government as well as over time (sustainable development)
Creating a set of values and a sense of direction, which leaves room for individual autonomy and creativity for mid-level managers and employees	Creating a set of values which are consistent with the expectations of citizens and other stakeholders, balancing their autonomy and creativity with their interdependence
Policy and strategy	*"Politicking": Balancing strategic interests*
Focus on the needs of customers	Activating civil society (through information, consultation and participation) in local policies and management
Separation of politics and administration	Governance as a process of interaction between elected officials, politically appointed officials, ad hoc advisors, career civil servants and external stakeholders
Annual plans, concentrating on current expenditure	Long-term plans, incorporating activity plans, capital budget plans and asset management for the whole community
People management	*Management of the labour market and its implications*
Increasing labour productivity through efficiency drives	Improving staff contribution to all the goals of the organization
Getting staff to focus on quality of service	Getting staff to focus on quality of life, in terms of quality of service outcomes for users and other stakeholders and also quality of working life for fellow staff
Motivation through more objective evaluation systems and more flexible pay systems	Motivation by allowing staff to contribute a wider range of their skills and aptitudes to the work of the organization and community
Recruiting and retaining qualified staff through transparent hiring processes	Recruiting, training and promoting staff in ways that increase the diversity of the public service in terms of gender, ethnicity, age, disabilities, etc.
Making better use of staff resources within the organization	Making better use of staff resources by increasing mobility within the public sector and also between other sectors and other areas
Resource management	*Resource and knowledge management*
Budget formulation as a top-down exercise (with fixed ceilings on total expenditures)	Preparation of local budgets with active participation of local community representatives, including councillors
Measurement of unit costs for performance improvement and performance monitoring	Measurement of money and time costs of the organization's activities, as experienced by both the organization and its stakeholders

(Continued)

Table 15.1 The move from local government to local governance (Continued)

Resource management	Resource and knowledge management
Transparent financial reporting	"Fiscal transparency" to communicate with external stakeholders (business, citizens, media, etc.) on the value-for-money of activities
Improving technical efficiency	Improving social efficiency, including equitable distribution of budgets and services
Making ICT available to all staff for efficiency-enhancement purposes	Generating and sustaining new knowledge through knowledge management, both for staff and for other stakeholders interacting with the organization (including making ICT available to all stakeholders to improve effectiveness)
Processes	**Internal and external relationships**
Internal improvement processes ("business process re-engineering")	Improved management of processes beyond organizational borders, including intergovernmental relations and constraints
Competing for tendered tasks	Managing multiple contracts and supplier relationships; building and maintaining accountable partnerships, with other organizations; co-production of services with users and communities
Measurement of objective and subjective results	**Measurement of multidimensional performance**
Reporting systems based on needs of public managers and government oversight bodies	Publishing of performance information, based on the needs of stakeholders in the community (environmental, social and governance reporting)
Benchmarking results, internal processes or organizational performance against other local authorities	Involving stakeholder groups in the definition of performance standards and comparison of performance against results achieved in other communities
Use of performance information for control purposes	Using performance data for innovation and learning at individual, organizational and network levels
Improving the functioning of the local authority	**Developing good local governance**
Improving the internal efficiency of local authorities	Improving the external effectiveness of local authorities and improving local outcomes and the quality of life
Increasing user satisfaction in relation to local services	Building citizen trust in local government through transparent processes and accountability and through democratic dialogue – but only where government is trustworthy
Serving the community by producing policies, services and knowledge (community leader)	Enabling the community to plan and manage its own affairs and co-produce its own services (community developer)

Source: Adapted from Bovaird and Loeffler, 2002: 21–23.

As part of this learning-based approach, public sector organizations increasingly recognize that they have to work together with their key stakeholders at all stages of the policy cycle in order to improve services and outcomes. This means that policy-making is no longer seen as a purely "top-down" process but rather as a negotiation between many interacting stakeholders. In practice, this means that public sector organizations have to share the activities of service commissioning, design, management, delivery and assessment with relevant stakeholders. When these other stakeholders are organizations, we will call such joint activities "collaboration" or "partnership" (see Chapter 16). Similarly, services are usually no longer simply delivered by professional and managerial staff in public agencies, but rather co-produced by users and their communities (see Chapter 23).

Forms of public governance

While trying to define public governance may appear like trying to "nail a pudding on the wall" it is helpful to distinguish between key approaches of public governance:

- chronological – the transition from "government" (Weberian bureaucracy) to "new public governance" (via "New Public Management") – see Chapter 4
- analytical – conceptualizing, identifying and working with different "modes of governance", including hierarchies, markets and networks – see Chapters 4 and 19
- normative – a better way of organizing public decision-making, institutions and services (see Box 15.2)

Furthermore, there are more specific forms of public governance, including:

- *urban and regional governance*: As Jon Pierre (2022: 519) points out, urban and regional levels of government are most immediately exposed to global economic pressures but are often constrained by rules and policy which subordinate them to national government. In order to overcome these constraints cities and regions seek to harness the resources of strategic stakeholders in the local community and economy
- *multi-level governance*: This focuses on inter-governmental relations between different levels of government but also governing arrangements in which the distribution of authority is more task-specific (e.g. to arm's length bodies and quangos) (Bache et al., 2022)
- *EU and supranational governance*: This may focus on supranational and intergovernmental decision-making as "ideal types", along with more informal types of governance, such as EU "governance by negotiation" or "governance by competition" (Panke and Haubrich-Seco, 2022)
- *transnational economic governance*: Here, transnational actors (NGOs, private standard setters, etc.) are co-opted by governments to manage the challenges of economic interdependence (Mattli and Seddon, 2022)

A public value framework for implementing governance

The Governance International Public Value Model provides a dynamic model as to how public governance can be put into practice. We define public value as the balance between the achievement of priority quality of life outcomes and priority governance principles in a resilient system (Loeffler and Bovaird, 2019: 242). This definition recognizes that trade-offs between quality of life outcomes and public governance principles needs to be made and that the balance may be changed over time, as contexts change.

Figure 15.1 demonstrates how the demands of citizens are prioritized through the political process and translated into needs, which are often met through public services from public, private or third sector providers, and their partnerships, bringing quality of life outcomes

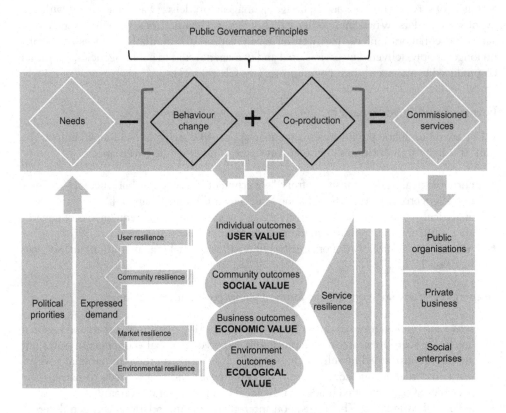

Figure 15.1 The Governance International Public Value Model.

Source: Governance International (Copyright © Governance International 2022).

for individual service users (user value), communities (social value), businesses (economic value) and the environment (ecological value). The upper line of the Public Value Model highlights that "needs" can be addressed in three ways – first, through behaviour change; second, through citizen co-production; and third, through commissioned public services, which themselves may incorporate elements of behaviour change and co-production.

Behaviour change and co-production are often closely linked. Both imply that citizens increase their contributions, which then constitute a higher proportion of the resources devoted to achieving desired outcomes. This is shown in the Public Value Model by the vertical arrow from behaviour change and co-production to user, social, economic and environmental value.

Three more important dimensions to public value are shown in Figure 15.1. First, public governance principles must inform the way in which services are commissioned and provided, and the ways in which co-production and behaviour change are mobilized by the public sector – this is a critically important difference between public value creation and the operation of private markets. It also means that the operation of co-production is fully subject to public governance principles.

Second, the sustainability of quality of life outcomes is promoted by appropriate resilience mechanisms (see Chapter 24). For example, a social care commissioner can arrange with a local café to deliver a light lunch at a discount price to clients whose normal meals-on-wheels provider does not turn up – this would be an example of single loop learning (Argyris and Schon, 1978). Double loop learning would occur where the meals-on-wheels provider installs a system to ensure that such delivery problems are much less likely in the future – and this would make the overall system even more resilient.

Last but not least, the Public Value Model represents a dynamic, cyclical process, going beyond common linear input-output-outcome chains, to take account of the way in which new demands, political priorities and intervention mechanisms emerge and interact.

Assessing public governance

By good governance, we mean:

the negotiation, by all the stakeholders in an issue or area, of improved public policy outcomes and agreed governance principles, which are both implemented and regularly evaluated by all stakeholders.

From this definition of good governance it is clear that there are two key types of outcomes which need to be assessed:

- improvements in "quality of life" outcomes from public interventions
- implementation by all stakeholders of a set of governance principles which will inform the design and implementation of all public interventions

Evaluating quality of life changes, rather than just the quality of the activities themselves, means assessing the improvements brought about by public interventions to:

- the level of community safety as seen by citizens, rather than the quality of policing
- the level of income and conditions of working life, rather than the performance of economic development programmes
- the level of health and social wellbeing experienced by citizens, rather than the quality of health and social care services
- the quality of environment which people experience rather than the quality of environmental protection services
- the level of access which people enjoy to facilities they wish to experience, rather than the quality of the roads or public transport services
- the comfort which people enjoy in their homes, rather than the quality of housing management services

Of course, this does not mean that there is no longer an interest in the quality or quantity of services provided by the public sector. However, these must be seen as instrumental, rather than as ends in themselves.

Building on categorizations of the main public governance principles and processes by Bovaird and Loeffler (2003), it seems likely that the following core principles of "good governance" need to be assessed:

- citizen engagement
- transparency
- accountability

- human rights, freedoms (freedom from … and freedom to …) and duties
- democracy
- the equalities agenda and social inclusion (gender, ethnicity, age, religion, etc.)
- ethical and honest behaviour
- equity (fair procedures and due process)
- respect for the rule of law
- fair conduct of elections, representation and participation
- sustainability
- privacy
- data security

It is important to note that these principles of public governance are generally not seen as absolute – their importance is likely to vary between contexts (e.g. the different levels of citizen engagement accepted in different public services) and over time (e.g. the slow movement to universal suffrage over the centuries), and different stakeholders are likely to have differing views on what they mean and how important they are in practice (e.g. businesses using "big data" tend to view citizen's privacy differently from citizens).

One example of how this approach can be used to assess the quality of public governance in practice is shown by the case of local governance in social housing estates in Carrick, a district council in the south-west of England (Bovaird and Loeffler, 2007). The methodology required measuring the gap between what local stakeholders expected and the outcomes which they perceived to have been achieved, both in terms of *quality of life* (against four key dimensions, namely liveable environment, community safety, health, social wellbeing and disability issues and education and training) and *principles of public governance* (including transparency, partnership working, sustainability and honest and fair behaviour). These dimensions of quality of life and principles of governance were selected as high priority in discussions with the Board of Carrick Housing and were subsequently confirmed in focus group discussions.

The core of the methodology was discussion in 12 focus groups with different stakeholders, centring around one quality of life issue and one governance principle, selected as particularly relevant to that focus group. Four key questions were addressed to each focus group in relation to each topic:

- the current *state* (e.g. "How safe do you feel on your estate?")
- the *trend* (e.g. "Has safety on this estate improved or got worse in the couple of years?")
- *proposals* (e.g. "What do you think communities and organizations in your area can do to deal with the community safety problems you have identified?")
- *commitment* of participants ("What would *you* be prepared to do in order to help these proposals to get implemented?")

The results of the discussions about the current state of the quality of life and governance issues are shown in Figure 15.2. The multi-stakeholder assessment process provided greater insights than are available from most measurement approaches and also brought the stakeholders into the process in such as a way as to increase their commitment to finding solutions to the problems identified.

The Governance Scorecard approach in Figure 15.2 has the conceptual advantage of covering the two key areas of governance identified earlier in this section where assessment is required, namely improvements in public policy outcomes and the implementation of a set of agreed governance principles and processes. However, in practice evaluations of outcomes

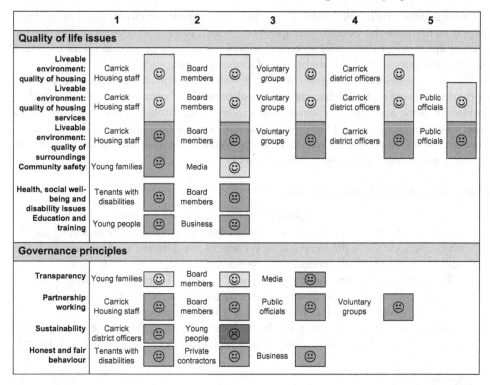

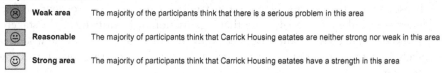

Key to present situation

☹	**Weak area**	The majority of the participants think that there is a serious problem in this area
☺	**Reasonable**	The majority of participants think that Carrick Housing eatates are neither strong nor weak in this area
☺	**Strong area**	The majority of participants think that Carrick Housing eatates have a strength in this area

Figure 15.2 Governance scorecard of quality of life and governance principles in Carrick public housing estates.

Source: Bovaird and Loeffler (2007) (unpublished annex).

have been undertaken rather more frequently than evaluations of how well governance principles have been implemented.

Summary

This chapter has stressed that the concepts of "governance" and "good governance" are contestable, but that they are central to an understanding of the way in which government and the public sector relate to their society and economy.

Government is not enough, since governance is enacted by many other stakeholders. However, good governance in society and in the polity will usually require good government. By the same token, of course, good governance will require positive contributions from all other important stakeholders.

The key question for government is: Which role should it adopt in which context? Whereas in some situations it may be appropriate to take a leadership role, there may be other contexts in which stakeholders do not trust government sufficiently, or where government does not have the necessary competence. In such cases, it may be more effective for government to adopt the role of an organizational partner or a co-producer with users and their communities, so that it is simply *part* of service planning and delivery.

The other question for government (and any other stakeholder) is to choose the right mechanism – market, hierarchy, organizational network or community – to deal with a problem. In some cases, the problem at stake can be solved through market mechanisms; in other cases, the problem should be delegated to groups in the community or other networks. But there are still issues, such as national defence, that are best dealt with by the hierarchical approach which still typifies much of government.

Questions for review and discussion

1   Select five readings from the reading list at the end of this chapter and compare their definitions of governance. What are the main differences between these definitions? To what extent do these differences arise because of the different contexts in which the authors are discussing the concept of governance?
2   What does "good governance" mean for you? In a public service with which you are familiar, specify the attributes of good governance which you think are most important and identify how well each of them is being achieved in practice.
3   How consistent with each other are the analyses of the characteristics of public governance which are to be found in different chapters of this book (e.g. Chapters 2, 4, 5, 18, 19)?

Reader exercises

1   Choose an organization with which you are familiar (e.g. your college or your employer). Undertake a stakeholder analysis for that organization by identifying all the stakeholders who have affected it or may be affected by it. In a second step, decide who are the stakeholders to whom most attention needs to be paid by allocating them into a power-interest matrix.
2   Think of one key public policy area that concerns you. What are the main mechanisms by which non-governmental stakeholders can influence the outcomes? What are the main ways in which their influence could be strengthened?
3   Take a copy of a serious newspaper (note: Be careful, this exercise could reveal a lot about you!) and identify the major public governance issues that are surfaced in its stories (e.g. transparency, integrity or honesty of staff in public agencies; engagement of non-governmental stakeholders in policy decisions; ability to work in partnership with other agencies). Do the stories suggest any mechanisms by which these governance issues might better be tackled?

Class exercises

1   Identify in class an important "wicked" public policy problem that affects your quality of life (such as high pollution in your city, high levels of crime in your neighbourhood, discriminatory behaviour against the group to which you belong, etc.). In groups, discuss which stakeholders are likely to be most successful in solving this problem. Then discuss the obstacles that exist to giving this stakeholder the power needed to allow them the opportunity to implement their solution. In the class plenary session, compare your analyses.

2   In groups, discuss which stakeholder(s) should take the lead in producing a healthier population in your city, and why. Compare your answers in a plenary session of the class.

Further reading

Christopher Ansell and Jacob Torfing (eds.) (2022), *Handbook of theories of governance*, Second edition. Cheltenham and Northampton, MA: Edward Elgar.

Tony Bovaird and Elke Loeffler (2002), "Moving from excellence models of local service delivery to benchmarking of "good local governance"", *International Review of Administrative Sciences*, 67(1): 9–24.

Tony Bovaird and Elke Loeffler (2003), "Evaluating the quality of public governance: Indicators, models and methodologies", *International Review of Administrative Sciences*, 69(3): 313–328.

References

Christopher Ansell and Jacob Torfing (2022), "Introduction to the handbook on theories of governance", in Christopher Ansell and Jacob Torfing (eds.), *Handbook on theories of governance*, Second edition. Cheltenham and Northampton, MA: Edward Elgar, pp. 1–16.

Chris Argyris and Donald Schon (1978), *Organizational learning: A theory of action perspective*. Reading, MA: Addison-Wesley.

Ian Bache, Ian Bartle and Matthew Flinders (2022), "Multi-level governance", in Christopher Ansell and Jacob Torfing (eds.), *Handbook on theories of governance*, Second edition. Cheltenham and Northampton, MA: Edward Elgar, pp. 528–539.

Tony Bovaird and Elke Loeffler (2007), "Assessing the quality of local governance: A case study of public services", *Public Money and Management*, 27(4): 293–300.

Liam Byrne (2022), *Reclaiming freedom: The case for a 21st century bill of powers and duties*. London: Fabian Society.

Merilee S. Grindle (2004), "Good enough governance: Poverty reduction and reform in developing countries", *Governance*, 17(4): 525–548. DOI: 10.1111/j.0952-1895.2004.00256.x.

Elke Loeffler and Tony Bovaird (2019), "Co-commissioning of public services and outcomes in the UK: Bringing co-production into the strategic commissioning cycle", *Public Money and Management*, 39(4): 241–252. DOI: 10.1080/09540962.2019.1592905.

Walter Mattli and Jack Seddon (2022), "Transnational economic governance", in Christopher Ansell and Jacob Torfing (eds.), *Handbook on theories of governance*, Second edition. Cheltenham and Northampton, MA: Edward Elgar, pp. 555–566.

Rebecca Minguela (2022), "This is not an ESG article", *Royal Society of Arts Journal*, 3(21 Sep 2022): pp. 32–35.

OECD (2022), *Anticipatory innovation governance model in Finland: Towards a new way of governing*. Paris: OECD.

OPM and CIPFA (2004), *The good governance standard of public services*. London: Hackney Press.

Diane Panke and Migual Haubrich-Seco (2022), "EU and supranational governance", in Christopher Ansell and Jacob Torfing (eds.), *Handbook on theories of governance*, Second edition. Cheltenham and Northampton, MA: Edward Elgar, pp. 540–554.

Jon Pierre (2022), "Urban and regional governance", in Christopher Ansell and Jacob Torfing (eds.), *Handbook on theories of governance*, Second edition. Cheltenham and Northampton, MA: Edward Elgar, pp. 519–527.

Jon Pierre and B. Guy Peters (2000), *Governance, politics and the state*. New York: St Martin"s Press.

Rod Rhodes (1997), *Understanding governance: Policy networks, governance, reflexivity and accountability*. Buckingham: Open University Press.

World Bank (1989), *Sub-Sahara Africa. From crisis to sustainable growth: A long-term perspective study*. Washington, DC: World Bank.

16 Partnership working across public and private sectors

Tony Bovaird and Erik Hans Klijn

Partnerships: Love them or hate them?

This chapter looks at partnership working within and across the public, private and third sectors, particularly (but not exclusively) between public sector and private sector organizations. So be careful – this topic can damage your health. There is probably no other issue in this book which is so prone to turn previously quiet, gentle citizens into apoplectic fire-breathing ideologues. A tip for starters, therefore – before you finally make up your mind about the issues considered here, read the chapter, dip into the further reading and do the exercises. And along the way, observe your own reactions, and ask yourself what exactly is it that drives most of us to feel passionately about these issues. In that way, there is a good chance that the energy you release will generate some light, and not just heat!

Learning objectives

This chapter is intended to help readers:

- To understand the different types of partnership that work within and across public, private and third sectors
- To understand their benefits and limitations
- To probe under their surface to see the level of 'jointness' which they exhibit
- To identify the key governance principles which underpin partnership working

Partnerships: Hang together or hang separately?

Now everyone wants to work in partnership. This has not always been so. Until the early 1990s it was common for public agencies to be inward-looking, assuming that their core task was to get right their *own* business, leaving others to stick closely to *their* businesses. And, if this inbred mindset dominated the public sector for so long, surely it is right to be suspicious of whether the recent outbreak of 'partnerships' and 'collaborations' is always as 'joined up' as it claims. This chapter will explore how and why the move to partnership has occurred, and whether it is always as thorough-going as it appears.

DOI: 10.4324/9781003282839-19

A typology of public-private partnerships

First, let us admit that public sector organizations form a huge number of different types of partnership – e.g. with organizations from the public sector, the private sector and the third sector (and even with groups of citizens). In this chapter, we will focus mainly on partnerships with the private sector – so-called public-private partnerships or PPPs. However, we will sometimes stretch the concept of 'private' in PPPs to cover also the third sector, especially where third sector involvement aims more to generate extra resources than to pursue its core social purposes.

The academic literature tends to focus on the form of organization on the one hand (is it strongly formalized, e.g. around a contract, or looser in form?) and whether the relationship between public and private actors is relatively equal (principal to principal) or more like a principal attempting to control its agents (Osborne, 2000; Hodge et al., 2010) – see Table 16.1.

When the form is tight and embodies a strong principal-agent relationship, we find approaches like the Design Finance, Building Operating (DFBO) contracts which are typical of the Private Finance Initiative (PFI) (Cell 1). Here, the contractual character of PPP is stressed, and the actors typically expect the partnership to lower costs (often expressed as 'efficiency' or 'value for money' gains). PFI partnerships originated in the UK, e.g. DFBO contracts for facilities like new motorways, private health clinics or secondary schools; by 2021 there were still over 700 PFI partnerships in the UK, many with at least a decade to run (see https://brodies.com/insights/infrastructure/pfi-project-handback-part-1-the-challenges-and-opportunities/).

As a private consortium typically gets a PFI contract for operating the facility for up to 30 years, it has an incentive to use more sustainable (expensive) inputs to save on future maintenance costs. The payment system from the public sector 'commissioner' to the private consortium usually rewards the quality of services from the infrastructure – e.g. the 'availability' of roads or the functionality of the buildings – rather than just paying the construction costs. It is hoped that the contractor's long-term commitment to the project promotes the search for innovative solutions and may circumvent typical public sector aversion to the risks of untested approaches. Of course, contracts tend to presuppose that the commissioner can specify the goals clearly at the beginning of the project – an assumption which is not always unproblematic. Indeed, it may be contradictory to seek both innovative approaches and also tight contractual procedures. In practice, the evidence on the success of PFI is still rather scant and some critics have asserted that PFI has been cumbersome, slow, unresponsive to the needs of public sector clients and over-expensive.

Table 16.1 A typology of PPP forms

Type of relation	A principal-agent relationship	More equal (principal-principal) relationship
Organizational form		
Tightly formalized	1. DFBO contracts (PFI-like partnerships)	2. Consortium (like an urban regeneration company)
Loosely coupled	3. Intensive general cooperation between public and private actors (e.g. in developing innovative policy programmes)	4. Network-like partnership

Source: Adapted from Klijn, 2010.

In Cell 2 of Table 16.1 we have a situation of a more equal principal-principal relationship between public and private actors but still in a tightly formalized arrangement – e.g. the type of urban regeneration company which was long exemplified by London Docklands Development Corporation or many university science parks.

In Cell 3, we have a much more loosely coupled form and a principle-agent relationship – e.g. where private or third sector agents provide services or policy outcomes specified clearly by the public principals. This is particularly important where potential mechanisms for achieving policy outcomes are highly unclear, so experimentation is required.

Cell 4 contains principal-principal relationships within a loosely coupled organizational form – here, we find network-like partnerships, with fairly intense interactions which only occasionally are concretized in contracts or other organizational forms. For example, in response to the UK government's Call to Action on Obesity, a voluntary partnership ('The Responsibility Deal') was formed among government, business, non-governmental organizations and public health bodies (see https://assets.publishing.service.gov.uk/ government/uploads/system/uploads/attachment_data/file/213720/dh_130487.pdf) . It provides an opportunity for businesses and other organizations to improve public health and support people to make informed choices – businesses make a public pledge to take action focused on one of four areas: food, alcohol, physical activity or health at work.

Why people like partnerships … and why they don't

Some people enthuse about partnerships (Box 16.1) – and some don't (Box 16.2).

Box 16.1 Partnerships are liked by organizations because…

- They help organizations to tackle 'wicked problems' they could not crack alone.
- They allow more integrated and comprehensive services to be delivered and better coordination of policy implementation.
- They reduce costs by sharing of expertise and other resources and by allowing economies of scale and scope not available to their individual members.
- They allow risk-sharing and therefore safer experimentation.
- Working with partners, especially from other sectors, may give access to organizational cultures and experiences that encourage learning in ways not otherwise available.

Box 16.2 Partnerships may be seen as undesirable because…

- They may lead to the fragmentation of structures and processes.
- …and this may lead to blurred responsibilities and accountabilities.
- Staff may lose their jobs or have worse conditions of service.
- Politicians may fear losing control over decisions on policy and services.
- Service users and citizens may fear services being run for profit rather than public value.
- NGOs drawn into service partnerships may fear losing their independence and critical roles.

Source: Adapted from Bovaird (2004).

Over time, the proponents of each set of arguments have learnt from each other and partly changed their positions. For example, many proponents of the public sector now advocate more risk-taking and innovation within public sector organizations, so cumbersome cross-organizational arrangements aren't needed for this. On the other side, legislation and regulation in the UK now provide some protection of employment rights for staff transferred or recruited to PPPs.

The context: The international emergence and growth of PPPs

Although public-public partnerships are a relatively recent phenomenon – associated with the 'joined-up government' movement in the UK (late 1990s), the 'whole of government' approach in Australia (after 2000) and the 'franchise government' movement in the US (1990) – public-private partnerships have a much longer history. During the seventeenth century one of the largest trading and shipping companies in the world was the United East Indian Company (VOC), a joint venture of merchants and the municipality of Amsterdam (which partly financed it). In the 1700s and 1800s, roads in both the UK and USA were funded and constructed by local turnpike trusts that charged tolls. In France many canals and bridges have been built since the seventeenth century by granting concessions, and this system still continues in much of the transport network, and many other public services such as water, sewage, refuse collection and treatment, urban transport, mass housing and facilities for culture, sports and social affairs have been operated by private companies since the nineteenth century, e.g. Compagnie Générale des Eauxs (called Vivendi since 1998) and the Lyonnaise des Eaux (later called Suez and then Engie).

However, it was only in the 1970s that PPPs began to attract much wider notice internationally as an alternative to the two main sectors. While the US public sector has a long history of contracting out to the private sector such activities as waste disposal, highways construction and maintenance, ambulance services, vehicle fleets and professional services (e.g. architecture, engineering and legal advice), these services were usually externalized through standard contracts. More recently, genuinely collaborative PPPs have become important in US transportation, water and many aspects of social policy.

Similarly, in the last two decades, there has been increasing interest in PPPs around the world (Bovaird, 2010), often promoted by major international financial institutions, such as the IMF, World Bank and European Bank for Reconstruction and Development. PPP growth has sometimes been dramatic, and they are now actually written into legislation in many countries (for example urban policy legislation in the UK and USA, into national industrial policies in France and into economic development policies in Italy, the Netherlands and the UK). While the route travelled in each EU country was significantly different, the destinations had strong similarities.

Many PPPs at the local level in the EU are transport projects, while many others deal with urban development, as in the US. Others typically deal with environmental issues, technology innovation and ICT. The mechanisms used for PPPs differ greatly. Spain, Portugal, Finland and the Netherlands have the most advanced PPPs of the PFI-type (Ball, 1999). The use of build-operate-transfer contracts (and its variants) is also quite popular in Europe, by which consortia of constructors and financiers can become involved in financing, constructing, operating and maintaining major infrastructure. However, these are not always 'partnerships' in the full sense, as many operate essentially on contract management lines.

In the EU the notion of partnership has become one of the organizing principles of the Structural Fund programmes, where 'partnership' refers to a broad local alliance between public authorities, private organizations, 'the social partners' and the population. Over time, the Commission has increasingly required the partnership principle to be taken into account in applications for funding. It now encourages PPPs in virtually every field and is willing to support them not only from the Structural Funds but also from many smaller initiatives (e.g. Interreg).

In practice, however, the main focus has been on trans-European networks (TENs) and, to a lesser extent, energy and telecommunications networks. Indeed, since the 1980s there have been a number of world-renowned PPPs in transport in Europe – the Channel Tunnel, the Oresund connection between Denmark and Sweden and some transnational high-speed railways and stations. Some of these are concessions, rewarding the private investor through customer payments. In other forms the public sector client partner pays the private sector partner directly.

However, EU projects make up only a small number of the PPPs in most member states and have not noticeably catalysed the major PPP developments in those states. Furthermore, since all EU member states have to follow EU legislation on PPPs, EU competition rules have proved a barrier to the development of partnership working in some cases.

From 2001 to 2007 the volume of PPPs (in euros) in EU member states more than doubled, then fell back during the financial crisis 2008–2009 (Tomasi, 2016), and essentially flatlined thereafter (albeit with jumps in 2013 and 2018), before falling back sharply from 2019 onwards (European PPP Expertise Centre, 2022). Since 2012, the UK, France and Germany have seen by far the largest volume of PPP activity (in euros), with France overtaking the UK in the latter part of this period.

While infrastructure projects have traditionally dominated PPPs in most countries, the Expert Centre also points to new initiatives in the field of social partnerships, e.g. in health and education, which became particularly common after 2010, as economic growth in the EU has faltered. However, in the five years to 2021, they were overtaken in importance by projects in telecoms and the environment, while transport continued to be the dominant sector for PPPs throughout the past 20 years.

Theoretical rationale of partnerships

In understanding the role of partnerships in the public sector, we need to examine the very different conceptual frameworks that are frequently used to examine inter-organizational behaviour in the public and private sectors.

Central to the new public management (NPM) is the traditional economic argument that resource allocation is most 'efficient' when arranged through markets in which potential suppliers compete with one another to cut costs and attract customers by improving the quality of the goods or services. When applied to the provision of public services from the 1980s onwards, this analysis gave rise to experiments in privatization, outsourcing and internal market mechanisms. Competition between providers was seen as key to achieving these cost and quality benefits, and collaboration was given a back seat.

However, in the NPM approach, commissioners or purchasers of public services were also seen to have the potential to achieve economies of scale or scope if they worked with one or more other agencies – e.g. economies of scale from buying in bulk through purchasing consortia for the purchase of paper, furniture, etc., or economies of scope through the sharing of some expertise, e.g. specialist music teachers, consumer fraud enforcement staff. Such partnerships were seen by economists as potentially efficient.

Consequently, many NPM proponents accept that partnerships can sometimes play a useful role, but partnership working must be scrutinized very carefully, to ascertain if it masks anti-competitive behaviour. Where private partners are brought in to provide public services, it is important to ensure that government is not simply trying to raise maximum revenues by granting monopolies to private firms (as was suspected in the case of some UK privatizations in the Thatcher era, notwithstanding the regulation of prices and quality). However, some public choice theorists continued to be sceptical of any argument for public sector intervention in markets, and therefore saw PPPs as only 'half-way' solutions, preferring outright privatization.

A key counter to NPM was transaction cost analysis (Williamson, 1996; Walsh, 1995), which argued that in complex contracts the high costs of designing, letting, monitoring and enforcing these contracts mean that organizations might well be better off undertaking many activities in-house (even where they are relatively bad at these activities), unless relational contracts can be set up. Relational contracts involve links between the contracting parties that are long-lasting and complex, so that the original agreement between the parties ceases to be important. In such cases, the relationship itself becomes the key focus – in a real sense, the parties 'make it up as they go along', rather than always seeking guidance from a specification (which is always incomplete and is likely to become increasingly out-of-date over time). Relational contracts therefore rely on trust (rather than the purely economic incentives in traditional or 'transactional' contracts), which forms the basis for these long-term relationships. Relational contracts can apply at all levels from strategic partnerships, right through to outsourcing small-scale services to sub-contractors – the basic criterion for moving to a relational contract is whether the transaction costs of detailed, specification-based contracts outweigh the likely benefits.

This analysis suggests that traditional public sector contracting has often been fundamentally misguided, leading to confrontational contracting based on the mutual attempt to take advantage each other (see Chapter 8) and on the assumption (from agency theory) that close monitoring of the partner is necessary. It suggests a new partnership-based approach to contracting, in which both parties may find it advantageous to find ways of helping each other to be more successful. Callens et al. (2022) conclude from their study of 24 PPPs in Belgium and the Netherlands that neither the logic of 'contracting for innovation' nor the logic of 'collaborative innovation' was, by itself, necessary for high levels of innovation – but, when occurring together, they did contribute to higher innovation.

This approach, though, only accepts the potential value of PPPs where it can be demonstrated that there is a complementarity of resources – in particular, it is highly suspicious of those UK PFI schemes that appear only to be proposed because private sector funding is made mandatory by public sector financing rules ('marrying for money'), rather than because there is any natural match between the different expertise brought by the public and private sector 'partners'.

Another theoretical justification of the value of partnerships comes from the 'resource dependency' perspective. This suggests that the more dependent partners are on each other for acquiring and sustaining resources key to their success, the greater the need for organizing the interactions between them (Mulford and Rogers, 1982). Partnerships are thus initiated because partners hope to harness each other's resources – and the stronger is the resource dependency, the tighter the form of organization which is needed. This is consistent with transactions cost analysis – partners investing heavily in a relationship are likely to maximize the transactions which are kept internal to this arrangement, rather than bought in from elsewhere in the market. However, it could be achieved either by 'tight' formal contracts (to stop partners capturing more than their 'fair share' of the resultant benefits of the partnership) or by relational contracts (where they trust each other to maximize the joint value created in the partnership).

Meanwhile, emphasis in the strategic management literature on strategic alliances, joint ventures and consortia (Bovaird, 2004) reinforced the importance of partnership and collaborative working, as opposed to competitive behaviour (although they can also provide opportunities for 'cost dumping' and 'benefits raiding'). This literature suggested (Bovaird, 2014) that partnerships can contribute to competitive (or collaborative) advantage by:

- Providing *economies of scale* (and perhaps critical mass) in the provision of services.
- Providing *economies of scope* (i.e. the ability to exploit more fully the complementary capabilities in the partner organization) in the provision of services.
- Providing *opportunities for mutual learning* between the partners (in the long-term dynamic process of interaction between the partners).

All partners may have to become expert in achieving 'collaborative advantage' if the partnership as a whole is to be able to gain competitive advantage over other rival partnerships (Huxham and Vangan, 2005). This has been the aim of some UK PPPs, in which local authorities have joined forces with major private sector suppliers of business services (such as contact centres, financial processing centres, etc.), hoping to win business from surrounding local authorities (and other public agencies) so that service costs fall, giving significant benefits to the local authority concerned and higher profits to the private partner.

From the mid-1990s, the emerging public governance and network paradigm reinterpreted key strategic management concepts in NPM. In this perspective, it is not so much the organizational characteristics (arm's-length relationships, the contractual form, contract monitoring and enforcement arrangements) which make partnership succeed but rather managerial efforts ('network management') (Klijn, 2010):

- *Decision-making has to become shared* within partnerships, which implies trust-building and capacity-building activities, so that different members of the partnerships and networks play their agreed roles.
- *Accountability has to become shared* within partnerships, so that both democratic accountability of politicians and managerial accountability are reinforced, not undermined, by the shared responsibilities for partnership activities.
- *Goals and plans have to become coordinated and integrated*, so that partners have to show sensitivity towards each other's goals, which may change over time. (This does not necessarily mean 'shared' goals – partnerships can succeed as long as goals are complementary, even if quite different.)
- *Extensive relationship contracting should be used, rather than in-house provision or transactional contracts with external providers*, so that there is less emphasis on 'clear divisions of labour for actors' and more on partnership working (see Chapter 8).
- *Management of the strategic change process should be joint*, typically in the form of cross-agency teams and project groups.

In summary, the mode of management in public governance has to change from attempting to impose strategic control on stakeholders towards negotiating overall strategies, within which decisions of partners will mutually influence each other, in a process of strategic experimentation and diversity. This may become more important if social and bottom-up partnerships become common in the future, instead of the large contractual partnerships which were common in previous decades.

Interestingly, recent research on PPPs also emphasizes that good PPP performance seems to stem from a mix of strict contractual measures (e.g. specifying collaborative working in the actual contract), combined with network governance and collaborative measures (see for instance Warsen et al., 2019; Callens et al., 2022), which underlines the argument that the governance of the partnership is likely to be more important than the specific contractual characteristics.

Governance of partnerships

Partnerships must not only help to deliver the objectives of the public sector and solve the 'wicked problems' with which they are faced, but their working has to be based on principles of good governance – the ends (public sector objectives, publicly desired quality of life outcomes) do not justify the means (through which objectives and outcomes are achieved). In Table 16.2 we set out some of the differences, from a governance perspective, which we would expect to see between genuinely collaborative partnerships (between any organizations, whatever their sector) and those relationships which simply involve the 'partners' respecting the contracts to which they are legally committed.

Obviously, the emphasis on the criteria by which good governance is judged may vary from partnership to partnership. The criteria highlighted in Table 16.2 have been selected as the 'lowest common denominator' from the approaches to good governance that have been advocated by major international and multinational agencies in recent years.

These criteria are demanding – as they are meant to be. It is therefore to be expected that, on occasion, they will bring howls of protest from partnerships which feel that it is too difficult to comply with them. However, the importance of these criteria is already being brought home to many partnerships that have suffered severe damage to their reputations, and lost the confidence of their funders and customers, because these principles have been ignored – e.g. through unfair employment practices for staff transferring into partnership bodies or lack of transparency on profits earned by private partners.

Interestingly, some recent research concludes that good governance practices, involving active network management (such as keeping partners well connected to each other, establishing agreed rules for internal decision processes, etc.) are related to good performance, whereas organizational characteristics are not (Warsen et al., 2019; Koppenjan et al. 2022).

Whatever criteria are given highest weight, public sector managers and politicians in every country can expect that their actions will be judged against good governance principles (Bovaird and Loeffler, 2007). However, the fact that these principles might differ significantly between different contexts in the public sector poses a major challenge. In particular, accountability in partnerships tends to be quite different from classic public accountability, where an elected office holder is held responsible for decisions made. A city council manager initiating a partnership, for instance for urban regeneration, is already accountable both to line managers in the bureaucracy and elected city politicians. Now, however, he/she is also accountable to the other actors in the network, e.g. to affected citizen/tenant groups, private investors, shop owners, etc. Moreover, this might involve quite different accountability mechanisms, some of which might be informal, such as an expectation by community

Table 16.2 Partnerships from a governance perspective

Governance principles	Transactional contractual relationships	Collaborative partnerships
Citizen engagement	Consultation with citizens and other stakeholders	Participation of citizens and other stakeholders in decision-making
Transparency	Limited to areas where stakeholders have a 'need to know' in order to monitor the contract – and, even then, limited by 'commercial confidentiality'	Open book working in respect of all partners (including user and citizen representatives, where appropriate) as a critical element of building trust
Accountability	The contractor must account to the purchaser in line with all performance reporting procedures agreed in the contract, particularly in relation to budgetary and cost control	Partners must be prepared to account to each other for their actions and performance on all issues that arise – and must be prepared to account to other stakeholders for the overall performance of the partnership
Equalities and social inclusion	These issues will only be considered in so far as they are included in the contract specification (although some organizations may independently be committed to improving their record of corporate social responsibility)	Accepted as core values in the working of the partnership – partners are expected actively to seek innovative ways of improving performance against these principles
Ethical and honest behaviour	Staff must act legally and within professional codes of conduct	Accepted as core values in the working of the partnership – partners must actively seek innovative ways of improving performance against these principles
Equity (fair procedures and due process)	Staff must act within organizational procedures, which must ensure consistent treatment of all individuals within any group and must accord priority to different groups as set out in the contract	Accepted as core values in the working of the partnership – partners must continuously seek innovative ways of improving performance against this principle
Willingness/ability to collaborate	Valuable but not essential characteristic of relationships with other parties (mainly means keeping to the contract)	Critical success factor for all partners, without which partnership is unlikely to continue
Ability to compete	Critical success factor for the provider in the contract (incorporating both cost consciousness and customer focus)	Critical success factor for the partnership as a whole (but not relevant to intra-partnership relationships)
Leadership	Necessary in each organization to ensure good contract management – timely, accurate and efficient meeting of contract specifications	Necessary at all levels of the partnership as a whole, in each of its constituent organizations and in the communities that it serves
Sustainability	The contractor must demonstrate conformity with all sustainability criteria set out in the contract	Partners must continuously seek improved ways of increasing the sustainability of policies and activities

groups for 'fair play' in negotiations – this, of course, makes accountability more complicated and can increase the (already large) potential for conflicts between governance principles.

From this, one lesson is immediately clear – partnerships usually mean heterogeneity, not tidiness. Indeed, some authors (e.g. Loeffler, 1999) have gone further, suggesting that a major problem with the partnership approach to public issues is that it brings *fragmentation of structures and processes*, which in turn leads to *blurring of responsibilities* and of *accountability* – as each agency has sacrificed some of its sovereignty in joining the partnership, it can also claim that the partnership, rather than itself, is the accountable body – yet there is often no direct mechanism by which these partnerships can be held accountable in a proper fashion. Such problems can be all the more acute when the partnership is reluctant to divulge information to outsiders on grounds of 'commercial confidentiality' (particularly in the case of partnerships that involve private firms) or 'data protection' (which can be used as a ground for secretiveness in virtually all partnerships – although this can also be true of networks and, indeed, individual public service organizations).

Moreover, ensuring achievement of the principles of good governance in Table 16.2 is often very difficult in practice, even if they are agreed by all the actors. For example, PPPs are often claimed to have a design that will ensure that the public sector procuring body remains ultimately accountable – e.g. because it has responsibility for specifying outcomes and standards and monitoring performance. However, the dynamics of organizational behaviour mean that the actual level of 'control' between the procurer and the provider is often difficult to establish, with plenty of room for games playing on both sides. We are still far from being able to assess the balance of achievements of partnerships in terms of 'good governance'. It is all the more difficult to judge the overall cost-effectiveness of partnerships, weighing up both the governance and service improvement dimensions. And even where there is no alternative to partnerships, e.g. because policy problems require 'joined-up' activities of various actors, we need to decide which forms of partnership are likely to achieve the right balance between service improvements and good governance principles.

Summary

This chapter has argued that there are major advantages to partnership working in the public domain – but also some important dangers. While many case studies demonstrate that partnerships can have very successful outcomes, and that some problems can probably only be tackled by partnerships, often involving private sector partners, there are also some horror stories where partnership working has gone wrong.

Since most public service partnerships are still young, and their success is not yet clear, it is important to experiment with them and to watch the results with care, not simply monitoring their efficiency and cost-effectiveness but also subjecting them to stringent tests of how well they comply with appropriate criteria of public governance.

As the novelty of the 'partnership' fad wears off, it is likely that many partnerships will be seen to have been inefficient, even unnecessary. We can therefore expect to hear more often in the future the advice 'Say "no" to partnerships, where they don't help!'. Similarly, strategic partnerships will have to learn to focus rather than trying to make partnerships cover all issues.

Moreover, there is a big question mark over the degree of genuine 'partnership' in many partnerships. While the language of 'partnering' may often be used, actual relationships often appear closer to traditional 'transactional' or even 'confrontational' contracting (Bovaird, 2004).

Perhaps the greatest challenge for partnership working is to demonstrate that it can achieve the potential arising from collaboration across many different types of organization, while still conforming to the basic principles of public governance.

Questions for review and discussion

1 What are the main reasons why partnerships may provide better results in the design and delivery of public services than agencies working alone?
2 What are the main governance issues that tend to make PPPs more controversial than other forms of public sector partnership working?

Reader exercises

1 Examine copies of high-quality newspapers in your country and identify stories about services that are being delivered by a public service partnership. Can you identify any ways in which the transparency of these services has been hindered by virtue of their partnership form?
2 In this chapter you will find many phrases which appear to praise PPPs and many which appear to criticize them. Examine them and try to identify the images which are used to make partnerships appear more – and less – attractive. How many of these images do you think could be justified by a rigorous evidence-based analysis – and which are likely to remain simply as 'nudges' to evoke emotional reactions in their audiences?

Class exercise

The class should break into groups of four to six people. Each group should identify a public service that is now being delivered by a partnership. For that partnership, the group should consider why a partnership might in theory be a better arrangement for the design and delivery of this service and should then collect evidence to see whether this potential has been borne out in practice. The groups should then compare their conclusions in a plenary discussion.

Further reading

G. Hodge, Greve, C. and Boardman, A.E. (2010), *International handbook of public-private partnerships*. Cheltenham: Edgar Elgar.
E.H. Klijn and Koppenjan, J.F.M. (2016), *Governance networks in the public sector*. London: Routledge.
Lester M. Salamon (1995), *Partners in public service: Government-nonprofit relations in the modern welfare state*. Baltimore, MD: Johns Hopkins University Press.
Helen Sullivan and Skelcher, Chris (2002), *Working across boundaries: Collaboration in public services*. Basingstoke: Palgrave Macmillan.

References

J. Ball (1999), 'Marketing a concept abroad', Project Finance, 193: 18–19. Cited in Akintola Akintoye, Matthias Beck and Cliff Hardcastle (eds) (2003), *Public-private partnerships: managing risks and opportunities*. Oxford: Blackwell.
Tony Bovaird (2004), "Public Private Partnerships: from contested concepts to prevalent practice". *International Review of Administrative Sciences*, 70(2): 199–215.
Tony Bovaird and Loeffler, Elke (2007), "Assessing the quality of local governance: A case study of public services". *Public Money and Management*, 27(4): 293–300.

Tony Bovaird (2010), "A brief intellectual history of the PPP movement". In Graeme Hodge, Carsten Greve and Anthony Boardman (Eds.), *International handbook on public-private-partnerships*. Cheltenham: Edward Elgar, pp. 43–67.

Tony Bovaird (2014), "Efficiency in third sector partnerships for delivering local government services: The role of economies of scale, scope and learning". *Public Management Review*, 16(8): 1067–1090.

C. Callens, Verhoest, K. and Boon, J. (2022), "Combined effects of procurement and collaboration on innovation in public-private-partnerships: A qualitative comparative analysis of 24 infrastructure projects". *Public Management Review*. DOI: 10.1080/14719037.2020.1867228.

European PPP Expertise Centre (2022), *Market update: Review of the European PPP market in 2021*. (Available at: https://www.eib.org/en/publications/epec-market-update-2021).

Chris Huxham and Vangen, Siv (2005), *Managing to collaborate: The theory and practice of collaborative advantage*. London: Routledge.

Erik-Hans Klijn (2010), "Public private partnerships: Deciphering meaning, message and phenomenon". In G. Hodge, C. Greve and A.E. Boardman (Eds.), *International Handbook of Public-Private Partnerships*. Cheltenham: Edgar Elgar, pp. 68–80.

J. Koppenjan, Klijn, E.-H., Verweij, S., Duijn, M., van Meerkerk, I., Metselar, S. and Warsen, R. (2022), "The performance of public–private partnerships: An evaluation of 15 years DBFM in Dutch infrastructure governance". *Public Performance and Management Review*. DOI: 10.1080/15309576.2022.2062399.

Elke Loeffler (1999), *Accountability management in intergovernmental partnerships*. Paris: OECD.

C. L. Mulford and D. L. Rogers (1982), 'Definitions and models'. In: D. L. Rogers and D. A. Whetten (eds), *Interorganizational coordination; theory, research and implementation*. Ames: Iowa State University Press.

Stephen Osborne (2000), *Public-private partnerships: theory and practice in international perspective*. London: Routledge.

Mirco Tomasi (2016), *Public private partnerships in member states*. https://ec.europa.eu/economy_finance /events/2016/20160302-pfn/documents/03_tomasi_presentation_on_en.pdf.

Kieron Walsh (1995), *Competition, contracting and the new public management*. Houndmills: Palgrave Macmillan.

R. Warsen, Klijn, E.H. and Koppenjan, J.F.M. (2019), "Mix and match: How contractual and relational conditions are combined in successful public–private partnerships". *Journal of Public Administration Research and Theory*, 29(3): 375–393.

O.E. Williamson (1996), *The mechanisms of governance*. Oxford: Oxford University Press.

17 Management at arm's length

Executive agencies and public bodies

Sandra van Thiel

Introduction

From the 1980s onwards, under the influence of the New Public Management (NPM), governments across the world started to disaggregate tasks and units, away from the government bureaucracy (Verhoest et al., 2012; Pollitt et al., 2004). Some of these tasks and units were no longer considered the responsibility of the government and were left to the market. They were privatized (i.e., sold) or outsourced to private companies. Other tasks and units were still considered to be important public tasks but were not seen as necessarily remaining within the government bureaucracy. In that case, units were hived off from the government bureaucracy and granted certain degrees of autonomy, while still receiving public funding to execute their public tasks. As a result, the core government apparatus was slimmed down, but a whole new range of semi-autonomous organizations was created that operates in the public domain but is not, or is no longer, part of the government bureaucracy. It is such types of organizations that will be discussed in this chapter.

We will begin this chapter by discussing a definition and different types of 'arm's length' organizations. While their establishment has been an international trend and all countries have them, there are also important differences in the pace of creation and the types of arm's length organizations. Some examples will be given to illustrate this variety. Next, we will go into the motives of governments for creating them and the results achieved – at least, in so far as we know, because unfortunately there have not been many evaluations done. What is clear is that many of the original expectations have not been realized. Although we know little about the actual results, we do know that the large-scale establishment of arm's length bodies has created some new governance dilemmas, in particular how governments can manage these organizations at arm's length. Questions have arisen about the use of management instruments, how to deal with democratic accountability and the lack of trust between governments and organizations at arm's length. We will then consider two theoretical models which are often used as a basis for arm's length management: the principal-agent and stewardship models.

Learning objectives

After reading this chapter you should be able to:

- Identify different types of arm's length bodies in your own country;
- Understand the motives behind the large-scale creation of arm's length bodies;
- Evaluate the evidence about this trend and its results;

DOI: 10.4324/9781003282839-20

- Reflect upon the new governance dilemmas this trend has created; and
- Offer advice to governments on how to manage bodies at arm's length.

Definition

There are many different labels in use for the creation of arm's length bodies: agencification, decentralization, autonomization, devolution, delegation, outsourcing, contracting out, quangocratization and many more. These labels actually mean different things, but are often mixed up by politicians, policy makers and the media. To be clear: this chapter deals with the creation of organizations at arm's length, not with selling off parts of the government (privatization) or with charging public tasks to private companies (contracting out, outsourcing), or with the delegation of power to lower levels of government (devolution, decentralization). Arm's length bodies have been given different labels over time (quango, hybrid organization) but are nowadays mostly known as 'agencies', sometimes as state agencies or executive agencies. And hence their creation is nowadays referred to in the academic literature as agencification (Pollitt et al., 2001).

There is much debate about a precise definition of an arm's length body, or agency. Because of the large variety, there is no comprehensive or exhaustive list of characteristics. Here we take a pragmatic approach and consider an arm's length body, or agency, to be an organization with the following characteristics:

- Operating at arm's length from the hierarchical government bureaucracy (like a ministry, or municipality);
- Carrying out a public task, like regulation, policy implementation, service delivery;
- Mostly financed from public means (such as the government budget but also social premiums or tariffs that customers pay); and
- Often having a legal basis of some sort, either with regard to its establishment and/or with regard to the authority needed to carry out its tasks.

A more precise definition is hard to give, as there is so much variety between different types of agencies, and between agencies in different countries, partly because of differences in their legal systems. To enable some comparability, a continuum of types of agencies was developed (Van Thiel, 2012). This continuum distinguishes three major categories, in which different legal types of organizations can be fitted, although exceptions are always present as well. The categories are, however, broad enough to encompass most types of arm's length bodies from different countries (see Verhoest et al., 2012, for an overview in 29 countries and the EU). In Table 17.1 we present an overview and some illustrative examples from different countries.

Type 1 agencies are closest to the government and have the least amount of freedom. Usually, they are allowed some leeway in financial decisions, for example to make investments for their own future or retain surpluses, but not in the area of personnel. Many organizations that fit into this category are literally referred to as an 'agency' (or the equivalent in that country's language), but that does not always hold true. If you really want to know what type of organization you are dealing with, you need to look into its legal status and competencies. Every organization can have its own mix of management autonomy, structural

Table 17.1 Types of arm's length bodies

Type	1	2	3
Label	*Executive agency*	*Public body*	*State-owned company*
Definition	Semi-autonomous organization without legal independence but some management autonomy (e.g., on financial issues)	Legally independent organization, based on statutes (public or private law based)	Independent organization, based on private law, established by or on behalf of the government as shareholder
Country examples	Nordic countries: State agency United Kingdom: Next Steps Agency Netherlands: *agentschap* Italy: *agenzia*	Southern European countries: public establishment New Zealand: Crown Entity Australia: statutory body UK: Non-Departmental Public Body Netherlands: ZBO	State-owned company (SOC) or state-owned enterprise (SOE)
Common tasks*	Taxes, prison service, prosecution office, meteorology, police, immigration	Social benefits, forestry, unemployment office, road maintenance, university	Railways, airport, broadcasting company, utilities, harbours

*Note that, while countries may differ in the type of agency in each policy sector, the table shows general patterns based on 21 tasks in 25 countries collected through an expert survey. Source: Based on Van Thiel, 2012: 20f.

autonomy, policy autonomy and so on (Verhoest et al., 2004). This also applies to the type 2 agencies. Type 2 agencies often have a more corporatized form than type 1 agencies, even though they are not officially companies like type 3 agencies. Public bodies have a legal basis (or statutes), which grants them certain degrees of freedom regarding personnel, finances and the ability to engage in legal agreements with other parties.

Type 3 agencies are the most well-known ones: they are companies, but with the government as shareholder. Countries differ in the number of state-owned companies (SOCs) they have; many of them were privatized under the influence of NPM or during the financial crisis in 2008 (see, for example, Greece, which was forced to sell many of its SOCs in exchange for EU financial support).

A final observation on this typology is that an organization's position on the continuum may shift over time, in both directions. For example, in some countries a trend is visible of de-agencification, with arm's length bodies being re-absorbed into the government apparatus – see Box 17.1 for an example.

Box 17.1 De-agencification: The bonfire of the quangos in the United Kingdom

In 2010 the UK government announced a reform operation which would be named 'the bonfire of the quangos' in the media. Out of the 901 quangos that had been counted, 192 were to be abolished, 118 merged into 57 bodies, 171 were to be substantially reformed and another 40 would be reviewed for further reforms. Ten years later a parliamentary committee concluded that the bonfire had not really been lit! In the end 263 bodies were affected: 192 (73%) were merged or changed into a different legal type. Only 8% of the organizations were abolished. Moreover, during this period, new arm's length bodies were established. This lack of success can be explained by political division, both between parties as well as between parliament and the ministries, which led to a lot of debate in parliament about the proposed changes on a case-by-case basis, and low numbers of agencies actually being abolished or reformed.

Source: Based on https://www.shrinkingthestate.org.uk/

Motives

The creation of agencies proliferated from the 1980s on, first in western countries (Anglo-Saxon and Continental Europe), later in transitional countries (Central and East Europe) and finally in developing countries (for an overview, see Verhoest et al., 2012). Arm's length organizations have been established at all levels of government: local, regional (county, province), state, national or federal and even international, as for example by the European Union. It would however be a mistake to think that agencies did not exist before the 1980s: in many countries agencies of some sort have been present for a long time already, as in Sweden and Australia (Verhoest et al., 2012). Their number increased strongly, however, when they were included in the toolbox of NPM reforms.

The most prominent reason for the creation of large numbers of arm's length organizations was the expected efficiency gains (Overman, 2016). It was believed that the granting of management autonomy would enable a more business-like way of working, which was equated with more efficiency and cost-effectiveness. Also, because the agencies would work in closer proximity to citizens (also known as 'customers'), it was expected that public services could be tailored more to the needs of the customer, thus getting better quality for less cost ('value for money'). Other aims related to the motivation on the part of workers within the arm's length organization, which was expected to improve because workers would have more autonomy and would feel more responsibility – which in turn would boost productivity. Finally, it was expected that because of the arm's length relationship, politicians would be less able to intervene or interfere with policy implementation, improving its quality and impartiality. Indeed, the decision to put public tasks at arm's length could be seen as contributing to politicians' credibility (Majone, 2001) because it showed that they were willing to ensure impartial policy implementation, even long after they had left office. Other authors point to another motive for politicians, though, namely that of blame avoidance (Hood, 2011): by charging public tasks to agencies, political accountability is reduced and if things go wrong, the agency is blamed and not the minister. Other less positive motives that have been ascribed to policy makers and politicians for the creation of arm's length organizations relate to the bypassing of other levels of government. For example, central government politicians may prefer to delegate tasks to an agency rather than to the municipal level, where many municipalities may be run by the opposition party. Or they may see agencies as more amenable to their patronage, for example by appointing friends as CEO and board members (Mair et al., 2012), or as an opportunity for personal gain, for example by later taking a well-paid top manager's position in the agency (James, 2003).

Results

The previous section showed that expectations underpinning the decision to create arm's length bodies were high (Overman, 2016). But what became of these expectations? We will now turn to what we know of the results, which is unfortunately not very much. There is a serious lack of evaluations of the results or performance of arm's length bodies. Pollitt and Dan (2013) analysed over 500 evaluation reports from 26 countries and the EU on the results of various NPM reforms, including the creation of arm's length bodies. They found that most studies (68%) were done by academics, not practitioners, indicating a serious lack of interest in evaluating the results of the reforms. Most studies (58%) focussed on processes rather than outputs or outcomes, showing improved results in about half of the cases, no change in about 30% and a decline in performance in 20%. Overman and Van Thiel (2016) show comparable findings specifically in relation to agencification: overall efficiency has not gone up in 20 countries (based on macro-level indicators).

This begs the question why there is so little interest in the results of agency creation, especially since expectations were very high. Perhaps blame avoidance could again be mentioned here as an explanation: by not knowing the results, there is also no risk of being blamed for a lack of results (Hood, 2011; van Thiel, 2021). In fact, avoiding blame was often the reason for putting the organization or task at arm's length in the first place. Another explanation points to the inclination of politicians – and the media – to pay attention only in cases where things have gone wrong, the so-called 'fire alarm oversight' (McCubbins and Schwartz, 1984). However, if there is an incident which involves an arm's length organization, the most prominent responses are to tighten control, dismiss the organization's leadership and/ or reorganize and reposition the organization. Such responses show a continued tendency to meddle on the part of politicians (Pollitt, 2005), despite the earlier decision to refrain from interference. Evaluation reports do not appear to play any role in the formulation of these responses, suggesting that politicians and top administrators may not have learnt from the failures (Van Thiel, 2021) (an issue which is further considered in Chapter 28).

New governance dilemmas

The lack of attention to the results of agencification, the focus on incidents where things have gone wrong and the type of responses to these incidents are all related to some new governance dilemmas that have developed as a result of the proliferation of arm's length organizations from the 1980s onwards. I will discuss three dilemmas here: loss of control, democratic deficit and the capacity to manage at arm's length.

Firstly, as more and more public tasks are carried out at arm's length, politicians have experienced a loss of control because they cannot, or can no longer, intervene directly. And although new mechanisms have been implemented to make sure that politicians get information about the agencies' performance, namely through the increased use of performance indicators and accountability requirements, this does not always lead to more insight into the performance of the organizations (Van Thiel and Leeuw, 2002). This so-called performance paradox has multiple causes (see also Chapter 12): (i) politicians are not always able (or interested) to process all the information; (ii) public tasks are difficult to measure, for example because of a lack of benchmarks or ambiguity of policy objectives; (iii) the chosen performance indicators are not always valid measurements of agencies' performance, for example because they only refer to quantitative aspects; and (iv) arm's length bodies can manipulate performance reports for their own benefit and reputation.

Secondly, the loss of control that politicians experience is exacerbated by the so-called democratic deficit: it is unclear, or less clear, who is responsible and can be held accountable for policy implementation. Depending on the type of agency, ministerial accountability is limited to small or larger degrees, but exact limitations are seldom described. New accountability mechanisms have sometimes been developed to compensate for this limited ministerial accountability. These new mechanisms are referred to as horizontal accountability (Schillemans, 2008) – think, for example, of the use of customer panels, peer review and client charters, but also agency CEOs appearing in parliament before a select committee to discuss the agency's performance (a practice which is customary in the UK, but not in many other countries).

Thirdly, the increased use of arm's length bodies has led to a hollowing out of the state, as government bureaucracies have lost units and personnel. In part this was intentional, but the concurrent loss of knowledge was perhaps less intended; as civil servants went off to work in the new organizations, they took their experience and expertise with them (James, 2003). This affected the ability of staff remaining in ministries and other government units to manage those arm's length organizations and to make sure that they performed their tasks as well as possible. To improve the governance capacity of governments to manage arm's length organizations, new models and instruments have been developed. They are the topic of the next section.

Management at arm's length

For the analysis of how governments can best manage organizations at arm's length, two theoretical models are nowadays used most often: principal-agent theory and stewardship theory (Van Thiel and Smullen, 2021; Schillemans and Bjurkstrøm, 2020). Both are economic models, based on the idea of rationality: all behaviour is targeted towards achieving the goals that are desired by the actors involved. Stewardship theory adds some concepts from psychology to this basic model, in particular about intrinsic motivation (Davis et al., 1997). Table 17.2 sets out an overview of both models.

Principal-agent theory starts with a dyadic relationship between a principal, or commissioner, and an agent – here, the organization at arm's length. In most countries the principal will be a parent department at national level, or a municipality at local level. The principal hires the agent to perform a particular task, as the agent is an expert at this task and the principal lacks the ability to do it personally or because the principal thinks that it is not his/

Table 17.2 Assumptions and instruments for the management of arm's length bodies in two models

	Principal-agent	*Stewardship*
Basic assumption	Goal divergence	Goal congruence
Degree of autonomy	Low	High
Instruments for management	Monitoring, performance indicators, vertical accountability requirements	Trust, results orientation, collaboration, horizontal accountability

her responsibility to do it personally (see above section on motives). However, the agent's expertise means that the agent knows more about the task at hand and what is necessary to do it well. This information asymmetry leads to uncertainty for the principal: how can the principal be certain that s/he has selected the best agent (adverse selection problem) and/ or that the agent will do its best (moral hazard problem)? In this economic model, agents are believed to have their own goals to pursue, different from the principal's. To reduce this uncertainty and prevent these problems, the principal will have to invest in monitoring, to make the agent account for its performance for example through the use of performance indicators. The use of monitoring is however costly and adds to the costs of hiring the agent.

Principal-agent theory assumes that principals and agents have different, contradictory, objectives: principals want the agent to perform as much and as well as possible for as little cost as possible, while the agent wants to do as little as possible for the highest price. This assumption – known as the economic model of human behaviour – has been criticized by many as not fitting with the way in which public sector organizations are oriented (Van Thiel, 2016). The critics argue that managers in public sector organizations are motivated by serving the public interest, just like the principal. Such an attitude would be more in line with stewardship theory, which is therefore nowadays considered more suitable as a model for the management of arm's length organizations (Van Thiel and Smullen, 2021; Schillemans and Bjurkstrøm, 2020).

Stewardship theory also starts from the dyadic relationship between a principal, or commissioner, and a 'steward', which is the arm's length organization (Davis et al., 1997). The information asymmetry still exists as the steward is also an expert, but because of the congruence in objectives the principal no longer has to be uncertain about the steward's actions. There is no need for monitoring any longer; in fact, a steward will consider extensive monitoring as a sign of distrust, which will negatively affect the relationship and thus potentially undermine the collaboration between principal and steward and hence the performance of the steward. Instead, trust and collaboration should be used to manage the arm's length body, as shown in the example of New Zealand in Box 17.2.

Box 17.2 It takes three: The operating expectations framework in New Zealand

The operating expectations framework is a tool for board members of Crown Entities (type 2 agencies), chief executives and staff of Crown Entities, and parent ministries to help build productive relationships between them. There are four guiding principles, which appear to be in line with a stewardship approach. First, all parties have clear roles and responsibilities, which are understood and maintained throughout the collaboration. There is a 'no surprises' principle, which means that each party informs the other of relevant information, in time. Second, policies are aligned in such a way that parties work together, and with other relevant agencies, to contribute to the same goals ('strategic alignment'). Third, monitoring is customized and proportional ('efficient and effective'). And fourth, all parties are committed to each other and there are trusting relationships ('trusted engagement').

Source: https://www.publicservice.govt.nz/guidance/
it-takes-three-operating-expectations-framework-for-statutory-crown-entities/

When stewardship theory was presented as an alternative to principal-agent theory, Davis et al. (1997) clearly stated that each model can work well, but a mixture of the models would lead to dysfunctional relationships between principals and agents/stewards. It is therefore essential that both parties, commissioners and arm's length organizations, choose the same model as a basis for their cooperation. In a principal-agent type of relationship this means that the commissioner will not grant the arm's length organization many degrees of freedom: there will be a strict regime of monitoring in place, with many performance indicators (input, output, throughput) and a frequent exchange of information. In a stewardship-type of relationship the commissioner will grant more freedom, for example regarding the legal type of agency and managerial decisions. But this does not mean that there is no interaction or exchange of information; however information will concern results (not input or throughput) and not go into detail. The commissioner will trust the steward and respect its autonomy. Horizontal accountability mechanisms fit into this kind of relationship as well.

Research into the management of arm's length bodies is still somewhat limited, particularly when it comes to the use of these two models. However, most evidence so far seems to point to a mixture of the two models, with the arm's length organization striving for stewardship, while the principal (e.g. a ministry) may apply many monitoring instruments from the principal-agent tool kit. The latter approach is often attributed to the negative role played by politicians and the media, calling for ministerial accountability and ministerial intervention in case of specific incidents or, more generally, attempting to counter their perceived loss of control and the consequent 'democratic deficit'. The mixing of the two models, however, leads, as predicted, to dysfunctional relationships, with distrust and conflict between principals and arm's length organizations, as shown by many evaluation studies (Van Thiel, 2021). This raises the question of whether there could be another, more effective model or whether we need to dig deeper into the conditions under which one or the other model would work best, or even if there are conditions under which a mixture would work without the predicted negative consequences. That is a topic for future research.

Summary

Turning government departments and units into 'arm's length' semi-autonomous organizations was expected to lead to more efficiency and less political interference, but neither of these happened. There is little evidence of improved performance in policy implementation, regulation and public service delivery. And politicians have not refrained from interference with public sector organizations, whether at arm's length or not. This has given rise to a new governance dilemma: how to manage organizations that are at arm's length? In this chapter, two models have been presented for this purpose: the principal-agent model and the stewardship model. Research is limited but indicates that the government often mixes these models, which has negative consequences for its relationship with the arm's length organizations.

Questions for review and discussion

1   Compare how a similar task – for example, the prison service, the postal service or the immigration office (or another task of your own choosing) – is set up in different countries. What type of agency are these organizations? And are they the same type? If not, why?

2   Look up an evaluation or annual report on an arm's length organization of your own choosing. Which elements of performance are reported on (input, output, throughput, outcome)? Are other topics also discussed in the report, such as the governance structure or the cooperation with the commissioner, and if so, which conclusions are drawn?

Reader exercises

1   Find an example of an arm's length organization in your country and examine it, for example by using information from the website, annual report or other sources (for example, the Ombudsman, political debate, legal statutes, newspapers). Find answers to the questions: what type of agency is it; how much autonomy does it have; what is the governance structure; how well does it perform; have there been any incidents?
2   Find an example of an arm's length organization and identify the top management, what their background is and how they were appointed (or elected) to this position. How different is their background from that of the top management of their 'home' ministry?

Class exercises

1   Find as many examples of arm's length organizations as you can and place them on the continuum set out in Table 17.1. (Tip: nowadays many governments have lists of agencies on their website.)
2   Some arm's length bodies have been de-agencified. Find an example (or use one from the 'bonfire of the quangos' in the UK). Which motives were given for re-absorbing the arm's length organization?

Further reading

Pollitt, C., J. Caulfield, A. Smullen & C. Talbot (2004). *How governments do things through semi-autonomous organizations*. Basingstoke: Palgrave MacMillan.
Schillemans, T. (2013). Moving beyond the clash of interests: On stewardship theory and the relationships between central government departments and public agencies. *Public Management Review*, 15(4), 541–562.
Verhoest, K., S. Thiel, G. Bouckaert & P. Laegreid (Eds.). (2012). *Government agencies: Practices and lessons from 30 countries*. Basingstoke: Palgrave MacMillan.

References

Davis, J.H., F.D. Schoorman & L. Donaldson (1997). Toward a stewardship theory of management. *The Academy of Management Review*, 22(1), 20–47.
Hood, C. (2011). *The blame game: Spin, bureaucracy, and self-preservation in government*. Princeton: Princeton University Press.
James, O. (2003). *The executive agency revolution in whitehall: Public interest versus bureau-shaping perspectives*. Basingstoke: Palgrave MacMillan.
Mair, P., P. Kopecky & M. Spirova (Eds.). (2012). *Party patronage and party government: Public appointments and political control in European democracies* (Comparative Politics Series). Oxford: Oxford University Press.
Majone, G. (2001). Two logics of delegation: Agency and fiduciary relations in EU governance. *European Union Politics*, 2(1), 103–122.

McCubbins, M.D. & T. Schwartz (1984). Congressional oversight overlooked: Police patrols versus fire alarms. *American Journal of Political Science*, 28(1), 165–179.

Overman, S. (2016). Great expectations of public service delegation: A systematic review. *Public Management Review*, 18(8), 1238–1262.

Overman, S. & S. van Thiel (2016). Agencification and public sector performance: A systematic comparison in 20 countries. *Public Management Review*, 18(4), 611–635.

Pollitt, C. (2005). Ministries and agencies: Steering, meddling, neglect and dependency. In M. Painter & J. Pierre (Eds.), *Challenges to state capacity: Global trends and comparative perspectives*. Basingstoke: Palgrave MacMillan, pp. 112–136.

Pollitt, C., K. Bathgate, J. Caulfield, A. Smullen & C. Talbot (2001). Agency fever? Analysis of an international policy fashion. *Journal of Comparative Policy Analysis: Research & Practice*, 3(3), 271–290.

Pollitt, C. & S. Dan (2013). Searching for impacts in performance-oriented management reform: A review of the European literature. *Public Performance & Management Review*, 37(1), 7–32.

Schillemans, T. (2008). Accountability in the shadow of hierarchy: The horizontal accountability of agencies. *Public Organization Review*, 8(2), 175–194.

Schillemans, T. & K. Bjurstrøm (2020). Trust and verification: Balancing agency and stewardship theory in the governance of agencies. *International Public Management Journal*, 23(5), 650–676.

Van Thiel, S. (2012). Comparing agencies across countries. In K. Verhoest, S. Van Thiel, G. Bouckaert, & P. Laegreid (Eds.), *Government agencies: Practices and lessons from 30 countries*. Basingstoke: Palgrave MacMillan, pp. 18–26.

Van Thiel, S. (2016). Principal-agent theory. In S. Van de Walle & S. Groeneveld (Eds.), *Perspectives on public sector reform*. Abingdon: Routledge, pp. 44–60.

Van Thiel, S. (2021, in press). Blame avoidance, scapegoats and spin: Why Dutch politicians don't evaluate ZBO-outcomes. *Public Policy & Administration*, online 18 June 2021.

Van Thiel, S. & F.L. Leeuw (2002). The performance paradox in the public sector. *Public Performance & Management Review*, 25(3), 267–281.

Van Thiel, S. & A. Smullen (2021). Principals and agents, or principals and stewards? Australian arm's length agencies' perceptions of arm's length government instruments. *Public Performance & Management Review*, 44(4), 758–784.

Verhoest, K., B.G. Peters, G. Bouckaert & B. Verschuere (2004). The study of organisational autonomy: A conceptual review. *Public Administration & Development*, 24(2), 101–118.

18 Managing 'wicked problems' through complex adaptive governance networks

Christopher Koliba and Joop Koppenjan

Introduction

In this chapter we address a persistent and often obtuse element of public administrative practice: grappling with 'wicked' problems in complex governance networks. We offer a deeper look at the nature of wicked problems, recommend complexity theory and governance networks frameworks as useful analytical tools and posit a definition of 'situational awareness' that provides practicing public managers with some avenues for negotiating the complex systems that confront them.

Learning objectives

In this chapter, you will learn:

- The distinction between 'wicked problems' and from those problems that can be understood through a 'linear' logic
- Core concepts and mechanisms that define governance networks that function as complex adaptive systems
- Managerial strategies that can be employed to harness complexity and steer governance networks towards optimal structures, functions and solutions

Governance networks as complex adaptive systems

The notion that the work undertaken by public managers unfolds amidst a complexity that defies simple steering and control has been with us for a very long time. Whether considering how best to balance administrative and political functions, how best to make decisions constrained by bounded rationalities or why policy solutions so often result in suboptimal results, public managers grapple with complexity. It is common knowledge in public administration that managing and leading any organization, particularly *public* organizations, is difficult because of the challenges posed by the very nature of public problem solving and service delivery.

Almost 50 years ago, Rittel and Webber (1973) coined the term 'wicked problem' to describe the persistent challenges posed by the nature of problems faced by public managers. Wicked problems are inherently nonlinear and are compounded by multiple perceptions of their nature and what policies might solve them. Wicked problems dominate many public managers' landscape, particularly in those areas where the challenges are especially steep:

DOI: 10.4324/9781003282839-21

public health, public safety, social service delivery, emergency management, transportation, land-use planning and environmental management. A good example is the challenge associated with water pollution, in which land uses for roads, agricultural production and development (paved surfaces) contribute to the transmission of nitrogen and phosphorus into waterways. The result: algae blooms that harm the health and wellbeing of local residents and wildlife. The wickedness of this problem lies in the trade-offs that exist in mitigating the drivers of the problem. Reducing nitrogen and phosphorus loading requires controlling the development and agricultural production in the region. The difficulty of explicitly identifying the sources of the pollution makes it very challenging to hold polluters accountable. To address this challenge, policy makers and public managers have turned to mobilizing networks of stakeholders to educate and gain voluntary compliance.

To address increasingly wicked problems, public officials have broken from the traditional paradigm of the single public organization or bureaucracy being tasked with implementing public policies to involving extra actors in the mix. Privatization and contracting-out have given actors from the private and non-profit/non-governmental sectors a governance role (Hughes, 2012). For instance, in delivering care to youngsters, disabled or elderly people, public managers may now be found working within nonprofit organizations, or interfacing with private contractors who deliver these public services. Similar developments can be seen in in other areas like health care, housing, public transportation, environmental policies and even in sectors traditionally seen as exclusively public, like public safety, justice and the management of prisons.

The rise of new intergovernmental arrangements, e.g. the United Nations, World Trade Organization and European Union, and the devolution of responsibilities to regional and local government have added layers of complexity, often facing public managers with tensions, conflicts and compromises between areas, agencies and groups. They also have to respond to emergent possibilities, including opportunities for partnership and collaboration, both simple and elaborate public-private partnerships (PPP) and collaborative governance arrangements that rely on the development and maintenance of inter-organizational networks (Klijn & Koppenjan, 2016; Koliba, Meek, Zia, & Mills, 2018). Consequently, public managers are pressured simultaneously to mobilize resources from multiple sources and also to facilitate collaborative arrangements, while balancing the needs and expectations of a myriad of public, private and nonprofit stakeholders. In other words, contemporary public management unfolds within a complex network of actors, organizations and interorganizational arrangements.

We argue that these networks can often be seen as 'complex adaptive systems' (CAS), an approach used to analyse social, biological and natural systems. This chapter shows how CASs can be viewed through the lens of public management. In particular, we take the 'governance network' as the unit of analysis, which public managers can harness to address wicked problems. We will show how the complexity of governance networks can constrain their effective management and governance. At the same time, recognizing this complexity opens up possibilities for innovation and adaptation. We will show that governing and managing networks is a dynamic process and that treating governance networks as complex adaptive systems helps in understanding the constraints and opportunities surrounding them.

Using a complexity lens to study systems was an approach pioneered within the natural sciences, including Edward Lorenz's ground-breaking work on the complexity of weather systems during the 1950s and 1960s, and within the field of computer science, where Holland defined CASs as 'systems that have a large number of components, that interact and adapt or learn' (2006: 1). Complexity theory attempts to capture the dynamic, adaptive and emergent properties of a system. Levy provides a definition of complex adaptive systems commonly found within the literature. CASs are 'robust patterns of organization and activity in systems that have no central control or authority'. A CAS is a system

> whose component parts interact with sufficient intricacy that they cannot be predicted by standard linear equations; so many variables are at work in the system that its overall behavior can only be understood as an emergent consequence of the holistic sum of all the myriad behaviors embedded within.
>
> (Levy, 1993: 34)

In social systems, individual people form groups, which in turn form whole organizations, which form networks of individuals, groups and organizations, resulting in nested social systems. Within these complex organizational arrangements, individuals, groups, organizations and coalition of organizations are actors involved in policy-making and public service delivery (Koliba, Meek, Zia, & Mills, 2018). In such social systems, there is heterogeneity in terms of agent goals, mission, resources, power and authority. Therefore, these systems function as complex adaptive systems.

The governance network as a unit of analysis and a space for action

Public managers design and implement policies and services to tackle wicked problems through the mobilization of networks of organizations and individuals. We describe these systems as 'governance networks', defined here as a

> relatively stable pattern of coordinated action and resource exchanges; involving policy actors crossing different policy areas, drawn from the public, private or non-profit sectors and across geographic levels; who interact through a variety of competitive, command and control, cooperative, and negotiated arrangements; in order to realize their objectives, which they cannot accomplish by their own given limited resources and interdependencies.
>
> (Koliba, Meek, Zia & Mills, 2018: 71–72)

Governance networks are comprised of 'nodes', 'resources' and 'ties' (see also Chapter 13). A network will have two or more nodes or actors – these are the entities who undertake actions, typically individuals, informal groups, organizations or sets of organizations. Interactions among actors result in resources flowing between these nodes over various types of 'ties'. These resources include funds, information, knowledge, human resources, material goods and services. Enduring interactions may result in the institutionalization of flows and the strengthening of ties (relationships), the development of joint arrangements, shared rules, joint outlooks, common language and mutual trust (or distrust).

Governance networks are complex adaptive systems because they possess the important property of self-organization. This means that they are not exclusively steered by some higher authority or control mechanism. How does this come about? In theoretical terms, the collective outcomes of a governance network emerge as the result of interactions between actors as they act upon their interdependencies by exchanging resources. In practice, the dense inter-connections between actors result in a form of 'social control' that may not be intentionally planned, or even explicitly formulated, but which can be very important to guide network activity.

As a result, the emergent behaviour of the network as a whole may differ greatly from that aimed at by any of its constituent actors. This self-organizing property of networks means that hierarchical interventions can be ineffective, since they can fail to account for the dynamics and emergent behaviours of network processes. In order to operate effectively within and manage these networks, public managers need to understand the workings of the governance network of which they are a part – and these workings are driven by substantive, strategic and institutional complexity.

Managerial constraints arising from complexity

The complexity of modern governance arrangements makes steering and controlling them difficult due to the presence of three forms of complexity – substantive complexity, strategic complexity and institutional complexity.

1   Substantive complexity

Substantive complexity refers to the wickedness of the problems with which governance networks are confronted (Klijn & Koppenjan, 2016). Simply conducting research and gathering information is not sufficient to deal with these problems, since they are not caused by information or knowledge shortages, but by a lack of agreement among actors on the nature of the problems and the values involved. In other words, substantive complexity stems from the uncertainty and conflicts over the nature of the problem itself, often exacerbated by the absence of consensus over the norms and values involved – here, it is hard to arrive at a joint problem definition.

Attempts to convince actors by information gathering and research may lead to knowledge conflicts, 'report wars' and information overload. Take, for instance, the debate on climate change: only over time – after various rounds of research resulting in piles of reports and counter reports – it still only gradually evolved towards a broader societal and political acknowledgement of the existence of this phenomenon. And 'climate change sceptics' still use the substantive complexity of climate change to refute the validity of concerns over climate change. Most problems within governance networks and complex adaptive systems are characterized by substantive uncertainty, in the sense that knowledge is uncertain and values are contested.

2   Strategic complexity

Another source of complexity derives from the complex set of actors involved, with their different interests, perceptions and strategies. These differences result in complex interaction processes in which actors try to gain support for their perceptions of the problem and the related solutions. In enacting their strategies, actors will use their resources to influence collective action and political decision-making. For instance, lobbyists of Big Pharma will come up with information and research to put pressure on governmental institutions to allow new medicines. Governments will use their authority, by giving or withholding permits to developers that want to develop real estate in inner cities. Truckers may drive their trucks to parliaments to prevent unfavourable regulations, as in the recent case of anti-vaccination mandates in Canada. Climate activists may disturb shareholder meetings of oil companies in order to gain media attention and the sympathy of the general public.

In enacting their strategies, actors frame problems in a certain way in order to gain support for their problem definition or solution and try to impose these perceptions upon others. This may result in the emergence of competing frames and frame conflicts (Rein & Schön, 1992). For instance, while some speak of a climate crisis, others see climate hysteria. These conflicts may be amplified by interactions on social media platforms, where like-minded people confirm each other's views within their own bubbles and disassociate themselves from people with different opinions.

The strategies of actors are far from static and, since actors also anticipate and respond to the strategies of other actors, behaviour becomes highly volatile and unpredictable and, in the parlance of complexity theory, 'stochastic'. These emergent and self-organizing behaviours of actors come together in an unpredictable way. Sometimes the strategies of actors and the forces that come along with them keep each other in balance. Sometimes the balance of power between various parties shifts and subsequently so does the support for certain solutions and policies. As a result, the ways that interaction processes evolve are hard to predict. During extended periods of time they may exhibit inertia and shut down opportunities for new solutions. At other moments new policies or solutions are suddenly adopted. All in all, strategic complexity results in interaction processes and outcomes that, to a large extent, are unpredictable, uncontrollable and unintended.

3   Institutional complexity

Governance networks are also often characterized by a high level of institutional complexity (Klijn & Koppenjan, 2016). This can be caused by the variety of organizational arrangements, cultures and regulations that govern the network. Since these institutions have emerged over time, and may stem from different sources, they are not necessarily compatible and may even be contradictory or competitive. For instance, legislation to safeguard the privacy of citizens may hinder the information exchange between various medical professionals or health bodies that have to coordinate the care they deliver to a specific patient.

The many regulations that often apply, for instance in the construction of a new highway, can make realizing solutions a time-consuming endeavour, often compounded by bureaucratic inertia and red tape. However, institutional complexity not only results from the sheer number of regulations and rules, but also from the fact that networks are embedded in a larger environment in which there are many other networks (Tsebelis, 1990). Fighting crime involves collaboration between many actors from various sectors: police and justice, education, employment, social work, housing authorities, etc. Indeed, dealing with wicked problems may involve actors coming from different societal sectors, policy domains, governmental jurisdictions and countries. Consequently, their varied backgrounds may severely hinder the interaction between them, since they work according to different institutional and professional logics, are differently financed, are supported by different information systems, etc.

For instance, due to climate change, making plans for water storage in the development of new urban neighbourhoods is important. In the Netherlands physical planners use maps in order to document their plans. Representatives from Water Boards typically do not use maps in developing their policies. Only when they started visualizing their claims in maps themselves, did they become more successful in convincing physical planners to adapt their plans and include water considerations.

Networks in which public and private sector actors seek partnerships, e.g. to redevelop an inner city, may result in what Jane Jacobs (1992) calls 'monstrous hybrids'. Private developers and construction firms seek profits. Cities are accountable for providing afford-able social housing and public infrastructure. Engaging in partnerships with strong private partners may result in the construction of expensive real estate that is profitable to private parties and leads to suboptimal public infrastructure, because private parties are not inter-ested in investing in the unprofitable public dimensions of the project.

Many wicked problems cut across jurisdictions and national borders, requiring collabora-tion, while adequate regional or international platforms are missing. Consequently, oppor-tunities for regional or international approaches are not pursued. In the case of the COVID pandemic, countries that could afford it competed for vaccines, leaving developing coun-tries with little access to them. While this allowed richer countries to offer vaccination pro-grammes to protect their population, people in the rest of the world remained unprotected. As a result, the virus was not contained and new variants could evolve, undermining the effectiveness of the vaccination programmes of the richer countries. The World Health Organization, with no decision-making power, could only call upon national governments to arrive at a more equal distribution of vaccines worldwide.

Managerial opportunities in complex adaptive governance networks

Despite the complexity of governance networks, it is possible for public managers to exert some influence over their operations. Several such strategies are discussed here.

1   Managing substantive complexity within governance networks

Relatively simple problems can be dealt with by the traditional methods of policy analysis: information gathering, clarification of the nature of the problem, setting goals, developing solutions, etc. However, wicked problems will not be tamed in this way, due to their dynam-ics and the absence of shared values and meanings among those impacted by and interested in them. To deal with these type of complexities, other approaches are necessary:

- *Learning about 'frames' can lead to consensus-building* – exploring the frames which actors use to think about a problem, and getting them to communicate about their frames, norms and values that underlie them. Often consensus-building proves dif-ficult, given the diversity of values and objectives of actors. Many specific tools have been developed to support processes of 'unfreezing', reflection about frames used and seeking common ground for joint action (Fischer, 2003). In the debate on the pros and cons of (COVID) vaccinations this could imply initiating a dialogue that goes beyond the attempt to convince people by evidence-based arguments, to one that unravels the motivations and concerns of anti-vaxxers. Eventually this may result in alternative courses of action, going beyond the narrow choice of getting a vaccine or not – e.g. in the case of COVID-19, using masks or encouraging social distancing and self-testing.
- *Win-win situations and enhancing variety.* Finding common interests and realizing win-win situations can circumvent the need for consensus or joint problem defini-tion. Innovative solutions can develop 'package deals' that succeed in meeting a variety of goals, while differences of opinions and a plurality of values and objec-tives persist. This requires strategies that are aimed at creating a variety of ideas and approaches. Instead of reducing substantive complexity these strategies seek to enhance and embrace complexity, since this widens the scope for finding solutions

(see Klijn & Koppenjan, 2016). For instance, road construction in densely built-up areas may result in resistance from residents and interest groups, due to the expected negative impacts, like noise, air pollution and lost space for housing. By organizing such a project as an area development project, in which road construction is combined with urban renewal, various problems, objectives and values can be served simultaneously, so that all stakeholders achieve some of their priorities and can agree to the overall project.

- *From evidence-based policy towards joint research.* In dealing with wicked problems, actors may be tempted to commission their own research and involve their own experts in order to convince others of what the problem is and what should be done. This strategy may not, however, reduce substantive complexities; actors with different opinions may not be convinced and trust in experts and science may be undermined. For example, residents who oppose road construction may not have much confidence in an environmental impact assessment conducted by the road or natural resource agency. Likewise, in terms of water quality mitigation, farmers may be suspicious of studies conducted by environmentalists. In order to enhance the probability that the outcomes of research will convince parties, accepting complexity and involving residents, farmers and other stakeholders in the research design and implementation may be the answer. Joint commissioning of research, joint selection of experts and joint data collection – rather than one sided fact-checking and pleas for evidence-based solutions – may increase the chance knowledge and experts will be considered trustworthy (Collins & Evans, 2007).

2 Managing strategic complexity

Addressing strategic complexity will not be solved by simply limiting the number of actors – especially in democratic societies that value equity and inclusion. Excluding some groups can lead to a series of trade-offs that ultimately end up harming those with less power. Rather, strategies should aim at collaboration and facilitating positive emergent behaviours and processes.

- *Collaboration and negotiation.* Since conflict, differences of opinion, goals and objectives are an inevitable feature of complex governance networks, public managers need to be skilled in the art and science of collaboration and negotiation. Skilled network managers seek to create value by crafting creative solutions that bridge differences, especially where agreement over coordinated action is likely to be difficult. They channel the flow of the negotiation process to build momentum in promising directions (Watkins, 1999). The construction of wind turbine parks, for instance, may trigger the resistance of residents who fear increased noise nuisance, resent the damage to the quality of the landscape or have other objections. This often results in escalating conflicts that delay or even prevent the realization of wind energy capacity. Negotiation with residents may result in adapting plans to reduce negative impacts, providing compensation by profit sharing or even making them shareholders or owners of windmills. The realization of these outcomes requires carefully facilitated negotiation processes between parties involved.
- *Facilitation of interaction processes.* Facilitation should be aimed at creating lasting and effective collaborations. To accomplish this, network managers need facilitation skills to bring actors together and ensure the proper flow of information and development of joint

actions between actors. This usually requires incentives and implicit agreements on common norms and standards. Successful facilitation skills can create 'procedures for ongoing
interaction, discussions, negotiations, and decision-making' to which agents feel bound
– these skills have also been referred to as 'reticulist' skills, i.e. skills in creating, servicing
and manipulating communication networks. There are many instances in which public
managers employ facilitation skills to ensure group processes and norms are observed. For
instance, in order to develop a regional, watershed scale plan for mitigating water pollution, a local water manager may staff a watershed planning council – developing collective norms for decision-making, setting meeting agendas and ensuring that stakeholder
voices are heard.

3   Managing institutional complexity

Management strategies may address institutional complexities by ensuring that the network
is structured well, bridging all organizational and cultural differences through the set of rules
that guide interactions among network actors and managing the feedback mechanisms.

- *Network formation and change by boundary spanning.* The art and science of building and
  maintaining networks of any kind hinge on the capacity of individuals within the networks to forge new ties and deepen others. The emergent behaviour of social networks
  depends on the skills and actions of 'boundary spanners', i.e. those people who link one
  network to another, creating new ties and making the assets found in one network more
  accessible to another network. The value of bridging networks is predicated on the
  notion of the 'strength of weak ties' (Granovetter, 1973). Weak ties open up new possibilities, new ways of doing things and new resources, without imposing major costs of
  interaction. The strategic establishment of new ties is one of the most critically important features of network management, so that knowing when, where and how to add
  new members to a network is a core competency for boundary spanners.

  The Dutch climate agreement of 2020 provides an example of network formation and
  boundary spanning. In realizing the climate policy objectives of the Paris climate agreement of 2015, far reaching adaptations are needed in various societal sectors: energy,
  housing, agriculture, mobility, industry, etc. The Dutch government initiated a process
  of building bridges to all of these sectors, which were invited to pursue targets specific
  to their sector. These debates, in which more than 100 parties were involved, representing business, natural and environmental organizations and citizens, were guided by
  mediators and supported by experts. This resulted in 2020 in the acceptance of a climate
  agreement in which parties committed themselves to realizing a 49% CO_2 reduction in
  2030, compared to 1990.
- *Enhancing and changing institutional rules.* In order to bridge institutional divides and
  overcome institutional complexity, network management may be aimed at stimulating actors to develop new rules ('rules of engagement') that are shared and guide their
  actions. Various categories of rules can be found in the literature; for example, Nobel
  prize laureate Elinor Ostrom (1990) distinguished between:
    - Position rules (rules that define roles);
    - Boundary rules (rules for entering/exiting roles);
    - Authority rules (rules that determine who is allowed to do what, when);
    - Aggregation rules (rules on how decisions are taken and conflicts are regulated);
    - Scope rules (rules that set the boundaries of the network);

- Information rules (rules on who get what information, from whom, in what way and when);
- Pay-off rules (rules on appropriation rights and provision duties).

These rules may be supported or codified in formal laws, contracts, covenants, charters, etc., or may just be agreed informally. Often tacit or informal rules simply emerge in repeated interactions. The absence of explicit rules, dysfunctional rules or confusion over rules may be a reason to enter into a dialogue about the rule structure and may lead to renegotiating them. The success of imposing rules or attempts at renegotiation is far from guaranteed, since rules have to accepted in practice. Therefore, effective network management is not only about initiating rules, but also about ensuring their ongoing use and refinement. For instance, in public-private partnerships – set up to realize public infrastructures like roads, waterways, energy plants, public buildings, etc. – contract partners commit themselves to a contract in which they promise to collaborate. In essence, the contract itself becomes the basis of the rule structure of the network. The success of the partnership largely depends on the extent to which they invest in collaboration and do not shift risks and costs to each other during contract implementation – even when problems arise.

4   Adaptive management

Having discussed strategies that deal with substantive, strategic and institutional complexities respectively, we want to we suggest at least three adaptive management principles that should be taken into account in choosing and elaborating these strategies: strategies should be flexible, and should either dampen or strengthen positive feedback, as the situation demands.

- *Flexibility.* Very often when confronted with particularly fluid situations, network public managers may need to 'surf along' with the changing dynamics that result from external and internal feedback, adapting strategies flexibly to the evolving system. For instance, in the policies to deal with the COVID crises, many governments decided to implement temporary lockdowns when infections were rising and the health system threatened to become overburdened, but then loosened these measures when peaks in the epidemic passed – and then reinstalled these measures in the next wave. These experiences also show the need to balance the extent of flexibility, as shop-keepers, restaurant owners, cultural institutions, etc., require some degree of certainty to be able to do business. Flexibility certainly is required in cases of natural disasters, like floods or earthquakes, where existing rule structures may need to be suspended in order to deliver unorthodox support to a hard-hit region.
- *When necessary, dampening positive feedback.* Positive feedback in a system means that the effects of a small disturbance are increased in magnitude in each succeeding round of changes, which can lead to destabilization (Baumgartner and Jones, 2009). In highly dynamic situations in which positive feedback builds up, e.g. where some stakeholders are mounting social media campaigns to influence the passage of particular public policies or raise public awareness that are going viral, it may be very hard to design a deliberate, well-informed managerial strategy. Here, it may be important to promote negative feedback loops, e.g. by establishing countervailing power in the network which uses other communication channels to challenge the social media 'feeding frenzy' or by incorporating regulatory constraints that stop or reduce the effects of the feedback. Governments can threaten to regulate social media platforms if they do not voluntarily

quell the spread of misinformation over their networks, as in instances of the propagation of hate speech, violence and misinformation. Positive feedback due to the connection to other systems may also be reduced by deliberately disconnecting the network from other systems, at least for a time. Monetary policy leaders, for instance, may temporarily shut down a downward cascading stock market to avoid panic.

- *When necessary, strengthen positive feedback.* The opposite strategy is that of creating 'disturbance' and enhancing positive feedback, particularly when the aim is to open up relatively closed networks and gain entrance or change their decisions. For instance, in stimulating the shift of the automotive industry away from its dependence on fossil energy sources, governments can create positive feedback by subsidizing the production of electric cars and their purchase by consumers. Such incentives are also being widely used to advance the renewable energy sector.

Each of the management strategies discussed here will generally not be applied in isolation, but in some combination. Nevertheless, there are no guarantees of success. What will work will be contingent on the context. Reading the context requires a level of situational awareness.

Conditions for managing complex adaptive networks: Situational awareness

Successful network managers must understand not only the current status of the governance network, but what its status *could be* in the future, and therefore how certain actions undertaken might influence the emergence of new situations. For this, they need *structural* knowledge, i.e. knowledge of how the variables in the system are related and how they influence one another. This knowledge can often be acquired using methods and tools such as social network analysis, stakeholder analysis, visualization techniques, computer-based modelling, serious gaming and the like.

An effective network manager will also need to have *tacit* knowledge: An informal, implicit and intuitive understanding of how processes and feedback mechanisms within networks evolve, acquired by intensive training and years of socialization and experience. This tacit knowledge has to be complemented with specific competences and skills.

What is more, network managers need 'situational awareness' to act within or steer a complex governance network. Situational awareness 'is the perception of the elements in the environment within a volume of time and space, the comprehension of their meaning, [and] the projection of their status in the near future' (Endsley, 1995: 34) – it should help in explaining which goals are selected and changed over time, in the light of critical cues from the current situation and expectations about future developments.

Situational awareness hinges on a combination of systems thinking, the acquisition and filtering of information and the ability to recognize patterns in debates, interactions and events in the wider environment, that is developed through extensive experience built up over time. Those with situational awareness rely on 'pattern-matching mechanisms to draw on long-term memory structures that allow ... them to quickly understand a given situation' (Endsley, 1995: 34).

Taken together, these qualities allow managers to take a context-driven approach within the very real constraints that complex governance networks impose. Network managers must have a desire to understand and learn about the complexity in such networks. In particular, they must have a positive attitude towards uncertainty and ambiguity and be able to exercise patience and some risk-taking. These same attitudes will also help in approaching the inevitable conflicts and other challenges associated with managing within a complex governance network. Since a network manager is but one person within the network, he or she must appreciate the limits imposed by bounded rationality and restricted authority. In the absence of 'control', an effective network manager will understand where power, resources and authority are concentrated in a specific complex governance network and how to mobilize and influence them to steer that network.

Summary

- Wicked problems are a consistent challenge facing many public managers.
- Complex governance networks are needed to address these problems.
- Most often the performance of these governance networks is suboptimal, as their emergent properties, structures and functions tend to arise organically, without the situational awareness of public managers responsible for their stewardship.
- Public managers may deepen their situational awareness by being able to gauge the substantive complexity inherent to the problems themselves, the strategic complexity inherent to the composition of the actors involved and the institutional complexity inherent in the prevailing rule structures and institutional norms.
- Such situational awareness can be used to design and govern more effective governance networks.

Questions for review and discussion

1   Think of a network of which you are a member (e.g. an association of sports clubs, your Facebook or Twitter account, an environmental lobbying network). Describe the network and how it functions by identifying who is involved, who has strong ties with whom and what members are after.
2   Does it have any characteristics of a complex adaptive system? To what extent do you think the members of this network can be influenced by 'strong leadership', as exercised by 'network managers'?
3   Take a wicked problem. Map out the range of actors involved in defining and solving the problem. Consider points of conflict that can arise among them. Can you also imagine their common interests? What strategies can be applied to enhance collaboration among them in order to address the problem? Assess their efficacy.

Reader exercises

1   From your experience, find examples of substantive complexity, strategic complexity and institutional complexity. What managerial strategies would you suggest for dealing with each of these examples?
2   Discuss how you would explore the success of the managerial strategies that you suggest in the previous exercise. How would you define success?

Class exercises

1   The class should select a topical policy issue. Working in groups of three or four, you should analyse the nature of the problem, why it is a problem, how it is caused and what the implications are. Who are affected, and who can affect the problem? What

can be done? How confident can you be in the success of the solutions you propose? In case different opinions exist, exchange arguments and try to get an understanding of alternative views on the topic.

2   In the class as a whole, each group should present its definition of the problem and its solutions. The class should discuss the differences and similarities between the various problem analyses and solutions presented. Do all definitions delineate the problem in the same way and see similar causes and implications? Do some problem definitions leave out some aspects of the problem? To what extent is knowledge claimed which is contestable? Consider the management strategies discussed in this chapter. What strategies would help to arrive at an agreement on what the problem is and how to deal with it?

Further reading

Eppel, E. A., & M. L. Rhodes (2018). Complexity theory and public management: A 'becoming' field. *Public Management Review*, 20(7), 949–959.

Head, B. W., & J. Alford (2015). Wicked problems: Implications for public policy and management. *Administration and Society*, 47(6), 711–739.

Koliba, C. (2013). Governance network performance: A complex adaptive systems approach. In R. Keast, M.P. Mandell, & R. Agranoff (Eds.), *Network Theory in the Public Sector*. Abington/New York: Routledge, pp. 98–116.

Koppenjan, J., & E. H. Klijn (2013). What can governance network theory learn from complexity theory? Mirroring two perspectives on complexity. In R. Keast, M.P. Mandell, & R. Agranoff (Eds.), *Network Theory in the Public Sector: Building New Theoretical Frameworks*. Abington/New York: Routledge, pp. 171–187.

References

Baumgartner, F. R., & B. Jones (2009). *Agendas and Instability in American Politics*. 2nd ed. Chicago, IL: University of Chicago Press.

Collins, H., & R. Evans (2007). *Rethinking Expertise*. Chicago, IL: The University of Chicago Press.

Endsley, M. R. (1995). Towards a theory of situational awareness in dynamic systems. *Human Factors*, 37(1), 32–64.

Fischer, F. (2003). *Reframing Public Policy: Discursive Politics and Deliberative Practices*. Oxford: Oxford University Press.

Granovetter, M. (1973). The strength of weak ties. *American Journal of Sociology*, 76(6), 1360–1380.

Holland, J. H. (2006). Studying complex adaptive systems. *Journal of Systems Science and Complexity*, 19(1), 1–8.

Hughes, O. (2012). *Public Management and Administration, An Introduction*. 4th ed. Basingstoke: Palgrave Macmillan.

Jacobs, J. (1992). *Systems of Survival*. Random House, Inc.

Klijn, E. H., & J. F. M. Koppenjan (2016). *Governance Networks in the Public Sector*. Abington/New York: Routledge.

Koliba, C., J. Meek, A. Zia, & R. Mills (2018). *Governance Networks in Public Administration and Public Policy*. 2nd ed. Boca Raton, FL: CRC Press/Taylor & Francis.

Levy, S. (1993). *Artificial Life: A Report from the Frontier Where Computers Meet Biology*. New York: Random House Inc.

Ostrom, E. (1990). *Governing the Commons. The Evolution of Institutions for Collective Action*. Cambridge: Cambridge University Press.

Rein, M., & D. A. Schön (1992). Reframing policy discourse. In F. Fischer & J. Forester (Eds.), *The Argumentative Turn in Policy Analysis and Planning*. Durham, NC: Duke University Press, pp. 145–166.

Rittel, H. W. J., & M. M. Webber (1973). Dilemmas in general theory of planning. *Policy Sciences*, 4(2), 155–169.

Tsebelis, G. (1990). *Nested Games: Rational Choice in Comparative Politics*. Berkeley, CA: University of California Press.

Watkins, M. (1999). Negotiating in a complex world. *Negotiation Journal*, 15(3), 245–270.

19 Innovation in public governance and management

Jacob Torfing

Introduction

This chapter explores the need for innovation in public governance and management and draws attention to some of the crucial innovations that we have seen in previous decades and that are likely to have a significant impact in coming years.

We focus in particular on innovations in the ways that public management and governance are practiced, rather than the specific social innovations and changes to public policy which result from these shifts in approach to public management and governance.

Learning objectives

This chapter will help readers to:

- Identify the key innovations in how public governance and public management have been considered and practiced over the past decades;
- Analyse the changing characteristics of the public sector which have shaped the kinds of innovations which have taken place; and
- Understand the drivers of innovation in the public domain.

The rise of the public governance orthodoxy and the need for innovation

This chapter looks at innovations in public governance and management. To provide a baseline against which to identify such innovations, it refers to the development of a public governance orthodoxy from the 1950s to the 1990s where liberal representative democracy and public bureaucracy were gradually supplemented by key elements of New Public Management such as the increased reliance on market governance and the introduction of performance management (Hood, 1991). Talking about public governance as an 'orthodoxy' serves to highlight the discursive embeddedness of the way governance is practiced in a particular period. An orthodoxy is a set of generally accepted ideas and practices that aspires to becoming an uncontested perspective (a 'totalizing discourse') that enjoys widespread support in spite of evidence that it does not always apply. Hence, a public governance orthodoxy can be defined as a hegemonic and relatively institutionalized discourse about how to govern and be governed.

Even the most entrenched public governance paradigm may be challenged by new events and developments, thus triggering innovations in governance and management. In times of

DOI: 10.4324/9781003282839-22

heightened societal turbulence, where unpredictable, uncertain, and changing events with inconsistent effects question the ability of the public sector to uphold its basic values, ambitions, and functions, we put a premium on stability and long for calm seas. However, the stable delivery of public service, regulation, and policy and the maintenance of social cohesion, democratic legitimacy, and trust in government often require changes in the way that service is delivered, society is governed, and the public sector is managed. We must change in order to preserve, and incremental changes aiming to foster continuous improvement will often prove insufficient. In short, we need to innovate when complex problems and challenges knock on our door.

This chapter aims to assess the need for innovation in public governance and management and to draw attention to some of the crucial innovations that we have seen in the last decade and that are likely to have a significant impact in coming years. There are many interesting 'first order' innovations in the public service, regulation, and policy that target individual citizens, private businesses, and local neighbourhoods. However, this chapter takes a 'second order view' on public sector innovation by looking at the innovations in public governance and management that condition these first order innovations which occur in the production of specific public services, regulation activities, and policy. This kind of second order innovation is less driven by popular needs and demands and more by political and administrative attempts to deal with emerging problems and challenges to public governance and to accomplish big societal missions such as putting an end to poverty or creating a more inclusive society.

Innovation is defined as the development and implementation of new and creative ideas and solutions that break with established practices and conventional thinking within a particular area (Torfing, 2016). Innovation may stem from the invention of entirely new and yet undiscovered solutions, or emerge as a result of the adoption and adaptation of solutions invented and tested elsewhere. Hence, if something appears to be new to the context in which it is implemented, it counts as an innovation. Although we sometimes encounter big bang innovations in the public sector that result from either a stroke of genius or a chance discovery, many innovations face political and administrative resistance, emerge in incomplete and embryonic forms, and take some time to mature and even longer to be considered as positive additions. The hesitant and gradual emergence and uptake of innovative solutions is explained by the institutional inertia and strong path-dependencies in the public sector characterized by centralized control, rule-following, and limited interorganizational competition (Pierson, 2000).

Although it sometimes takes time for new forms of governance and management to emerge and gain a foothold in the public sector, the public sector is perfectly capable of innovating itself. The traditional myth contrasting the dynamic and innovative private sector to the inert and ossified public sector has been effectively eliminated by the documentation of innovative capacities of the public sector (Ansell and Torfing, 2016). Still, the public sector has not yet become a serial innovator, permanently engaged in producing innovative solutions to challenges based on systematic methods and procedures and supported by an entrepreneurial learning culture.

Private firms are forced to innovate by fierce inter-firm competition. The public sector does not face noteworthy competitive pressures since it continues to have a near-monopoly on governance and regulation and the provision of public services, despite the recent spell of outsourcing. Nevertheless, innovations in governance and management are occurring, driven by emerging problems and challenges, along with big political and professional ambitions. We shall discuss five major governance and management innovations that have been underway for some time and are still developing, although unevenly across different countries. Two are related to governance, defined as the process through which actors aim to formulate and achieve common goals through different tools and mechanisms. Three other innovations are related to management, defined as the way that actors aim to achieve results with or through other actors. Each is illustrated by an empirical example.

From national government, via multilevel government, to multilevel governance

The Westphalian Peace Treaty of 1648 was a key point in the development of the international system of nation-states and triggered national efforts to form a protective army, link different parts of the national territory through a network of railroads, create an imagined national community, and improve the welfare of the population. In north-western Europe, North America, and the Antipodes, central government actors were in charge of developing and guiding Keynesian economic policies and social welfare policies that were pursued within a strategic framework provided by the relatively closed national economy and territorial boundaries of the state. Local and regional states were merely considered as vehicles of government policies and were not expected to make an independent contribution to public governance (Jessop, 2013).

The economic stagflation crisis from the 1970s onwards, and the demise of the Fordist system of mass production and mass consumption problematized the reign of the nation-state and put a squeeze on state finances. At the same time, the global circulation of goods, services, ideas, and policy agendas increased, and a new localism and regionalism emerged as people thought that their particular problems and needs were not properly dealt with by central government. Hence, a growing number of commentators thought that the nation-state had become too small to solve the world's big problems and too big to solve its little ones (Jessop, 2013). This recognition spurred the devolution of tasks to local and regional government and the growth of international collaboration. The nation-state aimed to stay in control by deciding what tasks and powers were to be shifted upwards and downwards. The predominance of intergovernmentalism in internal cooperation helped to ensure some degree of nation-state control. Interestingly, New Public Management (NPM) shaped the devolution of political and administrative competences by insisting on the formulation of national goals and targets that local and regional agencies had to meet. The neoliberal advocates of NPM also recommended that international markets be deregulated in order to avoid the creation of strong regulatory authorities beyond the nation-state. The result was the emergence of a system of multilevel government with a particular division of labour between different levels of government. The national system of governance and management was supplemented by new powers below and above it but could stay in control by building capacities to steer the other, partly competing, levels of governance.

The transformations in the 1980s and 1990s appear as a steppingstone to a major governance innovation that involves the formation of a complex system of multilevel governance, which went beyond the formal delegation of power to intergovernmental arenas and local and regional governments. Hence, multilevel governance facilitates relatively self-organized interactions between interdependent public and private actors at different levels and scales through crosscutting networks facilitating the uploading and downloading of policies (Tortola, 2017). These interactions may either be structured by formal and constitutional rules or may be a result of more flexible and adaptable ad hoc designs. While the European Union (EU) is clearly seen as the vanguard of the transformations described above, the concept of multilevel governance also seems to apply to governance transformations in other parts of the world and even in federal political systems (Tortola, 2017).

Within the EU, the Open Method of Coordination is a highly innovative way of governing policy areas where the EU cannot make binding decisions based on EU directives. The European active employment policy is a case in point. The Council of Ministers formulates some broad policy goals, and EU member states translate these supranational guidelines into national, regional, and local policies and use specific benchmarks and indicators to measure their performance against what is perceived as best practice. The results are reported back to the EU, which evaluates country performance and applies soft enforcement mechanisms such as 'naming and shaming' laggards. At all levels, social partners and civil society organizations collaborate with government actors to formulate, implement, evaluate, and revise the recommendations. This corporatist aspect of the system of multilevel governance helps to build a broad-based ownership of European-wide policies.

From unicentric governance, via market governance, to governance networks

In the post-1945 era, the fast-growing public sector was organized as a Weberian bureaucracy, based on a clear separation between politics and administration, centralized control in hierarchical organizations, horizontal specialization in line departments, implementation based on rule-following, and meritocratic recruitment of public administrators. In some countries, bureaucracy was combined with professional rule in decentralized welfare institutions where professionally trained public employees were given considerable autonomy in return for using their skills to produce high-quality services. The goal was to mass produce standardized services for growing and increasingly demanding populations. This goal was achieved through unicentric governance. Except for their participation in corporatist negotiations, private market actors played a limited role in public governance. Hence, the state was seen as the chief supplement and corrective to market forces within a mixed economy and civil society organizations were seen to have a limited impact beyond charity work.

The economic and fiscal crises in the 1970s and 1980s, combined with persistent criticisms of public bureaucracy for being too rigid, inefficient, and costly, paved the way for NPM reforms that aimed to replace bureaucratic control with efficiency-enhancing market governance combined with a new type of managerialism based on equal measures of deregulation, entrepreneurship, and performance management (Hood, 1991). The positive effects of the introduction of NPM-style public administration reforms include the new focus on producing results rather than slavishly following rules, the professionalization of public management, and the enhanced responsiveness to the demands of the service users. However, the gradual accumulation of unintended negative problems gradually eroded the political and administrative support for NPM. The creation of quasi-autonomous agencies and contracting out tended to enhance organizational fragmentation and the need for coordination. Control-based performance measurement crowded out the task motivation and public service motivation of public professionals. The competitive tendering of public services led to a race to the bottom, and the attempt to turn citizens into customers in newly created quasi-markets increased their service expectations and turned them into passive recipients with no obligation to contribute to service production. Finally, the attempt to run the public sector as a private enterprise based on competitive market governance undermined key public values such as transparency, legality, fairness, and equity.

In the last decade, the growing problems and broken promises of NPM have stimulated the search for alternative governance practices that can help to solve the problems associated with NPM by engaging a broad set of public and private actors in a coordinated and collaborative effort to tackle complex societal problems in innovative ways while building joint ownership over the new and bold solutions. Researchers all over the world have recommended a turn to collaborative governance (Emerson and Nabatchi, 2015) and network governance (Klijn and Koppenjan, 2015).

Collaborative governance involves affected actors in collaborative efforts to define common problems and develop and implement solutions that none of the actors could have produced alone. Trust-based collaboration between relevant and affected actors from the state, market, and civil society tends to stimulate knowledge-sharing, mutual learning, and creative problem solving and thus may produce innovative solutions that disrupt common wisdom and established practices. Finally, involving actors in collaborative problem solving tends to enhance the input and output legitimacy of public governance, because people feel that they have had a chance to influence outcomes and because the quality of the solutions is improved through problem-focused deliberation, scenario-building, and real-life testing of prototypes.

Collaborative governance takes place in and through networks and partnerships that bring together interdependent public and private actors in relatively self-organized governance processes through which resources are exchanged or pooled. Governance networks tend to be initiated and meta-governed by public authorities. They involve government agencies, private firms, interest organizations, and NGOs and tend to focus on interest mediation and policy alignment. However, some networks tend to become arenas for the co-creation of innovative solutions based on the involvement of a broader set of actors including users, citizens, and neighbourhoods in distributed actions – see Case Example 19.1.

Case Example 19.1 Governance networks to align private business actors with climate policy

In the city of Oslo in Norway, the Business for Climate Network involves almost 150 private businesses in achieving the locally formulated climate goals through the formation of a platform for joint problem solving and enhanced implementation capacity. Private businesses make either a basic level of commitment, where they meet a set of minimum criteria and the CEOs express their willingness to adjust their business model and operations to contribute achieving jointly formulated climate goals; or a more ambitious level, where they cut their own emissions and work to make other firms do the same. This illustrates how governance networks can help to mobilize resources and develop joint responsibility for policy implementation (Hofstad et al., 2021).

Source: The GREENGOV Project.

Governance networks may also spur the co-creation of environmental solutions. Inspired by programmes and campaigns launched by the government, the Youth Foundation of Bangladesh (YFB) has initiated an awareness raising and participatory action programme that seeks to reduce the catastrophic impact that single use plastic (SUP) from local water transport systems has on local rivers and marine life. YFB works closely with the local municipality, the city corporation, water transport lease-holders, and a range of businesses to create awareness amongst passengers of the environmental problems caused by SUP through information, signposting, and videos. It also tries to mitigate the problems by prompting relevant actors to provide additional waste bins, to keep launch areas and boats clean and tidy, to train transport personnel, and to monitor behaviour and results (United Nations SDG Partnership Platform, 2021).

From rule-based management, via result-driven management, to public value management

The rise of public bureaucracy was a gift to public governance and management that in the pre-bureaucracy period struggled with corruption, incompetence, nepotism, unequal treatment, and lack of predictability. Most of these problems were solved by the bureaucratization of the public sector, not least the new insistence that all administrative decisions should be based on written rules such as laws, executive orders, and administrative instructions and guidelines. Rule-following greatly improved administrative efficiency, since public employees no longer had to make an elaborate cost-benefit analysis every time they had to make a decision. Instead, they could identify, interpret, and apply the rules matching the situation in which they were placed. Over time, they would learn and internalize the rules and save lots of time making routinized decisions based on clear and legally valid instructions. Consequently, elected politicians could safely rely on the administrators to carry out political decisions and citizens were able to predict the result of public decisions.

However, this rule-based public sector soon became subject to fierce criticisms from public choice theorists, who accused the public sector of being rigid and inefficient and of delivering poor and costly services. Often, principal-agent theory was invoked to explain how self-interested public employees were capable of exploiting information asymmetries between themselves and their principal to act opportunistically, do less than expected of them, and spend more resources than necessary. The critics of bureaucracy compared the ossified and wasteful public sector to the flexible and efficient private sector. The frontal political attack on the public sector – epitomized by President Reagan's famous statement that 'government is not the solution, but the problem' – created an enduring inferiority complex within the public sector. Whereas the private sector was praised for its use of competition and innovation to produce private value for the customers and profit for the shareholders, public bureaucracy was depicted as an unimaginative and unproductive parasite, squandering value created by the wealth-producing private sector. Moreover, it was readily asserted that private contractors, in most cases, would be better at producing low-cost and high-quality services in response to the needs of private users, and that the implementation of a strict performance management system was necessary to secure goal attainment and reduce slack in public service organizations (Hood, 1991). Finally, public norms and values aiming to ensure the rules of law, equity, transparency, and accountability were depicted as red-tape rules preventing efficient problem solving and result-driven governance.

Against this background, the positive impact of the discovery and development of the public value perspective is self-evident. First, Mark Moore described the public sector as a unique type of organization with a distinct revenue source (taxation) and a distinct value form (public value) (Moore, 1995, 2000). Hence, instead of producing private value for a small group of shareholders, the public sector produces public value for specific groups of citizens and society at large.

Second, public managers are no longer portrayed as unimaginative and wasteful, but as imaginative explorers and entrepreneurs aiming to discover and define what would be valuable for the public sector to do to meet social needs and solve societal problems. Like managers in the private sector, public managers are inventive, well-intended, and mission-driven. As such, the public value perspective helps public managers to restore their self-worth as public managers (Rhodes and Wanna, 2007: 407).

Finally, the public value produced by public service organizations led by imaginative and proactive public managers is not supposed to be validated merely by individual consumers of innovative services, but is subject to democratic political debate between public managers, elected politicians, and relevant stakeholders, who jointly decide how the public sector shall contribute to public value creation.

While the strength of the public value perspective is that it revaluates the public sector, it has been criticized for being overly managerialist in praising the heroic actions of innovative public managers (Rhodes and Wanna, 2007). While this may be true, the public value perspective has been quite influential in the public sector in Australia, the Netherlands and North America, and some researchers have argued that it is a game changer because it opens up for appreciation how all kinds of public and private actors can contribute to public value creation in and through networks and partnerships (Stoker, 2006). For example, elected politicians may co-create public value together with public administrators and relevant and affected citizens – see Case Example 19.2

Case Example 19.2 Co-creation of public value is found in Gentofte Municipality, Denmark

Gentofte City Council has invented a new collaborative arena called a Task Committee, where typically five politicians and ten carefully selected citizens work together to solve pressing local problems assisted by three administrative facilitators and resource persons. For example, recently, a Task Committee was formed to develop a new youth policy that could help to improve the wellbeing of young people. It quickly became clear that the problems that the local youth were experiencing were different from what was originally thought, leading to the development of a rather innovative youth policy that was short and easy to read, and very different from what the council itself would have come up with. Two high school girls presented the new policy to the City Council, which was endorsed, and then toured schools and youth clubs to present it.

Source: Adapted from Sørensen and Torfing (2019).

From professional rule, via control-based management, to trust-based management

In response to the growth and appraisal of specialized professional knowledge in the modern welfare state, some public bureaucracies were supplemented by professional rule that assumes that well-educated professions such as doctors, nurses, school teachers, accountants, engineers etc., equipped with professional norms and specialized forms of knowledge should be trusted to govern themselves (Byrkeflot, 2011). Public professions are characterized by strong control over the entrance to the group, strong professional norms regulating the behaviour of professional individuals, and highly specialized knowledge about how to do things that outsiders have great difficulties understanding and assessing. This creates a huge dilemma for elected politicians and the generalist managers: They cannot control the professional service production, but the voters still hold them accountable for its availability and its quality. This dilemma can be solved by striking a tacit deal with public sectors professionals – the professions carry out their work in a self-managed way within an overall framework of centrally determined legal rules, public standards, and budgetary constraints.

Byrkeflot (2011) claims that NPM threatens the traditional forms of professional rule. For example, principal-agent theory questions the Weberian idea of public employees using their professional skills in a norm-based pursuit of public interests and the greater good. Instead, it paints a picture of self-serving public professions exploiting information asymmetries to engage in shirking. In this view, public employees cannot be trusted to do good work if they are not steered by clear goals and targets, constantly monitored, and assessed, and subjected to conditional rewards and punishment.

NPM adds a new layer of control-based performance management to an already existing layer of rule-based bureaucratic control, and the two forms of control seem to interact and construct a hybrid form of governance in the shape of a 'death spiral' where performance measurement results in the identification of problems, which leads to the formulation of new rules that stimulate further measurement of compliance, etc. The result is that frontline staff have little room for applying their energy, skills, and knowledge in the pursuit of continuous improvement and/or radical innovation of public services and in the development of empowering relations with users and stakeholders. Fortunately, the control-based approach and its foundation in principal-agent theory has been challenged by stewardship theory that supports the development of innovative forms of trust-based management (Torfing and Bentzen, 2020). Stewardship theory claims that public leaders and frontline staff share more or less the same policy goals and are driven by the same motivation to provide high-quality solutions that benefit citizens and society at large (Schillemans, 2008). As such, it is reasonable to expect nurses to be motivated by improving public health, elderly care assistants to be driven by the ambition to provide a dignified life for the elderly, schoolteachers to want to improve the writing and reading skills of their pupils, and social workers to strive to enhance the employability of the unemployed.

The potential agreement on goals between public leaders and public employees transforms the role of public managers from controllers ensuring compliance to partners in a trust-based and learning-focused dialogue with their employees about the organizational visions, goals, tools, and experiences – see Case Example 19.3. This dialogue calls for a combination of 'servant leadership', aiming to promote the self-development of employees, transformational leadership aiming to give direction to their efforts, and horizontal and distributed leadership facilitating team-based self-regulation. In sum, stewardship theory creates a foundation for rethinking and redesigning public management based on a trust relation between public leaders and employees, empowering the latter to collaborate in self-managing teams engaged in continuous improvement and creative innovation practices which influence the strategic decisions in the organization.

Case Example 19.3 Trust-based management in the Job and Activity Centre, Denmark

The Job and Activity Centre (JAC) organizes all of its employees in self-managing teams responsible for work planning, trouble-shooting, and recruitment, with their own local budget and power to decide on wages and bonuses. They contribute to strategic decisions through plenary debates and sometimes even through voting. JAC has reduced costs, enhanced the wellbeing of employees, and brought exceedingly high user satisfaction. It has won 'Best Workplace in Europe' several times (Bentzen and Torfing, 2020).

From bureaucratic management, via relational coordination, to mobilization leadership

The administrative staff in public bureaucracies are supposed to choose the most effective means for achieving political goals and then dutifully follow the new administrative rules, on pain of sanctions if they deviate. NPM gives public managers a more proactive role in leading their staff and organization, since, as we have seen, public employees are seen to be utility maximizing and, therefore, cannot be trusted to deliver effective and efficient solutions. Public managers are supposed to have all the knowledge and insight they need to manage their employees and incentivize their performance. They are expected to excise transactional leadership based on the conditional sanctioning of behaviour and results – and this is mainly within their own organization.

The intraorganizational management practices of professional public managers may boost productivity in public service organizations, but they are insufficient in the face of the dire need to deal with crosscutting societal problems and the ambition to deliver integrated and seamless services to citizens. Problems such as health pandemics and climate change cut across administrative units and call for interorganizational collaboration. Likewise, citizens with multiple problems should receive an integrated and well-coordinated service package, instead of facing a fragmented landscape of disjointed services and action plans sponsored by different agencies. The need to overcome the compartmentalization and fragmentation of public sector has led politicians to call for more 'joined-up' government. According to Pollitt (2003), joined-up government aspires to achieve horizontal as well as vertical coordination to eliminate inter-agency tensions, make better use of scarce resources, create synergies between free-flowing ideas and solutions, and provide citizens with more seamless service offers. Joined-up government prompts the development of new forms of interorganizational management that can help to facilitate interaction and build trust-based collaboration. In the public sector, there has been a growing appreciation of 'relational coordination', defined as a high-intensity communication enabling public stakeholders to effectively coordinate their work across boundaries. Theories of relational coordination argue that interorganizational collaboration requires the orchestration of frequent, timely, accurate, problem-solving communication based on shared goals, shared knowledge, and mutual respect between the involved actors.

While relational coordination helps to mobilize resources from different parts of the public sector, it remains focused on the public sector – an inward-looking form of public management that fails to reap the fruits of cross-sector collaboration with social and economic actors. This is highly problematic, as the public sector gets caught in a crossfire between growing citizens' expectations and scarce public resources. Citizens increasingly expect the public sector to deliver tailor-made high-quality services and to solve all kinds of problems from street crime and traffic congestion to climate change and the integration of immigrants. At the same time, there are limited public resources and no political will to raise taxes. One solution is to mobilize the resources of actors from the economy and civil society, recognizing that a growing number of citizens around the world are sufficiently competent, resourceful, and energetic to participate in networks and partnerships and co-produce and co-create solutions (Bovaird and Loeffler, 2021). This calls for a new type of mobilization leadership that starts by identifying a problem, task, or challenge and then convenes relevant and affected actors, spurs collaborative innovation, and tracks results (Torfing, 2016). Mobilization leadership highlights that public leadership not only involves a strategic effort to engage, inspire, and activate public and private actors possessing relevant assets including legitimacy, authority, ideas, and capabilities, but also seeks to align their understandings of what is valuable for the public – see Case Example 19.4.

Case Example 19.4 Mobilization leadership to achieve the UN's Sustainable Development Goals

In order to spur creative problem solving, and to build shared ownership of new and bold solutions, the Indonesian government sponsored a local peat restoration programme. In the process, it discovered that trust building and community participation were the critical factors for ensuring local support, which ultimately led to the programme's success (Moalliemi et al., 2020). Support from local residents was also a crucial factor in the small community of Feldheim, Germany, which succeeded in transitioning to 100% renewable energy. The success of the local de-carbonization programme has been attributed to the fact that citizens and the local government developed joint ownership of the green transition project (Young and Brans, 2017).

The drivers of innovations in public governance and management

Public governance and management have become increasingly politicized. Both the British PM Margaret Thatcher and the US president Ronald Reagan campaigned on a critique of classical bureaucracy and recommended the introduction of NPM reforms. Today, where the criticism of the public governance orthodoxy is mounting, governments, researchers, and think tanks are busy developing new ideas about how to govern and be governed in the future. The window of opportunity for innovation in public governance and management has opened.

Public leaders are frequently celebrated as the key drivers of governance and management reform. This is supported by the fact that newly appointed public leaders are often busy trying to demonstrate their resolve by embarking on governance and management reforms providing an idiosyncratic version of the current fad and fashion. However, successive top-down reforms seldom have any noteworthy impact beyond the production of reform fatigue. They tend to remain paper strategies, since there is no attempt to generate support from the rank and file (Ferlie and Ongaro, 2015).

By contrast, genuine governance and management innovation seems to be propelled by collaboration between manifold actors, including elected politicians, civil servants, policy analysts, researchers, consultancy firms, interest organizations, etc. Innovation is not driven by lone wolves but is a team sport, based on collective wisdom and 'swarm creativity'. Sustained interaction between diverse actors, who have different perspectives but a shared interest in solving a particular problem, facilitates the development of a nuanced problem diagnosis; the circulation, enrichment, and critical scrutiny of new ideas; the selection, testing, and revision of promising solutions; and the formation of a change coalition that can garner support for the implementation of new forms of governance and management (Torfing, 2016). The implementation of reform proposals resulting from collaboration may sometimes appear rather top-down and bureaucratic. However, implementation often requires critically important translation work, based on dialogue between administrative staff at different levels and in different units.

Public sector reforms aiming to spur governance and management innovation often build on a complex interaction between upstream and downstream actors. Central governments may form broad-based task forces that develop new and promising ideas that subsequently are tested in and through local experiments and then scaled if the positive expectations are confirmed. Sometimes, however, the innovation impulse come from local entrepreneurs who begin to do things in a new way in response to persistent problems and challenges and based on the translation of new global ideas and trends to the local level. These local changes may eventually form emerging patterns that are identified, evaluated, embraced, and given direction by public leaders at the apex of government, who finally broadcast the new ideas as official policy (Ferlie and Ongaro, 2015).

Public governance and management reform may emerge in a particular organization, sector, or country and then spread to other countries through isomorphic pressures that exploit the fact that many public organizations seek to appear legitimate by means of copying the governance and management practices of other similar organizations, responding to the recommendations of higher level authorities and getting inspiration from newly educated staff members who are supposed to know the latest organizational fashion.

In times of change where new distributed innovations emerge and begin to spread, there is an urgent need for a positive public administration that aims to identify promising new governance and management practices and seeks to scrutinize, conceptualize, and enlarge them. Hence, rather than looking for errors and things to criticize, we must look for new pioneering governance and management innovations, evaluate their impact, analyse the conditions for their success, and spread the news about how problems can be solved by adopting and adapting the new practices.

Summary

The impact of the kind of governance and management innovations described in this chapter is difficult to measure since, frequently, changing the existing forms of governance and management will not appear to have any direct effect on the efficiency, effectiveness, and quality of public sector. That said, it is important to recognize that second order innovations in governance and management will tend to have an indirect effect as they tend to create and improve the conditions for the improvement of and/or innovation in public service, regulation, and policy. Hence, the governance and management innovations described above are 'generative' innovations, as they tend to generate possibilities for spurring first order innovation in public services, regulatory regimes, and policy programmes.

In a turbulent world where everything solid melts into air, we will most likely see a dramatic increase in governance and management innovation because unpredictable social, economic, and political dynamics will tend to prompt institutional and practical changes to preserve goals, values, and functionalities that are deemed fundamental to the public sector but are threatened by new tumultuous events. This development calls for further studies of the emerging innovations in governance and management, the formative processes, and the impact of second order innovation on first order innovation.

Questions for review and discussion

1 What is the difference between 'first order' and 'second order' innovations? Which do you think is the harder type of innovation to achieve effectively?
2 Identify five major innovations which have occurred in the public sector in your country in the past three years and five major innovations which have occurred in the private sector in that time. What do you think this comparison says about the relative capacity of each sector to be innovative?

Reader exercises

1 Compare how two public agencies with which you are familiar (e.g. your local authority and your local hospital) have dealt with the COVID pandemic. What innovations have occurred in the way in which these public agencies have dealt with (a) local citizens, (b) local businesses and their staff, and (c) other public agencies in their area? Which agency do you consider has been the most successful in choosing effective innovations to rise to the challenges of the pandemic?
2 How would you propose to raise the level of innovativeness in the local authority and the hospital which you considered in Reader Exercise 1?

Class exercise

1 In the class, break into small groups. In each group, gather evidence from local newspapers and websites about innovative proposals from public service organizations in your area which have failed to be implemented. Compile a list of obstacles which appear to explain these failures. Compare these lists in the plenary session.

Further reading

Ferlie, E. & Ongaro, E. (2015). *Strategic Management in Public Services Organizations: Concepts, Schools and Contemporary Issues.* Abingdon: Routledge.
Torfing, J. (2016). *Collaborative Innovation in the Public Sector.* Washington, DC: Georgetown University Press.
Torfing, J. & Triantafillou, P. (Eds.). (2016). *Enhancing Public Innovation by Transforming Public Governance.* Cambridge: Cambridge University Press.

References

Ansell, C. & Torfing, J. (Eds.). (2016). *Handbook on Theories of Governance.* Cheltenham: Edward Elgar.

Bovaird, T. & Loeffler, E. (2021). Developing Evidence-Based Co-production: A Research Agenda. In Loeffler, E. & Bovaird, T. (Eds.), *The Palgrave Handbook of Co-production of Public Services and Outcomes* (pp. 693–713). Cham: Palgrave Macmillan.

Byrkjeflot, H. (2011). Healthcare States and Medical Professions: The Challenges from NPM. In Christensen, T. & Lægreid, P. (Eds.), *The Ashgate Research Companion to New Public Management* (pp. 147–160). London: Routledge.

Emerson, K. & Nabatchi, T. (2015). *Collaborative Governance Regimes.* Washington, DC: Georgetown University Press.

Hofstad, H., Sørensen, E., Torfing, J. and Vedeld, T. (2023). Leading co-creation for the green shift, *Public Money & Management*, 43:4, 357–366.

Hood, C. (1991). A Public Management for All Seasons? *Public Administration* 69: 3–19.

Jessop, B. (2013). Hollowing Out the "Nation-State" and Multi-level Governance. In Kennett, P. (Ed.), *A Handbook of Comparative Social Policy*. Cheltenham: Edward Elgar, pp. 11–26.

Klijn, E. H. & Koppenjan, J. (2015). *Governance Networks in the Public Sector*. Abingdon: Routledge.

Moallemi, E. A., Malekpour, S., Hadjikakou, M., Raven, R., Szetey, K., Ningrum, D., Dhiaulhaq, A. & Bryan, B. A. (2020). Achieving the Sustainable Development Goals Requires Transdisciplinary Innovation at the Local Scale. *One Earth*, 3(3), 300–313.

Moore, Mark H. (1995). *Creating public value*. Cambridge, MA: Harvard University Press.

Moore, Mark H. (2000), *Creating Public Value: Strategic Management in Government*, 5th ed. Cambridge: Harvard University Press.

Pierson, P. (2000). Increasing Returns, Path Dependence, and the Study of Politics. *American Political Science Review*, 94(2), 251–267.

Pollitt, C. (2003). Joined-Up Government: A Survey. *Political Studies Review*, 1(1), 34–49.

Rhodes, R. A. W. & Wanna, J. (2007). The Limits to Public Value, or Rescuing Responsible Government from the Platonic Guardians. *Australian Journal of Public Administration*, 66(4), 406–421.

Schillemans, Thomas (2008). Accountability in the Shadow of Hierarchy: The Horizontal Accountability of Agencies. *Public Organizations Review* 8: 175–94.

Sørensen, E. & Torfing, J. (2019). Designing Institutional Platforms and Arenas for Interactive Political Leadership. *Public Management Review*, 21(10), 1443–1463.

Stoker, G. (2006). Public Value Management: A New Narrative for Networked Governance? *The American Review of Public Administration*, 36(1), 41–57.

Torfing, J. (2016). *Collaborative Innovation in the Public Sector*. Washington, DC: Georgetown University Press.

Torfing, J. & Bentzen, T. Ø. (2020). Does Stewardship Theory Provide a Viable Alternative to Control-Fixated Performance Management? *Administrative Sciences*, 10(4), 86.

Tortola, P. D. (2017). Clarifying Multilevel Governance. *European Journal of Political Research*, 56(2), 234–250.

United Nations SDG Partnership Platform. (2021). https://sustainabledevelopment.un.org/partnership. Accessed August 22, 2021.

Young, J. & Brans, M. (2017). Analysis of Factors Affecting a Shift in a Local Energy System Towards 100% Renewable Energy Community. *Journal of Cleaner Production*, 169, 117–124.

20 E-governance

Concept, practice and ethics

Arman Behrooz and Albert Meijer

Introduction

Governments have arrived in the information age: Around the world they have transformed from paper-based bureaucracies to high-tech organizations. New technologies play a key role in internal processes (such as financial management) and external processes (such as service provision). Information and communication technologies are also increasingly used to support networked governance interactions in a variety of policy domains. Collaboration between the variety of public and private actors involved in urban governance, and also citizens and community groups, is increasingly supported by 'smart' technologies such as Internet platforms, sensor networks and collective databases, as in Barcelona – see Box 20.1.

Box 20.1 Barcelona: Digital platform for collaboration with citizens

Barcelona uses technology for knowledge exchange with and between citizens. *Decidim* (https://www.decidim.barcelona) is a digital platform through which residents may consider and directly decide on ideas, budgets and municipal plans, using computational features such as discussion threads. The *Metadecidim* lab provides a platform for collective learning and adaptation. *Metadecidim* examines *Decidim*'s usage trends and considers design modifications, institutional applications and new methods to connect the platform to other urban democracy-enhancing activities. Open development sessions are hosted on *Metadecidim*, where developers and democracy advocates cooperate to develop new ideas and ways to engage citizens (Smith & Martin, 2020).

While there has been a lot of research on e-government with a focus on internal government processes and government services, our academic understanding of e-governance as the transformation of governance interactions through the use of new information and communication technologies is still limited. This chapter aims to provide the reader with a conceptual and empirical understanding of the emerging field of e-governance.

Specifically, this chapter will answer the questions 'what is e-governance in theory' and 'how does e-governance manifest itself in practice'. A key point is that, while there are many practical advantages to using ICTs for governance processes, there are also many administrative, political, ethical and operational implications to consider. This means that e-governance demands the attention of not only information engineers and 'techies' but also of governance specialists. For this reason, e-governance as a field of expertise requires

DOI: 10.4324/9781003282839-23

interdisciplinary research across public management, public governance and computer sciences in order to ensure that e-governance supports the creation of equitable, collaborative and effective use of ICTs in public and private service delivery networks, as well as initiatives to solve contemporary social problems.

The chapter begins by providing a conceptual understanding of what e-governance is by discussing key definitions and outlining its historical progression. Subsequently, we analyse the value of e-governance based on two examples, namely smart cities and the COVID-19 pandemic. Finally, we discuss the ethical concerns that come with ICT usage by public service organizations. The chapter ends with conclusions and recommendations to policy makers and academics.

Learning objectives

After studying this chapter, you should understand:

- How e-governance has been shaped both by changing perspectives on government and new technological developments
- The main differences between e-government and e-governance
- How smart city governance has become a key manifestation of e-governance at the local level in order to tackle urban problems
- How COVID-19 stimulated governments around the world to develop innovative forms of e-governance to manage the crisis
- Ethical risks related to e-governance and how they can be minimized

What is e-governance?

In order to understand the term 'e-governance' (electronic governance), we first dissect and classify its two parts – 'electronic', and 'governance'.

- 'Electronic' can simply refer to technology, particularly communication and information technologies, such as web portals, social media applications, mobile phone applications or digital databases, etc. The ongoing technological dynamic keeps producing new technologies, such as algorithms and the Internet-of-Things.
- 'Governance' is the way an organization works with its partners, stakeholders and networks to influence the outcomes of public policies (see Chapter 15). The term governance highlights that governments need to collaborate with external stakeholders to solve societal problems. In e-governance, technologies are used to support these networked collaborations.

The term e-governance, then, entails a model of governance that seeks to utilize processes and structures to harness the potentialities of ICTs at various levels of government, working with partners, stakeholders and networks, including different sectors, in order to influence the outcomes of public policies (Saxena, 2005). Thus, we present the following definition:

E-governance is a combination of the process-oriented framework of governance, which considers duties, stakeholders and power dynamics, and information and communication technologies, which support and strengthen information and communications processes between multiple actors.

E-governance emerged over the past decade as a key domain of technology in the public sector. Globalization, liberalization, state reforms and technical advancements are just a few of the forces that later combined to strengthen the capabilities of ICTs for governance processes. Complex problems and the need to improve administration by modifying it at a systems level require effective e-governance (see Box 20.2).

Box 20.2 E-government (and how it is different from e-governance)

Building on the principles of New Public Management (NPM), e-government emerged as a way to improve the efficiency of public services for citizens and business and to strengthen the international coordination of government transactions such as international taxation. E-government allows public service providers to deliver public services and information electronically, enables online payments and applications and helps to streamline government processes and internal information exchange through ICTs (Saxena, 2005). As a result of e-government, transactions between government agencies (G2G), government and business (G2B) and government and citizens (G2C) are supposed to become more convenient, transparent and less costly. Moreover, e-government provides an alternative approach to government administration and service delivery and redefines the way in which governments interact with citizens and business. While e-governance has a wider focus on networked collaborations, e-government has a narrower focus on service delivery.

Access to open data is generally considered to be a core component of e-governance. Governments make data available on topics as diverse as land use, the performance of schools and urban safety. This data is used by individual citizens but also by companies, citizen groups and journalists for a variety of uses. Citizens can push for better school performance, companies can use weather data to develop commercial applications and journalists can use data on service procurement and political interactions to expose corruption. This variety of uses highlights how open data infrastructures can transform the process of governance into a more open process where information resources are used by a variety of actors for all kinds of different functions. Open data opens up the playing field of governance and can contribute significantly to the democratic process (see Box 20.3). At the same time, the potential for abuse of the technologies enabling e-governance requires vigilance and appropriate safeguards (see Box 20.4).

Box 20.3 From e-democracy to open governance

Since the 1980s, the promise of ICTs for strengthening democracy has been discussed. Technologies can be used to support democratic meetings and electoral processes. Webinars and online platforms for citizen engagement and citizens polls have come to play a growing role, especially in local democracy around the world. At the same time, the realization of this promise has been slow and most democratic processes still rely on old fashioned paper-based systems and in-person meetings. The Netherlands even decided to stop using voting machines after citizen groups had indicated that this was not a safe and secure system. More recently, authors have witnessed a next generation of e-democracy practices with a focus on open governance. In these new forms of citizen engagement, citizens are directly involved in solving societal problems by, for example, generating data about traffic jams or environmental pollution. Meijer, Lips and Chen (2019) even argue:

> The introduction of new tools for open collaboration in the public domain is rapidly changing the way collaborative action is organized. These technologies reduce the transaction costs for massive collaboration dramatically and facilitate new forms of collaboration that we could call 'open governance': new innovative forms of collective action aimed at solving complex public policy issues, contributing to public knowledge, or replacing traditional forms of public service provision.

Box 20.4 Governance *with* and *of* ICTs

While recent advances in ICT have created the need for e-governance, it is important to remember that there also comes a need for better governance of these technologies. Governance of ICTs is best encompassed by the term 'ICT governance', which is different from e-governance or governance with ICTs, which is the central focus of this chapter. ICT governance focuses solely on how ICT resources should be established, used and managed, whereas e-governance aims to use ICTs to alter governance processes and create new governance structures.

E-governance in smart cities

The previous sections have presented a conceptual understanding of e-governance. But what does it mean in practice? This section will focus on the smart city – an urban environment where technologies are used for multi-actor governance and services – as a key example of e-governance.

In 2022, 55% of the world's population lives in cities, with 80% of global GDP being generated in metropolises (World Bank, 2020). Therefore, developing urban e-governance solutions for tackling challenges related to urban life and the complex networks of ICT stakeholders becomes ever more important. Urban informatics is the study of urban issues using a data science framework with the purpose of resolving such challenges. Similar to policy informatics, urban informatics is interdisciplinary in its nature and aims to use new sources of data to improve operational decisions in governance and examine the use of ICTs in creating smart cities (Kontokosta, 2021).

The use of urban informatics is best seen in city planning (see Boxes 20.5–20.8). For example, in order to better analyse transportation routes and zoning/development recommendations, urban planners can employ geo-tagged social media data to produce population estimates and time dependent mobility behaviour. Another example is the use of video camera data, such as pedestrian counts or situation awareness and anomaly detection, to better understand city dynamics such as pedestrian behaviour (Kontokosta, 2021). The fundamental benefit of urban informatics is that it contributes to participatory planning processes through improved communication technologies. Specifically, by creating online platforms that enable feedback from local stakeholders, planners are able to understand and address grassroots requirements, creating a transparent and collaborative governance process.

Urban informatics contributes to what Meijer (2017) refers to as the 'datapolis', defined as the complex set of relations between the political communities of citizens and urban infrastructures. This perspective examines the roles and impacts of new technologies on the strategic interactions of different actors, as the best way to understand urban governance and to stimulate citizen engagement. In particular, initiatives such as open data can empower disadvantaged groups to bolster their political position. Furthermore, the datapolis imagines data infrastructures not as neutral tools but as mechanisms that can stimulate emergent structures for solving urban problems and improving the governance of citizens.

Box 20.5 Living Lab Stratumseind (Eindhoven, Netherlands)

The creation of the 'smart street' in the city of Eindhoven's entertainment area, called Stratumseind, is a real-world example of the certain benefits that e-governance can provide to cities. Stratumseind 2.0 was a collaboration between the local and municipal government, Eindhoven University of Technology, Philips's lighting company, local citizens of Stratumseind and businesses in the area. The smart street consists of a variety of technologies such as data from visual and auditive sensors, Wi-Fi points, social media sensoring, datasets about traffic and parking and private data from mobile telephones. A notable technology tested in this project is the 'smart lights' developed by Philips. Smart lights change colour and intensity depending on the nature of their surroundings (namely, time of day and number of people around them) with the aim of changing the atmosphere in the street and reducing aggression and violence in the area (for example, blue light can reduce people's heart rates, which is useful for reducing aggression). This project transformed Stratumseind into a 'quantified street', as ICT infrastructures collect large amounts of data that can inform goals/indicators for making the area safer and more attractive, with consequent economic development benefits.

Source: Meijer and Thaens (2016).

Box 20.6 Padova Smart City (Italy)

The collaboration between the University of Padova, the municipality of Padova and Patavina Technologies (a spin-off of the university) formed the basis for Padova Smart City. Technologies allowed them to collect environmental data and monitor public street lighting via wireless nodes equipped with sensors installed inside streetlight poles. This public-private partnership resulted in the collection of data on air quality, noise and vibrations, as well as a simple mechanism for ensuring the proper operation of the public lighting system. Furthermore, the data from these streetlamps led to the revelation that rainstorms temporarily obscure sunlight and induce traffic gridlock, which in turn produces pollution from idle automobiles. This discovery then informed future energy policy in the city.

Source: Zanella et al. (2014).

Box 20.7 Environmentally conscious transportation (Seattle)

Since the 1990s Seattle has experienced a significant intake of tech companies, which have been responsible for changes in tax laws, cost of living, housing market regulation and land development in the city (McGraw, 2021). Seattle's mass incorporation of tech companies into the city landscape began with Paul Allen, Microsoft's co-founder, who purchased a large piece of land in South Lake Union and developed it into a tech and life sciences cluster, which is now home to Amazon's headquarters and other tech firms, furthermore creating a strong collaborative regional innovation system (McGraw, 2021). With the aim of solving growing urban problems in the city, tech companies (such as Google, Microsoft and Tesla) have continually been invited to a City of Seattle roundtable to discuss the incorporation of new technology and data infrastructure to solve complex urban issues at technical, ethical and policy levels. The result of this e-governance contribution to the development of the city is best demonstrated through the new environmentally conscious Seattle transportation system, particularly the bike sharing service. Furthermore, the City of Seattle practices e-governance principles. The city's direct collaboration with these companies, and its encouragement of their collaboration with each other, demonstrates its appreciation of collective problem solving in this 'datafied' city.

Source: McGraw (2021).

Box 20.8 Citizens producing and generating urban data

While most analyses focus on governments producing and making data available, citizens also develop their own forms of data generation and management. A well-known example is Waze, a platform used to exchange information about traffic jams so that citizen can avoid them. Citizens produce and use the data and develop collective ways to use road infrastructures optimally by taking different routes or travelling at different times. The success of this platform also heralded its downfall – Waze proved so successful that Google bought the app and it now no longer exists as an independent citizen initiative.

Several critical analyses have highlighted the 'dark side' of the smart city. This can arise, for example, from citizens' loss of privacy through 24/7 surveillance, or from being subject to algorithms with biases and limitations that generate technological discrimination, or from facing unreliable technologies which generate unstable environments. More generally, this 'dark side' of the smart city consists of a loss of influence by citizens on the direct environment in which they live and work. Doorman and Poli (2021) argue that tech companies and policy makers are mistaken when they frame their use of smart technology as apolitical and beneficial for all of society. They emphasize that the very use of ICTs in a safety and security context permits the creation of boundaries between what/who is acceptable and what/who is 'dangerous', which is a socially constructed classification system that risks further perpetuating social inequalities, stigmatization and exclusion. In order to avoid the over-simplification of social life into questionable patterns, the authors take an e-governance stance in advocating that public institutions should adopt ethical regulations for the development of smart cities and resist prioritizing 'market objectives' (e.g. commercial benefits).

The rise of the smart city has often been connected to neo-liberal models in which the power of the state is reduced and corporate interests – connected to tech companies and companies that build their business models on new technologies – dominate the management of urban environments. In a very different context, smart city approaches have been promoted by authoritarian regimes that build environments for total surveillance. Both extremes, the market-driven smart city and the authoritarian smart city, have been presented as dystopian futures – clearly, using technology is not without risk. This highlights the need to position the smart city in democratic and collaborative models of governance, which Meijer (2017: 198) conceptualizes as the 'datapolis', recognizing how the complex set of relations between political communities of citizens and data infrastructures managed to create public value rather than dystopian outcomes.

Viewing Eindhoven, Padova, Barcelona and Seattle as examples of a datapolis helps us to understand how data infrastructure and technology can be embedded in strong democratic processes and can create public value through such mechanisms as regional innovation systems, citizen participation and improved policy formulation, while avoiding the risks of the 'dark side'.

E-governance for COVID-19 crisis management

A second example of the practice of e-governance can be found in the responses to the COVID-19 pandemic. The pandemic required a variety of new government strategies and collaborations but, at the same time, physical contacts needed to be kept at a minimum. The pandemic also highlighted the need for massive testing and for rapidly collecting, exchanging and visualizing information on dissemination patterns of COVID-19. Research on the pandemic has illustrated the rapid rise of the use of e-governance for crisis management, both in highly developed countries and in peripheral and semi-peripheral countries.

The pandemic resulted in 'hard' and 'soft' responses. Hard responses focus on monitoring patterns of infection to act directly on citizen movements. For example, Pakistan's implementation of the Geo-Tracking app, and the wide consensus on its use, helped the government to keep track of infected individuals and alerted authorities and residents when they came into contact with others (Ullah et al., 2020). Soft responses involved using digital technologies to keep society going and to provide services. Ullah et al. (2020) note that electronic identity record keeping has revolutionized the ability of governments worldwide to facilitate social services. Furthermore, virtual education and health services were developed in order to reduce the spread of COVID-19. Reaping the benefits of establishing e-services in different sectors and investing in the telecommunications sector since 2002, the Pakistan government was able to respond to COVID-19 more effectively than many of its neighbouring countries.

An overview of the variety of functions of ICTs for COVID-19 crisis management is provided by Meijer and Webster's (2020) study of 21 countries:

- Hard responses
  - Management of information for crisis management
  - Monitoring citizens in public space
- Soft responses
  - Publishing public information for citizens
  - Providing digital services to citizens
  - Facilitating information exchange between citizens

These functions are all connected and interlinked. Successful governments have found ways to combine these functions to make a significant contribution to public health policies – see Box 20.9.

Box 20.9 *Health Code* in China

An e-governance initiative related to the COVID-19 crisis that has proved to be useful – but which has also been criticized – is the Chinese digital contact tracing smartphone programme, *Health Code*. As a mini app embedded in Alipay and WeChat, *Health Code* used citizens' personal information and data collected from public services (specifically ICT providers) to calculate the level of virus risk and then assigned to each individual a coloured QR code that changed depending on their infection status. Essentially, these codes were mandatory for utilizing public amenities, such as public transportation. What differentiated this from the widely used 'vaccine-passport' was that citizens were constantly updating and announcing their infection status to those near them. In addition, their movements, namely where they have had contact with other people, were reported to the government. This quasi-mandatory programme embraced a preventative philosophy in that it evaluated a variety of data to determine the probability of an individual being infected and supported macro-preventative measures enforced by the Chinese government (e.g. lockdown) by using near real-time aggregated data as a basis for policy measures.

Health Code is an interesting case because it demonstrates that the success of e-governance can depend very much on the context in which it is being utilized. Although the programme emerged out of the need to prevent COVID-19 infection, its acceptance and implementation amongst a multitude of stakeholders can be accredited to the socio-political context of China. The social imposition of the *Health Code*, according to Cong (2021), supports the transformation of Chinese society's governance through ICTs by combining mass monitoring and basic public service provision. Additionally, years of close alliance between the government and private digital companies (Alibaba and Tencent) allowed this mass mobilization strategy. Specifically, because of the lack of a boundary between public and private stakeholders, and a relative lack of resistance from citizens, *Health Code* could be executed effectively. Although *Health Code* succeeded in the Chinese context, if it were implemented in other parts of the world, such as North America or Europe, Cong (2021) believes there would almost certainly be opposition from citizen and interest-groups. This is because of cultural differences between the two regions – in particular, privacy is a higher priority for citizens in North America and parts of Europe.

E-governance responses have demonstrated that established e-governance structures, such as digital services, electronic identity record keeping and the nature of relations between stakeholders, can support the crisis management of governments and can form the basis for both 'hard responses'(containing the pandemic) and 'soft responses' (facilitating the continuation of other public functions). In other words, the sooner that governments and private organizations consider the duties, stakeholders and power dynamics involved in ICT implementation, the sooner they will be able to establish structures that are functional enough to deal with crises such as global pandemics. However, different regions will respond to ICT-induced solutions differently, hence tailoring solutions to the socio-economic, political and legal context of regions is important.

Ethical issues in e-governance

The two examples above – urban informatics and information for managing the COVID-19 crisis – present interesting perspectives on the value of e-governance for tackling societal problems but also touch upon a range of sensitive issues related to privacy, solidarity, non-discrimination, human contact and many more. It is important to note that some scholars believe that we do not fully realize the implications of the use of data infrastructure, and its ability to reinforce social inequality. For these reasons, we need to discuss the ethics of e-governance.

The oldest ethical concern in e-governance – and also e-government – is the digital divide, which means that only certain citizens have the opportunities and skills to access e-services and to take part in digital forms of collaboration. The 'have nots' will then be excluded from a variety of services and interactions. This digital divide was a hotly debated topic in previous decades. Currently, there is less emphasis on the opportunities side of the digital divide but citizen skills are still receiving much attention. In addition, critics continue to highlight the need for providing non-digital venues for services and interactions, even if this is costly and only needed for a small group of citizens (Coglianese, 2021).

A specific ethical concern for smart cities is 'the right to the smart city' (Galič and Schuilenburg, 2021), a variation of Henri Lefebvre's 'right to the city'. From this perspective, cities are only acceptable places when they are flexible (so that public spaces allow free interpersonal communication and social encounters between strangers), when they allow difference (so that spaces are inclusive and avoid homogenization) and when they are participatory (meaning citizens have the right to occupy these spaces and modify them according to their needs). They suggest that in order to create open, flexible, diverse and participatory smart cities, we must first move beyond tokenistic civic engagement and include citizens as creators, members and leaders of smart city development (see Boxes 20.10 and 20.11). Although this can seem challenging, given that it requires technical expertise, it can be promoted by initiatives such as the right of citizens to produce information directly. This means moving beyond opaque behavioural data extracted *from* citizens (e.g. their location and habits) and allowing citizens to reappropriate and self-manage the information they produce to help them to improve the outcomes which they prioritize in their lives.

In sum, the ethical issues related to e-governance go much further than commonly identified issues such as privacy and surveillance. E-governance results in reconfigurations of social relations, and this may have a direct impact on complex issues, such as social equality. This requires governments to critically address these issues in collaboration with stakeholders and citizens to consider whether e-governance is appropriate and how e-governance can be positioned correctly to minimize ethical risks.

Box 20.10 Applying ethical principles to the use of drones in Enschede

In order to critically assess the impact of ICTs for society, government organizations need to identify ethical principles and organize a public debate on the question of how public values can be protected in e-governance. An example of a government organization that addressed these issues is the city of Enschede (Netherlands) in their policies for the use of drones for various public functions. For example, the city used drones during the corona pandemic for crowd management. The ethical committee of the city investigated this use and identified core values that needed to be protected – proportionality, justice, inclusivity, transparency, privacy, safety and autonomy – and operationalized these values for this specific case. The city then organized a public meeting with various stakeholders and citizens to debate this case and discuss how drones can be used in a responsible manner for public functions.

Source: https://www.enschede.nl/sites/default/files/Ethische-Analyse-van-drones-in-Enschede-2021.pdf.

Box 20.11 Tool for ethical deliberation on e-governance

There is clearly a need to address the ethical dilemmas connected to the use of technologies for governance. In response, several tools have been developed to facilitate ethical deliberation in groups of organizational actors and stakeholders. An example of such a tool is the Code *Good Digital Governance* that was developed by Utrecht University. This tool facilitates a debate about the key public values that may be impacted by the use of new technologies and helps actors to identify actions to tackle vulnerabilities. This tool has been applied, for example, to the use of data tools for crowd management that build upon data collected through the use of apps by citizens. The tool helped the government organization to identify the need for measures such as guaranteeing the privacy of citizens and communicating the use of this tool in an open manner to ensure legitimacy.

More information (in Dutch): https://www.uu.nl/sites/default/files/CODIO%20-%20Definitief%20-%20Opgemaakt%20-%2020210416.pdf.

Summary

The process-oriented framework of governance, which considers the interaction of duties, stakeholders and power dynamics with information and communication technologies can be defined as e-governance. We began this chapter by establishing that technological developments, global forces of change and an overall need for collaboration between complex networks of stakeholders have shifted the use of ICTs from solely the enhancement of service delivery, to enhancing structures and processes and creating value-oriented and collaborative forms of governance. We provided two examples of uses of ICTs for governance, namely through smart cities and the COVID-19 pandemic.

By contextualizing e-governance in an urban setting based on urban informatics, the datapolis and the smart city, we further place value on collaboration and strategic partnerships by different stakeholders at the local level. We specifically looked at the implementation of smart city concepts in Eindhoven, Padova, Barcelona and Seattle as datapolises, where strategic partnerships enable the development of data infrastructure and technology, based on democratic governance. In addition, we explored how e-governance structures and processes in China and Pakistan during the COVID-19 pandemic proved useful for the management of each country's COVID-19 crisis. These examples demonstrate that utilizing data infrastructures as tools for crisis management can prove beneficial. However, there is not a universal way of utilizing these technologies which can be replicated in every country. Specifically, public and private organizations within each country must consider their socio-economic, political and legal contexts when implementing ICT-induced solutions, as perceptions on topics such as privacy and compliancy vary.

Lastly, we explored the ethical implications of incorporating ICTs into governance networks and explored the problematic algorithm technology used by the Living Lab Stratumseind in Eindhoven. In addition, we explored the principle of 'the right to the smart city', which advocates making citizens creators, members and leaders in smart city development. We concluded that value-orientation and collaboration are a necessity if organizations wish to be ethical in their use of ICT infrastructure.

Given that technology provides value to government and governance, it is a surprise that both scientists and practitioners still pay little attention to the relation between policy and technology. As demonstrated by this chapter, whether we are considering the technicalities, real-life implementation, ethics or benefits of e-governance, we now understand that it is a complex and urgent subject that becomes more elaborate as time goes on. Therefore, we require more research on e-governance by scholars from a variety of disciplines, and more attention from practitioners in strategic positions, in order to harness the potential of ICTs and technologies to achieve the collective goal of improving our lives, when they are used in a responsible and ethical manner.

Questions for review and discussion

1   How would you distinguish between e-governance and e-government? (Hint: you could compare the approach in this chapter with that in Chapter 11 by Veiko Lember and Joep Crompvoets.)
2   Which aspects of technological change have been most important in driving the development of e-governance?
3   What are likely to be the main differences in the way e-governance is practiced in an NPM administrative culture, compared to a 'Rechtstaat' administrative culture?

Reader exercises

1 What impact has e-governance had on your life so far? Think about your personal inter-actions with government (at local, regional and national levels) and identify ways in which ICTs have changed those interactions. Then consider other interactions which would benefit from more ICT enablement – how would you suggest that the redesign of such interactions should be undertaken?

2 For each of the interactions you have identified in the previous exercise, consider the 'dark side' of the increasing use of ICTs by government – potential ways in which the digital approach may have had unwanted consequences.

Class exercises

1 In groups, identify examples of e-governance networks at the local level and discuss to what extent the selected networks have characteristics of a datapolis. Determine which conditions need to be in place in order to avoid authoritarian or strongly market-driven e-governance networks.

2 In groups, consider how important the 'digital divide' is in your country in relation to restricting the range of citizens who get involved in (a) influencing government policy; (b) joining social networks which seek to improve the quality of life of people suffer-ing from loneliness, isolation or mental health problems; (c) joining environmental networks which seek to improve the local environment in the area where they live.

In plenary session, compare the answers given by the different groups and discuss which of these effects of the digital divide is currently most important in your country.

3 In groups, propose ways of overcoming the effects of the digital divide which have been identified in the previous exercise.

In the plenary session, compare the answers given by the different groups and vote on which answers seem to be the most promising (You may decide to use – or not use – a digital voting platform to do this!').

Further reading

Bannister, F., & Connolly, R. (2012). Defining e-governance. *e-Service Journal: A Journal of Electronic Services in the Public and Private Sectors, 8*(2), 3–25.

Hollands, R. G. (2008). Will the real smart city please stand up? *City, 12*(3), 303–320.

Meijer, A., & Löfgren, K. (2015). The neglect of technology in theories of policy change. *International Journal of Public Administration in the Digital Age, 2*(1), 75–88.

References

Coglianese, C. (2021). Administrative law in the automated state. *Dædalus, 150*(3), 104–120.

Cong Wanshu (2021). From pandemic control to data-driven governance: The case of china's health code. *Frontiers in Political Science, 3*, https://www.frontiersin.org/articles/10.3389/fpos.2021.627959

Doorman, S., & Pali, B. (2021). Underneath the promise of safety and security in a 'smart city'. *Journal of Extreme Anthropology, 5*(1), 78–110.

Galič, M., & Schuilenburg, M. (2021). Reclaiming the smart city: Toward a new right to the city. In: J. C. Augusto (Ed.), *Handbook of Smart Cities*. Springer Nature Switzerland AG, pp. 1419–1436.

Kontokosta, C. E. (2021). Urban informatics in the science and practice of planning. *Journal of Planning Education and Research, 41*(4), 382–395.

McGraw, J. (2021). *Seattle's tech scene looks like San Francisco's did 10 years ago-what gives?* sf.citi. Retrieved from https://sfciti.org/news/blog/seattles-tech-scene-looks-like-san-franciscos-did-10-years-ago-what-gives/.

Meijer, A. (2017). Datapolis: A public governance perspective on 'smart cities'. *Perspectives on Public Management and Governance, 1*(3), 195–206.

Meijer, A. J., Lips, M., & Chen, K. (2019). Open governance: A new paradigm for understanding urban governance in an information age. *Frontiers in Sustainable Cities, 3.*

Meijer, A., & Thaens, M. (2016). Urban technological innovation: Developing and testing a sociotechnical framework for studying smart city projects. *Urban Affairs Review, 54*(2), 363–387.

Meijer, A., & Webster, C. W. R. (2020). The COVID-19-crisis and the information polity: An overview of responses and discussions in twenty-one countries from six continents. *Information Polity, 25*(3), 243–274.

Saxena, K. B. C. (2005). Towards excellence in e-governance. *International Journal of Public Sector Management, 18*(6), 498–513.

Smith, A., & Martín, P. P. (2020). Going beyond the smart city? Implementing technopolitical platforms for urban democracy in Madrid and Barcelona. *Journal of Urban Technology, 28*(1–2), 311–330.

Ullah, A., Pinglu, C., Ullah, S., Abbas, H. S., & Khan, S. (2020). The role of e-governance in combating Covid-19 and promoting sustainable development: A comparative study of China and Pakistan. *Chinese Political Science Review, 6*(1), 86–118.

World Bank. (2020). *Urban development.* World Bank. Retrieved from https://www.worldbank.org/en/topic/urbandevelopment/overview#1.

Zanella, A., Bui, N., Castellani, A., Vangelista, L., & Zorzi, M. (2014). Internet of things for smart cities. *IEEE Internet of Things Journal, 1*(1), 22–32.

21 Understanding public leadership

Jean Hartley

Introduction

Societies experiencing major challenges and changes often look to public leaders to make sense of what is happening and to offer solutions to end or at least reduce the problems – for example, climate change, wars, growing inequalities between rich and poor, homelessness, and much more (sometimes called "wicked problems" - see Chapter 18). Leadership is also sought where communities and public organizations make collective decisions and take action – so leadership is found in, for example, running hospitals and police forces, among groups protesting against a new road being built, or by an elected politician shaping new legislation.

So leadership is widely found – but often not well-understood. Bold claims are sometimes made about what is involved in effective leadership without recourse to evidence, analysis, or research. Furthermore, all sorts of dreams, dreads, hopes, and fears are invested in leadership. This applies especially to public leadership, where the purposes, roles, actions, and decisions of leadership may be contested by different groups in society.

There is a wide variety of types of public leadership in response to societal challenges. For example, "strong man" leadership (and it generally is very gendered) is the preferred way of acting for leaders like Donald Trump or Vladimir Putin, while political leaders like Jacinda Ardern of New Zealand or Nelson Mandela in South Africa showed a more participative, collective approach.

This chapter aims to unpack leadership – what do we mean by it? And how far is public leadership distinctive from leadership in other sectors (e.g. the private sector, where much commentary and research has focused until recently)? The chapter will address some key (and contrasting) conceptions of leadership and the evidence about leadership processes and outcomes – not swept along by current fashions but taking a hard analytical look at research and other evidence. In this way, the reader can engage in current debates about public governance, leadership, and management.

Learning objectives

- To recognize different roles and purposes of public leadership
- To understand the difference between leadership and management
- To be aware of key theoretical perspectives on leadership
- To understand how shared public leadership is exercised
- To be aware of how context shapes, and sometimes is shaped by, leadership
- To be aware of diversity and inclusion issues in leadership

DOI: 10.4324/9781003282839-24

What is leadership – and public leadership?

There are many definitions of leadership because there are so many different ways of thinking about leadership, both analytically and normatively. Rather than providing myriad definitions, each emphasizing slightly different aspects, this chapter starts off with a couple of definitions so that there is a shared understanding of the phenomenon. An early definition came from Stogdill (1950, p. 3): "Leadership may be considered as the process (act) of influencing the activities of an organized group in its efforts towards goal setting and goal achievement." This definition views leadership as a social and relational process, so it is not just about leader characteristics but what happens between people, and it links leadership to purpose. However, from a public leadership perspective, the emphasis on an organized group is not helpful – leadership may be with stakeholders and members of the public as well as those in organizations or formal partnerships. Hartley (2018, p. 203) suggested public leadership is "mobilising individuals, organisations and networks to formulate and/or enact purposes, values and actions which aim or claim to create valued outcomes for the public sphere."

Who exercises public leadership?

Earlier (Chapter 1), the public domain was outlined, as the arena in which public choices are made in order to achieve a collective purpose. This is particularly pertinent to democratic societies, though the public domain in authoritarian and anocratic (part democratic, part autocratic) societies may also be experienced collectively without the public being involved in making choices.

Public leadership was long equated with being a senior manager or professional within the public sector. Police officers, doctors, and highway engineers, for example, along with those in managerial roles in local and central government, prisons, public sector healthcare, nationalized railways, and so on were counted as public leaders, responsible for key public purposes, people, or resources. The generic leadership literature is dominated by studies of managers working in private business, so it is perhaps not surprising that public leadership studies originally focused on public managers.

However, while public managers are a notable category of public leader, there are others. Elected politicians (and, in some societies, appointed politicians) at all governmental levels (e.g. local, regional, federal/national) are also public leaders, exercising influence over the public domain through making laws and policy and through their shaping of debates and narratives about public matters, including the shape of the public domain itself. They may take the lead in a public crisis or in difficult longer-term policy development, where controversy and conflict is inherent in their work.

Both public managers and politicians derive their authority – their mandate to lead – from the institutions of the state. However, in democratic societies with polycentric governance a focus solely on state actors and state processes is insufficient to understand public leadership. Other stakeholders, including communities, groups, and individuals, may exercise leadership (often informally and without authority but sometimes in partnership with state bodies) in order to bring to public attention, protest, advocate, lobby, and problem-solve public issues. For example, Extinction Rebellion is an international social movement which exercises leadership through the power of collective action, bringing the climate crisis to public attention and advocating for greater public action from governments and individuals. Public leadership may also be exercised by business leaders, when they engage in debates or take actions which influence the public domain. For example, when the UK government was slow to impose lockdown during the 2020 coronavirus pandemic, two leaders influenced the Premier League to suspend football matches, thereby saving lives.

In summary, leadership may be exercised in, with, or against the state. It differs according to whether the leader can claim some legitimacy through the authority of the state or through other sources.

Thinking about leadership from different perspectives

Given the varied definitions and concepts of leadership in the academic literature, here we consider some contrasting lenses – leadership as person, position, projection, and process.

Leadership as person: Qualities and behaviours of the leader

A group of early (and still popular) theories about leadership clustered around whether there are distinctive features of the individual leader. Character, skills, or behaviour was either inbred or could be acquired over time – either way the leader stood out as head and shoulders (sometimes literally) above those around them and thus was able to shape events. It is relatively easy to think of distinctive leaders such as Nelson Mandela or Xi Jinping in this category – though the evidence is more complex both about individuals and those they interact with.

Initially, research on personal characteristics (sometimes called traits) was promising but, although the list of traits grew and grew, most were not supported by evidence. Also some leaders were judged to be successful in some contexts but not others. A famous example is Winston Churchill, who is hailed as a great war leader but who was roundly rejected from office when peace arrived. Research shows public managers can exercise successful leadership in one public organization but flatline when they move to another (Hartley and Benington, 2010). Clearly, something more than individual characteristics influences leadership.

However, research evidence shows that personal traits, such as intelligence, physical energy, self-confidence, self-awareness, and resilience, are important in many settings. In public leadership settings, these traits may help (but not determine) leaders to manage complex "wicked" problems and to handle the wide range of stakeholders acting in the public domain.

Given its limitations, research shifted from traits to behaviours, e.g. showing concern for people and having a clear sense of purpose. The distinction between transformational and transactional leadership, initially developed by Burns (1978) in relation to political leadership in the USA, has been taken up with gusto in wider leadership studies, across roles and sectors.

Transactional leadership is based on what the leader possesses or controls and what the "follower" (the person influenced by the leader) seeks in return. This is a social exchange view of leadership, where the exchange may be economic, political, or psychological (e.g. the leader may subtly offer promotion, interesting tasks, or approval among other things).

Transformational leadership, by contrast, is behaviour where the leader induces positive feelings in their followers which then motivates their high performance. The leader aims to inspire followers through arousing their strong emotions and their sense of identification with the leader; increase their awareness of problems and novel ways to tackle them; provide support, encouragement, and coaching to followers; and communicate an appealing vision to focus effort. Transformational leadership theory is part of a cluster of theories linked with charismatic leadership. It can be noted that both transactional and transformational leadership are not "pure" leader-focused theories because they depend crucially on the inter-actions with so-called followers.

From the 1990s onwards, transformational leadership was very popular and was some-times treated normatively (i.e. this is how leaders ought to behave). Detailed research then threw up more nuanced findings. First, transformational and transactional leadership are not discrete categories – leaders may display some behaviours from each approach. Second, con-text often affects leadership style – in complex organizational change settings, both transfor-mational (inspiring) and transactional (getting the nuts and bolts of implementation done) leadership can be important. Transactional leadership can sound rather basic, but being clear, focusing on expectations, and giving feedback are all important leadership behaviours. Third, arousing strong emotions may not always be compatible with the impartial work of public servants, so there can be tensions between charisma and sound policies. Finally, there can be downsides to charismatic leadership, e.g. in closed systems like children's homes or residential homes for the elderly, where charisma can lead to abuses of power and where loyalty can generate blind spots about negative aspects of leadership.

There are a number of other theories about who individual leaders are and what they do (personality, behaviours, and styles), but leader-focused models have a limited degree of explanatory power on their own, and can be uncomfortably close to the idea of the "strong leader" who will solve all the problems of society on their own. This is diametrically opposed to what is known about leadership for wicked problems.

Leadership as position

Leadership is sometimes associated with particular organizational roles on the assumption that having formal authority confers leadership on the individual. Prime minister, clinical director of a public hospital, army major, prison governor – these and others are assumed to be leaders simply by dint of their appointment. And, indeed, organizational position may confer authority and a particular set of powers (e.g. to make certain types of decisions, to allocate certain resources, to report to the public in particular ways) and may prompt citizens and others to look to that role holder to action public policies (e.g. bring down hospital waiting times or improve conviction rates in policing). Moreover, in the public sector, such authority may come through the state's monopoly of certain legal and regulatory powers.

However, the literature is sometimes confusing about whether managers are leaders or not, given their organizational positions. Some writers say these roles are distinctive, others say they overlap, others again see leadership as one function within wider managerial work. The early work on leadership was largely based on studies of managers but given that public leadership is about influencing the public domain, there is recognition that leadership is not solely associated with an organizational position – see Box 21.1.

Box 21.1 Management and leadership

Leaders require a blend of management skills (e.g., planning, organizing, budg-eting, staffing and directing), personal skills (e.g. the ability to communicate, motivate and inspire others), leadership skills (e.g. strategic focus, analytical com-petency and cognitive flexibility), and, in policing, a healthy dose of operational experience.

(Flynn and Herrington, 2015, p. 14)

However, even those who are office-holders may not necessarily show leadership, even if they have scope to do so. Some focus on managing or governing but not leading. And on the other hand, some public leadership is exercised without holding a formal position. An influential opinion leader in a team of public professionals, a social media commentator, or a public intellectual such as a writer or an academic may exercise leadership. Doreen Lawrence, for example, campaigned for better UK policing after the murder of her son was inadequately investigated by London's police. The young women Greta Thunberg and Malala Yousafzai are both influential leaders (about climate change, and about girls' education) although without organizational positions.

Heifetz (1994) valuably highlights that leaders with authority and leaders without authority may tackle leadership in different ways. Leaders with formal authority have formal powers and sometimes resources associated with their role (at least within particular contexts). Leaders without formal authority often lead because they care about an issue and they take the initiative to tackle it (e.g. reducing racism). For those working outside formal authority, their informal leadership can focus on all aspects of an issue, ignoring organizational constraints and using other sources of power, such as charisma and moral persuasion. More questionably, they may ignore their effects on the wider system beyond their chosen issue.

Overall, the positional approach to power, like the person perspective, provides only partial explanation of leadership – we must remain aware of leadership without or beyond authority.

Leadership as projection

Having examined leader-centric behaviour, let's now consider follower-centric views of leadership – that is, theories about the characteristics and behaviours of those who are being influenced by leaders. Meindl et al. (1985) coined the term "the romance of leadership" on noticing that followers and onlookers tended to refer to leadership mainly when events were going very well or very badly. So, leadership may sometimes be in the eyes of the beholders as much as reflecting how leaders present themselves or what they do.

Views of leaders may depend on how the beholder creates explanations for events and consequences, which they find plausible; and on how people interpret and read meaning into their collective experiences, along with psycho-dynamic processes about power, dependency, identity, and authority. There are many examples of projection by onlookers about leadership. Barack Obama was widely praised in his early days as US president but hope changed to disappointment over time even though he was essentially the same leader. In organizations, a new departmental leader is often initially viewed with excitement as they set out new plans but optimism may fade over time. On the other hand, a crisis can raise people's assessment of who has effective leadership qualities – the Ukrainian president, Volodymyr Zelenskyy, at the start of the war with Russia being a case in point.

Projection also provides insight into some of the gender and ethnicity differences found (or not found) in leadership studies. Reviews of gender and leadership repeatedly fail to find gender differences in leadership styles. In other words, the different perceptions of men and women, where they exist, are not explainable by who they are or what they do. However, people hold in their heads a set of beliefs about what distinguishes a good leader from a less effective one, shaped by their education and experiences. Schein et al. (1996) showed that the stereotype of an effective leader is more similar to a stereotypical male set of traits (e.g. strong, assertive) than to those of the stereotypical female. So, the views about men and women as leaders may be less to do with their inherent qualities and more to do with the way that society views leadership. This may, of course, change over time as society changes. A similar analysis has been found to apply to ethnic minorities.

Leadership as social process

Some perspectives on leadership emphasize that it is a social process, depending not only on how the leader "mobilizes", "influences", "motivates", and "sense-gives", but also on the characteristics and behaviours of those being influenced and what happens between the leaders and those being led. In this view, leadership is relational so that instead of analysing entities (leaders, followers, contexts) the focus is on processes (empathy, engagement, forging social identities, story-telling, sense-giving).

Adaptive leadership theory (Heifetz, 1994) is about the social processes of leading in the context of "adaptive" (wicked) problems, emphasizing that a leader must refuse to collude with the fantasy that he or she has magic solutions and instead must persuade those involved that they also need to help in tackling the issue (and indeed that they may be part of the problem). The leadership challenge is to confront the complexity of the problem and seek to orchestrate the work of a range of people to address it ("giving the work back to the people who have the problem") – an approach which is neither easy nor necessarily popular, given that we often prefer to blame our leaders rather than admit our own responsibility. The painful adaptations needed in tackling complex problems can be very emotionally demanding for all concerned. Heifetz outlines seven principles to keep attention on the adaptive challenge (not get distracted or side-tracked) and on a range of relevant voices and views. This can be seen as an approach which requires a whole-systems perspective (see Chapter 18).

The social identity theory of leadership is a further relational theory of leadership, based on social processes occurring within groups which share an identity (Hogg, 2001). Identity is fostered through a bias towards evaluating one's own-group members more highly than outgroup members, so leaders are more likely to be typical of the group's identity. For example, a group of doctors is likely to accept leadership more readily from a clinician than from a hospital manager.

However, some leaders aim to influence the outgroup as well as their own group, perhaps because they want to change existing relations in their society – e.g. leaders concerned with peacebuilding in violently divided societies need to gradually and sensitively reach out to "the opposite side." This can be fraught with danger – both hostility from the outgroup but also cries of betrayal from their own group. Such leaders require the skills and judgement to stay attached with their own group, while also being sufficiently different to be taken seriously by the other side (Khalil and Hartley, 2022). While not perhaps qualifying as "peacebuilders," many public leaders work across potentially or actually hostile divides, whether with youth gangs, with potential vigilante groups combatting rural crime or in societies at or recovering from war, or simply trying to run organizations in fragmented societies – see Box 21.2.

Box 21.2 Leadership beyond followers

Martin Luther King was one of the leaders of the US civil rights movement in the 1960s. His formal authority came as president of the Southern Christian Leadership Conference, but most of his leadership influence was through informal means – moral persuasion, charisma, and well-practised rhetoric. He was authorized by his supporters to champion a particular point of view – equal rights for black men and women in society. However, the people King wanted to lead were not people in his organization nor the groups of supporters. The people he wanted to lead were the great many people who couldn't care less about civil rights or who hated his ideas. These were the people he needed to provoke to rethink their values and their priorities.

See Heifetz (2011) for a short analysis of this case.

Box 21.2 shows clearly how the concept of "follower" is flawed. Many public leaders have to work with a variety of stakeholders who do not "follow" them but who may question them, oppose them, debate with them, undermine them, and/or try to exert leadership themselves. This is particularly so for politicians and for those involved in collaborative partnerships or working in the community, but it applies across all public leadership roles to some extent. A distinctive feature of public leadership is its concern with the public domain, so inevitably there is some contesting over values, priorities, goals, and means of achieving those goals.

All theories about leadership as social process have in common the need to take into account the leader, those being mobilized or influenced, the relationships between them, and to some extent the context in which these social processes take place. Leadership has got distinctly more complicated.

Taking an overview

The different concepts and theories of leadership considered so far illustrate that leadership is multi-faceted, so each may have something to offer in different situations and none is complete on its own. Personality, skills, and behaviour do matter to an extent (otherwise we wouldn't endlessly discuss our fears about what toxic national political leaders might do to society) but leadership is more than personality because the same person can be effective or not in different times or places. Those with an organizational position have particular resources with which to mobilize the time and attention of others, but many informal leaders are highly influential without or beyond an organizational role. Followers' and onlookers' perceptions can be important in some settings but not all. The social process approach to leadership looks at the whole relationship between leaders and those they try to influence, but it cannot capture all the nuances of leadership and by taking a relational approach can underplay the skills involved. The question perhaps is not which is the best way of conceptualizing leadership but which works in which contexts and with what strengths and limitations.

Box 21.3 The power behind (and below) leaders

Drath observes that leadership is like "the deep blue sea" – leaders are the white wave caps but the real power and momentum for action comes from the mass of water (the people) below, from which the white caps are created.

(Drath, 2001)

The contexts of public leadership

Context is especially important for public leaders, whose activities are more likely to affect the views and actions of a range of stakeholders than those of private sector leaders. Contingency and situational theories of leadership argue that the context affects what leadership style or approach is most effective. Crisis situations (e.g. a terrorist bombing, or a major fire) generally call for a command style of leadership, with clear, decisive action and little if any time for discussion. Other more everyday situations benefit from someone taking charge, managing known problems, and making the final decisions (although there may be some wider participation). However, wicked problems usually require detailed discussions and explorations to fully understand the problem and even more work to ensure appropriate joint action.

Contingency theories have been criticized for seeming to imply that context determines leadership behaviours (if X, then Y leadership approach) and for ignoring the role of leaders in actually constituting context through crafting a narrative, often in unclear situations, about what is going on, in a way acceptable to others.

"Reading" the complex context and judgement are important leadership skills, involving attention to context, including the variety of stakeholders and their diverse interests, values, and goals, and keeping a sense of which public goals to pursue. Arenas are not only about physical spaces, though some are identifiable as such (a council chamber, a citizens' jury, a climate change sit-in) but they are also social processes of mutual influence between stakeholders and public leaders (see Figure 21.1).

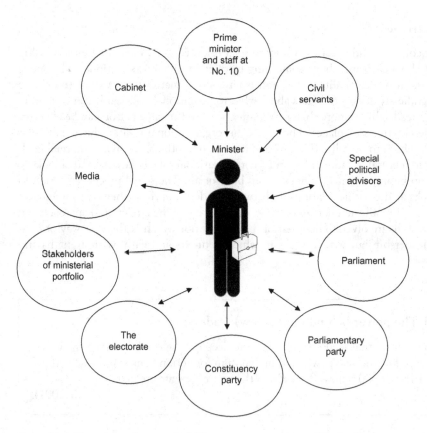

Figure 21.1 The principal arenas for UK government ministerial leadership.

Single and plural leadership

Early academic work on leadership focused on the single leader as though they exercised leadership alone – sometimes nowadays called heroic leadership. Current media portrayals tend to reinforce this, suggesting that the great leader works single-handedly.

Yet, although leadership can indeed be lonely (particularly in organizations), the reality is often that leadership is more distributed. For example, Nelson Mandela worked with a network of trusted compatriots and with politicians who initially opposed him, such as F. W. de Klerk, to achieve change in South Africa. All of them exercised leadership in different ways and were influential with different stakeholders. Malala Yousafzai's father worked hard to help her get a platform to promote girls' education around the world. A local authority political leader works closely and on a daily basis with the chief executive, the one exercising political leadership, the other organizational leadership.

A leadership constellation, particularly prevalent in public leadership, is where leadership is shared in different patterns. Leadership may be in constellation where there are interlinked roles to achieve complex change and/or where power is diffuse. Community leadership often involves a range of leaders working in concert across the public, private, and third sectors to try to achieve public purposes. Box 21.4 illustrates shared leadership to address youth issues in a Sydney suburb, orchestrated by a police leader but with key contributions from various other leaders. Often the first task is sense-giving – reframing a problem in ways which deal with root rather than surface problems. A second task is often convening a group to discuss the difficult issues – this is often a key role for public leaders. Both elements are illustrated in the case.

Box 21.4 Leading as reframing and mobilizing partners

Arriving as the new commander of western Sydney's Blacktown Police, Mark Wright was faced with burgeoning youth crime, and a central business district (CBD) that felt unsafe for local residents. Plus, the funding used to try to control groups of young people in the CBD was diverting resources from tackling more serious crimes elsewhere. The command and control options tried by his predecessors had failed and Mark realized he needed a partnership – the police could not tackle this complex social problem on their own.

Wright reframed the problem – youth disadvantage and social cohesion were at the root of the youth offending behaviours. This was far broader than just a police matter. Wright convened a group of key local decision-makers from all sectors, including several youth-focused NGOs, churches, the City Council, the state Department of Juvenile Justice, and the operations manager of Westpoint Shopping Centre, where much of the crime occurred. Many of these were initially suspicious of each other and not used to working together – in fact, they had often competed with each other for scarce funding. Mark chaired the meetings, and one member recalled how Mark's opening statement captured them all:

> Mark spoke about what he was trying to achieve, and that was about us all coming together to fill the gaps, and to really impact the youth and make them part of the community … And that's where the journey started.

Read Sophie Yates' full text of the case (including what Mark Wright and others did), at https://www.themandarin.com.au/87010-collaborative-innovation-shifting-dial-youth -crime-blacktown/.

One particular form of shared leadership, found widely in the public sector, is dual leadership at the top of the organization (e.g. government minister and permanent secretary; local government mayor/political leader and chief executive; university vice-chancellor and registrar). There are many studies of the "politics-administration dichotomy," though only a small number of articles consider this from the point of view of leadership. Hartley and Manzie (2020) show how senior civil servants in the UK succeed in both working closely with elected politicians, while also maintaining professional integrity and ethics.

Another form of shared leadership is relational leadership for co-producing public services and outcomes (Sancino et al., 2022). This involves collaboration between citizens and public officials (both politicians and managers), sometimes across the whole policy cycle from service design to service production and evaluation. The power dynamics can be complex and may create value for the public domain, though there can be a risk of capture by private interests where power imbalances predominate.

Public leadership to create public value

Leadership is sometimes defined as concerned with finding, shaping, agreeing, or pursuing particular goals. It sounds straightforward but in fact, research has illuminated the difficulties that leaders often have in finding, defining, or clarifying purpose, or in avoiding being distracted from key purpose. Purpose cannot be assumed but must be thought out, explored, and often refined. This involves learning and reflecting on a continual basis, moving between reading the context and judging the interests of stakeholders, while also reflecting on past patterns and future options for leadership. Leadership purpose may change over time as illustrated in Box 21.5.

Box 21.5

A case study of the policing of groups antagonistic to each other in Northern Ireland illustrates how leadership purpose may change over time, as leaders engage in sense-making and reframing. The police commander on the ground initially saw his role as keeping the peace through ensuring the two groups were separated from each other, but later reframed this as a different categorization – law-keepers and law-breakers. He then devised ways to encourage the two groups to undertake the policing of their own trouble-makers and encourage law-keeping.

Read the full case at Benington and Turbitt (2007).

Key to leadership purpose is discerning and creating public value (see also Chapters 7 and 15). For Benington (2011), public value is based on two inter-linked dimensions, concerned with what members of the public most value in this specific context and also what adds value to the public sphere – the wider and longer-term assessment of what benefits the whole society and future generations. These two dimensions are sometimes in tension and can be dynamic and changeable. Public leaders may need to discern public value themselves and also help stakeholders find sufficient agreement on what constitutes public value in order to take action.

Summary: Drawing threads together – the distinctiveness of public leadership

There is a vast literature about leadership but much of it is focused on private firms and in organizational settings. This is too narrow a perspective for understanding public leadership, so it is important to be clear about how public leadership is different. Public leadership involves a range of actors, including formal leaders such as politicians or public managers and professionals, but they can equally be informal leaders from any sector who are trying to have an impact on the public domain.

Public leadership is inevitably concerned with power and politics, judging between the differing and contested values, goals, and interests among different groups in a society. This means that it is exercised under scrutiny and controversy in many settings (although not in all – some public leadership, e.g. aspects of counter-terrorism or military special forces leadership, is hidden away). Therefore, most public leaders must think about a range of stakeholders – the public, lobby groups, etc. At more senior levels, they must lead with political astuteness – an awareness of the diverse and sometimes competing interests which have an impact on their work (Hartley, 2020). Furthermore, public leaders elected or appointed by the state (politicians and public managers) are expected – at least in democratic societies – to act on behalf of the public. They are expected to avoid pursuing sectional interests (personal interests, party political interests, interests which undermine social wellbeing), so that they can claim that they act on behalf of the whole of society and of future generations. Many democratic countries have a code of ethics for those working on behalf of the state. For example, in the UK, public office holders are expected to adhere to the seven 'Nolan principles' including selflessness, integrity, objectivity, accountability, openness, honesty, and leadership (see Chapter 27). Informal leaders are not bound by such authority and accountability structures and can be more single-minded in their goals and more partisan in how they exercise leadership. But even they will have to take account of particular stakeholders if they are to get their message across and achieve results.

The claims of public leaders to be creating a better future for their society are widely scrutinized and contested – that is the nature of the public domain. Context really matters in any kind of leadership, and the contexts of public leadership are distinctive – and especially challenging. The processes of influencing others through leadership are equally complex and often subtle, but it is hoped that this chapter has brought insights to help analyse how leadership can act for the benefit of the public domain.

Question for review and discussion

1. This chapter provides one leadership theory to help explain inequalities due to gender and diversity. Find one academic journal article which provides additional theories to explain discrimination and summarize the possible effects of these on leadership in a short report.

Reader exercises

1   Find a local public leader whom you can interview for about half an hour, e.g. a team leader in a local public service. How does that person think about their purposes and role as a leader? How do they assess their effectiveness as a leader? Who are they trying to influence? Now compare what they say with what you have read about public leadership.

2   Particularly in times of uncertainty, many people look to strong leaders to fulfil their greatest hopes, while others project onto them their intense fears. What are the risks and potential dark sides of charismatic leadership styles – and how can they be avoided?

Class exercises

1   The class should select a leader, whether local or national. Each group should gather information about this leader, identifying how their leadership is distinctive from the different perspectives of the person, their position, projection, and process and assessing the overall contribution of each perspective to their leadership. In plenary, compare your assessments.

2   Read and analyse the case study by Sophie Yates about leadership through partnership, found at https://www.themandarin.com.au/87010-collaborative-innovation-shifting -dial-youth-crime-blacktown/. Work in a small team to identify the leadership contributed by each of the partners. What were the risks and opportunities for Mark Wright in working in collaboration rather than leading the initiative on his own? In what ways is shared leadership a different set of processes compared with individual leadership?

Recommended reading and viewing

Crosby, B. and Bryson, J. (2018). Why Leadership of Public Leadership Research Matters: And What to Do About It. *Public Management Review*, 20(9), 1265–1286.

't Hart, P. and Tummers, L. (2019). *Understanding Public Leadership*. 2nd ed. Chapter 1: Introducing Public Leadership. London: Red Globe Press.

Hartley, J. (2018). Ten Propositions About Public Leadership. *International Journal of Public Leadership*, 14(4), 202–217.

Jackson, B. and Parry, K. (2018). *A Very Short, Fairly Interesting and Reasonably Cheap Book About Studying Leadership*. 3rd ed. London: Sage.

Step Up to Leadership. A free course from the Open University https://www.open.edu/openlearn/money -business/leadership-management/step-leadership/content-section-0?active-tab=description-tab

References

Benington, J. (2011). From Private Choice to Public Value. In J. Benington and M. Moore (eds), *Public Value: Theory and Practice*. Basingstoke: Palgrave Macmillan, pp. 31–51.

Benington, J. and Turbitt, I. (2007). Adaptive Leadership and the Policing of the Drumcree Demonstrations in Northern Ireland. *Leadership*, 3(4), 371–395.

Burns J. M. (1978). *Leadership*. New York: Harper Collins.

Drath W. (2001). *The Deep Blue Sea: Rethinking the Source of Leadership*. San Francisco, CA: Jossey Bass.

Flynn, E. A. and Herrington, V. (2015). Towards. A Profession of Police Leadership. *New Perspectives in Policing Bulletin*. Washington, DC: U.S. Department of Justice, National Institute of Justice, NCJ 248573.

Hartley, J. (2020). Leadership with Political Astuteness for Public Servants – and Why It Matters. In H. Sullivan, H. Dickinson and H. Henderson (eds), *The Palgrave Handbook of the Public Servant*. Cham, Switzerland: Palgrave Macmillan.

Hartley, J. and Benington, J. (2010). *Leadership for Healthcare*. Bristol: Policy Press.

Hartley, J. and Manzie, S. (2020). 'It's every breath we take here': Political astuteness and ethics in civil service leadership development. *Public Money and Management*, 40(8): 569–578.

Heifetz, R. (1994). *Leadership Without Easy Answers*. Cambridge, MA: Harvard University Press.

Heifetz, R. (2011). Debate: Leadership and Authority. *Public Money and Management*, 31(5), 305–308.

Hogg, M. (2001). A Social Identity Theory of Leadership. *Personality and Social, Psychology Review*, 5, 184–200.

Khalil L and Hartley J (2022). Public leadership to foster peacebuilding in violently divided societies. *Public Management Review*. https://doi.org/10.1080/14719037.2022.2116094

Meindl, J, Ehrlich, S. and Dukerich, J. (1985). The Romance of Leadership. *Administrative Science Quarterly*, 30(1), 78–102.

Sancino, A., Carli, G. and Giacomini, D. (2022). Relational Leadership in Local Governance: The Engagement of Mayors with Citizens, Public Managers and Politicians. *Public Management Review* (Early Access). https://doi.org/10.1080/14719037.2022.2039274

Schein, V., Mueller, R., Lituchy, T. and Liu, J. (1996). Think Manager, Think Male – a Global Phenomenon? *Journal of Organzational Behavior*, 17(1), 33–41.

Stogdill, R. (1950). Leadership, Membership and Organization. *Psychological Bulletin*, 47, 1–14.

22 Citizen engagement

Elke Loeffler and Steve Martin

Introduction

Citizen engagement has reached different levels of maturity in different contexts. Some approaches, such as participatory budgeting, have become common in many countries and in diverse policy areas and are apparently durable. Evaluations have provided evidence of the potential benefits of citizen engagement. However, some policy-makers and public managers remain unconvinced, and it has sometimes been seen as 'political window-dressing' and therefore has not succeeded in increasing the perceived legitimacy of government decisions.

Moreover, citizen engagement is viewed by some as a threat to the role of elected representatives and there is certainly a fuzzy relationship between representative, participatory and direct democracy. Particularly in highly unequal and divided societies there are critical questions as to who participates and who benefits most from citizen engagement initiatives. Recently, online initiatives such as crowdsourcing have allowed citizen engagement to be scaled at low cost but under the shadow of the digital divide.

In this chapter, we explore how these issues have been tackled in different contexts and the potential opportunities for new approaches in the future.

Learning objectives

This chapter considers five key issues:

- The concept of citizen engagement
- Forms of citizen engagement, especially in the digital age, including informing, consulting, participation and co-production
- Who to engage
- Arguments in favour of citizen engagement in public decisions and services
- Challenges to effective citizen engagement and ways of overcoming these

Forms of citizen engagement

Governments in liberal democracies have emphasized the importance of 'consultation', 'participation', 'listening', 'being in touch with the people', 'involving users', 'devolving power

DOI: 10.4324/9781003282839-25

to neighbourhoods', strengthening 'accountability to local people' and 'empowerment', as if these often very different types of activity were synonymous. In fact, they represent a wide spectrum of different types of engagement.

One of the most widely quoted typologies is the 'ladder of participation' devised by Sherry Arnstein (1969) (see Figure 22.1). On the lower rungs of the ladder are manipulation (getting citizens to think the way you want them to think) and therapy (telling them just enough to make them feel good). What Arnstein saw as 'tokenistic' activities – 'informing', 'consultation' and 'placation' – populate the middle section. At the upper end are three approaches that in her view genuinely empower the public – partnership, delegated power and citizen control.

This typology, however, implies that some forms of engagement are inherently superior. In practice, what matters is that the form of citizen engagement that is deployed is fit for purpose.

Moreover, not everybody wants to be engaged in everything at all times. Many citizens are content to let service providers 'get on with the job'. A less normative typology of citizen

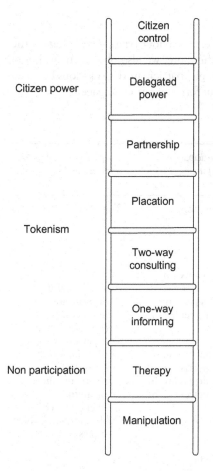

Figure 22.1 Ladder of engagement.

Source: Adapted from Arnstein (1969).

engagement is shown in Table 22.1, distinguishing between different intensities of citizen engagement:

(1) *Information* – a one-way relationship between governments and citizens. Traditionally, this meant governments providing citizens with information – but with social media citizens can now also send information to trigger government interventions.
(2) *Consultation* – a two-way dialogue between public organizations and citizens which gives citizens a voice on an issue and ideally feedback on the decision taken ('you said, we did'). There are, though, no guarantees that decision-makers will act on citizens' preferences.
(3) *Participation in public decision-making* – a more intense interaction between public organizations and citizens where each party has a role in decision-making (e.g. in relation to laws, policies, priorities). This may involve deliberative forums and/or direct democracy (e.g. referenda).
(4) *Co-production of public services and outcomes* – the most intensive form of engagement, where citizens and professionals harness each other's resources and capabilities to improve policy and/or public services through co-commissioning, co-design, co-delivery or co-assessment (the 4 Co's).

In most cases, citizens and governments move between these four types, depending on the willingness and ability of each party to engage. Furthermore, we also observe hybridity of practices across these forms of engagement – for example, participatory workshops between service providers and service users may include all four forms of citizen engagement.

Table 22.1 Forms of citizen engagement

	Information	Consultation	Participation in public decision-making	Co-production of public services and outcomes
Direction	One-way (from public service organization to citizens or vice versa)	Two-way	Two-way	Together
Contribution of public service organization	Giving or receiving information	Proposing, listening (and perhaps giving feedback)	Influence on decisions, depending on power balance	Joint action on the 4 Co's, using organizational resources, capabilities and expertise
Contribution of citizens	Receiving or giving information	Giving feedback	Influence on decisions, depending on power balance	Joint action on the 4 Co's, using citizen resources, capabilities, lived experience
Spaces where engagement takes place	Public and non-public spaces	Public spaces	Public spaces	Public and non-public spaces
Intensity of citizen engagement	Low	Low	Medium	High

Information: Approaches and evidence

It is clear that the provision of honest and effective information is a legitimate and necessary function, providing people with the means to engage effectively with public organizations. At the very least, citizens need clear information about issues such as the services for which they are eligible, complaints procedures, decisions which affect them that are being made by elected representatives, the issues on which they will be consulted (and the 'rules' of the engagement process) and, most importantly, the limits of engagement. Some rights to information are enshrined within Freedom of Information legislation in many countries. Nevertheless, research has suggested that, despite various initiatives to improve the quality and availability of health information, the public want more information than they currently receive and professionals tend to overestimate the amount of information they supply (Coulter and Ellins, 2006: 21).

Clearly, providing the right information on the right issues to the right people in the right language remains a challenge to most public organizations. There is now a strong drive by governments across the world to use 'accessible language', rather than professional jargon or bureaucratic terms which are incomprehensible to many citizens. The medium is also important – some groups understand an issue better and faster not through text but through graphics, videos and anecdotes, and some prefer oral to written communication. Policy-makers need good communication skills, and trusted intermediaries who can engage effectively with 'hard to reach' target groups play an important role. This can be key to tapping the potential power of 'nudge' – influencing people to change their behaviour by giving them information in psychologically influential ways (see Chapter 6).

Local and national governments have long used a wide variety of media to provide information to the public. Traditional methods include noticeboards, council newspapers, service directories and posters. Increasingly, digital approaches are used, including websites and mobile phone apps (see Chapters 11 and 20) – and the COVID-19 crisis accelerated the provision of online information. Governments have increasingly collected and published performance data in the name of transparency. However, it is important that the information and the way in which it is provided are 'fit for purpose' for the intended target group(s). This has not always been done well, as Case Example 22.1 demonstrates.

Case Example 22.1 Accessibility failures of local government websites in the UK

Accessibility tests of local government websites undertaken by the UK charity Scope in 2020 revealed that 9 out of 10 of England's largest local authorities were failing to meet new regulations regarding website accessibility. The issues identified included confusing layouts, problems enlarging text, poor colour contrasts and difficulties with screen reader accessibility and using keyboard navigation. This raised concerns about access of disabled people to public services.

Source: https://www.scope.org.uk/media/press-releases/councils-fail-public-sector-accessibility-duty/.

By contrast Case Example 22.2 highlights a public agency which provides clear information to citizens about engagement opportunities.

Case Example 22.2 Information about local projects and citizen engagement opportunities in the City of Heidelberg

Since 2012 the City of Heidelberg regularly publishes a list of local projects in order to trigger citizen engagement processes. Public officers and citizens define the methods, timeframe and costs of each engagement process, subject to approval by the council. Recommendations developed are considered by the local council in its decision-making process.

Source (in German): https://www.heidelberg.de/hd/HD/Rathaus/Vorhabenliste.html.

Consultation: Approaches and evidence

Consultation differs from information provision in that it involves two-way communication between governments/service providers and citizens. It covers a wide range of activities but typically involves public services or politicians requesting feedback or suggestions from citizens. Ideally, decision-makers provide feedback to consultees on what has subsequently been decided – 'You said, we did' – to reassure them that the exercise was worthwhile.

This is likely to be especially effective (and convincing) when people have an early chance to shape the consultation, e.g. by determining which issues are considered. However, where a public agency just wants to check that it has not forgotten anything or misinterpreted the public mood, it may be appropriate simply to invite public responses to well-developed proposals.

Although digital technologies have reduced the costs of large-scale consultations, they are still not universally used – according to a recent survey of UK local authorities on public engagement in climate change issues (APSE Energy and the Consultation Institute, 2021) fewer than half of respondents had a climate change engagement strategy, and most of their outreach activities involved 'communication' rather than meaningful consultation.

A wide range of approaches are used. A survey of UK public sector consultation specialists (Consultation Institute, 2012) found that traditional consultation methods still predominated – 93% reported use of written consultations and 83% reported use of public meetings. However, other consultative methods in use, although on a smaller scale, include focus group discussions, 'visioning exercises', 'listening days' (during which residents talk to senior managers and councillors in their neighbourhoods) and opening up council meetings with scheduled regular public question times. Moreover, almost all local councils, and many other local service providers, now conduct residents' and users' surveys to gauge public satisfaction with existing services.

So, does consultation make a difference? Strangely, this is not well researched. Two recent US survey experiments with nationally representative samples show that public consultations may reduce the blame attributed to elected representatives whose decisions end up backfiring (Kevins and Vis, 2021). However, more research is needed on the extent to which public managers and elected politicians make use of consultation results and what impact it has on their decisions.

There are indications that consultation is not always seen in a favourable light. In some cases, the public is presented with a narrow range of options to choose from, which may leave them feeling 'railroaded'. And while consultation has become mandatory for urban planning in most developed countries, and is a requirement for World Bank and other aid in developing countries (Baker, Coaffee, and Sherriff, 2007), many exercises appear tokenistic: consultation occurs at such a late stage that citizens believe that the key decisions have already been taken. Moreover, sometimes on grounds of cost, public agencies frequently fail to provide adequate feedback to consultees and explain how their views have influenced decisions.

All these problems mean that, in practice, 'consultation' can become a one-way flow of information. Worse still, many initiatives involve narrowly defined groups of the 'usual suspects'. There is often talk of 'consultation fatigue'. However, in practice, some groups are 'over-consulted', while the views of others are still not heard. Indeed, so-called 'hard to reach' groups often find that it is the public service providers who are 'hard to reach' – and even when they are contacted, public agencies may be perceived as wanting to keep control and have the last word.

Participation in public decision-making: Approaches and evidence

Earlier in this chapter, we defined participation as a more intense interaction between public organizations and citizens where each party has a role in decision-making (e.g. in relation to laws, policies, priorities, regulatory sanctions, etc.) and influence upon the final decision.

Case Example 22.3 The UK Climate Assembly

Six Select Committees of the UK Houses of Parliament commissioned Climate Assembly UK to bring together 108 people from across the UK, chosen to be representative of the population, to examine the question:

'*How should the UK meet its target of net zero greenhouse gas emissions by 2050?*'

The purpose was to issue recommendations about how the UK could satisfy the Climate Change Act amendment of 27 June 2019, which mandates that the country must reach net-zero carbon emissions by 2050.

The assembly met for six weekends between January and May 2020 and published its final report, *The Path to Net Zero*, in September 2020. This provides detailed recommendations across ten areas including how we travel, what we eat and how we use the land, what we buy, heat and energy use in the home, how we generate our electricity and greenhouse gas removals.

Select Committees intend to use the assembly's results to inform their work in scrutinizing government.

Source: https://www.parliament.uk/get-involved/committees/climate-assembly-uk/.

How common are such participation practices in public decision-making? The OECD (2020) reports that public agencies are increasingly using representative deliberative processes to involve citizens more directly in solving complex policy challenges. The tool-box contains a wide variety of approaches, including Citizens' Assemblies, Citizens' Juries/Panels, Consensus Conferences, Planning Cells, Citizens' Councils and Citizens' Dialogue. While only limited numbers of citizens can participate in such exercises, they are randomly selected, so can be seen as at least partly 'representative'. These 'mini-publics' have been used in diverse policy areas (e.g. health, environment, social policy, constitutional reform), at various stages of the policy process (from policy formulation to scrutiny) and across local, regional, national and transnational levels of governance (Elstub and Escobar, 2019: 25).

An example of a government embracing digital citizen participation is given in Case Example 22.4.

Case Example 22.4 Digital participation at national and local levels in Singapore

The UN E-Participation Index ranks Singapore 6th globally, and as particularly strong on using new media to gather a broader range of perspectives and insights from citizens. The government has made use of interactive methods such as dialogue sessions, straw polls, public forums, focus groups, telephone calls, email messages, faxes, internet relay conversations and SMS to engage the public.

In 2012, 'Our Singapore Conversation' was launched as a national dialogue on the country's future. Led by the Education Minister, a 26-member committee comprising Singaporeans from various backgrounds (e.g. the grassroots, private sector, non-profits, academics, the sports and arts communities) generated conversations with 47,000 citizens across 660 dialogues held in 75 different locations. Focus group discussions were held on housing, healthcare and education, and review committees were convened to discuss the necessary changes. Feedback from Singaporeans led to major policy changes. Reflecting on the intangible benefits of the Conversations, the Minister reported that they 'allowed citizens to appreciate one another's perspectives, put their own in a wider context, and build a common space'.

Source: https://ctic.nus.edu.sg/resources/CTIC-WP-03(2022).pdf.

However, citizens often remain sceptical about public participation. For example, an OECD survey shows that in all but 4 of 21 countries a majority of respondents actively disagree with the statement 'I feel the government incorporates the views of people like me when designing or reforming public benefits' (OECD, 2019).

Research by Gaventa and Barrett (2010: 3), which analysed 100 research studies of 4 kinds of citizen engagement in 20 countries, concluded that 'citizen participation produces positive effects across [several] outcome types, though in each category there are also examples of negative outcomes'. Benefits included the construction of citizenship, strengthened practices of participation, the building of responsive and accountable states and more inclusive and cohesive societies, but outcomes varied by type of citizen engagement and political context. Interestingly, participation 'success' was not strongly linked to 'level of democratisation' – nor was citizen engagement more likely to lead to government responses in more democratic than in less democratic states.

Although there is a lack of clear evidence about its impacts, there is now a stronger body of knowledge about how to implement public participation, its potential and its pitfalls in different contexts. Nevertheless, public sector organizations often fail to take account of good practice (see Chapter 28 on evidence-informed policy) or to experiment with democratic innovations (Elstub and Escobar, 2019) and, as a result, risk 're-inventing the wheel' and repeating mistakes made elsewhere.

Co-production

Public service co-production means providing services *with* and not just *to* citizens. This means treating citizens not as passive recipients of services but harnessing their knowledge, experience and skills to improve public services or outcomes. As shown in Table 22.1, this requires joint action, using the Four Co's (co-commissioning, co-design, co-delivery or co-assessment) which involves a closer and more intensive form of relationship. We will discuss this topic in detail in Chapter 23.

Engagement by whom?

Another important issue is *who* should engage with governments and service providers (see also Chapters 7, 15 and 26).

There are three key groups:

- *Customers* – in some cases the views of users/clients/customers (Simmons et al., 2009) will be the most valuable form of input to decision-making, e.g. in informing service providers about satisfaction with a service.
- *Citizens* – in other cases, citizens as a whole have an important stake in decisions – e.g. taxpayers who do not use a service themselves (such as prisons) nevertheless have a legitimate interest in its cost-effectiveness.
- *Communities* – many policies target specific communities (of place, identity or interest), which should be involved in policy design and delivery.

Combining the three types of interaction identified in Table 22.1 with this threefold categorization of the main stakeholder groups provides a useful typology of different modes of engagement (see Figure 22.2).

It is important to be clear from the outset about the objectives of each engagement initiative, because this ensures that the right groups are involved and the right tools and techniques are used. It can also clarify how much influence is on offer to the public, thus reducing the risk of disillusionment further down the line.

Drivers of citizen engagement

So, what are the drivers of citizen engagement? The OECD (2020, chapter 1) identifies economic, cultural, political, technological and environmental factors, including

- Rising economic and social inequalities
- Groups feeling 'left behind' and conflicts between those with different identities and values
- Pressure for greater participation by citizens who are 'dissatisfied democrats' (Webb, 2013)

- Declining trust in political institutions
- New technologies and social media enabling 'participation at scale'
- Wicked issues, such as climate change, requiring inputs of multiple stakeholders, including citizens

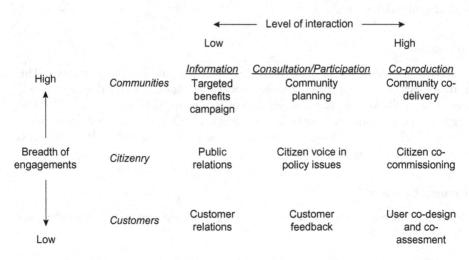

Figure 22.2 Examples of modes of citizen engagement.
Source: Adapted from Martin and Boaz (2000).

These trends imply that citizen engagement is being driven both top-down, e.g. by the desire of some politicians to reform democratic governance, and bottom-up, by citizens wishing to make their voices heard.

Potential benefits of citizen engagement

In order for citizen engagement to be sustainable, all key stakeholders need to benefit. The literature highlights several potential benefits:

- Improving policy-making by allowing government to tap wider sources of information, perspectives and potential solutions
- Facilitating greater and faster interaction between citizens and governments
- Increasing accountability and transparency, which in turn increase …
- … Representativeness, legitimacy and public confidence (therefore, serving as an antidote to rising 'anti-politics' sentiment).

However, these 'fuzzy' benefits are difficult to measure. For example, to test if citizen engagement produces better policy decisions, we would need experiments that compare similar policy processes with and without citizen engagement – which are difficult to enact. Consequently, it can be hard to make a business case for citizen engagement, and this may be one of the reasons for governments' patchy record when it comes to using it. For example, the Blair government required local governments in England to include consultation in reviews of services which had previously had little direct contact with the public, and this spawned new, more interactive approaches to reaching diverse communities (Martin et al., 2001). Similarly, the

Local Government and Public Involvement in Health Act 2007 placed on local authorities a new duty to 'inform, consult and involve' local people. However, the coalition government elected in 2010 abolished many of the key drivers of and instruments for engagement, including the duty to inform, consult and involve, the national survey of citizen satisfaction and the national collection of outcome indicators.

Obstacles to effective engagement

While the online platform Participedia (https://participedia.net/) and the OECD (2020) showcase a plethora of citizen engagement case studies, Stoker and Evans (2019) suggest that small-scale democratic innovations have had little impact on 'anti-politics' sentiment. So, what are the obstacles to effective engagement? Many are common to other forms of social innovation (see Chapter 19) – but some are more specific to engagement.

Power to the people?

As noted above, increased citizen engagement does not enjoy unqualified support among all public officials and politicians. Some see it as a threat to their professional judgement or democratic legitimacy. And there are legitimate concerns about the influence of self-appointed citizen 'experts' and the potential capture of participatory processes by unrepresentative activists or other vested interests (Cooke and Kothari, 2001). However, in practice, engagement with service users and citizens does not obviate the need for professional expertise or political judgement. It simply provides more information about the range of (often conflicting) views and priorities among the public.

Moreover, public service providers could benefit from increased engagement with their own workforce many of whom are well positioned to provide valuable feedback.

Have we got the right approach?

Many public sector organizations focus a great deal of effort on choosing the 'right' method(s) of engagement. In practice, there is rarely one correct approach. Some, for example public meetings, citizens' juries and focus groups, offer high levels of interaction but reach only a small proportion of the population. They are also relatively costly, time-consuming and require skilled facilitation. Other methods, such as referenda, which are widely used in European countries such as Switzerland, Italy, Liechtenstein and Lithuania (Geissel, 2019), engage larger numbers of citizens but provide less in-depth interaction.

In order to avoid duplication and bring together disparate initiatives, some organizations have developed databases of previous consultations. And in some areas joint consultation strategies are developed by local councils, health authorities, the police and other agencies to ensure that they coordinate their initiatives or, better still, pool their resources to conduct a combined exercise. However, it remains the case that in too many cases 'the infrastructure for participation is inefficient and outdated' (Nabatchi and Leihningher, 2015: 4).

We usually ask a question ten times and use the information once. We must learn to ask once and use the answer ten times in different settings.

                                                            Local authority chief executive

---

Making engagement relevant to citizens

One way of alleviating this problem is to focus on those policies and issues that matter most to citizens – usually very local issues such as community safety, street cleaning and facilities for young people. Almost all citizens care about at least one issue or service, but sometimes service providers do not ensure that they are consulting each citizen about the things that they are most interested in. Given that local supermarkets can now send customers highly relevant offers, based on their recent spending, it seems odd that many local councils don't use the information they hold to tailor communication and engagement strategies to individuals' needs and interests.

It is also important to use the consultation methods that members of the public are most comfortable with – and avoid those they dislike. For example, participatory budgeting in the UK often relies on public meetings, even though many people find meetings inconvenient and uninteresting.

Ensuring engagement makes a difference

A major obstacle to engagement is public scepticism about whether governments and public service providers will take any notice. And, indeed, in many cases the scope for action is constrained because an agency has only limited control over a policy area. Local authorities in the UK, for example, have limited direct influence over many of the issues which local people feel most strongly about – such as health, community safety and employment – and may have limited room for manoeuvre even when it comes to services they provide because of duties, standards and budgets determined by national government. Ken Livingstone, a former Mayor of London, questioned whether, in light of this, citizens can achieve meaningful change, quipping: 'If voting changed anything, they'd abolish it'.

It is therefore important to make clear at the outset what the parameters of engagement are, what issues are up for negotiation, what changes are possible and what is 'off-limits'. It is also crucial that there is effective communication with users and citizens throughout the process and, where possible, some early 'wins' are achieved and celebrated – communities often complain that decision-making processes are too slow, and lose interest if improvements do not materialize fairly rapidly. Therefore, although 'closing the loop' by giving feedback on how engagement results were used – what decisions were taken and why – may take time and money, it is invariably a price worth paying.

Making citizen engagement sustainable: The need for deeper democratic reforms

The debate about citizen engagement has evolved quickly across the globe. On the one hand, many policy-makers and senior public service managers in OECD countries like to portray themselves as 'listening to citizens' or even 'engaging citizens in public decision-making processes', resulting in a modern 'deliberative wave' (OECD, 2020). On the other hand, aggregate survey data show an overall decline of trust by citizens in politicians in liberal democracies since the 1990s, which might be directly affecting political engagement and is exploited by populist politicians (Stoker and Evans, 2019). In an age which is defined by 'anti-politics', where citizens are sceptical about traditional political institutions and processes (Flinders, Wood and Corbett, 2019: 148), we need deeper participatory democratic reforms, which go beyond isolated citizen engagement initiatives in order to rebuild trust in political institutions and improve the quality of public policies (Stoker and Evans, 2019).

In a number of countries, emphasis has been placed on strengthening 'deliberative democracy' by supporting processes and institutions which involve citizens in in-depth consideration of public issues. For example, deliberative polls supported by the Deliberative Democracy Lab led by Prof. James S. Fishkin have made a major impact on constitutional amendments in Mongolia in 2019 – see https://cdd.stanford.edu/. Tens of thousands of comments flowed from the meetings held by parliamentarians with citizens across Mongolia, which fed into the formulation of the new constitution.

However, not all citizen engagement approaches are embedded in political processes. Many democratic innovations remain ad-hoc and unsystematic, so there is a need for rules and regulations guaranteeing the implementation of direct democratic, as well as dialogue-oriented, procedures – Geissel (2019: 415), for example, recommends that the threshold for citizen petitions for policy change should not be too high (around 3% of the population) but, at the same time, there should be a reasonable threshold for making direct democratic decisions, e.g. at least 20% of citizens must agree with the proposal.

This is one example of the kind of 'hybrid' democratic innovation advocated by Fishkin (2009), who points out that participation is just one of a 'trilemma' of democratic values – (political) equality, (mass) participation and (meaningful) deliberation. Although they are each equally important for democracy, they are extremely difficult to achieve at the same time – trying to realize any two of them will necessarily undermine the third. For example, a strong focus on achieving mass participation may promote equal representation but is likely to be at the cost of in-depth citizen deliberation.

The right combination of these democratic values will depend on the context, which means that different hybrid approaches will be relevant in each country – the approach in East Belgium is illustrated in Case Example 22.5.

Case Example 22.5 The Permanent Citizen Dialogue in East Belgium

In 2019 the regional Parliament of the German-speaking Community in East Belgium passed a decree to establish a permanent citizen dialogue. Proposals for topics which fall under the responsibilities of the German-speaking Community can be submitted by various stakeholders, including by at least 100 citizens resident in East Belgium (about 0.12% of the population in the region). From these proposals, the Citizens' Council selects or formulates a concrete topic which is then dealt with by the Citizens' Assembly, consisting of 25 to 50 citizens living in the German-speaking communities, selected by lot and representative of age, place of residence, gender and socio-economic background. The Citizens' Council is made up of 24 former Citizen Assembly participants and monitors the subsequent implementation of the recommendations of the Citizens' Assembly.

Source (in German): https://www.buergerdialog.be/.

As Stoker and Evans (2019: 133) conclude: 'Participatory reforms can reinforce the quality of representative democracy and representative democracy can provide the basis for effective and legitimate public participation. It's about combining those things. It is the mix that matters'.

Finally, we should recognize a further type of citizen engagement, namely participation in protests, demonstrations, strikes, riots, sit-ins, boycott, petitions to Parliament, etc. – all of which we might classify as different kinds of 'social movement'. Prominent examples include Extinction Rebellion, #MeToo, Fridays for Future and #BlackLivesMatter. These movements generally have explicitly political purposes, aimed at changing public policy. In a sense, these activists represent the polar opposite of 'anti-politics', although citizens who have become entirely disenchanted with political processes also sometimes use these mechanisms to express their frustrations and seek change – e.g. the *gilet jaunes* in France since 2018. As these social movements are not specifically instigated, nor usually sanctioned, by public organizations, they fall outside the scope of this textbook but insightful treatments of their significance for public policy are given by Barnes et al. (2007) and MacNeil (2019).

Summary

Engaging service users and citizens in policy-making and in the design and delivery of public services can take many forms. Less interactive approaches involve a one-way flow of information from policy-makers and public service managers to the public. More interactive approaches include consultation – a two-way flow of information and views between policy-makers/managers and users/citizens – and participation in policy-making, with co-production being the most interactive approach.

Engagement may include a range of different stakeholder groups, from individual service users to the public as a whole.

There is a vast array of techniques for achieving citizen engagement. What matters most is that the tools used are fit for purpose and appropriate to the context.

Citizen engagement offers a range of potential benefits but also entails formidable challenges. Policy-makers, politicians and public service managers should take enough time and be sufficiently open-minded to draw upon the growing body of evidence, when developing their own organization's approach to public engagement.

Anti-political trends such as declining voter turnout and the rise of populist politicians point to a need to reinvent the relationship between the citizen and institutions of government, if a 'crisis of legitimacy' is to be averted. This will require more experimentation with democratic innovation.

Questions for review and discussion

1   In what ways can engagement with citizens enhance public policies and public services?
2   What are the benefits of representative democracy? How can these be reconciled with increasing citizen engagement in policy decisions?

Reader exercises

1   Think of your own experience as a user of public services. What services or issues would you like to have more influence over? How might the organization(s) responsible for these services engage most effectively with you?
2   Interview a local councillor to get his or her views on how his or her role has changed as a result of more public engagement.

Class exercise

Work in groups on this exercise.

Access information provided to residents by a local authority (ideally the council where you study, work or live) about a service of interest to your group.

Write a short report on the strengths and weaknesses of the council's communications, taking into account questions such as:

- How easy was it to obtain information?
- How user-friendly is it?
- Is it sufficiently comprehensive?
- Is there adequate provision for those with particular communication needs (e.g. translations, large-print versions)?
- Can people feed back their views to the council easily?
- Does it invite people to engage more intensively in further activities?

Draw up an action plan to address the weaknesses you have identified in the council's communications approach. Explain your proposals to the other groups.

Further reading

Stephen Elstub and Oliver Rodriguez Escobar (eds.) (2019), *Handbook of democratic innovation and governance*. Northampton: Edward Elgar

John Clayton Thomas (2012), *Citizen, customer, partner; Engaging the public in public management*. Abingdon, Oxon: M.E. Sharpe.

References

APSE Energy and the Consultation Institute (2021), *Climate emergency public engagement survey*, https://www.consultationinstitute.org/wp-content/uploads/2021/01/Climate-Emergency-Public -Engagement-Survey.pdf (accessed 26 July 2022).

Sherry Arnstein (1969), The ladder of citizen participation. *Journal of the American Institute of Planners*, 35(4): 216–24.

Mark Baker, Jon Coaffee and Graeme Sherriff (2007), Achieving successful participation in the new UK spatial planning system. *Planning Practice & Research*, 22: 79–93.

Marian Barnes, Janet Newman and Helen Sullivan (2007), *Power, participation and political renewal: Case studies in political renewal*. Bristol: Policy Press.

Bill Cooke and Uma Kothari (2001), *Participation: The new tyranny*. London: Zed Books.

Consultation Institute (2012), *The current state of public consultation in the public sector: Survey results*. Consultation Intitute available at http://www.communityresearch.co.uk/resources/assets/files/The _Public_Sector_Survey_Report_April_2012.pdf

Angela Coulter and Jo Ellins (2006), *Patient-focused interventions: A review of the evidence*. London: Health Foundation.

Stephen Elstub and Oliver Escobar (2019), Defining and typologising democratic innovations, in: Elstub, Stephen and Escobar, Oliver Rodriguez (eds.), *Handbook of democratic innovation and governance*. Northampton: Edward Elgar: pp. 11–31.

James Fishkin (2009), *When the people speak: Deliberative democracy and public consultation*. Oxford: Oxford University Press.

Matthew Flinders, Matthew Wood and Jack Corbett (2019), Anti-politics and democratic innovation, in: Elstub, Stephen and Escobar, Oliver Rodriguez (eds.), *Handbook of democratic innovation and governance*. Northampton: Edward Elgar: pp. 148–160.

John Gaventa and Gregory Barrett (2010), *So what difference does it make? Mapping the outcomes of citizen engagement*. IDS Working Paper 347 Brighton: Institute of Development Studies.

Brigitte Geissel (2019), Democratic innovations in Europe, in: Elstub, Stephen and Escobar, Oliver Rodriguez (eds.), *Handbook of democratic innovation and governance*. Northampton: Edward Elgar: pp. 404–420.

Anthony Kevins and Barbara Vis (2021), Do Public Consultations Reduce Blame Attribution? The Impact of Consultation Characteristics, Gender, and Gender Attitudes. *Political Behaviour*, https://doi.org/10.1007/s11109-021-09751-5

Kirsty MacNeil (2019), *We're in a movement moment but we need public service values more than ever* available at https://www.bsg.ox.ac.uk/blog/were-movement-moment-we-need-public-service-values-more-ever

Steve Martin and Annette Boaz (2000), Public participation and citizen-centred local government: lessons from the best value and better government for older people pilot programmes, *Public Money and Management*, 20(2): 47–54.

Steve Martin, Howard Davis, Tony Bovaird, James Downe, Mike Geddes, Jean Hartley, Michael Lewis, Ian Sanderson and Phil Sapwell (2001) *Improving local public services: final evaluation of the Best Value pilot programme*, London: Stationery Office.

Tina Nabatchi and Matt Leighninger (2015), *Public participation for 21st century democracy*. Hoboken, NJ: Jossey Bass.

OECD (2019). *Risks that Matter: Main Findings from the 2018 OECD Risks that Matter Survey*. Paris: OECD. www.oecd .org/social/risks-that-matter.htm

OECD (2020). *Innovative citizen participation and new democratic institutions: Catching the deliberative wave*. Paris: OECD. https://doi.org/10.1787/339306da-en

Richard Simmons, Martin Powell and Ian Greener (2009), *The consumer in public services: Choice, values and differences*. Bristol: Policy Press.

Gerry Stoker and Mark Evans (2019), Does political trust matter? in: Elstub, Stephen and Escobar, Oliver Rodriguez (eds.), *Handbook of democratic innovation and governance*. Northampton: Edward Elgar: pp. 120–134.

Paul Webb (2013), Who is willing to participate?. *European Journal of Political Research*, 52: 747–772.

WRR (2012), *Confidence in citizens*, Summary of Report No. 88, Scientific Council for Government Policy.

23 Co-production of public services and outcomes

Elke Loeffler

Introduction

Co-production is not a new concept. What is new, however, is the widespread interest in using co-production to extend involvement with service users and local communities to improve public services and outcomes. User and community co-production has become one of the most popular topics in public governance, as evidenced by an exponential growth of publications on different aspects of co-production since the third edition of this textbook. Furthermore, the term is also increasingly used by stakeholders in public policy and public services. For example, in the 2021 Adult Social Reform White Paper, *People at the Heart of Care*, the UK government's vision for adult social care highlights co-production as an important approach to enable innovation in the sector, e.g. contributing to improved design of social care services. Nor is this just "talk" – the growing interest in tele-health and peer group support has shown how service users can be helped to do more for themselves or others by harnessing their knowledge and expertise as "people with lived experience".

These examples represent different kinds of activity by citizens, working with the public sector. However, many such contributions made by citizens remain largely invisible. Indeed, a recent short study of public services for children and young people with special educational needs and disabilities (SEND) in Birmingham, UK, uncovered 48 revealing case studies of co-production in the city, although inspectors (and many managers in the SEND system) had previously concluded that co-production was an area of 'failing practice' (Bovaird and McCaffery, 2022).

Moreover, scaling of effective co-production initiatives has been slow. While there are fascinating case studies of co-production in a wide range of services, most initiatives have remained small-scale and ad-hoc. Although the use of digital technologies may in the future support the scaling of production, it has so far often simply led to more user or community self-help.

So, does the increased interest mean that co-production will be the future of all public services? Or is it just a cover for reduced public budgets under austerity? It is still too early to answer this question in respect of the longer-term future. However, in the context of current public policy, it is clear that there is an urgent need for policy makers to take more account of the existing empirical knowledge about co-production and for researchers to undertake more empirical research into its functioning, potential and limitations.

This chapter discusses definitions of co-production and differentiates it from citizen engagement (see Chapter 22), partnership working (Chapter 17) and social innovation (see Chapters 6 and 19). It explores the conceptual roots of co-production and identifies different approaches. It uses existing research evidence on co-production to highlight its enablers and

DOI: 10.4324/9781003282839-26

drivers, potential benefits and limitations and the likely barriers to scaling it – and finally it considers the potential pitfalls of co-production.

Learning objectives

This chapter will consider:

- Why has co-production become such a topical issue in the public domain?
- What are the conceptual roots of co-production and how does it differ from citizen engagement and partnership working?
- What are key co-production approaches? (The Four Co's Framework)
- What are the potential benefits of co-production?
- What are the barriers to spreading co-production across services and local areas?
- What are potential pitfalls of co-production?

Why has co-production become such a topical issue?

So, why co-production? And why now? Clearly, awareness has risen that policy agendas such as climate change, renewable energy and the reduction of health inequalities simply cannot be tackled by public agencies alone – they require contributions from active citizens. Here it is the public sector which has recognised that it needs to encourage more citizen co-production.

Cynics might suggest that interest in co-production follows the business cycle, with peaks during times of severe public sector austerity such as in the early 1980s and the recession after 2008. However, as Box 23.1 shows, co-production has more drivers than just austerity.

Box 23.1 Drivers of co-production may include…

- political need to reduce public budgets
- demographic change – the ageing society puts pressure on health and social care
- professionals becoming more willing to work with service users as 'experts by experience'
- citizens becoming more willing and confident to share their capabilities
- growth of "wicked problems" that cannot be solved by "experts" alone
- understanding by citizens and service professionals of the need for behaviour change in order to tackle health, social and environmental problems
- opportunities offered by digital technologies (tele-care, tele-health, social media) and open data

---

What is co-production?

The co-production discussed here is not about Hollywood films or TV shows (although you can read about such co-production in Wikipedia) but about relationships between citizens and public service organisations. There are many different definitions of co-production, as Box 23.2 shows.

Box 23.2 Co-production definitions

In pure coproduction ... the client does some of the ... work which could conceivably have been done by the service company.

(Normann, 1984: 81)

The process through which inputs used to produce a good or service are contributed by individuals who are not "in" the same organization.

(Ostrom, 1996: 1073)

Co-production is any active behaviour by anyone outside the government agency which:

- is conjoint with agency production, or is independent of it but prompted by some action of the agency;
- is at least partly voluntary;
- either intentionally or unintentionally creates private and/or public value, in the form of either outputs or outcomes.

(Alford, 2009: 23)

Coproduction is a relationship between a paid employee of an organisation and (groups of) individual citizens that requires a direct and active contribution from these citizens to the work of the organisation.

(Brandsen and Honingh, 2016: 431)

User and community co-production of public services and outcomes is about public service organisations and citizens making better use of each other's assets, resources and contributions to achieve better outcomes or improve efficiency.

(Governance International, https://www.govint.org/)

In each of these definitions, although they are quite different, the "co-" part of the word stresses that "it takes two to tango", i.e. professionals and citizens working together. This highlights that co-production is not only about "user involvement" but also about staff participation, which means that HR has a key role in enabling staff to make use of their own ideas, skills and experience and to support their users to make a contribution to improve outcomes (see Chapter 10).

The term "co-production" was coined originally at the University of Indiana in the 1970s when Professor Elinor Ostrom (the first woman to be awarded the Nobel Memorial Prize in Economic Sciences) and her colleagues were asked to explain to the Chicago police why the crime rate went up when police came off the beat and into (apparently more mobile) patrol cars. Her empirical research identified that this move broke the all-important link between the police and the public (Ostrom et al., 1977). With the police in their fast cars, the public seemed to feel that their intelligence, support and help were no longer needed. In fact, it turned out that the police needed the community as much as the community needed them – and Ostrom called this joint endeavour at the heart of all services *co-production*.

The positive analysis of co-production derives much from the services management literature – as Normann (1984) points out, the production and consumption of services are inseparable. From this perspective, quality in services is essentially secured during the act of service delivery (what Normann calls "the moment of truth"), in the interaction between the customer and provider, rather than just at the end of a series of "production" processes in which the service is performed "on" the customer. Because they are integral to the service production process, customers do not evaluate service quality solely on the outcomes (e.g. the success of a medical treatment in a hospital) – they also consider how the overall process felt (e.g. how friendly and responsive were the hospital medical staff and how comfortable was the ward). Co-production is therefore intimately related to quality management (see Chapter 13).

From this positivistic services management perspective, which assumes that all services require contributions from both service provider and service user, it is a natural conclusion that all services are co-produced (Osborne et al., 2013). However, this does not get us very far – the interesting questions from this perspective are whether greater or lesser contributions from citizens (or from service providers) would bring better results and how the interaction between citizens and staff can be made more effective. These are key questions to which we return later.

So far, we have described co-production as a positive concept. However, it is important to highlight that some proponents of co-production tend to see it as a normative concept, built upon desirable values, enshrined in a set of principles for how service providers and people using services should work together. We suggest a set of such principles in Box 23.3.

Box 23.3 Co-production principles

- *assets-based*: Citizens and communities are people with capabilities and resources, not just needs (this is also referred to as a "strengths-based" approach)
- *enabling*: Co-production requires co-producers to encourage and value each other's contributions
- *collaborative*: Elected politicians and public officers should work collaboratively with citizens and communities, rather than paternalistically
- *outcome-oriented*: Co-production puts the focus on public outcomes (quality-of-life outcomes and governance principles) rather than just public services
- *democratic*: In a representative democracy, co-production needs to contribute to the policies of elected politicians, which in turn need to pay attention to the needs and capabilities of citizens

Source: Adapted from Loeffler, 2021: 39.

As the term "co-production" becomes increasingly popular, it naturally also becomes blurred. For example, it is often used as a "catch-all" term for all forms of working together with partner organisations or all examples of citizen engagement. Using the term to describe relationships between organisations is unfortunate, given that we already have good terms for such relations – e.g. 'partnership' (see Chapter 16). So, in this chapter the use of the term co-production will be confined to collaborative relationships between public services (regardless of whether these are provided by public, private or third sector organisations) and citizens, either in their roles as individuals (e.g. service users) or as local communities.

Differentiating co-production from citizen engagement is more challenging. In Chapter 22 citizen "engagement" is explored as a generic concept, describing all forms of involvement of citizens with the public sector, even where citizens don't make any significant contribution (e.g. the "one-way informing" rung of the Arnstein (1969) ladder of participation, typified by the UK government sending letters to notify all 60+ year-olds of their forthcoming "winter fuel" subsidy payment). Co-production is a particular form of citizen engagement in which citizens *do* make significant contributions to activities which improve public services or publicly desired outcomes. So, co-production is a more intense form of engagement – consequently, it would usually be placed towards the top of the Arnstein ladder.

Most of the co-production literature has focussed on how public service providers can bring citizens into their services. However, there is an alternative to this traditional "inside-out" pathway to co-production. Table 23.1 shows different combinations of either citizens or public service staff exhibiting active or passive behaviours. Co-production (Cell A) occurs when both service providers and recipients are active and make a joint contribution to improving public services or outcomes. However, more common in public services is the scenario where professionals provide services for rather passive (or passively treated) service recipients (Cell B). In Cell C we find activities which achieve publicly desired outcomes through social groups organising themselves to provide self-help. Cell C also covers many cases of volunteering – only when volunteers work closely with service professionals does this become "co-production" (Cell A), rather than an aspect of self-organising communities. Cell D characterises scenarios where neither professionals nor citizens contribute much to publicly desired outcomes, e.g. where marginalised citizens suffer from low access to public services and social exclusion from their local community – these are people who are often regarded by public services as "hard-to-reach", although they themselves may rather perceive that it is the public services which are hard to reach.

When public service organisations bring citizens into their services, the "traditional" route to co-production, we are moving from Cell B to Cell A. However, as the arrow from Cell C to Cell A highlights, co-production may also emerge from citizen-led initiatives, which eventually also involve the public sector. For example, in Sweden 10–15% of all child care is provided by parents' cooperatives which rely heavily on parent participation

Table 23.1 Pathways to co-production

		Engagement of service users or communities	
		Active	**Passive**
Engagement of public service organisations	**Active**	A Co-production	B Professional-led service provision
	Passive	C Self-help and self-organising communities	D "Hard-to-reach" and vulnerable individuals or groups

Source: Adapted from Loeffler, 2021: 52.

(Vamstad, 2012). The open government movement has also promoted bottom-up forms of co-production, as open data made available by government allows users to create new content for each other – e.g. the interactive forum of the Dutch Agency for Unemployment Benefits (www.forum.werk.nl), which enables job seekers to answer each other's questions and discuss job-related issues with each other. So, are these examples 'co-production' – or just self-organising activities by citizens? Well, both are indeed co-production: the Swedish child care cooperatives get public funding, while the Dutch agency provides support from 14 staff members, who facilitate the discussion and provide answers to questions not answered by other users (Meijer, 2012).

Co-production approaches: The Four Co's

So far we have talked about co-production as an overall way for users and communities to contribute to public services and outcomes. However, it is useful to distinguish four different approaches to co-production – the Four Co's, as set out in Box 23.4 (see Loeffler, 2021).

Box 23.4 The Four Co's model

1. *co-commissioning* of priority outcomes: Citizens know best what matters to them (citizens as co-prioritisers and co-funders)
2. *co-design* of improved pathways to outcomes: Citizens know things which professionals don't know (citizens as co-innovators and co-improvers)
3. *co-delivery* of pathways to outcomes: Citizens have capabilities, skills, time and resources to improve public services and public outcomes (citizens as asset-holders) and can promote the value of public services they engage with (citizens as "legitimators"), so that other citizens are more likely to work closely with those services and agree to their (co-)funding (citizens as "co-workers")
4. *co-assessment* of public services, outcomes and governance principles: Citizens often know better than professionals whether a pathway works for them (citizens as co-evaluators)

Source: Adapted from Bovaird and Loeffler, 2013: 5.

Three of the Four Co's – namely, co-commissioning, co-design and co-assessment – mainly involve citizen voice. Co-delivery, on the other hand, is mainly about citizen action to improve public services and/or outcomes. This distinction is important, as many co-production initiatives have paid far more attention to citizen voice in public services and rather neglected the potential of citizen action to co-deliver both public services and publicly desired outcomes. We now look at each of the Four Co's in turn.

(1)   *co-commissioning* involves the public sector and citizens working together, using each other's knowledge and expertise, to plan and prioritise which services should be provided for which people, using public resources and the resources of communities. Examples include involving citizens in service planning, micro-commissioning by service users (using individual budgets given to them by the local authority) and participatory budgeting (see Case Example 23.1)

Case Example 23.1 Co-commissioning: Participatory budgeting in Brazil

The example of Brazil has inspired participatory budgeting (PB) exercises around the world since the 1980s. Indeed, the PB movement has spread to over a hundred cities across the country, with particularly famous examples in Sao Paolo, Belo Horizonte and Porto Alegre (although the latter was much diluted after the change in political control in 2004).

The Prefeitura (City Council) of Recife, a city of over 1 million residents in the state of Pernambuco, in the northeast of Brazil, is divided into six regions, each of which has three "micro-regions". The area-based discussions in PB take place in these 18 micro-regions. Citizens are involved in the four basic processes of PB in Recife:

A.   generating proposals for the most important projects or service changes to con-
     sider for the next year
B.   getting citizens to vote on these, so that the priorities can be established
C.   refining these priority projects/service changes, so that they are more practical
     and cost-effective
D.   monitoring the implementation of the agreed (and refined) priority projects

Source: Adapted from Bovaird (2012).

(2)   *co-design* offers a structured approach to harnessing the best ideas from the people who
      will ultimately use and deliver the service – e.g. personalisation in social care, website
      redesign and innovation labs with service users – see Case Example 23.2

**Case Example 23.2 Co-designing innovative solutions with jobseekers:
The Co-Production Labs of Offenbach Employment Agency, Germany**

The Offenbach Employment Agency *MainArbeit* embarked on a co-production journey in 2019, which started with the Co-production Star Action Learning Programme
delivered by the nonprofit organisation *Governance International*. This included an
action-learning programme to co-design innovative solutions with job seekers within
Co-Production Labs.

The Labs typically consisted of small teams of front-line staff, middle managers,
representatives of third sector providers and jobseekers, following a structured co-
design methodology. In Offenbach Employment Agency the Co-Production Labs were
given explicit permission to make mistakes but had the responsibility to document the
lessons learnt in a workbook and to share them within the organisation. Together
the five Labs which emerged covered all Four Co's, including co-commissioning, co-
design, co-delivery and co-assessment of employment services, which provided a rich
learning experience for *MainArbeit*.

Source: Adapted from Loeffler and Schulze-Böing, 2020.

(3) *co-delivery* is about citizens and the public sector working together to deliver services and improve outcomes – see Case Example 23.3. Other examples include community asset transfer, peer support groups and street champions (e.g. Neighbourhood Watch)

Case Example 23.3 Community Health Workers co-delivering malaria diagnosis and treatment in Tigray

The Tigray project, named after the Ethiopian region in which it took place from 2005 to 2009, aimed to address issues such as low access to health services, inadequate diagnosis and low provider and patient compliance with therapy in the region. These issues reduced the effectiveness of malaria drugs from 98% in clinical trials to 37% effectiveness.

A core element of the co-production approach was the training of Community Health Trainers from the farm community to provide diagnosis and treatment with the support of health professionals. This project was embedded in an international partnership between the WHO, a pharmaceutical company, public agencies in Italy and health agencies in Tigray.

The co-delivery approach led to a 40% reduction in malaria deaths, compared to the traditional hospital-based approach. The services provided by the Community Health Workers were not only much less expensive and easier to access for local people but also strengthened their self-efficacy.

Source: Adapted from Cepiku et al. (2021: 56–57).

(4) *co-assessment* involves citizens working with professionals and managers to give feedback on services and support received. It offers an "insider view" often lacking in formal assessment. Examples include user group reviews of public services, tenant inspectors of housing, social care users acting as care home inspectors and self-monitoring by people who use health and care services (see Case Example 23.4)

Case Example 23.4 Self-monitoring of patients in Highland Hospital, Sweden

In 2001, the gastroenterology unit at Highland Hospital had long waiting lists. Growing numbers of in-patients suggested a highly expensive new ward would be needed. However, a review of services, from a patient perspective, redefined the role of patients to give them greater responsibility for their health as members of a team, rather than just subjects of medical intervention. Patients were trained in self-monitoring – this proved much more effective than the previous check-ups, which generally did not coincide with times when patients were experiencing "flare-ups" in their condition.

The greater responsibility exercised by patients resulted in nearly 50% fewer hospitalisations over a seven-year period (compared to a national average of a 4% decrease) – and a bigger ward was no longer needed, a major saving in hospital costs.

Source: Adapted from Bovaird and Tholstrup (2010).

Potential benefits of co-production

Evaluations of co-production demonstrate that it has potentially many benefits in terms of better outcomes, service quality and efficiency. Figure 23.1 highlights that community co-production is likely to be even more beneficial than user co-production, as it increases social capital which is defined as the capacity of a social group or area to act together to achieve an agreed outcome. However, community co-production is also likely to be more challenging for public services organisations to initiate, requiring more inputs (e.g. staff time) to build trust between groups of citizens and also between citizens and public service providers.

There is also evidence that co-production increases service quality, objectively measured, when public services are more tailored to user needs (Loeffler, 2021). However, this does not always translate into increased user satisfaction (quality as a subjective experience), as co-production can also raise user expectations.

There is much less hard evidence on the effects of co-production on service efficiency. While, particularly in times of austerity, co-production may be introduced as a way to reduce staff inputs through increased citizen inputs (e.g. unpaid volunteers) many public agencies do not record properly how staff time is used and how it is affected by co-production, let alone measuring the inputs provided by citizen co-producers.

Of course, these benefits may be seen differently by different stakeholders – in Box 23.5 we set out reasons why various stakeholders might buy into user and community co-production.

Box 23.5 Benefits of co-production for different stakeholders

People who use services

- improved outcomes and quality of life
- higher quality public services and increased satisfaction

Communities

- increased social capital and resilience
- increased well-being

Front-line staff

- more responsibility and job satisfaction from working with empowered service users

Heads of services

- moving resources from problem-solving to prevention
- better collaboration with third sector organisations
- mobilising new resources and expertise for innovations

Top managers

- reducing the demand for services
- enabling the shift from a service provider to a service commissioner role

Politicians

- strategy to cope with reduced budgets and demographic change
- alternative to significant service cuts
- building trust with service users and communities
- improving the perceived legitimacy of public services

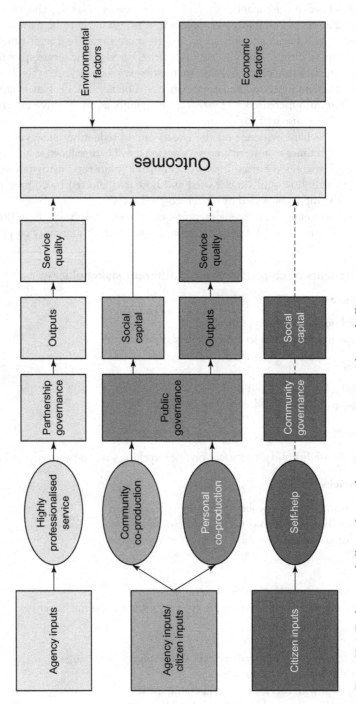

Figure 23.1 Evaluation of effects of co-production on outcomes, quality and efficiency.

Source: Adapted from Loeffler and Bovaird (2018: 270).

Overcoming the limitations and barriers

Research has demonstrated powerful cultural and systemic barriers to co-production (Loeffler, 2021, Chapter 5), which have to be overcome if co-production is to break into the mainstream and be scaled more widely in public services and local communities.

Figure 23.2 distinguishes between four types of barriers:

- barriers from user characteristics
- barriers from community characteristics
- barriers from organisational characteristics
- barriers from context

Barriers related to user and community characteristics typically involve a lack of ability or willingness to co-produce. This involves the need to better understand citizens' motivation for co-production (Steen, 2021). In the case of community co-production evidence often reveals a lack of community cohesion. In particular, vulnerable people may not be well integrated in their local community (Brandsen, 2021). Nevertheless, we should not assume that co-production mainly appeals to well-educated middle-class people. Empirical research on citizen co-production has shown that, particularly with preventative activities which involve "doing" and not just "talking", we should not make general assumptions about who is likely to co-produce – and who is not (Bovaird et al., 2021). Moreover, Brandsen (2021: 536) suggests that "co-production seems to have a better chance of involving vulnerable people than traditional types of participation, because it removes some of the elements that make the latter less accessible and attractive".

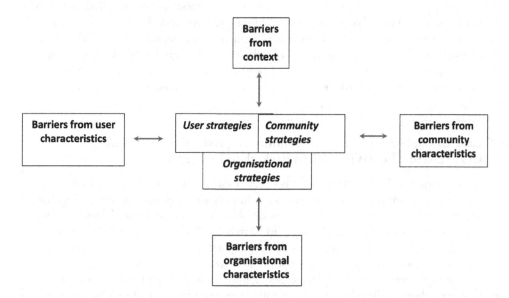

Figure 23.2 Barriers to co-production.

Organisational barriers to co-production typically include:

- **funding and commissioning barriers** – funders and commissioners often overlook the contributions citizens can make to improve public outcomes. Shifting toward outcomes-based commissioning should boost the potential for co-production by enabling interventions that range more widely than existing services (Loeffler, 2021) and by generating more relevant evidence about outcomes that matter (Durose et al., 2017)
- **inappropriate professional skills** – co-production requires staff to segment user and community groups in order to identify their assets and capabilities, as well as their special needs. Furthermore, staff need strong communication and enabling skills in order to support citizen co-producers and to facilitate their interaction with public service providers (Tuurnas, 2021). These skills may not be widespread
- **risk aversion** – co-production is still seen as highly risky by many politicians, managers and professionals. Traditional risk assessments are often carried out from the point of view of the commissioner or service provider, therefore often neglecting the risks (and potential benefits) perceived by users or communities (Loeffler, 2021, 267). Co-assessment provides one method for a more balanced risk assessment
- **political and professional seeking status and "control"** – if co-production is seen by politicians, managers and professionals as a loss of status or "control", a culture shift may be needed for co-production to succeed

In spite of 40 years of interest in user and community co-production of public services, there are still few examples of co-production being mainstreamed. Co-production initiatives still tend to be add-on, small-scale projects "complementing" traditional forms of public services. It is still not clear if this is because the above barriers are still very large in many organisations – or if public managers and elected politicians simply find the level of innovation required to be too daunting and the levels of risk to be too high (see Chapter 19).

Digitalisation has been seen as one way of overcoming many of these barriers (see Chapters 11 and 20) – nevertheless, it is still an open question how much impact it will have on the evolution of co-production. While some large-scale hackathons have shown that digital technologies enable mass engagement in co-production at relatively low cost (see Case Example 23.5), there are instances where digital technologies take over the role of citizens as co-producers and make co-production obsolete and other instances where digital technologies substitute the role of governments and enable community self-organisation.

Case Example 23.5 Digital community co-production to respond to COVID-19: The #WirVsVirus hackathon in Germany

Hackathons involve a competition between innovative ideas. They typically start with an open call by a government for solutions to a complex problem, inviting citizens to work in teams with other stakeholders through an online platform. The #WirVsVirus hackathon in Germany in March 2020 was special, judging from its size, scale and speed: More than 28,000 people participated as unpaid volunteers and generated about 1,500 project ideas within 48 hours.

It resulted from the Federal Chancellery joining up with seven third sector organisations specialising in digital services to organise a national response to the COVID-19 pandemic. As this initiative came from the "civictech community", this is a (rare) example of co-production, which followed the "outside-in" pathway to co-production, through which the public sector adds value to initiatives started in civil society, rather than the more traditional "inside-out" pathway to co-production, where public sector organisations invite citizens to co-produce better public services and outcomes (see Table 23.1).

However, while the hackathon incorporated elements of each of the Four Co's and was followed by an implementation phase, the support provided was considered insufficient and the time frame too short for scaling the innovations.

Source: Adapted from Loeffler and Masiga (2021).

Potential pitfalls of co-production and ways of addressing them

While the available evidence suggests that user and community co-production is still largely underused as an alternative service delivery approach, it is not a panacea. There is an increasing critical literature highlighting the potentially negative effects of co-production (Loeffler, 2021: 304–318) on both quality-of-life outcomes and on the achievement of key public governance principles.

For example, a specific co-production initiative may not achieve publicly desired outcomes or only with an unfavourable or negative cost-benefit ratio. Other negative outcomes can include professional job losses due to increased engagement of unpaid volunteers or perceived exploitation of citizen co-producers who may get pressed to take on an increasing number of tasks, some of which are inappropriate for them. Public governance pitfalls include lack of accountability, transparency, diversity and sustainable engagement of citizen co-producers.

In cases where co-production contravenes legal, regulatory or moral codes it is justified to speak of the "dark side" of co-production. An extreme example occurs when professionals and citizens engaged in co-production do not comply with the rule of law, for example when volunteers engaged in public safety co-production initiatives engage in vigilante behaviour, not recognising the limits to their contributions in improving public safety.

Summary

The conceptual roots of co-production go back to public sector economics (e.g. Elinor Ostrom), the services management literature (e.g. Richard Normann) and citizen engagement (e.g. Sherry Arnstein). From these varied sources has emerged an understanding of citizens as people with a potentially greater contribution to make to public outcomes, which can be harnessed when working together with public services.

User and community co-production of public services and outcomes is therefore different from simply "volunteering" in the community (where the public sector may not be involved) or "consultation" (where the contribution of citizens may be relatively small, especially where decisions are largely pre-decided). It is also different from inter-organisational collaboration, for which the word "partnership" is already available.

Why does co-production matter in public services? Quite simply because it opens up both new resources for public services, harnessing the strengths, assets and potential contributions of citizens, and it provides new expertise on ways of achieving outcomes which matter to citizens, based on experiences not available to service professionals – both of which are major benefits for public services under immense pressure.

There are a number of powerful cultural and systemic barriers to co-production that hinder its spread. While all of these barriers can in principle be overcome, they mean that there are still few examples of co-production being mainstreamed and taken to scale across public services – as with all social innovations, it meets with considerable resistance and takes time to become accepted, even where it appears to have high potential for success.

Questions for review and discussion

1   What makes co-production different from other forms of citizen engagement?
2   Which roles do the Four Co's offer to citizens as co-producers? Can you find examples of citizens performing these roles in other chapters of this book?

Reader exercises

1   Find examples from the literature of all the benefits of co-production listed in Box 23.5.
2   Consider the kinds of services and outcomes for which co-production is *not* likely to be appropriate in general. Are there some aspects of these services and outcomes for which some element of co-production might nevertheless be relevant?
3   Choose a community organisation which is based where you live. Discuss with members of their staff the extent to which they encourage local residents to co-produce better outcomes with the public services in the area.

Class exercise

Divide into small groups, half of which will consider some of the activities group members have undertaken in the past month in their university or college, while the other half will consider activities group members have undertaken in their private lives. How might these activities have resulted in better outcomes for group members or other citizens, if they had been done through a co-production approach? In plenary, discuss the implications for the way in which higher education and services in the public sector might be managed in the future.

Further reading

Tony Bovaird and Elke Loeffler (2012), From engagement to co-production: The contribution of users and communities to outcomes and public value. *Voluntas*, 23 (4): 1119–1138.
Elke Loeffler (2021), *Co-production of Public Services and Outcomes*. Cham: Palgrave Macmillan.
Elke Loeffler and Tony Bovaird (eds.) (2021), *The Palgrave Handbook of Co-Production of Public Services and Outcomes*. Cham: Palgrave Macmillan. https://doi.org/10.1007/978-3-030-53705-0.

References

John Alford (2009), *Engaging public sector clients. From Service Delivery to Co-Production*. Houndsmills: Palgrave Macmillan.
Sherry Arnstein (1969), The ladder of citizen participation, *Journal of the American Institute of Planners*, 35 (4): 216–24.

Tony Bovaird and Jörgen Tholstrup (2010), Collaborative governance between public sector, service users and their communities. In: *Repositioning Europe & America for Economic Growth: The Role of Governments & Private Actors in Key Policy Areas*, edited by E. Bohne. Berlin: LIT Verlag, pp. 3–25.

Tony Bovaird (2012), Participatory budgeting in the city of Recife, Brazil - the world's most participative public agency? *Governance International Case Study*. Birmingham: Governance International. https://www.govint.org/good-practice/case-studies/participatory-budgeting-in-the -city-of-recife-brazil-the-worldas-most-participative-public-agency/.

Tony Bovaird and Elke Loeffler (2013), "We're all in this together: Harnessing user and community co-production of public outcomes". In: *Making Sense of the Future: Do We Need a New Model of Public Services?* edited by Catherine Staite. Birmingham: University of Birmingham, pp. 1–13. https://www.birmingham.ac.uk/Documents/college-social-sciences/government-society/inlogov/ publications/2013/chapter-4-bovaird-loeffler.pdf.

Tony Bovaird, Elke Loeffler, Sophie Yates, Gregg Van Ryzin and John Alford (2021), International survey evidence on user and community co-delivery of prevention activities relevant to public services and outcomes. *Public Management Review*, pp. 1–23. https://doi.org/10.1080/14719037 .2021.1991665.

Tony Bovaird and Maria McCaffery (2022), *Mapping SEND Co-Production in Birmingham: The Current State of Play*. Birmingham: Governance International, Birmingham City Council and Birmingham Parent Carer Forum (with Maria McCaffery). https://www.localofferbirmingham.co.uk/wp-content /uploads/2022/07/Mapping-Send-Co-Production-in-Birmingham.pdf.

Taco Branden (2021), Vulnerabe citizens: Will co-production make a difference? In: *The Palgrave Handbook of Co-Production of Public Services and Outcomes*, edited by Elke Loeffler and Tony Bovaird. Cham: Palgrave Macmillan, pp. 527–540. https://doi.org/10.1007/978-3-030-53705-0.

Taco Brandsen and Marlies Honingh (2016), Distinguishing different types of coproduction. A conceptual analysis based on the classical definitions. *Public Administration Review*, 76, 427–435.

Denita Cepiku, Marta Marsilio, Mariafrancesca Sicilia and Milena Vainieri (2021), *The Co-production of Public Services: Management and Evaluation*. Cham: Palgrave Macmillan.

Catherine Durose, Catherine Needham, Catherine Mangan and James Rees (2017), Generating 'good enough' evidence for co-production. *Evidence & Policy: A Journal of Research, Debate and Practice*, 13 (1), 135–151.

Elke Loeffler and Tony Bovaird (2018). From participation to co-production: Widening and deepening the contributions of citizens to public services and outcomes. In: *The Palgrave Handbook of Public Administration and Management in Europe*, edited by Edoardo Ongaro and Sandra van Thiel. London: Palgrave, pp. 403–424.

Elke Loeffler and Matthias Schulze-Böing (2020), Co-producing better futures in employment services: The co-production labs of Offenbach employment agency. *Governance International Case Study*. Birmingham: Governance International. https://www.govint.org/good-practice/case-studies /co-productionlabs-of-offenbach/.

Elke Loeffler and Claudia Masiga (2021), Communities co-producing new solutions to meet Covid-19 challenges through a hackathon in Germany. In: *Covid-19 and Co-Production in Health and Social Care Research. Policy and Practice* (Vol. 2), edited by Oli Williams et al. Bristol: Policy Press, pp. 57–65.

Albert Meijer (2012), Co-Production in an Information Age. In: *New Public Governance, the Third Sector and Co-Production*, edited by Victor Pestoff, Taco Brandsen and Bram Verschuere. New York and London: Routledge, pp. 192–208.

Richard Normann (1984), *Service Management: Strategy and Leadership in Service Business*. 2nd ed. Chichester: John Wiley and Sons.

Stephen Osborne, Zoe Radnor and Greta Nasi (2013), A new theory for public service management? *American Review of Public Administration*, 2 (43): 135–158.

Elinor Ostrom, Roger B. Parks and Gordon P. Whitaker (1977), *Policing Metropolitan America*. Washington, DC: US Government Printing Office.

Elinor Ostrom (1996), Crossing the great divide: Co-production, synergy and development. *World Development* 24 (6), 1073–1087.

Trui Steen (2021), Citizens' motivation for co-production: Willingness, ability and opportunity at play. In: *The Palgrave Handbook of Co-Production of Public Services and Outcomes*, edited by Elke Loeffler and Tony Bovaird. Cham: Palgrave Macmillan, pp. 507–525. https://doi.org/10.1007/978 -3-030-53705-0.

Sanna Tuurnas (2021), Skilling and motivating staff for co-production. In: *The Palgrave Handbook of Co-Production of Public Services and Outcomes*, edited by Elke Loeffler and Tony Bovaird. Cham: Palgrave Macmillan, pp. 491–506. https://doi.org/10.1007/978-3-030-53705-0.

Johan Vamstad (2012), Co-production and service quality; A new perspective for the Swedish Welfare State. In: *New Public Governance, the Third Sector and Co-Production*, edited by Victor Pestoff, Taco Brandsen and Bram Verschuere. New York and London Routledge, pp. 297–316.

24 Managing risk and resilience in the public domain

Tony Bovaird and Elke Loeffler

Introduction

The world is an uncertain place – the only certainty appears to be that uncertainty will always be with us. Nevertheless, in virtually all chapters of this book there are discussions of "what is likely to happen if…", which demands that we explore these uncertainties in some detail. Furthermore, this word "likely" alerts us to the fact that we are often dealing with probabilities. And that, in turn, reminds us that in every model, in every analysis, there is a risk that the relationship being discussed will *not* work as expected. Some of these risks are bigger than others – and some are potentially more important than others. This chapter is about identifying these risks, mitigating them by deliberate actions and coping with the consequences, when these mitigating interventions don't work, by building resilience into the system, so that the level of welfare in the system does not suffer.

Learning objectives

The key learning objectives in this chapter are:

- To understand how risks can be identified and assessed
- To understand how the public service system can respond to risks
- To identify the options for strengthening the "whole systems resilience chain" for the public service system

Whose risk?

Economists have traditionally defined risk as those elements of uncertainty to which probability estimates can be attached. This makes risk easier to manage than uncertainty. However, the "risk assessment and management" industry is less precise – it is typically content to use the word "risk" to cover all of the factors which contribute to uncertainty, whether or not they can be captured by probability estimates.

The key lessons from classical risk analysis are highlighted in Figure 24.1. For events with a high probability and high potential impact, we need to maintain exceptional alertness, either to maximise the gain in the case of positive impact (positive risks) or minimise losses from negative impacts (negative risks).

DOI: 10.4324/9781003282839-27

	Low probability	Medium probability	High probability
High impact	Medium priority for action	High priority for action	Very high priority for action
Medium impact	Low priority for action	Medium priority for action	High priority for action
Low impact	Very low priority for action	Low priority for action	Medium priority for action

Figure 24.1 Priority for action in relation to any given event, given its probability and potential impact.

From the same analysis, it is clear that we don't have to worry about preventing every conceivable risk – little attention needs to be paid to low probability, low impact events. The problems, of course, are that it is difficult to know in advance either the probabilities in advance or potential impact – and that there are potentially dozens, if not hundreds, of events which fall into the "high" and "very high" categories.

Although risk can be found everywhere, it has a special character in public services. A core purpose of government is to minimise risks of harm to the public. Citizens – and media commentators – expect their government to counteract any important and potentially harmful risks, however they arise – and they are not forgiving when this doesn't happen. Consequently, politicians and public managers often seem highly risk averse.

This highlights the key point that risks to the public are not the same as risks faced by public organisations in delivering public services. Naturally, during a period of declining resources, public organisations tend to look inward – to avoid all identifiable risks to their services, their reputation and their existence. But, in the era of public governance, this is not enough – there is now a critical need to look outward – helping the public, individually and in communities, cope with the changing character and intensity of the risks they face.

Risk and the current era of potential public service failure

Dramatic failures in the private market system have been evident in recent decades, particularly since the global financial system crash in 2008. What has been new in recent decades is the prospect of public service failure in many countries, given government budgets rapidly declining in real terms, often driven by populist politicians railing against "profligate spending" and right-wing governments with a "small government" agenda. Radical cuts in public spending, service rationing and reductions in service standards now mean that there are real risks that public services are no longer delivered at an acceptable standard.

Speculation about the risks of failure of specific large-scale government programmes such as new ICT systems surfaces more and more often in the media. However, the contribution of risk assessment and management to the current debate has been rather meagre. Why is this? The profession of risk management, which has bombarded managers with its tools, frameworks, matrices and spreadsheets for emergency preparedness planning, disaster recovery and business continuity work, is a key element of public sector governance. So why has it made such a limited contribution? We suggest that most risk management approaches have developed from an audit approach that focuses mainly on the risk to specific public sector organisations. They therefore mirror the "blame-avoidance" and self-preservation strategies of public institutions more than they represent a thorough framework for reducing the risks experienced by the public.

This internally oriented approach is understandable but not adequate. Rather than opening up strategic options, these approaches often close them down, fostering a culture of paralysis focused fearfully on "what worst events might happen" and encouraging low risk appetites and risk averse behaviour.

However, this caution may well be misplaced in many cases. Taking our cue from the analysis of complex adaptive systems (see Chapter 18), we have to ask whether we are operating in the "simple", "complicated" or "complex" knowledge domains (Snowden and Boone, 2007). Current risk assessment tools may work well in the simple knowledge domain (where relationships are already well understood) but are much more suspect in the complicated knowledge domain (where our current knowledge is very limited and uncertainty is high) and are largely irrelevant in the complex knowledge domain, where uncertainty is all-pervading (Bovaird and Quirk, 2013). In this latter knowledge domain, which may be very important for many policy issues, the role of risk assessment and management is necessarily very different. By definition, we are dealing with variables which are only predictable to a very limited extent. Consequently, we cannot be sure of what undesirable events are likely to happen in the system, when they are likely to happen or what might be the results of action we take to prevent such things happening. The role of risk management in this domain is to warn against the temptation to look for facts, rather than allowing patterns to emerge (Snowden and Boone, 2007). This suggests that over-confident policy prescriptions should be avoided, that experimentation is likely to be fundamentally important and that a range of policy approaches is likely to be superior to "putting all your eggs in one basket".

Given the different knowledge domains in which risk managers operate, a proper risk management strategy needs to be multi-dimensional, allowing for these differences in knowledge domains and the cultures which they promote in organisations. The lack of understanding of this need for multiple risk strategies may be a key reason for risk assessment and management not being taken seriously in many organisations.

Strategies for managing risk

We can distinguish a range of quite distinct strategies towards risk in public services:

- *building low risk activity portfolios*: Choosing a portfolio of activities with lower risk attached and managing it to avoid future risks
- *risk reduction in the environment*: Either reducing the likelihood of key risks actually occurring or influencing them to reduce their particularly worrying features
- *building resilience into the service system*, including the activities of providers and the behaviours of service users, their support networks and their communities

- *risk enablement:* Encouraging decision makers throughout the service system to choose activities with appropriate levels of risk, rather than assuming that risk minimisation is always in order

We now look in turn at the key features of each of these strategies.

Building a low risk activity portfolio

The most cautious approach to managing risk is to ensure that all the activities which are undertaken are low risk. This does, of course, have the disadvantage of ruling out some highly promising activities which might achieve much higher results but which are are have higher risks attached.

There are, however, some ways in which this low-risk approach can be made more rewarding – primarily, by flexibility or diversification. Flexibility simply means that, when things begin to go badly, the organisation can switch out of the activity into an alternative – this has the disadvantage, of course, that it rules out full-blooded commitment to highly promising options. Diversification means that the portfolio of activities in total brings successful results, even though some individual activities fail or do badly. For example, when commissioning a range of social enterprises to provide short breaks for children with learning difficulties (as fun for the children and as respite for their parents and carers), social services departments sometimes contract with several social enterprises offering a more adventurous approach (e.g. "write and perform a group musical") for those families who are willing to try it. This means that everyone can learn from innovations on offer, but if the approach doesn't suit the families which have signed up for it, they can switch into more conventional activities, so that the risk of the overall programme of activities not working out well remains low.

Kaufmann (2019) suggests that an effective portfolio for tackling a complex system must be like a *managed forest* – the portfolio contains many individual contributions from various "categories" (e.g. energy production, efficiency, carbon capture), with many "species" in each category. Such a portfolio doesn't depend on any single "big bet", but thrives through the presence of "keystone species" which together provide fundamental infrastructure services, act in conjunction to distribute resources, but with no central planning (although the forest manager continually gives it small nudges). Variations are valuable – a "specimen" that fails provides valuable material for decomposition, while unexpected new species emerge and create new niches which enrich the whole portfolio. Altogether, this portfolio is even better than "robust" – it actually *benefits* from the unpredictable changes which occur.

A more specific example of a diversification strategy is to match up some risky approaches which are essentially alternatives to each other, known as "hedging" in the portfolio risk management literature (Roberts, 2019). This involves simultaneously investing in several options, especially if one is likely to work if the other fails (Stalk and Iyer, 2016), which is expensive but greatly lowers the uncertainty – e.g. contracting with both Real Madrid and Barcelona that they will do publicity for your organisation if they win La Liga next year!

It is also possible to devolve the risk to another stakeholder, so that the blame for failure is also deflected to that stakeholder – indeed, this is one of the attractions of contracting out risky activities to the private or third sector. The appropriate allocation of risk ownership is essential – this means that commissioners need to negotiate to transfer or share risk with service providers, in a way which is equitable and ensures that the risk is managed by the party most reasonably able to do so (rather than simply transferring as much risk as possible to providers) (OGC, no date). If risk allocation puts too much risk on providers, they are likely to charge a high premium (which means poor value for money for the commissioner) or to cut costs (which means poor quality of service) or to fail altogether.

Risk reduction in the environment

For this strategy to be successful, a public service organisation needs to be operating in the simple or complicated knowledge domain, where it can have some confidence that it can predict the consequences of its interventions to change the environment. In this case, it can draw up and test some pathways to outcomes (see Figure 24.2), highlighting how such a strategy is expected to work – and the tests should allow more specific and insightful pathways to be developed. However, this strategy will clearly often involve actions by many organisations and groups outside the organisation, whose behaviour may be difficult to influence.

Building resilience into the service system

A very different strategy involves making the service system more resilient. Here, we consider resilience to be the capacity for adaptation in the service system to recover to the same or higher outcomes after a disturbance (Bovaird and Quirk, 2017) – colloquially, often referred to as "bouncing back better". This distinguishes resilience from "robustness", which is the ability of a system to maintain its operations despite disruption.

When using the Public Value Model presented by Loeffler in Chapter 15 (Figure 15.1), it is essential to recognise that stakeholders' perceptions of their outcomes are influenced not only by the level of wellbeing which that outcome brings but also by the level of uncertainty attached to it – how stable these wellbeing outcomes are in the face of the risks to which they are subjected. For many stakeholders, a high level of instability of an outcome may

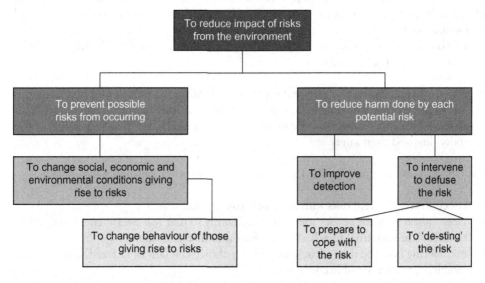

Figure 24.2 Pathways to risk reduction.

Source: Copyright © 2023 Governance International.

substantially reduce the benefit they perceive from an outcome, even one which has exhibited a relatively high average level over time. Public decision makers focused on a particular outcome therefore need to address the trade-off between the average level of wellbeing and the instability of that outcome when deciding their strategies for managing risk and achieving resilience on behalf of these different stakeholders (Bovaird and Quirk, 2017).

Consequently, a different form of resilience is required to cope with the risks which attach to each category of outcome – individual outcomes require *user resilience*, helping individuals to cope after their outcomes have been disrupted; community outcomes require *community resilience*, doing the same for communities; business outcomes require *organisational resilience*, doing the same for the overall set of firms in a specific service area and incorporating resilience on the part of each service provider, each of which is at risk of failing to provide the services expected from them; and environmental outcomes require *environmental resilience*, requiring attention to coping with risks caused by service interventions in the natural and built environments.

Risk enablement

The final strategy is risk enablement (Carr, 2010). This may seem paradoxical – in the discussion above, we have argued that risk strategies in public agencies need to focus more directly on decreasing the risks to users and communities, rather than organisations and their staff. However, there are risks to *all* activities, so this was simply a shorthand for saying "we need to focus more directly on achieving the appropriate level of risk" to users and communities. This will often be a lower level of risk – but not always. There are many enjoyable and valuable experiences which come with a level of risk attached – so a risk averse service provider may rule them out, "just in case something goes wrong". So old people may be banned from making a cup of tea for their friends in the kitchen of their care home, as there are risks of scalding from the boiling water, and young people with learning difficulties may be stopped from taking the bus from home to their care centres each morning, in case they get lost – in each case, denying them activities and a sense of achievement which would substantially increase their enjoyment of life and their ability to develop themselves and their social capabilities.

Such overcautious approaches are potentially damaging. As the UK Health and Safety Executive explains (HSE, no date):

> Often when assessing the care and support needs of an individual, everyday activities are identified that will benefit their lives, but also put them at some level of risk. This requires a balanced decision to be made between the needs, freedom and dignity of the individual and their safety.

The HSE goes on to argue that the key points to consider when balancing risk include:

- concentrating on real risks with a realistic risk of harm
- close liaison with the service user, carer and family so that risk assessments allow activities which are essential to achieve outcomes that matter to them
- considering how the risks of each individual's choice can best be reduced, as far as practicable, operating sensible controls
- organising group activities, so that the most vulnerable can be protected without unnecessarily restricting the freedoms of the most capable

Managing the "whole system resilience network"

These strategies are not mutually exclusive. The first two essentially seek to prevent risks associated with the organisation's activities, the third aims to mitigate risks and the fourth is about learning to live appropriately with the levels of risk which the organisation faces. As such, all could be pursued simultaneously.

In practice, the public sector often gives greater weight to the risk minimisation strategy than the others, thus ruling out activities which, although risky, also potentially bring major gains. This highlights the importance of incorporating at least some elements of a risk enablement strategy. However, in a risk averse world, risk enablement is more likely to be acceptable if there is some way of mitigating the potential harms which would arise if the negative risks which are identified were actually to occur. This need for mitigation, in turn, highlights the central role of resilience in putting together an overall risk strategy.

However, most approaches to resilience tend to be narrowly focused on the resilience of one set of stakeholders – service users, their communities, their service providers or the actors in their overall environment. Although each of these forms of resilience has been studied in some of the literature, there has not been a recognition that these four different types of resilience form a "whole system resilience network" – see Figure 24.3.

The "whole system resilience network" depends on each element in the network of user-community-provider-environment resilience being sound and well-balanced with the other elements. Each weak link in this system makes the system as a whole more vulnerable, as it puts more pressure on the remaining elements. Moreover, the resilience network constitutes a dynamic system, in which each of the stakeholder groups is always looking to learn and thus to improve, with the consequence that a weak link in the network reduces the overall capability of the system, both through interruptions to its dynamic development path and blockages in its capacity for learning.

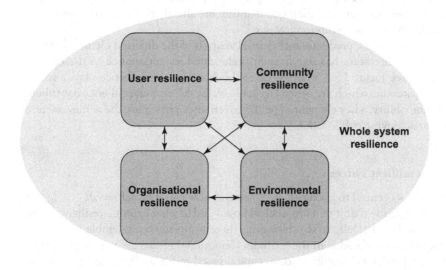

Figure 24.3 The "whole system resilience network" as a chain linking user-community-organisational-environment resilience.

Source: Copyright © 2023 Governance International.

This concept of the "whole system resilience network" has not previously been given sufficient attention. In practice, it is clear that public agencies have too often emphasised embedding resilience into the formal service provision process rather than strengthening all the links in the resilience network. For example, the Cabinet Office (2011) guidance on the resilience of critical infrastructure and essential services emphasises information sharing amongst organisational stakeholders but not activities for building service user or community resilience in the event of major crises. While understandable, given the potential for damage to agencies and their staff when their service provision fails, this narrow approach to resilience is logically indefensible. Similarly, some public service organisational briefing notes have discussed how community co-production can contribute to the resilience of community organisations but not its implications for resilience throughout the service system – e.g. Maguire and Cartwright (2008) for the Australian government; SCDC (2011) for Scottish public service organisations; CCCL (2018) for social care in Wales. While community resilience is desirable, its strengthening is not enough if service users or service provides are unable to cope with the crises which inevitably occur.

Moreover, it is essential to recognise that whole system resilience is not simply a set of additive resilience mechanisms. Each of its elements interacts with the other elements, as shown in Figure 24.3. For example, service users who become more resilient, and thereby more self-confident, are more likely to accept a wider range of paid carers supporting them – this in turn helps providers to build resilience into their service by allowing them to send a wider range of staff as cover for sick staff. Again, a community which increases its resilience by developing a "hyper-local" website connecting a wide range of local people will simultaneously increase service user resilience, since users can glean information and advice on how to support themselves over and beyond what they get from their commissioned services – and, simultaneously, service users who become more resilient are better placed to contribute to community activities, thereby strengthening community resilience. This interconnectedness even applies to organisational resilience – strengthening the resilience of an existing set of services by bringing in new providers to replace or supplement existing provision will be much less risky if service users and their communities are already resilient, so are more able to cope with the short-term disruption involved.

Finally, as a result of the predominantly partial analysis of the different elements of resilience, much of the literature has significantly understated its importance to the creation of public value – see Figure 15.1, where each of the four types of resilience plays a role in supporting the outcomes which are central to public value. Moreover, resilience contributes directly to sustainability, a key element of public governance principles, the achievement of which is key to achieving public value.

How to build a resilient system

So, if resilience is so central to good risk management, how can it be achieved?

We need to recognise that it remains unclear how – and to what extent – resilient organisations can be designed (Duit, 2016). However, there is already considerable research on how resilience can be embedded in the attitudes ("emotional resilience"), actions ("behavioural resilience") and relationships ("social capital-based resilience") of the agents within public service systems.

Building on process approaches, which conceptualise successive resilience stages (anticipation before the unexpected event, coping with it and adaptation after it) (Duchek, 2020), we can see public service organisations as promoting resilience through a range of different approaches (the six E's) – see Box 24.1.

Box 24.1 The six E's for building resilience

Public service organisations can promote stakeholder resilience by helping them to:

- *expect the worst*: The "surprise factor" can be removed from risk through forecasting what might happen and preparing scenarios of the consequences
- *educate themselves*: A range of instruction and training processes can give actors an understanding of risks which might occur – and how to cope with them
- *encourage others*: Public service organisations can nudge actors to change their behaviour, so negative risks become less likely or less dangerous
- *equip for change*: Actors can be prepared to cope with the circumstances which they may have to face when the negative risks occur
- *experience different situations*: Actors learn from actually experiencing what can go wrong – but only if supported to come through the experience
- *exercise their responses*: In different simulations, actors can try out and practice different responses to see what works best for them, given the need to learn from experience and break away from previous practices

Source: Copyright © 2023 Governance International.

These approaches each embed, to a greater or lesser degree, intensive collaboration by stakeholders, including co-production by service users and communities, whereby all stakeholders can use their knowledge and experience to protect themselves better from the problems caused by negative risks.

We now consider some of the key approaches available, for each of the four types of resilience.

User resilience: Helping a majority of citizens to develop greater resilience is likely to be important to public organisations (recognising that those who can buy alternative services when public services fail are already at least partly resilient). When the six E's (Box 24.1) are applied to service users, they embed user co-production, in which service users can be helped to use their knowledge and experience to protect themselves better from the problems which arise when negative risks actually eventuate. Service users know things that many professionals don't ("users as thinking people"), can make a service more effective by the extent to which they go along with its requirements ("users as critical success factors") and have energy and skills which they may be prepared to devote to ensuring higher outcomes from services, both for themselves and others ("users as resource-banks and asset-holders"). When these assets and potential contributions are identified and made use of, users are more able to take on some of the functions which professionals play, if those professionals become unavailable or are only able to play a more limited role. In this way, user co-production through co-commissioning, co-design, co-delivery and co-assessment of services can build up the capacity of service users to cope with less input from public services and to adapt to different configurations of services (see Chapter 23). In addition, it makes sense to build the capacity of the direct support network for users – their family, friends, neighbours and those who provide voluntary help to them. This "user and carer capacity building" is essentially developing "potential co-production", in case it is needed.

Community resilience: Communities, like users, know and understand things that go beyond the knowledge bases of professionals ("It takes a village to raise a child"), can exert social pressure to ensure community safety ("Notice: We report ALL anti-social behaviour in this pub to the police") and can mobilise effort and skills to help achieve publicly desired outcomes ("Emergencies and disasters bring out the best in folk"). Again, identifying these assets and potential contributions and mobilising them in community co-production means that communities are more able to cope when public services fail to deliver as expected. This is a role long played by community capacity building, which is once again becoming topical in the UK, although not yet widely funded from mainstream public agency budgets. As with service users, stakeholders in the community can be helped by public service organisations to anticipate, cope and adapt through the "six E's".

Organisational resilience: Service providers have an interest in ensuring their resilience in the face of potential service failure – as of course do the service commissioners who have commissioned these providers. Service provider organisations are likely to have internal mechanisms designed to flag up potential failure sufficiently early for appropriate avoiding steps to be taken – these are likely to include performance management frameworks and feedback channels from both users and staff. Indeed, service commissioners are likely to insist that organisations bidding to provide a service demonstrate that they have credible mechanisms such as these in place. Again, organisational actors can be helped to anticipate, cope and adapt through the "six E's". Moreover, service providers can also build resilience into their services partly by encouraging user and community resilience, as outlined above – this will minimise the damage from any service failures which occur and may decrease the likelihood of such failures occurring.

Service commissioners can also build organisational resilience, by designing and implementing market-wide mechanisms, such as those outlined in Box 24.2.

Box 24.2 Market-wide mechanisms for organisational resilience

- system entry barriers – e.g. restricting potential bidders to those who can prove financial stability, a successful track record and/or a high level of staff qualifications ("vigilant gatekeeping")
- structural solutions – e.g. having several suppliers, retainer arrangement with alternative suppliers, residual in-house capability or an emergency budget ("system redundancy")
- complexity solutions – e.g. acceptance of some promising "black box" approaches, where this is plausible narrative, with quasi-grants and rigorous evaluation ("meta-planning"), so that the system is more open to transformational innovations
- process solutions – e.g. compulsory insurance bonds or several different supply methodologies (i.e. different "pathways to outcomes") so that the system contains a variety of service mechanisms, in case there is complete failure in one type of mechanism ("built-in flexibility")

Adapted from Bovaird and Quirk (2013).

In line with the concerns outlined earlier about public agencies placing more weight on risks to public agencies and their staff than to users and communities, there must be at least some suspicion that public agencies have often given more emphasis to embedding resilience into the formal service provision process, given the potential for damage to agencies and their staff when service provision fails, and have, up to now, tended to underemphasise the resilience of service users and communities.

Environmental resilience: In many countries, by far the greatest attention in recent years has been devoted to achieving environmental resilience. However, much of this has focused on the macro-level, namely achieving global goals to minimise climate change. At the level of the individual public service organisation, the environmental risks are more micro-level – they are less about how the environment will be damaged by the organisation's activities and more about what environmental crises will mean for that organisation. Rather than global risks, the most serious such events faced by a public service organisation are those at national, regional or local levels, dependent on the reach of its activities. For example, for a national Ministry of Energy, key environmental resilience issues revolve around how energy provision can be maintained during and after major disruptions, such as climate events (e.g. floods) or political events (e.g. war in oil- or gas-producing states) or industrial disputes (e.g. strikes in nuclear- or electric-power plants). In the case of a local authority, key environmental resilience issues revolve around the threats to life from local climate events (a flood, a snowstorm) or risks to local employment from shifts in energy production (closure of coal mines) or to local farming from changes in consumer taste (switch to organic foods). In such cases, resilience can be, at least partially, assured by having a reserve of redundant resources – alternative energy provision, emergency service staffing, temporary employment opportunities, etc. – although this clearly implies a degree of short-term inefficiency, since it involves some resources being underused until the crisis occurs. Of course, both the macro-level and the micro-level environmental issues are important in the wider picture – but external pressure is likely to be necessary to make clear the importance of macro-level environmental resilience to a specific public service organisation, e.g. by imposing legal requirements or budgetary incentives or penalties.

Changing the organisational culture in relation to risk and resilience

Moving to a strategic focus on risk and resilience will represent a major change in public sector culture. However, it is not likely that public organisations or staff will be asked to launch into radically higher levels of risk – what we are discussing is much more likely to be a different portfolio of risks. The key is that the risks concerned are agreed by users and communities, not simply agreed strategically by leaders of the public agency and implemented by staff, both guided by their own self-interest. In any case, at least some parts of each public service organisation are already likely to be oriented to the achievement of user and community outcomes, so the agency only needs to rebalance its existing cultures to give more weight to such cultures, rather than creating a new culture outright (see Chapter 7). To help with this, the incentive structure in the organisation needs to be rebalanced, so that managers and professionals are more likely to choose activities with appropriate levels of risk, rather than assuming that risk minimisation is always in order.

Given that, in experimentation, some failure is inevitable, the key design principle of experimental approaches to policy and practice learning is: "Fail early, fail fast, fail cheap … learn … and put it right quickly". Experimentation is, however, hard to propose and to implement in the public sector. Each time failure occurs it is liable to be highlighted – by opponents and the media – as a "scandal" or evidence of incompetence. Moreover, multiple approaches to policy and service delivery can easily be parodied by opponents or the media as an admission of ignorance or dithering. So how can experimentation, which is fundamental in the complex and chaotic knowledge domains (and may even be valuable in the complicated domain), be protected and encouraged in this environment of risk averse public policy making?

First, we need to recognise that we are taking huge risks already, although we are often not owning up to them – and we also need to recognise that we are often focusing on minimising risk to public sector organisations and staff, not to service users and citizens. Both of these recognitions highlight the urgent need for a culture change. Second, we need to own up to the fact, often forgotten, that the role of public service organisation in reducing risks to the welfare of our service users and communities can be quite small – often much less than we like to think – so that, in many cases, the damage we can do through experimental approaches which turn out not to work is similarly quite small scale. Third, when we report "new risks" (e.g. from the public co-producing or self-organising), we need to be specific about how big will be the change to the risks to service users and citizens, compared to the risks of current ways of working. And, finally, we need to explore with citizens whether it's time to accept a different ratio of risks to costs in the future, rather than always choosing risk minimisation.

Of course, relying on resilience to cope with risks of service failure brings its own risks. Resilience can never be assumed to be complete and, however well we may have fashioned it in the light of past experience, new risks may be distinctively different, so some resilience mechanisms will no longer work (Duchek, 2020). It would be foolishly optimistic to believe that any method of dealing with uncertainty would be certain in its effects!

Summary

Risk management can do much more than it has to date – but it needs to do different things. It needs to focus more on risks to outcomes experienced by service users and communities and less on risks experienced by staff and the organisation.

There are four quite different strategies available to public service organisations to deal with risk – building low risk activity portfolios, risk reduction in the environment, building resilience into the service system and risk enablement. These strategies are not mutually exclusive – all can be pursued simultaneously.

In practice, the public sector has often given much greater weight to risk minimisation, thus ruling out activities which, although risky, also potentially bring major gains. This highlights the importance of a risk enablement strategy. However, in a risk averse world, risk enablement is more likely to be acceptable if the potential harms which might arise can be mitigated by a credible resilience strategy.

However, a different form of resilience is required to cope with the risks which attach to each category of outcome – individual outcomes require *user resilience*; community outcomes require *community resilience*; business outcomes require *organisational resilience* (incorporating *service provider resilience*); and environmental outcomes require *environmental resilience*. These different types of resilience together form a "whole system resilience network", which must be managed as a system, an approach which will usually require significant culture change on the part of public service organisations.

Questions for review and discussion

1   What is the difference between risk and uncertainty? And between "positive risks" and "negative risks"?

2 How might tools and techniques from other chapters in this book help to improve the identification and mitigation of risk?

Reader exercises

1 From the references at the end of this chapter, identify three definitions of "resilience". What are main differences and the main commonalities between these definitions? How would you define it?
2 Identify from your own experience a public service which has recently experienced a crisis or severe disruption. What evidence did you see of a resilience mechanism in that service which might have made the impact of the failures less severe? How would you suggest that the resilience of the service could be improved?

Class exercise

1 In groups, search the internet to find three case studies of resilience. Identify whether they cover user resilience, community resilience, organisational resilience and/or environmental resilience. Where they do not cover all four types of resilience, suggest how they could be extended to cover the missing types. In the plenary session, each group should present its suggestions for extensions and critique the suggestions from the other groups.

Further reading

Tony Bovaird and Barry Quirk (2017), "Resilience in public administration: Moving from risk avoidance to assuring public policy outcomes through the resilience chain", in Thomas R. Klassen, Denita Cepiku and T. J. Lah (Eds.), *Routledge Handbook of Global Public Policy and Administration*. London: Routledge.
Cabinet Office (2017), *Management of Risk in Government: A Framework for Boards and Examples of What Has Worked in Practice - A Non-Executives' Review*. London: Cabinet Office. https://assets .publishing.service.gov.uk/government/uploads/system/uploads/attachment_data/file/584363 /170110_Framework_for_Management_of_Risk_in_Govt__final_.pdf

References

Tony Bovaird and Barry Quirk (2013), "Reducing public risk and improving public resilience: An agenda for risk enablement strategies", in C. Staite (Ed.), *Making Sense of the Future: Do We Need a New Model of Public Services?* Birmingham: INLOGOV.
Sarah Carr (2010), *Enabling Risk, Ensuring Safety: Self-Directed Support and Personal Budgets*. London: Social Care Institute for Excellence.
CCCL (2018), *Approaches to community resilience*. Cardiff: Social Care Wales.
Stephanie Duchek (2020), "Organizational resilience: A capability-based conceptualization", *Business Research*, 13: 215–246. https://doi.org/10.1007/s40685-019-0085-7
Andreas Duit (2016), "Resilience thinking: Lessons for public administration", *Public Administration*, 94: 364–380.
HSE (n.d.), "Sensible risk taking in care settings", https://www.hse.gov.uk/healthservices/sensible-risk -assessment-care-settings.htm
Rafael Kaufmann (2019), *Saving the World: A Portfolio Approach*. https://medium.com/in-search-of -leverage/saving-the-world-a-portfolio-approach-e73d7853b893

Brigit Maguire and Sophie Cartwright (2008), *Assessing a community's capacity to manage change: A resilience approach to social assessment.* Canberra: Bureau of Rural Sciences, Australian Government.

OGC (n.d.), *Managing Risks with Delivery Partners: A Guide for Those Working Together to Deliver Better Public Services.* London: Office of Government Commerce (p. 3) https://assets.publishing.service.gov.uk/government/uploads/system/uploads/attachment_data/file/191515/Managing_risks_with_delivery_partners.pdf

Alex Roberts (2019), *Hedging Your Bets: Taking a Portfolio Approach to Innovation.* Paris: OPSI. https://oecd-opsi.org/blog/hedging-your-bets-taking-a-portfolio-approach-to-innovation/

SCDC (2008), *Community resilience and co-production: Getting to grips with the language.* A briefing paper. Glasgow: SCDC.

David Snowden and Mary Boone (2007), "A leader's framework for decision making", *Harvard Business Review*, 85(11): 68–76.

George Stalk Jnr and Ashish Iyer (2016), "How to hedge your bets", *Harvard Business Review*, 94(5): 80–86.

25 Transparency in government

Alasdair Roberts

Introduction

Today, talk about transparency has become ubiquitous. But what precisely does transparency mean, and how is the idea translated into rules that shape how governments operate? The purpose of this chapter is to answer these questions. We shall see that transparency in government is not universally regarded as an unalloyed virtue. There are good reasons to resist demands for transparency, and contexts in which the drive to promote transparency has met stiff resistance.

Learning objectives

The learning objectives for this chapter are that you should:

- Understand what the concept of transparency means, and how it has been translated into policy;
- Identify the main arguments that have been for and against policies that are intended to promote transparency;
- Understand the main contexts in which struggles over transparency have been fought and the policy disagreements that underlie those struggles.

Context

Suppose that a group of experts had been gathered in 1985 and asked to list the characteristics of a well-governed country. They might have said that the government in such a country should be responsive to the needs of citizens; that it should be able to assure public order and provide for the public welfare; and that it should be reasonably efficient, free of corruption and fair in its dealings with citizens and businesses. It is unlikely that the experts would have said that the government should be transparent. Many people cared about open government, but they would not have ranked it prominently as a key attribute of good governance. And almost certainly they would not have used the word "transparency" to describe that quality of openness.

Much changed in the three decades after 1985. Transparency entered the vocabulary of governance and became so widely used that, in 2003, lexicographers at *Webster's Dictionary* chose it as their word of the year. Transparency, they said, was "an answer to the public's impatience with secrecy and deceit on the part of leaders, institutions and processes everywhere" (Piotrowski, 2010: 1). In 2005, World Bank President James Wolfensohn insisted

DOI: 10.4324/9781003282839-28

that "transparency is essential to good governance" (World Bank, 2005). Transparency, said a senior official at the International Monetary Fund, "helps improve governance and reduce corruption – essential ingredients for better development and faster growth" (Kaufmann, 2005: 43).

Nevertheless, transparency is an idea that can be advocated by people with many different agendas, sometimes with starkly divergent views about the role of the state. Its role in good governance therefore needs to be analysed, not assumed.

Definition and applications of the idea

We should begin by clarifying precisely what we mean when we talk about transparency in government. Many authors have proposed definitions that are comparable in content, if different in phrasing. Ann Florini, for example, suggests that transparency "refers to the degree to which information is available to outsiders that enables them to have informed voice in decisions and/or to assess the decisions made by insiders" (Florini, 2007: 5). Obviously, if we are talking about transparency in the public sector, those insiders must be politicians, political advisers or bureaucrats within public agencies. Similarly, David Heald suggests that transparency is achieved "when those outside can observe what is going on inside the organization" (Heald, 2006: 28). Again, this might be applied to private as well as public institutions; since we are interested in transparency in government, we should apply the caveat that we are interested in the conduct only of *public* organizations. In a similar vein, Patrick Birkinshaw (2006: 4) suggests that transparency "entails conducting public affairs in the open or otherwise subject to public scrutiny".

In general, one wants to be on the watch for two potentially troublesome variations on the standard definition of transparency. The first variation is that which defines transparency narrowly as a condition in which governments actively disseminate information about their work. Consider a definition of transparency as "the publicizing of policy choices" by decision makers (Fox, 2005: 2). We would, no doubt, favour this sort of activity on the part of our leaders. But observe how the definition has omitted the idea of access to information about the *process* by which choices are made – or indeed, about any other aspect of the internal workings of government. And also observe how the task of judging whether transparency has been achieved has shifted subtly from outsiders to insiders. In the broader definitions, transparency is a project of *scrutiny by outsiders*; in the narrower definition, it is a project of *publicity by insiders*. Insiders tend to prefer this narrower definition of transparency precisely because it gives them more discretion in deciding when and how to release information.

Another troublesome variation on the standard definition of transparency is pitched too broadly. Consider, for example, this definition of "open government" proposed by the Organization for Economic Co-operation and Development in 2005:

> From the public's point of view, an open government is one where businesses, civil society organizations and citizens can "know things" – obtain relevant and understandable information; "get things" – obtain services from and undertake transactions with the government; and "create things" – take part in decision-making processes.
>
> (OECD, 2005: 1)

There is nothing intrinsically wrong with this definition – who, after all, could complain about improved access to essential services, or improved opportunities to participate in policymaking? But from the point of view of analysis it is unhelpfully wide. And it also creates an opportunity for policymakers to supplant one kind of "openness" for another – to assert, for example, that they are more open because they made certain services easier to use, rather than by improving the public's capacity to scrutinize government operations.

The idea of governmental transparency has been advanced in many different ways. For example, many countries have adopted archive laws that require public officials to preserve significant records and provide public access to some of those records after the passage of a specified number of years. Recently, dozens of countries have also adopted laws that provide members of the public with a broader right to obtain copies of records that have not yet been transferred to a government archive. These statutes, sometimes known as freedom of information or "right to information" laws, can be important tools for scrutinizing the activity of government agencies (see Case Example 25.1).

Case Example 25.1 Diffusion of freedom of information laws

The United States adopted its Freedom of Information Act (FOIA) in 1966. Like many of the laws that followed it, the US FOIA does four things: it affirms a right to acquire copies of records held by government agencies; establishes a process for making requests for information; identifies reasons (such as national security) that officials may give for refusing such requests; and establishes a right of appeal to an independent authority if officials are thought to have denied requests improperly.

Only a handful of countries had adopted statutes like the US FOIA before 1990. These included some of the states of northern Europe and the older Commonwealth countries. But the next two decades saw a remarkable diffusion of similar laws – to the newly democratized nations of central and Eastern Europe, several of the major OECD countries (such as Germany and the United Kingdom) and then to many developing countries, including India, which adopted a Right to Information Act in 2005. Even China adopted national regulations which acknowledged a qualified right to government-held information. By 2019, it was estimated that well over 100 countries, comprising most of the world's population, had acknowledged the right to information. Whether that right was effective in practice – in other words, whether the policy was effectively implemented – was another question entirely.

There are a host of other statutes that also promote openness. Administrative procedure laws (such as the American Administrative Procedure Act) usually require public agencies to publish regulations and provide reasons for decisions on matters such as requests for welfare benefits or licenses. Some jurisdictions also compel agencies to hold meetings by officials in public in certain circumstances. An increasing number of countries have also adopted public interest disclosure laws – popularly known as whistleblower laws – that provide protection for government employees who reveal information about corruption and other forms of misconduct within public agencies.

Sometimes statutory disclosure requirements are tied to specific policies. For example, India's National Rural Employment Guarantee Act, adopted in 2005, contains detailed provisions that are designed to assure access to information about money spent on public works projects. The aim is to deter corruption by allowing members of the public to monitor expenditure under the programme. The American Recovery and Reinvestment Act, adopted in the wake of the financial crisis of 2007–2008, also included detailed requirements for the electronic dissemination of information about the expenditure of funds on public works projects, in a bid to counter scepticism about the wisdom of the massive spending plan.

This hardly exhausts the ways transparency has been embedded in new policies. Many governments in richer countries have recently launched "open data" programmes that are intended to provide public access to certain large datasets that have been created by government agencies. The idea is that businesses and advocacy groups might find valuable new uses for such datasets – for example, by helping travellers to track the on-time performance of airlines. Meanwhile many poorer countries participate in the Extractive Industries Transparency Initiative, which promotes disclosure of information about the payment of royalties to governments by oil and mining industries. Many countries also participate in a programme led by the International Monetary Fund that promotes transparency in the conduct of national fiscal and monetary policies, as well as periodic reviews undertaken by the World Trade Organization that are intended to promote transparency in national practices affecting international trade.

We can see that transparency is a pliant idea – that is, it can be bent to many different purposes. Indeed, this is probably the main reason for the extraordinary popularity of the concept. Groups with radically different policy goals may still agree on the importance of transparency in the part of government that is of particular interest to them. In a sense, the term helps to create an illusory sense of consensus on policy. Everyone agrees that transparency is key to good governance. But this simply masks deeper disagreements about what the role of government should be.

Arguments for and against transparency

The arguments in favour of transparency seem straightforward. One approach is to regard transparency as an important mechanism for safeguarding various fundamental human rights. For example, it is widely recognized that people have a fundamental right to participate in the governance of their own country, and it is easy to argue that this right is meaningless if people cannot acquire information about what public agencies are up to. As the Indian Supreme Court explained in an important 1981 decision, "Where a society has chosen to accept democracy as its creedal faith, it is elementary that its citizens ought to know what its government is doing" (Roberts, 2001: 262). Transparency can also protect individuals against arbitrary state action that might affect their physical security (through arrest, for example) or their economic security (through the denial of educational or employment opportunities) or even their health (through denial of healthcare or failure to regulate polluters).

There are other arguments for transparency. Some advocates say that it promotes efficiency in government, by deterring corruption or the careless use of public resources (see Case Example 25.2). Yet others argue that it improves the legitimacy (or the degree of public support) of governmental action – on the premise that individuals are more likely to accept even adverse governmental decisions if they can see that they were based on sound reasons. And some advocates argue that government-held information is, by definition, the property of the people, and that consequently it should generally be accessible for public use.

Case Example 25.2 Helping India's poor

The National Rural Employment Guarantee Act (NREGA) was adopted by the government of India in 2005. It aimed to help India's poorest by providing them with a minimum level of paid manual work every year. In the past, relief programmes like NREGA have been badly weakened by "leakages" – that is, the diversion of funds through corruption.

NREGA uses transparency to reduce corruption in two ways. Much information about programme implementation is "proactively disclosed" – that is, released automatically without any request – on government websites. This includes information that would be protected by privacy rules in other countries, such as wages paid to named individuals. Activists argue that the disclosure of this information helps workers by allowing activists to check that workers actually received the money disbursed by government.

Transparency schemes often fail because there is no group with the capacity and motivation to make use of disclosed information. NREGA addresses this problem by establishing a system of "social audit". Investigators regularly visit villages to inspect projects and interview workers to determine whether official records are accurate. Audit teams hold village meetings to discuss their findings. These meetings are the second key technique for improving transparency.

Overall, NREGA has achieved mixed results. Not all Indian states have implemented the law with equal seriousness. In some parts of India, though, NREGA's transparency rules have reduced leakages significantly and empowered many poor and marginalized citizens.

Against this there are arrayed a powerful set of arguments against transparency. Several of these fall into the category of *raisons d'état* – state interests that could be jeopardized by openness. Prominent among these are considerations of national security and diplomatic relations, which could be endangered if defence capabilities or sensitive negotiations were exposed to public view. Political leaders and senior bureaucrats also argue that they need "space to think" creatively about the management of public affairs, and that this space would be eliminated if their internal deliberations were routinely disclosed. Many government leaders feel a rising sense of anxiety about their capacity to control the course of public affairs, because of trends such as globalization and the rise of new information technologies, and this has encouraged stronger resistance to transparency initiatives – since the public agenda can easily be upset by the untimely release of information about the inner workings of government. And finally, public agencies make their own arguments about efficiency. Transparency initiatives are not costless: on the contrary, it can be very expensive to organize and release information sought by the public. Agencies sometimes say that the cost of implementing new transparency policies outweighs any benefits that these programmes might produce.

Resistance to transparency does not hinge simply on *raisons d'état*. Much of the information that is held by government agencies has been collected by other parties – individuals, businesses and other governments. And each of these other parties can make their own arguments against disclosure. Individuals can say that the release of personal information would constitute a violation of their fundamental right to privacy. Businesses can argue that the release of information that they have been compelled to give to government might jeopardize hard-earned trade secrets. And other governments that have shared information can argue that they should be allowed, as sovereign entities, to make their own decisions about whether that information should be released.

The question of whether to adopt a particular transparency policy is rarely clear cut. More often, there are compelling arguments to be advanced for and against the disclosure of particular kinds of information. The design of transparency rules – and decisions about the release of specific pieces of information – almost always requires a careful balancing of the interests that will be advanced or harmed as a result of disclosure.

Recent battles over transparency

Perhaps the best way of appreciating the complexities that can surround transparency policies is by examining some of the most critical points of debate between transparency advocates and governments over the last few years.

Problems of implementation. In many countries, promises of increased transparency by public agencies have been confounded because of a simple failure by governments to take implementation seriously. Consider, for example, the steps that are required for a law like the United Kingdom's Freedom of Information Act (FOIA) to be put into force. Officials must be taught how to recognize a request for information and how to respond to it in accordance with the law. Agencies must develop procedures for assuring that the hundreds or thousands of requests which they receive are dealt with in a timely way. Internal record-keeping practices must be good enough to allow the quick retrieval of all documents that might be relevant to a request for information. And there must be some procedure for dealing quickly and fairly with complaints about the refusal to disclosure information. In a sense, an FOIA bureaucracy must be established. This requires time, money and the attention of agency leaders. If no investment is made in the training of staff, or the establishment of routines, or improvement of record-keeping, then requests for information are unlikely to be dealt with in accordance with the law. They might simply be ignored entirely.

In much of the world, the battle over "right to information" laws has devolved into a battle over the implementation of policy. Many governments have adopted a statute that promises a right of access to government records, but they have done little to make the law work in practice. In some instances, this is because governments were never serious about transparency in the first place. They adopted the law as a symbolic measure, to appease voters or international agencies that provide financial support.

In other instances, though, governments might have been serious about transparency, but limited in their capacity to implement a new law properly. Most of the countries that have recently adopted "right to information" laws are very poor. It is one thing to make a "right to information" law work in the United Kingdom, an affluent country with a highly educated and professionalized public service (although even the UK was criticized for flaws in implementation after its Freedom of Information Act went into force in 2005). It is another thing to make the law work in a country like India, where government budgets are much more tightly constrained and the public sector workforce is less skilled. There is a strong tendency for politicians and senior bureaucrats in these countries to argue that "right to information" laws are luxury goods – fine for wealthy countries, but a distraction in poorer countries with more pressing social needs.

The effect of crises. The willingness of governments to comply with transparency rules is tested even more severely during moments of crisis. For example, many Western governments adopted more restrictive policies on disclosure of information during a resurgence of domestic terror attacks from 2001 to 2005. Officials argued that terrorists might find ways of using disclosure requirements to discover vulnerabilities in public institutions and facilities. Seemingly innocuous information was sometimes withheld on the grounds that it might be combined in unexpected ways to reveal new opportunities for terror attacks.

The financial crisis of 2007–2008 impaired transparency in another way. This crisis caused public sector debt in many advanced economies to soar. Governments responded to this by adopting severe austerity programmes that threatened to have a disproportionate effect on transparency programmes that were not regarded as being part of the "core business" of government. At the same time, government enthusiasm for privatizing public functions – and thereby putting them beyond the reach of transparency laws – was rekindled (Roberts, 2012a: 4–5).

Governments often behave differently during crises, making major decisions more quickly and with less formality than usual. Officials may be too distracted to respond in a timely way to requests for information, and even if they do, the record of decision-making may be incomplete. The paradox is that crises may be just the moment when transparency is most important. Public trust in government may be tested when officials make unexpected choices that have profound effects on the lives of ordinary people, as during the pandemic of 2020–2022. In the United States, trust in the national government has plummeted as it has wrestled with one crisis after another over the last 20 years.

Effects of privatization. Concern about the effect of privatization on transparency is not new; it was a major concern in many advanced economies throughout the 1990s. The difficulty here is straightforward. In general, transparency policies are intended to promote the disclosure of information held by public agencies. But many governments have, over the last 30 years, reduced the range of activities performed by public agencies. The forms of privatization vary. In some instances, state owned enterprises have been sold to private investors. In other instances, public agencies have retained final responsibility for certain policies, but have delegated the implementation of those policies to private sector contractors. Some governments have also become enthusiastic proponents of "public-private partnerships" in which they enter into decades-long contracts with businesses to build and operate infrastructure such as highways, schools and hospitals. In all of these cases, the same question has been posed: should privatized functions be subject to newly adopted transparency policies?

There is no easy answer to this question. A few countries have taken a very expansive view of transparency rules. For example, South Africa's freedom of information act promises access to certain kinds of records held by all organizations, public or private. A more common approach, however, is one that excludes privatized enterprises and contractors from the ambit of transparency policies. The argument is that transparency would compromise the efficiency of private enterprises, which are in any case subject to other kinds of accountability, such as to shareholders or regulators. But many advocates of transparency are not persuaded by these arguments. They take the view that if private organizations wield power delegated by governments, or spend public money, or play a critical role in the formulation of public policy, they should still be subject to the same transparency rules that are applied to conventional public agencies.

National security considerations. Another difficult question regarding transparency policy has to do with the application of the concept to defence, intelligence and policing agencies – sometimes known as the security sector of government. The argument in favour of transparency is clear. These agencies exercise power in ways that can have an immediate and profound effect on the rights of citizens. And in some countries, the security sector spends a large part of the governmental budget. There is a strong case for accountability, which in turn requires access to information about the operations of these agencies. But the arguments against disclosure can be equally compelling. Security agencies worry that the disclosure of information will allow enemies – either external or internal – to undermine public order and threaten the stability of the state itself. Indeed, fears about the threat to public security are sometimes so deeply felt that security agencies are entirely excluded from the operation of transparency policies such as "right to information" laws (see https://ti-defence.org/gdi/).

It is important to recognize that concern about the preservation of secrecy is deeply embedded in the bureaucratic practice, as well as the organizational culture, of agencies in the security sector. Most security agencies have developed complex policies regarding "security of information" (SOI). These include rules about the screening, or clearance, of individuals to determine whether they can be trusted to handle sensitive security information. Governments are also bound by international agreements to maintain rigorous SOI policies in certain areas. And over time, SOI policies have assumed unintended functions: Security clearance has become a form of bureaucratic status, and a way of narrowing the number of people who are allowed to participate in policy debates. SOI policies are so deeply rooted in culture and practice that it would be difficult for even the best-intentioned leader to overturn them quickly.

Technological change and "radical" transparency. Recently, though, advocates of transparency have wondered whether technological changes might provide a way of overcoming bureaucratic inertia within the security sector of government. WikiLeaks is a non-governmental organization that came to prominence in 2007–2011. Its aim was to create a vehicle for the rapid dissemination of information leaked by individuals within security bureaucracies and other powerful institutions. The WikiLeaks project took advantage of technological innovations, such as the digitization of government-held information, improved encryption and the internet, all of which made it easier to contemplate the large-scale leaking and re-broadcasting of information. Some commentators thought that WikiLeaks had introduced a form of "radical transparency" that would bring an "end to secrecy" in its traditional form in government (Sifry, 2011).

There is no doubt that technological change has made it easier, in some circumstances, to leak and re-broadcast information. But claims about the transformative effect of WikiLeaks were vastly overstated. Many commentators underestimated the ability of security agencies in the United States to react against WikiLeaks following a series of damaging disclosures in 2010. The United States government took legal action against individuals implicated in the 2010 disclosures and tightened its internal practices to avoid similar leaks in the future. It argued that WikiLeaks had been careless in releasing information that harmed innocent third parties as well as important US national security interests. It may be that other organizations will find ways of circumventing these new restrictions in the future, but one of the main effects of the WikiLeaks affair was to demonstrate the power and resilience of the security sector of the US government (Roberts, 2012b).

Digitization. There are other respects in which technological change has altered the debate over transparency. In one sense it has made the task of achieving openness more difficult. Fifty years ago, recordkeeping in government was largely paper-based. Officials typed memos or reports that were stored in file cabinets and libraries. The available technology limited the amount of information that could be recorded within public agencies. Obviously, this has now changed. In the digital age it is vastly easier to capture the flow of information within government agencies. As a result, the volume of information that must be managed has grown explosively. This poses tremendous challenges for information specialists within government. They must decide how to separate significant information from insignificant, develop systems for organizing and retrieving information and anticipate how information can be retrieved in the future, when current technologies are superseded by new ones. If information specialists fail to meet these challenges, then transparency policies will fail. As a practical matter, information will not be accessible – either to officials within government, or stakeholders outside government.

There is a related challenge posed by digitization. Suppose that government agencies meet the challenge of preserving this vast new supply of digitized information, and that it actually becomes available to stakeholders outside of government. Will those stakeholders have the capacity to manage and interpret the supply of information that is available to them? This was an easy job when documents were printed on paper and limited in number. It is much harder when the stockpile of relevant materials may include tens of thousands of emails and other digitized records (see Case Example 25.3). To give a sense of the scale: it is estimated that the White House transferred 77 terabytes of data to the US National Archive at the end of the presidency of George W. Bush in 2009 – more than 30 times the amount of data transferred at the end of the Clinton administration eight years earlier.

Case Example 25.3 Journalists learn how to use "big data"

As government agencies have shifted from paper-based modes of recordkeeping to electronic modes, journalists have had to acquire new skills. In the United States, a non-governmental project – the National Institute for Computer-Assisted Reporting – was set up in 1989 to help journalists cope with "big data", the label frequently used to describe the mass of digitized information that is now being collected within government.

The appeal of computer-assisted reporting (CAR) lies in its ability to detect patterns of behaviour through analysis of big data. For example, the *New York Times* used a database maintained by the US Department of Transportation to demonstrate that fatal crashes involving Ford Explorer sport utility vehicles were three times as likely to be related to tyre failures as fatal crashes involving other brands. The *Times'* stories substantiated concerns about the reliability of Firestone tyres that were routinely installed on new Explorers. Federal regulators had not detected the pattern in their own database. A later *New York Times* analysis of data collected by the US Occupational Safety and Health Administration revealed a longstanding failure by regulators to seek criminal prosecution of employers whose wilful violation of safety rules had caused worker deaths.

CAR requires a significant investment of resources by media outlets. Unfortunately, it is increasingly difficult for traditional media outlets to make this investment. Bruce Ackerman has recently observed that "The internet is destroying the economic foundations of professional journalism" (Ackerman, 2010: 27). Advertising revenue for American newspapers declined by more than 70 percent between 2006 and 2019. As a result, the journalistic workforce has been cut back. There were 74,000 people working in newsrooms in 2006, and only 34,000 in 2019, according to the Pew Research Center.

There is an alternative and more optimistic view about the effect of digitization of transparency. It emphasizes the opportunities that might be created by allowing public access to the massive databases that have been created within government agencies as a result of digitization. It is this more optimistic view that drives recent open data initiatives in many countries. An early example of the potential of open data projects is provided by the Toxic Release Inventory (TRI), a database maintained by the US Environmental Protection Agency that tracks the use of hazardous chemicals by industrial facilities in the United States. Data collected within this database was made publicly accessible in the 1990s. Studies suggest that the use of hazardous chemicals dropped substantially after the public release of TRI data, even though there was no bar to the use of those chemicals under US law.

Civil society capacity. TRI did not have this effect simply because the EPA chose to make data available. The success of the TRI initiative hinged on the ability of well-funded non-government organizations to develop web-based applications that allowed citizens to track the behaviour of industrial facilities in their neighbourhoods. Disclosure of information was not enough. The goal of increased accountability could not be realized without the activity of those non-governmental organizations.

This suggests one final challenge that arises with regard to the implementation of transparency policies. It is not simply a matter of what the law says, or even a matter of whether governments take their laws seriously. Transparency policies will also fail if there is not a capacity within civil society – journalists, citizen groups, business associations – to seek government-held information and explain its meaning to a wider public. Indeed, this was true even before the digital age: in the era of paper-based records, we depended on the traditional media – newspapers and broadcast media – to obtain government records and interpret their meaning on our behalf.

However, there are some countries where this capacity within civil society is entirely lacking, either because of poverty or political repression. Even in advanced democracies, civil society capacity can be surprisingly limited. Ironically, technological change is undermining one of the main sources of this capacity – the old print and broadcast media. Optimists hope that the internet age will encourage new methods of "crowdsourced" analysis of information. But it is not yet clear that this will be an effective substitute for the sort of analysis once performed by old-style investigative journalists and well-funded interest groups.

Summary

The concept of transparency has enjoyed an extraordinary rise in popularity over the last 30 years. There are, as we have seen, many reasons why this is so. It is an idea that can be advocated by individuals and groups who pursue many different agendas, sometimes with starkly divergent views about the role of the state. An interesting question is whether the concept will enjoy similar popularity in the next quarter-century. Is transparency now permanently entrenched in our understanding of the core elements of good governance? Or will enthusiasm for the concept eventually be superseded by frustration over the long and difficult battles that have arisen over the translation of the concept into actual policy?

Questions for review and discussion

1   It is sometimes said that transparency is one of the key aspects of good governance. As you look at the challenges confronting government today, would you say this is the case? What other values might rank more highly?

2   There is a worldwide community of non-governmental organizations that campaigns in
    favour of various kinds of transparency policies. What kind of success do you think that
    this movement will achieve over the next 20 years? To put it another way, do you think
    that the trend will be toward more open government, or more secretive government,
    over these two decades?

Reader exercises

1   Look through the leading news stories on a major media website. To what extent did
    these news stories depend on information obtained from government agencies? And
    how does it appear that this information was obtained?
2   Make a list of the ways in which you depend on information provided to you by public
    agencies. How would your life change if this information was not accessible?

Class exercises

1   Pick a recent news report that appears to rely on a leak of information from a public
    agency. What arguments could be made in defence of that leak? What arguments could
    be made against it? On balance, was the disclosure was justified?
2   Pick a recent news controversy. Suppose you wanted to make a request for information
    from a public agency that was related to this controversy. Does the law in your country
    permit you to make such a request? Assuming it does, what information would you
    seek? What do you think the response would be?

Further reading

Christopher Hood and David Heald (2006), *Transparency: The Key to Better Governance?* New York,
    Oxford University Press.
Daniel Moynihan (1998), *Secrecy: The American Experience.* New Haven, CT, Yale University Press.
Suzanne J. Piotrowski (2010), *Transparency and Secrecy: A Reader Linking Literature and Contemporary
    Debate.* Lanham, MD, Lexington Books.
Alasdair Roberts (2006), *Blacked Out: Government Secrecy in the Information Age.* New York, Cambridge
    University Press.

References

Bruce Ackerman (2010), *The Decline and Fall of the American Republic.* Cambridge, MA, Belknap
    Press.
Patrick Birkinshaw (2006), "Freedom of Information and Openness: Fundamental Human Rights?"
    Administrative Law Review 58(1): 1177–218.
Ann Florini (Ed.) (2007), *The Right to Know: Transparency for an Open World.* New York, Columbia
    University Press.
Justin Fox (2005), *Government Transparency and Policymaking.* New Haven, CT, Yale University.
David Heald (2006), "Varieties of Transparency", in Christopher Hood and David Heald (Eds.),
    Transparency: The Key to Better Governance? New York, Oxford University Press.
Daniel Kaufmann (2005), "Ten Myths About Governance and Corruption", *Finance and Development*
    42(3): 41–43.
OECD (2005), *Public Sector Modernisation: Open Government.* Paris, Organisation for Economic
    Cooperation and Development.

Suzanne J. Piotrowski (2010), *Transparency and Secrecy: A Reader Linking Literature and Contemporary Debate*. Lanham, MD, Lexington Books.

Alasdair Roberts (2001), "Structural Pluralism and the Right to Information", *University of Toronto Law Journal* 51(3): 243–271.

Alasdair Roberts (2012a), *Transparency in Troubled Times*. Boston, MA, Suffolk University Law School.

Alasdair Roberts (2012b), "Wikileaks: The Illusion of Transparency", *International Review of Administrative Sciences* 78(1): 116–133.

Micah Sifry (2011, March 3), "In the Age of Wikileaks, the End of Secrecy?" *The Nation*. http://www.thenation.com/article/158988/age-wikileaks-end-secrecy?page=full.

World Bank (2005, March 17), *Press Release: World Bank Says Transparency Key to Development in Resource Rich Countries*. Washington, DC, World Bank.

26 Changing equalities

Politics, policies and practice

Rachel Ashworth

Introduction

Concepts of equality and inequality are fundamentally *political* concepts that have become institutionalized within the public service system in particular ways. Yet, along with concepts such as 'fairness', 'equity', social justice' or 'social inclusion', they are historically rooted and mutable. The meaning of such concepts has continued to shift in recent years, reflecting ever-changing social, economic and political conditions. These include the demise of taken-for-granted assumptions about the welfare state as the guarantor of universal rights and benefits; the changing role of women in the labour market and public life; growing evidence on the impact of intersectionality and the emergence of new social movements focused on race and ethnicity, disability, age and LGBTQ+.

Moreover, country-specific events and situations, such as the Macpherson Report into the death of black teenager Stephen Lawrence which identified institutional racism within the London Metropolitan Police, have been followed by worldwide reassessments of institutional cultures and practices. For example, the MeToo movement, which began when social activist Tarana Burke used the term 'MeToo' on My Space when highlighting the need for resources to enable women to recover from sexual harassment and assault experiences, prompted widespread calls for action in terms of greater mitigation, investigation and accountability for such incidents. Meanwhile, supporters of Black Lives Matter, a decentralised movement that emerged in 2013 after the acquittal of George Zimmerman for the murder of Trayvon Martin, have continued to lobby and protest against racial inequality, discrimination and violence. Each of these movements and events is framed in broader patterns of political change, notably the shift in language away from redistributive meanings of equality and towards the more cultural interpretations implied in the idea of social exclusion; and from the formalized concept of equality to more fluid notions of social diversity and inclusivity.

These dynamic transformations continue to produce major challenges for public service organizations. Their capacity to respond is influenced by a number of different issues, not least the politicization of equality; the adoption of new business and management practices; notions of consumerism, which have reshaped relationships between public services and the public; the effects of the emerging patterns of governance described in Chapters 2, 4, 5 and 15; and more recently the challenges of austerity and COVID-19. The pandemic has laid bare the nature and extent of inequality, both across and within nations, and underlined the role of public services in addressing these inequitable outcomes. What is the capacity of the public sector to deliver equality goals in the midst of these profound social and political transformations?

DOI: 10.4324/9781003282839-29

Learning objectives

- To understand the politics of equality, and the different notions of justice that it draws on;
- To understand how far equality, diversity and inclusion policies can be viewed as simply a matter of 'good business practice';
- To be able to identify the difficulties inherent in translating policy into practice;
- To reflect on how equality, diversity and inclusion might be re-framed within a context of current public policy challenges.

Changing politics: Administrative justice or social justice?

Equality is not an essential, unchanging and universal principle of public management. Equality legislation and equality policies continue to be the product of struggles by particular groups to overcome patterns of structural inequality – around social divisions such as class, gender, race, religion and belief, disability and sexual orientation. The politics of equality, diversity, inclusion and social justice is not settled, but is the continued focus of social action as groups face new forms of disadvantage or attempt to enlarge the opportunities open to them. It is also open to various forms of 'backlash', as those whose power bases are threatened mobilize their resources – ideological, legal and institutional – to resist change.

Box 26.1 Key terms

Social justice – the distribution of wealth, income, opportunities and privileges within a society.

Equality – the state of being equal, especially in status, rights, wealth, income or opportunities.

Equity – the situation in which everyone is treated fairly according to their needs, taking into account any unfair imbalance in starting points.

The form of equality that became enshrined in the UK public sector over recent decades was based on the concept of administrative justice – a concept that tended to strip it of these political inflections (see Box 26.2).

Box 26.2 The two principles of administrative justice

The first principle derives from the notion of citizenship in welfare democracies. All citizens are considered to have equal claims on welfare services, so that given the same circumstances, they could expect to receive the same benefits, wherever – and to whomever – they made their claims.

The second principle is that of the impartiality of public service officers – an impartiality guaranteed by the bureaucratic rules and norms of the organizations in which they work.

Administrative justice is, however, a poor means of redressing inequality. Subjecting everyone to the same rules is not enough to compensate for injustices inherited from the past. Administrative justice gives rise to an individualized and passive conception of equal opportunities that fails to address the sources and effects of discrimination and enables dominant cultures to reproduce themselves. That is, to succeed, individuals may take on the characteristics of the dominant groups in whose image organizational cultures have been moulded over successive generations. In this way, little structural change or shifting of power relations can take place, and the same groups of staff, users or citizens tend to remain excluded from power and decision-making. Despite the rules of impartiality and equality, some groups may perceive that their interests are marginalized, their voices unheard and/or that they are treated unjustly.

The politics of equality has been through three key shifts in recent years. The first has been an increasing emphasis on *diversity* – that is, a recognition of the need to respond to difference rather than simply providing equality of opportunity. The second – less embedded – has been an attempt to transcend the passive and formalized notion of equality with a more active and dynamic concept of *social justice* – see Box 26.3. This shifts attention to the outcomes of policies and practices rather than the processes through which they are delivered. Third, the concept of *inclusion* has gained greater prominence in recent times. While governments and public services have sought to address social inclusion in past decades, an explicit focus on inclusion can now be seen within public policy, organization and workplaces (Oswick and Noon, 2014; Shore et al., 2011).These three concepts are connected explicitly in a long-standing but recently resurgent body of literature on representative bureaucracy, which argues that public organizations should be both descriptively and actively representative of the societies they serve, so that policies can be designed to achieve desired and inclusive outcomes for diverse publics (Andrews and Ashworth, 2015).

Box 26.3 The difference between administrative and social justice

Administrative justice is about processes and rules – for example, the process of staff selection; the rules by which resources are distributed.
Social justice is about the outcomes of policies and practices – for example, the overall profile of a labour force; the extent to which resources are redistributed; and the degree to which policies achieve equitable outcomes.

Changing policies: Diversity as a business asset?

The diversity agenda

Public service organizations have experienced profound changes over the last 40 years due to a combination of an emphasis on marketization and efficiency, new forms of partnership and network collaborations and austerity policies which have prompted increasing downwards pressure on public sector budgets and pay levels and reductions in employment rights. Many organizations have responded by introducing flexibility strategies, such as the use of zero hour contracts, that adversely affect their lowest paid workers, among whom women and black and ethnic minorities are disproportionately represented. The global pandemic created additional, unprecedented pressures on governments and public organizations, placing them at the forefront of crisis management. This meant managing lockdowns, establishing testing and tracing and introducing vaccination programmes at speed. These developments mean that, despite some notable exceptions, equality goals have often become subordinated to 'core business' and efficiency goals.

Nevertheless, the HR literature has demonstrated a resurgence of interest in the possible benefits of diversity strategies for organizations across the private and public sectors aimed at 'managing diversity' (see Chapter 10; Conley and Page, 2014; Noon and Ogbonna, 2021). This agenda has been underpinned by a 'business case' that advocates the enlargement of recruitment pools, so that staff can be more representative of society and therefore more responsive to societal needs (Parken and Ashworth, 2019). In addition, public service organizations have been cast as the 'model employer', leading the way on equalities for their counterparts in the private sector to follow (see Case Example 26.1). However, this image has sometimes been threatened during austerity and the global pandemic, as budget cuts removed opportunities to recruit, whilst job losses had a disproportionate impact on particular communities – see Case Example 26.2.

While it is often suggested that equality and diversity are simply a case of being 'responsive' to the different needs of diverse groups of users or citizens (Cabinet Office, 2020), the academic literature suggests that responsiveness may not always deliver equality: The results of public consultation exercises may override professional notions of equality – and consumer power is weak as a driver of equality (Clarke et al., 2007).

Case Example 26.1 An anti-racist action plan for Wales

Aim: An anti-racist Wales by 2030

Already working towards 'a more equal Wales' as part of its *Future Generations for Wales* framework, the Welsh government has been prompted by the killing of George Floyd and a major investigation undertaken during COVID-19 to set out an ambitious new plan to become an anti-racist nation by 2030. Rather than a general strategy, a detailed action-oriented plan has been set out which recognizes the slow progress on tackling institutional racism in the UK since the Macpherson Report (1999) and initiates a more practical and proactive anti-racist response, allowing for a thorough audit of organizational practices and processes.

The plan outlines the following vision, purpose and objectives:

Vision – a Wales which is anti-racist.

Purpose – to make a meaningful change to the lives of Black, Asian and minority ethnic communities by tackling racism.
Values – lived experience, rights based, open and transparent.

The objectives for public service organizations include:

a) To provide demonstrable leadership at all levels to meet commitments on institutional racism;
b) To change the experience of education, job seeking and career progression for
ethnic minority people to bridge education attainment gaps and employment
reward gaps;
c) To provide equitable and culturally appropriate services that recognize intersectionality and differences among groups;
d) To provide a safe and nurturing workplace environment for ethnic minority people to thrive and flourish;
e) To implement policies they agree to deliver;
f) To collect the right data, establish baselines and use evidence to identify need for
action;
g) To recognize the differential impact of racism in different locations in Wales.

Source: Adapted from *An Anti-Racist Wales*, Welsh Government (Race Equality
Action Plan: An Anti-racist Wales | GOV.WALES).

**Case Example 26.2 Representation and reputation of public agencies
in Brazil**

Dantas Cabral et al., 2021, conducted a survey experiment to explore perceptions of
representation and effectiveness of government agencies within a Brazilian shanty-
town (*favela*), where citizens experience multiple and intersecting inequalities related
to race, class and geographical identity. The survey explored whether having a leader
representative of the local population influenced citizen perceptions of public agencies
with a positive reputation and those with a negative reputation.

The study showed that representation and reputation are connected and interact to
shape citizens' perspective on procedural justice. In the case of schools, communities
already expected to receive fair treatment from those organizations, irrespective of the
background of the local school leaders. When it came to the police, prior expectations
of fair treatment were much lower but were enhanced by the presence of a *favela*-born
resident as leader.

Source: Adapted from Dantas Cabral et al. (2021).

The solution to this dilemma is to develop strong, rather than weak, notions of diversity and forms of consultation, i.e. linked to concepts of social, rather than administrative justice (Young, 1990). A positive notion of diversity acknowledges the wide plurality of interests and complexity of identifications among the public, rather than resting on crude conceptions of 'consulting the whole (i.e. undifferentiated) community' or dividing the public into distinct categories ('the black and ethnic minority community', 'the elderly', 'LGBTQ+', etc.) (Barnes et al., 2007). Rather than simply sampling pre-formed 'opinions' through survey techniques, consultation should enable different groups to be informed about the issues and to engage in dialogue – with each other and with public agencies (see Chapter 22). For example, Elias (2020) highlights the urgent need for greater proactivity from local governments in the US to deliver policies, programmes and information for LGBTQ+ communities, identifying the need for greater adaptability, more accessibility and inclusive language.

Diversity policies have been criticized because of their focus on individuals, rather than groups, and because of their focus on assimilation. That is, diverse groups may be absorbed or incorporated into the mainstream and so lose their distinct forms of identity and patterns of allegiance (Prasad et al., 1997; Riccucci, 2021). The existence of a diverse workforce may not yield the benefits of enhanced innovation, responsiveness, market sensitivity and so on if the organization is modelled on an image of a holistic, consensual culture in which all sign up to the 'ownership' of the same goals and values and are expected to adopt the dominant ethos. A diverse organization is necessarily a dynamic organization: One in which there is likely to be conflict between different values and norms, in which minority voices are able to raise challenges to conventional practice and in which power imbalances and discriminatory practices can be recognized and discussed. That is, it is one that recognizes that change involves politics as well as management. Equally, there is a recognition that it is not always helpful to consider protected characteristics separately, as many citizens and employees experience multiple inequalities that intersect (Walby et al., 2012). This requires governments and public organizations to consider intersectional impacts in a much more meaningful way than they have previously.

As a result, attention has shifted recently away from equality and diversity and toward an explicit focus on 'inclusion' (Oswick and Noon, 2014). At the organizational or workplace level, the emphasis here is on the degree to which employees from all backgrounds 'experience treatment that satisfies his or her needs for belonging and uniqueness' (Shore et al., 2011, p. 1265). Shore and Chung (2021) highlight that much of the inclusive leadership research evaluates whether leaders are perceived to be inclusive by employees in general, whereas the test should be whether marginalized social identity groups agree. Encouragingly, research on public organizations shows that employees from more diverse public organizations report higher levels of inclusion and lower levels of discrimination and harassment (Andrews and Ashworth, 2015).

The links being made between equality, diversity and inclusion and organizational effectiveness potentially attempt to place equality agendas at the core of organizational strategies, rather than consigning them to the backwaters of HRM. Nevertheless, progress continues to be slow. Researchers who previously observed that equality policies often lack substance and are little more than 'an empty shell' have more recently noted that an emphasis on equality, diversity and inclusion may be confined to narrow management practices (Noon and Ogbonna, 2021). Clearly, it is important to hold on to the idea that equality and diversity are contested ideas around which a number of conflicts are played out. Only then can we understand why, while equality, diversity and inclusion are concepts to which everyone may ascribe in principle, few translate into practice in a way that makes a real and sustainable difference.

Changing practice: Barriers to change

Why, given the centrality of equality in public services over many decades, has so little been achieved (see Scott and Garman, 2010)?

Current approaches to equality in the UK, reflected in new legislative duties and the work of the Equality and Human Rights Commission, have placed a heavy emphasis on 'capabilities' – a person's ability to achieve a given state of well-being by combining the different 'functionings' available to them (e.g. meeting their basic physical needs, achieving social integration and self-respect) (Conley and Page, 2014). The capabilities approach moves beyond 'equal opportunities' by suggesting that some citizens will require additional support in order to take up opportunities such as, for example, extra resources for disabled people or childcare for working lone parents (Elias, 2020). However, despite these recent developments, progress on narrowing inequalities remains slow. We analyse potential explanations for this at three different levels: the institutional, the organizational and the personal.

Institutional explanations explore the ways in which organizations adopt norms and practices in order to enhance their legitimacy in the eyes of external stakeholders. Equality policies are part of a dominant 'logic of appropriate action' within public services. These logics are based on norms and conventions developed through interaction with peers and within particular professional groups (leadership teams, HR managers, equality officers, professional associations, trades unions, etc.). These norms differ subtly between different services (e.g. social service organizations talk about 'anti-oppressive practices', while police services may be oriented towards being 'anti-racist'). They also vary geographically, with a higher legitimacy afforded to equality issues in, say, metropolitan rather than rural areas, and often in larger rather than smaller jurisdictions (Elias, 2020).

Equality policies and programmes may be partly ceremonial, their function being to secure organizational legitimacy in the institutional environment, with a host of symbols (e.g. 'we value diversity' statements on job adverts, or perhaps a lone woman promoted to an otherwise all male senior management team). However, these symbols may be 'loosely coupled' to the realities of everyday practice. Loose coupling allows multiple goals to be pursued in different parts of the system independently of each other. A delicate balance has to be struck between being seen to support equality goals, while not allowing them to get in the way of operational efficiency. So, for example, there may be a formal job share policy, but an informal set of rules about where this policy can, and cannot, be applied. New 'efficient' working practices may be introduced that adversely affect the pay and conditions of low-paid workers, and so further disadvantage women and ethnic minority staff. The corporate centre may adopt a policy on social inclusion that has little impact on service planning or operational management. Tighter coupling warrants a more holistic approach with closer alignment between policies and outcomes, with outputs monitored and outcomes evaluated – often necessitating considerable effort by equality officers (Tatli et al., 2015).

Organizational explanations tend to focus on the intractability of organizational culture (Newman, 2002). This focus recognizes that individuals and groups may be disadvantaged not by overt discrimination (e.g. the former height eligibility for the UK police force or the bar on married women in the UK civil service) but by norms and practices that influ-ence their experience of the workplace. Expectations about working hours, access to flexible working (e.g. from home) and job sharing opportunities may all be applied 'fairly' (i.e. even-handedly) but may be profoundly discriminatory in their effects. Issues of language, humour and normative assumptions about lifestyle and relationships can all contribute to the mar-ginalization of particular groups and disable them from making an effective contribution. Assumptions about the characteristics of users and communities –young black males, Asian women, young single mothers, the unemployed, gays and lesbians, travellers, the homeless – may be enshrined in the culture and passed on from one generation of practitioners to the next. Many individuals may not consciously hold such assumptions but they may neverthe-less become institutionalized in the culture, influencing a myriad of informal practices that may be experienced as discriminatory by the groups concerned.

However, culture change strategies are rarely successful on their own – the hearts and minds of those whose power and status may be threatened by equality issues cannot necessar-ily be won by a succession of corporate documents. People may learn a new language without changing their behaviour. There may be a backlash against those promoting equality values and actions, coupled with subtle strategies of resistance. Culture change programmes need to be supported by 'harder' organizational change strategies, such as equality audits, targets linked to key performance indicators (KPIs), disciplinary procedures to signal unacceptable behaviours, resource allocation strategies that reward positive outcomes and the monitoring and evaluation of outcomes. Nevertheless, these actions can only reduce implementation gaps, never eliminate them (Noon and Ogbonna, 2021). 'Purpose' and 'values' driven organ-izations have recently offered some potential for change here – e.g. values-based recruitment processes have sometimes, at least temporarily, disrupted employment patterns and cultural norms and delivered desired equality outcomes (Parken and Ashworth, 2019).

Personal explanations explore how individuals experience the implementation of equal-ity policies. Enacting the equality agenda through one's own behaviour is threatening, not only to established power bases but also to workers' views of their own competence and professional expertise (Conley and Page, 2014). For example, a black hospital worker may experience racial abuse from a white patient, or a white worker may be asked to collude in racist comments about a black colleague, but neither may feel able to dissent because of their concern that they may, in so doing, undermine their own professional standards (and status) by showing lack of respect for the patient's vulnerable or dependent status. A white social work manager may feel that her authority is threatened by the claims of her 'multi-racial' team and may feel tentative about exercising proper performance management in the case of black colleagues. A male police officer may marginalize a gay or lesbian member of the team from the informal bonds of collegiality on which the team's proficiency depends. Such personal fears, emotions and responses tend to be viewed as outside the domain of rational management practice. Yet they may lead to strategies of avoidance that further marginalize groups that are already disadvantaged. Only in organizational cultures that acknowledge the emotional, as well as the managerial, dynamics of change, and where there is a culture of learning rather than blame, can these fears be confronted and addressed.

Changing forms of governance

In the new governance literature, notions of networks, partnerships, participation and involvement all tend to be conceptualized as predominantly optimistic drivers of change, i.e. as a welcome release from the inflexibilities of hierarchy or the fragmenting consequences of markets. However, more careful attention needs to be paid to the patterns of inclusion and exclusion that they may produce or reproduce.

Networks and partnerships are a response to the increasing complexity and ambiguity of the public realm, which similarly require the renegotiation of equality agendas. Newman (2002) suggests two alternative scenarios: the first is a pessimistic reading in which the power dominance of statutory agencies means that radical perspectives from 'outside' are absorbed, deflected or neutralized. For example, organizations may engage in forms of consultation in which the rules of debate are firmly set by the statutory body, thus excluding or marginalizing alternative forms of dialogue. Dissenting or difficult voices may be dismissed as 'unrepresentative', and groups likely to challenge the mainstream consensus may be excluded through a range of informal strategies. The second scenario is one in which the public service system becomes more open to challenges from groups historically marginalized, and socially oriented action is taken by public service workers committed to equality goals. The opening up of organizations to greater influence by users, citizens and communities – including community activists and politicized user groups – can be a major impetus for innovation (see Chapters 22 and 23) and also potentially legitimate action by those public service professionals seeking to engage with social and political change.

Recent developments

Here we examine recent developments on equality and diversity that have occurred at the three levels of analysis: the institutional, the organizational and the personal.

Institutional: New legislative developments

Despite considerable efforts, by late 2021 just over 30% of company board members across the EU were women, while 91.5% of board chairs were men. This has prompted EU member states to give initial approval to a proposal which will encourage firms with more than 250 employees to appoint women to at least 40% of non-executive and 33% of all board positions by 2027. This pressure to ensure that boards are more diverse could affect over 2000 employers in the EU. However, the nature and toughness of potential sanctions is still being disputed.

Outside the EU, much emphasis is being placed on UN Sustainable Development Goals as a key driver for greater equality, particularly in terms of gender (see Case Example 26.3).

Meanwhile, governments and public organizations have drawn on alternative levers in order to proactively deliver social justice and address inequalities. For example, public procurement has provided a mechanism that allows public bodies to enforce equality principles and practices through their supply chain, as Wright and Conley (2020) demonstrate in their study of women in construction.

Organizational: New approaches to equality

We have also seen developments in terms of new organizational approaches to equality, more specifically, a movement from a focus on equal treatment and positive action to 'mainstreaming' or 'transforming' equality (see Box 26.3).

This has been especially developed in relation to gender mainstreaming – see Box 26.4. Newman (2013) suggests that processes of gender mainstreaming have served not only to acknowledge but also partly to undermine feminist claims for equality. However, she stresses that both the equalities agenda and neoliberalism have changed as they have interacted with each other. For example, 'women's activism helped neoliberalism to adapt and flex, but also that activism successfully made new demands on capitalism (including those of equality, rights , welfare benefits and provision for "care")' (Newman, 2013, p. 210). Parken and Ashworth (2019) show how three public organizations – a health board, a local council and a university – took holistic, evidence-informed and effective action to reduce the gender segregation that resulted in significant gender pay gaps in their organizations by following a gender mainstreaming approach.

Personal: Firmer application of existing legislation

There is evidence to suggest that individuals and groups are using equalities legislation more than in the past with mixed success – e.g. concerted action on the part of women workers to tackle sex discrimination (see Box 26.5). High-profile cases relating to equal pay and the availability of overtime payments and bonuses are being won by women, with substantial compensation being awarded. These legal judgements are imposing substantial compensation payments on organizations ranging from the US retail giant Walmart to UK local councils such as Birmingham.

Latest developments have extended from legal disputes over rights to education and employment conditions to the right to engage in public protests focused on inequality. In 2020, a US Supreme Court judgment cleared a Black Lives Matter organizer from a legal claim by a police officer. The officer was injured at a protest which was held in response to a fatal police shooting and then sought recompense from the protest organizer. Meanwhile, the Metropolitan police in London were found to have breached the rights of the organizers of a planned vigil for Sarah Everard, a young women killed by a serving Metropolitan police officer. These kinds of cases have prompted debates across the world regarding the policing of public protests, placing public organizations in the forefront of balancing rights and responsibilities.

Case Example 26.3 Achieving gender equality through UN SDGs in Nigeria

About 6% of legislators in the Nigerian House of Representatives and 7% in the Nigerian Senate are women, while all state governors are male, leaving the country ranked 180/193 countries on gender equality. Meanwhile, the Gender Social Norms Index shows that 8/10 women and 9/10 men in Nigeria believe that men make better leaders than women and that equal rights between the two are not essential. This has raised serious concerns about whether issues of equality, such as sexual violence, can be sufficiently addressed by public organizations in such a context.

Keen to address this 'power gap', the African Union has made gender equality and empowerment one of its core priorities, while the UN and EU have been collaborating to ensure the Violence against Persons Prohibition (VAPP) Act is enforced. Working through the UN Sustainable Development Goals, and specifically UNSDG 5 which aims to achieve gender equality and empower all women and girls, actors are working to achieve the goal of 35% of elected and appointed positions held by women. It is hoped that the much-delayed Gender and Equal Opportunities Bill will be passed in the coming years.

Source: Women in Leadership: Achieving an Equal Future in a COVID-19 World | Africa Renewal (un.org).

Box 26.4 Models of equality

Equal treatment – 'tinkering':

- Focuses on individual rights
- Legal remedies.

Positive action – 'tailoring':

- Focuses on group disadvantage
- 'Special' projects and measures.

Mainstreaming – 'transforming':

- Focuses on systems and structures that give rise to group disadvantage
- Integrates equality into mainstream systems and structures.

Source: Adapted from Rees (2005, p. 557).

Box 26.5 Pay equity deal for social care workers in New Zealand delayed

A landmark Court of Appeal decision in New Zealand which established pay equity in social care and support is now under threat. Kristine Bartlett – a caregiver – was supported by the Service and Food Workers Union in her bid to secure equal pay. The case was deemed historic, as the Court suggested the Equal Pay Act was not limited to considering equal pay for the same or similar work within the same sector, since sometimes it was appropriate to consider evidence on wages paid by different employers in other sectors.

After the verdict Bartlett said:

> Caregiving is not recognized or paid fairly because most caregivers are women. I took this case, with the support of my union, not just for myself but for the tens of thousands of caregivers who get paid close to the minimum wage for doing one of the most important jobs in our society.

The national secretary of the Service and Food Workers Union, John Ryall, said, once implemented, the decision would help to close the gender pay gap in New Zealand.

The decision prompted considerable discussions between stakeholders to plan the implementation of new pay arrangements but these have proved challenging and there is a danger that these will take parties beyond the expiry date of 1 July 2022, without a resolution. As a result the Ministry of Health has proposed an 18-month extension on the implementation which Bartlett has described as 'heartbreaking'.

Source: Adapted from: Historic Care Workers Pay Equity Deal under Threat | Stuff. co.nz.

Summary

Concepts of equality and inequality are fundamentally *political* concepts. In recent years, the language has shifted away from redistributive meanings of equality and towards the more cultural interpretations implied in the idea of social exclusion; and from the formalized concept of equality to more fluid notions of social diversity and inclusion, i.e. a recognition of the need to build a sense of belonging, while responding to difference.

Equality is not an unchanging and universal principle of public management. Equality legislation and equality policies are the product of struggles by particular groups to overcome patterns of structural inequality – around social divisions such as class, gender, race, disability and sexuality.

As diversity begins to be seen as contributing to business effectiveness, equality agendas are more frequently to be found at the core of organizational strategies. However, equality and diversity remain contested ideas, which may be why less has been achieved than hoped in recent years. Barriers to change can be identified at three different levels of analysis: the institutional, the organizational and the personal. Recent developments at each of those levels of analysis include new legislative duties and a movement to 'mainstreaming' or 'transforming' equalities, but progress so far has been judged to be patchy.

Network forms of governance in the public sector mean that many actions are likely to be highly influential on patterns of equality and inequality – including representation on partnership bodies; selection of staff to develop new projects or initiatives; methods of developing community strategies and partnership strategies; and relationships with voluntary or community sector organizations (Barnes et al., 2007).

The recent period of financial austerity has presented new challenges for equality and diversity policy. Firstly, government cuts have led to reductions in recruitment, hampering efforts to improve the diversity of public organizations. Secondly, there has been some concern about the impact of government public spending cuts, in particular that these have disproportionately affected women. Finally, the COVID-19 pandemic has provided a paradox. On the one hand, it has presented stark evidence that across many countries inequality has contributed to the extent of illness and mortality, especially amongst black and ethnic minority groups, disabled people and disadvantaged groups. However, it also provided a new impetus to address inequalities and opened up greater scope for accessibility and flexibility due to the wide range of technological alternatives that have now been proven to enable wider engagement, including the opportunity to work from home across the economy.

Acknowledgement

Earlier versions of this chapter in previous editions of this textbook were written jointly by Prof. Rachel Ashworth with Prof. Janet Newman, Open University. Rachel wishes to acknowledge the contribution to this chapter by Janet, which is still evident in many parts of the chapter.

Questions for review and discussion

1   Why do policies or practices based on the concept of administrative justice fail to deliver change in historical patterns of discrimination or exclusion?
2   How might 'equality' and 'efficiency' goals be in conflict, and how might organizations attempt to reconcile them?

3   What specific challenges and opportunities might the COVID-19 pandemic present for equality, diversity and inclusion?

Reader exercises

1   What strategies or practices might your organization or service adopt to enhance its legitimacy in the eyes of particular groups who may have been subject to institutionalized patterns of discrimination or exclusion in the past?
2   The 'welfare state' is undergoing important shifts – some services are being targeted to particular (more narrowly defined) groups and some politicians have also argued that the receipt of services should be conditional on people behaving 'responsibly'. There is also a debate on the rebalancing of rights regarding public protests on inequalities. What ideas of equality or justice do you think underpin such measures? And what might be the implications for our understanding of citizenship in the twenty-first century?

Class exercises

1   In groups, research the way in which a sample of large public, private and third sector organizations develop and monitor their equality, diversity and inclusion policies. Are there any differences between the three sectors? In plenary session, discuss how might such differences be explained.

Further reading

Newman, J. and Yeates, N. (eds) 2008, *Social justice*. Buckingham: Open University Press/McGraw-Hill.
Noon, M. and Ogbonna, E. 2021. Controlling management to deliver diversity and inclusion: Prospects and limits. *Human Resource Management Journal*, 31(3), pp. 619–638.
Riccucci, N.M. 2021. *Managing diversity in public sector workforces*. New York, NY and Abingdon, Oxon: Routledge.
Shore, L.M., Randel, A.E., Chung, B.G., Dean, M.A., Holcombe Ehrhart, K. and Singh, G. 2011. Inclusion and diversity in work groups: A review and model for future research. *Journal of Management*, 37(4), pp. 1262–1289.

References

Andrews, R. and Ashworth, R. 2015. Representation and inclusion in public organizations: Evidence from the UK civil service. *Public Administration Review*, 75(2), pp. 279–288.
Barnes, M., Newman, J. and Sullivan, H. 2007. *Power, participation and political renewal*. Bristol: Policy Press.
Cabinet Office. 2020. Equality, Diversity and Inclusion Strategy 2020 to 2024 - GOV.UK (www.gov .uk) *Talent Action Plan: Removing the barriers to success*. London: Cabinet Office.
Clarke, J., Newman, J., Smith, N., Vidler, E. and Westmarland, L. 2007. *Creating citizen-consumers: Changing publics and changing public services*. London: Sage.
Conley, H. and Page, M. 2014. *Gender equality in public services: Chasing the dream*. London: Routledge.
Dantas Cabral, A., Peci, A. and Van Ryzin, G.G. 2021. Representation, reputation and expectations towards bureaucracy: Experimental findings from a favela in Brazil. *Public Management Review*, 24(9): pp. 1–26.

Elias, N.M. 2020. LGBTQ+ civil rights: Local government efforts in a volatile era. *Public Administration Review*, 80(6), pp. 1075–1086.

Sir Macpherson, W. 1999. *The Stephen Lawrence enquiry*. London: Stationery Office.

Newman, J. 2002. Changing governance, changing equality? New Labour, modernization and public services. *Public Money and Management*, 22(1), pp. 7–14.

Newman, J. 2013. Spaces of power: Feminism, neoliberalism and gendered labor. *Social Politics*, 20(2), pp. 200–221.

Noon, M. and Ogbonna, E. 2021. Controlling management to deliver diversity and inclusion: Prospects and limits. *Human Resource Management Journal*, 31(3), pp. 619–638.

Oswick, C. and Noon, M. 2014. Discourses of diversity, equality and inclusion: Trenchant formulations or transient fashions? *British Journal of Management*, 25(1), pp. 25–39.

Parken, A. and Ashworth, R. 2019. From evidence to action: Applying gender mainstreaming to pay gaps in the Welsh public sector. *Gender, Work and Organization*, 26(5), pp. 599–618.

Prasad, P., Mills, A., Elmes, M. and Prasad, A. 1997. *Managing the organizational melting pot: Dilemmas of workplace diversity*. Thousand Oaks, CA: Sage.

Rees, T. 2005. Reflections on the uneven development of gender mainstreaming in Europe. *International Feminist Journal of Politics*, 7(4), pp. 555–574.

Riccucci, N.M. 2021. *Managing diversity in public sector workforces*. New York: Routledge.

Shore, L.M., Randel, A.E., Chung, B.G., Dean, M.A., Holcombe Ehrhart, K. and Singh, G. 2011. Inclusion and diversity in work groups: A review and model for future research. *Journal of Management*, 37(4), pp. 1262–1289.

Shore, L.M. and Chung, B.G. 2021. Inclusive leadership: How leaders sustain or discourage work group inclusion. *Group and Organization Management*, 47(4), pp. 723–754.

Ahu Tatli, Katerina Nicolopoulou, Mustafa Özbilgin, Mine Karatas-Ozkan and Mustafa Bilgehan Öztürk (2015)Questioning impact: interconnection between extra-organizational resources and agency of equality and diversity officers, *International Journal of Human Resource Management*, 26(9), 1243–1258.

Walby, S., Armstrong, J. and Strid, S. 2012. Intersectionality: Multiple inequalities in social theory. *Sociology*, 46(2), pp. 224–240.

Wright, T. and Conley, H. 2020. Advancing gender equality in the construction sector through public procurement: Making effective use of responsive regulation. *Economic and Industrial Democracy*, 41(4), pp. 975–996.

Young, I. (1990). Justice and the politics of difference. In S. Fainstein and L. Servon (eds), *Gender and planning: A reader*. New Brunswick, NJ: Rutgers University Press, pp. 86–103.

27 Ethical considerations in the public sector

What is acceptable behaviour?

Howard Davis, Suzanne J. Piotrowski and Lois Warner

Introduction

Concern to ensure high standards of behaviour is by no means new. Indeed, demands for ethical conduct on the part of politicians and public officials predate the modern concern for the rule of law ('*Rechtsstaat*') and can be traced back at least to Greek and Roman times. These concerns have risen to prominence again in recent years, largely because of a series of scandals which have prompted changes in both management and governance arrangements in the public sector.

In spite of evidence of improved efficiency and service practices in public sector organisations (see Chapters 4 and 5), citizens' trust in government by and large has fallen in most industrialised countries in recent decades. One argument is that the public sector has become more transparent recently, so more cases of corruption have become exposed, even if corruption as a whole has not increased. On the other hand, it is possible that lower standards of conduct have indeed occurred, e.g. as a result of changed public management practices such as contracting, always an arena prone to corruption (see Chapter 8).

Whatever the reason for their growth, 'sleaze', corruption scandals and allegations of dishonesty have affected the confidence and trust that citizens have in public representatives and officials. This may, in turn, have affected the level of democratic activity in many OECD countries, particularly the low voter turnout at elections, sinking memberships of political parties, a general lack of interest in conventional politics and even disrespect and violence towards politicians. Balfour et al. (2019) argue that in an environment of extreme mistrust the tendency towards what they call 'administrative evil' is deeply woven into the identity of public affairs.

Ethics is on the agenda everywhere, supported by attention from international governmental organisations in promoting the formulation and implementation of Freedom of Information Acts, and continuous developments in information and communication technologies. With these developments raising expectations for accountability in the new millennium, public bodies now generally accept the need to increase transparency and take action to ensure fair and honest behaviour in the public domain.

DOI: 10.4324/9781003282839-30

Learning objectives

This chapter will help readers to identify:

- The reasons for the current emphasis on ethics and standards of conduct in the public sector
- The spectrum of unethical behaviour, from corruption to minor infringements of ethical codes
- The rationale behind the recent move to strengthened codes of conduct in the UK and elsewhere
- The pros and cons of control-oriented and prevention-oriented approaches to ensuring ethical behaviour
- The role of transparency as a mechanism for fighting unethical behaviour

Ethics as a key governance issue in the public sector

As Chapter 15 illustrates, ethics is considered a part of 'good governance'. How has the renewed emphasis in recent years on fair, just and ethical behaviour come about?

> In Brighton she was Brenda,
> She was Patsy up in Perth.
> In Cambridge she was Carina,
> The sweetest girl on Earth.
> In Stafford she was Stella,
> The pick of all the bunch,
> But down in his expenses,
> She was Petrol, Oil and Lunch.
>
> Source: Anon.

There are no empirical grounds for claiming that managerialism, as an ideology or a codified set of practices, has explicitly incentivised unethical behaviour. Nevertheless, it seems that the switch to a focus on results (outputs and outcomes), and away from processes, may have had some unfortunate side-effects. The simple truth that 'processes matter' (and that 'ends do not necessarily justify the means') seems sometimes to have been forgotten. Unregulated or under-regulated processes can lead to unfair and dishonest practices.

The focus on economically driven values and business management methods in the public sector – stronger in countries such as the UK but much weaker in countries such as France – has generated a new discussion about the values and norms of public service. Indeed, one must now ask, rather than assume, whether in any given country a public service ethos still exists or whether public service culture has become almost identical with business culture (see Case Example 27.1).

Furthermore, the introduction of contract management (see Chapter 8) and the increasing blurring of boundaries between various sectors (see Chapter 3) mean that decision-makers in the public sector face new, unfamiliar, situations and dilemmas, which require new ethical guidelines. Equally, those used to operating in business may find that practices acceptable in the private sector are unacceptable when working with public sector bodies.

In particular, the following changes in public management have raised questions as to what the new 'rules of the game' are:

- Greater intensity of interactions between the public, private and non-profit sectors has led to all kinds of partnership, and associated blurring of responsibilities – bringing a need for role clarity and transparency in decision-making, both inside partnerships and between partners and other stakeholders.
- The use of electronic mechanisms and the internet for documenting and storing public information increases governments' responsibility for privacy protection, for example, as it pertains to health and human services and public security.
- Managers – and also partly frontline staff – may have increased flexibility in the use of finance and staff resources. For example, in some EU countries, many public agencies such as utilities now operate within a private law framework, very different from the previous public sector framework with its rather rigid staff regulations and financial accounting systems.
- With deregulation in many OECD countries, including the UK, many new regulatory agencies have been created, often without clarity as to who actually holds the regulators themselves to account. Given their power, it is unsurprising that some individuals may occasionally abuse their position. For instance, there are recurring concerns worldwide about potential corruption in police drugs squads and in customs, both of which have access to high-value goods being traded illegally.
- Increased mobility of staff between different sectors introduces new values into the public sector. While this may usefully bring a more entrepreneurial spirit to the public sector, it may also dilute traditional understandings of 'public service'. It also raises the thorny issue of how staff treat confidential information, particularly when public officials and politicians later move on to jobs in the private sector.

Case Example 27.1 Standards in public life, UK

Decentralisation and contracting out have varied the format for organisations providing public services. There is greater interchange between sectors. There are more short-term contracts. There is scepticism about traditional institutions. Against that background it cannot be assumed that everyone in the public service will assimilate a public service culture unless they are told what is expected of them and the message is systematically reinforced. The principles inherent in the ethic of public service need to be set out afresh.

Source: *Committee on Standards in Public Life* (1995: 17).

The increasing use of contracting (particularly with the private sector) in the provision of public services has sharpened some ethical issues involved in inter-organisational relationships, emphasising the need for more accountable procedures and greater transparency in procurement processes, such as equal access to information about opportunities to tender for contracts, and contractual arrangements that represent the public interest.

Davis and Walker (1997, 1998) have argued that different parties in any contract inevitably have different primary objectives. The first objective for a contractor must be to survive. A contractor seeks ultimately not to provide the best possible public service but to provide the best possible public service *consistent with a profitable contract*, however this is dressed up.

Consequently, public officials and political representatives can find that it is no longer clear what constitutes proper behaviour. Of course, there are also cases of deliberate wrongdoing, in spite of clear guidance through legal regulations or standards of conduct, though many undesirable behaviours may occur more through ignorance or confusion. One proposed answer is increased ethics training and education of public employees, so that internal controls are embedded within the consciousness of decision-makers, to guide their individual decisions when external controls, such as ethics codes or laws, are not clear. The influential and inspirational role of ethical leadership is also an essential aspect in managing the effectiveness of ethics codes.

John Rohr changed the landscape of public administration literature by defining and introducing the concept of regime values in *Ethics for Bureaucrats* (1989), primarily focused on regime values in the USA but potentially with application elsewhere. Rohr stated:

> By 'regime values' I intend to suggest that the normative foundation of ethical standards for public servants in any regime is the values of that regime. In the United States the regime values happen to be constitutional values, but not every regime takes its constitution as seriously as Americans do.
>
> (Rohr, 1989: ix)

Rohr (1989: 68) laid out three characteristics of regime values, which he believed should be the basis of ethics courses for students of public administration:

1. That ethical norms should be derived from the salient values of the regime.
2. That these values are normative for bureaucrats because they have taken an oath to uphold the regime.
3. That these values can be discovered in the public law of the regime.

Corruption

Media attention tends to focus gleefully on corruption scandals – see Case Example 27.2 – but there are many other forms of unethical behaviour which are usually not reported by the media, such as disadvantaging citizens who do not have a strong voice or excluding certain user groups from access to public services. The question therefore arises as to what distinguishes corruption scandals from other forms of unethical behaviour?

Defining and measuring corruption is far from straightforward. While there is no easy and completely accurate way to measure corruption, the use of multiple data sources and triangulation does increase reliability and validity (Huberts et al., 2006).

Case Example 27.2 Local government corruption in the United States: 'The Jersey Sting'

The state of New Jersey in the United States has long had a reputation for being corrupt. Sadly, in 2009 New Jersey lived up to this reputation. Forty-four people were arrested in July of that year including three mayors, five Orthodox rabbis, two state legislators and the deputy mayor of Jersey City, Leona Beldini. Before Ms Beldini became deputy mayor she was a stripper using the stage name Hope Diamond. The details of the sting, initiated by Chris Christie, then US Attorney and later Governor of New Jersey and presidential candidate, were stranger than fiction, with the charges running from bribe-taking by politicians, money laundering by rabbis and the illicit market brokering of a kidney. Peter Cammarano was one of the mayors caught up in the sting. Cammarano was a young, promising politician who was sworn in as the mayor of Hoboken, New Jersey, just three weeks prior to his arrest. Cammarano took $25,000 over several months from an informant posing as a real estate developer. Much of the money was stuffed in cereal boxes and exchanged at a local diner in Hoboken, New Jersey. He was memorably caught on tape saying that the people in Hoboken who did not support him in the run-off election would be 'ground into powder'. Cammarano served two years in prison and was later disbarred by the state Supreme Court.

Source: Adapted from Fleisher (2011), McDonald (2019), and Sherman and Margolin (2011).

The legal definition of what constitutes corrupt practices varies from country to country, and what public opinion considers as 'corrupt practices' also varies from country to country. Typically, public views as to what is considered 'corrupt behaviour' go beyond what can be prosecuted as an offence under national criminal law.

The European Union Convention on the Fight Against Corruption (Council Act of 26 May 1997) defines active corruption as

> the deliberate action of whosoever promises or gives, directly or through an intermediary, an advantage of any kind whatsoever to an official for himself or for a third party for him to act or refrain from acting in accordance with his duty or in the exercise of his functions in breach of his official duties.
>
> (Article 3)

Passive corruption is defined along the same lines.

Source: www.conventions.coe.int/Treaty/ EN/Reports/HTML/173.htm (accessed 16 May 2008).

A key question must always be, in whose interest does a particular arrangement or relationship operate? In any relationship the full details, and what makes it work successfully, may well be opaque to outsiders. In the public service there is a continuing difficulty in ensuring that arrangements and relationships work in the public interest and are clearly seen to do so. The closer that any relationship becomes, the greater the potential for corrupt practice and corruption of purpose. Cosy and exclusive relationships sit uneasily with public probity expectations. The move from cliques to cosiness to collusion to corruption is all too easy without adequate safeguards.

It is also important to note, however, that double standards may sometimes apply, which could damage public service. Increasingly the public and media appear to demand that their politicians and public servants are totally without blemish in every regard, although the behaviour of those criticising slip-ups by public servants is often also far from perfect. If anyone putting themselves forward for public office is going to have their whole life history raked over in minute detail, this may discourage many from doing so and may result in 'blamelessness' rather than ability to contribute being the main criterion for achieving public office.

This leads to difficult dilemmas about balance. Are there ethically acceptable levels of corruption? Should the standards of conduct applied to those in public life and public service differ from those that the public and media apply to themselves?

The role of codes of conduct in the public sector

Because of the lack of a comprehensive legal framework for dealing with unethical behaviour, in recent years there has been an explosion of codes of conduct and/or expectations in countries with 'Westminster-type' governments.

A well-known example of such a code is the 'seven principles of public life' set out by the Committee on Standards in Public Life – see Case Example 27.3 below. This UK Committee, initially chaired by the judge Lord Nolan, was established in 1994, following a series of allegations about parliamentarians (such as 'cash for questions', sexual liaisons and alleged dishonesty) and concerns at the cumulative effect of these events on public confidence in politicians and the system of government. It was given a wide remit to examine concerns about standards of conduct of all holders of public office and to make recommendations on changes required.

The Nolan Committee stressed that none of these seven principles can be assumed to be in place – the onus is on demonstrating that they are honoured in practice.

Case Example 27.3 The seven principles of public life, UK

Selflessness	Holders of public office should take decisions solely in terms of the public interest. They should not do so in order to gain financial or other material benefits for themselves, their family or their friends.
Integrity	Holders of public office should not place themselves under any financial or other obligation to outside individuals or organisations that might influence them in the performance of their official duties.

Objectivity	In carrying out public business, including making public appointments, awarding contracts or recommending individuals for rewards and benefits, holders of public office should make choices on merit.
Accountability	Holders of public office are accountable for their decisions and actions to the public and must submit themselves to whatever scrutiny is appropriate to their office.
Openness	Holders of public office should be as open as possible about all decisions and actions that they take. They should give reasons for their decisions and restrict information only when the wider public interest clearly demands.
Honesty	Holders of public office have a duty to declare any private interests relating to their public duties and to take steps to resolve any conflicts arising in a way that protects the public interest.
Leadership	Holders of public office should promote and support these principles by leadership and example.

Source: *Committee on Standards in Public Life* (1995: 14).

Furthermore, such assessment often throws up systemic issues that need to be considered across the sector, not just in one organisation. For example, the first principle, 'selflessness' is undoubtedly threatened by some of the fragmented ways of working in the mixed economy of provision that now characterises public services in the UK, particularly where contracting is the norm.

It is interesting to note some omissions from these principles, e.g. *competence*, which is arguably central to 'proper' public service. There must be grave doubts about the ethics of an organisation providing a service where it no longer has the competence to deliver to the desired standard.

The above seven principles have strongly influenced codes of conduct in other countries. They have been adopted in particular in Central and Eastern Europe (in spite of the fact that most of these countries follow the German legalistic tradition), although their legal standing is often unclear.

Professional organisations frequently have their own ethics codes. The International City/County Management Association (ICMA) has a well-established Code of Ethics – originally adopted in 1924 and most recently amended in June 2020 and, unlike some other professional associations, with a formal enforcement mechanism and appeals procedure. Sanctions include public censure, private censure, membership suspension, suspension and membership bar (International City/County Management Association, 2022).

Some see the standards agenda as a new bureaucracy, or political window-dressing, but behind the agenda are concerns both to prevent corruption and improper behaviour and, in so doing, to bolster the regard in which politicians and public officials are held, with its consequent impact on both the credibility of government bodies and their ability to act. Svara (2022) identifies four sources for ideas in substantiating ethics – duties, virtues, principles and benefits to society through actions that produce the greatest good for the greatest number (Svara, 2022).

Another problem is 'ownership' of standards. In many cases, codes of conduct are drafted by a committee, the members of which may represent different backgrounds and values from those who have to conform to the standards. Glor (2001) stresses the differences in values between different generations, to which we might add the different value systems observed in people from different genders, races, religions, sexualities, regions, beliefs, etc. Clearly, getting ownership of a single set of standards may be difficult, and there may be a balance to be achieved between compliance and actual 'ownership' by individuals.

Control-oriented and prevention-oriented mechanisms

So what is defined as unethical behaviour is strongly culture-bound. Moreover, 'Western' countries also tend to have different traditions regarding the combatting of corruption and other forms of unethical behaviour. In particular, two major traditions can be identified: 'Westminster-type' countries such as the UK, New Zealand and Australia (and also the US) have a long tradition of addressing questions of values and moral behaviour directly on a case-by-case basis. In Continental European countries such as Germany and France, ethical issues are more normally addressed indirectly through general laws. In particular, the French Napoleonic Code of 1810 is a landmark, introducing penalties to combat corruption in public life, and even today France is renowned for its emphasis on professional ethics and the study of duties (the so-called *déontologie*) in various sectors (Vigouroux, 1995). In Germany, the rule of law (*Rechtsstaat*) was codified in the Prussian state in the nineteenth century, and the ethos of the civil service that it embodied has been further codified in Article 33 of the modern German constitution. Although the values of German civil servants have greatly changed from those of the Prussian state, the legal tradition is still strong today.

There is general agreement that ethics management should always involve both control-oriented and prevention-oriented mechanisms – controls include mechanisms for ensuring accountability and limiting and clarifying discretion (see Case Example 27.4), while prevention concentrates on increasing transparency and awareness of unethical behaviour.

An OECD survey in 1999 showed that control-oriented mechanisms, such as independent financial and legal scrutiny, were considered to be the most important mechanisms for combating corruption (OECD, 1999: 22). Many OECD countries have also taken measures to protect 'whistleblowers' and to encourage staff to report wrongdoing. Much less common are participatory approaches to counter unethical behaviour by involving citizens in the policing of public activity.

Case Example 27.4 Political corruption in New South Wales, Australia

Although maintaining she had always acted with integrity, in October 2021, Gladys Berejiklian, the Premier of New South Wales (NSW), resigned. She had become ensnared in the sensational Independent Commission Against Corruption (ICAC) hearings into alleged corruption by former fellow State Member of Parliament, Daryl Maguire, with whom she had admitted having a close personal relationship. Mr. Maguire admitted to using his parliamentary office and resources to conduct private business dealings, including receiving thousands of dollars in cash as part of a visa scam. Corruption has been ingrained in the political culture of NSW from the days of its founding in the nineteenth century. This is the very reason ICAC was formed in 1988. Before NSW began governing itself in 1856, the colony was run for many years by the upright, dedicated and incorruptible Colonial Secretary Edward Deas Thomson. With a fully elected parliament and premier, however, things changed and democratic politics attracted corruption from the beginning. A sleazy subterranean network developed of fixers and door-openers able to influence decisions for the right price. The early years of NSW thus set the stage for a long history of political and public corruption. In recent years ICAC itself has come under scrutiny, having been accused of overreach. As a result, ICAC was restructured in 2016. The existing single commissioner was replaced by a panel of three, and a decision to proceed to a compulsory examination or public inquiry needed majority approval of the three commissioners. More emphasis was also placed on procedural fairness in inquiries.

Source: Adapted from Clune (2020) at www.abc.net.au/news/2020-10-15/nsw-history-of-corruption-icac/12767346 accessed 21 January 2022, www.abc.net.au.news/various dates, www.icac.nsw.gov.au/.

Controls are costly and can never be watertight. Consequently, most countries have focused their efforts on risk management, with particularly frequent and intensive controls in areas where the risk of corruption is high, such as in public procurement and public finance. For example, most organisations place ceilings on the expenditure that can be authorised by any individual manager, and contracts invariably have to be awarded by more than one person.

Besides more effective controls, many countries have also taken prevention measures, including measures to avoid conflicts of interest, affirmative action and public and professional education programmes.

This latter group of prevention measures reminds us that ethics always involves values. All control mechanisms will fail if actors do not try to live up to the values that are implicit or explicit in various standards of conduct. It is important to be informed about how these continue to be shared, for example across generations. Can values be taught? Both in the US and in the UK it appears that academics, at least, think so – ethics typically forms an important part of public management education and training curricula.

Transparency

There is common agreement that transparency is important in order to fight corruption and other forms of unethical behaviour (see Case Example 27.5 and Chapter 5). While this is a common assumption, it should be noted that there has been little empirical evidence to confirm this relationship.

Case Example 27.5 Corruption and technology in India

In 2021, Transparency International ranked India 86th out of 180 countries on their perceived level of public sector corruption. On Transparency International's Corruption Perception Index, India scored 40 out of 100 (0 being highly corrupt). In a 2022 report on the Corruption Perception Index for Asia Pacific, it was concluded that

> The case of India is particularly worrying. While the country's score has remained stagnant over the past decade, some of the mechanisms that could help rein in corruption are weakening. There are concerns over the country's democratic status, as fundamental freedoms and institutional checks and balances decay.

The creative use of technology is trying to change the secretive nature of bribery in India. A non-profit organisation in Bangalore called Janaagraha, which translates as 'people power', launched a website called IPaidABribe.com. Individuals post information on the site when they pay a bribe and for what service. While the website has not stopped bribery in India, there is some evidence that it has made a small difference, with some people using the information on the site to avoid paying bribes. The State Transport Department of Karnataka was repeatedly cited on IPaidABribe.com. The transportation commissioner invited the *I Paid a Bribe* team to report their findings to employees, who realised that their actions were being broadcast around the world. Changes were made in the department, such as the introduction of online applications for driver's licences and an automated driving test centre. Both of these changes reduced the opportunities for employees to solicit bribes.

Source: Adapted from Campion (2011), Harris (2013), and Transparency International (2022).

Most OECD countries have passed freedom of information laws that give third parties access to government information. However, this is just one of the possible avenues for giving access to government information (Piotrowski, 2010). They include:

1. *Proactive dissemination* – governments distribute information that has not been formally requested, e.g. by posting information on websites, depositing reports in archives or libraries or mailing newsletters.
2. *Requestor model* – associated with freedom of information laws, under which individuals can ask an agency formally for information, which may or may not be released, depending on whether it falls under one of the exemptions listed in the law (usually subject to appeals mechanisms for contesting denied requests). Governments have a range of fee structures based on the requestor's affiliation and the scope and mode of the release.
3. *Open public meetings* – which provide both a mechanism for participation but also for citizens or journalists to learn about the inner workings of government, such as proposed contracts and ordinances, etc.
4. *Whistleblowing and leaks* – which, unlike the other three avenues of access to information, may be illegal, e.g. when the information revealed by the whistleblower threatens or compromises national security, including the safety of those responsible for protecting it. In whistleblowing, an individual goes through formal or informal channels to make an ethical issue known to organisational leaders or the public directly. Leaking, however, is done anonymously, e.g. providing information to a news outlet or a non-profit advocacy group.

In many cases, freedom of information laws also provide remedies for citizens who believe that their right of access to information has not been respected – in some cases, citizens may complain to an information officer or an ombudsman or ask courts to enforce their access rights (see Case Example 27.6). Clearly, in each case a balance needs to be struck between the public interest and the need to protect personal privacy and to respect confidentiality of information. For example, in Canada, most freedom of information legislation does not apply to public-private partnerships. It is argued that this could impinge on private interests and endanger the confidentiality of commercial information.

Again, the degree to which various stakeholders in different countries wish to be transparent is culture-bound. Scandinavian countries have a comparatively high degree of transparency in the public sector. For example, the Swedish 'principle of public access' means that the general public and the media are, with few exceptions, guaranteed an unimpeded view of activities pursued by the government and local authorities.

Case Example 27.6 The Swedish Parliamentary Ombudsmen – Riksdagens Ombudsmän

Sweden has had an Ombudsman institution since 1809. An Ombudsman is an individual appointed directly by the Swedish Parliament (Riksdag) to ensure that public authorities and their staff comply with the laws and statutes governing their actions. The Ombudsmen form one pillar of constitutional protection for the basic freedoms and rights of individuals. The four Ombudsmen are independent in their decisions and answer directly to the Riksdag. The Ombudsmen's inquiries are prompted by complaints from the public or are initiated by the Ombudsmen themselves. Regular inspections are made of various public authorities and courts in the country. Fundamentally, the Ombudsmen are there to ensure that public authorities treat individuals lawfully and correctly.

Source: Riksdagens Ombudsmän (Sweden), www.jo.se/en/About-JO/ (accessed 21 January 2022).

In Finland, transparency even extends to tax information. Although there has been some discussion in Finland about the privacy issues arising, so far the principle of transparency has supported publication of this information, which would be regarded as an intrusion into privacy in most other countries and be socially and politically unacceptable.

Without doubt, the media also play an important role in this context. In particular, in the information age, they are often considered as the 'fourth estate' in the political system. Of course, the media themselves come under attack when they abuse the freedom of the press to violate personal rights to privacy. Indeed the boundary between transparency, which supports ethical standards, and intrusion, which undermines privacy, is a very fine line, and it is not always easy to strike an appropriate balance. What disclosures are in the public interest can be far from straightforward to define.

E-government may also be used to increase the degree of transparency, at least for those who have electronic access, as entire documents and accounts can now be disseminated easily and widely, e.g. by Wikileaks – an international non-profit organisation that publishes leaked news items and classified (secret) information on its website. Electronic security is therefore a recurring concern, and cross-border 'scams' or cyber-attacks can also potentially take place with great ease and speed. Software developers are consequently challenged to create systems that can provide more robust protection against unauthorised access and pirating.

Summary

The standards and conduct of public representatives and officials significantly affect the standing in which they are held. That in turn affects the confidence and respect in which governmental systems are held. High standards of conduct and public confidence go hand in hand. Many people in public life maintain these standards most of the time. Nevertheless, the need to remain vigilant and alert remains as important today as ever. At the same time, there is a need to balance transparency with the right to privacy of individuals, even those in public office.

Questions for review and discussion

1 Why are high standards of conduct thought to be important for those in public life?
2 What degree of disclosure of private interests is needed from those in public life? How far should such expectations extend to their friends and families?
3 Are ethics and standards of conduct matters for enforcement or education and guidance?
4 What values do you expect would strengthen ethical behaviour, and how might they be fostered in public organisations?

Reader exercises

1 Is it right to expect higher standards of conduct from those in public life than we would apply to ourselves?
2 Can you provide a 'watertight' definition of 'conflicts of interest'? Are there any circumstances in which this definition might be relaxed?

Class exercises

1 Consider the 'seven principles of public life' (see Case Example 27.4). Are there any principles that you consider inappropriate? Are there any additional principles that you would include? Can these principles be defined in a meaningful way?
2 (In groups): All students in the group should find a set of standards of conduct (or ethics code) from a public organisation. What is similar about the things contained in these standards or codes? What is different? What is missing?

References

Danny L. Balfour, Guy B. Adams and Ashley E. Nickels (2019), *Unmasking Administrative Evil* (5th ed.). New York: Routledge.
Mukti Jain Campion (2011), Bribery in India: A Website for Whistleblowers Retrieved January 8, 2013, from http://www.bbc.co.uk/news/world-south-asia-13616123.
David Clune (2020), The Long History of Political Corruption in NSW. www.abc.net.au/news/2020 -10-15/nsw-history-of-corruption-icac/12767346 accessed 21 January 2022.
Committee on Standards in Public Life (1995), *First report*, Cm 2850–1. London: Stationery Office.
Howard Davis and Bruce Walker (1997), Trust Based Relationships in Local Government Contracting. *Public Money and Management*, 7(4), 47–54.
Howard Davis and Bruce Walker (1998), Trust and Competition: Blue Collar Services in Local Government. In Andrew Coulson (ed.), *Trust and Contracts: Relationships in Local Government, Health and Public Services*. Bristol: Policy Press.

Lisa Fleisher (2011), 'The Jersey Sting', *Two Years Later*. January 7. Ic Retrieved from http://blogs.wsj .com/metropolis/2011/07/25/the-jersey-sting-two-years-later/.

Eleanor Glor (2001), Codes of Conduct and Generations of Public Servants. *International Review of Administrative Sciences*, 67(3) (September), 524–541.

Gardiner Harris (2013), India Aims to Keep Money for Poor Out of Others' Pockets, *New York Times*. January 5. Retrieved January 8, 2013, from http://www.nytimes.com/2013/01/06/world/asia/india -takes-aim-at-poverty-with-cash-transfer-program.html?ref=asia.

Leo Huberts, Karin Lasthuizen and Carel Peeters (2006), 'Measuring corruption: Exploring the Iceburg', In C. Sampford, A. Shacklock, C. Connors & F. Gaining (Eds.), *Measuring Corruption*. Burlington, VT: Ashgate, pp. 265–293.

International City/County Management Association (2022), ICMA Code of Ethics. Retrieved February 2, 2022, from https://icma.org/icma-code-ethics.

Terrence McDonald (2019), NJ Supreme Court Disbars Ex-Hoboken Mayor Who Admitted Taking Bribes. Retrieved from https://www.nj.com/hudson/2014/09/nj_supreme_court_disbars_ex -hoboken_mayor_who_admitted_taking_bribes.html.

OECD (1999), *Public Sector Corruption: An International Survey of Prevention Measures*. Paris: OECD.

Suzanne Piotrowski (2010), *Transparency and Secrecy: A Reader Linking Literature and Contemporary Debate*. Lanham, MD: Lexington Books.

John Rohr (1989), *Ethics for Bureaucrats: An Essay on Law and Values* (2nd ed.). New York: Marcel Dekker.

Ted Sherman and Josh Margolin (2011), *The Jersey Sting: A True Story of Crooked Pols, Money-Laundering Rabbis, Black Market Kidneys, and the Informant Who Brought It All Down*. New York: St. Martin's Press.

James H. Svara (2022), *The Ethics Primer for Administrators in Government and Nonprofit Organizations* (3rd ed.). Burlington, MA: Jones and Barlett Learning.

Transparency International (2022), CPI 2021 for Asia Pacific: Grand Corruption and Lack of Freedoms Holding Back Progress Retrieved from https://www.transparency.org/en/news/cpi-2021 -for-asia-pacific-grand-corruption-holding-back-progress.

Christian Vigouroux (1995), *Déontologie des Fonctions Publiques*. Paris: Dalloz.

28 Evidence-informed policy and practice

Annette Boaz and Sandra Nutley

Introduction

In many countries there is widespread interest in the use of evidence to improve policy-making and public service delivery (Boaz et al. 2019). The 1990s saw reduced public confidence in public service professionals. Moreover, educated, informed and questioning service users demanded more information about service choices and their effectiveness. The move to evidence-informed practice addressed such concerns. National governments began to promote the mantra that *'what matters is what works'* and to invest in an evidence infrastructure to support this. For example, a decade ago a US report (Baron and Haskins 2011: 28) concluded 'the Obama administration has created the most expansive opportunity for rigorous evidence to influence social policy in the history of the U.S. government'.

While we have seen challenges to the role of evidence and expertise in national policy debates (most notably in Trump's America, but also elsewhere), many practitioners and policymakers still seek research guidance and support, as shown recently by many politicians claiming they are 'following the evidence' in their responses to the COVID-19 pandemic. Public interest in evidence also continues, and initiatives to engage the public in research and make research outputs more accessible to them have grown.

This chapter aims to demonstrate that it is desirable and practical to ground policy and practice in more reliable evidence about social problems and what works in tackling them. We unpack what we know about how to mobilize evidence effectively for policy and practice. This does not mean that we have simple faith in the achievement of progress by logical reasoning and evidence – rather, we believe that effective governance of complex social systems requires opportunities for learning, which in turn rely on systems for gathering and using evidence.

Learning objectives

- To understand what counts as evidence for what purposes
- To understand how evidence can be used to improve public services
- To be aware of the obstacles to, and facilitators of, improved evidence use
- To understand how evidence-informed policy and practice can be encouraged

DOI: 10.4324/9781003282839-31

What counts as evidence for what purposes?

Two main forms of evidence are required to improve governmental effectiveness (Sanderson 2002) – evidence to improve *accountability* (information about the performance of government) and evidence to promote *improvement* (knowledge that enables the design and delivery of more effective policies and programmes). Chapters 12 and 15 have looked at several aspects of accountability and how performance information can facilitate this. Here we consider the use of evidence for improvement purposes – originally referred to as 'evidence-based policy and practice' but increasingly described as 'evidence-informed policy and practice' (EIPP).

Discussion of EIPP has been focused predominantly on the question of 'what works' – what interventions or strategies should be used to meet specified policy goals and identified client needs (Nutley et al. 2007). However, policy and practice improvement entail a broader range of evidence than this, including evidence about the nature of social problems, how potentially effective interventions can be implemented, what the likely effects of innovative interventions are and who needs to be involved in these processes. Furthermore, evidence is also required about the costs of action and the balance between costs and likely benefits.

Evidence about some of these issues is often based more on tacit understandings than on research based on systematic investigations, and thus what counts as good evidence is a subject of debate (Nutley et al. 2019). A broad and eclectic definition of evidence is needed, which includes routine monitoring data, stakeholder consultations and expert opinion.

How can evidence be used to improve public policy and practice?

In this section we focus on three main uses of research and evaluation evidence:

- To design and develop public policy
- To assess the effectiveness of policy interventions and improve policy implementation
- To identify tomorrow's issues

Using evidence right from the start: To design and develop public policy

Research can help to identify the policy issues to be addressed and whether there are interventions that are likely to be effective in tackling recognized problems. The choice of policy direction should be informed by existing evidence on what has been tried elsewhere and whether it has been demonstrated to deliver the desired benefits. Typically, this involves commissioning literature reviews. There are now a wide range of techniques for undertaking these reviews in a more systematic and robust way than was previously the case (Fraser and Davies 2019).

A distinct feature of systematic literature reviews is that they are carried out to a set of pre-agreed standards. The main standards are as follows:

- Focus on answering a specific question(s).
- Use protocols to guide the review process.

- Seek to identify as much of the relevant research as possible.
- Appraise the quality of the research included in the review.
- Synthesize the research findings in the studies included.
- Update in order to remain relevant.

Although there are benefits of such a process, in terms of its coverage and replicability, a study of evidence use in UK policy-making found that policymakers were concerned about the time involved in conducting systematic reviews and, hence, their utility (Campbell et al. 2007). There are also concerns that the outputs of such reviews are not always as useful as they need to be. Methodological innovations such as the development of 'living systematic reviews', which are constantly updated, may help to address some of these concerns. 'Best practice' (perhaps better thought of as 'revealing practice') reviews are also commonly undertaken in policy development, although there are fewer guidelines for how these can be carried out systematically or rigorously. Despite these concerns, research reviews can have considerable impact. For example, researchers in the UK and Australia consolidated the evidence on effective reading approaches by drawing together more than 300 studies. Their research is credited with ending the 'reading wars' and transforming the way reading is taught in classrooms around the world (Castles et al. 2018).

Consultation exercises and market research are often used to explore the views and priorities of key stakeholders and the public (see Chapter 22). Research can also explore the context and challenges facing a proposed policy. Techniques may include forecasting specific impacts of a proposed policy, such as regulatory impact assessments (see Case Example 28.1). Research into the potential risks of new approaches is needed where innovative interventions are proposed and no existing evidence is available. Moreover, it is important to initiate mechanisms to gather relevant evidence at an early stage when such innovations are implemented.

Policy pilots are often used in the design and development of public services. A policy can be trialled with a small group of organizations to identify potential problems and refine it before wider implementation. Pilots are often evaluated to distil the learning and feed this into subsequent roll-out of the policy. Examples of policy development through evaluated pilots include Best Value (Sanderson 2002). Although the potential benefits of policy pilots are clear, policy decisions often seem to be made prior to evaluation results becoming available.

Finally, the design of policy implementation needs to consider how to change practice. Research on alternative strategies can help to identify the available options and what seems to work best in what circumstances. Here again, there have been systematic reviews of the options available. For example, the Cochrane Effective Practice and Organisation of Care Group (EPOC) draws together international evidence on the effectiveness of different strategies for changing the behaviour of health care practitioners, such as issuing practice guidelines or using financial incentives. The relatively new field of implementation science has also generated a large number of models and frameworks to visualize and study the implementation of evidence into practice (Nilsen 2015).

Case Example 28.1 Improving the quality of regulations through regulatory impact analysis

Regulatory impact analysis (RIA) is a multiple stakeholder assessment of the economic, environmental and social impact of regulations. The OECD and European Union have strongly promoted this evidence-informed approach to legislation. An OECD survey revealed that, in 2005, all member countries used some form of RIA on new regulations.

OECD assessed the effectiveness of various RIA systems and developed a set of best-practice guidelines for the design and development of RIA systems, which recommends:

1   Maximize political commitment to RIA.
2   Allocate responsibilities for RIA programme elements carefully.
3   Train the regulators.
4   Use a consistent but flexible analytical method.
5   Develop and implement data collection strategies.
6   Target RIA efforts.
7   Integrate RIA with the policy-making process, beginning as early as possible.
8   Communicate the results.
9   Involve the public extensively.
10 Apply RIA to existing as well as new regulation.

However, as OECD admits, there are 'significant challenges' to measuring the benefits of tools such as RIA, since the links between improved outcomes in terms of improved productivity or investments and the quality of regulations tend to be weak.

Source: OECD 2020

Using evidence right to the end: Evidence on effectiveness/impact and policy implementation

Existing knowledge about the effectiveness of many policy and practice interventions is partial at best (see also Chapter 12). Hence, while systematic reviews of the knowledge base may suggest promising policy directions, there is still a need to evaluate their impact in specific contexts, which in turn adds to the evidence base. Evaluating effectiveness may involve the use of experimental methods, such as randomized control trials (RCTs). These have mainly been used to measure the effectiveness of clinical interventions. However, they have also been applied in other areas, including the assessment of continuing education programmes, offender rehabilitation programmes and alternative welfare regimes. There is also interest in 'meta-evaluation', which generally focuses on bringing together similar evaluations on a topic to aggregate data and/or research findings. It can provide an overview of evidence which is useful for policy and practice.

Knowledge of what works in social policy tends to be provisional and highly context-dependent. This has led to calls for a realist approach to social policy evaluations (Pawson and Tilley 1997), which begins with a theory of causal explanation and gives research the task of testing theories on how programme outcomes are generated by specific mechanisms in given contexts (Bovaird 2012). Theory development draws on the knowledge of different stakeholders in the policy process, getting them to articulate their views of what works for whom in what circumstances. Subsequent evaluation involves making inter- and intra-programme comparisons to see which configurations of context-mechanism-outcome are efficacious.

Regardless of the evaluation methodology employed, a key challenge facing those tasked with evaluating effectiveness is the difficulty of measuring the outcomes of many social interventions (see Chapter 12), since many outcomes are only really understood by those experiencing them. This has led to calls for the involvement of a wide range of stakeholders in evaluation processes, and the need to respect different forms of knowledge (e.g. involving the knowledge of indigenous peoples in countries such as Canada and New Zealand). Knowledge of what works tends to be influenced greatly by the kinds of question asked, who is asked and when they are asked. The answer also depends on context.

Impact studies need to be complemented by research that explores and improves policy implementation and progress towards goals. This calls for ongoing monitoring of progress and evaluation of the process of implementation throughout the life of a policy or programme. A wide variety of research methods and approaches are used. For example, action research – which involves multiple cycles of action, evaluation and critical reflection – can enable ongoing learning and timely adjustment to policy implementation plans by engaging practitioners in the research process. One of the strengths of this approach is that the practitioner does not have to wait for a final research report, but is able to integrate learning into their work as it emerges.

Using evidence to break the mould: Identifying tomorrow's issues

It is important for researchers to also explore a wider set of ideas than those defined by the current policy agenda. Research can consider 'blue skies' thinking, look more widely for ideas and problems and challenge current thinking. For example, research has prompted challenges to the traditional medical model of suicide prevention. By drawing on service user perspectives and the example of the Maytree crisis support service it has argued that a broader, social approach to the care of persons who are suicidal is needed (Fitzpatrick and River 2018).

Because of their distance from policy and practice, academic researchers are in a good position to challenge current thinking. Research councils and independent organizations, such as the Joseph Rowntree Foundation in the UK and the Rockefeller Foundation in the USA, currently take a lead role in supporting and nurturing curiosity-driven research.

Overall, we can see that research and evaluation can be used for many different purposes, each requiring somewhat different evidence-gathering approaches (see Table 28.1).

What are the obstacles to and facilitators of evidence use?

Although policy and practice benefit from being more rather than less informed by evidence, studies have frequently expressed concern about the apparent under-use of research, where findings are either not applied or are not applied successfully (Weiss 1998). How should

Table 28.1 Evidence uses and methods

Purposes	Methods and approaches might include:
Identify and prioritize key issues	Review existing literature, surveys, group discussions, interviews
Understand the views of stakeholders	Interviews, group discussions, surveys
Explore contextual factors (including analysis, opportunities and costs)	Impact assessment, cost benefit interviews and discussion groups
Prepare guidance for those implementing, a policy	Synthesizing the best available evidence, consulting key stakeholders, cost benefit analysis
Evaluate the effectiveness of a policy intervention to understand what works with whom and in what circumstances	Experimental and quasi-experimental studies, economic evaluations, realist evaluations, evaluations of pilots
Evaluate the processes and issues involved in implementing the policy	Case studies, observations, documentary analysis, interviews, group discussions, surveys and action research
Monitor progress	Management data, surveys and interviews
Generate new ideas and alternatives, highlight issues for future consideration	'Blue skies' research, syntheses of existing research, interviews, group discussions

this problem be tackled? And, conversely, should we also be concerned about the *overuse* of research – e.g. the rapid spread of tentative findings – and about *misuse*, especially where evidence is taken out of context and misrepresented (see Case Example 28.2) or is entirely false (such as fake news – stories created to deliberately misinform or deceive readers).

Case Example 28.2 The curious incident of research in the papers

On Thursday, 8 July 2004, the *London Evening Standard* ran its lead story on research into children in childcare and the government's cautious response. For nearly three weeks there was a flurry of press interest, largely around the issue of whether very young children are more aggressive if looked after in day nurseries, rather than by their mothers.

What was going on in this curious incident of research in the news? Certainly, many contributions to public debate. But also contributions where everyone – journalists, lobbyists, politicians and researchers – used all the rhetorical tricks in the book: Loaded words, selective quotation, reframing the issue, attribution of unseemly motives to opponents, generalizing from personal experience, accusations of misrepresentation, concealment of interests and false modesty. It should remind those of us who look to research and evaluation to improve the quality of public debate and decisions of a few home truths:

- The development of policy is largely achieved through argumentation, often behind closed doors, with policymakers compelled to act before the evidence is in – researchers must take their chances as they occur.
- How the argument is joined is unlikely to be of our choosing – we either have to go with how others choose to frame the debate or, more boldly, seek to change the terms of engagement by seeking a public platform ourselves.

- Let's not kid ourselves that our contribution will be seen as more objective than that of others – the media care little for academics' much vaunted quality control procedures.
- The scope for misrepresentation is immense by mediators who have other ambitions than ours. We should think twice about intentionally choosing the media as a channel for communicating our research to policymakers, programme managers, lobbyists, consumers. Better to find some direct, unmediated, channel for that purpose.

Source: Adapted from William Solesbury (2004).

Nutley et al. (2007), in a review of ways of increasing the impact of research, identified several barriers to and enablers of increased research use (see Box 28.1). The problem of under-use is frequently considered to stem from the fact that researchers and research users (policymakers and practitioners) occupy different worlds: they operate on different time-scales, use different languages, have different needs and respond to different incentive systems (Locock and Boaz 2004). This leads to calls for better dissemination strategies to bridge the gap between these two communities.

Box 28.1 Barriers to and enablers of the use of research

The nature of the research

Research is more likely to be used if it:

- Is high quality and comes from a credible source
- Provides clear and uncontested findings
- Has been commissioned by, or carries, high-level political support
- Is aligned with local priorities, needs and contexts
- Is timely and relevant to policymakers' and practitioners' requirements
- Is presented in a 'user-friendly' way – concise, jargon-free and visually appealing

The personal characteristics of both researchers and potential research users

- Policymakers and practitioners with higher levels of education or some experience of research are more likely to be research users.
- Lack of skills to interpret and appraise research can inhibit research use.
- Some individuals may be hostile towards the use of research.
- Researchers may lack the knowledge and skills to engage effectively in dissemination and research use activities.

The links between research and its users

- Research use may be inhibited where policymakers and practitioners have limited access to research.

- Knowledge brokers – both individuals and agencies – can play an effective 'bridging' role between research and potential users.
- Direct links between researchers and policymakers or practitioners – e.g. face-to-face interactions – are most likely to encourage the use of research.

The context for the use of research

Context plays a key role in shaping the uptake of research.

- In policy contexts, research is more likely to be used where:
  - It is aligned with current ideology and individual and agency interests
  - Its findings fit with existing ways of thinking or acting
  - Open political systems exist
  - Institutions and structures bring researchers and policymakers into contact
  - At local level, the organizational culture is broadly supportive of evidence use
- In practice contexts, local organizational, structural and cultural issues may limit the use of research, for example:
  - Lack of time to read research
  - Lack of autonomy to implement the findings from research
  - Lack of support – financial, administrative and personal – to develop research-based practice change
  - Local cultural resistance to research and its use
- In research contexts, a number of barriers inhibit the flow of findings to policymakers and practitioners:
  - Lack of incentive or reward for engaging in dissemination and research use activities
  - High value placed on traditional academic journal publications at the expense of 'user-friendly' research outputs
  - Lack of time and financial resources for research use activities
  - Attitudes among some academic researchers that dissemination is not part of their role

Source: Adapted from Nutley et al. (2007: 81–83).

While helpful in some ways, the 'two communities' view tends to imply homogeneity in each community, which contrasts with the considerable diversity within both the research, and the policy and practice, communities. It is also in danger of over-simplifying the political landscape by ignoring others involved in policy development. Potential sources for new policy ideas include political parties, ministers, pressure groups, lobbyists, international bodies, academics and the research community. These groups may draw on research evidence to develop their ideas, but other forms of knowledge may play a more prominent role. For example, a minister is likely to be influenced not only by formal research, but also by the views of constituents, the results of opinion polls, the party manifesto on which he or she was elected, his or her formal learning and knowledge gained through both work and personal experience. One of the problems facing decision-makers is the sheer volume of information available to them.

In addition to information overload, decision-makers must wrestle with political and organizational factors, particularly the need to conciliate between all of the interests in the policy-making process. While it might be tempting to think of evidence being used directly to make rational and informed decisions, reality is often far more messy and overtly political.

There are at least four ways in which evidence might influence policy (see Box 28.2), and the direct (instrumental) use of research in decision-making may be quite rare. It is most likely where the research findings are non-controversial, require only limited change and will be implemented within a supportive environment: in other words, when they do not upset the *status quo* (Weiss 1998). A set of research findings may be used in different ways over time and by different groups. In general, there is more cause for optimism about the use of evidence if we define research use more broadly than simply its direct use in making decisions.

Box 28.2 Four main types of research use

1   Instrumental use
    Research feeds directly into decision-making for policy and practice.
2   Conceptual use
    Even where findings are not used directly, research can provide new ways of thinking and offer insights into the strengths and weaknesses of particular courses of action. New conceptual understandings may then be used in instrumental ways.
3   Mobilization of support
    Here, research becomes an instrument of persuasion. Findings – or simply the act of research – can be used as a political tool, to legitimate particular courses of action or inaction.
4   Wider influence
    Research can have an influence beyond the institutions and events being studied. Research adds to the accumulation of knowledge which ultimately contributes to large-scale shifts in thinking, and sometimes action.

Source: Adapted from Weiss (1998).

How can evidence-informed policy and practice be encouraged?

As our understanding of the varied ways in which research is used has developed (Box 28.1), so too has our thinking about ways of improving its use. Best and Holmes (2010) argue that models for improving research use have shifted through three generations of thinking:

- First generation models envisage research being 'pushed' to research users – researchers produce evidence, which gets disseminated to end-users and then incorporated into policy and practice based on rational decision-making.
- Second generation models emphasize the importance of two-way dialogue and collaboration between the producers and users of evidence, including the development of

research-practice partnerships and fostering of networks of stakeholders with common interests.

- Third generation models pay greater attention to whole systems thinking – identifying and addressing the system elements that shape research use interactions and actions.

Initiatives on the ground to increase research use are many and varied (see Box 28.3 for some generic examples). They range from national centres/clearing houses that produce, synthe-size and disseminate research evidence (often based on first generation models of research use) to local initiatives that encourage researchers and practitioners to work together in knowledge co-producing partnerships (based more on second generation thinking). Despite this diversity, strategies that push evidence are still more prevalent than those that try to increase capacity for research use, build engagement in research and change systems in order to support evidence use (Powell et al. 2017).

Box 28.3 Examples of initiatives designed to promote research use

- **Evidence synthesis centres**, such as clearing houses and What Works centres, are funded to produce and disseminate high-quality syntheses of evidence.
- **Evidence guideline centres** translate evidence syntheses into practice guidelines and evidence-informed protocols for practitioners.
- **Research training programmes** for policymakers and practitioners build capacity to do and/or use research.
- **Knowledge brokers** connect research producers and end-users to support the use of research.
- **Research networks** provide opportunities for knowledge exchange and facilitate research-related interactions between individuals and organizations.
- **Research-practice partnerships** are long-term collaborations between specific researchers and practitioners. They work together to identify problems, conduct studies and apply findings.

Source: Adapted from Boaz and Nutley 2019.

There is increasing interest in the potential of research networks and research-practice part-nerships to improve the use of research, as in Case Example 28.3.

Case Example 28.3 Making connections and building collaborations for evidence-informed public management across Africa

The Africa Evidence Network (AEN) (www.africaevidencenetwork.org) was formed in 2012 to support evidence-informed decision-making and has grown from a membership of 20 to over 3500, supported by the Africa Centre for Evidence at the University of Johannesburg. The network supports the sharing of news, activi-ties, innovations and learning, as well as arranging in-person and virtual events. Based on a belief that only by working together can evidence-informed decision-making become a reality, the membership spans governments, academia and many in-between. It is cross-disciplinary and cross-sector and avoids association with any specific form of evidence. Over the last decade it has successfully formed and strengthened connections within and across countries, facilitating new collaborations to enable greater use of evidence in decision-making at various levels. It has raised the profile of evidence-informed decision-making across the continent and disseminated these innovations in global forums. The combination of colleagues who work directly in public management with those who aim to support better public policy outcomes through the generation of useful evidence makes the network a valuable learning community.

Capturing the impacts of networks is challenging. The AEN routinely captures qualitative Stories of Change, and is working to apply Most Significant Change methodology more routinely. However, assessing the value of the network for public policy outcomes and for the evidence ecosystem more broadly remains work in progress.

Source: The Africa Evidence Network founding chair, Ruth Stewart (https://www. africaevidencenetwork.org).

Many initiatives to encourage research use have not been evaluated, and the evidence base on effective approaches is relatively weak. Different approaches are likely to be more or less helpful at various points in policy-making and implementation (indicating, for example, the need for both national clearing houses and local partnerships). This links to more general ideas about knowledge management in organizations and networks (Box 28.4), which emphasizes the benefits and limitations of a codification approach to managing knowledge. The creation of accessible and interlinked databases of key information and evidence is often necessary and helpful, but there is also a need to complement this with a more personalized approach to sharing knowledge.

The importance of blending different approaches has prompted interest in identifying the key features of a well-functioning 'evidence ecosystem' – a system of interconnected elements that interact in the process of evidence generation, synthesis and use. We would expect such a system to include the initiatives listed in Box 28.3, but it would also need to consider the wider aspect of incentives that encourage relevant stakeholders (individuals and organizations) to engage appropriately with that system. These might include financial incentives (such as research engagement grants) and career development incentives (such as incorporating evidence use into competency and promotion frameworks and professional registration requirements). Incentives for researchers and their institutions to contribute to EIPP tend to centre on the design of research grant systems and assessments of research impact. For example, the UK Research Excellence Framework aims to assess not only research quality but also its impact. How each university performs in this assessment is linked to subsequent research funding allocations. As with all incentive systems, it is important to consider whether and how they work, and if they produce worrying unintended consequences.

Concerns about evidence misuse also indicate a need for arrangements that seek to hold others to account for their use of evidence. Organizations, such as Full Fact (https://fullfact.org) and Sense about Science (https://senseaboutscience.org), aim to raise the standard of evidence use in public life, including highlighting misrepresentations of evidence for political purposes and fake news stories. Some inspection bodies have also conducted periodic assessments of the extent to which specific policies and practices are informed by evidence.

Overall, there has been significant investment in a range of initiatives aimed at encouraging and supporting EIPP. Many appear promising, but there is a need to continue to build an evidence base on what works to improve evidence use.

Box 28.4 Knowledge management

Knowledge management is concerned with developing robust systems for storing and communicating knowledge. There are two main approaches: a codification strategy and a personalization approach (Hansen et al. 1999). Codification strategies tend to be computer-centred: knowledge is carefully codified and stored in databases. In a personalization approach it is recognized that knowledge is closely tied to the person who develops it, and, hence, what is needed are enhanced opportunities for sharing knowledge through direct person-to-person contact. The role of information and communication technology within this is to help people communicate knowledge, not to store it.

Summary

We have argued in this chapter that evidence can be used to facilitate *accountability* and to promote *improvement* in policy-making, programme development and service delivery. We have focused on the latter and have considered three main uses of research for policy and practice:

- To design and develop public policy
- To assess the impact of policy intervention and improve policy implementation
- To identify tomorrow's issues

Research has important insights to offer in each of these areas. Each requires different forms of evidence, which in turn employ different methods for gathering evidence. We therefore need to work with inclusive definitions of both evidence and research and to emphasize a 'horses for courses' approach, adapting our evidence-gathering approaches to specific policy and practice issues.

Research evidence must, of course, compete with other forms of knowledge and experience, so it must be actively and persuasively disseminated. There is a need for better ongoing interactions between researchers and research users, in long-term partnerships that span the entire research process, from the definition of the problem to the application of findings. We also need to adapt systems to support research use. This includes the academic systems that produce research and the policy and practice systems that manage and make use of research (Boaz et al. 2019).

Overall, the emerging lesson is that there are many challenges facing EIPP. There are good reasons why policymakers and practitioners should rise to these challenges, but evidence will and should remain just one of the influences that shape policy development and service delivery.

Questions for review and discussion

1 Why is evidence a useful resource for policymakers?
2 What are the main obstacles to, and enablers of, EIPP?
3 How might the concept of knowledge management inform thinking about how to change service delivery practice so that it is more evidence-informed?

Reader exercises

1 Identify a policy or practice initiative that has been labelled as being based on good evidence (e.g. many early years interventions). Search for information on this initiative (via websites and journal articles) and write a report that describes and appraises its use of evidence.
2 Scan newspapers for a high-profile report of a research project. Consider how the research has been presented and how it might be used by different stakeholders (e.g. policymakers, researchers, journalists, professional bodies and other interest groups).

Class exercises

1 You are a cross-government group brought together to take a fresh look at policy development in relation to smoking. You have been asked to consider how smoking should be framed as a policy problem. For example, it might be viewed as a health problem, as a fiscal matter or as an environmental/regulatory issue.
   - If seen as a health problem, then the focus is likely to be on the relationship between smoking and ill-health.
   - If viewed as a fiscal issue, then the focus might be on ensuring that tobacco taxes cover the social and health costs of smoking, or interest might lie in addressing issues such as smuggling and duty avoidance.
   - If seen as an environmental/regulatory problem then the focus might be on passive smoking and the regulation of smoking at work and in public places.
        Discuss in class what sorts of evidence you would need to help you determine the most appropriate ways of framing smoking as a policy problem.
2 You are a group of government staff with responsibility for primary school education policy. A recent review of the evidence on how to teach mathematics at primary school level has concluded that one particular approach is more effective than others. Discuss how you would go about trying to change teaching practice so that it is in line with the recommended approach. Reflect upon your initial thoughts by considering how they fit with the ideas outlined in this chapter.

Further reading

Simon Bastow, Patrick Dunleavy and Jane Tinkler (2014), *The impact of the social sciences: How academics and their research make a difference.* London: Sage Publications.
Annette Boaz, Alec Fraser Huw Davies and Sandra Nutley (2019), *What works now? Evidence-informed policy and practice.* Bristol: Policy Press.
Louise Locock and Annette Boaz (2004), 'Research, policy and practice? Worlds apart?'. *Journal of Society and Social Policy*, 3(4): 375–384.

Sandra Nutley, Isabel Walter and Huw Davies (2007), *Using evidence: How research can inform public services*. Bristol: Policy Press.

Further information and suggested reading are also available from three key websites:

Transforming Evidence is an open access community promoting the use of evidence in policy and practice through publications, events and other networking opportunities – see: transforming-evidence.org.

The UK government currently funds seven 'What Works' centres to improve how government and other organizations create, share and use evidence in a range of policy areas, including education, crime reduction and wellbeing. See: https://www.gov.uk/what-works-network.

The international journal *Evidence & Policy* publishes research, debate and practice papers in this field – see: http://www.policypress.co.uk/journals_eap.asp.

References

Jon Baron and Ron Haskins (2011), 'The Obama administration's evidence-based social policy initiatives: An overview'. In NESTA, *Evidence for social policy and practice (pdf)*. London: National Endowment for Science, Technology and the Arts (nesta.org.uk).

Allan Best and Bev Holmes (2010), 'Systems thinking, knowledge and action: Towards better models and methods'. *Evidence and Policy*, 6(2): 145–159.

Annette Boaz and Sandra Nutley (2019), 'Using evidence'. In Boaz, et al. *What works now? Evidence-informed policy and practice*. Bristol: Policy Press.

Tony Bovaird (2012), 'Attributing outcomes to social policy interventions – 'gold standard' or 'fool's gold' in public policy and management?'. *Social Policy and Administration*, 48(1): 1–23.

Siobhan Campbell, Siobhan Benita, Elizabeth Coates, Phil Davies and Gemma Penn (2007), *Analysis for policy: Evidence based policy in practice*. London: Government Social Research Unit.

Ann Castles, Kathy Rastle and Katie Nation (2018), 'Ending the reading wars: Reading acquisition from novice to expert'. *Psychological Science in the Public Interest*, 19(1): 5–51. doi: 10.1177/1529100618772271.

Scott Fitzpatrick and Jo River (2018), 'Beyond the medical model: Future directions for suicide intervention services'. *International Journal of Health Services: Planning, Administration, Evaluation*, 48(1): 189–203. doi: 10.1177/0020731417716086. Epub 2017 Jun 26. PMID: 28649928.

Alec Fraser and Huw Davies (2019), 'Systematic approaches to generating evidence'. In Boaz, et al. *What works now? Evidence-informed policy and practice*. Bristol: Policy Press.

Morten Hansen, Nitin Nohria and Thomas Tierney (1999), 'What's your strategy for managing knowledge?' *Harvard Business Review*, March-April, 77(2): 106–116.

Per Nilsen (2015), 'Making sense of implementation theories, models and frameworks'. *Implementation Science*, 21(10:53). doi: 10.1186/s13012-015-0242-0. PMID: 25895742. PMCID: PMC4406164.

Sandra Nutley, Huw Davies and Judith Hughes (2019), 'Assessing and labelling evidence'. In Boaz, et al. *What works now? Evidence-Informed policy and practice*. Bristol: Policy Press.

OECD (2008), *Measuring regulatory quality*, Policy Brief. Paris: OECD.

OECD (2020), *Regulatory Impact Assessment, Best Practice Principles for Regulatory Policy*. Paris: OECD.

Ray Pawson and Nick Tilley (1997), *Realistic evaluation*. London: Sage.

Alison Powell, Huw Davies and Sandra Nutley (2017), Missing in Action? The role of knowledge mobilisation literature in developing knowledge mobilisation practices. *Evidence & Policy: A Journal of Research, Debate and Practice*, 13, 201–223.

Ian Sanderson (2002), 'Evaluation, policy learning and evidence-based policy-making'. *Public Administration*, 80(1): 1–22.

William Solesbury (2004), 'The curious incident of the research in the papers'. *The Evaluator*, Winter: 15–16.

Carol Weiss (1998), 'Have we learned anything new about the use of evaluation?' *American Journal of Evaluation*, 19(1): 21–33.

Part IV

... and finally

The fourth part of this book (Chapter 29) attempts to look into the future, highlighting forecasts made in different chapters of the book and suggesting that the public sector will continue to be important, providing socially valuable public services, so that public management and governance will also remain relevant to society.

However, it warns that some aspects of public management and governance are complex and even chaotic, so that we may never be able to understand them in any systematic way. It suggests, finally, that understanding how to tackle public issues in a context where some issues are simple, others are complicated, and yet others lie in the complex or chaotic knowledge domains, requires not simply scientific understanding, but mastery of both the craft and the art of public management and governance.

DOI: 10.4324/9781003282839-32

29 Public management and governance: The future?

Tony Bovaird and Elke Loeffler

Introduction

We have already covered a long time span in this book. Some of the early chapters explored trends in the public sector and in public services over the past century. Some chapters have explored topics which have excited interest more recently (such as co-production in the past 45 years and e-government in the past 25 years).

During this travel in time, we have explored how analysis of the public sector has mutated, from "old public administration" to "new public management", and then to "public governance".

Has this been a one-way street to greater understanding? Can we expect "public management and governance" to demonstrate an "ever onwards and upwards" trajectory? Or is it simply a circle – or better, a spiral – in which new understandings lead us inevitably back to some old understandings, albeit in a new context?

While being optimists about the human potential for learning (and therefore natural believers in "progress" in human affairs), we do not buy the "ever onwards and upwards" storyline. A credible approach to public management and governance has to accept and try to explain the serious lurches backwards which have continually been experienced. Of course, by using a term such as "backwards", we imply that it is possible to discern what a "forwards" movement looks like in public management and governance. This is what this chapter will seek to explore.

Learning objectives

The key points which we hope students will take away from this chapter are:

- In the future, there will continue to be an important public sector, with socially valuable public services – and therefore public management and governance will also continue to be important
- Most of the key issues in public management and governance remain the same over time, whatever we call the subject which we are studying
- The key players who excite most interest will vary from time to time and from place to place – as we change the focus on key players, so we change the issues which have highest priority in our study of public management and governance
- There are some aspects of public management and governance which are simple to understand, some are complicated and some are complex. Beyond these issues lie some chaotic and entirely disordered realms of human behaviour which we may never be able to understand in any systematic way

DOI: 10.4324/9781003282839-33

- We do not know what the next trends are likely to be – but we can have a strong suspicion of the set of issues around which the debates on public management and governance are likely to revolve, at least in the medium term
- Understanding how to tackle public issues in this context of multiple knowledge domains requires not simply scientific understanding, but mastery of both the craft and the art of public management and governance

Future of the public sector

Warnings about the death of the public sector have often been sounded in the past. However, it has always turned out, as Mark Twain once observed in relation to himself, that the report of death has been exaggerated. At the moment, as several chapters in this volume indicate, the public sector is under attack and is being reduced in size in many countries. However, we are confident that this is a passing phase, not its death throes.

This is for two major – but very different – reasons. First, the current attack on the public sector is extraordinarily inappropriate. After all, governments are tackling several global crises which threaten not only the livelihoods but also the lives of citizens all over the world. The financial crisis in the private sector of the major OECD countries in 2008 has caused long-lasting problems and highlighted the extent of ineffective and inefficient private sector markets across the global economy. The subsequent recession wiped out a much higher proportion of the private sector economy than the public sector economy in most OECD countries – revealing that much of this private sector activity was inefficient and low value-added. The different private sector firms which grew to take their place often had very low wages, "zero-hours contracts" and low security of job tenure, so they still made a relatively small contribution to the overall economy. The subsequent COVID-19 pandemic highlighted that governments are fundamental to coping with health crises – while many different approaches have been used to deal with COVID-19, no country has successfully relied on private sector responses to prevent its spread and treat its consequences. Meanwhile, the climate crisis continues to demonstrate that governments across the globe are weak and ineffective – but that the private sector is actually contributing more to the problem than the solution. Similarly, misuse of 'big data' is mainly driven by the profit motive of private firms.

Therefore, to suggest that the solution to current financial, economic, social and environmental crises lies in radical cuts to the public sector shows a political and economic naïveté which, we believe, will be viewed with incredulity in the future. We therefore expect that most OECD governments will eventually seek to follow a balanced approach to achieving stability, which recognises the value of the public sector and does not simply see it as a burden upon the rich and upon private firms.

Second, and perhaps more importantly, concerns with private market inefficiency have grown significantly since the global "great recession" in 2008. Nearly 25 years after Francis Fukuyama (1989) declared the "end of history" as we know it, namely the endless battle between private and public sectors, his claim that markets had finally and fully prevailed over the social economy is in tatters. Never has the need for government intervention been so obvious throughout the world. In particular, much more emphasis is being given to regulation in many countries, particularly around issues of global warming and pollution, and the role of public services in tackling inequality is being rediscovered in many countries.

However, this reassertion of the role of government intervention is not simply the reappearance of "big government". Indeed, the sectors have begun to merge into each other in some ways:

- the provision of public services is undertaken by private and third sector organisations, as well as public sector organisations
- user and community co-production of public value and publicly desired outcomes are now seen to be an important complement to public sector activity
- not only are public services now subject to close inspection and audit but stronger regulation has been introduced into many private sector markets, especially since the scandals of the "great boom" after 1998 and the "great recession" from 2008
- corporate social responsibility (sometimes packaged as "economic, social and governance" concerns) is now a common theme among successful private companies, particularly encompassing concerns with environmental sustainability, equal opportunities for all employees and sensitivity to impacts on local communities
- many third sector organisations have grown in importance in the delivery of public services, often espousing aims at least as "social" as those of their public sector commissioners
- the campaign against corruption in many countries, particularly in the developing world, is now understood to necessitate control not only over public corruption ("the abuse of public power for personal gain") but also over private sector corruption ("the abuse of power within private sector organizations") (Sartor and Beamish, 2020), especially as "public sector corruption" is usually fuelled by private sector payments to public officials

For all of these reasons, we believe that there will still be a strong and important public sector in the future and that it will continue to require strong and effective public management and governance. So, be prepared for further editions of this book – and for many similar books to appear!

Exploring the dynamics of public management and governance

The ongoing need for strong and effective public management and governance does not imply, however, that it will not change in character – indeed, history has demonstrated that public management and governance change constantly and we have no reason to believe that this will now stop.

What are the drivers of this constant change in public administration and governance? Clearly, one driver is the continual emergence of new policy issues which matter to the public – or the reappearance of old issues in a new form. These public issues are mediated, of course, by politicians, whose careers are partly dependent upon being seen to respond successfully to issues as they emerge, and who are therefore careful about the policy issues with which they become identified. Moreover, the media (in particular, social media) play an important role in the presentation of these policy issues and the expectations which develop amongst the public about how they will be tackled by government. Quite rightly, the way the public sector is managed and governed will be different, depending on whether it is focusing on getting jobs for disadvantaged young people or on promoting economic growth through tax breaks for companies.

However, in practice, the key policy issues tend not to change very significantly over time. Take one of the key social policy textbooks of the 1970s: Cooper (1973) contains chapters on education, health, social security (e.g. welfare payments and pensions), housing, probation, elderly people and child care. Of course, there are some differences – a modern textbook would be likely to place much more emphasis on inequality, diversity and migration. However, these differences in emphasis on priority policy issues over the decades do not seem likely to explain many of the changes in public management and governance recorded in the earlier chapters of this book.

One might argue that not only policy issues but also most of the key issues in public management and governance have remained the same over time, although with changing emphasis from time to time. And it is certainly true that most of the chapters in this book relate to similar chapters in public management and governance textbooks of earlier decades. Consider, for example, the chapter titles in the first edition of Norman Flynn's classic textbook, *Public Sector Management*, in 1990 – after the introductory section, there were six core chapters in the first edition – "Markets, Prices and Competition", "Managing and Measuring Performance", "The Impact of Competition", "A User-Oriented Service", "Organisational Structures" and "The Future of Public Sector Management". Again, no surprise here – each of these merits at least one chapter in the book you are reading (and sometimes several chapters, as in the case of "A User-Oriented Service").

However, we don't entirely buy this story. We believe that the study of public management and governance has indeed altered considerably over the past three decades. (Indeed, that is also clear from considering Norman Flynn's first edition, which had no chapters on partnership/collaboration, on e-government or audit/inspection, all of which only appeared in subsequent editions.) And we think there are two key reasons for this alteration. One is the developing scholarship in the field – now covering a much wider range of disciplines and perspectives than ever before and also benefiting from much deeper empirical testing than was previously available. This scholarship has also deepened our understanding of each aspect of the field – and this has revealed that some issues are more complicated than first thought, so that we no longer believe that performance management should mean "driving the car by looking in the rear-view mirror" or that we can "market brotherhood like soap" or that we can look forward to "evidence-based" policy and practice, as opposed to "evidence-informed" policy and practice (as pointed out by Boaz and Nutley in Chapter 28). We believe that the previous chapters in this book demonstrate this increasing range of well-founded scholarship.

A second key reason has been the change of the practice of public management and governance, largely driven by the changing balance of power in our society, as different groups have grown or declined in their capacity to deliver positive improvements through their contributions to public policy and public services. This is perhaps most evident in relation to the increased interest in the potential of user and community co-production to improve public outcomes, as shown in Chapter 23. Other chapters have demonstrated the increased recognition in recent decades of the potential contribution which the removal of discrimination against women, ethnic minority groups, etc., can make to improving the practice of public management and governance. Further, in many countries the private sector is now looked upon more suspiciously by the public when it wins contracts to deliver public services than was the case in the early years of the Thatcher government in the UK – whether fairly or unfairly, the highly publicised failure of many private sector outsourcing deals has raised considerable doubt and even resentment against privatisation. Taking these factors together, in any given period those who seem able to deliver positive improvements to public value, and have gained sufficient trust from the public to act accordingly, have often been able to gain more power for their vision – and therefore to shape public management and governance to their own liking.

From this perspective, the move in OECD countries from "old public administration" to "public governance" was not simply a change in the ideas espoused by scholars. It was also partly a shift in the power balance, away from the internally focused public sector in which politicians and public administrators were preoccupied with their own struggle for dominance in policy making. It constituted a clear shift towards a more externally focused public sector, in which many stakeholders vied with each other for dominance in policy making. In public governance, both politicians and paid public administrators have to share power with other actors, who might include (depending on the issue and the time concerned) the private sector, the third sector, service users or citizens generally. The intermediate epoch of "new public management" marked the start of this shift, in which public sector organisations began to cede power to external providers (often in the private sector but sometimes also in the third sector) but before service users and citizens generally began to play more important roles.

So, the question naturally arises: what does this mean for the future of public management and governance?

What can we know about public management and governance?

So, as you will already have noticed, in this final chapter, after having been cautious throughout the book, we are finally going to allow ourselves to make some predictions. Isn't this a potentially fatal error for authors, since readers will quickly have the chance to notice how adrift these predictions are from what actually happens after the book is published?

Well, we accept the risks involved. This is mainly because we believe that there are some things which can be known with some confidence in the social sciences, as well as many things which are inherently unknowable. And we intend to confine our predictions to areas of knowledge where we believe there is already some well-founded understanding of the factors influencing public management and governance, and where these factors are likely to continue, at least for a while.

The stance we are taking here derives from the Cynefin framework developed by Snowden and Boone (2007) – see Bovaird (2013) and Chapter 18. It suggests that some aspects of behaviour (e.g. in public management and governance) lie in the simple knowledge domain, some in the complicated domain and some in the complex domain. Beyond these domains lie some chaotic and entirely disordered realms of human behaviour which we may never be able to understand in any systematic way. Our predictions are naturally going to be most bold where we are dealing with issues in the simple and complicated domains, where we have at least some knowledge of relevant patterns, and we will be most cautious when discussing issues in the complex domain, where trial and error through thoughtful experimentation is usually the key learning mechanism.

We will seek to avoid altogether predictions about issues lying in the fourth ("chaos") or fifth ("disorder") domains. While politicians may get away with bluster rather than owning up to such a situation, claiming confidence in any propositions here is essentially indefensible.

What are the next trends likely to be?

We do not know what the next trends are likely to be – the future always carries surprises. However, we can use our existing knowledge to forecast some of the issues around which the debates on public management and governance are likely to revolve, at least in the medium term. This can be done by a range of methods – projections based on time series analysis, econometric models suggesting correlations between forecastable variables, analogies with phenomena in comparable situations, simulations of outcomes from different future situations, Delphi methods (getting experts to interact to come up with a forecast), scenario-writing of likely and unlikely developments, etc. Here, we mainly project from existing trends, using our knowledge of existing correlations between variables, and exercising judgement on comparability across different situations.

It is important, of course, to stay realistic. We remain sceptical of being able to predict future trends across a wide range of dissimilar countries – we think predictions are only likely to be of any use where the specific conditions of a country are taken into account (and even within a single country, we may need to take account of significant variations from place to place, from sector to sector, from stakeholder group to stakeholder group, etc.). Some of the bases on which trends might be projected for a specific country are:

- the extent to which current initiatives appear to be working well (since successful initiatives are likely to continue) or badly (since unsuccessful ones are likely to be halted or reversed)
- the extent to which some current trends, apparently successful in similar countries, have been under-developed in our country (since they are likely to percolate slowly into our country, too)
- the extent to which some past trends in public management and governance have run into difficulty in similar countries (since they are likely to experience similar difficulties in our country, too)
- the policy issues on which change seems most strongly desired by powerful stakeholder groups, e.g. voters, political parties, big business, the media (since they are particularly likely to influence decisions on public management and governance approaches)
- the changing balance of power of different stakeholders in our government (which will favour some approaches to public management and governance and disadvantage other approaches)

Let us look in more detail at one of these approaches, namely the approach in the final bullet point, to see how this might be done. Changes in the balance of power between different actors in public management and governance will vary from country to country, which has implications for changing political priorities. As a general rule, it is probably safe to forecast that actors whose problems appear to be largely ignored in current policy agendas are likely to play a stronger role in the future, if their numbers are sufficiently large. What does that mean in particular? Well, this will vary from country to country. In the UK, we suggest that inequalities will become an even more important issue given that the economic recession after 2010, the subsequent decade of austerity and the savage effects of COVID-19 have particularly disadvantaged people in economically and socially deprived groups. In Germany, however, its rapidly ageing population means that issues concerning older people are likely to get more attention from policy-makers. In Spain, by contrast, the reduction of youth unemployment is likely to be a high priority for future governments. More generally, it seems likely that in many OECD countries, private sector service providers will have rather less influence on government over the next decade, as the obsession of governments from the early 1980s until recently with private sector management has to face the reality that it has not delivered as much as it promised. Finally, in spite of a short period (1998–2013) in which, according to the World Bank, extreme poverty in the Global South was halved (mainly but not exclusively in China), inequality in the Global South has reached such a level as to produce an "explosive situation" (Therborn, 2022: 63–64), in which the average person in the richest tenth of the world's population now has an income 38 times larger than the average person in the poorer 50%, at a time when "the wretched of the earth" are more connected to what is happening elsewhere in the world than ever before.

These developments will, if they do indeed come about, imply certain changes in the public management issues which are given most priority. In the UK, for example, this implies a need to experiment with new approaches to welfare policies and social care such as social impact bonds. In Germany, urban development is faced with the issue of how to adapt public infrastructure and services to an older population. In many parts of the Global South even greater political turbulence seems likely, with major pressures for increased public sector intervention to tackle inequality.

Again, we have proposed earlier that there are also some areas of knowledge which are not likely to be subject to any clear understanding or confident predictions of this type. This is particularly the case in the complex and chaotic knowledge domains, characterised by densely interconnected variables which have non-linear relationships. This is likely to mean, for example, that the management of multi-outcome programmes and the governance of multi-organisation partnerships will always be inherently difficult, their trajectories will be predictable only to a very limited extent (e.g. perhaps only the outer limits of their achievements may be predictable, not the optimum pathways to outcomes) and any attempt to set detailed strategies in these cases should be taken with a large pinch of salt (Bovaird and Kenny, 2015; Foresight, 2007).

What have previous chapters said about the future? In Table 29.1 we list many of the comments made in different chapters about how the authors see future developments in relation to the topic of that chapter. As you will see, quite a few of our authors have been careful not to make explicit predictions, while others have made quite a few. And just to add to your interest (and, no doubt, hilarity in some cases) as you read this final chapter, the editors have added in some further predictions related to these chapters. You might like to speculate on which forecasting approaches these different authors have used in making these predictions.

Of course, it is always dangerous to make predictions like this. They may well turn out to be misguided. That's why one of the exercises at the end of this chapter asks you to update the evidence on these predictions and to then replace them with your own predictions for what might happen in the following decade!

Are public management and governance a branch of science, craft or art?

Finally, after 29 chapters, let us discuss more openly what we have been trying to do in this book. Has this long examination of issues in public management and governance been a scientific study, to take forward theory and conceptual understanding? Or has it been a craft manual, to improve practice? Well, we would answer "yes" to both of these – but only in part. Actually, we believe this book has been very ambitious – it has studied public management and governance in the round, considering these concepts as science, craft and … art.

As academics, we might be expected to focus most on public management and governance as a social science. And certainly this has been a key theme of the book – for example, we have looked at many social science theories around public finance, performance management, partnership working, the equalities agenda, etc., and have examined the evidence for these theories. This is part of the scientific approach. However, our authors have not rested at that – just as well, you might say, since the body of knowledge in public management and

Table 29.1 Predictions in previous chapters on likely future developments in public management and governance

Chapter	Predictions by chapter author	Some supplementary predictions from the editors
2	"As public policy contexts become more differentiated in the future, the variety of governance reforms is likely to be much greater than in the NPM era".	Democratisation of information, through 24/7 news channels and social media, will bring more informed and sceptical publics throughout OECD countries. At the same time, there will be more fake news and conspiracy theories.
4	"Continuing fiscal pressures suggest that OECD governments will inevitably find themselves pushed to greater efforts to do more with less. Government concerns for improved responsiveness and performance are doubtless here to stay as key concerns for the future public management reform agenda".	Public scepticism of how much politicians understand about policy interventions will lead to fewer sweeping, nation-wide reforms in OECD countries – innovation will be more common at regional and local levels, where powerful politicians can convince their electorates that there is a different, locally relevant way.
	"Making painful choices about who gets what from the state (e.g. limiting access to certain treatments) will be inevitable and such efforts cannot be limited to technical exercises and will require strong political buy-in and prioritisation".	The limitations of outsourcing will become more apparent. There will be a move back to giving grants to organisations (especially in the third sector) which promise high levels of outcomes for high priority groups – only renewed if later achieved.
	"The public sector is about much more than delivering services efficiently – and its broader political significance in society will ensure that the drive to institute reforms will continue, even if perhaps more cautiously than in the recent past".	Mainstreaming public sector innovations continues to be a challenge in pluralistic democracies. Even successful pilots are often not scaled up and job cuts and outsourcing lead to loss of "institutional memory", so resources will continue to be invested in "reinventing the wheel".
5	"GDUs (Government Delivery Units) may be more relevant and sustainable if they sharply focus on carefully prioritized flagship government programmes and also lead to tangible development outcomes and dividends to citizens".	As part of an increased citizen orientation, governments will more often seek to promote citizen co-delivery of public services.
	"Going forward, it is likely to be a different kind of government and state that will matter to citizens in dealing with crisis – government that listens and can be trusted by citizens, the private sector, and communities".	As social media proliferate, and fake news becomes ever more common, citizens will become more divided as to which governments, which politicians and which media they believe to be telling the truth.
	"Technology will also play an increasingly greater role in public service delivery and in government business, building on the positive developments of increase in online service delivery and remote working prior to and during COVID-19".	As IT becomes more central to everyday life, two contrasting tendencies will arise – more help will be available to the less "IT-literate" and more crime will focus on exploiting IT loopholes.

(Continued)

Table 29.1 Predictions in previous chapters on likely future developments in public management and governance (Continued)

Chapter	Predictions by chapter author	Some supplementary predictions from the editors
9	"The next conceptual breakthrough will likely be accrual budgeting, which could transform the budget document from focusing only on flows into (eventually) a comprehensive prospective statement of both stock and flow measures".	Alternative budgeting approaches are likely to try to find convincing ways to incorporate financial valuation of non-financial flows, such as social capital creation.
14	"Increasing financial pressure on governments is likely to lead to a squeeze on resources available for regulatory inspection, with agencies having to make difficult decisions about where to allocate limited funds. This could mean that regulators are less able to conduct in-depth inspections, and instead focus on areas that present the greatest risk to public safety ... In the context of shrinking budgets, regulatory agencies will be under increasing pressure to justify the costs of their work. This is likely to lead to a more focussed approach, concentrating on areas where they can have the greatest impact and paying less attention to areas that are considered low risk, or where rigorous inspections and audits are difficult".	Citizen inspectors, particularly through the internet, will become the norm for all public services, leading to an elaborate system of accreditation of "citizen inspectors" and validation of online service reviews. Citizens will be encouraged to spy on each other and report to the authorities any breaches of regulations' which they observe
16	"The mode of management in public governance has to change from attempting to impose strategic control on stakeholders towards negotiating overall strategies, within which decisions of partners will mutually influence each other, in a process of strategic experimentation and diversity. This may become more important if social and bottom-up partnerships become common in the future, instead of the large contractual partnerships which were common in previous decades".	Partnerships will become seen as a form of working "above and beyond the contract", based on personal and organisational relationships, so that many partnerships, where they continue, will become looser and more informal.
	"As the novelty of the 'partnership' fad wears off, it is likely that many partnerships will be seen to have been inefficient, even unnecessary. We can therefore expect to hear more often in the future the advice 'Say "no" to partnerships, where they don't help!'".	OECD governments will come to recognise partnership working as high cost, so much of it will disappear – but, unfortunately, even many partnerships which are cost-effective will be tarred with the same brush.

(Continued)

Table 29.1 Predictions in previous chapters on likely future developments in public management and governance (Continued)

Chapter	Predictions by chapter author	Some supplementary predictions from the editors
19	"In a turbulent world where everything solid melts into air, we will most likely see a dramatic increase in governance and management innovation because unpredictable social, economic and political dynamics will tend to prompt institutional and practical changes to preserve goals, values and functionalities that are deemed fundamental to the public sector but are threatened by new tumultuous events".	In many OECD countries the perceived failure of many governments, in the face of multiple crises, will bring into power a range of much more radical administrations (both of the right and left), which are likely to experiment with much more innovative policies than have been normal in recent decades – many of which will, in turn, fail dramatically.
29	"In the future, the public sector will remain important, running socially valuable public services. Public management and governance will therefore also continue to be important, although the priority between the key issues in public management and governance will change from time to time. The key players who excite most interest will also vary from time to time and from place to place, demanding flexibility in how we conceptualise and treat public issues".	

governance which passes strict "scientific" standards (or, from a Popperian perspective, is "tested and non-disproven") is still quite limited. If you check back, few of the recommendations made in previous chapters have been made solely on the basis of scientifically tested evidence. In many cases, authors have fallen back on the "craft" of public management and governance, from their own experience or from their interpretation of the literature. And in some cases authors have highlighted how an actor must tailor practice creatively to specific situations, rather than claiming general applicability of statements made. This creative ability to tailor practice to specific and unique circumstances is an example of the "art" of public management and governance, in a way which may be non-replicable but which builds upon both the scientific and craft knowledge of the actors involved (Bovaird, 2009).

The point is that, while a scientific treatise focuses basically on the "proven" results of empirical research, and a craft manual distils the lessons from countless experiences of actually undertaking the practice in question, a textbook has to attempt to bring these together in a "state-of-the-art" compendium, which allows its readers to learn what is currently believed about the subject, while encouraging them to be sceptical. This scepticism requires them to remain on the lookout for contradictory evidence (which will always be available) and continually to construct alternative ways of explaining observable behaviours, and then subjecting these alternative conceptual approaches to empirical testing. However, even more is expected of readers. If they are academics, they have to teach students and advise practitioners on how the evidence currently looks, imperfect though it is. If they are practitioners, they have to make decisions in the meantime, without fully tested scientific knowledge. In both cases, then, an understanding of the craft of public management and governance is needed – and this textbook has attempted to summarise some of its key elements. Finally, some practitioners will need to develop and improve the art of public management and governance – where the craft isn't enough to carry them through uncharted problems and behaviours – here our textbook has given some tips but, in truth, art requires artists and the best that education can do is to make these artists fully familiar with their craft, allowing their creativity to take over at that point.

So now, over to you. Having read this textbook – or, perhaps, having skipped to this final chapter – you now have a better idea of what is widely believed to drive public management and governance and to lie in store for its future. This should help you to improve the existing practice of public management and governance – but beware! Some of what you have learnt here will have to be unlearnt, as new evidence and more convincing theories emerge over time. And our hope is that you, too, will in future play a role in making public management and governance better understood in theory and more successful in practice. And, of course, we hope that some of you will turn out to be masters of the art of public management and governance, perhaps the hardest task of all!

Summary

In the future, we predict that the public sector will remain important, running socially valuable public services. Public management and governance will therefore also continue to be important, although the priority between the key issues in public management and governance will change from time to time. The key players who excite most interest will also vary from time to time and from place to place, demanding flexibility in how we conceptualise and treat public issues. And the effectiveness of public management and governance will greatly depend on how trusted – and trustworthy – are the key stakeholders (Holzer, 2022) – an area in which many governments currently score badly in the eyes of citizens.

Clearly, prediction, always difficult and liable to making serious mistakes, should be confined to the simple and complicated realms of knowledge – people who attempt to predict behaviours in the complex or chaotic realms are simply charlatans. However, it is not always easy to differentiate between these realms of knowledge, so a sceptical approach to prediction is in order.

We do not know what the next trends are likely to be – but we can have a strong suspicion of the set of issues around which the debates on public management and governance are likely to revolve, at least in the medium term. This can prime us to be ready to react, if these trends do indeed occur. However, we also need to be on the lookout for new trends, and for the non-appearance of the trends we expect. The Scouts have a motto: "Be prepared!" We would suggest an extension of this motto: "Be prepared for what is likely to happen – and be ready to deal with things you didn't think to be likely!"

Finally, understanding how to tackle public issues requires not simply scientific understanding, but mastery of both the craft and the art of public management and governance. You are free to choose which role you most want to play – scientist, craftsperson or artist. But beware – no matter how hard you try to stick to your chosen role, you are likely to find yourself becoming involved in all three roles from time to time, if you really care about improving the outcomes experienced by those citizens who matter most to you. We hope this book will help you.

Questions for review and discussion

1   What are the implications for policy-makers when they move from dealing with issues where the evidence comes mainly from the simple knowledge domain to dealing with issues where the evidence comes mainly from the complicated or complex knowledge domains?

2   What are the different ways in which trends might be projected? Give an example of the kind of evidence which might be used in each case – and discuss how reliable such evidence is likely to be.

Reader exercises

1   Get from your library the first edition of this textbook (*Public Management and Governance*, Routledge, 2003) and compare the chapter headings in it with those in this edition. What changes do you detect? What do you think that says about how public management and governance have changed in the intervening years?

2   Update the evidence on the predictions in Table 29.1 and replace them with your own predictions for what might happen in the following decade.

Class exercises

1   "As a general rule, it is probably safe to forecast that actors whose problems appear to be largely ignored in current policy agendas are likely to play a stronger role in the future, if their numbers are sufficiently large". Divide into groups and discuss whether there is evidence for this assertion. Discuss your conclusions in a plenary session.

2   Divide into three groups to consider different aspects of public management and governance. One group should identify the three most influential "scientists" in this field; the second group should identify three people highly expert in its "craft"; and the third group should identify three people skilled in the "art" of public management and governance. In the plenary session, discuss which is the most important – the art, craft or science of public management and governance?

Further reading

Dion Curry (2014), *Trends for the Future of Public Sector Reform: A Critical Review of Future-Looking Research in Public Administration*. COCOPS. Available at http://www.cocops.eu/wp-content/uploads/2014/04/TrendsForTheFutureOfPublicSectorReform.pdf. Accessed 27/01/2015.

Marc Holzer (2022), "The future of public administration", *Public Integrity*, 24(1): 102–104. DOI: 10.1080/10999922.2022.2003153.

References

Tony Bovaird (2009), "Public administration through the lens of strategic management: The art, craft and science of improving the public domain", Paper delivered at conference: *The Future of Governance in Europe and the U.S.*, 11–13 June 2009, Washington, DC.

Tony Bovaird (2013), "Context in public policy: Implications of complexity theory", In Christopher Pollitt (Ed.), *Context in Public Policy and Management: The Missing Link?* Cheltenham: Edward Elgar, pp. 157–177.

Tony Bovaird and Richard Kenny (2015), "Managing complex adaptive systems to produce public outcomes in Birmingham, UK", In Paul Cairney and Robert Geyer (Eds.), *Handbook of Complexity and Public Administration*. Cheltenham: Edward Elgar, 261–283.

Michael H. Cooper (Ed.) (1973), *Social Policy: A Survey of Recent Developments*. Oxford: Basil Blackwell.

Foresight (2007), *Tackling Obesities: Future Choices – Project Report*, 2nd edition. London: Foresight, Government Office for Science.

Norman Flynn (1990), *Public Sector Management*. London: Harvester Wheatsheaf.

Francis Fukuyama (1989), "The end of history?", *The National Interest*, Summer: 3–18.

M.A. Sartor and P.W. Beamish (2020), "Private sector corruption, public sector corruption and the organizational structure of foreign subsidiaries", *Journal of Business Ethics*, 167(4): 725–744. DOI: 10.1007/s10551-019-04148-1.

David Snowden and M. Boone (2007), "A leader's framework for decision making", *Harvard Business Review*, November: 69–76.

Göran Therborn (2022), "The world and the left", *New Left Review*, 137: 23–73.

Index

Note: Page numbers in *italics* indicate figures, and page numbers in **bold** indicate tables in the text

Printed in the United States
by Baker & Taylor Publisher Services